The Funeral Home Records

Of

Fielden Funeral Home

Jefferson County Tennessee

New Market

Transcribed from the original records by Wayne Shaw

To my Grand children

Kiera, Bonnie and Allen

2013

Fielden Funeral Home White Pine

Legend

M- Married

S-Single

W- Widowed

FBLOC-Fathers Birth Location

MBLOC- Mothers Birth Location

By- Who Paid For Funeral

NAME	DDATE	AGE	DPLACE	BPLACE	BDATE	FATHER	FBPLACE	MOTHER	MBPLACE	SPOUSE	MILITARY	DAUG	SON	SISTER	BROTHER	BY	BURIAL
Aaron, Mae Currie	May 25, 1997	85	Jeff City	Orange Co., Nc	Oct 22, 1911	Qualls, James		Riley, Lucy	Aaron, Jesse [D]				James-Ronald [Nc]		Rainey-David [Nc]	Son	Forrest Hill - Llington, Nc
Abel, Kenneth Allie Jr.	Sep 7, 1987	11	J.M.H.	Jeff City	Apr 27, 1976	Abel, Kenneth Allen Sr.	Mc Nish, Vickie Lynn Spencer					Abel, Christianna Michelle			Spencer, Michael [Step-Father]		Kitts- Grainger Co.
Acuff, Charles Clarence	Apr 13, 1994	73	Morristown, Tn	Grainger Co.	Aug 7, 1920	Acuff, Pryor		Millticoat, Mattie	Whitlock, Jean	Army		Sharps, Janette- Johnson, Louise	Jerry	Breeding, French- Shnups, Nelle	Jerry	Willis	East View
Acuff, Herbert Sidney	Apr 29, 1999	47	Knoxville, Tn	Feb 21, 1952	Acuff, V.I.		James, Mary		Div	Navy	Cirsty-Kim	Jeremy	England, Marilyn King, Melissa			East View
Adkins, Eugene	Dec 13, 1996		Maryville, Tn	Rockford, Ky	Mar 27, 1916	Adkins, Marion		Deats, Annory						Coleman, Elizabeth	Sister - Willis	West View
Adkins, Viola Marie	Jul 15, 1993	71	Knoxville, Tn	Jeff City	Dec 23, 1921	Strange, Earnest		Smith, Parolee	Adkins, Eugene			Robinson, Lena Mae - Trent, Mary Ann - Herrell, Christine	Charles Lee	Wright, Lanada	Eugene-Jim- Leroy-Floyd- Lloyd-Gilbert- Harvey-Bill- Dexter [D]- Samuel [D]	Son - [Ples] Adkins, Lena - Wrangler, Keith-Dan - Mutter, Marion - Strange, Leroy	West View
Alley, Arthur Rudolph	Nov 10, 1987	88	New Market	Dandridge, Tn	Jan 10, 1909	Alley, Arthur		Newman, Lula	Newman, Maude B.					Morris, Ruby [Nc]- Alley, Beulah [D] - Hosharis, Arlene A.	Bates, Donald [Friend]		J.M.G.
Alley, Bettie Ann	Aug 10, 1998	73	Knoxville, Tn	Knox Co	May 24, 1925	Easterday, Thomas		Mell, Anna Laura	Alley, Curtis A.					Goldman, Della Mae [OH]	Jack & Carol- Frank & Brenda	East View
Alley, Bobbie Lee	Aug 10, 1994	75	S.M.H.	Jeff City	Dec 26, 106	Wagner, Samuel		Branson, Mary	Alley, Robert L. Sr.		French, Christine	Patsy- Childress, Jean	Robert [Butch]	Davis, Lowtha	[1/2] Marshall, Ed	[Ples] Wagner, John-Dale-Charlie- Ralph-Luther Jr. - French, Bob - Cox, Tom - Norton, Joe	Strawberry Plains
Alley, Curtis Alfred	Oct 20, 1998	82	F.S.H.	Jeff Co	Jul 31, 1916	Alley, Arnold		Newman, Laura	Easterday, Bettie [D]					Lawrence, Ruby [D]- Elmore, Beulah	Oscar [D]- Arvel [D]- Robert [Dal]	East View
Alley, Dean Christine [Tina]	Oct 20, 1999	59	F.S.H.	Lincoln Co., Nc	Mar 28, 1940	Richard, Marion G.		Beal, Dorothy E.	Alley, Everett Denver			Randy & Lette- Dan		Caldwell, Libby & Steve	Richard [Nc]- Bill [Nc]	J.M.G.
Alley, James Vincent	Mar 4, 1996	82	J.M.H.	Dandridge, Tn	Mar 10, 1913	Alley, Henry H.		Acrey, Mary	Denton, Louise			Shockley, Barbara - Barbee, Mary Frances - Breeden, Elobie		Alley, Freda	Charles	[Ples] Lindsey, Fred-Billy- Forrestine, Donald- Charles - Opp, Ervil-Jr. Donald, May - Horton, Billy - Horton, Herold - Patterson, Dan [in-Law]	J.M.G.
Alley, Josie Mae	May 24, 1981	82	F.S.H.	Jeff Co	Apr 2, 1919	Patterson, Earnest		Hurst, Barbara	Ng		Forrester, Margie	Richard-Vineyard Eugene	Lovell, Edna - Newman, Ruby- Gladys - Manning, Ruth	Garfield-L.P.- Curtis		J.M.G.
Alley, Mack	Oct 16, 1992	84	Dandridge, Tn	Jun 8, 1906	Alley, Kerwod		Gaddis, Margaret		Patterson, Josie [D]		Forrester, Margie	Vineyard-Richard Eugene	Richard, Mattie [Ind]- [In-Law] Bodkin, Grace [Ind]-Kate	Alley, Dolly [Daug- In-Law]		J.M.G.
Alley, Maude	Apr 2, 1991	82	New Market	Dandridge, Tn	Oct 8, 1908	Boden, Green		Boden, Emmie	Alley, Rudolph						Husband	J.M.G.

Name	Date	Age		Birthplace	Date				War				
Alsrd, Rhoda Genevieve	Sep 14, 1999	81	Jeff City	Sevier Co	Feb 9, 1918	Mc Clara William L.		Alsrd, William Howard		Jack & Garry - [Step] Alsrd, W.C. & Dorothy - R.B. & Traudten	Carney, Jane		[Pals] Alexander, James~ Tommy-Millie - Milner, Steve - Eslinger, Mark	J.M.G.
Alexander, Ethel Mae	Nov 5, 1983	82	J.M.H.	Blue Ridge, Ga	Nov 14, 1900	Pierce, Glass	Jones, Callie	Alexander, J.I. Sr.		Irwin Jr.	Hawkins, Blanche - Jones, Anna Belle		[Pals] Alexander, James~Tommy - Tommy-Millie - Milner, Steve - Eslinger, Mark	Trentville - Straw Plains
Alexander, Irwin Jr.	Oct 10, 1992	69	J.M.H.	Blandridge, Ga	Jul 11, 1923	Alexander, J.I. Sr.	Pierce, Ethel Mae	Eslinger, Anita - Veeser, Sari??	WW 2	Eslinger, Anita - Veeser, Sari??			Doug	East View
Alexander, J.I. Sr.	Jun 14, 1985	91		Sequatia, Tn	Nov 14, 1895	Alexander, John	Pierce, Ethel Mae [D]	Milner, Virginia	WW 1	Milner, Virginia			[Pals] Alexander, James~Tommy - Tim~Millie - Tom - Eslinger, Mark	Trentville
Alexander, Lynn Suzanne	May 3, 1996	46		Dayton, Ohio	Aug 2, 1949	Griggs, Donald	Curtis, Geraldine	Alexander, Danny D.					Husband - Irwin	New Market
Allen, Arnel	Aug 30, 1989	57	J.M.H.	Somerville, Tn	Dec 1, 1930	Allen, Bates	Barker, Nancy	Fritts, Margaret		[Step] William, Jean	Dwight-Ronnie [Step] Wilburn, Kenneth - Hodge, Franklin~James~ Terry Wayne	Lowdsey, Marie - Bailey, Alf - Folbrit, Lillie	Arnel	J.M.G.
Allen, Nancy E.	Jun 24, 1982	80	Sevierville, Tn	Sevier Co	Jan 17, 1902	Barker, Bill	Raymond, Perable	Allen, Bates	Army		Russell, Man - Whitehead, Asenia - Thomas, Fanny - Vann, June		Boucher, Homer	J.M.G.
Allison, Charles Lee	Jan 16, 1998	59	U.T.H.	Loudon Co, Tn	Sep 24, 1926	Allison, Garnet Lee	Miller, Elizabeth Ann	Ward, Sally [D]		Jackie	Jason~Jeffery		Arnel - Anel	Shiloh
Allsup, Doris Lillian	Nov 18, 1998	67	B.H.	New Market	Mar 1, 1931	Young, Guy	Ballinger, Eula	Allsup, William A.		Gary	Hickle, Alice		Bill - Bob [Dol] - Paul - Lynn	White Pine
Allsup, Geneva Ella	Jul 10, 1997	69	Morristown, Tn	New Market	Mar 1, 1906	Alexander, J.I.	Mc Nish, Carrie	Allsup, Ray [D]		Gib [D] - Bill & Garrett, Genevieve & Fred - Cox, Lois & David	Gib [D] - Bill & Garrett, Genevieve & Fred - Cox, Lois & David			Pleasant Grove
Allsup, Girl G.	Jul 26, 1996	62	F.S.H.	New Market	Mar 22, 1934	Allsup, Leonard	Mc Ghee, Genova	Allsup, Ray		Ree	Roderick, Vickie~White, Pattie	Garrett, Genevieve - Cox, Lois	Don - Bill	Pleasant Grove
Alsup, William Ray	Aug 23, 1961	57	New Market	Jeff Co	Sep 22, 1907	Allsup, Ray	Mc Ghee, Genova	Fielden, Marlene		Nash, Genevieve - Cox, Lois			Genova [Wife]	Pleasant Grove
Anderson, Charles Curtis	Oct 28, 1998	68	U.T.H.	Lee Co, Va	Mar 15, 1930	Anderson, Marshall	Testerman, Bernice	Campbell, Lula		Billy - Girl - Don	Gary & Helen [In- Law] Messer, Kinsler, Annette	Nichols, Mary Jane - Hoover - Jackson~Grady~ Olen	Lonzo [D] - Herbert - Hoover - Austin - Franklin, Charles - Richard, David - Allsup, Don - Rogers, Ron - Norris, Eddie	J.M.G.
Anderson, Clara Mae	Oct 25, 1989	82	J.M.H.	New Market	Jun 5, 1907	Miller, George A.	Carter, Nora	Anderson, Floyd R. [D]		Willis - Paul - John	Daniel, Maria	Smith, Gertrude - Whitlock, Naomi - Bales, Kathlene - Shelton, Nellie	George Jr.	Nances Grove
Anderson, Claude	Sep 23, 1982	62	F.S.H.	Kyle Ford, Tn	Dec 17, 1929	Anderson, Harvey	Martha L.	Williams, Ora	Korea	Tim	Quillen, Minnie		Livesay, Ernie	J.M.G.

Anderson, Donald Richard	Sep 18, 1987	69	Jeff City	Jul 17, 1928	Alcox, Ethel Mae	Clark, Ethel Mae	Alcox, Elsie Pauline	Fox, Sharon Paulette	Duncan, James Michael - William David	Dennis, Hazel - Gibson, Hattie - Gilstrp, Dallas - Prettipo, Audrey - Alexander, Wanda	William	East View
Anderson, Elsie Blanche	Mar 23, 1976	75	Knoxville, Tn	Tn	Apr 12, 1900	Satterfield, Horace A.	Hodge, Aurinda					Narrows Grove
Anderson, Floyd Rodgers	Jul 15, 1976	96		Roane Co	Oct 28, 1889	Anderson, John W.	Rodgers, Ollie	Miller, Clara	Daniel, Marie	Willie-Pat-John	Knudsen, Irene		Narrows Grove
Anderson, Hugh Kyle Sr.	Mar 15, 1981	43	J.M.H.	Hancock Co	Feb 26, 1938	Anderson, Ezra C.	Buchsel, Hattie	Relia Emma	Susan	Jack-Hugh Jr.	Batis, Pearl - Gray, Geraldine - Brooks, Pauline = Johnson, Isell	Clay-Jay	Hopewell
Anderson, James M.	May 12, 1958	63	Knoxville, Tn	Rogersville, Tn				Davis, Lucy Kate		Houston, Mrs. W.A. - Glover, Mrs. V.G. (Dayton, OH)	Willie	Straw Plains
Anderson, John Newell	Sep 12, 1970	84	New Market, Tn	Tn	May 24, 1906	Anderson, John Samuel	Griffin, Nellie	Satterfield, Elsie	Cain, Ruth	Mink, Ora - Murphy, Anna	Tom		
Anderson, Katharine Louise	Apr 17, 2000	88	New Market	Knox Co	Jun 13, 1931	Miller, Horace	Seaborn, Eva	Anderson, Paul	Kathy	Roger [D] - Franklin & Monica	Miller, I. Lucille [D] - Hill, Edith [D] - Longmire, Maggie [D] - Collins, Opal [D]	Earl [D] - Bob [P]	Narrows Grove
Anderson, Lucy Jane	May 28, 1985	62	Jeff City	Ky	Jun 2, 1902	Lloyd, Jim	Johnson, Maggie E.	Anderson, W.M.		Churchman, Mrs. George - Duncan, Mrs. A.C. - Newton, Mrs. A.Z. - George, Mrs. George C. - Brown, Mrs. A.P. - Trent, Mrs. Taylor	Golden, George - Guy Jr. [McA.]	George-Agusta - P.L.	Husband	J.M.G.
Anderson, Robert Frank Sr.	Apr 13, 1996	57	S.M.H.	Union Co	Dec 18, 1938	Anderson, Frank	Hankey, Mildred	Pierce, Mary Sue	Tonya Jean	Robert Frank Jr. - Michael Allen	Roberts, Ella - Baker, Lavern - Terrence - Tyrone, Sheryl & Wilbur - Kittis, Maryll & Boyd - Brown, Jimmy	Paul & Judy - Lynn-Junie & Sarah-Jimmy & Mickie	East View
Anderson, Shirley Carmella	Oct 6, 1975	40	Strawberry Plains		Nov 24, 1934	Gann, Clyde	Gibson, Dollie	Anderson, Hugh		Jeff	Thelma - Hewitt, Elsie & James - Petty, Linda & Doyle	Wayne	Hobston View
Anderson, Wilma Sue	Nov 7, 1978	28	J.M.H.		Feb 25, 1950	Depew, John	Lee, Rachel	Anderson, Clay Jr.	Elizabeth Jo Ann	Perry, Jaunita [Pat]	Sanyer, Kathy	Jenny-David-Ronnie	Hopewell
Anderson, Ruth	Nov 26, 1995	90	Hill Haven	Rutledge, Tn	Nov 17, 1905	Gillaa, George W.	Lee, Richard	Anderson, Hubert [D]	Perry, Jaunita [Pat]	Roach, Paul - Loy, Norman	[In-Law] Gilles, Nadine	Anderson, Clay A. Sr.	Son	Sunrise

Name	Date	Age	Place	Location	Date	Father		Mother	Spouse		Children	Other	Notes	Burial
Angel, Billy Edward	Nov 27, 1960	19	U.T.H.	Talbott, Tn	Apr 30, 1941	Angel, W.B.	Tn	Myers, Ethel						New Market
Angel, Willie B.	May 17, 1984	70	J.M.H.	Tn	May 17, 1914	Angel, George		Bond, Anna	Myers, Ethel		Pierce, Grace (Alb)	[H-Lacy] Carr, John		New Market
Angel, Willie Ethel	Sep 1, 1988	79	J.M.H.	Sevier Co.	Feb 7, 1909	Myers, Luther		Crowson, Sable	Angel, Willie B. [D]		Carr, Litha - Bolden, Nell - Flynn, Zora	[Pals] Bales, Don - Livesay, Steven - Belin, Dexter		New Market
Armican, Aaron	May 10, 1971			Tn	Aug 23, 1902	Armican, Harrison		Seals, Hannah	S		Wolf, Eula & Crews, Ida - [Weah] Mahan, Ethel - Kessel, Sarah	Roberts, Mary - Mc Coy, Martha	W.M.	Armican - Sneedville, Tn
Armican, John Allen	May 15, 1987	45		Hancock Co., Tn	Dec 13, 1940	Armican, Aaron		Yount, May	S					Armican - Hancock Co
Armican, May	Jan 13, 1978	75		Jeff Co.	Apr 17, 1902	Yount, John		Becker, Martha	S		Janice-Rhonda- Wolf, Eula & Marshall - Kessel, Susan [Weah] - Crews, Ida & Clarence - Mc Mahan, Ethel & Raymond	Fred-Kyle- Raymond-Neal- John-Jack- [Foster] Armican, Bruce	[1/2] 3	Armican - Sneedville, Tn
Armican, New Rubin	Feb 18, 1990	54	New Market	Sneedville, Tn	Mar 27, 1935	Armican, Aaron		Yount, May	S		Armican, Janice, Rhonda - Wolf, Eula - Crews, Ida - Mahan, Ethel - Kessel, Sarah	Raymond, Jack Fred Kyle, Bruce	[Pals] Nephews	Armican - Sneedville, Tn
Armstrong, Henry Charles	Jan 4, 1989	81	J.M.H.	Hawkins Co., Tn	Feb 12, 1907	Armstrong, N.H.		Balns, Fanny D.	Wrampler, Lena Mae		Hunt, Charolotte - Robinson, Judith A.	Wrampler, Anna Lee	Son	Edgewood - Gallaher Rd. Knox Co.
Armican, Bert Houston	Dec 7, 1972	77	Jeff Co.	Tn	Oct 28, 1896	Armican, William B.	WW 1	Riddle, Leah	Wilson, Jessie		Daily, Madeline - Harris, Nina - Welcher, Betty & Larry	Bert Jr.-William B.-John L. [Jed]- Kenneth	Wife	Friends Station
Armed, Dona M.	Jan 27, 1982	78	St. Petersburg, Fl	Tn	Sep 17, 1903	Armed, Flem		Unk	Sue		Donna M.- Flanigan, Hazel (Mo)	Winter, Margaret [Pa]	Otis, Clinton	Wooten Chapel [B]
Armed, Flem	Jan 27, 1982	89	M.C.	Tn	Dec 27, 1892	Unk		Unk	Sue		Donna M.- Stephens, Gwen - Adams, June	H.-Arnold	Armed, Otis [Son]	Friends Station
Arnold, Hubert Glenn	Jan 18, 1981	66	New Market	Tn	Apr 16, 1913	Armed, Jeff		Moore, Nora	Ruby [D]			Bill	Arnold, Ralph	Friends Station
Arnold, John M.	Nov 16, 1984	83	F.S.H.	Tn	Aug 31, 1901	Wilson, John L.		Donna, Marie	Sue			Jack	Arnold, Kenneth	Friends Station
Arnold, John H.	Jan 26, 1983	92	Norfolk, Va	New Market	Apr 26, 1900				Arnold, Marie [Ft]			Sullivan, Nancy - Winters, Maggie [Ft]	Oliver F.H. [Norfolk, Va]	Friends Station
Arnold, John H.	Jan 26, 1983		New Market						Marie H. [Ft]				Mathews F.H. [Sr. Pete, Fl]	
Arnold, Kenneth Terry	Apr 6, 1979	20	Jeff City	Grainger Co.	Sep 30, 1958	Arnold, Kenneth		Tucker, Racheal	Nancy Irene			Daniel Bert		
Arnold, Nora Bell	Apr 16, 1980	97	J.M.H.	Hamblen Co.	Oct 14, 1882	Moore, Joe		Sarlin, Mary Elizabeth	Arnold, William A. [D]			Glenn-William	Vineyard, Sallie	Jerry-Gary	Friends Station

Name	Date	Age	Place	Place 2	Date 2											
Arnold, Ruby E.	Mar 3, 1981	64	J.M.H.	Talbott, Tn	Sep 6, 1916	Elder, Will				Arnold, Glenn	Adams, June - Stapleton, Jean	Arthur - H.S.	Chambers, Mary Ruth - Whaley, Gladys	Elta, John (Pels) Vinson, Roger - Lowrary, Ralph - Brick, Roy - Kirkwood, Earl - Arnold, Kenneth	Friends Station
Arnold, Sue	Oct 4, 1954	73	Fairfax, Mo		Feb 8, 1881					Drackie - Frazier, Hazel (Ma)	Nixson, Mrs. Albert	Whitsers, Margaret (Fl) - Sullivan, Nancy (Fl)	Arnold, Olie (Step)	Arnold, Glenn (Son)	Friends Station
Arnold, William A.I. Sr.	Sep 6, 1950	61	Blount Co, Tn	Blount Co, Tn	Sep 30, 1888	Arnold, William R.	Tn	Tn		Chramer, Miss Dorothy			Arnold, Olie (Step) John (Fl) - Bert		Friends Station
Arwood, Virgie E.	May 4, 1979		Morristown, Tn	Jeff Co	Dec 14, 1903	Young, J.G.			Clevenger, Mollie	Arwood, Tom (D)	Nora	Jernigan, Frances	Northern, J.W. - Riley, Edward	Collins, Georgia	(Paul) Kelly, David - Jimmy - Collins, Glenny - Brown, Jimmy - Young, McNeal - Bill	Mill Springs
Asbury, James W.	Jul 23, 1960	28	Newport, Tn	Carryville, Tn	May 25, 1932	Asbury, W. Raymond			Russell, Lucille	Cynthia		Norma Jean	Ralph - Maurice/former Rhee-Harold	Ralph - Maurice/former Rhee-Harold		Woodlawn
Asbury, Susan Renea	Aug 7, 1967		F.S.H.		Aug 5, 1967	Asbury, Ward		Ruby						Parents - Kevin, Dessie-Ashley, C.P. (G-Parents)	New Market
Atchley, Benjamin J.	Aug 8, 1964	77	Knox Co.	Tn	Apr 13, 1886	Atchley, Ben J.		Beulah					Russell, W.D. (G-Parents)	Russell, W.D. (G-Parents)	New Market
Atchley, William J.	Mar 17, 1983	70	U.T.H.	New Market, Tn	Jan 7, 1913	Atchley, Ben J.		Franklin, Nancy			Hammond, Elsie		Hammond, Elsie	Kay (Fla)-Harry	Willie	Lyndhurst - Knoxville, Tn
Atchley, Dona C.	Aug 15, 1899	96	J..Mh.	Sevier Co	Sep 15, 1899	Atchley, Palmer		Carter, Martha		S	Basset, Nancy	W.K.-W.J.-Harry D.	Basset, Nancy	Mc Campbell, Naomi	Willie	Piedmont
Atchley, Charles A.	Jan 18, 1954	64	Jeff City	Tn	Feb 4, 1889			Unk		Bell, Mary	Harris, Mrs. J.A. - Graves, Mrs. Marion - (Step) Spradlen, Mrs. Buford - White, Mrs. D.E. - Wheelock, Mrs. Paul - French, Mrs. Edgar - Seale, Mrs. Raymond	Scriven-Fambley - (Step) Clark, Condon	1	4	Atkins, Mrs. C.A. - Epperson, Mrs. Margaret (Step - Daugl)	Kittis - Granger Co
Atkins, Ed (Col)	May 19, 1965	84	New Market	Ga	Dec 11, 1980	Unk		Unk		Jennie	Henderson, Ruth & John H. (Dal - Smith, Myrtle & Abraham - Holderfied, Leola & Grady - Brown, Georgia & Joe - Lewis, Mrs. Addie (Wk) - Green, Mrs. Jennie				Wife	West View
Atkins, Jeanie (Negro)	Mar 10, 1972		Knoxville, Tn		Jul 3, 1899			W						Brown, Georgia (Daug)	West View

Name	Date	Age	Place	County/State	Birth	Father	St	Mother	St	Mil.	Spouse/Children				Burial
Atkins, Solom Melton	Sep 29, 1999	84	J.M.H.	Granger Co	Mar 31, 1915	Atkins, Charlie		Hopson, Tina			Turley, Sue	M.L. & Norma Fae/Vic	French, Wanda - Whitlock, Myrtis - Adrian, Felicia & Jonathan - [In-Law] Margaret - [In Law] Atkins, Mabel Jo [See Obit For D]	[D-See Obit]	Charles-Kenneth	Trent, Claude - Lafayette, John - Austin [G-Parents]	J.M.G.
Ault, William Henry	May 21, 1996	75	U.T.H.	Knoxville, Tn	Apr 4, 1921	Ault, Henry	Tn	Wright, Mill		Navy					J.M.G.
Austin, Danny Flitcher	May 11, 1949	1d	Knoxville, Tn		May 10, 1949	Austin, M.L.		Trent, Jewell	Tn						Nances Grove
Babcock, Hugh C.	Jul 30, 1997	81	Jeff City	Iowa	Dec 3, 1915	Babcock, Warren		Hewn, Edna			Shaggs, Lorraine	Ron H. [N Marc] - Brett R. [New]	Babcock, Marion [Cal]	Mervin [Cal] - Wendell [DL]	New Market
Bacon, Mary Emma	Jun 4, 1988	81	Hamblen Co		Apr 9, 1907	Lilly, R.B.		Pierce, Nola			Carter, Nola L. - Brock, Mary Ruth	Bacon, Howard [D]	Horner, Cora	Lilly, Sam	Dangs	Pleasant View
Bailey, Albert A.	May 8, 1985	89	J.M.H.	Granger Co	Aug 12, 1895	Bailey, Henry		Helton, Julie			Kelsey, Sarah	Solomon, Lucille - Sherrod, Mary Ruth - Wise, Pauline - Bradshaw, Ada - Lane, Allene	James-Henry	Collins, Vallie	[Pats] Bailey, Frank - Ken-Benny-Rickey - Wade, Merrill - Lewis, Robert	New Market
Bailey, Charlie Robert	Dec 9, 1975	80	J.M.H.	Jeff Co	Sep 26, 1895	Bailey, Sam		Rudder, Mattie	W		Whitlock, Martha			Claude	Didgmas, Mary & Bill [Daug]	Pleasant Grove
Bailey, Clara Lou	Dec 31, 1981	63	J.M.H.	Hamblen Co	Sep 30, 1918	Stump, Edgar		Williams, Martha Eva	W		Bailey, Rex Eugene [D]		Donald-Jackie	Price, Beulah - Bergh, Frances - Elmore, Elizabeth	Ralph-Charles-Jamie-Eugene-Danny-Freddie-Eddie	J.M.G.
Bailey, Eula	Feb 12, 1989	85	Jeff City	Alabama	Apr 10, 1912	Painter, W. John		Mixsay, Pearl			Bailey, Mark P.			Woodruff, Lillian [Cal]	Ralph - Br - Luther H. - [Lee] Bailey, Luther H.	[Pats] Guinn, Jim - Franklin, David - French, Tom - Young, Mack - Carpenter, Rich - Bailey, Dennis - McGhee, Luther	Strawberry Plains
Bailey, Florence Elizabeth	Dec 27, 1986	85	J.M.H.	Granger Co	Nov 14, 1901	Howell, William Luther		Howell, Florence			Bailey, Joe [D]		Hat-Gene	Hal-Gene	[Pats] Taylor Jr. - Cain, Fred - Franklin, David - Young, Mack - Moats, Greg	Strawberry Plains
Bailey, Herbert E.	Jul 19, 1990	48	J.M.H.	Tn	Mar 27, 1930	Bailey, Joe		Howell, Florence			D., Judy [Roy]	army	Jamie-Sharon	Hal-Gene	Frazier, Mildred	[Pats] Loy, G.W. - Bill - Frazier, Ralph-Fred	Strawberry Plains
Bailey, J. Will	Feb 4, 1990	66	J.M.H.	New Market	Jun 14, 1923	Bailey, Claude		Lytle, Beatrice			Wilson, Lillie Mae	WW 1	Buckner, Debbie & Bobby - Konell, Jamie & Gene	Sam-David - William Eddie - Rickey	Frazier, Mildred	Valley View
Bailey, Joe	Jun 27, 1954	67	J.M.H.	Tn	Dec 27, 1886	Bailey, William		Williams, Amanda			Howell, Florence	WW 1		Herbert-Luther-Eugene-J.T.	Floyd-Elvin	Willie	Strawberry Plains
Bailey, Joe Calvin	Jan 15, 1995	67	Strawberry Plains	Jeff Co	Apr 25, 1927	Bailey, Floyd		McGhee, Lucy		WW 2	Cain, Mary Ellen	Smith, Darlene - Deluck, Lori Ann - Neal, Peggy - Leftoo, Anny	Joey	Long, Nina B. - Winsted, Elizabeth	Clint	[Jarrigan City Med. Center]
Bailey, Joe Calvin	Nov 26, 1995		J.M.H.	Tn	Nov 25, 1995	Bailey, Joe Calvin		Cain, Mary Ellen						Darlene-Peggy-Laura Ann	Cain, Jakie - Bailey, Floyd [G-Parents]	Strawberry Plains
Bailey, Lester Grant	Nov 26, 1995		J.M.H.	Tn												

Name	Death Date	Age	Place	Residence	Birth Date	Father	Mother	Spouse / Notes	(cont.)	(cont.)	(cont.)	(cont.)	Cemetery
Bailey, Lillie Mae	Nov 25, 1993	70	U.T.H.	New Market	May 7, 1923	Wilson, Robert	Lyle, Ruby	Bailey, J. Will [D]	unk	Knott, Janie- Buckner, Debbie	Stan-David-Ed- Rick	[Pals] Knott, Gene- Buckner, Bob- Solomon, Stan- Lloyd- Holland, Stacy- Frazier, Ralph	Valley View
Bailey, Lucy Lane	May 31, 1998	88	F.S.H.	Sevier Co.	Dec 25, 1909	Lane, Charlie	Underwood, Frances	Bailey, Robert Earl		Bailey, Robert [D]-Corrine [D]-Geneva & Larry	Perty, Virgie [D]	Atchley, Eldridge	Beech Springs
Bailey, Luther Hall	Dec 25, 1999	65	J.M.H.	Jeff City	Feb 27, 1934	Bailey, Joe T.	Howell, Florence [D]	Boley, Deborah [D]		Richard Troy & Colleen- Dennis C.	Norland, Bonnie	Luther	New Market
Bailey, Mark P.	Mar 8, 1996	84	Jeff City	Strawberry Plains	Aug 4, 1913	Bailey, Luther Sr.	Philbeck, Eda	Painter, Eula [D]	unk			Luther	Strawberry Plains
Bailey, Rex Eugene	Dec 12, 1974	59		Seymour, Tn	Apr 27, 1915	Bailey, Arthur	Jeff Co	Van Dyke, Sue	Jeff Co	WW2	Donald E.-Jack [Calif]- Davis, Extra- Treese, Bulah	James-Hal	J.M.G.
Bailey, Sam	Sep 2, 1977	82	S.M.H.	Dowell, Tn	Oct 31, 1894	Bailey, Marion	Kerr, Annie	Mee		Trent, Maudie- Workman, Bertha- Frances, Ruby & Gurge- Tipton, Zora & Ernest- Ballinger, Mary & Doyle- Phipps, Betty & Howard [Miss]	[Step] Younger, Harold [Calif]	[1/2] Hubbard, Minnie & Jim- Seals, Bulah & Grant	Strawberry Plains
Bailey, Trula	Apr 7, 1990	82	Hill Haven	New Market	Oct 6, 1907	Lowery, George	Newman, Cordia	Bailey, Charlie [D]		Whitlock, Martha- Dulgnan, Mary		Eanie-Earl	Friends Station
Bailey, Vida Lucille	Aug 21, 1995	59	B.H.	Jeff Co.	Apr 19, 1936	Elmore, Paul	Griffin, Willie Pauline		Kinkead, Regina Brown, Paula- Bailey, Tina	Michael [Cal]	Diamond, Alma [Cal]- David	Orvalle-William- David	Piney
Baird, Charles Winston	Aug 29, 1992	41	Asheville, Nc	Knoxville, Tn	Dec 26, 1949	Baird, Aaron	Hearn, Anna Rae	Div			Hinchey, Joyce Faye & Sam W.	Sister	
Baker, Bessie	Jan 21, 1997	93	Sevier Co	White Pine, Tn	Jun 15, 1903	Smith, Steve	Reed, Mary	Baker, Ray H. [D]			Bumgardner, Kim- Baker, Amanda	Helton, Louise & Howard [G-Mother]- Allen, Teresa	Flat Gap
Baker, Christopher Eugene	Feb 6, 1995	20	U.T.H.	Jeff City	Jan 25, 1975	Baker, Jack	Quinn, Patricia Mae	S				Parents	J.M.G.
Baker, Leon Shelton	Mar 28, 1998	75	Jeff City	Jeff City	May 5, 1922	Baker, Harrison	Lunos, Mary	Cox, Blanche	Army	Williams, Carolyn & Roger	Marshall, Inez	Williams, Carolyn L. [G-Doug]	J.M.G.
Baker, Mary Frances	Mar 19, 1992	90	Sullivan Co. Tn	Sullivan Co. Tn	Sep 8, 1901	Lunos, Jake	Woods, Margaret	Baker, Harrison			Leon	Fred	Mt. View
Baker, Ray H.	Sep 1, 1978	64	Care Inn	Tn	Jun 13, 1913	Bailey, Jim	Gettis, Lizzie	Bessie S.			[Step] Howell, Bob	Chester- Herbert	New Market
Bales, Agnes	Feb 8, 1991	65	S.M.H.	Jeff Co	Jan 6, 1926	Jenkins, Robert V.	Glenn, Iva	Bates, Clinton		Coltey, Patricia Gwy	Strange, Robert- Hal-Sammy-Gary	Finley, Gladys	Chester- Herbert

Name	Date	Age	Place	City/County	Birth Date	Father		Mother	Spouse						Cemetery
Bates, Boyd E.	Dec 23, 1982	55	Morristown, Tn	Jeff Co	Nov 15, 1926	Bates, Floyd E. Sr.		Thornton, Bertha	Brinkman, Ruth [Dix]	Ruthie [Columbus, Oh] - [In-Law] Bates, Bonnie [Cleveland, Oh]	Marcus-John [Cleveland, Ohio]	Lawson, Alma	Bruce	Lawson, Alma - [Pete] Loy, G.W. Jr., Bates, Curtis - Cannon, Ken - Cate, James H. - [Pete] Strange, Frank - Bates, Gray - Donnie - Sharp, Guy - Brock, Paul	Cremated
Bates, Bruce Jesse	May 1, 1982	63	J.M.H.	Jeff Co	May 20, 1928	Bates, Floyd E.		Thornton, Bertha	Cole, Yvone	Allen, Beverly - Nannastad, Karen	Doug	Lawson, Alma	Douglas	Paula	Pinny
Bates, Carrie Lois	Oct 14, 1990	78	J.M.H.	Jeff Co	Jul 27, 1912	Heaton, William Henry		Mc Collum, Minnie Louise	W	Sharp, Grace, Nadine - Masengill, Opal	J.R.-Clinton-Don-Roy-Troy	Sharp, Grace - Wilson, Nadine - Masengill, Opal	J.R.-Don-Roy-Troy	Strange, Hattie E. Jr.	Friends Station
Bates, Clinton Boyd	Nov 16, 1983	59	Talbott, Tn	New Market	Aug 21, 1924	Bates, James R.		Huffaker, Bernice	Jenkins, Agnes	Gay	Hal	Gay	John	Paula	Friends Station
Bates, Emma Pauline	Sep 12, 1996	86	Knox Co	Jeff City	Sep 10, 1910	Grubb, Phess P.		Burchell, Maude	Bates, Erwin D. Sr.	Dunlap, Shirley - Martin, Agnes - Brock, Paula	Robert	Miller, Obbie - Jackson, Robie - Peck, Mary - Reeta, Betty	Paula	Paula	Union - Knoxville, Tn
Bates, Erwin O. Sr.	Aug., 1970	65	S.M.H.	Tn	May 30, 1905	Bates, Oscar K.		Brown, Mollie	Grubb, Emma	Mills, Paula - Martin, Agnes - Dunlap, Shirley - [In-Law] Bates, Mrs. E.O.	Robert L.	Simpson, Mrs. Vaughn - Mayes, Mrs. Cecle - Sherrod, Mrs. Herbert - Finelly, Mrs. Albert			Newport, Tn
Bates, James Curtis	Dec 22, 1994	42	U.T.H.	Jeff City	Oct 31, 1952	Bates, James Randy		Cox, Sylvia	Waddell, Wilman Glay	Army		Bates, Teresa - [Step] Osborne, Amanda	Bates, Jason [Step] Osborne, Danny		John	Friends Station
Bates, James R.	Aug 14, 1977		J.M.H.	Tn	Nov 6, 1895	Bates, William Thomas		Arnold, Nancy	Heaton, Carrie	U.S.A.F	Sharp, Grace - Wilson, Nadine - Sperice, Opal	Mc Glamery, Edith, Howard, Anna Bell	Paul	Friends Station
Bates, James Randy	Jul 25, 1986	17	B.H.	Hamblen Co	May 1, 1971	Bates, Edward C. Jr.		Lumpkin, Mary Bates Wolfe	S			Janice	Douglas	Willis - [Pete] Stapleton, Dwight - Whitlock, Curtis - S. David - Courtney, Connie - Steve - Bates, Lynn-David	J.M.G.
Bates, Karen Diane														Wills - Edward & Joyce - Wolfe, Earnest & Mary - [Pale] Brooks, Pete - Dean, Hattie - Coomer, Steve - Bates, Mc Campbell,	
Bates, Lincoln H.	Dec 21, 1974	76	Jeff Co			Bates, J.R.							John T.		Presbyterian - New Market
Bates, Marvin Edward	Jun 14, 1994	40	Dandridge, Tn	Jeff City	Oct 3, 1953	Bates, J.R.		Cox, Sylvia	Hendrick, Nancy	Mc Glamery, Mary		Cristy - [Step] Warren, Tina	Michael-Timothy-Marty-Brandon- [Step] Warren, Bob-Sam-Allen	Carroll, Collie & J.A. - Sharp, Lucy & C.S. - Shonn, Gertrude & Jack	Friends Station

Name	Death Date	Age	Place	County	Birth Date	Father	Mother	Spouse	Mil.	Relatives / Children				Cemetery
Bales, Mary Eliza	Nov 28, 1995	94	Dandridge, Tn	Jeff Co	Dec 5, 1900	Mc Glamery, Andrew B.	Glenn, Blanche	Bales, Lincoln H.				Hood	New Market	Piney
Bales, Nola Bell	Jan 7, 1965	79	Knoxville, Tn	Tn	Oct 6, 1885	Dance, James Bedford	Jeot, Texanna	Bales, Walter Emerson [br]		Hutton, Tmda - Dockery, Lois - Spencer, Mrs. James	Willis-Raymond-James	Widner, Mattie - Johnson, Mrs. Eddie	Raymond	Piney
Bales, Sallie Elizabeth	Sep 21, 1989	83	Morristown, Tn	Sevier Co	Dec 13, 1905	Huffaker, Samuel N.	Griffey, Annie	Bales, Alex		Nesles, Leona [Oh] - Petti, Edna [Oh] - Witha, Anna L. - Underwood, Charlotte		Norton, Pauline	Charlie	J.M.G.
Bales, Wayne Herbert	Apr 26, 1976	46	New Market, Tn	F.S.H.	Aug 21, 1929	Bales, J.R. Sr.	Huffaker, Bernice			Mary Ann - Hawk, Cora - Hale, Jill		Sharp, Grace - Wilson, Nadine - Spence, Opal	B.B. J.R. Jr. - Clburn-Dub-Troy-Ray	[Field] Bales, L.N. - Thomas-Eddie - Sharp, Ricky - Gray, Glenn - Strange, Junior → Friends Station
Bales, William S.	Jul 3, 1984	80	V.A. Hosp-Nashville, Tn	Jeff Co	May 26, 1924	Bales, James R. [Cef] (Tn)	Huffaker, Mamice	King, Mary Ruth	Tn	Bowman, Julia - Massey, Betty	Raymond	Sharpe, Grace - Wilson, Nadine - Massengill, Opal	Don-Clarice-Troy-Roy-J.R. Jr.	[Field] Vols → Friends Station
Bales, Luther Clay	Mar 13, 1956	83	Tn	Tn	Feb 17, 1956	Bailey, Walter (Tn)	Burchell, Betty Jane	Susie	Tn	Brown, Mary [Ga] - Vineyard, Carolyn	Alfred-James	Ole	Bailey, Walter	Walnut Grove
Bell, B.J.	Apr 28, 1979	83	S.M.H.	Tn		Bell, William J.	Huffaker, Betty Jane	S		Vineyard, Carolyn	Bell, Mike-Don-Frank		Bell, Fred-John	Highland Memorial
Bell, Ellis Joy	May 22, 1983	75	White Pine, Tn	J.M.H.	Jul 16, 1917	Bell, William J.	Garner, Mary	S		Vineyard, Carolyn	Bell, Mike-Don-Frank		Bell, Fred-John	French Broad Brethren
Bell, Ellie	May 4, 1961	61		Grainger Co	May 10, 1899	Hammer, Joseph	Clevenger, Lucy	Bell, B.J.		Vineyard, Cunningham, Mary Jane	Alfred-James	Elliston, Georgia	C.W.	Highland Memorial
Ballard, Paul Raymond	May 25, 1997	71	Straw Plains	Whitesburg Hawkins Co	Nov 16, 1925	Ballard, Floyd	Elkins, Ollie	Sneed, Judy Ann		Whitlock, Hazel - Sandra-Kathy - Carla, Angela - Goosnell, Martha - Powell, Joyce [Sd]	Deegree-David-Dale	1	7	Strawberry Plains
Ballinger, Ada M.	Jan 22, 1981	73	M.C.	Grainger Co, Tn	Mar 22, 1887	Hall, Leslie	Ballinger, J. Henry			Whitlock, Hazel - Trent, Edith - Fielden, Stella - Kinder, Della	Lucian-Floyd	Bailey, Eula	Ralph-Buddy-Robert-Roger	Pleasant Grove
Ballinger, Austin Elmer Jr.	May 16, 1999	74	J.M.H.	New Market	Dec 7, 1924	Ballinger, Elmer	Foster, Carrie Mae	Taylor, Eva Sue [br]	Army	Phillip-Deon	Dalton, Edmonds - Turner, Phyllis	Ballinger, Claude - Nell, James	Mill Springs
Ballinger, Ben	Aug -, 1989			New Market						Dalton, Mrs. - Edwards - Turner, Mrs. - Phillip-Gibson, Dorothy - Haworth, Ella - Young, Ena - Whitley, Erma - Rose, Lillian - Hessly, Mary	Austin-Doyle-Jack	Clarence-Guy-Donald-Gerald - [Step] Clowers, Howard	Ballinger, Claude - Nell, James	Mill Springs
Ballinger, Carrie Mae	Nov 25, 1982	63	M.C.	Jeff Co	Mar 1, 1919			Ballinger, Elmer				Austin-Doyle-Jack	Sam Shafe-Jess	Husband → Mill Springs
Ballinger, Charles Henry	Jun 20, 1958	77	New Market	Tn	Jun 16, 1884		Foster, James					Clarence-Guy-Raymond-Mongo	J.H.-Elmer-Raymond-Mongo	Ballinger, Claude - Nell [Wife] → Family

Name	Death Date	Age	Death Place	Birth Place	Birth Date	Father	Co.	Mother	Spouse	Military	Children / Relatives	Siblings	Pallbearers	Cemetery
Ballinger, Clarence Edward	Jan 24, 1990	69	Jeff City	New Market	Aug 16, 1920	Ballinger, Raymond		Carroll, Myrtie	Slover, Aileen	WW 2	Hobbs, Cindy	Charles; Waldrop, Katherine; Alvin-Gary	[Pete] Newby, Harvey - Preston, Roy - Jones, Paul - Woods, Harold - Byrd, Roger	Mill Springs
Ballinger, Claude R.	Nov 18, 1994	66	New Market	New Market	Mar 9, 1918	Ballinger, Raymond		Carroll, Myrtie	Mc Mahan, Marjorie	navy	Kenny-C.R.	Waldrop, Katherine; Edd-Gary-Alvin; Minton, Josephine - Burnette, Edna - Rose, Edd Mae - Trotter, Agnes	Doug - [Pete] Bixler, Warren - Minton, Roy - Nathan - Killen, John - Miller, Jimmy	Mill Springs
Ballinger, Clifford Chester	May 23, 1989	58	U.T.H.	New Market, Tn	Nov 18, 1930	Ballinger, U.G.		Everhart, Louise	Div	korea	Grant, Patricia	Michael-Darrell; Paul-Grant	Ballinger - New Market, Tn	Mill Springs
Ballinger, Dora Myrtle	Aug 5, 1983	87	New Market	New Market	Jun 2, 1896			Carroll, Nannie	Ballinger, Raymond [D]		Waldrop, Katherine - Poore, Cynthia - Ford, Lisa - Wettenbarger, Sheila	Claude-Ed-Alvin-Gary; Fielden, Margaret		Pleasant Grove
Ballinger, Doyle Leon	Feb 16, 1998	66	S.M.H.	New Market	Jun 29, 1931	Ballinger, Elmer		Foster, Carrie	Bailey, Mary	Army	Minton, Darrell	Dirk; Dalton, Edwardo - Reed, Phyllis	Austin	Mill Springs
Ballinger, Floyd H. [Bud]	Feb 5, 1976	53	New Market, Tn	New Market, Tn	Jun 23, 1922	Ballinger, J. Harvey		Haworth, Dorthy		WW 2	Tennessee-Christy - Lindsey, Sue & Ted	Jackie-Doyle-Austin; Whitlock, Hazel - Trent, Edith & Arlie - Kinder, Della & Earl	Lucian	Pleasant Grove
Ballinger, Gary Wade	Sep 23, 1993	49	Newport, Tn	New Market	Dec 9, 1943	Ballinger, Raymond		Carroll, Myrtel	Unk	army	Karen, Jacqueline-Teressa	Danny & Anita [Pete] Galein, Koontz, Denise [Step-See Obit]; Waldrop, Katherine; Alvin	Brother	Mill Springs
Ballinger, Guy Charles	Dec 19, 1997	74	Rutledge, Tn	New Market	May 20, 1923	Ballinger, Charles H.		Young, Lela	Brady, Thelma J.		Chastity - Cole, Janell & Harry - Koontz, Denise [Step-See Obit]	Roos, Lillian [D] - Young, Eula [D] - Hawley, Mary - Whatley, Emma; Bobby, Gene [D]-Clarence [D]-Gerald-Donald [bro]	Willie	Unk
Ballinger, Houston Elmer Sr.	Nov 24, 1973	80	Tn	Tn	Oct 17, 1893	Ballinger, William	Jeff Co	Clawson, Sarah	W	WW 2	Kinder, Della - Trent, Edith - Wheelock, Hazel	Floyd-Lucian; Morgan	Brother	Unk
Ballinger, J. Harvey	Aug 24, 1969	94	Jeff City			Ballinger, William		Clawson, Susie	W			Morgan; Elmer-Raymond		Pleasant Grove
Ballinger, Jackie	Feb 15, 1982	41	J.M.H.	New Market	Sep 27, 1940	Ballinger, Elmer		Foster, Carrie	Trent, Margie	army	Karen, Jacqueline-Teressa	Gibson, Dorthay - Turner, Phillis; Austin-Doyle	[Pete] Gilbert, Tommy- Dukin, Bobby- Snead- Jay-Wayne- Tolliver, Herman- Herman	Mill Springs
Ballinger, John Earnest Jr.	Jan 14, 1972	67	Jeff City	Tn	May 4, 1904	Ballinger, John E.		Daniel, Lera	Mc Curry, Julia		Hicks, Mrs.- Jerry - Purkey, Ollie Jo	Mc Curry, Edith [1/2] - Turner, Mrs. Louie	Willie	West View
Ballinger, Julia Augusta	Feb 12, 1997	88	Jeff City	Cooke Co., Tn	Oct 7, 1907	Mc Curry, William Lee		Coglitti, Dora	Ballinger, John Ernest Jr. [D]		Purkey, Olivia - Josephine [D] - Lancaster, J. - Geraldine & Gene	John E. 3rd - Jr- Lew), Purkey, Don; Finley, Beryl [TX]	Doug	West View
Ballinger, Lela	Nov 20, 1978	79	Jeff Co				Jeff Co					Young, Guy		Mill Springs
Ballinger, Lela	Nov 18, 1978	79	Dandridge, Tn	Jeff Co	Dec 27, 1898	Young, William	Jeff Co	Pratt, Mary	Ballinger, C.H. [D]		Hendy, Mary	Gerald-Guy-Donald; Guy	[Pete] Allbaun, Bill- Gill - Hensley, K.B.- Ballinger, Rileys- Austin - Kidde, Pete	Mill Springs

Name	Death Date	Age	Death Place	Birthplace	Birth Date	Father	Mother	Spouse	Svc	Relatives			Pallbearers / Relatives	Cemetery
Ballinger, Margaret Louise	Feb 6, 1982	82	Knoxville, Tn	Bristol, Tn	Aug 10, 1899	Everhart, Henderson	Stroabig, Oma	Ballinger, U.G. [D]					[Pete] Ballinger, David-Mille-David - Ross, Tony - Melton, Jerry - Melton, Bennie-Steve - Elmore, Barry	West View
Ballinger, Margie Elizabeth	Dec 5, 1989	70	New Market	Newport, Tn	Mar 18, 1919	Farmer, Jessie	Ballinger, Ross	Ballinger, Claude [D]			C.R. Jr.-Kenneth			Mill Spring
Ballinger, Nancy Elizabeth	Oct 13, 1967	82	S.M.H.	Tn	Sep 19, 1885	Foster, Melton D.	Acuff, Savanah	Ballinger, Ross		Watkins, Mrs. Bill-Howell, Mrs. H.E.			Ballinger, Amnon, [Pete] Newman, Bill - Conwell, J.C. - Hicks, Clifford - Hicks, James - Lowery, Rea - Turley, Andy	Mill Spring
Ballinger, Pauline	Dec 23, 1981	70	J.M.H.	Jeff Co	Sep 8, 1911	Fielden, Nancy	N., Kate	W			Lisa			Pleasant Grove
Ballinger, Raymond	Aug 20, 1971	76	J.M.H.	Ky			Myrtle	Waldrop, Katherine	WW 1					Pleasant Grove
Ballinger, Tilda	Nov 11, 1994	90	J.M.H.	New Market	Feb 5, 1904	Quinn, James	Kerr, Kate	Ballinger, Joe [D]			Campbell, Lula		Neal, Imogene [Niece]	New Market
Ballinger, William Lucian	Feb 19, 1978	67	New Market		Feb 14, 1911		Vinyard, Ada	Pauline F.		Finley, Edna - Sherrod, Larone - Carothers, Helen	Amnon	Whitlock, Hazel - Trent, Edith - Ballinger, Mrs. Della	Ballinger, Amnon - Trent - Harold Glenn - Everett - Whitlock, Ed	Pleasant Grove
Ballinger, Ulyssee Grant	May 20, 1965	77	J.M.H.	Ky	Sep 6, 1897	Ballinger, F. Marion		Everhart, Louise	Div	Minton, Josephine - Burnette, Edna Faye - Roots, Eula Mae - Trotter, Agnes	Lee, Nancy - Malone, Janice - Robidoux, Tricia - Seals, Connie	Robert Jr.	Ballinger, Riley [Son]	West View
Banks, Robert Lee	Mar 10, 1999	71	F.S.H.	Shaw Plains	Apr 5, 1927	Banks, Perry	Dockins, Nancy	Div		Dix	Rush	Ronnie	Groves, Gladys	West View
Banks, Wallace	Oct 19, 1987	67	V.A.-Mt. Home	Jeff Co	Sep 2, 1920	Banks, Perry	Dockins, Nancy	Ruth	WW 2		Ronnie	Groves, Gladys	Tommy-Lee	West View
Banks, William Michael	Jun 6, 1978	16	Knoxville, Tn	Tn	Jan 21, 1961	Banks, Tommy	Bolin, Dorothy	Bolin, Dorothy			Lisa	Darrell		West View
Banks, William Tommy	Apr 3, 1988	55	S.M.H.	Jeff Co	Sep 3, 1932	Banks, Perry	Dockins, Nancy	Bolin, Dorothy		Lisa	Darrell	Groves, Gladys	Lee	West View
Barbee, Dora	Jul 14, 1979	92	J.M.H.	Sevier Co	Mar 12, 1887	Jones, Thomas	Bailey, Sarah	Barbee, W.T. [D]		Purkey, Catherine	Winifred-Curtis			Mill Springs
Barbee, Nancy Sue	Sep 5, 1995	55	S.M.H.	Jeff City	Aug 25, 1940	Epps, Mack	Kinder, Billie	Barbee, William B.			Gary	Kinster, Jean		West View
Barbee, Rebecca Ann	Feb 2, 1951	2-7-3	Jeff City	Jeff City	Jun 29, 1948	Barbee, Curtis	Baumgardener, Martha Ann		Tn				Barbee, Curtis - Baumgardener, J.C. [G-Father]	Rosebarry
Barbee, Thomas Brelner	Jan 17, 1969	75	Jeff Co	Tn	Jul 2, 1893	Barbee, Charles	Fielden, Darithula	Barbee, Viola	unk				V.A.	Friends Station

Name	Date	Age	Place	County				Mil.					Cemetery
Barbee, Viola	Jun 20, 1987	85	Jeff Co		Boden, James Albert	Brooks, Deborah	Barbour, Thomas [D]		Stutherland, Terri	James-Bill-Roy-Troy	Dickinson, Peggy & Ed [New] - Gaston, Ann & Wes [Pal]	[Pals] Barbour, Randy-David-Gary-Craig-Lee-Bob-Oliver, Harrell	Friends Station
Barbour, Mary M.	Mar 2, 1998	67	J.M.H.										
Barker, Dorothy Lee	Sep 9, 1998	88	Jeff City	Henderson, Nc	Mc Ghee, Roy	Hopkins, Mattie	Barker, Willie [D]		Barbour, Stephen R. [Sd]	Barbour, Stephen R. [Sd]	Ballinger, Aileen [Niece]	[Pals] Smith, Bill - Bates, Ray-Jean - Pratt, George - Evans, John - Glover, St. Clair - Procunior, Roy	Mill Springs
Barnard, Kenneth Earl	Sep 11, 1985	48	U.T.H.	Strawberry Plains	Barnard, Perry	Atchison, Nancy		army		Troy-Eddie Lee	Cain, Sylvia - Berry, Elizabeth - Glover, Matlie - Fritz, Mary - Glover, Jo Ann - Benson, Lillie	Cain, Sylvia - Berry, Elizabeth - Glover, Matlie - Penn, Matlie - Fritz, Mary - Glover, St. Clair - Procunior, Roy	J.M.G.
Barnard, Nancy	Jun 18, 1971	65	S.M.H.	Tn	Dec 15 1906	Anderson, Flora	Yount, Nancy		Barnard, Perry		Carroll-William-Kenneth-James Jr. [Mach]		Jo Ann	Strawberry Plains
Barrett, Everett Wesley	May 4, 2000	67	Jeff City	Sc	Jul 31, 1932	Barrett, Chloie	Minors, Rula ?	unk	Lauderdale, Deborah - House, Bridget	Ross, Michael	Gaylon, Frances			Lauderdale
Bateman, Kenneth Maynard	Nov 28, 1981	49	Cleveland, Ohio	Tn	Mar 20, 1932	Bateman, Chorley T.	Williamson, Ruby Spencer	W			Rhymer, Helen - Malone, Allen - Livingston, Peggy	[Pals] Watson, Swan - Spencer, Jay Ralph-Ronnie-Lloyd - Gass, Bob - Lockhart, Jerry	Stitch
Bates, Clinton	Nov 25, 1971	65		Tn	Feb 24, 1906	Bates, Glass	Binley, Etta		Cain, Carolyn	Bates, Cecil [Ga]		Bates, Carroll C. [Son] - Cochran, Lawrence [Cousin-Son Obid]	Nances Grove
Bates, Etta	Sep 18, 1990	83	M.C.	Grainger Co., Tn	Jul 26, 1877	Byerly, James	Stape, Mary	Army	Cecil	Paul-James O.	Mc Bee, Ella	Bates, Carroll C. [Son]	Nances Grove
Bates, Joseph Donald	Jun 26, 1987	56	Jeff City	Knoxville, Tn	Aug 26, 1940	Bates, Paul S.	Kettle, Lucille	S			Brackett, Mrs. C.E. - Marry, Mrs. V.H.	Cochran, Lawrence [Cousin-Son Obid]	Nances Grove
Bates, Lucille	Nov 21, 1978	67	U.T.H.		Oct 10, 1911			Army	Don			Nances Grove	
Bates, Obed Leland	Jan 21, 1966	80	Knoxville, Tn	Tn	Mar 9, 1885	Bates, Obed	Hawkins, Martha		Moore, Helen - Cain, Hazel [Step] Bains, Edith			[Pals] Moore, Jean-Harrold - Bains, Ben - Zimmer, Clifton - Beckenham, William	Nances Grove
Bates, Paul Stanley	Nov 6, 1963	56	J.M.H.	Tn	Sep 2, 1907	Bates, Glass G.	Byerley, Etta	Tn	Lucille	Don	Cecil	Carroll-James - Willie - Bates, Carroll C. - Cooper, James, Melinda	Nances Grove
Bates, Perry Malcolm	Dec 15, 1951	39	Johnson City, Tn	New Market, Tn	Jul 4, 1912	Bates, Leland		WW 2				Father - Bertha [Step-Mother]	Nances Grove
Bates, Ruth	Jun 18, 1998	93	North Haven H.C., Tn	Grainger Co	Oct 11, 1894	Gilmore, Henry E.	Greenlee, Nettie E.		Bates, William George [D]			Moore, Helen - King, Hazel	Cruze, Nadine [Cleveland, Tn]	Buffalo Rutledge, Tn
Batts, Harry B. [Col]	Jan 21, 1979	78	Jeff City					W				Patton F.H. [Cleveland, Tn]	
Baumgardner, Cloy	Feb 24, 1986	80	F.S.H.	Knox Co	Dec 11, 1915	Baumgardner, Tipton	Plount, Reva		Lawson, Gladys	Oglesby, Sharon		Mack L.	Willie	Strawberry Plains

Name	Death Date	Age	Death Place	Origin	Birth Date	Father	Mother	Spouse	Relations / Children	Cemetery
Baumgardner, Grace Bell	Dec 25, 1983	77	Knoxville, Tn	Knox Co	Oct 10, 1906	Sherrod, Phillip	Oates, Hazen	Baumgardner, Calvin [D]	Barbee, Martha Ann - Purkey, Hazel; Jim; Simmons, Zelma - Sexton, Frankie - Burris, Sara Lou; Mutt-Ross; [Pike] Baumgardner, Jay - Purkey, Mike - Tony - Mehrcents, John	Roseberry - Knoxville, Tn
Baumgardner, James Calvin	Mar 24, 1959	59	Knoxville, Tn	Tn	Feb 18, 1900	Baumgardner, John W.	Mc Cracken, Susan	Sherrod, Grace	Barbee, Mrs. Curtis - Purkey, Hazel B.; James H.; Hayes, Mrs. G.W.; Charles A.; Willis; Daug	Roseberry
Baysinger, Daisy	Dec 12, 1992	71	Jeff City	Sevier Co	Nov 1, 1921	Hulsey, William	Bolden, Ada Birtie	Baysinger, Lloyd	Baysinger, Lloyd	Oakland
Baysinger, Joel William	Sep 28, 1999	59	F.S.H.	New Market	Feb 9, 1940	Baysinger, Lloyd	Hulsey, Daisy	Morgan, Wanda Sue	Charles-Carl; Hargus, Bertie - Ortield, Wanda Faye	J.M.G.
Beal, Michael Bradley	Dec 3, 2000	20	Rutledge, Tn	Knoxville, Tn	Nov 16, 1980	Beal, Robert	Neves, Linda	S	Beal, Brittany-Amy-Missy - Compton, Jessica-Brittany; Beal, Josh; Compton, John [Step-Father]	Caldonia
Beeler, Ada Mae	Aug 22, 1981	70	J.M.H.	Copper Hill, Tn	Nov 15, 1910	Guy, John	Robinson, Lydia	Beeler, James Edward [D]	Slagle, Ada Geraldine [Pansy]; Maurice [Az]-Willard [Cal]-James [Alb]; Parr, Florance [Cal]; Johnson, Hal	West View
Beeler, Carl Dean	Feb 18, 1982	47	J.M.H.	Treadway- Hancock Co.	Nov 7, 1944	Beeler, Kay	Trent, Pearl	Wright, Shirley	unk; Kenneth-Ernie-Tom; Eskander, Karen; Kyle	Hamblen Memorial
Beeler, Joseph Hilliard	Jan 4, 1992	79	F.S.H.	Cocke Co, Tn	Oct 12, 1912	Beeler, William	Presley, Polly	Daniels, Myrtle [D]	Smith, Betty & Harley; Lee, Georgia; Elbert	Wesleys Chapel
Beeler, Herman L.	Jan 11, 1956	63	Tn		Jul 27, 1892				Bellinger, Bernice - Howard, Pearlie Mae - Coy, Gladys [Val]; Dallas	Pleasant Grove
Beeler, John	Sept -, 1969	23	Jeff City					Nora Mae	Franklin, Brenda; Linda-Helen-Darlene-Myrtle; Osborn-Roger-Billy; Beeler, Myrtle [G-Mother]	Pleasant Grove
Beeler, Murphy R. Jr.	Jul 7, 1969	76	U.T.H.	Maynardville	Oct 1, 1922	Beeler, Murphy R. Sr.	Chambers, Zetta R.	Carroll, Margaret	Army; Lewis, Patricia & Ray-Bryan, Sue & Tom; Donald & Janice	Mill Springs
Beeler, Myrtle	Dec 2, 1979	84	Cane Inn	Claiborne Co	Dec 24, 1894	Hurst, John	Bunch, Sarah	Beeler, Herman [D]	Gladys-Bernice-Howard, Pearlie Mae; Dallas [D]; Presley, Lettie; Beeler, Mrs. Nora Mae	Pleasant Grove
Beeson, Anna Belle	Mar 23, 1959	42	Knoxville, Tn	Tn	Aug 30, 1916	Hurst, H.L.	Mills, Viola	Beeson, Walter L. [D]	Hullafiser, Joyce; Profitt, Eddie; Presley, Lettie; Beeler, John	Pleasant Grove
Beeson, Osborne Della	Dec 22, 2000	82	Tn	Jeff Co	Jul 8, 1918	Anderson, Claude O.		Beeson, Walter L.	Hullafiser, Joyce - Jayne - Thorne, Sharine & Raymond - Funderbunk, Lynn - [Step] Hullafiser, Joyce & Marvin; Profitt, Eddie [D]; Presley, Lettie; Beeler, Mrs. Nora Mae	Ebenezer
Beeson, Walter Leroy	Aug 21, 1998	77	Talbott, Tn	Brookhaven, Miss	Mar 1, 1921	Beeson, Walter Loy	Humphill, Mary	Anderson, Anna Belle	Navy; Lewis...; [Step] Profitt, Eddy; Waldrop, Geneva - Proctor, Althea - Freeman, Vera; Charles-J.L.	Pleasant Grove
Bell, Doss	Apr 25, 1992		Hancock Co		Jan 13, 1893	Bell, Hilton	Dinnero, Mary	Pelney, Lora	WW 1; Earwood, Ada - Smith, Bobbie - Meade, Genes - Johnson, Carolyn; Jack-John-Lennie-Smith-Alfred; Dieltman, Minnie	New Market

Name	Death Date	Age	Place	County/Origin	Birth Date	Father	Mother	Spouse	Service	Children/Relatives			Notes	Cemetery
Bell, Jackie [M]	Oct 15, 1991	45	V.A. - Mt. Home	Hancock Co.	Feb 27, 1946	Bell, Doss	Penny, Lora	Hilton, Brenda	Army	Steven-Jack	Earwood, Ada - Smith, Bobbie - Meade, Gennee - Johnson, Carolyn	Smith-John - Lonnie-Alfred	Wife	V.A. - Mt. Home
Bell, Lora	Aug 7, 1998	88	Harrogate, Tn	Knox Co	Jun 3, 1910	Peters, William	Minton, Minnie	Bell, Doss [D]						New Market
Bell, Owen	Jul 1, —	44	Sneedville, Tn		Nov 2, 1934	Bell, Doss	Claiborne Co, Monroe, Blanche	Penny, Lura						New Market
Bell, Peggy Ann	Jul 1, 1988	41	J.M.H.	Tazewell, Tn	Apr 19, 1945	Bell, Doss	Hancock Co	Griffin, Nan	Bell, Alfred					New Market
Bell, Roy Otis	Feb 12, 1995	54	B.H.	Richmond, Tn	Oct 13, 1940	Bell, Hugh Lynn	Nelson, Gertrude	Snyder, Trula		Huffner, Tammy Bell, Pam	Ronnie-Donnie	Cribb, Sylvia [Sic] - Smith, Joye	Wife - [Pals] Bell, Randy - Huffner, Calvin - Snyder, Tommy - Trobb, Watt - Collins, Bobby	Mc Campbells Chapel
Bell, Lester	Aug 5, 1979	46	Morristown, Tn	Hancock Co	Oct 13, 1900	Bell, Doss	Penny, Lora	Div	army				Father	New Market
Bellamy, Garrett Hobert	Sep 27, 1970	72	Jeff Co	Va	Oct 13, 1897	Bellamy, Harvey	Mc Murray, Josephine	Hodam, Nina			Gerald		Bellamy, G.H. [Son]	New Market
Bellamy, Josephine	Dec 23, 1981	93	Morristown, Tn	Virginia	Feb 22, 1888	Unk		Va						New Market
Bellamy, Nina	Nov 23, 1994	90	S.M.H.	Scott Co, Va	Jun 26, 1904	Hickam, Ewell		Bellamy, Hobert [D]			Gerald H.	Hale, Thelma [Va]		New Market
Benett, Marchie	Dec 19, 1998	79	Athens, Tn		Mar 11, 1909	Farris, John	Benton, Elizabeth	Benett, Anthony [D]		Cillick, Jewell - Snodgrass, Bonnie L - Atkins, Alice	Thurman, Newell - Bill [Calif]	Wilson, Mandy		J.M.G.
Bender, Eugene Franklin	Aug 16, 1997	78	Arkton, W. Va		May 29, 1919	Bender, Neal	Rothe	Shelton, Louis	Navy				Wife	Nances Grove
Bender, Louis	Dec 14, 1999	85	J.M.H.	Tazewell, Tn	Mar 2, 1914	Shelton, A.J.	Keck, Isabell	Bender, Eugene			Weyer	Oaly-White [Da] Carl-Weyer-Roy		Nances Grove
Bernard, James Perry	Mar 22, 1976	42	Strawberry Plains	Mascot, Tn	Jun 18, 1933	Barnard, Perry B.		Hickey, Christine		Seale, Janiel & Ronnie	Bryan	Caine, Sylvia - Glenn, Mrs. Ray - Fritz, Mary Bailey - Benson, Mrs. James - Caruzo, Vern [Nj] - Collins, Georgia	Mathews, Lura[D] - Paladino, Norma [D] - Massieri - Lunsor - Poone, Mrs. Tom - Berry, Mrs. Marion - Clonce, Mrs. Vaughan [Mich]	Hobson

Name	Date	Age	Abbr.	Place	Date 2	Name 2		Name 3		Relatives					Cemetery
Bernard, Perry	Jul 18, 1971	69	S.M.H.		Nov 30, 1901			Antioch, Nancy [D]		Garn, Joanne & Ray - Fritts, Mary - Bailey - Cates, Sylvia & Junior - Brenon, Lillie & James - Poore, Mattie & Tommie - Berry, Elizabeth - Glover, Lixie - & Vaughn	Carroll-William-Kenneth-James Jr.	Atkins, Nellie	Harrison-Samuel-Clarence-Roe-William		Strawberry Plains
Berry, Daisy	Dec 17, 1982	73	F.S.H.	New Market	Feb 18, 1919	Lewis, Henry		Berry, Avis [B]			David	Bradley, Helen - Arthur, Gladys	Son		J.M.G.
Berry, David Avis	Dec 28, 1991	69	J.M.H.	Union Co	Sep 7, 1922	Berry, Frank		Lewis, Daisy			David	Wright, Dorothy B.	Clyde	Willie - [Pals] Newman, Frank - Whitaker, Christine - Shelton, Claude - Tittle, Claude - Nancie, Harold	New Market
Berry, Gertrude Arietta	May 31, 1992	76	J.M.H.	Sharps Chapel, Union Co	Sep 17, 1915	Ervin, Isaac Thomas		Berry, Willard E. Sr.		Sitton, Mildred - James, Edna - Roberts, Ann	Willard Jr.-Tom	Clabough, Doll		[Pals] Berry, Michael-James - Pitts, Richard - Cable-Steve - Woodsworth, Clayton	New Market
Berry, Joseph L.	Dec 9, 1976	68	Battle Creek, Mich.	Sharps Union Co				Becker, Sallie Elizabeth [D-Age 73]		Malone, Mrs. Howard - Duncan, Mrs. George	Gaylord-Joseph-Frank [Mich]	Cameron, Mrs. Hassie	Berry, M.W.		New Market
Berry, Maggie Jane	May 19, 1956	54	M.C.	Tn	Jun 8, 1901	Kivett, E.M.	Tn	Kivett, Connie	Tn	Duncan, Betty - Malone, Mrs. Howard	[Step] Naish, Bob	Rose - Moyers, Mrs. U.S. - Tarbett, Mrs. S.F. - Ijams, Pearl	Conley-Ethel		New Market
Berry, Milburd W.		68		Tn				Imogene		Duncan, Mrs. Howard		Rhode - Herron, Mary - Creech, Talitha		[Pals] Berry, Foster-Clyde - Corum-Lee - Herron, Paul - Creech, Arthur	New Market
Berry, Sallie E.	Jun 3, 1969	75	Knox Co	Tn	Jan 15, 1894	Becker, Alford		Sharp, Katherine	Berry, Joseph					Son [Pals] Berry, David Sr.-Jr. - Roberts, Anderson - Sitton, Leon - Clabough, Roy	Strawberry Plains
Berry, Willard Esco	Jun 1, 1991	81	J.M.H.	Union Co	Dec 1, 1909	Berry, Frank		Braden, Dora	Ervin, Gertie	Roberts, Ann - Sitton, Mildred - James, Edna	Willard Jr - Tommy	Wright, Dorothy	Clyde-Avis	Willie - [Pals] Newman, Frank - Whitaker, Christine - Shelton, Leon - Clabough, Roy	New Market
Bettis, Doris Jane	May 3, 1995	80	B.H.	Belton, Jackson Co, Nc	Feb 16, 1916	Tittle, Paul H.		Tittle, Lillie May	Bettis, James Harley [D]	Duncan, Ruth	Pray, John Walter			Bettis, Mrs. Mack H. - Turner, James H.-Elmer [Cleveland, Oh]	Piedmont
Bettis, Hattie Pearl	Jun 13, 1996	80	E.T.H.	Tn	Jan 4, 1886	Owens, Samuel		Johnson, Martha	W				Bob	[Pals] Moore, Bill - Greenlee, Richard-Bruce - Wright, Howard - Shackleford, Ed	Piedmont
Bettis, James Harley	Dec 25, 1987	70	B.H.	Jeff Co	Jan 8, 1977	Bettis, Mack H.		Owens, Hattie P.	Brenon, Doris Jane				Paul T.-Elmer E.	Carl	Piedmont
Bickel, George Edworth	Aug 24, 1995	55	S.M.H.	Ft. Wayne, Ind	Apr 8, 1939	Bickel, Russell		Mandle	Webb, Mary	Broughton, Tracy & Jerry	[Step] Hanlon, John		Carl	Willie	Piedmont

Name	Death Date	Age	Place 1	Place 2	Birth Date	Father	Mother	Spouse	Svc	Parents	Survivors	Other	Son	Buried
Biddle, William Buford Sr.	Sep 21, 1995	96	Morristown, Tn	Jeff City	Nov 2, 1906	Biddle, Jerry Franklin	Cate, Lovella	Maples, Thelma [D]		William & Catherine	Gladys [D]+Edith [D]- Homer, Cora - Odom, Virginia - Gibson, Winifred - Smith, Alma Greenway, Dorothy	Dale [D]-Tom [D]+Houston [D]+George	Son	Friends Station
Biddle, Willie Thelma	Dec 8, 1994	82	S.Mh.	New Market	Jan 26, 1912	Maples, W.M.	Robbins, Dora	Biddle, W.B. [D]		William	Jones, Mary [Daug] Jones, Clyde - Culver F.H.		Son	Friends Station
Black, Iva Angela	Apr 25, 1996	80	F.S.H.		Dec 13, 1905									Springfield, Mo
Black, Marion J.	Feb 20, 1971	75	Mo		Apr 23, 1895						Jones, Mary & Clyde- Culver F.H.			Pilllot - Barry Co
Blackburn, Margrate	Feb 5, 1965	44	Tn		Jan 10, 1921	Talbert, K.P.	Burchfield, Johnnie	Blackburn, Orel			Brenda	Kidd, Blanche	Charles / Bill B. [Son]	Lynnhurst
Blackburn, William Orel	Sep 26, 1994	43	F.S.H.	Tn	Feb 13, 1921	Blackburn, Samuel Howard	Wheeler, Callie	Talbert, Irene			Brenda	Bill	Price, Sara / J.W.	Willie / Lynnhurst
Blair, Robert Lee	Jun 22, 1989	0	Knoxville, Tn	Sevierville, Tn	Oct 10, 1988	Blair, McMaster H.				Herman B. & Louise		Herman		Holly Hills - Knoxville, Tn
Bohanan, Mary Ica	Mar 22, 1985	105	Rutledge, Tn	Jeff City	Dec 10, 1957	Collins, Jennifer Ion	Walls, Mary Manis	Bohanan, Doss [D]		Vada		Mother		Cremated
Boley, Deborah Kay	Jan 23, 1996	38	New Market	Jeff City	Oct 22, 1999	Yarberry, Barry	Cain, Faye	Div		Pratt, Martessa - Boley, Jamie	Stansberford, Jesse Lee	Richard - Dennis	Mother	Nances Grove
Boley, Deloris Denise	Dec 20, 1994	38	Morristown, Tn	Granger Co	May 25, 1956	Bryant, Roy Earnest	Meyes, Rabb	Boley, Bobby R.		Boley, Jamie Lynn - [Step] Boley, Donnie	Boley, Susie - Atkins, Jamie	Earnie	Husband	Buffalo
Boley, Fred Edward	Aug 28, 1982	29	Morristown, Tn	New Market	Jun 28, 1953	Boley, Walter	Burchell, Betty	Div		Mc Clain, Martessa Gail	Nancy - Courtney, Linda - Whitehead, Jeanie	Alvin-Bobby	Pleasant Grove
Boley, Fredie L.	Nov 10, 1966	72	Dandridge, Tn	Tn	Sep 17, 1894	Boley, Jack	Turner, Minnie	Div		Shultz, Minnie	Walter-Jack	Alvin-Bobby	Willis	New Market
Boley, Jack	Mar 20, 1993	68	New Market	Newport, Tn	Dec 1, 1925	Boley, Fred	Styles, Rendie	Hensley, Kathleen		Lyla, Mary Ann	Jack-Jerry-Mike	Shultz, Minnie	Walter	New Market
Boley, Walter	Jun 9, 2000	72	Jeff Co	Newport, Tn	Nov 27, 1927	Bryant, Roy Earnest	Stiles, Rinda	Boley, Betty		Linda - Hailey, Nancy - Mitchell, Jeanie [Cath]	Kivett, Nellie - Shultz, Minnie	Earnie	Willis	J.M.G.
Bolin, Allie Mae	Apr 10, 1985	83	S.M.H.	Shady Grove, Tn	Jul 17, 1901	Bolden, Elijah	Cross, Katherine	Moore, Peggy		Mc Clain, Martessa Gail	H.T.	Kivett, Nellie - Shultz, Minnie	[Pete] Bolin, H.T. Jr. - Williams, Terry-Owen - Bettis, Carl - Kenneth - Bolden, Roger	Highland Memorial East
Bolin, Carol C.	Aug 31, 1979	73	Siluria, Alabama							Bolin, Mrs. Clyde - Spencer, Wanda - Buster, Mrs. S.G.	Billy Don-Charles Ralph	Solomon, Ruth - Brooks, Imogene - Martin, Geneve	Roy	Piney
Bolin, Charles Wayne	May 30, 1970	44	Nt		Jun 5, 1925			WW 2				Banks, Dorothy - Young, Mary Ruth - Morrison, Florence - Brewer, Gladys	Dexter-Haskell	Mt. Campbells Chapel
Bolin, Edith	May 12, 1986	82	J.M.H.	Knox Co	Dec 11, 1903	Ramsey, James A.	Perry, Mary C.	Bolin, Howard		Martin, Geneva & Cecil - Solomon, Ruth - Brooks, Imogene	S			Piney
Bolin, Ethel	Mar 18, 1979	95	Dandridge, Tn	Knox Co, Tn	Feb 7, 1883	Wagman, John	Susie	Bolin, Sam [D]					Willie	Strawberry Plains
Bolin, George Raymond	Nov 24, 1965	33	J.M.H.	Tn	May 28, 1932	Bolin, Ray	Whitaker, Ruth	Bely Joe A.		Raymond Lee	Roy-Carroll	Banks, Dorothy - Young, Mary Ruth	Willie	Mt. Campbells

Name	Date	Age											
Bells, Hobart Tilman	Oct 13, 1990	65	Strawberry Plains	Jeff Co	Aug 30, 1925	Bells, Bilshid Monroe		Bolin, Allie Mae	Bolen, Lillie Bell	WW 2	Henderson, Cheryl - Anderson, Becky [K]	H.T. Jr.-Frank	Moore, Peggy	Wife [Pat] Elmore, Wade-Rose-Scot - Butler, Bill - Ward, Carl - Mc- Closkey, Kenneth - Smith, Herman	Piney
Bells, Raymond	Aug 6, 1954	52	Jeff Co												
Bells, Raymond Howard	Jun 14, 1976	82	Jeff Co	Aug 2, 1893	Bells, Joshua		Snyder, Mattie	Ramsey, Edith	[Foster] Luretha, Sally & Jack [Val] Ruth - Wadkins, Dunty & Juanita	Wayne-Dexter-George-Haskell	Cates, Ellis - Woodson, Pauline	Clarence-Jack-Enos	Mc Campbells Chapel
Bells, Ruth A.	Mar 18, 1990	54	M.C.	Tn	Mar 25, 1905	Whittaker, Chorley	Tn	Alsup, Minnie	Tn			Wayne-Dexter- George-Haskell	Wife	Pleasant Grove
Bocker, Tarance Allen	Oct 9, 1990	60	New Market	Union Co, Tn	Jan 26, 1933	Bocker, Arthur		Rhea, Mae	Richard, Virginia Pauline	Korea		Richard-David	Whaley, Judy Dall, Reba	Graves, Mrs. Irving	East View
Bostic, Tina	May 27, 1979	87	J.M.H.	Claborne Co	Mar 28, 1892	Walker, Henry		Collins, Sarah	W				Graves, Mrs. Irving	New Market
Boswell, Gladys E. [Black]	Feb 3, 2000	86	Morristown, Tn	New Market		Armstrong, Alex		Davis, Ida	Boswell, Mack [B]	W		Mack Jr. [B] - Stewart, William		West View
Boswell, Mack A. [Black]	Apr 18, 1990	40	J.M.H.		Dec 28, 1949	Boswell, Mack Sr.		Davis, Gladys	Cubberson, Gloria [Div]		Tanya		Brooks, Martha Lee - Breedlove, Mary A. - Hooker, Betty Ann	Mary [Sister]	West View
Bowlin, Jennifer Roberts	Feb 2, 1988		J.M.H.		Feb 2, 1988	Bowlin, Donald Maurice		Roberts, Vivian						Parents - Roberts, H.G. Sr.-Roberts, D.L. [G-Parents]	J.M.G.
Bowling, Evelyn Pauline	Dec 23, 1987	54	Jeff City	Jeff City	Feb 2, 1933	Kanjoe, V.P.		Griffin, Zula	W		Bullock, Cheryl - Atkins, Mary	Thomas W.-Josh	Southerland, Bonnie - Fidden, Jean	Jeffery-Jerry-Ricky	J.M.G.
Bowling, Paul R.	Feb 21, 1985	64	J.M.H.	Knoxville, Tn	Apr 14, 1933			Roberts, Vivian	W	WW 2	Bullock, Cheryl - Atkins, Mary	Thomas W.-Josh	Southerland, Bonnie - Fidden, Jean	W.R.	J.M.G.
Bozeman, Arthur Jr.	Aug 2, 1990	70	S.M.H.	Mascot, Tn	Dec 26, 1919	Bozeman, Arthur Reggie Sr.		Shumaker, Merrita	Jones, Louise	WW 2	[Step] Henson, Jauntia - Cline, Judy - Denton, Wanda	[Step] Thomas, Edd Jr.	Trevon, Katherine - Bozeman, Jewell - Stevens, Jene - Hembree, Nadine - Dennison, Betty Jo	J.T.	J.M.G.
Bozeman, Paul Lovelace	Apr 1, 1998	86	J.M.H.	Blaine, Tn	Apr 17, 1911	Bozeman, James Alexander		Skipo, Margaret	Mc Gill, Charlie Mae	WW 2	Paulette - Hodges, Mary & James		Clanton, Ruth - Boruff, Margaret		J.M.G.
Bradshaw, Clarence William	May 19, 1979	81	J.M.H.	Grainger Co	Oct 26, 1897	Bradshaw, Nathan		Mayes, Martha	Bailey, Ada	WW 2	Brenda-Martha-Peria	William-Clyde	Underwood, Sadie - Eldridge, Cora - Vincent, Lena	Marr, Charlie-Bradshaw, Clifford	[Feb] Nance, Wilson-Len - Moody, Lester- Sam-Lesley- Osteen, Luther	New Market

Name	Date	Age	Place	State	Birth	Father	Mother	Other	Spouse	War	Children / Relations	Children	Cemetery
Brady, Ida	Nov 8, 1957	84	New Market	Tn	Dec 6, 1872	Unk					Solomon, Joe- Murphy - Brady, Joe T.-Alex; W.R.		New Market
Branam, Anna	Jan 10, 1968	79	Tn	Tn	Oct 3, 1888	Goss, James T.	Corbett, Fannie	W			Cochran, Edna	Cochran, Edna	Hebron
Brashears, Martha Jane	Dec 5, 1996	53	U.T.H.	Tn	Mar 20, 1943	Hoffman, John Richard	Maurkie, Mary Ellen		Patterson, Joseph [Dr]		Patterson, Michael	Thomas Lee; Brother	Cremated
Brazelton, Lionel Doyle [Black]	Dec 7, 1980	83	Care Inn	Jeff Co	Oct 28, 1897	Brazelton, Edgar	Martin, Laura		Rhod, Mary		Morrison, Carzell	Miles, Modest - Fitzgerald, Vivian	St. Lukes Presby.
Brazelton, Nellie [Col]	Nov 17, 1979	84	New Market, Tn	Tn	May 9, 1895	Brazelton, Russell	Mellin, Mary		Nellie M.		General	Mynatt, Ruby; Brazelton, Calbert - Lewis, Robert - Phipps, Augaline - Scruggs, Calvin - Simon, Johnny - Johnson, Samnel	Younga Memorial
Brazelton, Rosa A. [Black]	Nov 11, 1979	62	Knoxville, Tn	New Market, Tn	Jan 30, 1911	Brazelton, Edgar	Martin, Laura	Div	WW 2		Miles, Modest - Fitzgerald, Vivian	Lionel	St. Lukes Presby.
Brazelton, Alax T.	Nov 17, 1979	84	New Market, Tn		May 9, 1895		Mellin, Mary		Nellie M.			Taylor, Nadine [9] - Presby. - New Market	Presbyterian
Brazelton, Hoyle	Dec 24, 1968	69	Knoxville, Tn										
Brazelton, Mary [Black]	Jul 1, 1990	92	New Market		Sep 22, 1897	Reed, Powell	Reed, Ellen	Brazelton, Lionel			Miles, Modest - Duffy, Dorothy - Fitzgerald, Vivian	Lionel-Ross	Younga Memorial - New Market
Brazelton, Mary [Col]	May 17, 1984	62	J.M.H.	Tn	Jul 27, 1901	Mitchell, Thomas	Patton, Sara	Brazelton, Alex	WW 2		Mynatt, Ruby & Carl - [In-Law] Brazelton, Margaret	General	Husband	Younga Memorial
Breeden, Erwin H.	Dec 3, 1991	66	New Market	Sevier Co	Apr 16, 1925	Breeden, Harrison	Lovsley, Stella	Vance, Wilma	WW 2		Linda	Bill-Jim-David-John	Collins, Gerraldine-Poore, Edith	George- Harrison	St. Lukes Presby.
Brewer, Mary Agnes	Jan 24, 1990	66	New Market		Feb 22, 1925	Stallard, George	Pretzr, Nellie	Brewer, Paul [D]			Norton, Barbara - Jean	George Franklin-Paul Riley	Norton, Barbara J.	Son
Brewer, Paul Ray Jr.	Feb 22, 1925	56	New Market		Feb 23, 1940	Brewer, Paul R. Sr.	Stallard, Mary	Div			Riggs, Paulette		George Franklin	Friends Station
Brewer, Paul Ray Jr.	Jan 27, 1994	54	New Market		Feb 23, 1940	Brewer, Paul R. Sr.	Stallard, Mary	Div			Riggs, Paulette	Norton, Barbara J.	Friends Station
Brisker, Dom Leroy Jr.	Mar 22, 1993	69	Salem, Ohio		Sep 20, 1933	Brisker, Dom Leroy Sr.	Shackley, Kay	Fetters, Jo Ann	Navy		Dunn 3rd-Michael	Kidd, Dixie [Mich]	Ken [Mich]	Cremated
Briskey, Ray Glenn	Sep 24, 1986	74	Sumerset Co., Pa		Sep 16, 1912	Briskey, Henry	Shumaker, Lucinda	Briskey, Lucille					Pa
Britt, Edwin	Aug 20, 1976	43	New Market, Tn	Ft. Valley, Ga	Mar 26, 1933	Britt, Henry	Eslinger, Maxine	Korea			Kathy-Vickie	Roy-Steve	H.N. [Gh] - William - Franklin E.	Clingmans F.H. [Patterson, Ga]; Wife - [Pala] O' Dell, Charles - Dell, Charles - Batley, Mack - Cammon, Handal - Nichols, Floyd - Houk, James	Blue Springs
Bradsock, Thelma H.	Jul 12, 1997	78	Jeff City	Ball Co, Ky	Jun 28, 1919	Hill, Tolliver	Wollen, Bertha	Brodsock, Gurney J. [D]			Loy, Annette	Lyon, Myrtie - Harvey, Pearl [Ky]	Oakview - Middlesboro, Ky
Brock, Anna Lee	Sep 22, 1978	67	J.M.H.	Tn	Feb 6, 1911	Lane, Swannie		W			Hensley, Geraldine - Warren, Betty	[1/2] Douglas, L.D. - Lane, Dave & Junior - Snyder, Bill; [1/2] Lane, Maggie	Pleasant Grove
													Brock, Troy H. [Son]

Name	Date	Age	Place 1	Place 2	Date 2	Father	Mother	Spouse	Relations	Relations	Relations	Relations	Cemetery
Brock, David Eugene	Mar 30, 2000	31	Knoxville, Tn	Seagus, Calif	Sep 11, 1968	Brock, Monroe	Caldwell, Nettie	Rickard, Tracy				Chassidy-Tennah-Tiffany-Miranda-Devin [Children]	J.M.G.
Brock, Nettie	Oct 31, 1996	62	J.S.H.	Helen Co., Ky	Nov 19, 1923	Caldwell, Jack	Mosley, Mollie	Ng	Martin, Grace- Greene, Mollie- Messey, Sue- Hammer, Faye &	Howard, Stella- Sprvirbs, Frances- Gibson, Dorothy- Kathhone- Sexton, Amanda	Waller- Charlee-Elmer	[Pals] Tohbl, Michael-Messey, Chris-Robert- Trujillo, Toby- Caldwell, Walter- Tony- Whitehead, John	J.G.
Brock, Tony Sr.	Feb 1, 1996	48	Jeff Co	Tn	Feb 5, 1937	Brock, Remus	Ng	Ng	Hargus, Karen	Tony-Dwayne-Billy	Henry	Hensley, Geraldine - [Pals] Hensley, Harold- Gass, Jerry- Snyder, Frank- Young, Frank- West, Paul - Fisher, Jim	Piney
Brock, Albert Calloway	Oct 7, 1994	58	J.M.H.	Tn	Nov, 1905	Brock, Fate	Miller, Rebeca	Lurie	[Shep] Gunn, Mrs. J.D.	[Shep] Jarnigan, Joe-Ray	Leon-Hubert- Gifford	Willie	New Market
Brock, Arthur E. Sr.	Dec 26, 1977	67	J.M.H.	Jeff Co	Apr 11, 1910	Brock, William L.	Snyder, Rachael	Bertie	Mc Millan, Mary Ruth - Roderick, Mable - Welch, Betty Jo - Mills, Juanita [D]	Arthur Jr. [Fla]- Ralph D.	C.H. [Nc]- Willie F.	Blue Springs	Blue Springs
Brooks, Ellie Belle	Jul 28, 1965	90	Strawberry Plains	Mascot, Tn	Mar 17, 1905	Stallings, James	Maples, Minnie	Brooks, Willie Francis [D]	Elmore, Ruby- Cook, Helen	Robert-Bobby- Franklin	Helen	Mc Campbells Chapel	Mc Campbells Chapel
Brooks, Frank	Mar 22, 1959		Jeff Co	Jeff Co		Brooks, Sam	Weyman, Sthel	Brooks, Luther	Davidson, Hazel Shelluck, Dorothy-Lee, Shirley	David B.	Martin, Genena	Roy	Pleasant Grove
Brooks, Imogene	Sep 13, 1906	81	Hill Haven	Jeff Co	Feb 13, 1906	Brock, Sam	Weyman, Sthel	Brooks, Luther	Harris, Mary [Ga]		Martin, Genena	Brooks, Charles [Toledo, OH]- [Pals] Solomon, Lloyd - Myers, Glenwood - Morgan, Bill - Robinson, Jay - Rangel, Tony Jr.	Strawberry Plains
Brooks, Jasper Eugene	Oct 12, 2000	80	Jeff City	Dandridge, Tn	Feb 21, 1920	Brock, Henry H.	Lemon, Mattie	S				[Pals] Griffey, James - Hicun, Burt-Jay - Roach, Deep-Dean Jr. - Mills, Mike	Wesleys Chapel
Brooks, Laura	Oct 27, 1999	82	Sneedville, Tn	New Market	Mar 1, 1910	Willard, Thomas	Willard, Mollie	Brooks, Leon [D]	Mc Bee, Leona	Billy Neal		Brooks, Laura - Duene - Brooks, Jay - Mildred - Rebba - Deep - Hensley, Denny	Pleasant Grove
Brooks, Leon	May 2, 1972		J.M.H.				Cross, Imilly	Laura	Mc Bee, Leona	Bill	Hubert	[Pals] Wellers, Bill - Young, Mack - Gunn, Carl - Leon-Jr. - Brown, Jim	New Market
Brooks, Lurlie Lee	Aug 22, 1982	91	Care Inn	Shady Grove, Tn	Jan 6, 1891	Lowery, Alexander	Cross, Imilly	Brooks, Albert C. [D]	Guinn, Mary E.	Jarnigan, Joe-Roy Jr.	Solomon, Molly	Pleasant Grove
Brooks, Luther Milton	Dec 15, 1973	70	Jeff Co	Tn	Jan 27, 1903	Brooks, William	Snyder, Rachael	Imogene	Davidson, Hazel [Fla] - Shelluck, Dorothy - Lee, Ruby	Edward-Dayton-David	Mc Ghon, Mrs. Jessie - Shillart, Emma [Ind]	New Market
Brooks, Mattie	Nov 8, 1954	90	Knox Co, Tn		Jan 8, 1864	Brooks, William	Snyder, Rachael	Imogene	Cook, Helen - Morgan, Mildred - Elmore, Ruby	Franklin-Robert- Bobby	Willie F. - Arthur-C.H. [Nc]	St. Pl.
Brooks, Willie F.	Jan 26, 1981	77	F.S.H.	Sevier Co	Oct 8, 1903		Stallings, Ellie Belle	Stallings, Ellie Belle	Franklin-Robert- Bobby			Brooks, Laura - [Pals] Morgan, Jay - Mitchell - Mc Campbells Chapel	[Willard Town] Pleasant Grove

Name	Death Date	Age	Place of Death	Residence	Birth Date	Father	Mother	Spouse	War	Children / Notes	Cemetery
Brodry, Joseph Anthony Jr.	Feb 15, 1999	70	Mt. Pleasant, Pa	White Pine, Tn	Apr 9, 1928	Brodry, Joseph A.	Helen	Cox, Jean	Navy	Patricia Ann - Goldie, Pamela Jo [St]; Joseph A. 3rd; Willie	Cremated - At Sea
Brown, Charles William	Jun 17, 1993	60	S.M.H.	White Pine, Tn	Apr 22, 1932	Brown, Henry	Jones, Mae	Cox, Jean		Ford, Sharon Dawn; William L.; [Pals] Parker, Gerald - Bobby - Steve - Victor - Hodge, Harold - Walbre, Tom	Mt. View
Brown, Hester	Oct 27, 1983	75	B.H.	Jeff Co	Aug 23, 1908	Parker, James B.	Brown, Florence	Div		Hodges, Guide - Parker, Jessie	Mill Springs
Brown, Jeanette	Nov 28, 1996	59	Blaine, Tn	Jeff Co	Feb 9, 1937	Smith, Robert	Lowery, Sarah	Brown, James Clarence		James Robert - Jerry Lynn - Clarance Donald - Daniel Glenn; Lowery, Irene - Cole, Nadine; Husband	Zion - Blount Co, Tn
Brown, Jeanette Walker	Feb 2, 1974	96	Florida		Jul 12, 1912	Brown, Tom		Brown, Thomas G. [D-1272]		Cox-Parker F.H. [Winter Park, Fla]	New Market
Brown, Maggie Lucille	Jan 19, 1997	84	Jeff City	Jeff Co	Aug 2, 1912	Edmonds, Susie		Brown, Mela [D]		Doug	Rays Chapel
Brown, Shirley Ann	Oct 11, 1998	54	New Market	Newport, Tn	Aug 2, 1944	Stewart, Ira		Brown, Edward		Hensley, Louise Quinn; Free, Maude	Mt. View
Brown, Thomas G.	Feb -, 1973	93	Orlando, Florida					Walker, Jeannette		Cox-Parker F.H. [Orlando, Fla]	New Market
Brown, William Clayton	Dec 30, 1974	35	Dayton, Ohio	Tn	Aug 12, 1939	Brown, John L.	Parker, Hester	Div		Henshall, Trena - Charles - Daniel; Valentine, Will - Crown, Ralph - Edward - Curtis Jo [CH]; Henshall, William Charles - Dewayne Edward - Curtis Jo [CH]; May, Jean - Mela - Gertrude - Helskey Grace - Greenlee, Maude - Young, Mary; Joe [D]-Buddy-Fred-James	Mill Springs
Brundige, Robert Henry	Feb 27, 1994	67	Des Moines, Iowa	J.M.H.	May 27, 1926	Brundige, William H.		Johnston, Dora Carolyn	WW 2	Charles Dale - Brian Thomas; Collins, Nettie - Blair, Rosa Lee - Hammond, Imogene	Summit F.H. [El Mirage, Az] Father	J.M.G.
Bruner, Infant Twins	Sept 18, 196		J.M.H.	J.M.H.	Sept 19, 196	Bruner, Edgar		Henderson, H.			J.M.G.
Bruner, Arley William	Nov 22, 1985	68	J.S.H.	Union Co, Tn	Jul 18, 1917	Bruner, Wert	Savage, Janie	Elmore, Ola Mae		Samuel Calvin; Wright, Wanda	Otter Springs - Mascot, Tn
Bryan, Fred R.	Oct 10, 1986	78	U.T.H.	Sevier Co	Feb 15, 1910			Odom, Mary Sue	WW 2	[Nieces] Carr, Elizabeth - Smith, Helen; [Nephew] Bryan, George L.	J.M.G.
Bryant, Earl Marcel	May 2, 1995	17	U.T.H.	Knoxville, Tn	Mar 20, 1978	Bryant, Burl H.	Mills, Barbara			See Obit	Bryant - Union Co, Tn
Bryant, Ronald Allen	Aug 25, 1996	18	Morristown, Tn	Knoxville, Tn	Apr 28, 1978	Boley, Alvin	Bryant, Virginia			None	Buffalo
Bryant, Sancho P. [Black]	May 19, 1979	67	U.T.H.	Knoxville, Tn	Mar 31, 1912	Bryant, Roy L.	McCowan, Elisy G.	Sancho Jr.		Phipps, Annie	Younger Memorial
Bushler, Scott Allen	Nov 24, 1997	55	New Market	Bay Shore, Ny	Feb 9, 1982	Bushler, Wayne	Dominguez, Rose Marie	Panequinno, Danielle		Zack, Rose Marie [Mother]	Cremated

Name	Date	Age	Place	Birth Date	Father	Mother	Spouse					Relatives	Burial
Bullion, Carroll E.	Sep 25, 1971	23				Bullion, Mc Kinley	Tolliver, Sue Ellen		Cline, Dot - John, Jo Anne		Jackie-Larry-Lynn	Bullion, Pryor [B-Father]	Courtney - Hawkins Co
Bullion, Michael	Sep 25, 1971	6w				Bullion, Carroll E.	Tolliver, Sue Ellen					Tolliver, Herman - Bullion, Mc Kinley [G-Parents] - Frt., M.B. [G-G-Parents]	Courtney - Hawkins Co
Bullion, Sue Ellen	Sep 25, 1971	18			Tolliver, Herman		Bullion, Carroll E.			Sandra	Jackie-Larry-Lynn	Parents - Tolliver, Mary - Burchett, John [G-Parents]	Courtney - Hawkins Co
Bumgarner, James Lester	Jan 23, 2000	82	Rutledge, Tn	Nov 11, 1917	Bumgarner, Lee	Div			Gowen, Hazel [Nd] - Roberts, Myrtle [Od] Paul [Nd]-Guy [Nd]-Carroll [Od]		Emil-Wallace-Freman-Paul	Reichmann - Cocke Co.
Bunch, Herman Charles	Mar 11, 1974	72	Jeff Co.	Nov 3, 1901	Bunch, Charles	Moody, Hattie	Div				Nickey, Nell - Hyde, Velma, Nell - Pertree, Helen	Willis	New Market
Bunch, Lawrence Eance	Dec 7, 1988	67	F.S.H.	Jan 1, 1921	Bunch, Sherion P.	Jones, Bonnie			Jack-Steve-Joe			Wife	Mill Springs
Bunch, Rose	Dec 12, 1983	70	Buffalo, Ny	Mar 12, 1913	Jeffrey, John	Virginia		Bunch, Herman [Joe - D]				Moody, Lawrence - Bunch, Elizabeth F. [Buffalo, Ny]	New Market
Burchell, Donald Ray	Dec 2, 1975	18	Knox Co.	Feb 11, 1959	Burchell, Ray	S					Wadell, Jane & Chester Jr.	Parents	J.M.G.
Burchell, Henry Lee	May 25, 1986	76	Grainger Co.	Aug 3, 1909	Burchell, Henry	Lizzie	Mc Daniel, Mary Lou		Hazel, Leona - Matheney, Betty - Carr, Beatrice - Elmore, Virginia		Ward, Helen	Kenneth	Sunderland
Burchell, Mary Lou	Dec 11, 1990	81	Jeff City	Sep 17, 1909	Mc Daniel, Pies	Morgan, Nola	Burchell, Henry [D]		Matheney, Betty - Leonard, Hazel - Carr, Beatrice - Elmore, Virginia			Sunderland
Burgin, George Edward	Sep 25, 1991	62	White Pine, Tn	Sep 8, 1929	Burgin, L.G.	Voiles, Elisabeth	Anderson, Mary		Katy-Patsy - Mc Intosh, Linda		Harrell, Mary	Monroe-Eugene-Joseph-Vernon-Bobby	Blue Springs
Burkhart, Albert Mayford	Dec 23, 1997	83	Knoxville, Tn	May 9, 1914	Burkhart, Albert M. Sr.	Chenoweth, Grace Alma	Morgan, Pearl		Larson, Nancy [OH] - Framingler, Carol [Kansas] - Mennon, Judy [OH] - Williams, Leanna [Nd]		Elppert, Mildford [Pa]	Kenneth-Clifford	J.M.G.
Burnette, Imogene	Jan 22, 1996	69	Knoxville, Tn		Hulbert, Tom	Glass, Mabel	Burnette, J.B.		Denton, Sharon Grace	Randal	Swaggerty, Grace	Wife	Strawberry Plains
Burnette, Ronald Stephen	Apr 30, 1950	1d	Jeff City		Burnette, J.B.	Hulbert, Imogene						Husband - (Pete) Dillard, James - Mc Coll, Wayne - Newman, Alben - Stooksbury, Hugh - Carr, Cloy - Turner, Charlie	New Market
Buser, Lillian	Dec 14, 1959	65	M.C.	Tn	Mc Bride, Brazell	Tryon, Emma						J.F.-J.C.	Father	Dutch, W. Va
Byrd, Abe	May 2, 1977	66	F.S.H.	Oct 30, 1910	Byrd, James L.	Phillips, Hattie	Hammer, Ruby		Profitt, Velma - Roach, Aileen		Morgan, Hazle	Lawrence-Lester	Willis	New Market
Byrd, Dwight Allen	Apr 3, 1998	65	B.H.	Nov 21, 1932	Byrd, Howard H.	Bright, Rose	Burnette, Marietta	Navy	Delora M. [Sally]	James E - Lloyd	Rickert, John	Axel, Mildred [Nd] - Degroe, Ann [Oh]	Bradley, Mrs. Grady	Henderson	East View

Name	Date	Age	Place 1	Place 2	Date 2	Father		Mother		Spouse						Burial
Byrd, Howard William	Oct 16, 1995	81	Knoxville, Tn	Nc	Sep 25, 1904	Byrd, Stan		Byrd, Anna		Bright, Rose [D]			Byrd, Henderson			[Pals] Johnson, Leonard - Denning, Jack - Hammar, Jack - Woods, Rick - Byrd, Ronald	Greenwood - Knoxville, Tn
Byrd, James Lawrence	Oct 6, 1979	59	J.M.H.	Nc	May 10, 1920	Byrd, James		Phillips, Hattie		Hammon, Georgia			Eddie-Lonnie-Benny-Roger	Lester	[Pals] Korn, Larry - Hammar, Ralph Jr. - Byrd, Lloyd - Eugene-Mike - Morgan, Junior	J.M.G.
Byrd, Rose Matilda	Oct 23, 1981	70	Greenville, Tn		Feb 10, 1911	Bright, George		Yoiell, R. Matilda		Byrd, Howard			Oxer, Mitford - Hoskins, Pearl	Dwight A.- Henderson	Mother - [Pals] Mieells, Ralph Jr. - Monroe, Cottis - Reech, Dwain - Griffey, Ed-Rick- Steve-Ruble-Alvin	Greenwood - Knoxville, Tn
Cadle, James Michael	Feb 7, 1991	37	Hollywood, Calif.	Jeff City	Sep 12, 1953	Cadle, John		Griffey, Elizabeth		Div				Johnson, Hazel C.	Wife - [Pk-S] Johnson, J.R. - Cadle, Bill - Griffey, Steve-Rick-Alvin-Don- Junior	J.M.G.
Cadle, John Cecil	Jan 31, 1994	70	F.S.H.	Fork Ridge, Tn	Oct 10, 1923	Cadle, James F.		Hurst, Melissa		Griffey, Elizabeth				Johnson, Hazel C.	[Pals] Cameron, Allen-Danny - Pierce, L.E. - Seale, Don - Reposs, P.V.	J.M.G.
Cadle, Ruby	Nov 14, 1994	74	Dandridge, Tn	Union Co	Oct 3, 1910	Harron, Hubert Sr.		Berry, Mary		Cadle, Alfred		Cameron, Anna Mae & George - Nutting, Wanda & Wendall	Seale, Edith - Herron, Lorene	Find-Thurman- Clarence- Oscar-Carroll		Strawberry Plains
Cadle, Betty Lois	Apr 4, 1999	66	B.H.	Greenville, Tn	Jun 23, 1932	Leonard, M.F.		Deen, Leona		Cadle, James - [D]	Evelyn [D]	Eddie & Angelia- Boone-Kenneth [Step] Bartes, Bobby & Debbie	Glenn, Mary - Poe, Anna Belle	Father		Strawberry Plains
Cain, Bryant Allen	Apr 21, 1995	43	J.M.H.	J.M.H.	Nov 12, 1955	Cain, John Robert	Tn	Leonard, Betty		Cain, Angela		Mindy	John-Jacob	[1/2] Banks, Bobby & Deborah	Father	East View
Cain, Eddie Lee	Jun 24, 1999	43	Jeff City	Jeff City		Cain, Jimmy Larry [Age-28]	Tn	Wonda Faye [Age-24]		Cain, Angela						Strawberry Plains
Cain, Hazel	Oct 3, 1987	77	New Market, Tn	Grainger Co	Jul 30, 1910	Shockley, John		Morgan, Hattie Bell		Cain, Buford		Davis, Peggy- Poore, Betty- Buckner, Shirley & Freeman	Brady, Ruth	Atkridge, Howard-Jackie- Arthur-Dexter- Clifford	[Pals] Cain, Jim- Berry, Jim - Jett, Terry - Buckner, Tim-Jeff - Davis, Greg & Bradley- Wayne	J.M.G.
Cain, Hazel Virginia	Nov 11, 1994	75	Strawberry Plains	Jeff Co	Apr 25, 1909	Bates, Leland		Boyd, Emma		Cain, Carl E. [D]			Adkins, Helen	Sister		Nances, Grove
Cain, Herbert	Oct 3, 1998	75	J.M.H.	Jeff Co	Mar 9, 1913	Cain, Edd		Elmore, Rebecca		Norton, Mattie	Nc	Sams, Anna Lou	Greenes, Bonnie- Humbard, Dorothy- Russell, Merris	Ralph-Bill	Willie	Friends Station
Cain, Infant Female	Jan 11, 1959		Jeff Co	Jeff Co	Jan 11, 1959	Cain, John R.	Tn	Leonard, Betty	Nc					Father		Strawberry Plains
Cain, Infant Female	Jun 14, 1954	66	Straw Plains	Ky	Aug 4, 1877	Cain, Daniel		Holt, Jennie		Lora L.				Willie		Strawberry Plains
Cain, Jacob Calvin	Jul 2, 1985	59	S.M.H.	Strawberry Plains	Aug 29, 1934	Cain, Jacob Calvin		Hill, Evelyn		Leonard, Betty	unk	Evelyn	Daniel B.- Kenneth F.- Eddie L.-Bobby Ray	Stipes, Gladys - Bailey, Mary Ellen	Jimmy-Tommy	[Pals] Breden, Denis - William, Max - Fultz, Ron - James- Sam - Eldridge, Junior - Edmunds, Dewey	Strawberry Plains

Name	Death Date	Age	Place	County	Birth Date	Father		Mother	Spouse						Cemetery
Cain, Lora L.	Aug 22, 1994	84	S.M.H.	Union Co.	Jun 2, 1910	Fultz, James		Cook, Rachael V.	Cain, Jake [D]	Mary Ellen	Jim-Tom E.	Pollard, Bea - Henry, Elizabeth	Jack Jr. [TA]- Bill [list]-John [list]-Frank	Son - [Pals] Cloninger, Dale - Cain, Ronald- Cain, James - Tolliver, Kyle	Strawberry Plains
Cain, Lula Mae	Apr 28, 1973	39	Knox Co	Tn	Nov 28, 1933	Young, Jack Sr.		Buckman, Cora	Cain, Robert Jr.	Cindy	Ruety-Ricky	Prince, Barbara Jean - Peterman, Jo Ann	Remus	Husband	Friends Station
Cain, Mahala Evelyn	Nov 12, 1984	74	J.M.H.	Knox Co	May 5, 1910	Sellers, Edd		Evans, Tennessee	Cain, Ralph Sr.	Cheryle-Donald- Jim	Ruety-Ricky	Sanders, Larry - Hutchinson, Irene		Wife - [Pals] Lynn, Catherine - Nutt, David - Franklin, Robert - Prince, George - Fultz, James - Gann, Frank	Friends Station
Cain, Ralph Wade	Aug 7, 1977	42	Jeff Co	Tn	Dec 6, 1934	Cain, Ralph Sr.	Tn	Wadek, Ann	Sellers, -		Douglas, Imogene - Haverly, Elsie	Douglas, Imogene [DN] - Haverly, Elsie	Claude-Donald- Jimmy		
Cain, Ralph Woods [Rubber Jaw]	Aug 3, 1998	87	Jeff City	New Market	Feb 4, 1909	Cain, Edd		Elmore, Jane Rebecca	Sellers, Mahala		Douglas, Imogene- Haverly, Elsie	Claud-Donald- Jim - Ralph Wade [Scoot-D]	Green, Bonnie - Humbard, Dorothy - Russell, Martha	Cain, Herbert - [Pals] Claude G.- Jackie G.- Rance G.- Russell, Eddie - Green, Joe	
Cain, Ruby	Apr 22, 1975	84	J.M.H.	Tn	Feb 6, 1911	Cain, Ed		Elmore, Rebecca	S		Pocza, Betty- Buckner, Shirley - Davis, Peggy	Greene, Bonnie - Humbard, Dorothy - Russell, Martha		Buckner, Jeff-Tam- Davis, Greg - Cain, Jim - Russell, Jack	Friends Station
Cain, William Buford	May 13, 1987	83		Tn	Aug 16, 1903	Cain, Ed		Elmore, Rebecca	Newman, Kizy			Greene, Bonnie - Humbard, Dorothy - Russell, Martha	Ralph - Herbert - Edd	[Pals] Herbert - Claude G.- Ralph Sr.- Edd	J.M.G.
Caldwell, Charles Thomas	Nov 12, 1984	89	Hillcrest N.H.	Tn	Nov 17, 1874	Caldwell, Sam		Rush, Cora	Caldwell, Charles T.		Minnie, Blanche R.	Lucy E. - Manston, Mrs. Charles - Manston, Mrs. Charles	Husband	Talley, Alice	New Market
Caldwell, Cora L.	Sep 27, 1954	80	New Market	Tn	Apr 6, 1873	Rush, Henry		Caldwell, Charles T.					Fred C.	Husband	New Market
Caldwell, Faye V.	Mar 13, 1957	79	M.C.	Tn	Dec 19, 1877	Caldwell, David M.E.	Tn	Johnson, Mary					Fred C.	Caldwell, Ralph	New Market
Caldwell, Lucy E.	Mar 11, 1982	86	U.T.H.	Tn	Feb 27, 1876	Carroll, Will	Tn	Northam, Mary		Tn				Doug - [Pals] Calloway, Paul Jr.- Vineyard, J.P.- Ramsey, Paul- Don-Jim	New Market
Calloway, Bessie Dollie	Jan 2, 1988	83	F.S.H.	Jeff Co	Jan 21, 1904	Fielden, Arlie		Foster, Mamie	Calloway, Ralph [D]		Charon, Amani- Leonra, Lorena	Elsie - Nickey, Grace - Nance, Helen	Earnest	Doug - [Pals] Calloway, Paul Jr.- Vineyard, J.P.- Ramsey, Paul- Don-Jim	Indian Ridge - Vineyard, J.P.- Ramsey, Paul- Donald-Jimmy
Calloway, Claudine	Jan 28, 2000	87	F.S.H.	Knox Co	Jul 28, 1912	Calloway, James A.		Mitchell, Lissie	Calloway, Ralph [D]		Martin, Dottie		Flynn, Dorothy	Martin, Dottie	Indian Ridge
Calloway, Hugh James	Jun 17, 1992	88	Knox Co	Rutledge, Tn	Aug 26, 1903	Calloway, James A.		Mitchell, Lissie	Leo H. [D]			James Allen	Flynn, Dorothy		Indian Ridge
Calloway, Jewell	May 4, 1992	77	Morristown, Tn	Grainger Co	Oct 26, 1914	Moody, Gorace C.		Cameron, Harriett	Calloway, Charles			Bobby		Husband- Calloway, R.C.- Hammer, Dallas - Atkins, M.L.- Husband- Calloway, R.C.- [Son]- [Pals] Turley, Ray - Atkins, M.L.- Hammer, Dallas - Vineyard, J.P.- Ramsey, Paul- Elmore, Barry	J.M.G.
Calloway, Joe Alfred	Jan 16, 1987	86	S.M.H.	Grainger Co	Mar 10, 1900	Calloway, James Alford		Mitchell, Lessie	Carroll, Bessie		Calloway, Charles			Charon, Amanell & Von D. [Niece]- Moody, Horace	Indian Ridge

Name	Death Date	Age	Place of Death	Birthplace	Birth Date	Father	Mother	War/Status	Spouse	Children	Grandchildren/Daughters	Sisters	Brothers	Relation	Cemetery
Calloway, John Isaac	Dec 19, 1977	85	J.M.H.	Grainger Co.	Jun 19, 1892	Calloway, Jim	Mitchell, Lissie	W		Cochran, Ruby & Chester Allin, Herb & Susie - Ballinger, Marie & Clifford	Ralph-Charlie-John Jr.	Vineyard, Mrs. Pres	Frank-Joe-Hugh		J.M.G.
Calloway, Mary Elsie	Mar 21, 1999	89	Jeff City	New Market	Feb 12, 1910	Carroll, William	Northern, Mary		Calloway, William Frank [D]			Nance, Helen - Nunley, Grace	John		Indian Ridge
Calloway, Ralph James	Dec 20, 1991	75	J.M.H.	New Market	Oct 16, 1916	Calloway, John	Davis, Edna	WW 2	Martin, Dottie	Paul & Opal		Cochran, Ruby - Elmore, Marie - Atkins, Helen	John Jr.- Charles		J.M.G.
Calloway, William T. Sr.	Jan 31, 1979	65	Nashville, Tn	New Market			Arnold, Anna Laura		Cartwright, Pam [K] - Wright, Alma [K]	W.T. Jr.-John [Aig]-Walter		Howard, Larry- Rod-Edwin - Miller, George - McClain, Willie - Nance, Harold			Nances Grove
Cameron, Eula Mae	Apr 1, 1976	48	J.M.H.		Apr 15, 1927	Cameron, W.B.	Berry, Hessie	S		Eula Mae [D] - Lowry, Esther & Ernie - Green, Juanita	James Allen				Little Flat Creek
Cameron, Hassie Melinda	Mar 22, 1996	96	Dandridge, Tn	Union Co.	Apr 18, 1899	Berry, Andy	Wyrick, Mary Ann	S		Von [D]-Leland & Delores			Mother		
Cameron, James Oscar	Jul 20, 1999	82	Jeff City		Jun 15, 1937	Cameron, Lee	Mc Carter, Barbara		Cameron, Allin [D]	Donald-Gary & Linda	Harville, Easter	Robert			J.M.G.
Cameron, John Arthur	Jul 3, 1989	33	Talbott, Tn	Jeff Co	Jul 17, 1955	Cameron, Manuel A.	Gibbons, Irene	S			Vance, Mae Belle - Bales, Mary - Katherine - Bales, Shirley	Sister [Pals] Cameron, Don - Wolfe, George - Everhart, Greg - Breeden, John - Lowry, Grant - Norton, James			J.M.G.
Cameron, Kenneth James	Dec 30, 1981	47	J.M.H.	Jeff Co	Jun 14, 1934	Cameron, Lee	Rosie		Hazelwood, Linda		Miller, Lou Ella - Chambers, Sonnie - Simms, Elsie - Guinn, Willie Mae - Harvell, Easter	James-Robert - Cameron, Donnie - Williams, Thomas - Donnie - Lawson, Loona			Mt. Pleasant
Cameron, Manuel Arthur	May 27, 1987	76	Humana Hosp	Jeff Co	Mar 2, 1911	Cameron, War E.	Nolan, Elizabeth						French, Elizabeth [Pals] Brendon, John-Jim-Yance, David-Courtney, Charles - Everhart, Greg		J.M.G.
Cameron, Reginald James	May 6, 1999	31	Rutledge, Tn	Jeff Co	Jul 1, 1967	Cameron, Ronnie James	Mc Vey, Margaret			Reginald-James Jr.-[Skeg] Humbard, Frank-James	Angie E.-Precious E.-Lessen		Cameron, W. Louise [G-Mother]		J.M.G.
Cameron, Vaughn DeLone	Jul 20, 1981	60		Knox Co	May 25, 1921	Cameron, W.B.	Berry, Hessie	WW 2	Bailey, Louise		Lowry, Ester-Green, Juanita-Bourff, Minnie	Leland-Sam-Hugh	[Pals] Cameron, Steve-J.C.-Thomas-David - Lowry, Earnest-Freshie		Hamblen Memorial
Campbell, Cecil L [F]	Oct 7, 1973	72	Jeff Co	Tn	Mar 11, 1901	Campbell, William C.	Meadows, Margaret		Campbell, James A.	Margaret - Gray, James-Ruby	James W.-Ralph- Hugh-John	Robinson, Daisy- Johnson, Edith [Pals]	Eugene-Arthur- King	Husband	Corinth - Loudon Co

Name	Death Date	Age	Place of Death	Funeral Home	County	Birth Date	Father	Mother	Spouse	War / Notes	Daughters	Sons	Sisters / Relatives	Brothers / Pallbearers	Cemetery
Campbell, Charles Amos (Tommy)	May 31, 1993	56	Knoxville, Tn	New Market		Jan 19, 1937	Campbell, Porter	Pitts, Beulah	Whitehead, Virginia [DM]	S	Davis, M. Geneva - Mott, Margaret - Jessie, Betty Ruth	John - James	Doug	[Pals] Holloway, Gary - Hubbard, Lester - Williams, Erley - Cammon - Ellis - Watkins, Tom - Johnson, Ralph	Flat Gap
Campbell, Earl Eugene	Mar 6, 1995	63	Knoxville, Tn	J.M.H.	Elizabethton, Tn	Dec 2, 1931	Campbell, Ralph	Carden, Ida		Korea	Crouch, Kin			Doug	J.M.G.
Campbell, James Abraham	Sep 27, 1979	83		J.M.H.	Giles Co	Sep 18, 1886	Campbell, Samuel A.	Eely, Hanna	Black, Cecil		Margaret - Young, Ruby	John James - Ralph Hugh	Newton, Sandra - Ford, Ruby	David - John - Hubert	City - Loudon, Tn
Campbell, Joseph	Dec 15, 1966	70	Strawberry Plains			Unk	Unk	Unk	Unk	S	17-19	S		V.A.	Piney
Campbell, Luke Levi	Apr 26, 1973	70		J.M.H.	Tn	Jan 28, 1903	Campbell, William	Smith, Cora	Payne, Ollie		Province, Marie	Bud - A.W.	Finchum, Minnie - Trout, Anna Lee - Deatherage, Mary; Bill - Don	Campbell, Luther [Son]; [Pals] Province, Bill - Province, Larry - Owens, Robert - Mark - Glenn, Scott	J.M.G.
Campbell, Ollie L.	Jan 10, 1967	78		J.M.H.	Tn	Jan 28, 1908	Payne, Luther	Hines, Jennie	Campbell, Luke L. [D]		Province, Marie	Bud - A.W.	Finchum, Minnie - Trout, Anna Lee - Deatherage, Mary; Bill - Don	Wife	J.M.G.
Campbell, Van Robert	Sep 13, 1981	82	New Market	Cocke Co		Aug 21, 1899	Campbell, Elex	Breeden, Mate	Ng		Cannon, Violet				Creech Chapel
Cannon, Beatrice Kaye	Apr -, 1967	18	New Market				Cannon, Robert	Cannon, Violet					Rowlett, Pauline [Cal]	Johnson, Walter J. - Cochran, Ben F. [G-Fathers]	Lebanon
Cannon, Luella May	Jul 25, 1965	89		S.M.H.	Tn	Nov 10, 1875	Lyle, John	Newman, Margret	Cannon, Robert V.				Miller, Mrs. R.B. - Garber, Mrs. John	Cannon, Cecil	Mt. View
Cannon, Mack Lawson Cecil	Feb 21, 1973	59	Jeff City		Tn	Feb 1, 1914	Cannon, Robert	Lyle, Mae	Cannon, Robert [D]		Cecil	Welch, Mrs. Lloyd - Knight, Mrs. Haynes	Welch, Edna - Knight, Rowena	Cannon, Cecil	J.M.G.
Cannon, Mina Erskine	Oct 28, 1999	82		S.M.H.	Talbott, Tn	Oct 28, 1917	Quarles, William E.	Watkins, Trophia	Cannon, Cecil [D]		Daniel [Ind] - Wendell	Cannon, Wendell	Cannon, Diary & Kitty		J.M.G.
Cantrell, Mattie M.	Sep 12, 1985	92	Troublesome, Ky			Apr 17, 1893	McDaniel, Robert	Terry, Suddy	Cantrell, John [S]		Sweeten, Janie			[Pals] Quinn, Jimmy - Riley, Jody - Riley, Bradley - James - Collins, Benny - Ean	Indian Ridge - Blaine, Tn
Caruthers, George Harold	Oct 24, 1988	55		J.M.H.	Jeff Co	Sep 26, 1933	Caruthers, George Holly	Jones, Ida Mae	Ballinger, Helen			George Jr.	Leslie [Mo] - Ed - Gene [Ala] - Sam	[Pals-G-Sons-Step-G-Sons] Hall, Danny - Parkison, Dennis - Gray, Jack - Watson, Darrel - Ballinger, Jim - Ron; Father - Cato, Tom - Smith, Cecil [G-Fathers]	Pleasant Grove
Care, Cynthia Jane	Apr 27, 1973	0				Apr 27, 1973	Cate, Thomas Richard Jr.	Smith, Wanda Faye [Age 16]							Cato
Carl, Mary Edna Kooch	Dec 5, 1991	87	Mascot, Tn	J.M.H.		Jun 2, 1904	Nos, Frank	Roach, Themla	Carl, R.H.		Lowery, Louise - Porter, Elizabeth - Wright, Mary - Nell - Wichner, Addie	William - Thomas - Bennie C. - Kenneth W. - Roland Marion	M.T.	Husband - [Pals] Nos, Ken - Kooch, Ken - Jeff - Lehr, Tom - Wright, Mike - Porter, Carl	New Market
Carman, Patsy Maxine	Jan 27, 1995	47	Knoxville, Tn	J.M.H.			Martin, Mack Preston	Riley, Gladys Genevieve	Carman, Harold			Connie Star	Manley, Caroline Val	Wood, Earl - Martin, Tony [D] - Marlin, Drury; Harold	Hillcrest
Carmichael, Charles Floyd	Oct 28, 1991	90	Sevier Co	J.M.H.		Sep 20, 1901	Carmichael, John D.	Ellis, May	French, Sally				Joslin, Dora		U.T. Memphis

Name	Date	Age	Place	County/Place	Date	Father	Mother	Spouse						Cemetery
Carnes, George Washington	Jan 28, 1986	70	S.M.H.	Knoxville, Tn	Apr 27, 1917	Carnes, Dock	Collins, Mary Jane	Thrasher, Hazel	WW 2				Howard	Piney
Carpenter, Mell Dona	Jan 22, 1982	94	Dandridge, Tn	Pulaski, Va	Nov 21, 1887	Lester, Johnson A.	Boyd, Virginia	Carpenter, T.C. [D]					Lee, Mrs. Fred L. (Neva); Lee, Mrs. Fred L. - Gene - Glenn; Davy - Carol; Terry - Russell; Oliver	West View
Carr, Artie	Feb 8, 1979	68	Strawberry Plains	Sevier Co	Jul 19, 1910	Carr, John	Sevier Co	Trotham, Mary	Quillians, -		McMahan, Gladys - Nations, Bess (½)		Herman	Strawberry Plains
Carr, Bessie Gladys	Feb 23, 1975		J.M.H.	Granger Co	Feb 26, 1904	Roach, Derek	Byrd, Rachael A.	Carr, George William [D]		Lowe, Nettie Pearl - Moore, Mary - Scarlett, Sarah	Russell, Mrs. Hugh P. - Ackley, Sarah (Cal)	Frank [Cal]	[Pals] Scarlett, Velma - Stephs, Bruce - Shelton, William, Eastinger, Alger - Courtney, Hugh	Sunderland
Carr, Billy P.	Feb 19, 1986	62	Knoxville	Knoxville	Jan 21, 1936	Carr, William Levi	Cook, Leona Belle	Div		Stamm, Sherry - Lee, Sandy - Hicks, Sandra [Ind]	Billy	3	1	Bookwalter
Carr, Charles Ray	Oct 19, 1981	69	Maryville, Tn	Sevier Co	Jan 7, 1912	Carr, Marion	Maples, Rosan	w	WW 2		Huff, Rose - Moore, Lydia - Morelli, Fred - Jernigan, Harold -Green, Neil	T.N.-Richard-Mitchell	Wife - [Pals] Bates, Don - Bayles, Jeff - Maples, Carl - Roach, Fred - Maples, Fred - Kinder, Robert - Jeffers, Jim	Mt. View
Carr, John Newton	Apr 19, 1991	82	U.T.H.	Gatlinburg, Tn	Apr 11, 1909	Carr, Nicholas	Owmby, Litha	Myers, Lithia	[In-Law] Elly	John N.	Green, Cora - Paschal, Martha	Ezra	Wife - [Pals] Bates, Don - Bayles, Jeff - Maples, Carl - Roach	J.M.G.
Carr, Audrey C.	May 27, 1996	69	New Market, Tn	Alabama	Nov 26, 1897			Carroll, Mack Conklin				Husband	Pleasant Grove
Carroll, Clarence Arcil	May 11, 1979	76	New Market, Tn	Northern, Nannie	Apr 7, 1903			Foster, Mae [D]		Haworth, Juanita (Carl)			[Pals] Ballinger, C.R.-Kemp-Charles - Waldroyp, Bob - Albaugh, Old	Pleasant Grove
Carroll, Jerry Marshall	Sep 1, 19-	12	Pontiac, Mich		Dec 23, 1975	Carroll, Jerry	Lowe, Sue	S					Voorhees-Spite F.H. (Pontiac, Mich) - Father	Beech Springs - Kodak, Tn
Carroll, Mack	Oct 14, 1971	73	Knoxville, Tn	Tn	Jul 8, 1898							[Step] 1	[Pals] Bauer - Eidd-Kerry-Kenny (Nephews)	Pleasant Grove
Carroll, Pearl	Dec 11, 1994	93	Jeff City	New Market	Nov 3, 1901	Northern, Adam	Talley, Anna				Ballinger, Myrtie - Fielden, Margaret - [Step] 5		Jones, Elaine (Nana)	Mill Springs
Carroll, Thomas	Oct 12, 1986	63	S.M.H.	New Market	Apr 1, 1923	Carroll, Dewey	Laymon, Julie	S		Carroll, Ross [D]	[1/2] Bolin, Rosa - Ward, Imogene	Carroll, Willis - [1/2] Ozmn, Lee	Carroll, Willis - [Uncle] - [Pals] Nance, Harold - Carroll, Ernest [Uncle] - L.C. - Carroll, Jr.- Charles - Mc Daniel, Roy	Oakland

Name	Date	Age	FH	Location	Birth Date	Father	Mother	Cemetery
Carroll, William Clarkie	Jun 2, 1999	61		Rutledge, Tn				J.M.G.
Carroll, Willis Dee	Jun 1, 1997	69	J.M.H.	New Market	May 15, 1938	Carroll, Charles S.	Smith, Hattie	Mill Springs
Carson, Earl Jones	Sep 2, 1998	62		Sevierville, Tn	May 16, 1926	Carson, Herbert	Jones, Bertie Mae	Phillips - Bulls Gap, Green Co
Carson, Lillian Frances	Mar 1, 1982	55	J.M.H.	Jeff City	Aug 6, 1925	James, Louis F. Sr.	Milksalik, Mary	J.M.G.
Carson, Minnie Rosaline	Jul 25, 1998	82		Jeff City	Dec 27, 1915	Prince, James R.	Blackson, Addie Potter	West View
Carter, Alice Corene	Dec 28, 1999	85	J.M.H.	Lincoln Co. Tn	Apr 9, 1914	Posey, Jim	Webb, Willie	
Carter, Eli Henderson	Feb 3, 1998	71	J.M.H.	Knoxville, Tn	Dec 17, 1924	Carter, William H.	Johnson, Margaret	Beaver Creek
Carter, Lillie Ruth	Oct 6, 1976	50	F.S.H.	Jeff Co	Dec 26, 1925	Theodore, Joseph C. [Dock]	James, Flora M.	Piney
Carter, Mary Elizabeth	Feb 7, 1997	73	New Market	Strawberry Plains	Jul 3, 1923	Laudendale, Elmer	Pierces, Pearl	Beaver Creek
Carter, Nola Lee	Aug 17, 1995	65	J.M.H.	Talbot, Tn	Aug 30, 1929	Bacon, Howard	Lilly, Mary	Eden
Carton, Sarah Dustle	Jan 29, 1995	82		Anderson Co. Tn	Mar 3, 1913	Raby, Austin Green	Ray, Rachael	J.M.G.
Carton, Ralph Raymond	Jul 17, 1992	70	M.C.		Feb 3, 1922	French, Ruth		J.M.G.
Case, Eddie Wayne	Jun 3, 2000	42	Monroe, Ohio		Apr 26, 1958	Case, Paul	Caughron, Wanda	Hills Union
Case, Larry Eugene	Apr 25, 1999	40	Church Hill, Tn	Jeff City	Nov 19, 1958	Case, Robert E.	Gray, Wilma E.	J.M.G.
Case, Wilma L. Billie	Nov 23, 1993	60	J.M.H.	Jeff City	Nov 13, 1933	Gray, Buford	Cockburn, Blanche	Pleasant Grove
Case, Cecil Montgomery	Sep 9, 1987	58	B.H.	Jeff Co	Dec 8, 1928	Cate, Arthur	Wolford, Mae	Pleasant Grove
Case, Lissie T.	Apr 5, 2000	87	New Market	Jeff Co	Dec 25, 1912	Lindsey, Albert	Bailey, Molly M.	Pollards
Cate, Ollie L.	Feb 6, 1980	79	J.M.H.	New Market	May 12, 1900	Elmore, W.W.		Pleasant Grove
Cate, Thomas Richard Sr.	Nov 29, 1992	69	J.M.H.	Dumplin Valley	Aug 6, 1923	Cate, Tilman	Fielden, Sarah Elizabeth	Cate - Dandridge, Tn

Name	Date	Age			Date								
Cate, William Mc Kinley	Jan 18, 1904	96	New Market, Tn	Knox Co, Tn	Mar 19, 1897	Cate, Lon	Smith, Mollie	Elmore, Ollie [D]	Poore, Pauline - Cureton, Frye - Cate, Ruth - Wolfe, Rozella [Nc] - Schultz, Jo	Ray Jack-Sidney Gerald		Son - [Pals] Cate, Cureton-Cory-Rick-Chris-Tony-Chris - Aundel, Ron	Pleasant Grove
Caudill, Roy	Mar 27, 1996	72	U.T.H.	Edin, Ky	Jan 8, 1924	Caudill, William	Bowman, Margie N.		Wilson, Barbara Ann		Wilkey, Gladys		Hiram Of Rest - Letcher, Ky
Chambers, Dorothy Elizabeth	Sep 17, 1999	66	J.M.H.	Chestnut Hill, Tn	Dec 12, 1932	Chambers, Walter	Henry, Ellen	S	Chambers, Douglas-Ray-James Sonny [Park]		Stidham, Gabrielle C. - Smith, Barbara Jane - Strange, Mildred - Dungan, Hazel - Davis, Anna Mae [Oh]	Roger-Pat-Coy	Hills Union
Chambers, Delma Ellen	Feb 23, 1983	81	Talbott, Tn	Sevierville, Tn	Nov 26, 1911	Henry, William D.	Fincham, Ethel	Chambers, Walter [J]	Sandra-Dorothy-Smith, Barbara - Mott, Dora - Strange, Mildred - Dungan, Hazel - Davis, Anna	Roger-Pubk-Ray-Floyd-Edd	O' Dell, Josie Lee - Forest, Aileen - Larbotte, Sue	Sandra	Hills Union
Chambers, Eugene F.	May 5, 1977	88	Morristown, Tn	Knox Co, Tn	Sep 10, 1908	Chambers, Isaac T.	Williams, Ida	Neal [Ind] -Robert	Zane, Marjorie [G] Grimes, Lynn - Zane - Enid, Donna Zane	Ray		Wilie	Valley View
Chambers, James Walter	May 25, 1978	75	Tn		Sep 16, 1903	Chambers, Bill	Layman, Betty	Ellen	Dorothy-Sandra-Styawaka, Hazel [Oh] - Strange, Mildred - Davis, Anna Mae ? [Oh] - Smith, Barbara - Mott, Dora	Edward-Floyd- Roger-Ray-Sonny	Dockery, Martha - O' Dell, Lockie	Wilie - [Pals] Chambers, J.L.- Von-J.P.-R.A.- Dockery, Robert - O' Dell, Ray	Hills Union
Chambers, Julia	Jan 11, 1971			Tn	Oct 25, 1886	Reac	Manning, Annie	Ng					Batch
Chambers, Margaret Doris Turk [Black]	Oct 27, 1981	69	J.M.H.	Tn	Sep 10, 1912	Wm. G.	Falls, Iva	Ng		Robert Jr.	Mc Farland, Anna Bell	Roger Ray-George-Douglas-John- Cunningham, R. Jr. - Brazelton, J.L. - Gilbert - Davis, Eugene - Phipps, Leroy	Batch
Chambers, Mary Adelia	Jun 13, 1989	81	S.M.H.	New Market	May 26, 1908	Bull, W.M. Sr.	Wolford, Nora Martha	Ng	Horner, Marjorie		Wilson, Kate - Doyle, Connie	Doug [Pals] Moore, Jim- Carter, Charlie- Alley, Rudolph - Loy, G.W.- Bull, Bill	Valley View
Chambers, Mary Ruth	Dec 8, 1991	67	J.M.H.	Talbott, Tn	Jan 31, 1924	Eller, Will	Richard, Leola		Chambers, W.T. [Bull]		Neal-Robert	W.M. Jr.	J.M.O.
Chambers, Neal Floyd	Feb 4, 2000	69	S.M.H.	Jeff Co	Jan 23, 1931	Chambers, Eugene	Bull, Mary	Mc Curry, Lorraine		Garry	Whitley, Gladys	Heaband	East View
Chambers, Robert B. [Black]	Aug 29, 1991	89	J.M.H.	Luxville, Sc	Aug 3, 1902	Chambers, John	Essie	Army		Robert Calvin	Mc Bride, Josephine - Marjorie		Young Memorial
Chambers, Sandra Lynn	Sep 19, 1999	49	J.M.H.	Dandridge, Tn	Sep 23, 1949	Chambers, Walter	Henry, Ellen	S	Gipson, Phyllis [Peanut] - Gibson, Sheela	Chambers, Dorothy- Mott, Dora - Smith, Barbara Jane - Strange, Mildred - Dungan, Hazel - Davis, Anna [Oh]		Hills Union

Name	Date	Age	Place	Place	Date									Cemetery
Chambers, Sinnie Elizabeth	Dec 10, 1993	69	Jeff City	Jeff City	May 26, 1924	Cameron, Lee	Cameron, Rosie	Chambers, Charles [Dy]	Baxley, Magie	John	Harvell, Ester	Robert-James	Doug - [Pds] Houston, Fred - Davis, Fred - Johnson, David - Simms, Lewis - Hatfield, Tom	Lebanon
Chancey,Laura	Sep 26, 1979	37	Ft. Lauderdale, Fl	Lauderdale, Fl	Apr 18, 1942	Muffin, Lewis Mack	Miller, Carolyn	Chancey, Russell M.	Brenda Sue - Tucker, Debbie	Jim-Bobby-Roger	Courtney, Mrs. B.I.			New Market
Chandler, Charley Shannon	Mar 27, 1997		U.T.H.	Knoxville, Tn	May 27, 1997	Chandler, Charles	Norton, Mary		Davidson, Sandra - James - Marilyn		Sipps, Mattie			Piedmont
Chandler, Lizzie Lee [Black]	Feb 13, 1998	64	Jeff City	Birmingham, Ala	Dec 27, 1933		W		Jones, Edward - Chandler, Terry					West View
Channer, Donald F.	Apr 22, 1983	73	Detroit, Michigan	Detroit, Michigan	Aug 21, 1909	Channer, Charles	Donald, Mabel		Bob-Arnold Beard				[Pds] Arnold, Arthur-Billy-H.G. - Adams, Robt - Charles - Stapleton, J.H.	Friends Station
Channer, Dorothy Arnold	Mar 13, 1979		Beverly Hills, Fl	Tn	Jan 30, 1918		Arnold, Dorothy	Channer, Donald	Arnold-Robert			Arnold, Glenn-William	[Pds] Arnold, Arthur-Kenneth-J.A. - Adams, Charles - Vance, Roger	Friends Station
Charles, Judy Karen	Apr 11, 1984	15	Valparaiso, Fl	Tn	Mar 27, 1949	Charles, Jack	Noe, Thenia Louise	S					Watchous, Thenia - Cliff - Blanchard [Fa] - Father	New Market
Chavis, Willie B.	Dec 10, 1996	98	Dandridge, Tn	Ohio Co, Ky	Mar 5, 1898	Lindby, Nat	Ashby, Mattie	Chavis, Alexander [D]	Arbin, Martha - Blandey, Carolyn - Williamson, Barbara	Charles L. [Miss] - James D. [Ky]	Lindby, Geneva [Ky]	Doug	Jackie - [1/2] Noe, Terri - Watchous, Tina	West View
Chester, Buelah	Jan 4, 1971	72		Tn	Jun 6, 1898	Tom	Lambdin, Lucy	Div					Kinder, Mary - Lambdin, Joe - [Bros] [Pds] Ort, Lawson - Cliff - W.H. - Swan, Will - Quarles, Lawrence - Turner, R.R	West View
Chon, Dessie	Aug 2, 1982	86	Houston, Texas	Blountsvill, Ky	Feb 26, 1896	Davis, Helen		Chon, Martin W.	Long, Betty [TX]	Allen-James [Call]	Houston, Marie [Va]			J.M.G.
Churchman, Flossie Ruth	Nov 2, 1995	50	J.M.H.	Morristown, Tn	Aug 11, 1945	Collins, Carroll A.	Henson, Alice E.	Churchman, Frank	Johnson, Sherry - Snyder, Brenda	Mike	Arbe, Beatrice - Glassone, Carol - Collins, Barbara	Husband - [Pds] Wright, Mike - Johnson, Jerry - Churchman, Allen - Todd - Burchell, Jr. - Stapleton, J.A.		J.M.G.
Churchman, Ruby Naomi	Mar 28, 1996	75	J.M.H.	Greene Co.	Apr 9, 1920	Lloyd, Lucy Jane		Churchman, George R.	Betty		Duncan, Lula - Suronc, Irea - Trent, Carol	Guy Jr.	Doug	J.M.G.
Clapp, Melvyn D.	Mar 27, 1998	60	F.S.H.	Knoxville, Tn	Oct 1, 1937	Clapp, Edwin	Donaldson, Lucille	Div	Roger & Debbie [Fa]-Christopher	Mike	Baldwin, Edwina	Jack & Lisa - Thomas Sr & Dell	Husband - [Pds] Rice, Marie-Jeff-Tn - Johnson, Jerry - Burton, Junior - Bush, Bobby - Partum, Junior - Brannon, Nelson	Tn Vets - Knoxville, Tn
Clark, Condon Cecil			Oak Ridge, Tn	Tn	Jan 21, 1914	Clark, Conan	Acuff, Mary	Air Force		Cecil		Guy Jr.	Willis	J.M.G.
Clark, Irene	Aug 31, 1990	67	Hill Haven	London, Ky	Feb 17, 1923	Rice, Banner	Mc Knight, Pearlie Mae	French, Hilda	Marsh, Dorothy L. - Bierston, Shirley	Coach, Evelyn [Ind] Bush, Dorothy [Ky]	Daniel-James-John [TX] - Rice, Mark-Jeff-Tom-Junior - Sexton [Ill] - Willard [Ind] - Virgil [Ind]	Husband - [Pds] Rice, Mark-Jeff- Tom - Junior - Bush, Bobby - Partum, Junior - Brannon, Nelson		West View

Name	Date	Age	Place	Location	Birth Date	Father	Mother		Mil.				Relation	Cemetery
Clark, James Willie	Jun 8, 1998	76	Jeff City	Harlan, Hy	Oct 15, 1921	Clark, Ansley	Bush, Cora			Maish, Dorothy - Blanton, Shirley	Cecil	Bush, Gracie - Jordan Helen - Baldwin, Pauline - [Pd] Bush, Gennelda [bd]	Son	West View
Clark, William Bell	Aug 24, 1990	79	J.M.H.	Rutledge, Tn	Oct 6, 1910	Clark, Dan L.	Roberts, Kate / Townsend, Attilee Beatrice			Griglen, Maxralee [D]	Raymond	Jones, Lena Mae		Central Point
Chilsbough, Margaret Ann	Oct 9, 1949	8b	E.T.H.	E.T.H.	Oct 6, 1949	Chilsbough, W.C.		Tn	Tn			Chilsbough, W.C.	Son	Hinshons Chapel
Clevenger, Ralph Lawrence	Jun 17, 1977	61	F.S.H.	Grainger Co.	May 28, 1916	Clevenger, William B.	Wells, Mary			Sloan, Mrs. Mason - Johnson, Mrs. Ray	Ralph Jr.-Vernon-W.-Fayne-Wayne-Steve	Crossley, Velma - Soloman, Mrs. Henry	Curtis-Donald	Oakland
Clevenger, Rose Antionette	Oct 11, 1976	58	J.M.H.	Grainger Co	Aug 28, 1918					Clevenger, Ralph	Ralph Jr.-Vernon-Wayne-Fayne-Steve	Stagle, Virgie - Widner, Allene - Cox, Dorothy	[Pds] Purkey, Winchert - Cooper, Tex - Grant, Jimmy - Williams, Paul - Arthur - Stanton, Riley	Oakland - Grainger Co
Clevenger, Sam F.	Jan., 1967	50												Oakland
Clevenger, Steven Edward	Sep 5, 1999	48	Jeff City	Jeff City	Apr 23, 1951	Clevenger, Ralph	White, Rose		S	Grace	Gayle	Grady-Henry	Johnson, Wilma - Vernon-Fayne-Sloan, Wanda / Ralph Jr.-Vernon-Fayne-Wayne / V.A.-Willis	Oakland
Clevenger, William Ralph	Feb 25, 2000	38	Jeff City	Cocke Co. Tn	Mar 15, 1961	Clevenger, Ralph Jr.	Mason, Patsy Carol	Cocke Co			Justin	Green, Cindy	Lindsey, Neeta	West View
Click, Clifford Lester	Mar 28, 1983	72	Strawberry Plains	Cocke Co. Tn	Oct 13, 1911	Click, Joseph	Sweeten, Carrie J.		WW 2	Thurman, Jewell Mae	Billy Eugene			West View
Cline, Almer Eugene	Apr 14, 1990	83	J.M.H.	Faligation, Sevier Co.	Dec 25, 1906	Cline, David P.	Bettis, Viola			Jones, Betty - Howard, Linda - Williams, Robbie	David	Lline, Inez - Collins, Ruth	Neff-Neill- Daniel P. / Husband	J.M.G.
Cline, Artie Mae	Feb 9, 1994	80	New Market	Oct 28, 1913		Esllinger, G.P.	Cline, Artie Esllinger			Cline, Gene [D]	David	Horner, Pauline	Bruce Algor	J.M.G.
Cloninger, Frank Willis	Oct 29, 1975	44	U.T.H.	Sevier Co	Oct 11, 1930	Cloninger, James Adam	Brody, Johnnie			Francis, Evelyn	Frank Steven	Russell, Millie	James F.-John C. / Luther	Holston View
Clowers, Lonzo	Apr 27, 1985	74	Jeff Co	Tn	Sep 15, 1880								Clowers, Lucy [Willis]	Mill Springs
Clowers, Luther	Feb 27, 1990	69	County Home	1891									Clowers, Howard [Son]	Mill Springs
Coats, Ryan Christopher [Balck]	Jul 25, 1995		S.M.H.	Knoxville, Tn	Jul 25, 1995	Coats, Charles	Thomas, Tanya						Thomas, Thomas E.S. [G-Father] / Younge	Younge Memorial
Cochran, Anita Jean	Mar 4, 1996	71	Knoxville, Tn	Akron, Ohio	Sep 7, 1924	Repass, Paul	Elmore, Arminda		navy	Cochran, Charles [D]	Kanipe, Charolette		P.V.	New Market
Cochran, Anthony Lee	Oct 24, 1980	23	Morristown, Tn	Jeff Co	Jul 14, 1957	Cochran, Jones	Whaley, Elsie		S		Myrtie-Diane-Tona ?	Myrtie-Diane-Tona ?	J Jr. [Phil]-Ronnie	New Market
Cochran, Bert Cleveland	Dec 13, 1967	77	Tn	Feb 27, 1890		Cochran, Patton	Hodge, Mollie			Lockhart, Mrs. Elbert [Ola] - Loy, Mary [Sd] - Holland, Angel - Colleen & Todd	B.C. Jr.-Edward-James F.-Loyd-Jesse-John		Doug - [Pds] Williams, Cena - Deas-Jeff - Jones, Tom - Turner, Travis - Cline, Robert	Mill Springs
Cochran, Betty Jean	Dec 12, 2000	57	J.M.H.	May 2, 1943		West, Charles	Wright, Ruth M.			Cochran, Paul [D]	Tim-Jeff-Shawn			Mill Springs
Cochran, Charles Ancil	Dec 12, 1994	67	New Market	Nov 28, 1924		Wright, Ruth M.				Cochran, Charlie D.	Vineyard, Hazel - Vineyard, Margaret	Kanipe, Charolette		J.M.G.
Cochran, Charles Richard	Oct 17, 1984	37	V.A. Hosp.-Mt. Home	Jeff Co	Dec 20, 1946	Cochran, Charles A.	Foster, Minnie Bell		Air Force	Nos, Katherine	Chuck-Charles	Kanipe, Charolette	Willis	New Market

Name	Death Date	Age	Place	Origin	Birth Date	Father	Mother	Spouse	Relatives / Survivors / Pallbearers	Cemetery
Cochran, Charles D.	Jan 18, 1990	58	M.C.		Aug 24, 1901	Cochran, Patton (Tn)	Hodge, Mary (Tn)	Cochran, Charles	Vineyard, Hazel-Margaret [Step]; Blanchard, Mrs. L.E.- Brodsy, Mrs. Joe - Rogers, Mrs. Johnnie; Charles A-Fred-Steve; John-B.C.; Cochran, Edna [Wife]	Mill Springs
Cochran, Edna Mae	Jul 1, 1984	72	J.M.H.	Dandridge, Tn	Jan 3, 1912	Branam, Walter R.	Gass, Anna	Cochran, Charles [D]	Schlemmer, Mildred - Brodsy, Jean - Rogers, Martha; Stephen; Robert; [Pds] Lowe, Jackie-Danny-Jodie-Fred - Shrader, Mike - Jones, Ed [S]- Wattis, Tracy Felton, Jr. - Father	Batch - Dandridge, Tn
Cochran, Edward Eugene	Jan 5, 1967	33	Knoxville, Tn	Tn	Apr 3, 1933	Cochran, John Loyd	Dawson, Ella Dean		[Pds] Lowe, Tom - Southern, Ron - Jeffey, Dwayne - Foster, Donnie - Larry-Michael	J.M.G.
Cochran, Gladys Leota	Mar 1, 1986	77	J.M.H.	New Market, Tn	Jun 25, 1910	Jones, Edward	Young, Lucy	Cochran, John [D]	Givin, Bernice; French, Eula - Foster, Dorcas; Douglas	J.M.G.
Cochran, John Loyd	Apr 2, 1980	84	J.M.H.	New Market, Tn	Mar 30, 1896	Cochran, Patton	Hodge, Molly	Jones, Gladys	Russell, Bernice & Perry; Tarwater, Mildred; Hugh [Pts]- George- Kenneth- Earnest-John- Jim	New Market, Tn
Cochran, Jonas Patton	Sep 17, 1965	57	J.M.H.	New Market	Nov 4, 1937	Sr.	Whaley, Elsie	West, Betty	Holland, Angel; Timothy-Jeff- Shawn; Ronald	Mill Springs
Cochran, Lucy Irene	May 29, 1986	77	J.M.H.	W. Va	Aug 12, 1908	Lawson, Robert	Pruitt, Virginia	Cochran, Samuel Lee [D]	Nash, Lorraine; Joe-Cecil - Archer, Ralph; Bill; Joe-Lorraine	Blue Springs
Cochran, Mary Katherine	Jan 9, 2000	74	S.M.H.	Mascot, Tn	Jun 11, 1925	Noe, Odes	Luttrell, Sadie E.	Cochran, Charles A. [D]	De Baets, Linda Kay; Tarwater, Mildred; Hugh [Pts]- George- Kenneth- Earnest-John- Jim	J.M.G.
Cochran, Parable	Nov 21, 1961	71	J.M.H.	Sevier Co, Tn	Apr 20, 1890	Jones, Thomas	Bailey, Sarah	Cochran, Bert C. [Rev.]	Todd, Beatrice - Mayo/short, Lou- Lloyd-Bert C. Jr.- Berta Lee; Laughery, Cordie- Barlow, Dora - Nelson, Addie- Potete, Diana - Bingham, Iowa- Preston, Martha; Ed-Walter-Will; Kasterson, Thomas O.	New Market
Cochran, Phillip [Billie]	Aug -, 1966	18	Wilmington, Nc			Cochran, Jonas			Turley, Margaret - Spencer, Lurena - Vest, Elizabeth; Fred W.-George P.; James Jr.- Ronald Torry; Lee	Mill Springs
Cockrum, Albert Wallace	Jan 31, 1988	80	J.M.H.	Grainger Co	Jun 7, 1930	Cockrum, Milford P.	Newman, Blanch		Henry, Agnes - Schwarz, Kenneth - Cochran, Kathleen; George-James; Lee	J.M.G.
Cockrum, Robert	May 25, 1981		Knoxville, Tn	Jeff Co		Cockrum, Robert W.	Helm, Nora	S	George-James; [Pds] Henry, Bill - Young, Don - Patter, Harold - Peoples, Paul	J.M.G.
Cockrum, Walter Loyd					Nov 28, 1914			40-45	Todd, Mrs. Edward [Sd]- Loy, Mary E. [Sd]- Locklard, Mrs. Elbert; Jones-B.C.; [Pds] Cochran, Ronnie-Robert- Fred-Billy-Chester- Heskel	New Market
Coller, Jeffery Matthew	Apr 15, 1999	35	J.M.H.	Chattanooga, Tn	May 20, 1963	Coller, Ned A. Sr.	Matthews, Carol L. Puckett	Sharon K. [Div]	Patricia [D]- Puckett, Shirley & Bill - Brooks, Jamie & Paul - Williams, Amy & Keith; Andrew A- William Matthew; Mayo, Pamela; Ned A. Jr. Shawn-Brian; [Pds] Henry, Don - Young, Bill - Patter, Harold - Peoples, Paul; [Pds] Cochran, Ronnie-Robert-Fred-Billy-Chester-Heskel	Mill Springs
Colbaugh, Mildred Louise	Aug 17, 1987	72	New Market		Apr 27, 1777	Kerr, William A.	French, Myrtie	Div	Bill & Debbie; William [D]- Jim & Ann- Alger & Shirley [Gs]; Collette, Kenneth L. [D]	Piedmont
Collette, Vive Kate	Jul 29, 1998	88	Jeff City	Jeff City	Feb 1, 1910	Collette, Thomas A.	Branam, Vertie	S	Div	West View
Colley, Mary Gladys	Nov 21, 1985	66	Knoxville, Tn	Knox Co	Nov 18, 1919	Thomas, George W.	Breeden, Sarah E.	Colley, Palmer [D]	Lowry, Debra; Henry F.-Larry-Joe; Miller, Dorothy- Sellers, Ellen - Metheny, Bess; Johnson, Mary [Council]; [Pds] Thomas, Jim-Bill - Sellers, Mike-Eddie- Crawford, Mike- Colley, Mike	Highland Memorial East

Name	Date	Age	Place	County/Inst.	Birth Date	Father	Mother	Spouse	Relatives / Survivors	Cemetery
Collins, Ada Rose	Jan 14, 1993	69	Jeff City	Knox Co	Mar 24, 1903	Oddins, William Rice	Houser, Myrtie Lee	Collins, Mack	Perry, Mary - Gonzales, Linda - Carter, Lena; Brother	West View
Collins, Alvin	Nov 3, 1996	76	Jeff Co	Tn	Sep 7, 1894	Collins, John	Webb, Sarah	Ollie	Hazel [Mahh] - Grant, Mrs. B.E. [Mich] - Dukes, Mrs. Jim [Dal] - Mrs. Ron; Wife	West View
Collins, Beony Lavern	Jun 1, 1995	53	Jeff City	Jefferson	Mar 31, 1942	Collins, Carroll A.	Horner, Zona	Div	Brand-Jackie; Brad-David; Whitley, Shirley - Brown, Joyce; Dean; Joyce	J.M.G.
Collins, Betty Jean	Jan 10, 2000	50	Talbott, Tn	Jeff Co	Nov 4, 1949	Gann, Benjamin F.	Parker, Lucy Evelyn	Collins, Calvin R.	Greggs, Rebecca; Danie; Woods, Mary; Willie-Bond-Henry	Mt. View
Collins, Denny Ray	Jun 28, 1992	54	Tazewell, Tn	F.S.H.	Sep 16, 1937	Collins, Thurl	Lee, Luvenie	Marvilla	David Rick - Randy Christopher Dean; Ross, Margaret - Bradston, Eula Mae; Willie-Bond-Henry; Ruby	J.M.G.
Collins, Helen Estelle	Aug 24, 1964	77	Dandridge, Tn	Tn	May 1, 1887	Collins, Jack	Webb, Sarah	Collins, Thomas A. [D] (Nc)	Locke, Mary; Charlie; Alvin	Belch - Jeff Co
Collins, Georgia Leona	May 1, 1994	70	B.H.	Nc	Jun 6, 1914	Hahn, Robert	Rollins, Jessie A. [D]	w	Lee, Kathy - Tate, Cindy; David	Mill Springs
Collins, Fred Marvin	Oct 22, 1995	70	S.M.H.	Cuyahoga Falls, Oh	Jan 18, 1925	Collins, Willie	Holcomb, Alice Ellen	Kennedy, Nellie [Div]; Air Force	McCoy, Dorothy [Pa] - Wolverton, Edna [Oh] - Painter, Laurie [Wood] - Decker, Gazie [Tn]; Henry, Duane [Oh] - Smith, Jerry [Ariz?] - Collins, Earl; Ruby	J.M.G.
Collins, Hilliard	Jun 13, 1992	78	Hill Haven	Tn	May 1, 1917	Collins, Jack	Webb, Sarah	Collins, Lizzie (Nc)	Locke, Mary; Charlie; Alvin	Belch - Jeff Co
Collins, Houston Floyd	Jan 18, 1990	66	J.M.H.	Luttrell, Tn	Jan 18, 1923	Collins, William Andy	Kells, Bertie	Stephenson, Laura	Kelley, Jim D. - David - Collins, Gary [Sc] - Tomas A. Jr. - Eddie L.; James Mack - Joseph Mack; David	J.M.G.
Collins, Junior E.	Feb 1, 1993	66	Jeff City	New Market	Aug 30, 1917	Collins, Esam	Northern, Edith	Smith, Lillie	Morgan, Leona - Tankersley, Emma - Lyle, Chelsey - Walker, Dorothy - Seals, Betty - Hamilton, Hazel - Grant, Margaret - Smith, Edith - Elkins, Kathy; Moore, Robert - Phillip; Wife	J.M.G.
Collins, Laura Jo	Apr 29, 1995	69	Sevierville, Tn	Speedwell, Tn	Jan 6, 1927	Stephenson, Robert C.	Green, Birdis	Collins, Houston F. [D]	Smith, Cindy; Smacker, Diana & Wygand; Gary; Hubbell, Joe & Bertha; Lyle-Luke-Dame-Kyle-J.A.; Doug	J.M.G.
Collins, Juanita Jeanette	Jan 24, 1981	46	Care Inn	Grainger Co	Mar 11, 1934	Hubbard, Hubert	Jernigan, Ira	Collins, Huston	Floyd; Wife	J.M.G.
Collins, Mack	Jul 23, 1993	58	Dandridge, Tn	New Market	Feb 6, 1935	Collins, Alvin	Bailey, Ollie Mae	Ada; U.S.A.F.	Frank-Donald; Brother	West View
Collins, Muriel L.	Jun 10, 1998	91	Jeff City	Lenior Co., Ky	May 2, 1907			Collins, James Auby	Moore, Mrs. Pauline [Doug] Br.; Husband	Lynnhurst
Collins, Nannie A.	Jan 6, 1954	78	Knoxville, Tn	Tn	Oct 26, 1877			Lindsey, Pearl	Brother	Union - Newport, Tn

Name	Date	Age												Cemetery
Collins, Nellie	Sep 7, 1999	98	Sevierville, Tn	Morristown-Union Co.	Aug 1, 1911	Bruner, Samuel W.		Selvey, Jamie		Holsman, Bonnie	Cardwell, Billy [D]-Cardwell, Leon Jr.-Paul-Bruner, Gene-Collins, Paul-James P.-Lawson, Jim			J.M.G.
Collins, Pero David	May 5, 2000	89	F.S.H.	Lone Mt. Tn	May 23, 191	Collins, Eli Olendin	Posey, Ruth	Edmonds, Nina [D] Bruner, Nellie [D]		Lawson, Mary-Hickman, Bonnie	Collins, James P. & Sandra-Collins, Paul & Gene	Cochran, Bertha	Lum	Blue Springs
Collins, Ray Mack	Dec 13, 1983	57	J.M.H.	Jeff Co	Oct 6, 1926	Collins, Fred		McSpadin, Katherine	Pauline	Whitlock, Brenda K.	Ronald Ray-David Michael-Dana Beth-Phillip Larry-Marvin	Thomas, Hollis-Turpin, Nancy-Gatlin, Sue-Carrol, Linda	Robert-Frankie-Donnie	J.M.G.
Collins, Sandra Faye	May 23, 1993	47	J.M.H.	New Market	Apr 3, 1946	Lawrence, Roy		Smith, Mary	Collins, Denny Ray [D]		Christopher	Whaley, Betty-Murray, Jewell-Roach, Brenda-Collins, Jana-Lawrence, Shirley	Bill Donald-Jim	J.M.G.
Collins, Susan E. Reimer	Oct 28, 1978		Jeff City	Tn	Jul 14, 1887	Reimer, James W.		Whitfield, Katherine					Reimer, Glen (nephew)	Batch
Collins, Taylor Willard	Nov 23, 1983	81	J.M.H.	New Market	Aug 23, 1912	Collins, William H.		Collins, Elizabeth A.	Mc Campbell, Jeanette Elizabeth	Hill, Lonna-Smith, Barbara			Bruce	Campbell, Steve-Chamberlain, Gary-Parker, Don	J.M.G.
Collins, Thomas A.	Jan 21, 1984	72	J.M.H.	Madison Co, Nc	Apr 6, 1911	Collins, T.A.		Candler, Maggie	Nc	Talley, Helen	Eddie L.-"Tommy A.	4	[Pals] McCarter, E.J.-Crooks, Ted-Jones, Gary-Williams, Jim-Hodges, Curt	J.M.G.
Collins, Tommy Carroll	Dec 6, 1983	36	Jeff City	Jeff City	Dec 8, 1945	Collins, John James		Collins, Leona Ruth	Div	navy		Seale, Billie Jean-Morgan, Anna Lee-Eldridge, Mary Lois	John E.-Harold	[Pals] Collins, John-David Don-Sonsky, Langston, Robery-Ray, Jerry	J.M.G.
Collins, William Everett	Nov 7, 1981	75	Greinger Co	Tn	Apr 2, 1877	Collins, W.A.		Link						Union- Newport, Tn
Collins, William A.	Jan 13, 1992	38	Jeff City	Jeff City	May 19, 1950	Collins, Bill		Shoun, Emma Glenn	S	Linzey, Pearl-Moore, Pauline [Chicago]			Vergil-Billy-Johnny-Joe	Collins, Mrs. Nannie A. [Wife]	Blue Springs
Collins, Willis A.	Jul 25, 1954	22	Jeff Co	Tn	Jul 2, 1932	Collins, Alvin	Tn	Bailey, Ollis May	Tn			Bailey, Vivian & Boyce - Cook, Roberta & Roy - Huff, Jewell & Bob - Ogle, Alvice & Marvin - Chapplemen, Carolyn & Leo - [Step] Huffaker, Rosemary & James	Bailey, Ruth-Dorothy-Lee-Katherine-Vaughn, Nora-Grant, Margaret-Smith, Edith	Father	Blue Springs
Colyer, Elsie Mae Brooks	Apr 3, 1997	86	F.S.H.	Somerset, Ky	Mar 25, 1911	Mc Ginney, Milford ?		Meece, Martha A.		Colyer, William B. Brooks, Robert H. [D]	Colyer, William B. Brooks, Robert H. [D]	[In-Law] Mainer, Charles Jr.	Frank Mack-Donald	East View

Name	Date	Age	Place	Birthplace	Birth Date	Father	Mother								Burial
Condell, Linda Lorraine	May 4, 1995	37	U.T.H.	Jeff City	Sep 2, 1957	Brooks, Arthur E. Jr.	Anderson, Pauline		Div	King, Tracy	King, Kevin	Brooks, Diana - Wilhite, Kelly		[Pale] Brooks, Rae - Doyle, Don - Grimes, Carl - Wilhite, Tony - Anderson, Mike	Blue Springs
Conner, Jesse Green	May 17, 1994	83	J.M.G.	Knox Co.	Oct 30, 1910	Conner, Alex	Palmer, Laura		Army	Kefner, Lois & Eugene	Kefner, Lois & Kay-A.J. & Barbara			[S-Children] Franklin, Debbie & Larry - Cochran, Kim & Scott - Treadway, Kelly & Wayne - Detmer, Amy & Tom - Conner, Paula & Mike	Highland Memorial East
Cook, Andrew L.	Jun 22, 1997	84	Jeff City	Straw Plains	Jul 6, 1902	Cook, Abraham	Lawson, Jennie			Johnson, Grace	Cook, Ron				
Cook, Carrie Lou	Nov 18, 2000	90	Straw Plains	Straw Plains	Aug 12 1910	Dugman, Charlie	Rudder, Jenney	Cook, Scott [D]		Satterfield, Mary Lou	Ed & Mary Ruth- Bill & Cathy-Roy Ralph - [In-Law] Dugman, Thelma - Luttrell, Donna - Dugman, Pauline	Dammerwood, Ruth & Richard - [In-Law] Bailey, John - W. Sr.- Satterfield, E.K. Sr.			Strawberry Plains
Cook, David Dora	Feb 26, 1991	73	F.S.H.	Hammond, Okla.	Apr 23, 1917	Winstead, Thomas	Hayes, Elizabeth	Cook, Andrew L.		Johnson, Grace	Ronald-Jack	[None] Daugherty, Rue - Fleming, James - Greene, Pauline - Dinnon, Edna	Jim		Piney
Cook, George B.	Aug. - 1988	66					Sarah			Green, Mrs. Ralph - Kefner, Mrs. Earl	Ronald-William [Pat]		Husband		Willis
Cook, Herbert Bernard	Sep 1, 1977		F.S.H.	Union Col.	Oct 13, 1891	Cook, Richard	Marsh, Irene						Wiley	Wiley	Willie
Cook, Homer Herman	Oct 18, 1981	85	Strawberry Plains	Union Co.	Nov 18, 1895	John O.	Cook, Nellis	Alfred, Mary				Shoun, Bertie Lou [None]	Cook, Curtis	[Pale] Cook, A.C.- Johny-Eddie - Lawson, Harold - Luttrell, Frank - Edmonds, Dewey	Strawberry Plains
Cook, Irene M.	Oct 31, 1994	84	J.M.H.	New Market	Sep 29, 1910	Marsh, G.V.	Lytle, Luis	Cook, Herbert B. [D]					H.B. Wiley		Pleasant View Union-Maynardville
Cook, Leila Maude	Mar 24, 1973	98	J.M.H.	Tn	Feb 7, 1915	Cook, R.C.	Cook, Sarah M.	S				Luttrell, Donna	Sister		Strawberry Plains
Cook, Martin Curtis	Nov 22, 1991	79	Mt. Home	Strawberry Plains	May 7, 1912	Cook, J.O.	Cook, Lissie	Div	WW 2						Strawberry Plains
Cook, Mary A.	Sep 18, 1988	85	Sevierville, Tn	Tn	Apr 16, 1903	Alfred, Jim	Cannon, -	Cook, Homer [D]				[Niece] Dougherty, Rue - Fleming, James - Greene, Pauline - Relationship - P.O.A.I		Cran, Mary [Niece, Tn - Relationship - P.O.A.I]	Strawberry Plains
Cook, Sarah Jane	Nov 1, 1982	81	J.M.H.	Hancock Co.	Jan 1, 1901	Adams, John O.	Trout, Adaline	Cook, George [D]		Kefner, Tillie - Greene, Hazel	Ronald-William			[Pale] Adams, Clara - Bates, Buddy - Cannon, Jim - Kefner, Eugene - Cheasney, Gene - Long, Gene	J.M.G.
Cook, William Robert Jr.	Dec 25, 1996	75	J.M.H.	Muncie, Ind	Nov 26, 1921	Cook, William Sr.	Zelma	Guinn, Barbara [Div]	Army	Misty Dawn - Dunbar, Carol & Mike [17x]	[Step] Ambrose, Jamer-William			[Step] Ambrose, Jamer-William	Cremated - New Market
Cooke, Wylie Alden	Jun 3, 1985	90	Mt. Home - Greene Co	Union Co	Dec 22, 1894	Cooke, Richard D.	Miller, Sarah	Horine, Ruby	army					Lambert, Betty Cook [None]	Hamblen Memorial Gardens

Name	Death Date	Age	Place	Birth Date	Father	Mother	Spouse / Relations	Notes	Cemetery
Cooley, David Anthony Jr.	Jul 24, 1965	6m	Jeff City	Jan 22, 1965	Cooley, James Amos	Combs, Jo Ann			J.M.G.
Cornett, Grant Odell Jr.	Jul 27, 1993	52	Tn	Aug 13, 1941	Cornett, Grant Odell Sr.	Campbell, Kitty Frances	Lee Co., Va	Kitty F. (M) - Betty Frances; Horton, Peggy - [1/2] Cornett, Darrell - [1/2] Shelton, Peggy	J.M.G.
Cotter, Oscar Arlen	Apr 6, 1983	81	Cosby, Ky	Nov 25, 1901	Cotter, Winden	Mc Garha, Amanda	Webb, Sallie	Earl N. [if still]; Mc Carter, Nora	J.M.G.
Cotter, Sallie	Feb 14, 1987	85	Rutledge, Tn	May 17, 101	Gilles, Mack	Gilles, Margaret	Cotter, O.A. ? [D]	Holsworth, Eva; Earl; Baxter, Malver; Welch, Willie - Edgar; Doug	J.M.G.
Cotter, Trennis Harrison	Feb 2, 1979	78	Jeff Co	Nov 23, 1901	Cotter, William H.	Corbett, Alice	S	Kern; Brother - Cranford, Tom - Laird, Claude - Seals, Robert - Sellers, Terry - Thorpe, Wayne - Manning, David	Lebanon Cumberland
Cotter, Charles Jesse	Jan 22, 1998	54	J.M.H.	Aug 22, 1943	Cotter, William H.	Klepper, Edith E.	Mary E.		Lebanon Cumberland Presby.
Cotter, Coy Henry	Oct 22, 1994	71	Jeff Co	Sep 10, 1923	Cotter, Frank	Cameron, Zelma	Smith, Jessie Lou	Frank-Robbery; West, Jeannette; Frank, C. Jr. - Walter-Coy; Willie	J.M.G.
Cotter, Danny Walter	Feb 12, 1987	29	Hamblen Co	Aug 21, 1957	Cotter, Walter J.	Button, Ora Mae	Franklin, Vinkie Sue	Shell-Stacy; Willie - [Pals] Cotter, Robert - Houston - Seils, Danny - Swingood, Jeff - Minutt, Robert	J.M.G.
Cotter, Edith Elizabeth	Feb 25, 1988	74	J.M.H.	Dec 20, 1913	Klepper, James	Maddox, Queenie	Cotter, William H. [D]	Whitlock, Carolyn ? - J.M.; Collins, Mary Ruth & Eddie - Ashley, Ann & Gary; Charles; [Niece] Whitlock, Carolyn - Collins, Mary Ruth - Ashley, Ann]	Lebanon Cumberland - Jeff City
Cotter, Kermit L.	Feb 7, 1999	96	Jeff City	Mar 27, 1902	Cotter, William H.	Corbett, Alice Maude	S		J.M.G.
Cotter, Louis Charlie	Dec 15, 1989	84	Hill Haven, Jeff City	May 10, 1925	Cotter, Frank	Cameron, Zelma	Osborne, Ruth [Div]	Cannon, Dorothy; Doyle; Wrott, Grace - Burchfield, Remonda - Coley, Ruby - Hinds, Hazel	Lebanon Cumberland Presby
Cotter, Mary Evelyn	Jan 30, 1994	73	Sevier Co	Oct 26, 1920	Gray, Dan	Whistley, Martha	Cotter, Charles J.	Hodges, Robert; Haven, Martha - Fox, Edith; Husband	Lebanon Cumberland

Name	Date	Age	Place	County/State	Date	Father	Mother							Cemetery
Cotter, Thales	Feb 6, 1977	59	Morristown, Tn		Feb 27, 1917	Cotter, Frank	Cameron, Zelma	S						Lebanon Cumberland Presby.
Cotter, Zelma	Sep 14, 1976		Care Inn - Jeff City	Jeff Co	May 14, 1898	Cameron, War	Nolan, Elizabeth	W		Hinds, Rosie [Val] - Hinds, Mrs. Douglas [Val] - Burchell, Mrs. Ramona - Cotley, Mrs. Ruby - Smith, Mrs. Grace	Jones, Lora Mae - Cotter, Mrs. Ludo - Brown, Mrs. Miller, Pearl	[Pals] Burchell, Donnie - Hinds, Vernon - Cotter, Doyle - Franklin - Robert-Allen	[Pals] Cotter, Franklin-Allen - Doyle - Hinds, Benson - McGill, Joe - Cramm, Ralph	Lebanon Cumberland Presby.
Cox, David Lynn	Mar 31, 1999	46	Jeff City	Jeff Co	Aug 25, 1952	Cox, Joe F.	Lockhart, Mildred		Melinda	Matthew		Bill Dale		J.M.G.
Cox, Gena Rena	May 1, 1985		Morristown, Tn	Morristown, Tn	May 11, 1985	Cox, Daniel Glen	Allsup, Lois Irene	Tn	Tn					J.M.G.
Cox, Infant Male	Apr 18, 1998		F.S.H.		Apr 18, 1998	Cox, Harold					Lisa	Roger	Parents - Nox, M.T.-Newman, Blanche [G-Parents]	J.M.G.
Cox, Mary Alstair	Jan 31, 1992	95	J.M.H.	Jeff Co	Apr 24, 1925	Cameron, Porter J.	Cox, Von V.				Gann, Armanda - Nox, Nina Mae	Sinnie	[Pals] Cameron, Lenance - Nox, David - Large, Allen - Donald-Michael-Larry-Roger-Mark	J.M.G.
Cox, Von Vergil	Aug 14, 1983	64	J.M.H.	Jeff Co	Oct 8, 1916	Cox, Eck	Rogers, Minnie		Navy			[1/2] Dockery, Earl	[Pals] Koker, Bill - Commer, A.J. - Hodge, Guy - Ballinger, Glenn-Whaley, Donald	J.M.G.
Coy, Ira Dancil	May 5, 1998	55	J.M.H.	Galton, Ohio	Mar 27, 1931	Coy, Guy M.	Shadowblad, Jennie				7	1	West View
Craig, Margaret Louise	Nov 8, 1999	64	Morristown, Tn	Knoxville, Tn	Aug 18, 1935	Beck, William	Armstrong, Vernie	Army	Craig, Hershel	Mayes, Mary Etta - Craig, Carolyn-Brown, Libby	Beck, Clarence	Father	J.M.G.
Crespo, Kenneth C.	Aug 19, 1996	30	Rutledge, Tn	Bridgeport, Conn	Nov 18, 1964	Crespo, Luis A. Sr.	Medina, Carmen	S		Cotter, Lonnie	Lisa Jr.-Orlando-Kevin	Father	J.M.G.
Crewsonberry, David Walter	Jul 19, 1996	79	S.M.H.	Rutledge, Tn	Aug 13, 1915	Crewsonberry, William	Rankin, Josie		WW 2	Reeves, Mildred	William-Phillip	Parker, Elsa - Grindstaff, Georgia		Roseberry
Crockes, David N.	Jul 23, 1972	73	New Market, Tn	Tn	Jul 19, 1899	Crockes, Franklin A.	Crofton, Lou Ellen [Lillie]			Ruth	Higgins, Lillie & W.A.	[1/2] Franklin [Delhi]	Wife	Mill Springs
Crockes, Fred Franklin	Dec 20, 1991	83	Jeff City	Nc	Aug 29, 1908	Crockes, Walter	Draper, Grace			Varnell, Bonnie	Gary-Dennis	Walter-Ted	Parents - [Pals] Crockes, Bud-Crewsonberry, Robert-Danel-Steve-Larry, Ron-Gene	Flat Gap
Crockes, Herbert Walter	Apr 24, 1996	79	Knoxville, Tn	Nc	Mar 23, 1907	Crockes, Walter	Draper, Grace	S	J		Moody, Fern - Crockes, Ruth	Fred Wayne-Ted	Brother [Pals] Crockes, Gary-Dennis-Don-Mark-Steve-Roger	Mill Springs
Crockes, Ruth Mae	Nov 1, 1991	88	Hill Haven	Nc	Apr 19, 1903	Crockes, Walter	Draper, Grace			Crockes, David	Moody, Fern	Ted-Walter	Brother [Pals] Crockes, Dennis-Don-Mark-Steve-Roger	Mill Springs

Name	Date	Age	Place	Place 2	Birth	Father	Mother	Spouse					Cemetery
Cross, Bessie Lula Belle Lowe	Sep 1, 1989	65	J.M.H.	Greene Co.	Apr 24, 1924	Danielle, George Willard	Payne, Gerthie	Cross, Fred [D] - Lowe, Arlie [D]	Booth, Elizabeth - Lowell, Shirley - Young, Geraldine - Denton, Florence	Booth, Elizabeth - Mott, Polly - Owens, Mattie - Bell - Green, Janice [Step] - Booth, Elizabeth - Lowell, Shirley - Young, Geraldine - Denton, Florence	Glass, Gladys-Dolly 0 Denolle, Rosa Lee - Cox, Dorothy - Bell, Ruth - Stanquiales, Ruby	James-Charles- Edward-Joe- Floyd-Paul- David	Mt. View
Cross, Fred Edgar	May 25, 1988	76	J.M.H.	Jeff City	Jun 1, 1911	Cross, John	Cross, Madge	Cross, Fred [D] - Lowe, Arlie [D]					West View
Cross, Lilly Mae	Nov 13, 1995	69	J.M.H.	W. Frankfort, Ill	Jul 11, 1926	Minnelsos, James	Sheppard, Ines Awbry	Cross, Silas [D]	WW 2	Quinn, Barbara Cook & Wayne [Step] Bradley, Francise & Gary	Booth, William Craven [D]	Turner Family - Middleton, Ky	Turner Family - Middleton, Ky
Crowe, Addie Ariona	Nov 17, 1987	66	J.M.H.	Strawberry Plains	Jul 24, 1921	Lauderdale, Wilmer	Compton, Ellis	Crowe, William C. [D-3/9/68]		Powell-Ralph			Strawberry Plains
Crowe, Cora Lillian	Jun 17, 1989	59	J.M.H.	Grainger Co	Jun 12, 1930	Mc Bee, Thomas	Danielle, Leroy	Crowe, Raymond		Roach, Cora - Bates, Betty - Crowe, Norma	Buddy-Donnie- Rennie-David	Hill, Bernita - Lowe, Dorothy	New Blackwell
Cross, Darold Ray (Tony)	Feb 13, 1997	56	S.M.H.	Corryton, Tn	Feb 20, 1940	Crowe, Omer H.	Lakins, Martha	Barnard, Janet Yvonne		Boatman, Ruth - Lowe, Helen - Berry Ann	Corey Allen-Tony Lynn	Walker, Kay - Wolfes, Pauline - Gentry, Blanche	Strawberry Plains
Cross, Frank Hodge	Nov 13, 1965	45	J.M.H.	Tn	1900	Crowe, Henry	Williams, Sarah	Myers, Jennie			Henry-Steve- Bobby	William - Johnny-Fred	J.M.G.
Crowe, Ralph Earl	Mar 23, 1991	47	New Market	New Market	Apr 17, 1943	Crowe, William C.	Lauderdale, Addie Ariona	Same, Shirley					Rhys Chapel - Newport, Tn
Crowe, Raymond Ancel	Jun 5, 1993	64	Rutledge, Tn	Blaine, Tn	Aug 4, 1928	Crowe, Earl	Patterson, Felba	Mc Bee, Cora [D]		Whitt, Cora - Bates, Betty - Ferrell, Norma	Raymond Jr.- Donnie-Ronnie- David	Sharp, Evelyn	New Blackwell
Crowe, Virginia Ann Miller	Nov 11, 1995	37	J.M.H.	Jeff City	Nov 30, 1957	Fritz, Warren	Shelton, Sallie	Crowe, William Powell	1943	Gardner, Lisa	Massengill, Larry	Allen	East View
Crowe, William Cedric	Mar 8, 1968	49	Jeff Co		Aug 19, 1918	Quinn, Harvey	Williams, Sarah	Fritz, Virginia Ann	Army	Seels, Janet	William P.-Ralph	Husband	Holston View
Crowe, William Powell	May 29, 1999	58	Dandridge, Tn	New Market	Jun 29, 1940	Crowe, William Cedric	Lauderdale, Addie Ariona	Fritz, Virginia Ann	Army	1943	Gregory & Kim		East View
Crye, Ted Roosevelt	Jul 29, 1993	82	Jeff City	Cleveland, Tn	Jul 14, 1911	Crye, Graceville	Unk	Vaughn, Maude	Bradley Co	Gibbons, Bundie		Wayne	J.M.G.

Name	Death Date	Age	Death Place	County/State	Birth Date	Father	Mother	Spouse	War	Relatives / Survivors	Pallbearers & Notes	Burial
Cunningham, Geneva [Black]	Jan 2, 1999	83	J.M.H.	New Market	Sep 4, 1915	Fain, E.W.	Davis, Ida	Cunningham, Ross Sr. [D]		Nixon, Eldise & Halsie; Ross Jr. & Sonnie		J.M.G.
Cunningham, Loy Myrtl Jr. [Black]	Nov 4, 1994	67	New Market	New Market	Jun 17, 1927	Cunningham, Loy M.Sr.	Jackson, Mildred					Younge Memorial
Cunningham, Loy Myrtl [Black]	Jul 28, 1995	91	Hill Haven	New Market	Nov 26, 1903	Cunningham, William	Johnson, Harriett	Mc Farland, Myrtle		Willie-Donald [Dayton, OR]; Cunningham, Willis	Cunningham, Loy Myrtl 3rd-Wayne [B-Sonj] - Harry, Helen - Bennie, Beatrice [B-Deggs]	Younge Memorial
Cunningham, Mollie Cecil [Negro]	Dec 16, 1998	78	Jeff Co	Tn	Oct 2, 1890	Davis, Dave	Davis, Eliza	W		Cunningham, Willis		Younge Memorial
Cunningham, Myrtle Shannock [Black]	May 22, 1996	91	F.S.H.	New Market	Feb 17, 1905	Mc Farland, Will	Messengill, Nannie	Cunningham, Lloyd Sr. [D]		Chesney, Ruby; Sister		Younge Memorial
Cunningham, Oneatus [CM]	Jul 13, 1987	41	Jeff City	Tn	Jan 14, 1926	Cunningham, Willie C.	Davis, Mollie	Div		Willis, Donald [Dayton, Ohio]; Oneatus Jr. - David; Mother		Younge Memorial
Cunningham, Ross O' Dell	Dec 17, 1993	83	New Market	Mascot, Tn	Sep 3, 1910	Cunningham, William	Johnson, Harriett	Davis, Geneva		Nixon, Elsie; Ross Jr.; Wife		J.M.G.
Cunningham, Sanford Nathaniel [Black]	Aug 17, 1984	28	J.M.H.	New Market	Jun 26, 1959	Cunningham, Loy Jr.	Yearly, Sherry	Yeary, Sherry		Sherry; Beatrice - Williams, Helen; Wayne-Myart	[Pas] Jarntgan, Jim - Cammie, James - Willie, Melvin - Hodges, Charles - Williams, Greg - Huff, Robert	Younge Memorial
Cunningham, Willie C. [CM]	Apr 23, 1950	49	New Market, Tn	Tn	Jun 6, 1900		Johnson, Harriett	Jossie [D]		Rada - Lewis, Marta; Loy-Ross		New Market
Cupp, James Nelson	Jan 21, 1992	76	J.M.H.	Jeff Co	Dec 9, 1915	Cupp, Jade	Vaughn, Martha E.	Cupp, Josie		Mc Kinley, Susie; Wayne; Doug		J.M.G.
Cupp, Josie Myrtleben	Apr 15, 1998	91	B.H.	Hamblen Co	Jun 10, 1916	Holifield, Rod H.	Stoyers, Mary Lou	Cupp, James Nelson		Mc Kinley, Susie; Wayne; Johnson, Bessie - Ridley, Viola - Long, Elsie; Rudfield	Husband - [Pas] Cleavinger, Guy - Carr, Frank - Purkey, Micky - Cooper, Tex - Broyles, Jeff	J.M.G.
Curl, Mossie C.	Jun 24, 1998	72	Morristown, Tn	Grainger Co	Jan 8, 1907	Curl, Leonard	Mayes, Cordia	Curl, Howard Boyce [D]		Cleavinger, Georgia - Johnson, Eva; David-Eugene	Wife - [Pas] Levin, James - George - Long, Remus - Langston, Lowery - Stooksbury, Miles	Oakland
Curl, William Kenneth	Nov 7, 1993	65	Strawberry Plains	Straw Plains	Apr 18, 1928	Curl, Earnest	Conn, Faye		U.S.A.F.	Ben; Schrader, Minnie - Maxine; Jim-David-Burl-Albert	Wife - [Pas]	Piney
Curtis, Laura	Jan 28, 1958	75	Strawberry Plains	Nc	Feb 14, 1883	King, Elijah	Donaldson, Nancy	Unk	Nc	Queen, Ola		West View
Dale, James William	May 9, 1997	59	New Market	New Market	Nov 24, 1937	Mc Nish, James C.	Morgan, Mary	Speos, Betty Lou	Navy	Seals, Mary; Thomas; Imogene [D] - Lyons, Georgia [D] - Simmons, Belle; Glenn-Ezra	Doug - [Pas] Patterson, John - Henry, George - Morgan, Tim - Glenn, Charles - Love, Bob - Harding, Fred	Pleasant Grove
Dalton, Colbia Sr. [M]	Mar 5, 1992	75	V.A.-Mt. Home	Grainger Co	Jan 5, 1916	Dalton, P.T.	Darling, Viola	Kidwell, Pauline	WW 2	Thomas; Son-Doug		New Blackwell
Dalton, General Gilmore	May 10, 1986	73	Knoxville, Tn	Piney Flats, Tn	Oct 2, 1912	Dalton, Rubin		Delaney, Elizabeth	Navy	Richards, Martha - Morgan, Dorothy; Conroy, Trula ?; James Taylor; Hardin, Vira; William		Chota Masonic - Concord, Tn
Dalton, Jack Otto	Nov 30, 1982	76	Jeff City	Grainger Co	Feb 6, 1906	Dalton, John H.	Henry, Eppie	Mabel K.		Jack [Ya]-William		Cremated

Name	Death Date	Age	Place of Death	Place of Birth	Date of Birth	Father	Military	Mother	Spouse	Children / Relatives	Notes	Cemetery
Dalton, Minerva Arlene	Oct 11, 1995	59	Rutledge, Tn	Jeff City	May 27, 1955	Byrd, Lester		Wright, Pauline	Dalton, Johnny	Dalton, Messy; Tony; Morgan, Judy; Tyek-Doug-Milo-Ron-	Husband- [Pals] Byrd, Jeremy - Profit, Randall - Daniel & Chris - Medina, Roger	J.M.G.
Dalton, Virginia Pauline	Aug 21, 1990	70	F.S.H.	Rutledge, Tn	Apr 23, 1920	Kidwell, Lon		Berkley, Wilda Mae	Dalton, Cottle	Saski, Mary - Shores, Linda; Ogan, John - George - Lawrence - Eugene - Dalton, Greenlee, Rosalee; White, Stella; Zelma - Hancock, Irene - Tom-Cobie Jr.	Husband- [Pals] Turley, Avery - Combs, Harold - Sam - Sophie - Steve - Mattie, Roger - Lamplin, Darrell - Bishop, Rick - Frame, Lee	New Blackwell
Dennwood, Jerry	Feb 9, 1979	0	Knoxville, Tn		Feb 9, 1979	Dennwood, James E.		Ragan, Charlotte				
Dance, Chet B. [M]	Oct 14, 1980	57	Mascot, Tn	Knoxville, Tn	May 24, 1923	Dance, Charlie	WW 2	Gilbert, Phoebe	Wright, Frances	Wilson, Kellie Sue - Deane, Georgie Gail	Bobby-Jimmy-Timmy	Swann [1/2] Burton, Charles / Son / Youngs Memorial
Darby, Fannie Mae	Aug 12, 1995	93	Walton, Ga		Apr 28, 1902	Frankston, Roscoe		Kitchen, Jeanni	Dotby, James Leroy [2]		Arthur T.	Son / Darbysburg, Tn - Covington, Ga.
Dumbauld, Viola	Nov 30, 1988	82	Sevier Co		Jun 17, 1906	Kerr, Hugh		Wilson, Ella Mae	Dumbauld, Harm [2]	Newman, Dorothy - Jordan, Ella Vee	Reese, Conley; Slatworth, Ruth - Hodge, Frick - Bateman, Ann	[Pals] Newman, Steve - Laws, Dan - Jordan, Larry E. - Reese, Rene-Han Allen / Nances Grove
Davidson, Earl Mahle	Jun 18, 1983	87	J.M.H.	Hobbridge, Nebraska	May 29, 1896	Davidson, Andrew	WW 1	Martha	Sylvester, Nina B.		Terry	Son / West View
Davidson, Nina B.	Oct 20, 1993	94	Jeff City	Fort Worth, Tx	Jan 4, 1899	Silvester, W. W.		Laura	Davidson, Earl [D]	Freeman, Lou Edd	Snodgrass, William Richard - Hall, Elisha Newton	Son / Young Memorial
Davis, Alberta	Jan 20, 1977	53	F.S.H.	New Market, Tn	Aug 23, 1923	Davis, Robert		Walker, Gertrude		Brenda	Ruth-Ellen	Archie-John / Sunderland
Davis, Anna Lynn	1969	72		Roane Co.	Mar 11, 1897	Byrd, John		Cook, Dora		Taylor, Sarah Lynn	Richard-Gilbert	Walter
Davis, Arthur Eugene [Black]	Dec 18, 1996	65	New Market	New Market	May 28, 1931	Mack, Dan	Army	Davis, Ruth	Ethel E.	Hill, Diana & Marvin [Va] - Williams, Pam & Greg [Nc] Evelyn	Steve & Cynthia - Tony-Eugene Jr.; Williamson, Elizabeth [2]	Davis, Ethel [Aunt] / Youngs Memorial
Davis, Arvard	May 19, 1963		Tn	Tn	May 29, 1894	Davis, James Nelson		Gaines, Teailtha	Gladys	Allen A.-James H.	Myrtle	Willie / Willie
Davis, Clarence A. [Black]	Apr 28, 1987	72	J.M.H.	New Market	Jun 22, 1914	Davis, James		Hodge, Laura	Me Bee, Dolly	Layne, Ivory	Clarence-James-William; Sisson, Ruth	George / Youngs Memorial
Davis, Clarence Edward	Aug 10, 1995		Chicago, Ill		Oct 27, 1940	Davis, Clarence [Chick]		Dolly		Layne, Ivory - [Br-Law] Davis, Gwen	Davis, William - Stephens, Katherine - Mainard, Precious [Aunts]	James A.- William F. / Youngs Memorial

Name	Death Date	Age	Place of Death	Origin	Birth Date	Father	Mother	Spouse	Status/Other	Children	Relatives	Note	Cemetery
Davis, Dollie [Black]	Dec 5, 1988	67	S.M.H.	Whitesburg, Tn	Dec 5, 1921	Mc Bee, Hal	Kyle, Florence	Davis, Clarence A. Sr.	Layne, Ivory	Clarence-James- Stephens, Katherine - Munford, Precious		Doug [Pals] Simon, John - Jennigan, Jimmy - Phipps, Alex. - Lewis, Bobby - Cunningham, Ross Jr. - Camp, Eugene	Youngs Memorial
Davis, Flussie Marie Trent [Pooly]	May 10, 1993	68	S.M.H.	Knoxville, Tn	Sep 15, 1924	Hall, John M.	Rymer, Peggy Ann	Davis, Elmo	Smith, Sue - Rushing, Patt	Trent, D.M.-Tim-Thomas F.-Tony B.	Pickel, Elsie - Cook, Oma	Son	Strawberry Plains
Davis, Gladys Ruth	Jan 28, 1996	88	S.M.H.	Jeff Co.	Spe 19, 1909	Fielden, Henry Taylor	Newman, Kate	Davis, Arvard A. [2]	Dawson, Evelyn	Allen & Peggy [Ala]-James & Barbara	Robert [Nd]-Marvel [Ye]		Nances Grove
Davis, Grace	Jul 21, 1975	81	Morristown, Tn	Granger Co.	May 21, 1894	Moyers, Sam		Davis, Rufus			Victor-Clyde-Harold [1/2] Everett		Buffalo
Davis, Jerry Dennis	Apr 19, 1996	40	Strawberry Plains	Jeff Co	Oct 7, 1945	Trent, Ella			S		Mc Clain, Faye		Strawberry Plains
Davis, John Rufus	Dec 15, 1977	81	S.M.H.	Tn	Jan 26, 1896	Davis, Joe	Galyon, Eliza				[Br-Law] Davis, Mrs. Sam-Mrs. Tom [Okla]	Mc Ghee, Sam Moyers, Clyde-Everett	Buffalo - Granger Co
Davis, Myrtie	Oct 23, 1985	77	Tn	Tn					Vietnam			Davis, Gladys [Sister-in-Law]	Indian Ridge
Davis, Pearl	Jun 20, 1997	79	S.M.H.	Iowa City, Iowa	May 10, 1918	Ball, James Edgar	Austin, Mary Estella	Davis, Gilbert			Clyde & Margie [Che]-David & Nancy [Tx]	Husband	New Market
Davis, Robert Brent	Feb 15, 1998	49	New Market	Rutledge, Tn	Oct 6, 1948	Davis, Arthur Brent	Farrar, Lucille Swann	Div	Allor, Kristie	Robbie & Cindy	Yates, Anita & Rod		Shiloh
Davis, Ronald Gregory	Sep 24, 1951	1d	Jeff City	Jeff City	Sep 24, 1951	Davis, James	Plett, Louise	New Married				Father	Presbyterian
Davis, Ruth [Black]	Dec 14, 1996	77	J.M.H.	New Market	Oct 25, 1909	Davis, Robert	Davis, Gertie		Davis, Walter-Eugene		Davis, Walter-Eugene	[Pals] Scruggs, Colon-Rogers, Simon, John - Cunningham, Lucy Jr.-Palis, Ed	Youngs Memorial
Davis, Samuel Wesley	Nov 9, 1971		Jeff Co	Tn	Jan 15, 1888	Davis, Joseph	Galyon, Eliza	Bettis, Ada				Wife	West View
Davis, John Thomas [Bug]	Jan 20, 2000	66	Rutledge, Tn	Rutledge, Tn	Jun 24, 1933	Davis, John Thomas	Looney, Helen	Earl	Whitlow, Barbara - Tolley, Diane		Davis, Betty Jean - [1/2] Norton, Anna	Rufus	Tempico
Davison, Curtis Earl	Aug 20, 1989	22	Ocala, Florida	Jeff City	Jul 3, 1967	Davison, Curtis Joe	Mc Nish, Shirley	S				Mother - [Pals] Flournoy, Michelle - Cavalcante, Nicholas - Sterling, Troy - Wimmer, Corby - Shaffer, Bobby - Muncey, James	Valley View
Davison, Martha	Jun 1, 1967	100	Knoxville, Tn	Tn	Aug 23, 1866	Davison, Curtis	Mc Nish, Shirley	W	Houser, Mrs. Artie - Rentro, Minnie		Mother		Nances Grove
Davison, Richard Joe	Dec 30, 1991	22	U.T.H.	Knox Co	Oct 3, 1969	Davison, Curtis	Mc Nish, Shirley	S					New Market

Name	Death Date	Age	Location	Birth Place	Birth Date	Father	State	Mother	Spouse	Svc	Relatives / Children	Cemetery
Dennison, Lowell Edward	May 16, 1992	54	Jeff Co	Knox Co	Dec 29, 1937	Dennison, Hugh	Tn	Scull, --				Strawberry Plains
Denton, Anna V.	Dec 31, 1963	61	B.H.	Tn	Sep 14, 1902	Martin, Jim	Tn		Denton, W.R.		Chuck — Miller, Mrs. Hobart — Willis — Husband	J.M.G.
Denton, Charles Virgil	Mar 14, 1990	85	Newport, Tn	Sevier Co	Mar 17, 1904	Denton, Henry		Harris, Lula	Harrington, Maude		Charles H. — Chambers, Nannie — Son	New Market
Denton, Frances Lorenza	Sep 17, 1997	97	J.M.H.	Dandridge, Tn	Mar 9, 1900	Hicks, John C.			Denton, Mell M. [D.]		Alley, Louise — Myers, Deanna — Phillips, Eleanor — Watts, Jane — Holbert, Jean; Roger-Paul Shields-John E. — Ben	
Denton, Franklin Eugene	Mar 1, 1992	58	U.T.H.	Strawberry Plains	May 10, 1933	Denton, Orville		Lee, Alma	Tipton, Margaret Opal		Tolison, Regina; England, Shirley; Clark-David-Stan; Willie-[Pals] Lusk-Artie-Elmore-Ross-Scott-Denton, Will-Colfier, Ron	Beech Springs-Kodak, Tn
Denton, Hall H.	Feb 9, 1987	83	New Market	Sevier Co	Aug 22, 1903	Denton, Johnston		Inman, Julia Ann			Roderick, Frances — Elmore, Betty — McCalnahan, Helen — Dixon, Shirley; Charles-Pete-Donald-Robert; Parker, Estelle; Vato; Willie-[Pals] Elmore, Wade-Scott-Norman-Roderick, Charles-Denton, John-Clark	New Market
Denton, Lula Virginia	Jan 11, 1968	94	J.M.H.	Virginia	Aug 31, 1912	Wollard, Earl		Wilson, Frances	Wollard, Lucy		Roderick, Mary Frances — Elmore, Betty — McCalnahan, Helen — Dixon, Shirley; Robert-Donald-Clarance-Marshall-Charles; Roderick, Hazel	Widley View
Denton, Lucy Lizzy Bell	Nov 6, 1991	79	J.M.H.	Tn	Sep 29, 1873	Williams, W.O.		Early, Martha J.	Denton, Hall [D]			
Denton, Margaret Opal	Aug 25, 1996	56	Corryton, Tn	Knox Co	Sep 21, 1939	Tipton, Dennis B.		Whittaker, Gertrude	Denton, Eugene		Tolison, Regina & Mathew; Dennis A.-Troy; Doug; Husband-[Pals] Harrington, Bruce D.-Bruce Jr.-Hathway, Garry-Cook, Randy-Cobb, Mack-Randy-Darren-Pettijin, Lenny	New Market
Denton, Maude Anna	Nov 30, 1996	61	White Pine, Tn	Tn	Jun 29, 1907	Harrington, John		Wicely, Polly Jane	Denton, Virgil		Charles H.; Bruce; New Market	New Market
Denton, Mildred Maude	Feb 10, 1993	80	New Market	Blaine, Tn	Mar 26, 1912	Slabsworth, John		Pate, Gertrude	Denton, Melvin Willis		Glenn-Harold; Husband; New Market	New Market
Denton, Ronald Earl	Sep 19, 1999	75	Jeff City	Jeff Co	Sep 26, 1935	Denton, Earl		Hicks, Frances	Div		Paul L. [Sr]-Jerry, Tony [Nc]; Phillips, Eleanor [D]; Jim [D]-Bill [D]-Jack-Roger; Husband	J.M.G.
Denton, Paul Shields	Sep 8, 2000	64	Jeff City	Jeff Co		Denton, Earl		Phillips, Mildred	Denton, Shirley J.	Army	Gray, Caroline & Keith; Mark & Sharon-Phillip Earl & Ronnie; Richard, Katherine; Roger; Hillcrest	Hillcrest
Denton, William Robert	Mar 23, 1996	60	Sevier Co, Tn		Sep 26, 1905	Denton, William Eli		Brimer, Ronda P.	Ann V.		Harold Dwight; Audrey-Julia-Martin, Mrs. Noah-Swann, Mrs. Samuel; Boyd R.; Denton, Dwight-[Pals] Brimer, [Pals] Buster Walter-Donohue Bill-Richard	J.M.G.
Diamond, Charlie Greene	Apr 29, 1992	80	Lake City, Tn	Mascot, Tn	Apr 25, 1912	Keezner, Charles		Foust, Elizabeth	Diamond, Oscar		Carr, Linda-Carr, Marjorie; J.R.-Ray; Boyd R.; Dawg	Strawberry Plains
Diamond, Frances Louise	Sep 9, 1995	58	S.M.H.	Mascot, Tn	Jun 13, 1937	Dockery, Richard		Walker, Callie	Diamond, Ray		Reach, Ann-Howard, Emma; Frank-Ray-Pat-Robert-Jim-Jerry; Roger; Husband	Strawberry Plains

Name	Date	Age	Place	Birthplace	Birth Date	Father	Mother	Notes				Cemetery
Dillon, Hester Elizabeth	Jan 16, 1971	88			Dec 18, 1882					Smith, Harley - [1/2] Smith, George [TX]	Son	Beaver Creek
Dinwiddie, Clyde H.	Mar 30, 1986	89	J.M.H.	Jeff Co	Apr 24, 1896	Dinwiddie, David M.		W		Johnson, Clara [Cha.] - Gibson, Bertha		
Dinwiddie, Fannie V.	Aug 15, 1972	74	Jeff City	Knoxville, Tn	Jul 8, 1898	Northern, Tina			Winsjun - Farmer, Mary & Roy	Weeks, Mary Ellie [TX] - Hood, Pearl [Pa] - Greer, Anna [Cal]	Virgil	Pleasant Grove
Dirl, Bob Lee [Black]	Sep 15, 1988	74	Jeff City	Jeff City	Nov 17 1913	Dirl, Thomas	Massingill, Mary	navy	Bryant, Leoda - Mills, Linda	Albert	Gilbreath, Mattie - Shanks, Gertrude	Wife	J.M.G.
Disney, Martha French [Polly]	Nov 28, 1971	53	Decatur, Ga			French, -	Mattie	French [Cal]	Foust, Patsy	Billie [Fla]	Lewis, Brenda [Cal] - Steele, Jean [Mich]	Sherman - Hurds S. Ward, Inc [Decatur, Ga]	New Market
Dixon, David Gugman	Jan 25, 1998	59	Morristown, Tn	Greeneville, Tn	Jul 22, 1938	Dixon, Andrew	Rader, Merida Jo	Div	Army	Perra, Lois - Spire, Ruth - Wilson, Nancy - Webb, Gail [Fla]	David Andrew	Kuykendall, Josephine - Carroll, Dorothy	Clifford	Timber Ridge - Greeneville, Tn
Dixon, James Silas Wade	Oct 10, 1992	50	Jeff City	Blaine, Tn	Feb 9, 1942	Dixon, Willis S.	Vineyard, Linia	Div			Johnson, Mary		J.M.G.
Doane, Addie	Feb -, 1967	93	M.C.	Tn	Oct 16, 1973	Crowder, John E.	Anderson, Rachel			J.N.-N.M.	Newman, Mrs. J.C. [Conn.]		Friends Station
Doane, William E.	Jun 28, 1967	90	Jeff Co	Wallace Switch, Pa	Nov 7, 1876	Parles, William	Keller, -		Doane, Robert H. [D]		Doane, Mattie - Newman, Mrs. J.C. [Conn.]	Hicks, Robert T. - Patterson, Troy	T.S.
Dockery, Asa Woodrow	May 15, 1983	70	Care Inn	Sevier Co	Sep 28, 1912	Dockery, Mitchell	Baker, Florence		Mc Daniel, Bonnie	Leon-Roy	Hubbard, Lillian - Hubbard, Ellen	Hicks, Robert T. - Patterson, Troy	Valley View
Dockery, Edgar Leon	Sep 30, 2000	64	New Market	New Market	May 15, 1936	Dockery, Asa	Bales, Emma Lois	Div		Aaron-Mitchell	Mc Daniel, Bonnie		Valley View
Dockery, Roy Mitchell	Oct 17, 1994	47	U.T.H.	Jeff Co	Jul 5, 1947	Dockery, Asa	Bales, Emma L.		Knight, Michelle	Mary-Eric-Marcus	Mc Daniel, Bonnie	Leon	Valley View
Dockins, Lurco Tracey	Aug 4, 1990	74	J.M.H.	Dandridge, Tn	Feb 26, 1916	Dockins, Del	Osborne, Mary				Mc Mahan, Gladys		Hills Union
Dockins, Lora Tracey	Aug 6, 1981	89	New Market	Jeff Co	Apr 25, 1882	Case, Henry	Presly, R.		Osborne, Wanda			Wife	Hills Union
Dockins, Mary Katherine	Jan 1, 1996	82	Jeff City	Jeff Co	Jul 25, 1913	Russell, Tom	Cutshaw, Mattie Jane	Dockins, Charles [D] - Dockins, James Henry [D]	Meyer, Gloria - Crooke, Ruth	Ralph-James [Bath-D]	Mc Mahan, Gladys		Hills Union

Name	Date	Age			Date										Cemetery
Douglas, Charles Henry	Aug 14, 1985	61	F.S.H.	Knoxville, Tn	Apr 7, 1924	Dodgin, Jim	Leona		Perry, Esther	army	Ritz-Reba [Step] Moody, Sandra	Robert-Roy- Ronnie-Raymond [Step] Spoon, Terry F- Foster, David	Jay	[Phil] Vets	Central Point - Rutledge, Tn
Dodson, Joyce Beverly	May 7, 1990	10m	M.C.	Tn	Jan 11, 1959	Dodson, Bobbie	Tn							Dodson, Bobbie Billy-Steve	New Market
Donaldson, Irene	Nov 8, 1982	64	J.M.H.	Pulaski Co, Ky	Nov 4, 1918	Kerr, Hugh	Jordan, Ada		Donaldson, John T.		Allen, Patricia	John T. 3rd	Scarlett, Bonnie - Liane, Michell	Bronco-Roy- H.H. Jr	J.M.G.
Donaldson, John Tudor	Mar 3, 1985	70	Bossier City, La	Fountain City, Tn	Sep 13 1914	Donaldson, Robert	Kerr, Irene	WW 2			Allen, Pat	[Step] Mc Nish, Billie	John Tudor Jr.		J.M.G.
Donaldson, Misty Leanne	Jan 23, 1977	0	Morristown, Tn	Morristown, Tn	Jan 23, 1977	Donaldson, Ralph T.	Welch, Kathy								Mill Springs
Donaldson, Richard Theodore (Bud)	Mar 21, 1993	78	S.M.H.	Knoxville, Tn	Jul 3, 1914	Donaldson, Richard B.	Young, Lola				Kee, Zora	Ralph	Reed, Beunie - Henry, Katie - Ruder, June - Walker, Evelyn	Son - [Phil] Rucker, Ken - Roberts, Scott- Steve - Taylor, Bill - Young, Bill - Lane, Earl	J.M.G.
Donaldson, Zora Versie	May 28, 1998	82	Morristown, Tn	Granger Co	Feb 6, 1916	Kee, Jordan	Collins, Ida Evelyn		Donaldson, Richard T. [D]			Ralph T.			J.M.G.
Dotson, Barbara Jean	Dec 23, 1998	54	Dandridge, Tn	Knoxville, Tn	Jul 11, 1944	Bell, Arthur	Edwards, Evelyn		Dotson, Steve G.		Strange, Rebecca Ann - Dotson, Janice	Steven			New Market
Dotson, Lucille T.	Jul 25, 1978	57		Tn	Jul 18, ----	Tipton, George	Herron, Stella	W			Whaley, Mrs. Troy - Foland, Mrs. Kenneth - Emory, Mrs. Albert	Robert Jr.-Bruce [Wesh b.C.]- Steven - William	Oscar-Ralph	[Phil] Bozeman, Frank - Solomon, Franklin - Welch, Bill - Collins, John - Elder, Freddie - Kerr.	New Market
Dotson, Robert	Sep 4, 1982	46	Jeff Co	Jeff Co	Sep 15, 1915						Patsy-Janie-Jeanette	Robert Jr.- Steve-Billy	Raymond-George-James	Lucille [Wife]	New Market
Dotson, Roberta Lynn	Sep 15, 1974	0	Jeff Co	Jeff Co	Sep 15, 1974	Dotson, Robert	Clarkson, Sheila								New Market
Dotson, Twa Ray	Oct 3, 1992	64	Jeff City	Jeff City	Jul 2, 1928	Dotson, William	Scott, Willie		Scott, Julia Faye		Dotson, Carrie			Lowe, Victor - Dotson, Mrs. L. [3-Parents] Scott, Lucy [S-Law] - [Phil] Elmore, Wade- Ross-Scott- Amburn, Kevin - Scott, Carol - Dotson, Robert - Blair, Charles - Kerr.	New Market
Douglas, Charlie Newman	Feb 5, 1951	62	New Market, Tn	Tn	Apr 9, 1888	Douglas, G.A.	Privette, Elizabeth	Tn					French, Mrs. W.A. - French, Mrs. Mary - Lewis, Mrs. Dow - Henry, Mrs. Ralph	[In-Laws] Kirwick, Phoebe - Douglas, Frances	Piedmont
Douglas, Hazel Mahinda	Apr 19, 2000	85	J.M.H.	Sevier Co	Mar 19, 1915	Chesney, R.N.	Huffaker, Mary		Douglas, James L. [D]				Tillett, Geneva Edith James & Mary- John C. & Linda	Douglas, N.O. [Brother] Andy-Harley	Paw Paw Hollow
Douglas, Leona K. [Louis]	Sep 20, 1992	84	J.M.H.	Hamblen Co	Nov 29, 1907	Kinnick, James Vincent	Hooper, Della		Douglas, N.O. [D]					Roy Brother	New Market

Name	Date	Age	Place	Birth Date	Father	Mother	Mil.	Children / Survivors			Cemetery
Douglas, Roger William	Apr 2, 1981	83	Sevier Co	Nov 13, 1897	Douglas, Floyd	Bailey, Janice	S	Roberts, John-Jerry [Ste]-Douglas, Eddie	Huffaker, Zona		Chilhowee - Seymour, Tn
Douglas, Ruby Catherine	Apr 18, 1996	82	J.M.H.	Mar 31, 1934	Whaley, Aaron	Mc Carter, Ines				Hugh-Glenn	Beech Springs - Sevier Co
Doyle, Thomas Jackson	Aug 25, 1993	62	New Market	Mar 11, 1931	Doyle, Lawrence C. Sr.	Price, Katherine	Army	Riley, Rejeyna	Charles T.	Wife	White
Drake, Leroy Clark	Feb 15, 1996	70	Morristown, Tn	May 3, 1915	Drake, Charles	Ham, Ida	Ruth	Carmichael, Ardshley - Stanmore, Lisa [Ste] - Tisey, Barbara [Ste]	Lynn M [Pat] - [Step] Smith, Lawrence [Pat]	Mc Crustey, May - Goodman, Allen	V.F.W. — Hamblen Memorial
Duck, Harvey Clyde	Oct 14, 1996	77	F.S.H.	May 15, 1921	Duck, Jess E.	Sweet, Lydia		Roach, Grace	Gordon, Carolyn - Wronds, Sandy & Proper - Oliver, Diane & Jerry	Donald C. — Robinson, Thelia [Nc]	Ove-Tom — Oakland
Duckworth, Nell Grant	Jan 19, 1990	80	Anderson, Sc	Jan 30, 1913	Burgess, John Mack	Stone, Essie		Duckworth, Edrew H.			Greenwood - Easley, Sc
Douglas, Ruth Elizabeth	Mar 22, 1996	92	Hill Haven	Apr 26, 1903	Repass, Emory S.	Dutton, Lucy Jane		Douglas, Harve [D]	House, Virginia - Oates, Mona - Kidwell, Zollie - Linear-Colston, Bonnie Kate [Tr] - Reese, Ruth	Pat Hatchet - James Earl		Highland Memorial
Dugnan, George Mike	May 9, 1984	79	J.M.H.	Oct 18, 1904	Duignan, Charlie	Rudder, Jennie			French, Pauletie	Jack [Sc]-David — Cook, Carrie Lou - Wood, Ruth Dane	Hugh — Strawberry Plains
Duignan, Hugh Monroe	Feb 24, 1995		Strawberry Plains	Sep 20, 1916	Duignan, Charlie	Rudder, Jennie		Hicks, Jennie	French, Pauletie	Bill D.-Duvan D.	Pauline — J.M.G.
Dukes, Bessie	Mar 30, 1987	84	Jeff City	Sep 19, 1902	Dumbush, Robert	Gillian, Julie		Hicks, Jennie	Dukes, Margin M. [D]	French, Pauletie	Pauline — New Market
Dukes, Conrad A.	Oct 17, 1993	69	M.C.	Jul 12, 1894	Dukes, J.A.	Northern, Julia	Tn		Wright, Mrs. James - [G] Brenda-Sandra-Jane	Hicks, Mrs. M.L.-Trent, Mrs. C.L.	Family — Twin Hollow - Grainger Co
Dukes, William Chester	Jan 10, 1985	75	Gregar	Oct 8, 1890	Dukes, Joe	Northern, Julia		Nellis Dettilna [G]	[G] J.C.-Steve	Hicks, Mrs. Smith - Griffin, Mrs. J.T. [Calif]	Nances Grove
Duncan, Thomas Mack	Apr 25, 1981	82	Washington Co, Tn	May 17, 1898	Duncan, John	Sheil, Martha		Tallent, Marie			Oak Grove
Duncan, Rollie Ray	Feb 16, 1996	59	B.H.	Feb 1, 1939	Duncan, Jessie	Wells, Jessie		Petty, Nadine	[Step] Hale, James	Bobbie-Pat-Donna - Vogt, Billis [Mach]	
Dunn, Floyd Harrison	Feb 8, 1964	63	Columbus, Ohio	Jan 7, 1920	Dunn, Mansfield	Burnett, Adeline		Lako, Elizabeth	WW 2 — Wood, Brenda - Parker, Patty		[Pat] Cunningham, Fred-Allen - Yardley, Clarence - Besler, Bob - White, John - Murray, E.P. — Friends Station
Dunn, Mary Morgan	Jan 18, 1980	80	Grainger Co	Jul 8, 1899	Morgan, Joe	Greenlee, Cordelia		Dunn, Gate [D]		Spoon, Paul	Blackwell - Ruthledge, Tn

Name	Date	Age	Place	City	Birth Date	Father		Mother	Spouse						Cemetery
Dunsmore, Henry Allison	Jan 5, 1990	81	New Market	Jeff Co	Jul 11, 1899	Dunsmore, Henry Clifton		Sharp, Pettie Jane	Foster, Stella Mae					[Pial] Dunsmore, Allison-Dwayne-Eddie-Roma..., Shaw-, Gossard-Donnie-, Hall, Buddy-, Gordon, Dale-, Halfner, Bob-A.J.	Piedmont
Dunsmore, Stella Mae	Aug 26, 1997	81	Jeff City	New Market	Apr 1, 1916	Foster, Charles A.		Everhart, Edna Pearl	Dunsmore, Henry [D]	Hickman, Betty & Bill - Smith, Doris & Eddie - [Step-See Child]	Thomas [D]-Jack & Laura [Nc] - [Step-See Child]	Charles [D]- Ralph [D]- Grover [D]-James	Betty	Piedmont
Dunwoody, Elizabeth [Col]	Jul 20, 1955	44	M.C.	New Market	Sep 10, 1910	Johnson, Eli	Nc	Howell, Addie	Dunwoody, Carl	3	6	2	Father	West View
Dyke, Louie [F]	May 3, 1959	76	M.C.	Tn	Nov 30, 1872	Wright, ?		Dyke, Mary	W			Foster, Mrs. Jess	J.C.-Dave	Husband	Piedmont
Dyke, Will H.	Oct 14, 1962	73	M.C.	Tn	Jul 23, 1889	Dyke, Dewitt	Tn	Roach, Mary	Tn	WW 2				Baker, Mrs. George	Piedmont
Easley, James Edwin	Apr 2, 1977	69	J.M.H.	Jeff Co	Aug 2/2,190	Easley, James		Ellis			[Nephews] Easley, Clifford - Jimmy Joe [All-Kd]	Victor-Robert T. - [Step] Brandon, Jr.-Robert Lynn-Jeffery-Donald	[Pals] Foster, Fred, Simpson, Earl-Conner, Guy - Wright, Charles - Walker, John - Hodge, Edward	West View
Edmonds, Robert Jr.	Mar 11, 1987	60	New Market	Dandridge, Tn	May 15, 1936	Edmonds, Robert F.		Hale, Jancy Jane	Hubbard, Peggy	Dalton, Nancy K. - Henry, Peggy F. - Dalton, Helen J.	Moody, Agnes	George-James Paul	Willie	Hills Union
Eled, Andrew	Jan 22, 1963	48	J.M.H.	Jeff Co	Jan -, -	Eled, Robert M.		Brown, Candy L.						Brown, James & Violet - Eled, Richard & Vivien [G-Parents]	New Market
Eldridge, Mary Lois	Nov 16, 1988	48	U.T.H.	Jeff City	Apr 5, 1940	Collins, John		Collins, Leona	Eldridge, Andrew [Pie]				Harold-John Ernest	Sexts, Bille Jean [Pals] Collins, Don - Dopley-Kenneth - Dale-Matthew - Moore, Robert	West View
Elem, Emily Jane Hopson	Feb 21, 1991	30	U.T.H.	Jeff City	Aug 6, 1960	Moore, Wayne [Step]		Hopson, Martha	Elem, James		Dawn		Carroll, Nancy & Charles - Le Claire, Connie & Raymond	Sexts, Bille Jean - Morgan, Anna	Sunderland
Elkins, Ronald C. Jr.	Dec -, 1968	3	Madison Hts., Mich.			Elkins, Ronald		Collins, Katherine	Tn				Husband	West View
Eller, Charles James	Oct 17, 1992	38	White Pine, Tn	White Pine, Tn	Jan 18, 1954	Eller, Charles Leonard		Carpenter, Bonnie	Thomas, Brenda		Kevin-Chad	Runda	Tom	Willie	Mt. Pleasant Methodist
Ellis, Carolyn Rose	Jan 22, 1992	51	F.S.H.	Jeff Co	Jul 28, 1940	Clark, Cordon C.		French, Hilda	Ellis, Robert H.	Betts, Connie	Robb	Allen, Shirley	Tom	Hopcroft F.H. [Husband] Fra-, Mott J.-Collins, Ms. Allen- Haynes, Thelma [G-Mothers]	J.M.G.
Ellis, Edna Louise	May 6, 1992	71	F.S.H.	Sevier Co	Jan 3, 1921	Kooch, Fred A.		Nob, Mary Edna	Tn			Widner, Adde - Davis, Mary Nellie - Porter, Elizabeth	William-Thomas-Ben-Kenneth-Richard	[Pals] French, Ron - Elwood, Robert - Ballantyne, Millie - Palmer, David - Sexts, Robert - Bounds, Mark	New Market
Ellis, Myrtle Mae	Apr 19, 1990	74	Knoxville, Tn		Aug 27, 1915	Newman, Luther	Tn	Haynes, Mattie	Tn	Marshoth, Dorothy	Bill-Gene	Clery, Ann	Husband	Brother	Mullins Chapel - Dandridge, Tn

Name	Death Date	Age	Place	Birthplace	Birth Date	Father	Mother	St	Spouse	Mil	Daughters	Sons	Sisters	Brothers	Pallbearers	Burial
Ellis, William Aaron	Feb 14, 1990	73	U.T.H.	Arkansas	Nov 11, 1906	Ellis, Wiley	Collins, Ida		Kooch, Edna Louise		Westervelt, Mrs. Robert	Daniel-William A. Jr.-Jerry	Walker, Mrs. Virgil	Mason	[Pals] Wright, Luther-Freddy- Wickner, Jack - Moore, David - Porter, Frank - Ashbrook, Doug	New Market
Ellison, Corum Seals	May 20, 1999	77	Grainger Co.	Tn	Jan 16, 1922	Clark, Corum	Acuff, Mary	Tn	Ellison, Carroll [D]				Seale, Robert H.			
Ellison, George C.	Jan 11, 1962	67	S.M.H.	Tn	Aug 22, 1896	Ellison, James P.	Keener, Mary A.	Tn			Hull, Mrs. Hugh			Ellison, Mrs. J.S.		Lebanon Baptist
Ellison, Louise	May 4, 1981	64	Riverdale, Georgia	Tn	Nov 25, 1916	Thomas, Floyd	Templin, Della		Ellison, Carroll [DM]		Harris, Barbara - Rice, Darlene			Helen-Betty	Harris, Homer- Daniel - Rice, Kenneth - Novak, Chuck - Smith, Glen - Overton, Andrew	
Ellison, Mary	Feb 10, 1969	78	Jeff City	Tn	Sep 20, 1890	Ellison, Sherman	Wilkerson, Ann	S					Scarlett, Edna - Flynn, Kate	Bufford-Ben [Ark.]		Deep Springs
Ellison, Paul Hale	Mar 1, 1981		U.T.H.	New Market, Tn	May 2, 1917	Ellison, Charlie B.	Van Dyke, Nellie		Witt, Gladys				Smith, Lula - Hurst, Chad - Ellison, Mary - Brown, Lucy - Bradley, Louise		[Pals] Akter, Earl - Lindsey, Robert - Love, Cecil - Witt, James - Riley, Robert-Willis	Highland Memorial East
Ellis, Granville Lee	Jul 18, 1991	76	Chestnut Hill, Tn	Tn	Oct 14, 1914	Ellis, William	Profitt, Sarah		Newman, Myrtle Mae [D]		Mantooth, Dorothy			Doug	[Pals] Mantooth, Jim - Chuck-Jack - Ellis, Gary-Todd- Ken - Blanchard, Jeff	Mullins Chapel - Dandridge, Tn
Elmore, Alfred Eugene	May 4, 1965	35	Winton-Salem, Nc	Tn	Mar 7, 1929	Elmore, Raymond	Lewis, Pearl		Calloway, Marie		Vivian-Denise	Barry		Willis		J.M.G.
Elmore, Betty Lou	Apr 9, 2000	64	Jeff City	New Market	Jan 18, 1936	Guinn, Frank	Solomon, Molly Lowery	Div			Kidwell, Donna - Housewright, Vicky - Ownby, Sylvia			J.F.-Wayne		Pleasant Grove
Elmore, Billy Dean	Oct 9, 1965	53	B.H.	Jeff Co	Sep 24, 1942	Elmore, Lee	Smith, Mattie		Denton, Carolyn			Randy	John-H.L.		[Pals] Brown, Don - Elmore, Sam - Fred - Widner, Dan - Dials, Ezra - Denton, Dwight	Westleys Chapel
Elmore, Emma Lee	Mar 30, 1999		Knox Co	Tn	Mar 24, 1895	Fielden, Alex	Cole, Sarah	W			[Step] Lewis, Bonnie - Cates, Mrs. Bill	[Nephew] Kelsie Fielden [III]		Elmore, Hulbert		Pleasant Grove
Elmore, Harold W.	Jun 26, 1983	21	Jeff Co	Tn	Feb 9, 1932	Elmore, Linden	Cole, Demurcus	Tn						Donald-Lueben Philip	Elmore, Mrs. Linden - Kate, Andrew [G-Father]	Nances Grove
Elmore, Harvey Carol [Bill]	Feb 23, 1983	72	Knoxville, Tn	Jeff Co	Feb 26, 1910	Elmore, Sam	Russell, Stacy	S		WW 2				Raymond	[Pals] Elmore, Billy-Johnny-H.L.- Laymon-Freddie- Jerry	Friends Station
Elmore, Howard	Dec 17, 1996	64	Dandridge, Tn	Tn	1963	Elmore, Sam	Russell, Stacey	S			Blair - Hazel	Earl-Raymond		Willie - [G-Children] Margaret, Gay- Brent - Hicks, Collen [Sis]		Friends Station
Elmore, Hubert Carlile	Mar 3, 1971	70	Jeff City	Tn	Jan 22, 1901	Elmore, John T.	Fielden, Laura		Lillie		[Foster] Minton, Georgia Lou		Vineyard, Middie - Skelts, Wilma			J.M.G.
Elmore, J.W.	Oct 3, 1972		New Market, Tn		Mar 21, 1904	Elmore, Sam	Brazelton, Harriet									New Market
Elmore, Joe Conley	Oct 19, 1998	79	M.C.	Tn	Nov 2, 1878	Elmore, William	Lewis, Pearl	Tn	Russell, Willie				Repass, Mrs. Paul	Willie	Wife	New Market
Elmore, John Franklin	Dec 4, 1969	39	Knox Co	Tn	Oct 11, 1930	Elmore, Raymond	Fielden, Fannie	Tn	Kyle, Wilma		Angela	Tim-Mark		Wayne	Wife	Pleasant Grove

Name	Death Date	Age	Place	County / Birthplace	Birth Date	Father	Mother	Code	Spouse / Family			Relatives	Cemetery
Elmore, John Henry	Jun 12, 1983	65	F.S.H.		Apr 5, 1918	Elmore, Caleb	Banks, Aveline	S	Bruner, Ola Mae	Frank-Isaac-Edgar		[Pat] Arnold, Arthur, J.A. - Hodge, N.M. - Vance, Roger - Shelton, Roy	Clear Springs
Elmore, Lee Taylor	Apr 27, 1975	65	F.S.H.	Jeff Co	Feb 16, 1900	Elmore, Sam	Russell, Stacey	Div	Layman-Johnny Bill-H.L.	Blair, Hazel	Raymond-Bill	[Pat] Jones, Bill - White, Danny - Howell, Charles - Ogle, Ezra - Brown, Clarence [Dau] Milton, Georgia L.	Friends Station
Elmore, Lillie	Jun 7, 1976	81	Jeff City	Knox Co, Tn	Nov 10, 1894	Faulkner, Albert H.	Nora	W					Nances Grove
Elmore, Linden P.	Nov 8, 1951	52	Jeff City	Tn	Jan 30, 1899	Elmore, J.T.	Fielden, Laura		Cole, Demetrius [D]	Mildred-Lucille - Hickman, Willard, Dora	Donald-Phillip-Lucian-Harold	Edgar-Marsh-Herbert-Raymond	Nances Grove
Elmore, Mary Demetrius	Dec 15, 1997	92	U.T.H.	Sevier Co	Sep 4, 1905	Cole, Andrew	Bradley, Sarah	W	Elmore, Linden P. [D]	Lowery, Mildred - Hickman, Lucille	Eugenia Marion - Spruling, Judy Ann	Phillip-Lucian	Wyrick, Ruby	Nances Grove
Elmore, Mildred Louise	Dec 1, 1994	63	F.S.H.	Mascot, Tn	Jun 1, 1931	Mc Cann, Cory	Brabson, Lula		Elmore, Ralph Eulene	Cameron, Barbara	Vineyard, Mabel - Steck, Wilma	Gray, Margaret	Husband	New Market
Elmore, Merrell H.	Oct 17, 1981	64	J.M.H.	Jeff Co	Dec 6, 1896								New Market
Elmore, Myrtle Mae	Nov 8, 1996	82	B.H.	Sevier Co	Feb 10, 1914	Quillums, Andrew	Mc Carter, Eliza		Elmore, Otha Cleo	Wilson, Lillian P. [D]	Loneday, Otis - Carr, Matison	Gratdell [D]- Jake	Wilson, Mackly - [Pat] France, Bill - Wilson, Little - Melton, Sam - Burnette, Bud-Earl	Strawberry Plains
Elmore, Nellie Grace	Mar 11, 1995	67		Sevier Co, Tn	Jan 14, 1898	Mc Nabb, Tipton	James, Sarah Addie		Elmore, Edgar [D]	Mc Daniel, Helen - Louise & Glenn - Hinson, Versia Ruth & John	Murry, Edith - Smart, Mrs. J. Hugh [Hattie]	Mc Nabb, George	Nances Grove
Elmore, Nina Pearl	May 12, 1996	75	J.M.H.	Jeff Co	Jan 28, 1911	Lewis, Frank	Shiglia, Aliha		Elmore, Raymond [D]		J.D.-Carl Edward	Wayne	Stpplin, Ruby	Son	J.M.G.
Elmore, Norman Eric	Oct 30, 1989	24	U.T.H.	Jeff City	Sep 12, 1965	Denton, Benjy Ann	Bates, Nancy Michelle			Paul		Wade-Scott- Ross-William	[1/2] Bates, Jason-Chad - Edington, Danny - Lonnell, Rocky - Hook, Greg-Scott	Valley View
Elmore, Otha Cleo	Mar 6, 1996	84	J.M.H.	Sevier Co	Feb 18, 1912	Elmore, Henry	Ernert, Kattie	W	Quillums, Myrtle Mae	Wilson, Lillian P. [D]	[1/2] Bates, Coy Evelyn	Wade-Scott- Ross-William	Willis - [Pat] Bates, Jason-Chad - Edington, Danny - Lonnell, Rocky - Hook, Greg-Scott	Strawberry Plains
Elmore, Raymond E.	Feb 2, 1991	85	J.M.H.	Jeff Co	Feb 17, 1905	Elmore, Sam	Russell, Stacey	Tn	Morgan, Pearl	Ray [Ray]			Elmore, Wayne [Son] - Stallings, Wife	J.M.G.
Elmore, Raymond Leslie	Sep 23, 1985	82	J.M.H.	Jeff Co	May 2, 1903	Elmore, John Thomas	Fielden, Laurel	Tn	Lewis, Pearl				Wife	J.M.G.
Elmore, Roy Layman	Nov 25, 1993	56	S.M.H.	New Market	Nov 11, 1937	Elmore, Lee	Smith, Mattie	W	Metcalf, Beverly	Meribeth, Judy		Randele, Eva - Sauceman, Mrs. C.H.	Cameron, Barbara & Ellis [Dau]	New Market
Elmore, Sallie Kate	Jan 21, 1975	74	S.M.H.	Green Co	May 12, 1900	Fulton, Gudger	Sams, Julia	W				Massey, Mary-Kermit [III]	Cameron, Barbara & Ellis [Dau]	New Market
Elmore, Theis Irene	Mar 8, 1999	84	New Market	Parrottsville, Tn	Sep 1, 1914	Buster, Will	Minnie A.		Elmore, Isaac D.		Hubie-Ralph- Lonnie			Beaver Creek
Elmore, W.W. [Doc]	Jul 27, 1959	89	New Market	Tn	Apr 26, 1870	Elmore, Thomas	Renfro, Emily	Tn	Fielden, Emma Lee			Vineyard, Mrs. M.F. - Carr, Adaline - Steck, Wilma	Willis	Pleasant Grove
Elmore, William Edgar	May 3, 1955	69	New Market	Tn	Aug 26, 1894								Elmore, Nellie G. [Wife]	Nances Grove
English, Dorothy Irene	Feb 12, 1990	68	Morristown, Tn		Sep 28, 1921	Givens, William			English, Guy Edward		Gary E.		Husband	Husband
English, William Edgar		60	South Range, Mich											J.M.G.

Name	Died	Age	Place	Born	Father	Mother	Spouse	Children / Relatives / Notes	Cemetery
English, Guy E.	Aug 19, 1934	74	Marshall Co., Ky	May 29, 1920	English, Fred	Dodge, Etta Mae	Givens, Dorothy [D]	Gary; Edwards, Jean [Ky] - Green, Emma Lou [Ky] - Margrove, Jewell [Fla]; Frederick; Gary	J.M.G.
Epps, Edith	Jun 24, 1982	71	Jeff City	May 23, 1911	Talley, W.A.	Ballinger, Minnie	Epps, Meck		J.M.G.
Epps, Meck	Mar 18, 1974	60	Jeff City	Jun 26, 1913	Epps, Thomas	Carum, Delia	Talley, Edith		J.M.G.
Ervin, Blanche Louise	Dec 8, 1967	57	Tampa, Fla.	May 23, 1917	James C.	Smith, Mrs. Maude	Denton, Callie V.	Kinzler, Jean Ann - Barbee, Nancy; Morgan, Leila Mae; Robert [Fla] - William - Hubert; Epps, Hubert - Kinzler, Ellis - Barbee, Bill; Sheriff [Fla]; Smith, Maude	Mills Spring
Eslinger, Edna Vicka	May 13, 1974		New Market					Smith, Frank [Mich.]	Mills Spring
Eslinger, James Monroe	Jun 10, 1990	41	Tn	Jul 19, 1948			Owens, Virginia Kay	Melissa Ruth; James Fredrick; Britt, Melvin - Houser, Sue [Fla] - Heath, Betty J. [Ind] - Betty-Jo [Ind]	J.M.G.
Eslinger, Marjorie Ruth	Mar 19, 1976	64	New Market	Apr 24, 1911	Oaks, Luther	Oaks, Ruth	Eslinger, Ralph [Jack Rock]	Langston, Rachel - Wollenberger, Trula - Heath, Margaret	Piney
Eslinger, Ralph Talbert	Apr 18, 1998	88	J.M.H.	May 11, 1911	Eslinger, James	Reed, Nettie		Charles-Billy- Don-Gene; Britt, Maxine - Houser, Sue [Fla] - Heath, Betty-Jo [Ind]	Piney
Eslinger, Violet	May 26, 1954	86	M.C.	Feb 8, 1906	Eslinger, James	Reno, Mary	Tn	Ruth [D]; Jody [D]-Charlie-Billy	Pleasant Grove
Eslinger, William Alger	Jan 16, 1998	71	New Market	Nov 4, 1926	Patterson, George	Ellison, Allie	Turner, Verna	Willers, Ginger & Jody - Hutchison, Shella; H.C.-J.G.-G.P. P.M [S. America]; Foster, Arnold - Essary, Carroll & Patricia-Ronald & Nancy-Roger & Sharon; Homer, Pauline; Bruce; Ellsie	New Market
Essary, Edna Pauline	Oct 24, 2000	80	Knoxville, Tn	Feb 29, 1920	Luttrell, Aaron Mc Millan	Moore, Minnie Belle	Essary, Otto Brown [D]	Ingram, Cordelia; John-Jim; Eslinger, G.P.	Caldonia
Estepp, Lucille	Aug 27, 1985	72	U.T.H.	Jan 15, 1913	Boy, Hugh Luttrell	Lee, Lenora Tennie	Estepp, Carl	Stinnett, Helen; Graham, Maynie - Wrangler, Uma Mae - Frazier, Molly Jo; Paul-Carl- Hugh L.	J.M.G.
Estes, Betty Joe	Dec 31, 1996	65	Dandridge, Tn	Jun 24, 1931	Kerr, Nielson A.	Woods, Carrie	Estes, Paul P.	Seals, Bobbie [1/2] - Denton, Nell - Peters, Mary - Rowe, Cindy [OK]; Kerr, Don; Kerr, Don	Hillcrest
Estes, Thomas Foley	Oct 18, 1997	69	Jeff City	May 27, 1928	Estes, Lynn Smith	Foley, Nancy Annie	Div	Key - Belch, Nancy; Thomas F., Jr.- Lynn; U.S.A.F.; Bill & Virginia [Ohio]; Sister; [Pals] Frazier, John-Gary- Boy, Riley - Wrangler, Jim - Snodgrass, Jack - Bales, Don - Tunnell, Ken	Pineville - Bell Memorial Co., Ky

Name	Death	Age	Place	Origin	Birth	Father		Mother					E.P.	Burial
Estes, Virgil Sterling Brown	Feb 11, 1990	71	J.M.H.	Whitley Co., Ky	Sep 30, 1908	Estes, Alfred J.		Deeds, Helen	S			Chow, Dessie - Houston, Marie - Trapp, Ina - Hackler, Mary Alice		New Market
Etheridge, Ernest St. Clair	May 17, 1995	51	Talbott, Tn	Portsmouth, Va	Jun 2, 1943	Etheridge, Charles St. Clair		Weaver, Dorothy	Div		Scott-Mark-Brett			Cremated
Evans, Ray Harvey	Sep 30, 1999	80	Dandridge, Tn	Portsmouth, Oh	Dec 28, 1918	Evans, Wyatt Blair		Luster, Ollie		Hensley, Dorcas - Preston, Sue - Merrell, Lynda [Oh] - Winemy, Ronda [Calif] - Booth, Donna [Minne] - [Step] Denton, Brenda [M]	Ray Jr. - [Step] Mc-George, Steve			Cedar Hill - Trotwood, Oh
Everhart, Alma	Sep 24, 1974	84	Morristown, Tn	Ky	Aug 23, 1890	Day, John B.		Day, Jo Ann	W	Gass, Cora - Johnson, Lillie B. [M]				New Market
Everhart, Arlie Mae	Nov 11, 1971	66	J.M.H.	Tn	Oct 8, 1905	Dille, John		Rice, Eliza		Everhart, J.F.	R.H.-J.T.	Husband		New Market
Everhart, George Robert	Feb 5, 1956	78	V.A. - Mt. Home	Tn	Feb 11, 1880	Everhart, James		Kyle, Martha	Tn	Day, Alma	spanish am	Stroud, Minnie	George-Lee	New Market
Everhart, Joseph F.	Oct 10, 1980	73	New Market, Tn	Greene Co.	Jun 17, 1907	Everhart, Robert		Day, Alma		Dille, Arlie [D]	R.H.-J.T.	Gass, Cora - Johnson, Lillie [Cal]	Rufe-Homer	New Market
Everhart, L.V.	Jan 30, 1966	49	Jeff City	Jr	Aug 14, 1915	Everhart, George R.		Day, Alma	Tn	Mc-Nish, Pauline	unk			Husband	New Market
Ezelle, Ina	Oct 11, 1962	21	New Market	Tn	---	Moore, John W.	Tn	Jernigan, Ina	Tn	Ezelle, Robert L.	Carol			West View
Ezelle, Sheryl Lynn	Oct 11, 1962		J.M.H.	Tn		Ezelle, Robert L.	La	Moore, Ira	Tn			Gunn, Wilma [1/2], Webb, Ann - Morgan, Leona	Robert-Philip [1/2] White, Walter Collins, Junior	West View
Fain, E.W. [Col]	Apr 19, 1963	66	New Market	Tn	Feb 2, --97	Fain, William	Tn	Brazelton, Laura	Tn	Cunningham, Mrs; Ross - Mc-Clendon, Mrs; Von - Hawkins, Mrs; Oliver - Berry, Mrs; Sylvania - Conley, Mrs; Lillian - Rogers, Mrs; Mamie - White, Juanita - Fells, Juna	Rogers, Ott-Jackson	Turk, Iva	Earl-Mack-Roosevelt	Fain, Mrs. Lelah	Youngs Memorial
Fain, Earl Edger [Black]	Aug 13, 1991	92	J.M.H.	New Market	Dec 5, 1998	Fain, Will	Tn	Brazelton, Lena	Tn	Jernigan, Odessa Marie		Rooseveit-Cecil	Willie	Youngs Memorial
Fails, Bertha	Sep 28, 195_		New Market	Tn				Moore, Ira						
Farrar, Dorsie Lena	May 6, 1996		Rutledge, Tn	Grainger Co.	Sep 24, 1902	Farrar, Samuel	Tn	Roach, Sarah Elizabeth	Tn	S		Turk, Iva	Kitchen Bros. [Brooklyn, NY] - Farrar, Traylor [Nephew]	Grainger Memorial
Farrar, Grace	Oct 17, 1984	77	Rutledge, Tn	Grainger Co.	Jan 4, 1907	Hodge, Jessie	Tn	Bidde, Emma Alice	Tn	Farrar, Thomas Tipton	Rule, Evelyn	Kennedy, Manna	Farrar, Delma	Oakland
Farrar, Thomas Tipton	Feb 9, 1995	90	J.M.H.	Grainger Co.	Apr 30, 1905	Farrar, Samuel	Tn	Roach, Sarah Elizabeth	Tn	Hodge, Grace [D]	Rule, Evelyn	Delamar E.	Edward-Jody-Ray	Farrar, Delma	Oakland
Ferris, Ora Kirkland	Feb 7, 1969		Morristown, Tn	Tn	Sep 6, 1882	Stewart, Langard		Pendleton, Rose	W	Haggard, Mildred - Standridge, Eula	Kirkland, Roger - John-Earl-Whitney, Paul	Flavous, Mrs. Bobby - Price, Sue - Owens, Pearl	Kirkland, Earl	Mills Spring

Name	Date	Age	Place	County	DOB	Father		Mother		Spouse	War	Notes / Relations	Cemetery
Fennell, Emma Edna	Dec 26, 1998	82	F.S.H.	Grainger Co	Nov 14, 1906	Mitchell, Charlie		Campbell, Sam Viney		Fennell, Thomas Boyd [D]		Spoons, Barbara -[Step] Spnrues, Loucila; [Step] Fennell, Arthur; Hodge, Mrs. Will [Sister] - Fielden, Elbert; [Pals] Mitchell, C.R. - Ramsey, Donald Paul - Spoons, Leon - Fennell, Roger	Indian Ridge
Fielden, Aileen [Dirkie]	Oct 19, 1975	38	J.M.H.	Jeff Co	May 23, 1937	Oakenberry, William Amos		Vesser, Alice		Fielden, James [Bud]		Spoons, Barbara -[Step] Spruras, Loucila; Alice; Bill; Rice, Ruby; William; Husband	Pleasant Grove Baptist
Fielden, Benjamin Bailey	May 28, 1992	77	New Market		Sep 19, —								Owensburg, Ky
Fielden, Carlos Winton	Aug 13, 1970	68	J.M.H.		Oct 27, 101	Fielden, Robert		Ballinger, Essie		Northern, Margaret		Glass, Vorellis & Elmer - Allsup, Marlene & Girl - Hensel, Carolyn & Jim; James-David [Gal]; Conley-Mack; Husband	Pleasant Grove
Fielden, Clyde H.	Nov 24, 1983	90	B.H.	Tn	Nov 10, 1913	Fielden, Henry T.	Tn	Newman, Mary C.	Tn	Northern, Margaret		Jerry-Everett-Millard; Adams, Paola L.; Robert-Marvel; Husband	Pleasant Grove
Fielden, David Earl	May 30, 1991	47	Atlanta, Ga	New Market	Mar 24, 1944	Fielden, Carl		Northern, Margaret		S	Army	Mother	Pleasant Grove
Fielden, Edgar A.							Tn		Tn		WW 1	Lucas, Ora; Frank	Nances Grove
Fielden, Edgar L.	Apr 26, 1960	60	Knoxville, Tn	Tn	Mar 6, 1900	Fielden, Robert		Ballinger, Essie		Kelly, Gladys		[Step] Kelley, Kenneth - Kelly, Pat [MF?]; Linn, Mrs. L.E.; Carl-Conley-Mack; Wife	Pleasant Grove
Fielden, Henry Taylor	Dec 14, 1966	83	Tn	Tn	Sep 1, - 83	Fielden, Luther		Howorth, Jane		Newman, Kate		Robert-Marvel; Howorth, Martha [IV] - Locust, Mrs. M.A.; William [N.M.] - Frank-Edgar - Carl [Chld]; Husband	Pleasant Grove
Fielden, Jerry W.	May 16, 2000		Ringgold, Ga	New Market	Feb 18, 1942	Fielden, Clyde Henry		Ballinger, Stella		Williams, Jean		Amanda - Lebuven, Kim [Mq] - Dee Ann [Gal] - Burrett, Melissa [Gal] - Byrd, Roberta; Everett-Millard; Husband	Pleasant Grove
Fielden, Kate	Sep 27, 1970	83	Knoxville, Tn	Tn	Apr 16, 1887	Fielden, Luther		Ballinger, Stella		W		Davis, Gladys - Ballinger, Pauline; Robert [N.M.] - Marvel [Va]; Davis, Gladys; Wife	Nances Grove
Fielden, Luther Frank	Mar 16, 1981	95	New Market, Tn		Dec 20, 1905	Newman, Robert		Lawrence, Sarah		W		Charlene; Everett-Millard; Davis, Gladys	Nances Grove
Fielden, Mack Arthur	Mar 31, 1983	75	Knoxville, Tn	New Market	Jun 20, 1907	Fielden, Robert		Ballinger, Essie		Howard, Ruth	WW 2	[Pals] Bonds, Ken - Day, Kan - Lowe, A.W. - Jones, J.T. - King, John - Howard, Wesley; Mill Springs	Mill Springs
Fielden, Margaret Pearl	May 7, 1992	83	J.M.H.	Mill Springs, Tn	Aug 26, 1908	Carroll, Nannie J.		Carroll, Nannie J.		Fielden, Carl [D]		Glass, Vorellis - Allsup, Marlene - Hensel, Carolyn; James W.; Allen, Nola; Doug	Pleasant Grove
Fielden, Rhoda Rebecca	Aug 19, 1997	77	Richmond, Va	Lockhart, Joe Henry	Apr 22, 1920	Lockhart, Joe Henry		Sitex, Mary Lee		Fielden, Marvel L.		Joseph T. & Georgia; Adams, Paola L.; Roger & Betty-Roger & Bernie; Husband	Nances Grove
Fielden, Rosa Ellen	Jul 2, 1998	95	Conway, Ky		Nov 11, 1902	Dalton, Thomas		Callahan, Jenny		Fielden, Luther Frank		Fielden, Martha Charleren; Byrd, Roberta; Whitlock, Hazel Trent, Edith - Kinder, Della; Nances Grove	Nances Grove
Fielden, Stella Mae	Sep 23, 1962		J.M.H.	Tn		Ballinger, J.H.	Tn	Vineyard, Ada		Fielden, Clyde		Byrd, Roberta; Jerry-Everett-Millard; Lucien-Floyd; Husband	Pleasant Grove
Finchum, Bill	Dec 19, 1998	79	Straw Plains	Sevier Co	Jul 12, 1919	Finchum, Roy		Fennell, Laura		Vineyard, Mary	Navy	Billie Sue - Scarbrough; Roy & Linda - James Allen & Becky-Phillip & Elizabeth [T.N]; Magna, Margaret Leonard - Hammer, Jean; [Pals] Finchum, Don - Scarbrough, Byron - Shrader, Robert; Husband	Banner Creek

Name		Age											
Finchum, Hope	May 19, 1982	82	J.M.H.	Mega Co	Apr 23, 1900	Underwood, William		Finchum, Jess [D]	Hallmaher, Mary - Lows, Dorthy	Floyd O.- Lawrence	Miller, Gertrude	[Pals] Finchum, David-Jack-Bell- Jim-Theller-Tony- Lows, Danny	J.M.G.
Finchum, Jess Ulyses	May 23 1981	81	J.M.H.	Sevier Co	Oct 19, 1899	Finchum, Joseph		Underwood, Hope	Lows, Dot.- Hallmaher, Mary	Floyd [D]- Lawrence		[Pals] Brooks, Dadd - Lows..., Finchum, Ralph - Lowry, Joey	J.M.G.
Finchum, Margaret Louise	Feb 4, 1970	82	Jeff Co	Jeff Co	Aug 9, 1887	Henry, J.W.		Finchum, William	Schneider, Mrs. Hammer, Mrs. Jean	Bill	Grover	Husband	Beaver Creek
Finchum, Roy	Apr 12, 1959	64	Strawberry Plains	Sevier Co. Tn	Dec 5, 1894	Finchum, Roxen	Tn	Patterson, Elizabeth	[Step] Schneider, Mrs. Henry	Bill	Finchum, Mrs. A.C.- Atchley, Gladys - Cheney, Lucile - Meeks-Bush, Reva- Thomas, Imogene	Finchum, Margaret [Wife]	Beaver Creek
Fine, Mildred	Apr 22, 1995	65	New Market	Chestnut Hill, Tn	Jun 27, 1909	Shrader, Robert E.		Finchum, Pearl	Fine, Fred [D]	William F.		Daug	J.M.G.
Fine, Mrs. Roe	Apr 17, 1995	88	New Market	Tn		Speed, Julia	Tn		Walker, Julia			Fine, Fred	Fine
Fine, William Fred	Dec 15, 1999	70	Jeff Co	Tn	Dec 12, 1899	Speed, Roe		Shrader, Mildred	Dide - Watson, Addie Vine [Cal.]	Paul-Fred-Loyd [Mich.]		Fine, Fred	Fine
Finley, Everett Coy	Mar 7, 1983	78	J.M.H.	Grainger Co	Apr 12, 1914	Finley, Lon		Davis, Ollie	Walker, Julia	Bill [Ky]	Olie - Watson, Addie [Calif.]	Loyd-Paul	West View
Finley, James Edward	Nov 3, 1983	60	Massey Creek, Tn	Jeff City	May 25, 1923	Finley, Lon	WW 2	Prince, Ruby Allen	Parker, Brenda	Donald-George D.-David	Lawson, Katherine	Everett	West View
Finley, Lester	Jan 18, 1985	79	J.M.H.	Grainger Co	Oct 13, 1905	Brewer, Franie		Edna B.	Scroggins, Almeta - [Step] White, Jamise	John Grady [PH] [Step] Watson, Darrell	Buckner, Microllee	Son	Highland - Oak Hill, W. Va
Fiorucci, Vincenzo	Sep 22, 1980	96	Jeff City	Italy	Apr 27, 1894	Fiorucci, Vlabaldo		Giroloma	Placidi, Mary	Jerry		Fiorucci, Lincdo [Son]	Hillcrest
Fisher, Samuel Lynn	Oct 20, 1999	0	Morristown	Morristown	Oct 20, 1999	Fisher, Terry Lynn		Heaton, Ruby				Heaton, Richard-Christopher-Fisher, Terry E.	Wesleys Chapel
Fleming, Joe	Apr 28, 1980	81	Union Co, Tn	Union Co, Tn	Jan 1, 1912	Unk		Unk		Fleming, David [Orange, Calif]		Gray, Joe [Legal Guardian]	Tn Vets
Flourney, Pauline Magdalene	May 14, 1984	69	Humana Hosp.	Piqua, Ohio	Nov 16, 1914	Unk		Unk	Flourney, Fred F. [D]			Care Inn	New Market
Folster, Clarence Joseph	Jun 18, 1985	77	J.M.H.	Maryville, Tn	Jan 21, 1918	Folster, Thomas E.	Army	Campbell, Margaret	Howell, Betty - Stewart, Elizabeth - Miller, Deborah	Martin-Stephen- Joseph C.-Carl	Wampler, Bertha Mae	Ralph	J.M.G.
Foland, Juanita Gail	Jun 13, 1996	35	S.M.H.	Jeff City	Feb 23, 1961	Dobson, Bobby		Foland, Kenneth F.	Sharon-April		Whaley, Patsy - Emery, Jamie	Bill-Bob-Steve- Bruce [TX]	New Market
Ford, Albert	Jan 25, 1990		J.M.H.	Union Co, Tn	Apr 25, 1894	Ford, John		Berry, Susan	Weaver, Rachel	Charlie Eugene- Henry Robert		[Pals] Graves, Ervin - Downs, J.N.- Odom, Neil - Graham, Charley - Nichols, Hood	J.M.G.
Ford, Albert		71	J.M.H.	Knox Co	Jul 6, 1920	Ford, Albert		Weaver, Rachel	Div			Charlie & Loraine Henry	J.M.G.
Ford, Henry Robert	Dec 4, 1995	71		Knox Co	Aug 7, 1891	Weaver, John		Glenn, Amanda	Weaver, Rachel		Watson, Susie	Charles	J.M.G.
Ford, Rachel	Mar 18, 1972	80	J.M.H.			Ford, Albert		Ford, Alfred				Brother	J.M.G.

Name	Death Date	Age	Place	Place	Birth Date	Father	Mother	Spouse	Svc						Cemetery
Forgety, Bessie Pearl	Nov 9, 1995	80	J.M.H.	Dandridge, Tn	Jun 24, 1915	Williamson, Oscar	Chambers, Phalby	Forgety, Leonard		Holloway, Vicki - Sands, Betsy [D]	Mc Daniel, Vicki - James Phillip [D]			Doug - [Pals] Barhee, Gerald - Hale, Glenn - Repass, P.V. - Morgan, Raymond - Solomon, Tom - Betts, Tom	West View
Forgety, Leonard R.	Jul 10, 1998	75	Dandridge, Tn	Jeff City	Jan 22, 1923	Forgety, Will	Underwood, Mattie	Bess [D]		[Step] Holloway, Vicki & Gary	Gray, Tillis [Fla] - Carter, Agnes - Forgety, Emma Lee		Joe	[Pals] Alley, Vineyard-Richard Sr. & Jr. - Forrester, Charles - Den Sr. & Jr.	Buffalo Grove
Forrester, Ermel Leroy	Nov 10, 1992	50	Talbott, Tn	Maryville, Tn	Feb -, 1942	Forrester, Frank Richard	Harmon, Helen	Margie A.	Army	Mc Corkle, Loretta	Hunt, Louise - Righie, Marie - Sneed, Linda	Handt-Gene-Roy	[Pals] Forrester, Richard Jr.		J.M.G.
Foster, Charles Elmer	Feb 21, 1984	44	Jeff Co	Tn	Aug 11, 1919	Foster, Charlie A.	Everhart, Pearl	Lowry, Helen		Janie-Vivian - Fincham, Mrs. - Chyde - Turbey, Mrs, Billy- Rhodes, Mrs. Bobby	Charles Jr.	Dunsmore, Mrs. H.A.	James T. - Grover-Ralph	Wife	J.M.G.
Foster, Donald Clifton	Feb 12, 1988	53	New Market	Tn	Oct 17, 1934	Foster, Earl	Ellison, Leah V.	Brown, Nora		Denton - Ronda, Mrs. - Jean - Witt, Donna - Lewis, Rebecca	David-Ronald-John				Mill Springs
Foster, Earl Clifton	Jan 25, 1986	79	J.M.H.	New Market	Jan 26, 1906	Foster, John	Ballinger, Minnie	Ellison, Lee			Donald C.	Hodge, Grace - Northam, Maude		[Pals] Foster, P.V. - Ballinger, Austin-Doyl - Foster, Kenneth - Bailey, Jack - Tolliver, Ronnie	Mill Springs
Foster, Elizabeth Louise	Feb 2, 1983	85	Knoxville, Tn	Tn	Dec 7, 1896	Foster, John	Brooks, Nola	Foster, Sam		Newton, Ollie - Lowry, Mary Kate - Little, Ruth - Cross, Truda	Paul Edward-Fred				Mill Springs
Foster, Fred	Oct 2, 2000	84	Jeff City	Knox Co	Aug 27, 1916	Foster, John Thomas	Wilkerson, Delta	Wilson, Mary Helen		Shelton, Mary Edith - Matthews, Margaret - Humbard, Reva - Clower, Catherine	Skinner, Truda Foster [OH]				East View
Foster, Grover Winton	Jan 22, 1997	71	J.M.H.	New Market	Mar 6, 1925	Foster, Charlie	Everhart, Cona	Lumbdin, Louise	Army	[Step] Greenlee, Carolyn-Maxine - Brownfield, Brenda [Fla] - Dunsmore, Stella Mae			James T.	Wife	Mill Springs
Foster, Harold Eugene [Butch]	Feb 7, 1973	18	New Market	Tn	Jan 6, 1955	Foster, Ralph	Munn, Loreta		S			Mary	Coy [D]-Floyd	Foster, - Murry, Etta - Williams, Pearl [Gr-Mothers]	New Market
Foster, Hazel Lucinda	Apr 26, 1997	82	Jeff City	New Market	Oct 28, 1914	Sellers, Albert	White, Sarah [Selling]	Foster, William A. [D]		Dinnatte, Sonja & Roland [Mich]		Waggoner, Mae [D] - Riley, Lee [D] - Shipe, Verna [D]		Cantwell, Imogene [Mother] - Cantwell, Carl [Step-Father] - Wright, D.W. [Gr-Father]	Piedmont
Foster, James Michael	Oct 9, 1989	6	Green Co	Tn	Nov 17, 1982	Foster, Donald	Wright, Imogene					[1/2] Foster, Rhonda Jean	[1/2] Foster, David Lee-Ronald	Cantwell, Imogene [Mother] - Cantwell, Carl [Step-Father] - Wright, D.W. [Gr-Father]	Mill Springs

Name	Date	Age	Place	County	Date	Name	Name								Cemetery
Foster, James S.	Aug 27, 1981	74	Jeff City	New Market, Tn	Jun 20, 1907	Foster, James Thomas	Bowen, Mary Olevia	Pauline	Hernsley, Bobbie	Kenny			[Pala] Foster, James-Grover-Fred-Balinger-Jodie-Balinger-Doyle		Mill Springs
Foster, Jessie	May 23, 1975		J.M.H.	Tn		Foster, James T.	West, Mary	W	Howard, Gladis-Sellers, Buelah		[1/2] Howarth, Ella		[Pala] Vineyard, Robert - Henley, K.B. - Balinger, Austin-Riley - Clifford - Bailey, Jack		Mill Springs
Foster, Leon Vina	Dec 30, 1976	72	Care Inn	Jeff Co	Sep 26, 1986	Elliott, Charlel	Van Dyke, Nellie			Donald			Foster, Hattie-Jo [Pala] Prad-Shelton, Charles - Prad-Charles - Anderson, Charle		J.M.G.
Foster, Osee Lee	Oct 22, 1987	83	U.T.H.	Jeff Co	Oct 17, 1904	Foster, Frank	Hawkins, Rushia				Mary - Smith, Mrs. Conard - Hunt, Mrs. Frank - Brown, Mrs. Louise [Lisle]	Willis [Ne] - Robert-Paul	[Pala] Henley, Robert - Henley, K.B. - Balinger, Clifford - Bailey, Jack		Mill Springs
Foster, Paul Edward	Mar 25, 1983	65	J.M.H.	Jeff Co	Jul 20, 1917	Foster, Sam	Lowery, Elizabeth	S			Shelton, Edith - Balinger, Ruby - Kirkwood, Lola - French, Naomi	Fred	[Pala] Balinger, Paul - Shelton, Thurman - Foster, Ken-Fred-Mike		Mill Springs
Foster, Ralph Eugene	Jan 8, 1965	66	J.M.H.	New Market		Foster, Charlie	Everhart, Pearl				Dunamore, Stella Mae	James-Grover	[Pala]		New Market
Foster, Rushie	Feb 15, 1960	82	New Market	Tn	Mar 2, 1928	Hamlen, Lyle	Lewis, Amanda	W		Shumate, Mrs. Edgar - Balinger, Mrs. Sherman - French, Naomi & Mack	Hurton, Reessa - Margaret - Clower, Katherine		Willie		Mill Springs
Foster, Sam H.	May 13, 1969	76	S.M.H.	Tn	Oct 3, 1882	Foster, Jim	Merlin, Le Vi	W				Fred-Eddie	Elmer-Wayne-Otis		Mill Spring
Foster, William Arles	May 25, 1987	70	F.S.H.	Tn	Dec 24, 1950			Army		Donatties, Sonja		John	[Pala] Dunatties, Roland - Wagner, Cornelious, Wm. - Lathous, Teonie - Mills, W.A. - Green, Robert		Piedmont
Foster, James Garfield	Mar 14, 1982	74	Jeff City	Sevier Co	Dec 4, 1907	Foster, Floyd	Ellis, Janie	Lindsey, Lucy Bell		Hatmaker, Margie - Purkey, Burnice - Rector, Carolyn - Bowman, Penny	Foland, Lula - Simms, Bell - Hack, Estelle		[Pala] White, Bob - Densison, Ronnie - Elmore, Harold - Ewing, Balsir - Hatmaker, Carl - Mary, Julio		West View
Foster, Lucy Belle	Dec 23, 1982	82	J.M.H.	Dumplin, Tn	May 11, 1910	Lindsey, John	Elder, Mary	Foster, Garfield [2]		Hatmaker, Margie - Purkey, Burnice - Rector, Carolyn - Long, Penny	King, Mary Kate		[Pala] Hatmaker, Margie - Purkey, Burnice - Rector, Carolyn - Long, Penny		West View

Name	Date	Age	Place	County / City	St	Date	Father	St	Mother	St	Spouse	Mil	Children				Info	Cemetery
Francis, Garge Walker	Jun 15, 1998	74	S.M.H.	Sevier Co		Apr 25, 1924	Francis, Mark		Lewis, Nannie		Bailey, Ruby		Maples, Linda & Roger	Gary & Faye	Humphry, Christine & Roy - Johnson, Bonnie & Carroll - Thomas, Helen & Norman - Miller, Evelyn & Jim - Guillams, Lucille	Bill & Elsie - Charles & Betty - John & Elizabeth		East View
Franklin, Robert Austin	Oct 30, 2000	65	J.M.H.	Jeff Co		Apr 7, 1935	Franklin, Kenneth		Cox, Reba		Grover, Myrtle	Marines	Howard, Diane & Ronnie - Russell, Linda & Ronnie - Hannel, Robin & Jeff	Larry & Debbie	Mc Craig, Lois	Franklin, Lon [R]- Cate, Roy		Friends Station
Franklin, Bonnie	Mar 3, 1982	86	S.M.H.	Grainger Co		Oct 25, 1925	Finley, Archie		Farrow, Maude		Franklin, Hubert		Cob, Brenda - Robin - Murphy, Leas		Nelson, Ruby	Fred	Husband	J.M.G.
Franklin, Dwayen	Jun 15, 1989		Jeff Co	Jeff Co	Tn	Jun 15, 1989	Franklin, George Lawrence [Age 42]	Tn	Estinger, Mary D. [Age 42]	Tn	Franklin, Hubert						Father	
Franklin, George L.	Feb 25, 1990	52	J.M.H.	Lanier City, Tn		Mar 25, 1927	Franklin, Lewis		Evans, Olice L.		Leisinger, Mary	unk	Reads, Elizabeth - Shininer, Judy [Step] Herrell, Sheila - Totliver, Sonja - Plughin, Brenda	Paul-Richard - [Step] Herrell, Freddie-Donnie	Brown, Agnes - Kelly, Baby-Mott, Bobbie			New Market
Franklin, Hubert Glenmore	Nov 14, 1999	78	J.M.H.	Jacksonville, II		Nov 2, 1921	Franklin, James H.		Jarnigan, Martha		Finley, Bonnie	Army	Cole, Brenda & John - Murphy, Lisa & Mark - Franklin, Sandy & Robin		Bolin, Ruth - Woods, Juanita	Frank		J.M.G.
Franklin, Mary Dowie [F]	Nov 23, 1997	70	S.M.H.	Concord, Tn		May 23, 1927	Leisinger, C.W.		Sutton, Trula		Franklin, George L. [R]		Phillips, Brenda - Totliver, Sonja - Bryan, Sheila - Guinn, Brenda	Herrell, Jamie - Donald	Parker, Barbara - Leisinger, Kitty	James		Friendship
Frazier, Jack Arnold	Feb 1 1981	51	New Market	Sevier Co		Dec 3, 19129	Frazier, Howard		Sutton, Viola		Shelfy, Ola						Buehler, Scott A.	Friendship
Free, Emma Lee	Mar 25, 1986	71	F.S.H.	Jeff Co		Apr 5, 1926	Kenjos, Thula		Free, Nicholas [D]		Moore, Mary L.[R]- Maples, Curtis		Lunsford, Sarah				Ed	J.M.G.
Free, Harry Dean	Nov 15, 1998	52	Jeff City	Jeff Ctty		Jun 23, 1946	Free, Nicholas		Gruner, Peggy Jane		Gruner, Peggy Jane		Williamson, Brenda & Donnie	Jeff & Lucy-Tony & Kim	Maples, Joyce	Fere-James		J.M.G.
Free, Nicholas	Jul 9, 1983	63	J.M.H.	Knox Co		Feb 17, 1920	Free, Arch		Shelbr, Fannie		Glass, Emma Lee		Moore, Mary - Maples, Rita	Fred-Harry- William-James	Oliver, Ollie - Rediund, Lucille	Arthur		J.M.G.
French, Agnes L.	Oct 26, 1979	71	Jeff City	Jeff Co		Jan 6, 1908	French, Crockett B.		Douglas, Mary Jane		S		French, C.G.		Graves Naomi	Moore-Carroll- Ray		J.M.G.
French, Carroll Charlie	Oct 31, 1990	81	Hill Haven	Drutridge, Tn		Aug 31, 1909	French, C.G.		Douglas, Mary		S				Ray, Mose	Brother		Piedmont
French, Charlotte Geraldine	Apr 20, 1997	77	New Market	New Market		May 17, 1919	Hawkin, Owen		Smolcher, Lella		French, Sherman [D]		Virginia Lee [D]- Lane, Baby Jane & Robert	Charles		Bill Jim		New Market
French, Darrell Stephen	Oct 9, 1982	2	Childrens Hosp.	Tn		May 30, 1959	French, Larry	Tn	Cameron, Elizabeth	Tn	French, Larry						Father - Cameron, Mamull [G-Father]	Friends Station
French, Dexter Carl [Doss]	Mar 13, 2000	89	New Market	Piedmont		Dec 2, 1910	French, Hugh		Snyder, Minnie		Mc Nish, Katherine	WW 2	Kerr, Myrtle [D]- Elder, Hazel	W.J.[R]- Leonard [D]- Herman [D]- Hazel [D]	[Pele] Carr, Frank- Lunsford, Leo - Brown, Charlie- Wayne - Shelfer, Hoss			Piedmont

Name	Date	Age	Place	Location	Date	Father		Mother		Spouse		Relatives	Relatives	Relatives	Relatives	Cemetery
French, Elizabeth	Oct 17, 1988	48	S.M.H.	Jeff Co	Feb 5, 1940	Cameron, Manuel A.		Gibbons, Irene		French, Steve [Div]		Vance, New Belle - Bates, Mary - Katherine- Bates, Shirley	Brother - [Pete] Everhart, Greg - Courtney, Charles - Wells, George - Cameron, Frank - Lowry, Frank - Norton, James			J.M.G.
French, Georgia Ellen Douglas	Oct 29, 1975	89	J.M.H.	Jeff Co	Feb 9, 1886	French, George		Privette, Eliza		French, W.A. [D]		Horner, Lois & Robert - Clark, Hilda	Taft-Edgar [Both D]	Henry, Polly & R.E.		Piedmont
French, Jasper Gordon	Sep 17, 1967	51	Pontiac, Mich.					French, Mattie				Steele, Mrs. Emmett - Disney, Mrs. A.E.	Fred-Paul-Sherman-Thomas	Frank	Barsley F.H. [Pontiac, Mich.] - French, Paul-Fred [Mich.] - Steele, Emmett [Mich.]	Piedmont
French, Katherine Irene	May 2, 1962	73	J.M.H.	Jeff Co	May 22, 1916	Mc Nish, Rufus		Satterfield, Delia		French, Dexter C. [Dece]				Husband		Piedmont
French, Mary Jane	Feb 9, 1957	72	M.C.	Jonesboro, Tn	Jul 13, 1884	Privette, Elizabeth	Tn		Tn	French, Paul [D]		Agnes - Graves, Mrs. Oliver	Carroll-Mose-Ray Lewis, Mayne - Henry, Ralph	Andy-Harley [Springfield, Ohio]	French, Marshall [Son]	Piedmont
French, Linnie L.	Feb 23, 1998	88	Dandridge, Tn	Sevierville, Tn	Feb 11, 1910	Sims, John		Wiomas, Hulda		French, Turner S.		French, Mrs. W.A. - Lewis, Mayne - Huff, Mildred - Woods, Wilma	Ogle, Ezra Lee - Fox, Ruby - Hill, Ruth - Butcher, Gladis -	Robert		J.M.G.
French, Mattie Lucille	Oct 29, 1998	88	New Market, Tn	Jonesboro, Tn	Mar 21, 1900	Keen, John B.		Johnson, Artie		French, Paul [D]		Steele, Imogene Lowe, Brenda	Fred-Tom	Peach, Viola	French, Marshall [Son]	New Market
French, Paul R.	Oct 31, 1954	64	New Market	Tn	Jan 2, 1890	French, James	Tn	Daniels, Mattie	Tn	Mattie		Brenda - Disney, Mrs. A.E. [Val] - Walton, Mrs. William E. [Tx] -	Arwin, Mrs. Lee - Dalton, Mrs. John	James	Children	New Market
French, Paul R.	Mar 5, 1974	52	Jeff City	Tn	Nov 30, 1921					Jones, Eula	WW 2	Deal, Shirley	John Paul-David [Mich]	Steele, Imogene [Mich] - Lowe, Brenda [Cal]	Tommy-Sherman-Fred [Mich]	New Market
French, Sherman	Feb 5, 1978	57	J.M.H.					Mattie		Mattie		Jones, Florence	Charles	Ogle, Mary Sue	[Pete] Cowan, Fred - Johnson, Kenneth - Hale - Trent, Larry - Slagle, Vernon - Taylor, Junior	New Market
French, Turner Jones	Aug 7, 1996	87	Jeff City	Dandridge, Tn	Jan 7, 1911	French, James Albert		Jones, Florence		Sims, Linnie		Clark, Mrs. Gordon - Horner, Mrs. R.G.	Taft-Edgar	Ogle, Mary Sue	[Pete] Cowan, Fred - Grenebee, Don - Burngardner, Jim - Mc Carter, Jim - French, Ricky - Haworth, Billy	J.M.G.
French, William Austin	Feb 9, 1963	84	M.C.	Tn	Oct 7, 1878	French, William	Tn	Mertt, Mary	Tn	Douglas, Georgia		Clark, Mrs. Gordon - Horner, Mrs. R.G.	Taft-Edgar	Franklin Mrs. John - Mowery, Mrs. Sidney	Wills	Piedmont
Frison, David l Lamonte [Back]	Jun 1, 1995	19	F.S.H.	Knoxville, Tn	Jun 1, 1985	Peters, Frank		Frison, Tamela S.	Tn	Frison, Tamela S.		Bailey, Johnny - Franklin-Ralph H.	Benson, Lilly Ruth - Genn, Jo Ann - Cutler, Sylvia	Frison, Peggy	Wills	Humboldt Memorial Gardens
Fritts, Mary Katherine	Oct 16, 1995	66	Jeff City	Strawberry Plains	Jun 30, 1928	Barnard, Perry		Anderson, Nancy		Fritts, Warren		Bailey, Nancy - Howard, Kathy	Benson, Lilly Ruth - Genn, Jo Ann - Cutler, Sylvia	William [Mich] - Carroll	John	Strawberry Plains

Name	Date	Age	Place 1	Place 2	Birth Date	Father	Mother						Burial
Fritts, Sally Blair Shelton	Oct -, 1970	39	Jeff City			Shelton, -	Mc. Daniel, Mrs. Pearl	Virginia Ann	Warren Allen	Barnett, Pauline - Shelton, Nelle - Bowman, Helen - Daniels, Helen - Orr, - Phillips, Virginia - Clark, Margaret - Spencer, Georgia	Shelton, Norman	Husband	New Market
Fritts, Warren Elbert	Jul 16, 1987	75	Jeff City	Washington Co	Oct 12, 1921	Fritts, Tom	Yates, Etta	Army	(Step) Bailey, Nancy - Howard, Kathy	Warren Allen - (Step) Bailey, John - Ralph - Franklin		Fultz, Loren	Strawberry Plains
Fritts, Brenda Kay	Nov 13, 1954	1m	Knoxville, Tn	Jeff Co	Oct 4, 1954	Fultz, Loren	Tn	Tn	Lauderdale, Pauline Voilea				Beaver Creek
Fultz, James R.	Sep 17, 1998	55	Maryville, Tn	Straw Plains	Nov 14, 1942	Fultz, Loren	Lauderdale, Pauline Voilea		Smiens, Barbara	Fultz, Rick - Peaock, Larry - Clark, Larry & Christy - Robert & James - Roger & Sheila	Ritta Jane [D] - [Cotton-D] - Bro - Lee - Shane, Hugh - Fultz, Sam & Sue		Cedarville
Fultz, Willie Mae	Nov 11, 1999	66	Strawberry Plains	Tn	May 2, 1921	Smith, Roy Cecil	Minton, Lena			Warren Allen - (Step) Bailey, John - Ralph - Franklin	Nicely, Jeanette - Smith, Mattie - Hazlock, Evelyn - Anderson, Reba - Shackeford, Jean - Miller, Margaret	Roy Jr.-Lynn	New Hopewell
Galbraith, Lula Mae	Jul 22, 1988	83	Morristown, Tn	Talbott, Tn	May 17, 1905	James, John J.	Cockrum, Virginia		Galbraith, Winton [D]			James, Edd - Ramsey, B.J.	
Galey, Joyce Reuss	Feb 21, 1985	35	California		May 2, 1949	Galey, James	Scott, Bonnie		S	Harrell, Elsie & James - Hath, Thelma & William - Petty, Linda & Doyle - Anderson, Shirley [D]		Griffin, Ann - Fremont Mortuary Mem. - Fremont, California	Islington Mem. - Alameda Co.
Gann, Clyde William	Dec 5, 1977	71	F.S.H.	Tn	Nov 22, 1906	Gann, William N.	Lindsey, Debbie		Gibson, Dollie	Harrell, Elsie & Hathcock, Thelma - Petty, Linda	Wayne	Dee	
Gann, Dollie Ann	Mar 19, 1980	77	J.M.H.	Washington Co	Jul 17, 1902	Gibson, John	Hammit, Lucy		Gann, Clyde W. [D]	Morgan, Doris J. - Booth, Dolly J. - James, Ann - Morgan, Nor Lee	Henderlight, Pearl	Jerry	
Gann, Edith Mae	Dec 5, 1980	66	Morristown, Tn	Jeff City	Sep 26, 1921	Phillips, Nora			Gann, Ralph [D]	Frank [Gap] Andy- Ralph Jr.-John	Gilbert, Agnes	[Pais] Morgan, Dean-Allen - Prescott, Victor - Hall, Richard - Cline, George-J.V.	J.M.G.
Gann, Jess Ray	1976	74	Bluffs, Illinois						Ollie	Knocke, Sara [III] - Street, Edna [III]	Charles [III]	Lon [Mack]-Clyde-Nathan	Laurel Hill
Gann, Mary Agnes	May 20, 1975	44	Lee Co, Va.	Apr 6, 1931	Fleenor, Rudell	Jones, Opal		Gann, Frank	Frank-Bobby	Moore, Irwe [Tn]	Huband - Rominies, James - Rominies, Opal & E.P. [Step-Father]	J.M.G.
Gann, Maud Elizabeth	Dec 14, 1994	71	J.M.H.	Strawberry Plains	Dec 18, 1922	Walker, Bessie		Gann, Walsey B. [D]	Collins, Emma - Shaver, Loretta	Hubert-Charles	Ogletroy, Lucille	Doug - [Pais] Anderson, Hugh - Bailey, Mack - Hanley, Clarence - Gann, Andrew - Wayne - Curt, Jim	Piney
Gann, Nathan Dennis	Nov 22, 1997	82	Jeff City	Jeff Co	May 6, 1915	Gann, William H.	Lindsey, Debbie	Layman, Ruth	Hodges, Helen	Dennis-Carl			Strawberry Plains

Name	Date	Age	Place	Place	Date				WW 2					
Gann, Ralph	Nov 5, 1976	64	J.M.H.	Oklahoma	Jan 26, 1912	Gann, George	Fincham, Dicie	Spencer, Edith	WW 2	Anna Faye - Morgan, Doris Jean - Morgan, Morgan, Mrs. - Morgan, Mrs. - Nora Lee	John W. - Frank - Ralph Jr. - Andy Roy	Brown, Addie Sue - Etherton, Pauline - Kennedy, Ruth	Jack [Bud]	Willie
Gann, Ruth Allewee	Dec 30, 1999	80	U.T.H.	Jeff Co	Jan 12, 1919	Layman, William Mitchell	Faith, Sarah	Gann, Nathan D. [0]		Hodges, Helen	Dennis-Carl			Strawberry Plains
Gardner, Daniel W.	Jul 3, 1969	80	U.T.H.	Tn	Jan 22, 1889	Gardner, Joseph E.	Ramey, C.			Clemmensen, Mrs. Paul - Sadie	James G.		Willie	New Market
Gardner, Fern	Aug 20, 1980	95	Jeff City							Wilson, Mrs. Homer	James	Wooten, Maggie - Hudley, Marime	Son	New Market
Gardner, J.P.	Apr 30, 1957	79	M.C.	Tn	Feb 12, 1878	Gardner, Joe	Kern, Ronnie	Tn		Gardner, Fern	Joe-Ray		D.W.-Lee	Gardner, Ray	Friends Station
Gardner, Jennie	Nov 8, 1954	69	Knoxville, Tn	W. Va	Feb 7, 1885	Bill, John	Va	Kern, Elisabeth	W. Va				Gardner, J.P.	Friends Station
Garland, Timothy Ray	Dec 4, 1990	27	U.T.H.	Jeff City	May 10, 1989	Garland, Ralph	Rosenbaum, Sandra Kay	Thacker, Angela Lee						Cremated
Gass, Buford	Feb 3, 1978	75	J.M.H.	Tn	May 10, 1902	Gass, John P.	Gass, Ida Jane	W		Loy, Wanda	Fred Dale	Cleo	Sen- [Pete] Mitchell, Tred - Barnett, J.B. - Cobb, Mack - Hobbert, Julie - Moody, Lawrence - Gass, Elmer Jr.	New Market
Gass, Cleo P.	Oct 12, 1981	85	Jeff Co	Jeff Co	Sep 10, 1896	Gass, John P.	Gass, Ida	S						New Market
Gass, Cora Alice	Jan 5, 1988	78	S.M.H.	Greene Co., Tn	Apr 22, 1909	Everhart, Robert	Day, Alma	Gass, Elmer H. Sr. [0]			Elmer Jr.	Johnson, Lillie [Gal]		New Market
Gass, Elmer Halk	Dec 21, 1965	81	Jeff City	Tn	Oct 25, 1901	Gass, John	Ida	Everhart, Cora			Elmer, Jr.	Cleo	Buford	Willie [Pete] Bates, Floyd- Jones, Jesse - Denton, Virgil- Willis - Kirkland, Frank - Loy, Wanda [Doug] - [Pete] Mitchell, Tred - Barnett, J.B. - Cobb, Mac- Moody, Lawrence- Gass, Elmer Jr	New Market
Gass, Helen Mae	Oct 9, 1977	69	New Market, Tn	Tn	Feb 15, 1908	Neal, Frank	Neal, Flora	Gass, Buford		Fred Dale	Cecil-Earnest	Cobb, Mac	New Market
Gaut, Joseph Edward	Mar 3, 1976	87	Knox Co	Jeff Co	May 23, 1888	Gaut, John	Rutherford, Mary	W		Williams, Sarah & George - Gibson, Mary Lou & George- John W. [Vic]- Nina & Coy	Kennette, [Ale]- Tommy Joe [Tk]- John [Vic]- Charles	Mills, Ida - Pleniston, Ethel	Strawberry Plains
Gaut, Lou	Mar 25, 1971	76	Knoxville, Tn	Tn	Oct 25, 1895	Bailey, William	Williams, Mandy	Gaut, Joe Edward		Williams, Mrs. George [Ind]- Long, Nina- Gibson, Mrs. George [Mary]- Merrill	Kenneth [Ale]- Tommy Joe [Tk]- John [Vic]- Charles	Simpson, Bessie	Husband	Strawberry Plains
Gentry, Bonnie Rovella	Mar 7, 2000	68	S.M.H.	Cocke Co., Tn	Feb 23, 1932	Orr, Milford		Beeler, Annie		Gentry, Joe Edward	Stuffer, Agnes & Don - Adkins, Ann & Chuck	J.C. & Tina		Jack [Vic]	J.M.G.

Name	Death Date	Age	Death Place	Residence	Birth Date	Father	Mother	Spouse	Notes	Relations	Relations	Relations	Cemetery
Gentry, James Henry Earl	Apr 22, 1990	82	F.S.H.	Knox Co	Oct 22, 1907	Gentry, John	Thomas, Laura Ellen			Curtis-Ralph-Herbert-Henry-Bryant-Cecil	[Pals] Shaffer, Donny-Ronnie-Wayne-Kenneth-Hayes, Johnny		Shiloh
Gentry, Laura Ellen	May 31, 1995	82	J.M.H.	Dandridge, Tn	Apr 17, 1913	Unk	Thomas, Sarah	Gentry, J. Henry Earl [D]		Clabourn, Debbie [Step]-Kiwit, Carolyn	Kenneth - [Step] Crook, Don-Larry	Son	Shiloh
Gentry, Ralph Kenneth	Aug 30, 1995	63	U.T.H.	Rutledge, Tn	Jul 24, 1932	Gentry, Henry Earl	Thomas, Laura	Smith, Ruby		Clabourn, Debbie [Step]-Kiwit, Carolyn	Curtis-Herbert-Cecil [TX]-Henry [TX]	Willie	Shiloh
Ghenn, Lon S.	Feb 9, 1961	82								[Flown In]			
Gibbons, Mary Kate	Jul 14, 1977	91	J.M.H.	Jeff Co	Nov 26, 1885	Cameron, Frank	Newman, Betty			Witaker, Ollie-Crye, Barshie-Thompson, Bessie-Brock, Minnie-Hubbard, Margaret -Cupp, Kathryn-Sellers, Irene	Marshall [W. Va]		M. Pleasant
Gilbert, Alice Ruth	Jul 9, 2000	73	S.M.H.	Straw Plains	Nov 23, 1926	Gilbert, William	Seymour, Nola	S		Hazel-Edna - Collins, Thelma [In-Law] Gilbert, Connie	LA, [D] - [In-Law] Collins, Earl [D]		Strawberry Plains
Gilbert, Earl James	Mar 8, 1975		J.M.H.	Tn	Oct 1, 1920	Gilbert, Charles	James, Betty		WW 2	Vermillion, Geraldine-Tolliver - Tipton, Betty Faye-Workman, Mary Jane	Cochran, Minnie [Ind] - Cochran, Nellie [Ind] - Tommy-Earl Jr.-Cox, Porter	J.W.-Bruce-Cochran, Lee-Brown, Frank-Hurst, Roy - Pratt, Kenneth	J.M.G.
Gilbert, Lewis Alfred	Oct 18, 1983	60	Strawberry Plains	Strawberry Plains	Nov 3, 1922	Gilbert, William	Seymour, Nola				Billy Lewis-Jimmy Alfred	Hazel-Edna-Ruthcollins, Thelma	Strawberry Plains
Gilliard, Lena Mae	May 17, 1979	39	White Pine, Tn	Morristown, Tn	Jul 9, 1939	Sizemon, W.T.	Kinsler, Pearl	Gilliard, Billy E.				Mother - [Pals] Kinsler, George-Williams, D.J.-E.R. - Sizemon, Fred-Albert - Wills, J.W.	J.M.G.
Gilmore, Edgar R.	Dec 9, 1974	71	Knoxville, Tn	Tn	Apr 11, 1903	Gilmore, Henry L.	Greenlee, Nellie	W	All	Curtis, Madine - Forrester, Jane [So]	Jack	Herbert-Roy	[Pals] Griffin, Earl-Evans - Glass, Johnnie - Alsup, Bill - Houser, Ralph - Gilmore, Ellen - Whitted, Kenneth	Pleasant Grove
Gilmore, Lucy	Jan 14, 1969	57	Jeff City	Tn	Aug 4, 1911	Mc Ghee, Lenard	Mc Nish, Gertrude	W			Jack	Alsup, News - Hamblen, Bessie - Palenska, Edith	Husband-Forrester, Jane [Bil]	Pleasant Grove
Gilmore, Maude	May 28, 1999	103	Rutledge, Tn	Rutledge, Tn	Feb 12, 1896	Gilmore, Henry Lee	Greenlee, Nellie Ester	S		[Nephew] Gilmore, Melvin [Step]-Jack-Blazier, Ray [Calif]	Gilmore, Maude-Lou, Nellie	[In-Law] Blazier, Frank	Buffalo
Gilmore, Roy Glenn	Jan 13, 1987	95	Rutledge, Tn	Rutledge, Tn	Apr 11, 1901	Gilmore, Henry Lee	Greenlee, Nellie Ester	Finley, Margaret [D]	[Niece] Forrester, Jane	[Nephew] Gilmore, Melvin [Step]-Jack-Blazier, Ray [Calif]	Gilmore, Maude-Lou, Nellie	[In-Law] Blazier, Frank	Buffalo Baptist

Name	Date	Age	Place	Place 2	Date 2	Father	State	Mother	State	Status	Mil	Children	col	col	col	Cemetery
Glenn, Bob [Col]	Nov 10, 1973	58	J.M.H.	Mississippi	Aug 1, 1915		Glenn, Sam		Martha B.		Edna		Jennifer - George, Mary Ruth - Thompson, Anna - Jones, Jo Anne	Bob Jr. [BL]- Michael [Russ]	Baron, Mrs. J.A.- Dance, Mrs. J.C.	Diamstein, Lawton & John [Male]- Woodrow [Colp]+Henry [Colp]+David [Ch]+Roosevelt [Ird]	Helia, J.D.	Bradford, Charles [Father-in-Law]	West View
Glenn, Sam A.	Mar 2, 1936	85	J.M.H.	Tn	Oct 31, 1872		Glenn, John	Tn	Hodge, Mary	Tn								Manley, Mrs. J.D.	West View
Godden, Maude	Mar 6, 1971	86	Wabash, Indiana	Tn	Dec 16, 1884		Manley, James			W			[Step] Manley, Nellie [Ird] - Dance, Bessie				Raymond [Niece - Ird]	Shiloh - Grainger Co.
Godsen, Mary Louise	Aug 3, 1985	89	Knoxville, Tn	Mascot, Tn	Jan 18, 1926		Walfore, Albert		Grove, Lou Bell		Div		Lisa Jo	Paul E. - William [Phil] - Ricky Leo	Butterer, Francis Samuel, John Priest, Billie Sue	Sons	Shiloh
Godwin, Robert Hood Jr.	Jul 12, 1967	74	U.T.H.	Jeff City	Feb 8, 1923		Godwin, R.H. Sr.		Irwin, Ora Lee				Roggli, Helen Meany, Diane - Larman, Stephanie - Johnson, Lisa	R.H. 3rd [AM]- [Step] Johnson, Gary				West View
Goin, Doyle M.	Aug 6, 1967	63	Danridge, Tn	Tazewell, Tn	May 1, 1934		Goin, William D.		Adkins, Mary S. Demps		W		Doub, Donna Marie	Acuff, Judy - Goin, Angie	Danny [D]- Nichole, Catlenne [Mich]- Ewugien [Mich]	Pomeville, Dorothy - Nichole, Calienne [Mich]- Marlow, Ewugien [Mich]			J.M.G.
Goin, Frazier Leon	Dec. , 1968	54	New Lebanon, Oh.	Claiborne Co., Tn						W		Goin, Lora		Wager-Dayne Richard, Elaine- Hoyle-Kirby Wade [Ne]	Wager-Dayne Richard, Elaine- Hoyle-Kirby Wade [Ne]	Hoyt-Kirby Wade [Ne]		West View
Goin, Lora C.	Aug 28, 1974	77	J.M.H.	Tn	Jul 5, 1897		Cole, William		Lyons, Martha		W							J.M.G.
Goin, John Clayton	Jan 19, 1990	75	Campbell Co	Aug 28, 1914			Goins, Whit		Mc Nealey, Florence		WW 2		Hutton, Cathy - Crooks, Teresa		Parker, Reba		Goin, Hoyle		J.M.G.
Goins, Ruth Groendsoo	Apr - , 1972	52	Huntsville, Alabama	Groendsoo, W.M.									Carol	Kenny [Als]	Dale, Jane	W.M.	Wife	J.M.G.
Goins, Verlin Tecumseh	Apr 27, 1967		J.M.H.	Tn	Jun 15, 1893		Goin, A.C.		Rouse, Nora		Cole, Lora		Goins, Samuel K.	Leon-Hoyle-Kirby- Keck, Eva [Mich.]- Beason, Ohio- Johnson, Edna [Ird]	Manley, Little [Wyo.]- Keck, Eva [Mich.]- Beason, Ohio- Johnson, Edna [Ird]	Joshua [Male]	Husband	Willie	J.M.G.
Godin, George Guy	Nov 9, 1960	62	U.T.H.	Tn	May 2, 1898	Tn	Dyer, Mettie J.	Tn			Churchman, Mrs. George - Duncan, Mrs. A.C. - Newsom, Mrs. A.Z. - Mc Cosh, Mrs. John Trent, Mrs. Taylor	G.J.-Guy Jr.	Dogley, Mrs. Fred - Owens, Mrs. S.D. - Hurst, Mrs. Willard	Ernest	Lucy [Wife]	J.M.G.
Grant, Charles William	Jan 6, 1967	61	J.M.H.	Jeff Co	Aug 17, 1925		Grant, Ernest		Glass, Etta				Looney, Pollie - Price, Carolyn	Billy Charles	Blevins, Eva Nell - Stanat, Luna - Stanat, Dorothy	[Phils] Loeld, Tom - Klovid, Gene- Talbert - Beaver, Dorothy - Anderson, Robert	Billy Charles	New Market
Graves, Alma June	Jul 22, 1985	65	New Market	Toledo, Ohio	Jan 18, 1930		Sims, Irvin		Willard, Caroline		Graves, Earl			Eric-Earl Jr.				Husband	J.M.G.
Graves, Edward [Black]	Jan 12, 1992	90	Hill Haven	New Market	Aug 4, 1901		Unk		Hodge, Hollie		S						Brazelton, Margaret [Cousin]- Dial, Marion [Cousin]	J.M.G.

Name	Date	Age	Place 1	Place 2	Date 2	Father	Mother	Spouse					Cemetery
Graves, Horace Irvin	Apr 10, 1988	55	S.M.H.	Union Co, Tn	Jul 18, 1932	Graves, Irvin	Bostic, Lillian	Walker, Lillian Williford	Kansas		Earl-Kenneth	Brother - [Pals] Denton, Jack - Foster, Terry - Weaver, - Cowan, Eric-Creasy, - Holmes, Wayne - Clevenger, Jim - Liebickner, Jerry	J.M.G.
Graves, Irvin James	Jan 12, 1998	86	J.M.H.	Speedwell, Tn	Jan 20, 1911	Graves, M.P.	Calloway, Della	Lillian [D]				Thomas-Horace-Ed-Michael	J.M.G.
Graves, Juanita Hellen Pierce	Jul 3, 1987	72	Knoxville, Tn	Bull Run - Union Co	Aug 18, 1924	Pierce, Robert [Div-D]	Hensley, Elizabeth	Pierce, Sue Pierce - Brickley, Bobbie Pierce & Edward	Anderson, Mary [In-Law]	Anderson, Robert Sr. [D]		Reacon-Harvey-Cecil [Fla]	East View
Graves, Lillian Overa	Feb 15, 1995	81	J.M.H.	Goin, Tn	Jul 13, 1913	Bostic, Olsen	Walker, Tina	Graves, Irvin			Earl-Kenneth	Earl	J.M.G.
Graves, Lura B. Atkins	Mar 5, 1977	53	Monroe, Mich			Atkins, --		Graves, Marion	Peggy-Charlene Ortewood, Diane Kay & Ronald [Mich]	Dale	Harris, Sybil - Whittle, Ina - Whitlock, Myrtle - Ellison, Mrs. Coram - Spradlin, Mrs. Era - Epperson, Margaret	Eddie Little F.H. [Mich] Atkins, Charlie - Clark, Mary	J.M.G.
Graves, Naomi	Sep 17, 1986		J.M.H.	Jeff Co	Sep 9, 1911	French, Crocket		Douglas, Mary Jane	S		Randolph, Shirley	Carroll-Ray-Mae	Piedmont
Graves, Almond Junior	Oct 13, 1988	47	New Market, Tn	Tn	Mar 17, 1922	Gray, William A.	Franklin, Ruby Mae	S		Everett	Hobach, Alice [ING] - Hamley, Irene	Roach, Robert [Pal] - Raymond [Ind]- Lester [Coll]	Reach, Ruby - Clifford-Austin- Lucian Claude- Edd
Graves, Archie Everett	Jan 20, 1982	65	Knoxville, Tn	Sevier Co	May 17, 1916	Gray, Henry	Ogle, Sarah		Hodges, Linda	Everett	Miles, Myrtle	Artis	Oakland - Granger Co
Gray, Arlie Alson	Jan 23, 2000	80	Rutledge, Tn	Selverville, Tn	Sep 22, 1919	Gray, Henry	Ogle, Sarah	Hampton, Grace		Jack & Dianne-Frank		[Pals] Gray, Roy- Franklin - Mies, Clevenger, Don	Oakland
Gray, Arthur	Oct 3, 1984	79	VA - Mt. Home, Tn	Dec 28, 1984		Gray, Aden	Ballinger, Lavena	Mollie K.	unk			[1/2] Gray, John	West View
Gray, Bessie Kate	Jan 30, 1997	98	Rutledge, Tn	Va	Aug 14, 1898	Riner, George	Honeycutt, Jemimiah	Gray, Ray Herman [D]	unk	Lyle-William		Willie	Strawberry Plains
Gray, Buford Clyde	Jun 19, 1992	83	J.M.H.	Grainger Co	Sep 3, 1908	Gray, George W.	Mc Nish, Anna Lee	Foster, Virginia Ross	Cass, Wilma Lee - Hill, Mary Agnes - Sellers, Eula Jacquline			Willis-Doug	Oakland
Gray, Henry Harrison	Aug 9, 1980	89	J.M.H.	Grainger Co, Tn	Oct 19, 1890	Gray, Jim	Nos, Lizzie	Sarah	Miles, Myrtle	Archie-Arlie		[Pals] Grandsons	Oakland
Gray, Jarred Riley	Jul 23, 2000	28d	Nashville, Tn	Nashville, Tn	Jun 26, 2000	Gray, Ronnie Glenn	Cook, Theresa Ann	Sarah				Andrew	Hubbard, Leon & Linda-Gray, Glenn & Robin-Cook, Terry [Gr-Parents] Wright, Wesley & Elizabeth [Gr-G-Parents]
Gray, Michael Joseph	1967		J.M.H.	Knoxville, Tn	Nov 6, 1978	Gray, Michael E.	Green, Judy						Nichols, Paul [Nephew-Fla]
Gray, Mollie	Jan 12, 1995	16				Gray, Arthur [D]		S	Gray, Arthur [D]		Kathryn - Amanda	Mother	West View

Name	Death Date	Age	Death Place	Birth Place	Birth Date	Father	Mother	Spouse	Children/Relatives	Sons	Cemetery
Gray, Cias Mae Mc-Carter	Oct 13, 1989	71	J.M.H.	Wiedabe Creek, Tn	Nov 27, 1917	Reagan, Homer D.	Ramsey, Orlee	Gray, Don T.	[Step] Williantke, Jane Gray; Mc Carter, Frank- Jim; Watson, Gladys - Mc Gaha, Edith; Judd	Doug - [Pals-G-Sons] Witt, Allen-Sam - Gray, John-Dwayne-Edward-James	Tampico Baptist - Rutledge, Tn
Gray, Roy Herman	May 23 1993	96	Rutledge, Tn	Sneedville, Tn	Nov 13, 1896	Gray, William	Drake, Ida Belle	Witt, Evelyn	Lyle-William; Rick, Lizzie	Doug	Strawberry Plains
Gray, Bonnie May	Jul 30, 2000	94	Dandridge, Tn	New Market	Feb 13, 1906	Cain, Ed	Elmore, Rebecca	Green, Bessie Kate	Franklin, Myrtle & Robert - [In-Law] Green, Juanita; Joe [D]-Jack & Sharon-Rance & Blanche; Russell, Martha - Humbard, Dorothy		Friends Station
Green, Elmer	Dec 22, 1990	63	S.M.H.	New Market	Sep 4, 1927	Green, James A.	Cameron, Juanita		Murphy, Joe Ann Ramsey, Judy & Dennis - Charles - Calloway, Debbie; Myrtle; Jack-Rance	Wilie	Friends Station
Green, James Albert	Oct 22, 1996	95	J.M.H.	New Market	Oct 14, 1901	Green, Anderson	Humbard, Sallie	Cain, Bonnie	Franklin, Martha - Jackie & Sharon; Rance & Blanche - Jackie & Sharon	Lloyd	Friends Station
Greene, Delola Geneva	Dec 21, 1982	84	U.T.H.	Hancock Co	May 25, 1898	Seals, Oliver	Smiley, Ruhama	Greene, Walter [D]	Frazier, Ruby - Shelton, Irene - Doyle, Betty; Donald-Arnold-Edgar	Doug	
Greene, Donald Doris	Jul 8, 1992	72	Morristown, Tn	Sneedville, Tn	Jul 2, 1920	Greene, W.B.	Seals, Delsie	Cross, Margaret [D-1983]	Burch, Barbara Jean	Frazier, Ruby - Shelton, Irene - Doyle, Betty	Son / West View
Greene, Glen B.	Mar 23, 1998	67	S.M.H.	Hancock Co.	Jan 4, 1931	Greene, James L.	Hurley, Lucy	Sisley, Dorothy A.	Army [POW]; James Larry [D]-Jerry	Cameron, Dorothy	Wayne-Dean / J.M.G.
Greene, James Larry	Apr 20, 1996	33	Jeff City	Jeff City	Jul 4 1962	Greene, Glen	Sisley, Dorothy	Greene, Donald	Lori Beth	Fred	Jerry / West View
Greene, Margaret Cross	Apr 6, 1983	53	Jeff Co.	Jeff Co	Feb 8, 1930	Cross, Fred	Spencer, Hattie	Greene, Donald	Betty - Frazier, Ruby - Owens, Mattie Belle - Taylor, Virginia; Donald-Arnold-Edgar	Greene, W.B.	J.M.G.
Greene, Omer P.	Sep 17, 1957	23	Junction City, Kansas	Tn	Apr 8, 1934	Greene, William B.	Tn	Delores J.	Fort Riley	Fred	[Pals] Mott, Allen- Vernon-Terry - Shelton, Clair - Taylor, Jeffrey - Gene	
Greene, Walter Brunstow	Jul 17, 1977		New Market, Tn	Tn	Aug 12, 1889	Greene, Plas	Trent, Betty	Delsia			Blackwell
Greene, Agnes Virginia	Dec 20, 1997	71	B.H	Rutledge, Tn	May 14, 1926	Lambden, William Clay	Wilmouth, Carrie	Greene, Garland D.	Jeff, Shirley - Watkins, Diane - [In-Law] Greenlee, Kathy; Foster, Louise - Nelson, Velma [D] - Sharrod, Janie [D]	Charles [D]	Blackwell
Greene, David Wayne	Mar 10, 2000	37	J.M.H.	Jeff City	Apr 13, 1962	Greene, Wesley	Murray, Juanita	Wilson, Renee	Kenny-James-Aaron	Donna	New Market
Greene, Don E.	Oct 25, 1997	58	Morristown, Tn	Granger Co	Jan 18, 1939	Greene, H.M.	Nash, Lou Etta	Roberts, Tina & Eddie	Jim-Bill-Jack [D]	Metcalf, Rose Mary	Myrt-Darrell[Dll] / New Blackwell

Name	Date	Age	Place	Location	Birth	Father	Mother						Cemetery
Greenlee, Floyd C.	Oct 17, 1997	73	F.S.H.	Rutledge, Tn	Sep 18, 1924	Greenlee, H.M.	Potter, Minnie	Velma [D]					New Blackwell
Greenlee, Howard Jr.	Sdt 3, 1981	52	S.M.H.	Greenlee Co.	Dec 22, 1928	Greenlee, William Howard	Gipson, Nola	Div					New Blackwell
Greenlee, Juanita	Jan 2, 1994	59	U.T.H.	Mt. Swan, Tn	Jul 9, 1934	Murray, Liza	Greenlee, Wesley	Donna		Miltie, Gladys - Foster, Lucitta	Husband		New Market
Greenlee, Lloyd L.	Mar 27, 1994	38	Akron, Ohio	Akron, Ohio	Jun 10, 1954	Greenlee, Floyd C.	Dunathe, Velma	Div		Michael	Boot, Linda - Greenlee, Lou Ann		New Blackwell
Greenlee, Minnie Estelle	Mar 12, 1984	80	J.M.H.	Greenlee Co.	Apr 14 1903	Potter, James N.	Boyd, Lucy L.	Greenlee, Horace [D]	Metcalfe, Rose Mary	Boyd-Lloyd-Myrtle-Dave-Don	[Pete] Roberts, Ed Anderson - Metcalfe, Burl - Baumgartner, William - Greenlee, Adam		New Blackwell - Rutledge, Tn
Greenlee, Ricky Lynn	Nov 17, 1989	0	Morristown, Tn	Morristown, Tn	Nov 17, 1989	Greenlee, David	Greenlee, Tina Renee						New Market
Greenlee, Wesley	Feb 24, 1997	82	Jeff City	Greenlee Co. Jeff City	Jun 18, 1934	Greenlee, Dudley	Murray, Juanita	S	Donna	David		Mother	New Market
Gregory, James Ray	Aug 20, 1993	38	Jeff City	Ft. Benning, Ga	Oct 14, 1954	Gregory, James Ray	Howard, Rose Ann	S			Mother		Cremated
Gregory, Rose Ann	Feb 21, 1996		Dandridge, Tn	Jeff Co	Oct 21, 1932	Howard, Bert	Miller, Rosa	Div			John		Mill Springs
Griffey, Dortha Louise	Sep 7, 1983	53	Knoxville, Tn	Knox Co	Sep 25, 1929	Griffey, J.W.		S					Pollards - Tn
Griffey, Sallie H.	Jun 29, 1977	88	F.S.H.	Sevier Co	Dec 12, 1887	Rufus	Atchley, -	W	Dorothy - Cadle, Elizabeth & John - Herron, Isabella & Paul	Rufus	[Pete] Griffin, Alvin-Donald - Steve-Rickie- Cadle, Jimmy		Pollards
Griffin, Easter Zelma	Apr 8, 1999	94	J.M.H.	Knox Co	Jul 7, 1904	King, Willis	Hickman, Alice	Griffin, Robert D. [D]	Gibson, June R.	Bob L.-Charles G.-Lay Jake-Vernon P.			Pollards
Griffin, Everett Dillon	Nov 27, 1986	81	J.M.H.	Jeff City	Feb 18, 1907	Griffin, William	West, Caroline		Murph, Novella	Vineyard, Gertrude	Novella - [Pete] Wells, Floyd - Mitchell, Ted - Shipe, Fain - Lexington, Kenneth-Gene - Williams, Roger		J.M.G.
Griffin, Fred	Oct 30, 1986	79	Knoxville, Tn	Jeff Co	Aug 10, 1907	Griffin, Frank	Jones, Dellie	Nichols, Anna	Darlene - Jones, Charlene		Fisher, George - Day, Lucille	[Pete] Elsworth, William-David - Griffin, Ken - Nichols, Floyd-Charles - Anderson, Jerry	Blue Springs
Griffin, Marjorie L.	Feb 28, 1998	91	Dandridge, Tn	Elyria, Ohio	Dec 10, 1906	Wagner, August	Bauer, Josephine A.				Carl [D]	Bauer F.H. [Elyria, Ohio]	Brookdale - Elyria, Oh
Griffin, Novella N.	Jul 5, 1989	81	F.S.H.	Granger Co	May 15, 1906	Murph, William Thomas	Gobble, Louise	Griffin, Everett [D]	Myers, Nancy		Strorn, Barbara L.[D] - Hicks, Maureen [D] - Lanes, Kathleen G. [Pe] - Strorn, Marjorie G. [Cel]	Williams, Mattie - Shipe, Alta - [Pete] Myers, Bryan - Murph, Bobby-Lewis - Delete - Shipe, Eddie	J.M.G.

Name	Date	Age	Place	Location	Birth Date									Cemetery
Griffin, William A.	Nov 17, 1994	89	J.M.H.	Henry Co. Ohio	May 19, 1905	Griffin, William		Alexander	Henry Co. Oh	Wagner, Marjorie L.	Stism, Marjorie G. [Calif]- Lubans, Kathleen [Re]- Hicks, Maureen G.- Stism, Barbara G. [B]	Bill	Calvert, Lucille [Re]	Edward [Dhl]	Brookdale- Elyria, Oh
Grigsby, Irene	May 9, 1979	87	Greenville, Tn	Athens, Tn	Jan 11, 1892	Lowry, --			Grigsby, Fred O. [D]			Bobby [Re]	Price, Buzzsll [Re]- Stewart, Donald [Re]	John Jr [Re]	Grigsby, Fred [3- Son]	Hawkins Co, Tn
Grindstaff, Bruce	Apr 24, 1987	75	J.M.H.	Newport, Tn	Jul 15, 1911	Grindstaff, John		Fine, Leola	Army		Hearn, Milla [G]- Hearn, Tonna- Tracy - [Step] Gibson, Rita [Re]	Donald [Re]	Son	J.M.G.
Grindstaff, Georgia Flora	May 23, 1996	77	New Market	Jeff City	Jan 2, 1919	Quisenberry, William B.		Rankin, Josie		Grindstaff, Bruce	[Step] Grindstaff, Donald [Re]	Parker, Elsa		Husband	J.M.G.
Grindstaff, Kittie	Oct 27, 1985	92	Knoxville, Tn	Jeff Co	Oct 28, 1893	Thomas, Isaac		Head, Mollie		Grindstaff, David - Julias, Hill	Mrs, Evelyn	Grindstaff, Clifton L.- Julias, Homer M.- Roy C.		Julias, Roy C.	New Market
Groner, James Franklin	Nov 21, 1993	46	Jeff City	Powell, Tn	Jan 17, 1947	Groner, James D.		Phillips, Fleo				Bobby [R/r]	Frak, Peggy & Harry Mouzart, Imogene	Thomas D.	Sister - Moore, Marion	Bell Campground - Powell, Tn
Grosclose, Marie Leona	Jan 18, 1983	90	J.M.H.	Grainger Co.	Mar 3, 1893	Spencer, Barton		Mc Nish, Mary Jane	Grosclose, W.M. [D]		Davis, Jane	Marion	Ballinger, Grace	Thomas D.	Frek, Duncan- Mike - Paysse, P.V. - Paysse, A.E. - Grodie, Walter	Pleasant Grove
Grosclose, Shirley [M]	Aug 11, 1996	73	New Market	Va	Aug 31, 1892	Grosclose, James Thomas	Va	Repass, Rhoda Jane	Collins, Lela P.		Pauline - Walker, Ruby	Mrs. J.A. [Mo]	Caldcott, Mrs. J.A. [Mo]		Grosclose, Frank [Son - Dayton, Oh]	Pleasant Grove
Grosclose, William Marion	Aug 21, 1990	70	Virginia		Aug 14, 1910	Grosclose, J.T.	Va	Repass, Rhoda	Va		Greene, Ruth - Davis, Jane	William Jr.	Cadcott, Flora Greene, Mrs. Dean - Walker, Mrs. Troy	Sid-John	Mamie [Wife]- Greene, Sam K.	Mill Springs
Groves, Fred C.	Mar 11, 1992	48	M.C.	Tn	May 13, 1913			Adkins, Mary			Dean - Walker, Mrs. Troy	Jimmy	Price, Mrs George- Stout, Mrs. Zeno- [1/2] Mills, Mary	John - Rufus	Groves, Pearl L. [Wife]	Flat Gap
Groves, Jamie Louise	Jul 21, 2000	59	Jeff City	Knoxville, Tn	Feb 19, 1941	Collins, Robert			Groves, Jim	Newman, Colonnia - Yeary, Kimberly	Long, Kathryn - Cobb, Evelyn - Beckman, Grace - Longo, Sue	Jim Jr.	Turner, Bobbie	Danny		J.M.G.
Grubaugh, Joshua Willis	Sep 18, 1981	89	B.H.	Camden Co. Mo	Feb 14, 1912	Grubaugh, Brice		Mc Clure, Ethel Mee			Long, Kathryn - Cobb, Evelyn - Longo, Sue	Charles	Newcomb, Emma - Bright, Mary		Piney	Piney
Grubaugh, Mattie Mildred	Jan 18, 1996	83	Jeff City	Jeff Co	Nov 21, 1912	Foster, Charles		Wigmon, Mary	Grubaugh, Jack [D]	Beckman, Friend - Cobb, Evelyn - Longo, Katherine - Longo, Sue		Bill	Newcomb, Emma - Bright, Mary		Piney
Grubb, Carol Millard	May 28, 1990	43	J.M.H.	Grainger Co.	Apr 22, 1937	Millard, Arthur		Helton, Katherin	Riggs, Wanda [D]	Melissa		Tony		Dad	Indian Ridge
Guinn, Carl E.	Oct 11, 1992	46	S.M.H.	New Market	Nov 23, 1933	Guinn, Frank		Lowry, Mollie	Moore, Wilma			William E.- Timothy	Betty		[Feb] Keys, Gene- Charles, Rodney- Price, Tracy- Fleenory, Glen- White, Larry - Smith, C.F.	J.M.G.

Name	Date	Age	Place	Place 2	Birth Date	Father	Mother	Spouse / Family						Relatives	Cemetery
Guinn, Clarence Leon [Wee] (Husband)	Sep 5, 1990	57	St. Louis, Mo		May 7, 1933	Guinn, Jess	Wise, Elsie	Guinn, Tracy	Danny - [Step] Swab, Roney W.	Waddell, Ima Grace	Carl-James W.-Jess Jr.			Step-Son [Pals] Bejsvonger, Joe - Becker, Roger - Wise, Dan - Brown, Stanley - Wright, Billy	New Market
Guinn, Deborah Lynn	Nov 2, 1993	38	J.M.H.	Dandridge, Tn	Nov 6, 1954	Hill, Buford	Gray, Agnes (W)	Guinn, James E.						Husband	J.M.G.
Guinn, Elsie Nora	Feb 29, 1996	53	J.M.H.	Tn	Jun 8, 1916	Wise, Jim	Lane, Annie	Guinn, James E.	Jessie-J.D.-Leon-Carl	Loveday, Ross	Hubert-Dwerty-Fred			Guinn, J.D.	New Market
Guinn, Harvey	Dec 27, 1998	90	Talbott, Tn	New Market	Mar 22, 1908	Kerr, Mary	Wuendsman, Mary -?, Sarah [D] (Army)	Kinder, Pattey & Gene	Ballinger, Titta [D] - Campbell, Lula	Jess-William-Frank				Guinn, J.D.	J.M.G.
Guinn, Jack William	Dec 15, 1995	65	F.S.H.	New Market	Sep 8, 1930	Guinn, Frank	Lowery, Mottie	Guinn, Marina [D]	McGhee, Shelly	Elmore, Betty				Doug	J.M.G.
Guinn, James Wesley	Feb 19, 1996	65	Jeff Co	New Market	May 5, 1932	Guinn, Jesse J. (Tn)	Wise, Elsie	Jernigan, Mary E.	Kathy	James E.	Carl-Junior			Guinn, Elsie [Wife]	New Market
Guinn, Jesse James	Jan 12, 1982	82	J.M.H.	Tn	Dec 16, 1898	Guinn, James (Tn)	Crumley, Mattie (Tn)		Ima Grace	James-Leon-Carl-Jesse Jr.	Campbell, Lula	Harve-William		Guinn, Elsie [Wife]	New Market
Guinn, John William [Bud]	Sep 6, 1996	66	Morristown, Tn	Mascot, Tn	Jul 6, 1932	Guinn, William	Shores, Leona	Keys, Laquietta	Pryor, Debra - Maples, Suzanne & Roger	Ina Grace	John P. & Faye			Jim [D]- Charlie-Frank [Ma]-David	J.M.G.
Guinn, Laquietta Mareen	Jan 27, 1996	59	Morristown, Tn	Knoxville, Tn	Jan 13, 1939	Keys, Jack	Wuendman, Mary Jane Whitt	Guinn, John			Pryor, Debra - Maples, Suzanne & Roger	John P & Faye		Kinder, Patsy & Eugene	J.M.G.
Guinn, Leona	Jan 26, 1994	79	J.M.H.	Mascot, Tn	Jul 7, 1914	Shores, John W.	Lowery, Nell	Guinn, William [Gus]	Lowery, Hazel - Oxies, Mary Nell - Oxies, Katharine - Lowry, Linda	Charlie-Bud-Frank-David			Howard, Rose Lee	John-Frank	New Market
Guinn, Michael Lee	1968	21m	Jeff Co				Guinn, Leon							Seymour, Floyd [G-Father - Grandmother]	New Market
Guinn, Sarah Elizabeth Cowee	Apr 17, 1975		New Market, Tn	Rutledge, Tn	Jan 22, 1896	Williams, Frank	Satterfield, Dory	Guinn, Harvey							J.M.G.
Guinn, Tommy Allen	Jul 27, 1966	23	White Pine, Tn	White Pine, Tn	Jul 27, 1968	Guinn, Leon [Age 35] (Tn)	Seymour, Louise [Adopted] (Tn)	S	Brown, Ashely-Angel					Helms, Tangie	New Market
Guinn, Tracy Lee Anne	Jul 2, 1992	84	U.T.H.	Newport, Tn	Mar 26, 1969	Guinn, Clarence Leon	Shores, Leona	Guinn, Payne			Brown, Michael-Tyler			Guinn, Dennie	New Market
Guinn, William [Bass]	Feb 25, 1997	52	New Market	New Market	Aug 25, 1912	Guinn, James K.	Kerr, Mary							Harvey (Mother)	New Market
Guinn, Willie Mae [Col]	Mar 14, 1985	92	J.M.H.	Rutledge, Tn	Jun 3, 1932	Cameron, Lee	Ross	Guinn, Payne	Junior				Sims, Evelyn - Chambers, Christie - Harvel, Ester	Robert-James [Pals] Jernigan, Joe - Guinn, Bob - Otis - West, Robert - Wood, Oscar - Robertson, Terry	Mt. Pleasant

Name	Date	Age	Place		Birth Date											Cemetery
Haag, Rosa Woods	Mar 18, 1987	89	S.M.H.		Oct 28, 1987	White, Rosa		Lina, Florence	Haag, John [D]-Woods, Carl C. [D]	Osick, Lois [M]-Cox, Betty Jean-Hartley, Helen-Pridemore, Gienera-Stevens, Marjorie [Mo]	Dobson, Kathleen-Cox, Betty Jean-Carl Jr.-George-Smith, Nettie	Woods, Clifford-Carl Jr.-George-Ray L.-James		Frank	Cox, Betty	Mt. Horeb-Talbot, Tn
Hackler, Mary Alice	Oct 17, 1978	80	Kingsport, Tn	Ky	May 16, 1898	Alfred J.		Davis, Helen	W		Houston, Merle [Va]-Chew, Dassel [TX]-Tresp, Iva	John [Ga]-Bill [Cali]Perry	[In-Law] Weddies, Bernard-Don	Frank		J.M.G.
Haggard, James M.	Mar 21, 1980	70	U.T.H.	Knox Co.	Feb 24, 1910	Murphy, Carl								Son		Strawberry Plains
Haggard, Mildred Elnor	Jul 6, 1993	77	Morristown, Tn	Sturgisville Hawkins	May 5, 1916	Kirkland, John		Pendelton, Ona	Coiley, Linda		Jimmy R.	Sandage, Kate	Paul	Son		
Hall, Celdous Wayne	Aug 2, 1967	21	Morristown, Tn			Hall, Reid			Coiley, Linda		1					J.M.G.
Hall, Deward Burl	Sep 4, 1987	33	Jeff City		Mar 18, 1964	Hall, William E.		Broadwater, Evelyn	Osborne, Ruby [Osie]	Karen-Amanda-Wendy	Osborne, Tim-Kaiser, David	Bailey, Patricia	Broadwater, Eugene-Walker, Billy Jr. [Moth]-Hall, Daniel Ray	Walker, Evelyn & Bill [Mother & Step Father]	Mill Springs
Hall, Edith Lutchia	Sep 12, 1993	68	Maryville, Tn	California	Dec 22, 1924	Walker, George Sr.		Strange, Anie Mae	Hall, Ruel	Jenkins, Reba Ann	Sturgil, Betty-Meler, Gertrude	George Jr.	Husband-[Pds]-Walker, Scottie-Stanley-Ed-Poteat, Dave-Summerfield, John-Osborne, Curtis		J.M.G.
Hall, Hattie Elizabeth	Dec 18, 1954	66	Mascot, Tn	Tn	Feb 11, 1878	Hall, Theodeus		Hall, Catherine	Hall, Arthur Carnel		Floyd	Elmore, Press-Judd-Walter	Morgan, Kathryn [Daug]		Friends Station
Hamblin, Carl Dean	Mar 6, 1988	52	Teaberry, Ky	Teaberry, Ky	May 21, 1936	Hamblin, Evan V.		Della	Collins, Hazel			Hamblin, Little [Ky]-Clark, Marie [Ky]	Roland [Mo]-John H. [Mo]	Watts-Clark, Mr. & Mrs. Carnel [Ky]	Samatta-Teabury, Ky
Hamilton, John Charles	Oct 13, 1997	19	Jeff City	Baltimore, Md	Sep 19, 1978	Daughrity, Virgil		Dasher, Susan	S		Amanda Ashley		Mother	Dasher, Wayne & Betty-Daughrity, Eugene & Betty [Grandparents]	J.M.G.
Hamilton, William Robert Jr.	Mar 24, 2000	50	Nashville, Tn	Matewan, W. Va	Sep 11, 1949	Hamilton, William A. Sr.		Workman, Dorothy	Bradshaw, Brenda	Dempsey, Tammma Lynn [Ga]	William R. 3rd-[Step] Chambers, Chris	Dean, Mira [W. Va]-Frazer, Sharon [W. Va]-Vannoy, Darlene [Ga]-Chambers, Lori-Vannoy, Rhonda [W. Va]	Medlock, Charlie [Gr-Father]-[Pds]-Morgan, Johnny Ray-Watson, Ernest Jr.-Bailey, Bob-Oscar Smith, Johnny-Jerry		Caledonia
Hammer, Charles J.W.	Jan 21, 1973		Knoxville, Tn		Jan 21, 1933	Hammer, Roy		Medlock, Ruby	Large, Patsy	Ikonsa					Oakland
Hammer, Herman C.	Dec 29, 1948	35	Evarts, Ky		Apr 21, 1913	Hammer, J.A.	Granger Co. Tn	Clevenger, Lucy	Clevenger, Lucy	Granger Co. Tn				Cecil		Oakland
Handy, Dottie Mae	Jul 16, 1996	79	J.M.H.	Thornhill, Tn	Mar 22, 1917	Collins, Henry		Hipshire, Nellie	Patterson, Inez	Handy, Woodrow [D]-Cox, Houston N.[D]	Handy, Sandra		Cox, Kenneth [Fig]-Stanley-Harold	Collins, Pauline-Atkins, Jessie [D]	Doug	Hammer, Edna J. Lebanon Baptist	J.M.G.

Name	Date	Age	Place	Location	Birth	Father	Mother		WW 2				Burial
Hardy, Woodrow Wilson	Aug 13, 1988	75	J.M.H.	Tn	Feb 4, 1913	Hardy, Isaac	Harper, Martha	Collins, Dollie Cox				Hardy, Dollie	J.M.G.
Harvey, Carl Ray	Jan 12, 1999	54	Jeff City	Knoxville, Tn	Apr 16, 1944	Harvey, Amos C.	Latham, Troy	Beck, Mildred Louise	Whitehead, Carla & John - Whitehead, Carla	Carl Jr. & Lisa - Steve & Pat - Carl Ray Jr - Steven Wayne	Barnes, Brenda - Cinnamon, Mary Frances	Gene	J.M.G.
Harvey, Mildred Louise	May 25, 1997	52	Jeff City	Knoxville	Jan 13, 1945	Beck, Clarence	Harvey, Carl		Whitehead, Carla & John - Whitehead, Carla			Edward Carl - J.B. [TX]-Larry	J.M.G.
Harvey, Steven Wayne Jr.	Jul 30, 1993	0	Morristown, Tn	Morristown, Tn	Jul 30, 1993	Harvey, Steven Wayne Sr.	Francis, Patricia Darlene					Henry, Carl &Mildred - Francis, Parents] - Howell, Martha [G-G-Mother]	New Market
Hankins, Bessie M.	Aug 31, 1978		Care Inn	Jeff Co	Dec 30, 1898	Lenard	Mc Nish, ??	Hankins, Joe [D]				Morgan, Pamela [G-Daug] - [Pats] Hankins, Don - Goss, J.R. - Ballinger, Riley - Ellis, Neil	Pleasant Grove
Hankins, Glenna S.	Mar 31, 1978		S.M.H.	Tn	Aug 15, 1927	Shelton, —	Curts M.	Hankin, James H. [Di]		Maples, Judy & Daniel; Blackburn, Christy; Blackburn, Janice	Margaret, Denton/Roach [2nd Husband]-Robinson, Edith	[Pats] Shelton, Jimmy Ray - James Haskell - Jackie Dwayne - Dale-Gary - Martin, Jim - Ballinger, David - Maples, Ricky	Forden
Hankins, James Haskell	Apr 4, 1986	60	New Market, Tn	New Market, Tn	Jul 1, 1925	Hankin, Sam Mc Kinley	Neal, Lillie	Shelton, Glenda			Jonathan Mc Kinley	Frank-Elmer-Jim+Haskell- R.D.	Franklin - Promiseville, Tn
Hankins, Jo Alfonso	Dec 21, 1971	72	Jeff City	Tn	May 18, 1899	Hankins, Alex	Howard, Laura	Mc Bessie			W.R.	Howard, Mrs. Minnie	Pleasant Grove
Hankins, Lillie Maude	May 29, 1977	78	Jeff Co	Jeff Co	Jul 26, 1898	Neal, Thomas	Green, Nannie	W		Ballinger, Frances & Riley-Johnson, Leona	Haskell-Donald	Ballinger, Frances - Johnson, Leona	Pleasant Grove
Hankins, Paralee	May 12, 1993	73	Knoxville, Tn	Liberty Hill, Tn	Mar 25, 1920	Loy, Paris E.	Wolfe, Alice	Hankins, W.R.	Tn	Sellers, Doris - Morgan, Pam & Dale; Johnson, Mrs. Alfred R.[Mich.]; Ballinger, Mrs. Riley E.	Bobby Joe & Gina	Watson, Opal - Reddy, Bobbie	Pleasant Grove
Hankins, Sam Mc Kinley	Apr 7, 1957	59	E.S.H.	Tn	Nov 4, 1897	Hankins, Alec	Howard, Laura	Neal, Lilly	Tn		Donald E.-James H. [Fl.]	Loy, Paul & Betty	Buffalo
Hanna, Abraham	Apr 5, 1962	74	Morristown, Tn	Akron, Ohio	Jan 5, 1908	Hanna, George	Helene Owyens	Nellie O.		Trent, Martha [D]-Carolyn [D] - Trent, Glenda - Lentz, Mary; Jayne & Tony	Hannal, Jim & Carolyn	Miller, Freida - Brant, Nellie	West View
Hamal, Helene Mae	Jan 2, 2000	80	J.M.H.	Morristown, Tn	May 1, 1919	Caruthers, Newton	Melone, Louise	Hamal, Lloyd [D]			Hannal, Jim & Carolyn	Fralix, Laura	J.M.G.

Name	Date	Age	Location 1	Location 2	Date 2								Cemetery
Harrell, Lloyd E.	Oct 31, 1989	78	Morristown, Tn	Warrensburg, Tn	Jan 9, 1911	Harrell, Christopher Hale	Wilson, Jennie	Helen C.	Trent, Carolyn-Glenda - Lamb, Mary Jane	Jimmy	Gadsen, Sally - Anderson, Beatrice	Wills - [Pals] Trent, Glenn-Dean-Chris - Harrell, Jeff-David - Lamb, Jared-Marc	J.M.G.
Hardin, L.C. [F]	Jan 18, 1999	67	Rutledge, Tn	Thorn Hill, Tn	Mar 2, 1931	Lamb, Walter	Steele, Rutha	Hardin, Jakie			Tate, Jean - Dean, Ethel	O.C.	Hargas, Mrs. Dora	Narrow Valley
Hargas, Brad L.	Nov 5, 1958		Jeff City										New Market
Hargas, Leonard A.	Jan 3, 1987	57	Holston Valley Hosp.	Jeff Co	Nov 29, 1929	Hargas, Boyd	Baker, Dora	Hudley, Daisy			Sohn Sr.	Brother - [Pals] Murray, Robert - Orfield, Jerry - Dixon, James - Harrell, Carl - Bible, Dexter - Hargas, John Jr.	Flat Gap
Harmon, Jeffrey Waylan	Dec 11, 1997	33	Chattanooga, Tn	Knoxville, Tn	Oct 10, 1964	Harmon, Wayland R.	Cox, Phyllis	Div			Balson, Gidget - Harmon, Nancy [B]-Brad[D]	Curtis R. [CR] - Ray [CR] - Bruce	Father	New Market
Harmon, Mary Evelyn	Jul 9, 1996	68	Strawberry Plains	Strawberry Plains	Jan 18, 1928	Smith, Roy Sr.	Morton, Lena	Harmon, Billy Joe [D]			Nicely, Juanita - Smith, Martha - Anderson, Reba - Miller, Margaret - Fultz, Willie [D] - Shackelford, Joan [D]	Roy C. Jr. - Lynn W. - Norman [D] (Neice)	Anderson, Michelle & Jeff (Neice)	Hopewell - Mascot, Tn
Harness, Floyd	Dec 7, 1985	83	J.M.H.	Anderson Co	Apr 1, 1902	Harness, Lum	Hendricks, Leona	Houser, Mary		Floyd E.	Powell, Edith - Long, Bonnie - Bracken, Magdaline	Elmer	[Pals] Hobbs, Floyd-Verble-Brandon-Dwight-Della-Sharp, Jim	Caledonia
Harness, Mary Sue	Feb 22, 1997	68	Knoxville, Tn	Knox Co	Mar 19, 1907	Houser, Dave	Shook, Lucy	Harness, Floyd [D]	Hubbs, Juanita - Ramsey, Lee Wanda	Little Floyd [D]-Floyd E. [VA]	Kynshndoll, Gayna [D] - Mills, Bertie Mae [D] - Roach, Georgia [Ohio] - Stahl, Rose [Fla], Conrad, Marie	Ocie [D]-Frank	Smelcer, Violet & Don [G-Daug]	Caledonia
Harper, Paul J.	Jun 9, 1987	72						Verta		Patricia [Fla]	Jerry	Sweet, Ilea		Pleasant Grove
Harper, Verta	Feb 2, 1982	82	J.M.H.	Tn	Jan 31, 1900	Mynatt, William T.	Boles, Mary	Harper, Paul	Carey, Patricia	Jerry	Stokes, Hazel			Pleasant Grove
Harrell, Bruce Albert	Ded 1, 1994	72	Hill Haven	Burnsville, Nc	Nov 5, 1922	Harrell, Roy	Harris, Altha	Standifer, Jacinta [D]	C. Guard				Harrell, Roy Edward Sr. (Nephew)	Cremated
Harrell, James Haldew	Mar 6, 1995		V.A.-Mt. Home	Russellville, Tn	Sep 21, 1922	Harrell, Nessie	Howerton, Martha	Glann, Elsie	Army				Wills	Strawberry Plains
Harrell, Mary Catherine	Sep 22, 1994	69	U.T.H.	Hamblen Co	Jun 11, 1925	Burgin, L.G.	Vallee, Elizabeth	Harrell, James					Monroe-Eugene-Joseph-Vernon-Bobby Husband	J.M.G.

Name	Date	Age	Place	State	Birth	Father	Mother	Spouse	WW	In-Law				Cemetery
Harris, David Mc. Conrad [Chapadoras]	Apr 18, 1999	76	New Market	Antioville, Nc	Oct 11, 1922	Harris, David M.	Johnson, Josephine	Mullins, B.A.	WW 2	[In-Law] Chancey, Hope - Williams, Becky & Jon [Jo] - Grady, Lynn & Greg - Allen, Susan & Jim [Jal] - Jamroz, Brenda & Mike - Taylor, Debbie & Gary [Fla]	Chancey, Jim- Bobby-Roger [Tn] - Moore, Greg	Strow, Joan - Kornagay, Patty- Friona, Peggy- Henry, Lynda	Spruke, Jean [D] - Spours, Martha	Cremated
Harris, Dorothy Lamar [Black]	Oct 24, 1999	55	New Market	Asheville, Nc										Youngs Memorial
Hamburger, Roby	Sep 17, 1980		Care Inn	Sullivan Co	Jun 27, 1902	Hamburger, Zach S.	Mings, Mattie	Div						Strawberry Plains
Hart, Frank Eugene [Tobe]	Nov 26, 1999	72	Sevierville, Tn	Knoxville, Tn	Mar 18, 1927	Hart, John	Price, Patsy	Stines, Betty J.	Navy					East View
Hartley, Woodson R.	May 26, 1982	73	Jeff City	Oklahoma	Jul 21, 1906	Hartley, Sam	Walker, Georgia	Bailey, Hazel		[Step] Drinnon, Mrs. Robert- [Step] Walker, Mrs. Ronnie	Woodson R. Jr.- [Step] Walker, Fred	Mc Cracken, Laverna	John Howard	Highland Memorial East
Hatmaker, Christie Mae	Feb 16, 2000	74	J.M.H.	Norfolk, Va	Sep 3, 1925	Richardson, George	Murray, Charlotte	Hatmaker, Edward [D]		West, Christie Mae & James	Coblt, Ruth	Willis		J.M.G.
Hatmaker, Edward Avery	Dec 18, 1994	67	Morristown, Tn / Lafollette, Tn		Apr 2, 1907	Hatmaker, Fletcher	Pengel, Columbia Anna	Richardson, Christie	Navy					J.M.G.
Haworth, Angie Elizabeth	Jan 1, 1996	60	New Market, Tn		Nov 15, 1925	Bates, Lee H.	Moore, Lydia L.	Haworth, W.T. Sr.		W.T. Jr.				Friends Station
Haworth, Bessie	Jun 9, 1971	82	Knoxville, Tn	Tn	Mar 29, 1889	Neal, Thomas	Green, Nancy	Haworth, Horace E. [D]		Bollinger, Dorothy	Ralph [Dayton, Oh]-James W.	Hopkins, Lillie	Frank	William I. [Son] / Pleasant Grove
Haworth, Carl Martin	Nov 8, 2000	64	Jeff City	New Market	Feb 10, 1936	Haworth, Golden	Williams, Ruby	Melton, Ruby [D]		Pigsbee, Lawata H.	Richard [D]	Everhart, Olis Mae & R.H.-Kerr, Condia Fae		J.M.G.
Haworth, Clarence Edgar	Jan 21, 1995	92	New Market	Tn	Mar 9, 1902	Haworth, Dillon	Campbell, Lillie	Whitlock, Pearl [D]					Nances Grove
Haworth, Cornelia	Jul 21, 1991	74	B.H.	Jeff City	May 6, 1917	Combs, John C.	Moore, Emma E.	Haworth, Raymond				Newman, Blanche	Husband	West View
Haworth, Esther Emma Haynes	Jun 1, 1999	90	J.M.H.	New Market	Apr 14, 1909	Smith, Carl N.	Groves, Emma	Haworth, Marshall [D]		Whan, Mary Taylor [Cal]	Haynes, Larry [Cal]	Howard, Agnes	[Pals?] Dale, Glen - Howard, Jim - Ballinger, Charles - Young, Paul - Wood, Hendi- Michelle	J.M.G.
Haworth, Henry H. [Negro]	Aug 2, 1977	66	U.T.H.	Tn	Dec 31, 1910	Haworth, Sam	Nance, Lena	Div		Gloria [Va]		Wilkerson, Flora	Jones, Anfina [Ala] - Boatwright, Peggy	Youngs Memorial
Haworth, Horace Edgar	Oct 6, 1965	78	J.M.H.	Tn	May 14, 1889	Haworth, David Thomas	Dinwiddie, Cordie	Neal, Bessie Belle		Ballinger, Mrs. Boyd	Ralph [Dayton, Oh]-Bill-James W.-Neal [Cal]	Northam, Mrs. J.W.-Fennell, Mrs. C.C. [Dayton, Oh]	Haworth, Bill	Pleasant Grove
Haworth, Lelia Mae	Apr 27, 1996		Jeff City	Tn	Dec 8, 1886	Smelcher, Fred	Baughard, Elizabeth	Haworth, Owen Lee		French, Mrs. Sherman	William-James			
Haworth, Lillie A.	May 7, 1957	92	Tn	Tn	Nov 5, 1864	Campbell, John	Shell, Harriet	Tn		Slagle, Blanche	Golden-Clarence		Haworth, Clarence	Nances Grove

Name	Date	Age	Place	State/Birthplace	Birth Date	Father	Mother	Spouse	Military	Notes 1	Notes 2	Notes 3	Cemetery
Haworth, Owen Lee	Apr 30, 1996	78	Jeff City	Tn	Oct 23, 1887	Haworth, Richard	Smicher, Lelia			Carroll, Mrs. Tadwell		Haworth, James	New Market
Haworth, Pearl Ethel	Jul 20, 1989	86	Knoxville, Tn	Tn	Sep 17, 1902	Whitlock, Oscar	Lara	Smicher, Clarence		Rigsbee, Lavada			Nances Grove
Haworth, Ralph E.	Jan 13, 1984	73	Centerville, Ohio	New Market, Tn		Haworth, Horace	Neal, Bessie	Howard, Louise	WW 2	Gene	Ballinger, Dorthy	Flit Wilfred	Pleasant Grove
Haworth, Richard Godwin	May 19, 1991	91	J.M.H.	New Market	Mar 3, 1900	Haworth, Dillon	Campbell, Lillie	Williams, Ruby				Clarence	J.M.H.
Haworth, Richard Marion	Oct 26, 1999	40	New Market	Jeff City	Nov 25, 1959	Haworth, Carl Marion	S				Carl M. [Tom]	Cox Marion [G-Mother]	J.M.G.
Haworth, Ruby Jean	Apr 10, 1998	61	New Market	Pinville, Ky	Jan 26, 1937	Maiden, William	Haworth, Mildred Cox	Haworth, Carl M. [Tom]		Richard M.	Richard M.	Clarence	J.M.G.
Haworth, Ruby Mae	Aug 3, 1998	82	New Market	New Market	Aug 18, 1915	Williams, George	Forgey, Ora	Haworth, Richard R. [D]		Carl Martin [Tom]	Ruth, Ethel Frazier [D] - Everhart, Ola Mae & R.H. - Kerr, Clauda Fae	Walter [D] - Roy Mae & R.H. & Ola	J.M.G.
Haworth, William Marshall	May 5, 1991	84	Knoxville, Tn	Jeff Folly	Oct 18, 1906	Haworth, George	Esther	West, Ellen				Willie	J.M.G.
Haworth, William Taylor Sr.	Mar 27, 2000	74	S.M.H.	New Market	Jul 13, 1925	Haworth, Owen	Betes, Elizabeth [D]	unk	unk	W.T. Jr.	French, Charlotte [D]	Jim & Mary	Glenwood - Knoxville, Tn
Hayes, Clyde	Sep 7, 1994	83	Benton, Tn	Ocoee, Tn	Oct 22, 1910	Hayes, John C.	Ballow, Harriet	Hodges, Rena	Navy	Nicholas	Miller, Minnie	Norris, Patricia	Oakland
Haynes, Beryl	Apr 3, 1996	62	Tn		Jun 26, 1933	Haynes, James	Gass, Verna Lou	Smith, Ester E.	unk	Barbee, Mary Taylor	Larry	Northern, Mrs. Jennie - Clemens, Mrs. Herbert	Earl [Twin] - Raymond	J.M.G.
Hector, Valdrid George [Swedish]	Aug 26, 2000	94	New Market	Georgetown, Co	Feb 22, 1906	Hector, Peter	Gustafson, Eva	Schwartz, Lillian Virginia [D]		Robert-David & Peggy Mars & Judy	Rockhesner, Anna	V.A.	Cremated
Hedrick, John Allen Sr.	Apr 2, 1986	35	J.M.H.	Morristown, Tn	Jan 12, 1950	Hedrick, Thomas E.	Imes, Jennie E.	Quinn, Brenda Sue	Nat. Guard	Angela Dianne	John Jr.	Allice S.	William D.	West View
Helm, Augustus George Jr.	Aug 18, 1994	69	Rutledge, Tn	Rutledge, Tn	Jul 21, 1925	Helm, A.G. Sr.	Farrar, Etta Pearl	Sarbin, Azelea	Army		Mary	Willie	Ross	Shiloh
Helton, Carmel Eugene	Nov 2, 1993	71	J.M.H.	Hawkins Co, Tn	Jan 21, 1922	Helton, Joseph	Wallen, Annie	Booker, Penny - Carter, Carmela		Mary	Wife	3	Rosaberry - Mascot, Tn
Henry, Ada (Polly)	Apr 21, 1990	95	Jeff Co		May 3, 1894	Douglas, George W.	Privette, Liza	Henry, Ralph E. [D]		John Jr.	Allice S.	Randolph, Shirley G. [G-Nancy]	New Market
Henry, Donald Perry	Jul 4, 1993	41	Jeff City	Knoxville, Tn	Nov 23, 1951	Henry, Horace W.	Cochran, Agnes	S	Marines	Matthew	Loy, Linda & John	Loy, John Jr. - Joe [Nephews] - Mother	J.M.G.

Name	Date	Age			Date	Father	Mother	Spouse							Burial
Henry, Grover Cleveland	Jul 19, 1981	86			Feb 17, 1895	Henry, J.W.	Baker, Cordelia	Marshall, Mary Lou	Hammer, Jean						Hills Union
Henry, Susan Alice	Mar 14, 1975	80	New Market, Tn	Sevier Co	Jan 18, 1895	Loveday, Mitchell	Atchley, Margaret			Williard, Mae [Nc] - Thomas, Stella		Clifford	[Pals] Catlin, Charlie - Spencer, Don - Denton, Dale - Alley, Butch - Norton, Bill - Mc George Johnny		New Market
Hensley, Amanda Elizabeth	Jan 15, 1984	74	J.M.H.	Union Co	May 8, 1909	Atkins, Volk	Collins, Viola			Mc Ginnis, Mary - Fields, Opal - Selvy, Polly - Russell, Bertha - Turner, Shirley	Troy-Ray	Adams, Parlee	[Pals] Hensley - David-Mille- Gregory - Owens, James - Russell, Allen - Selvy, Rick		Hillcrest
Hensley, Anna Mae	Jul 31, 1999	61	Dandridge, Tn	Knoxville, Tn	Apr 27, 1938	Poore, James	Roderick, Mary Ellis	Hensley, Curtis E. [D]	Pollard, Patricia - Dawson, Darlene	Michael-Greg					
Hensley, Curtis E.	Jul 22, 1980	82	Charlotteville, Va	Union Co	Mar 15, 1933	Hensley, Phillip	Adkins, Amanda	Anna Mae	Patricia - Bowman, Darlene	Mille-Greg	Mc Ginnis, Mary - Russell, Bertha - Turner, Shirley - Selvy, Polly	Troy-Ray	Hawkins F.H. [Charlotteville, Va]		
Hensley, Dana Harmon	Dec 2, 1986	84	J.M.H.	Hawkins Co, Tn	Nov 2, 1904	Hensley, Phillip	Sapphire, Hulda	Smith, Lois [D]	Bailey, Bobbie Jean - Mc Daniel, Clara Nell - Brown, Carolyn		Mc Ghee, Mae - Looney, Mary - White, Ethel - Bull, Crowe, Natalie Lee	Jim	Brown, Carolyn [Nc]		Tangelo - Rutledge, Tn
Hensley, David Vasco	Jul 9, 1986	94	S.M.H.	Union Co	Jun 3, 1902	Hensley, John	Cox, Melisa	Adkins, Elizabeth [D]	Brown, Betty - Jones, Mary Ruth - Evans, Donna - Bevry, Kathleen [B]	K.B. Jr.	Mc Nutt, Mrs. Vick - Trish, Florence		Baker - Union Co		Shiloh
Hensley, Janie Ada	May 30, 1997	88	Jeff City	Rutledge, Tn	Apr 4, 1908	Curt, J.T.	Moody, Tina	Hensley, Kyle [D]	Cook, Mary Ruth - Mc George, Douglas - Kerr, Kathleen - Kemp, Roberta - Russell, Betty [B]	K.B. Jr.	Looney, Mary - Mc Ghee, Mae - Crowe, Heddie - Bull, Esther - Selvy, Callie - White, Ethel - Nash, Titta	Dana-Jim	[Pals] Shiltz, Curtis - Devils, Frank - Combs, Hobb - Moody, Ralph - Helm, Fritz - Kissell, Lon		Shiloh
Hensley, Kyle B.	May 2, 1981	79	J.M.H.	Hawkins Co	Feb 14, 1902	Hensley, Phillip	Shropshire, Hulda	Curt, Ada							
Hensley, Sherial Inez	Feb 24, 1963					Hensley, Ray Edward			Cutshaw, Helen & Eugene - Lauderdale, Dorothy & Stewart - Maples, Diana & David - Richard		Bertis Elizabeth - Owens, Patricia Ann	Owens, James Wayne	Hensley, David D. - Thompson, Lon [G-Fathers]		Friends Station
Hensley, Troy Lee	Sep 6, 2000	75	S.M.H.	Union Co	May 8, 1925	Hensley, David	Collins, Amanda E.	Cannon, Virginia [D]	Cutshaw, Helen - Lauderdale, Dorothy & Stewart - Williams, Diana - Maples, Betty & Richard	David & Judy - Troy & Kelly	Mc Ginnis, Mary - Fields, Opal - Russell, Bertha - Turner, Shirley - Selvy, Polly	Curtis [D]-Ray			East View
Hensley, Virginia Merlah	May 27, 1995	70	F.S.H.	W. Va	Mar 14, 1926	Cannon, Frank	Lawson, Minie	Hensley, Troy Lee	Lauderdale, Dorothy - Cutshaw, Helen - Williams, Diana - Maples, Betty	Elwood, Margaret - Blair, Frances - Faulkner, Juanita - Mize, Evelyn	Frank-Harold	Husband			East View

Name	Date	Age		Place	Date	Father	Mother	Spouse							Burial
Herndon, William	Apr 15, 1999	83	Morristown, Tn	Seperts, Ga	Dec 19, 1915	Herndon, James	Price, Inez	Needham, Edith		Peck, Martha - Sue - Wallenberger, Barbara - Mellicoat, Sherry	Larry		2		Mitchell Springs
Herrell, Helen Ruth	Jan 11, 1997	65	Knoxville, Tn	Gatlin, Tn	Nov 7, 1931	Shelton, Roscoe	Moore, Laura	Herrell, Lynn D.		Rena - Courtney; Janice	Tyler, Elda [Mich] - Neal, Laura - Phelps, Jeanne	Ray Austin - Webb-Felton W.	Husband - [Fiel] Shelton, Wesley - Roger-Rodney - Greg-Wayne-Junior-Carol - Courtney, Charles		Indian Ridge
Herron, Earl	Jul 5, 1993	78	J.M.H.	Sharp Chapel- Union Co.	Jun 12, 1915	Herron, H.B.	Berry, Mary	S	Swann, Geneva Aileen	WW 2		Seale, Edith	Hubert Jr.	Seale, Jennifer - [Fiel] Seale, Albert-Tim-Jim - Cenonna, Stan - Herron, Mike - Nuthing, Windell	J.M.G.
Herron, Loree	Jun 24, 1990	63	F.S.H.	Sharp Chapel- Union Co.	Jan 17, 1927	Herron, H.B.	Berry, Mary	S				Seale, Edith	Earl-Hubert Jr.		J.M.G.
Herron, Mary Kate Marr	Apr 27, 1993	77/78	New Market	New Market	May 13, 1915	Pitts, Charles	Murray, Maddie	Herron, Palmer [D]		Barbara Sue	Michael-Craig	Murt, Pauline - Renor, Ruth - Petros, Amanda	Doug	Wife - [Fiel] Seale, Albert-Tim- Cenonna, Allen - Danny-Murry, Tobert - Morrow, Cecilia	New Market
Herron, Palmer	Feb 1, 1975	57	New Market	Union Co.	Aug 18, 1917	Herron, Bart	Berry, Mary	Pitts, Mary Kate		[Step] Howell, Mrs. Bob	Mike-Craig	Lorane - Cadle, Mrs. Riley - Seale, Edith	Earl-Paul-H.B.	Husband - [Fiel] Morgan, Jim - Hickey, Wayne - Kimbrough, Don	J.M.G.
Hickey, Bessie Mae	Oct 9, 1995	80	U.T.H.	Hamblen Co.	Jul 25, 1906	Kimbrough, Mack	Davidson, Margaret	Hickey, James T.							Strawberry Plains
Hickey, James Thurman	Jan 15, 1999	87	J.M.H.	Tn	Dec 20, 1901	Hickey, Andrew	Smith, Kate	Kimbrough, Bessie [D]		Barbara - Pratt, Christine - Kerner, Phillis	Lawrence-Robert [D]	White, Cora	Ralph	[Fiel] Smith, Billy - Bill - Lees, Cecil - Bennett, Bryon - Gann, Wayne - Denton, Jim	Strawberry Plains
Hickey, Lawrence Gordon	Mar 19, 1998	60	F.S.H.	Knoxville	Jan 27, 1938	Hickey, James Thurman	Kimbrough, Bessie	Kimbrough, Grace M.		Jeannie [D] Pwn [Mich]-Lisa [Mich]	Tom [TX]-Jerry		Robert [D]	Sister	Trenville
Hickey, Robert Lynn	Aug 3, 1987	55	Strawberry Plains	Morristown, Tn	Sep 10, 1931	Hickey, James T.	Kimbrough, Bessie May	Proctor, Adveny Jean		Hickey, Tracy [Mich]	Robert-Michael - Larry-[All- Oregon]-Steve- Gary [All-Mich]	Barbara - Pratt, Christine - Kerner, Phylis	Lawrence [Mich]		Ormsford- Strawberry Plains
Hickle, Ernest John	Oct 14, 2000	77	F.S.H.	Grainger Co.	Feb 11, 1925	Hickle, Maynard L.	Dukes, Sernith	Young, Alice		Collins, Robin & Floyd	Ernest & Faye- Charles & Monny	Howard, Pansy- Hastings, Elsie - Bunting, Edna [Mich]	Earl [D]		Mill Springs
Hickle, Margaret Anna Mae	Jul 6, 1989	63	B.H.	New Market, Tn	Sep 15, 1925	Hickle, Luther	Reed, Nettie	Div			Earnest J. Jr.			Son - [Fiel] Wollenbarger, Rick - Clarkston, Bill - Smith, Eugene - Ervin, Eugene - Oats, Luthur-Elmer	Pleasant Grove

Name	Date	Age	Place 1	Place 2	Date										Cemetery
Hicks, Maynard L.	Jul 23, 1990	68	M.C.	Tn	Jul 3, 1922	Hicks, Thorn				Howard, Mrs. Raymond - Hastings, Mrs. Kenneth - Bunting, Mrs. John A.	Ernest-John	Hensley, Pauline	Annie-Oscar	Hicks, Sarah [Wife]	Nances Grove
Hicks, Sanith Athea	Apr 17, 1987	88	U.T.H.	Tn	May 11, 1898	Dukes, Joe		Northern, Julia			E.J. [Pink]				Nances Grove
Hickman, James Dewey	Oct 3, 1997	61	Sevierville, Tn	Kodak, Tn	Jan 13, 1936	Hickman, James Dewey Sr.		Parker, Mabel B.	Collins, Bonnie Jean	Juanita - Henry, Dorothy [In-Law] Hickman, Dollie	Oliver-Kenneth - J.D.-Jr.	Williams, Elizabeth - Wade, Gladys - Vaughn, Hazel	James	Hickman, James Jr. - Mc Ghee, Allen - Henry, David - Collins, Jim - Cobb, Gary - Atwood, James	Shady - Kodak, Tn
Hickman, Mabel B.	Apr 17, 1996	87	Strawberry Plains		Jan 23, 1909	Parker, Fonzo		Brock, Artie	Hickman, Dewey [D]				James	Son	Piney Flats Hollow - Kodak, Tn
Hickman, Robert Samuel	Jan 19, 1982	61	Sevier Co.	Kodak, Tn	Oct 3, 1930	Hickman, Dewey		Parker, Mabel	Korea	Lane, Dorothy - Mc Geei, Darlene	Jeff-Joey	Henry, Dot - Juanita	J.D.-Ollie-Earl	Drug	East View
Hickman, James Dewey	May 28, 1979	55	Orlando, Florida	Jeff Co	Jul 24, 1923	Stallings, Mack Alexander		Koontz, Sallie	Hicks, Ira Lee	Faye - Dugman, Thelma-Pauline - Wollard, Jean	John	Denton, Frances	Ben	Seawolt, B. Koye	East View
Hicks, William Maynard	Jul 23, 1984	88	Morristown, Tn	Newport, Tn	? 24, 1896	Merle, Maggie			Ruth [D]	S		Yeary, Lynn	Jackie	Hill, Agnes Gray [S-Mother]	J.M.G.
Hicks, Kathleen	Jan 14, 1995	14	J.M.H.	Jeff Co	Dec 5, 1908	Rosch, Judy			S	Seals, Polly - Baker, Bobbie		Sellers, Mrs. Robert - Rutledge, Mrs. Charles	Bill	Hill, Agnes Gray [S-Mother]	Oakland
Hill, Dan Allen Jr.	May 9, 1993	82	Jeff City	Newport, Tn	Jun 30, 1910	Hill, Ben D.		Raines, Hattie	Howard, Ruby	Seals, Polly - Baker, Bobbie			Wife	Hill, Ruby L. [Daug]	J.M.G.
Hill, James F.	Aug 18, 1995	83	J.M.H.	Tn	Oct 23, 1882	Hill, Ira		Ida		Seals, Polly - Baker, Bobbie		Hurst, Helen - Fielden, James, Evelyn		Hill, Ruby L. [Daug]-Donald - Howard - Frazer, Jack - Johnson, Walter	Lebanon
Hill, Jesse Franklin	Dec 3, 1985	86	Morristown, Tn	New Market	Apr 25, 1908	Howard, Richard T.	Ayres, Ruby	Hilton, Josephine	Seals, Polly - Baker, Bobbie					Doug	J.M.G.
Hill, Ruby Ayres	Apr 25, 1999	86	S.M.H.	Jeff Co	Mar 20, 1913	Hill, Jesse Franklin			[In-Law] Hill, Lillian-Frances					Hawk, Martha & Walter - Hill, Corley - Hill, Joe & Tina [Nieces-Nephews]	West View
Hill, Willie Ray	Oct 18, 1977	61	J.M.H.		Oct 10, 1915	Hill, Jess	Gladis, Ida	Gladis, Ida Belle	Mary Frances		Corley	Ruby	Donald	Hill, Corley E.	New Market
Hill, Ruby Lee	Oct 29, 1993	32	Jeff City	Knoxville, Tn	Jul 4, 1981	Hilliard, Herman Mc Coray		Hancock, Elizabeth Bernetta	S		Corley		Donald	Mother	Strawberry Plains
Hilliard, Larry Michael	Aug 14, 1996	35	Jeff City	Knoxville, Tn	Dec 20, 1959	Hilliard, Herman Mc Coray		Hancock, Elizabeth Bernetta	Div	Army	Stephanie [One]	Justin [One]	Larry [D]-Tony-Scott	Mother	Strawberry Plains
Hilliard, Stephen Mc Ray	Nov 19, 1995	86	Jeff City	Chestnut Hill, Tn	Jul 21, 1909	Profitt, Samuel W.		Strange, Sarah	Hinchey, Marshall	Shands, Patsy - Lockhart, Kathleen	Justin [One]			Willie - [Pink] Hinchey, Jim - Profitt, Eddy - C.N.-Wesley - Williams, Eddie - Seals, Donald	Flat Gap
Hinchey, Alma Jane	Jun 24, 1993	80	J.M.H.	Jeff City	Jan 8, 1913	Hinchey, Robert P.		Clevenger, Margaret Bertha	Profitt, Alma	Lockhart, Kathleen - Shands, Patsy	Sam-Max-Albert	Seals, Ollie Kate	Robert	Willie - [Pink] Shaw, Leonard - Hinchey, Jim - Cecil - Corbooth, Bruce 7 - Seals, Bobby - Williams, Edie	Flat Gap

Name	Death Date	Age	Place	County/State	Birth Date	Father	Mother	Spouse					Siblings / Pallbearers	Cemetery
Hinchey, Max Caldwell	Dec. 1, 1999	57	Jeff Co	Jeff City	Oct 14, 1942	Hinchey, Marshall Houston	Profitt, Alma Jane	Rosenheim, Sylvia Ann	Davis, Kimberly Ann - Edmonds, Lindsey Rae	Swann, Mary Frances [New Carlisle, OH] - Mayo, Betty Jean	Kenneth James- Marshall Craig- Christopher Max	Lockhart, Kathleen & Don - Shands, Pat & Bill	Hipsher, J.B. [Pals] Hipsher, Herbert-Robert- Swann, David - Roth, Jerry - Garrett, Michael - Pierce, Marcus - Willie - [Pals] McDaniel, Steve - Barnett, Leo C. - Tolley, Harriet - Hipshire, Carroll - Greenlee, Floyd - Don	Flat Gap
Hipsher, Herbert	Aug 14, 1986	89	J.M.H.	Tn	Oct 13, 1898	Hipsher, Burton	Shockley, Cynthia	Bailey, Ada L. [D]	Navy			McDonald, Grace [Kinsaw]	Bridgewater, Curt	J.M.G.
Hixon, Otis Bryant [Trest]	Jun 25, 1994	61	New Market		Sep 26, 1932	Hixon, Otis	Daniel, Donna			Charlotte, Donna	Patterson, Virginia Marie	Gurtie Mae - Ethel Dallas- Jackson, Peggy	Tatt-J.S.- Burt	Hixon - New Market
Hixon, Roy Tatt	Jan 9, 2000	84	Rutledge, Tn	Rutledge, Tn	Sep 24, 1935	Hixon, Obel	Daniel, Louella	McDaniel, Estelle			Charnelle, Donna	Hixon, Gurtie Mae- Jones, Peggy- Hixon, Gladys [D]	Junior [D]-Burt- J.S.	Mitchell Springs
Hodge, Benjamin Jeffery	Apr 23, 1982	29	F.S.H.	Jeff City	Jun 2, 1982	Hodge, Bobby	Suddarth, Melba	S		Hodge, Mary Ruth & Kenneth - French, Lois & Thomas - Kerr, Anna Lyman & James		Ernest & Gwen- Tina & Tammy	Jolene	Father- [Pals]- Kerr, Mike- Hodge, Bobby- Billy-Harold- Gary- French, Ricky
Hodge, Bertha	Feb 28, 1978	82	Jeff Co			Hodge, William	Neal, Mary Angeline	Hodge, W.H. [D]					Jewel-Kenneth- Edward	Pleasant Grove
Hodge, Charles Benton	Nov 20, 1986	71	Strawberry Plains	Texas	Aug 1, 1915	Hodge, Charles B.	Hunt, Ella	Shackelford, Lorene				Brown, Fred- Lunsford, Mrs. Earl	Wife- [Pals] Brown, Fred-Mike- Denton, Clark- Shackelford, Sam- Hamilton, John- Ron	Piney
Hodge, Charlie Haskel	Feb 28, 1974	66	Nashville, Tn	Tn	Mar 11, 1917	Hodge, Joe	Haworth, Maggie					Milburn-Roy	Fielden, Eugene [Admin]- [Pals] Fielden, Bill- Haworth, Marshall- Franklin, Charles	Mill Springs
Hodge, Cora Mae	Jul 27, 1976	78	Granger Co	Granger Co	Sep 22, 1897	Mynatt, Shade D.	Wynick, Alice				Jett, Bertha- Farrow, Juanita	Hodge, Mrs. Lula Theodore- Coolidge-Carroll- B.H.-Lonas- Kenneth	Elmer	Blue Spring
Hodge, Debbie Lee	Sep 27, 1977	57	J.M.H.	Tn	Apr 17, 1920	Parker, Ralph Ray	McCollick, Gurtie	Hodge, Paul		Hodge, Paul		Harold Wayne	[1/2] Parker, Victor	Husband - Parker, Blanche [Step- Mother] - [Pals] Parker, Gordon - Davis, Joe - Stroupe, Ed - Denton, Jim	J.M.G.
Hodge, Fred Elbert	Jun 11, 1982	87	J.M.H.	Jeff Co	Dec 7, 1894	Hodge, J.T.	Kinser, Annie	Fielden, Ollie Mae	Ira			Hixon, Curtie Mae- Deitas, Ethel	Father- [Pals] Hodge, Bobby- Parker, Gordon- Davis, Joe- Stroupe, Ed- Denton, Jim- [Pals] Brockway, R.B.- Watkins, Bass, W.W.- Johnson, Ralph	West View
Hodge, Ida	Nov 3, 1973	90	Morristown, Tn	Tn	Oct 15, 1883	Longmire, Frank	Smith, Rachael	Hodge, J.H. [D]		Kadigan, Mrs. W.P. [Olda]	Ira	Roy	Wallace, Mary - [1/2] Greenlee, Bonnie	Central Point - Rutledge

Name	Date	Age		Location	Birth	Father	Mother	Spouse						Cemetery
Hodge, Irene Edith	Aug 18, 1998	67	U.T.H.	Grainger Co.	Mar 30, 1931	Patterson, Clyde	Dalton, Vesta	Hodge, Benjamin H.	Kirby, Cathy & Randall	Jim [D]-Steve & Ramona	Bishop, Kathleen & Lois - Meyers, Polly & Sam - Smith, Patsy & James - [In-Law] Jones, Evelee Pearl	Hodge, W.H. [Fla] Hodge, Michael-Roger J. Ralph-Terry-Dean		West View
Hodge, John A.	Oct 31, 1955	72	E.S.H.											Sunrise
Hodge, John Luther	Mar 24, 1994	98	F.S.H.	Jeff Co.	Jan 2, 1896	Hodge, Tom	French, Cecelia	Sarah Maude	Jones, Golda - Costner, Gladys Pappas, Mrs. Jessie	Jewel T.-Nash-Ralph-Hal	Paul-John-Max-Buford [D]			Piedmont
Hodge, Julia	Mar 4, 1977	93	J.M.H.	Sevier Co.	Dec 12, 1883	Kerr, Daniel W.	W		Mary Ruth - French, Lula - Kerr, Anna Lynn			[Pels] Hodge, Jackie-Harold Donald-Bobby-Donnie - Kerr, Mike - French, Rick		Mill Springs
Hodge, Kenneth Lester	Apr 20, 1983	63	Jeff City	Jeff Co.	Jun 19, 1919	Hodge, William H.	Fielden, Bertha	Goins, Vola			Jewel F.	[Pels] Hodge, Jackie-Harold David-Bobby-Donnie - Kerr, Mike - French, Rick		J.M.G.
Hodge, Nina Trula	Jul 10, 1991	81	J.M.H.	Knoxville, Tn	Jan 5, 1910	Cain, Samuel	Underwood, Martha C.	Fielden, Jewell [DM]	Steen, Sue & Zack - Denton, Shirley & Harold	Bobby Joe-Bill	Cain, Jessie	Joe		Beaver Creek
Hodge, Ollie Mae	Dec 27, 1983	89	J.M.H.	Jeff Co.	Apr 13, 1894	Fielden, Jacob Berry	Howard, Elnora	Hodge, Fred E. [D]		Ira	Colfe, Jessie	Vernon		West View
Hodge, Pearl M.	Oct 24, 1985	82	New Market	New Market	Nov 26, 1902	Hodge, Luther	Julia K.	Parker, Debbie	S	Pappas, Jessie	[In-Law] Hodge, Mrs. Will	Max-John	Hodge, Harold Wayne [Son]	Pleasant Grove
Hodge, Pearl	Feb 5, 1996	72	Knoxville, Tn	Tn	Jan 15, 1898	Hodge, Edward	Collins, Amanda	Hodge, John Luther						J.M.G.
Hodge, Sarah Maude	Jul 18, 1979	89	F.S.H.	Jeff Co.	Apr 12, 1890	Lamaron, Jim	Atchley, Julia	Hodge, John Luther			Jett, Bertha - Fencon, Jaunita	Coddington-Ken-Carroll-Benjamin H.-Lonas	[Pels] Jett, Barry-Hodge, Randy-Frank-Lonchny-Pancon, Johnny-Costner, David	
Hodge, Theodore Roosevelt	Dec 15, 1992	73	S.M.H.	Rutledge, Tn	Oct 31, 1919	Hodge, Ben H.	Mynatt, Cora	Hillard, Jessie [D]					[Pels] Hodge, Randy-Frank-Lonchny-Franz-Bob - Wilson, Herman Jr.	Blue Springs-Rutledge, Tn
Hodge, Vola C.	Jul 10, 1996	77	Care Inn	La Fa, Tn	Jul 26, 1908	Goins, Whitt	Mc Nealey, Florence	Hodge, Kenneth [D]	Hodge, Christine		Parker, Rheta	John	Brother [Pels] Preston-Debbie-Goins, Wallace-Goins, Whit-[Pels] French-[Pels] Hodge-[Pels] Hodge-Bobby Joe-Billy Ray-Donnie-Kerr, Mike	J.M.G.
Hodge, W.R. [Dub]	Aug 15, 1975	50	Jeff Co		May 10, 1925		Bertha	Christine	[Step] Hodge, Rosa Mary-Johnson, Mrs. Kermit-Smith, Mrs. John [Fla]	Jackie-Harold	French, Mrs. Tom - Hodge, Mrs. Kermit-Kerr, Mrs. Jim	Jewell Edward-Kenneth	French, [Pels] French-[Pels] Hodge-[Pels] Hodge-Bobby Joe-Billy Ray-Donnie-Kerr, Mike	Nances Grove

Name	Date	Age	Place	County	Birth	Father	Mother		Note	Relations				Cemetery
Hodge, William Edward	Aug 15, 1978		Colorado	Tn	Mar 1, 1922	Hodge, W.H.	F., Bertha		Brandon, Ruth	WW 2	Baker, Joyce & Warren - Bailey, Linda & Donald - ?, Kirkland, Mary Lynn & Bob - ?, Jessica & Troy Tillery, Barbara Anna Lynn Kerr, Mrs. Jim - French, Mrs. Thomas - Hodge, Mrs. Kenneth	Donald [Gal-Gary] Lawrence [Alli] - Jewel		Craighen Mortuaries [Denver, Colorado]	Pleasant Grove
Hodge, William Harrison	Jul 3 1966	75	New Market, Tn	Tn	Oct 28, 1890	Hodge, Edward	Collins, Amanda			WW 2		W.P.-Edward [Chicago]-Kenneth Jewel	Willis		Pleasant Grove
Hodge, William Melburn	Sep 30, 1988	76	V.A.-Mt. Home	Jeff Co	Nov 18, 1909	Hodge, Joe	Haworth, Maggie			WW 2		Bill	Roy	Hodges, Mrs. Mollie	Mill Springs
Hodges, Andy Edward	Mar 15, 2000	96	New Market	Washburn, Tn	Aug 28, 1913	Hodges, James	Seymour, Ethel		Williams, Sarah Virginia	WW 2		Ed & Tanya	Conard [D]- Robert [D]- Charles [D]- Edgar-Edit- J.A.	Wills - [Pals] Bunch, Lawrence - Stephen - Howard, Marshall - Craig, Joe - Thomas, Darrell - Slagle, Herman Jr.	J.M.G.
Hodges, Buford Randle	Feb 17, 1950	72	New Market, Tn	Jeff Co	Sep 27, 1877	Hodges, Thomas	French, Celia A.	Tn		Tn	Hux, Mrs. Ross - Porter, Mrs. K.C.	Harry [Ali]-Jerry & Mary	Luke-Frank- Perry-Temp	Hodges, Mrs. Mollie	New Market
Hodges, Charles Lewis	Oct 5, 1991	69	S.M.H.	Granger Co	Nov 6, 1921	Hodges, James A.	Seymour, Ethel		Seats, Ruby		Anderson, Charlotte [Gal]-Wright, James-McDaniel, Carolyn	Billy Lee-Kenneth	Edgar-Edward- Robert-Emil- J.A.	Anderson, Justin - Craig, Jim - David Glen - Wright, Ray Sr. -	J.M.G.
Hodges, Conard Edwin	May 20, 1981	66	S.M.H.	Granger Co	Apr 28, 1915	Hodges, James A.	Seymour, Ethel		Newby, Aileen	unk	Alley, Mrs. Robert Jr.		Hayes, Rena & Clyde	Edgar-Charles- Glenn-David- Edit-Jeff- Robert-Edward	[Pals - Nephews] Hodges, Edit- Glenn-David - Newby, Wallace - Bradley - Hayes, Nick	J.M.G.
Hodges, Mollie	Sep 20, 1980	75	New Market	Jeff Co	Oct 14, 1904	Bettis, George	Remmer, Frances				Porter, Mrs. K.C.	Harry-Frank- Vaughn		Hux, Mrs. Ross [Pals]	New Market
Hodges, Ruby Beatrice	Apr 6, 1995	59	Rutledge, Tn	Morristown, Tn	May 25, 1930	Seats, John C.	Bowlin, Mattie		Hodges, Charles [D]		Wright, James - McDaniel, Carolyn	Hemsley, Kenneth - Hodges, Billy	John	Son [Pals] Smith, David-Bill-Frank- Young, Raymond - Hodges, Bob Jr. - Wright, Allen-Ray	J.M.G.
Hodges, Von Oliver	Jan 25, 1973	64	Detroit, Mich.	Tn	Nv 15, 1913	Hodges, Buford Randle	Bettis, Mollie			? - 43			Henry [Ali]- Frank	Yerington F.H. [Detroit, Mich]	New Market
Hodgins, Frodd K.	Sep 12, 1990	61	New Market, Tn	Crown Pt., Ny	Jan 11, 1889	Unk	Unk		S				Henry [Ali]- Frank	Hux, Ross [Admin]	New Market
Hodgson, Anna Lynn	Oct 5, 1995	76	U.T.H.	Dandridge, Tn	Jan 30, 1919	Nicholson, Ward	Elder, Sallie May		Hodgson, Avery Hunter		Gale		Cooley, Ruby	Husband - [Pals] Nicholson, Walter- Milne-Jean-Joe - Cooley, David - Hodge, Frank	J.M.G.

Name	Death Date	Age	Place	Birth Place	Birth Date	Father	Mother	Spouse	War	Children	Others	Siblings / In-Laws	Pallbearers	Cemetery
Hodgson, Avery H.	Apr 15, 1998	81	Jeff City	Jeff City	Dec 12, 1916	Hodgson, Thomas R.	Monday, Daisy	Lynn, Anna		Gary [D]-Gale & Donna	Lila [D] - Cannon, Lucy [D] - Fraker, Deena [D]	Jack [D]-Tom [D]- Bill [D]- Charles [D]- King [D]- Ellis	Ellis M. Sr.- Avery-Hal King	J.M.G.
Hodgson, Charles Emmett	May 14, 1993	83	F.S.H.	Jeff City	Aug 17, 1909	Hodgson, Tom	Monday, Daisy	Williamson, Faye	Navy	Solomon, Frankie	Fraker, Dena	Wife - [Pala] Fraker, Tom - Hodgson, Hollis	William H.-Galle- Fraker, Scott - Cannon, J.T., Jr. - Whitlock, L.M. - Solomon, Kenneth	J.M.G.
Hodgson, Hollis Wilson	Mar 25, 1999		New Market	Jeff City	Oct 22, 1923	Hodgson, Ellis	Wilson, Elizabeth	Shirley, Hazel [Div D]	Navy	Hutzka, Vickie & Dan	Galey, Jane - Shanda, Joyce	Paul Jr. [D]- Sherman [D]- Jack [D]- [In-Law] French Opal [D]	Lowe, Howard [Ga-D]	West View
Hodgson, Imogene F.	Jul 28, 1999	74	J.M.H.	New Market	May 10, 1925	French, Paul R.	Kiein, Mattie L.	Hodgson, Ellis	vietnam		Disney, Polly [D]	[In-Law] French Opal [D]	Howard [Ga-D]	New Market
Hodgson, James Gary	Oct 6, 1998	42	Jeff City	Jeff City	Jun 22, 1946	Hodgson, Avery Hunter	Nicholson, Anna Lynn	Brickmeier, Vickie [D]		Brashears, Martha Jane - Hendrix, Nancy Kaye - Cummins, Cathy Mae [Miss] - Watson, Mary Ellen		Burnett, Imogene - Swaggerty, Grace	[Pala] Orr, Lamar - Lawrence, Horace - Stella, Bob - Turley, Amos - Green, Richard - Mc Ghee, Ray	J.M.G.
Hoffman, John Richard	Jun 9, 1996	76	Talbott, Tn	Altoona, Pa	Jan 13, 1920	Hoffman, Milton	Camp, Gertrude	Mantele, Mary Ellen		Thomas Lee [Md]			Milton C. [Pa]	J.M.G.
Holbert, James Alexander (Able)	Sep 15, 1982	63	New Market	New Market	Sep 24, 1929	Holbert, John	Glass, Mable	Denton, Jean			Doug-Steve- Stacy-Halbert		Son	Flat Gap
Holbert, Thelma S.	Dec 25, 1996	72	J.M.H.	Rutledge, Tn	Aug 2, 1924	Spoon, Pryor E.	Daniel, Meta	Holbert, Cecel [D]				Silver, James & Katherine		Pleasant Hill Knox Co.
Hornback, Elva	Nov 25, 1980		Knoxville, Tn	Knox Co	Apr 23, 1904	Plumlee, Joe	Evans, Lucy	Hornback, Harold H. [Jim]		Pratt, Gene - Hornback, Jack	Lewis, Marie - Bailey, Rose - Carey, Edna		[Pala] Smith, Tommy- Newman, Lester - Sutton, Danny- Heison, Jerry- Brian - Feavrer, Clay	Pleasant Hill
Hornback, Harold H. [Jim]	Mar 27, 1998	86	S.M.H.	Knox Co	Jul 17, 1901	Hornback, Albert	Riggs, Lillie Mae	Elva [D]	WW 2	Kirk, Retha - Young, Marie - Snyder, Frances	Pratt, Gene - Hornback, Jack		Jack - [Pala] Newman, Lester - Sutton, Danny- Heisman, Mitch- Joe - Blake, Kenneth- Charles	J.M.G.
Horner, George Washington	Jul 13, 1983	79	Mo	Mo	May 19, 1904	Horner, Joe	Livesay, Sara	Philbeck, Lella Mae		Campbell, Katie [Foster] - Longmire, Minnie	Philbeck, Lella Mae		Willis	Nances Grove
Horner, Joe	Jan 18, 1973	82	M.C.	Tn	Apr 21, 1890			Minnie B.		Campbell, Katie & Van - [Foster] Longmire, Mrs. Roy	Ray, Peggy			West View
Horner, Merrie B.			J.M.H.	Tn		Epps, James	Brown, Corbis	W			Frank		Milam, Ina - Houn, Mrs. Sanford	Creech- Hamblen Co
Horner, Tiffany Leann	Aug 7, 1993	0	Knoxville, Tn	Knoxville, Tn	Aug 7, 1993	Horner, Tom	Bowman, Michelle						Abe-Pete [Nc]	West View

Name	Date	Age	Place	County	Date	Father	Mother	Spouse	War	Children / Relatives	Burial
Hoskins, Dewey Palmer	May 14, 1990	65	J.M.H.	Jeff Co	Oct 23, 1924	Hoskins, Dewey	Palmer, Leslie	s	WW 2	Hoskins, John [Polson - Polly], Willard - Fred, Stoddard, Mel - Paul J. Hensley, Paula	Pleasant Grove
Hoskins, Dorothy Elizabeth	Sep 5, 1995	76	J.M.H.	New Market	Feb 19, 1919	Hoskins, George	Williater, Elizabeth	s		Ellon, Gail [Bob] Mc Mitzy, Betty	Pleasant Hill
Hoskins, Leslie M.	Aug 16, 1989	84	New Market, Tn	New Market, Tn	Nov 17, 1904	Palmer, Mack	Adcock, Nora	Hoskins, Dewey P.		[In-Law] Nash, Lorraine — Dewey	Piney
Hoskins, Mc Cleary Edward	Jul 14, 1978	27	Dandridge, Tn	Tn	Apr 10, 1951	Hoskins, William E.	Fischer, Lorraine	Thelma [Dis]	Angie	Tammy - Clark, Marilyn [Dot]	Blue Springs
Hoskins, William Edward	Feb 12, 1983	81	New Market, Tn	Jeff Co	Dec 19, 1921	Hoskins, Dewey P.	Archer, Lorraine	Palmer, Leslie	John	Tammy - Clark, Marilyn [Dot], Dewey	Blue Springs
Holtz, Gerald Eugene	Jun 13, 1996	84	Jeff City	Edwardsville, Ill	May 28, 1912	Holtz, Clarence	Redding, Roschelle	Peck, Virginia Lewis		Bruce & Donna [Calif], Willis	J.M.G.
Houser, Artie Mae	Oct 27, 1984	79	New Market	New Market	Jul 20, 1905	Davidson, Ben	Mc Ghee, Martha	Houser, Otis [S]		Hayes, Mamie Ann, Remben, Minnie, Vlad	Caldonia
Houser, Gladys Virginia	Feb 21, 1998	69	U.T.H.	Blount Co., Tn	Nov 23, 1918	Duke, Morgin	Dumbach, Bessie	Houser, Frank		Ferguson, Joyce Bona, Frankie, John Franklin, Pat Hack - James	J.M.G.
Houser, Otis L.	Aug 8, 1983	79	New Market	Knox Co	Feb 1, 1904	Houser, Dave Franklin	Shook, Lucy Frances	Davidson, Artie Mae		Hayes, Ann, Frank Sonny	Caledonia - Knox Co
Houston, Johnnie Gladys	Mar 18, 1953	70	Wattega, Tn	Wattega, Tn	Nov 24, 1882	Houston, J.B.		Houston, William Avery		Florence - Kate - Cooper, Mrs. Will - Mc Falls, Mrs. Ralph - Adkins, Mrs. Sam, Houston, Mrs. W.A.	New Market
Houston, Samuel Avery	May 14, 1992	77	New Market	New Market	Dec 6, 1914	Houston, William Avery	Anderson, Johnnie Goldie	S	Army		New Market
Houston, William Avery	Mar 18, 1984	78	Jeff Co	Tn	May 2, 1887	Anderson, Thomas J.	Laskt, Matilda	Houston, William Avery		Houston, W.B. & Samuel [Sons], Houston, William C. [Nephew]	New Market
Houston, William Baxter	Apr 17, 1985	55	J.M.H.	Tn	Oct 3, 1909	Houston, William	Anderson, Johnnie G.	Pugsley, Dorothy	42-45	William Charles, Samuel A.	New Market
Howard, Raymond Earl	Feb 11, 1991	82	F.S.H.	New Market	Jun 30, 1906	Howard, Sam	Hankins, Hannah	Sartin, Pansy Viola		Vineyard, Pauline, William-Earl, Shernod-Fisher A.H.	New Market
Howard, Edwin Todd	Jul 26, 1970		F.S.H.	F.S.H.	Jul 20, 1970	Howard, Lloyd Edwin [Age 27]	Dockery, Emma Lou [Age 22]	Mascot, Tn		Father - Dockery, Richard [G-Father]	Proffit - Dandridge, Tn
Howard, Ellie Beulah	May 17, 1982	83	New Market	New Market	Jun 5, 1896	Hamilton, Tilman	Mc Prentidge, Eldora	Howard, Sam		Lowe, Eldora - Newman, Laverne, Bixley, Ruth - Jones, Jonnie-Buckman, Pearl - Nellie, Nellie, Bixley-Ralph-T.L., Chris, Howard, Sam	Pleasant Grove

Name	Death Date	Age	Place	Res.	Birth Date								Cemetery
Howard, George	Jun 5, 1968	78	New Market, Tn	Tn	Oct 30, 1889	Hankins, Hannah	Whitlock, Mary	Frances	Mc Daniel, Rula - Vineyard, Pauline	Tolliver-Taylor-[Sherod]-Alfonzo	Howard, Lufford [Sion]		Pleasant Grove
Howard, Gladis L.	Jun 16, 1999	84	Jeff City	Tn	May 4, 1915	Wright, Vina	Howard, Herbert [D]		Jim & Barbara	Armholds		Willie	Mill Springs
Howard, Halmond L.	Apr 7, 1991	87	New Market	Tn	May 23, 1903	Howard, Walter	Northern, Dona	Howard, Mary C.	William-Robert-Larry-Rod-Edwin			Willie	Pleasant Grove
Howard, Herbert Clarence	Oct 10, 1970		Hamblen Co	Tn	Aug 3, 1914	Howard, Richard T.	Ruby R.	Will, Mary Lou - Hews, Dorcus - Boruff, Betty [Daugh] Howard, Miss Helen - Brock, Mrs. Thelmer ?	Jimmy [G] Zane-Todd	James, Evelyn - Hill, Ruby & James - Fielden, Ruth	Willie		Mills Spring
Howard, John Wesley	Dec 26, 1977	87	J.M.H.			Neal, Mae [D]		Frances	Lufford	Howard, Mrs. Hannah			Pleasant Grove
Howard, Mary Emily	Dec 9, 1970	73	New Market, Tn	Tn	Dec 25, 1897	Whitlock, Lufford	French, Hailey Jane	W	Frances	Lufford	Howard, Mrs. Hannah	Andy	Pleasant Grove
Howard, Minnie	May 12, 1979	84	Knoxville, Tn	Tn	Feb 14, 1895	Hankins, Alex	Howard, Elizabeth	Howard, Tolliver [D]	Haworth, Louise [OR] - Ellis, Shirley		[Phil] Ellis, Howard - Hankins, Gine - Hankins, W.R - Don - Mc Daniel, Rufus Jr. - Howard, J.W.		Pleasant Grove
Howard, Samuel F.	Jul 21, 1982	89	New Market	Tn	Sep 24, 1892	Howard, Sam	Hankins, Hannah	Beeler, Pauline Mae	WW 1	Lowe, Eldora - Newman, Laverne	Ray Wesley-Corroll	A.H.-Raymond Sherrod-Taylor	Pleasant Grove
Howard, Samuel Lelford	May 6, 1996	69	Knoxville, Tn	New Market	Jun 21, 1926	Howard, George	Whitlock, Mary	Hankins, Hannah	Hubbard, Lois	Kenneth	Frances		Pleasant Grove
Howard, Tolliver W.	Mar 18, 1972	36	New Market	Tn	Sep 18, 1894	Howard, Sam	Hankins, Hannah	Howard, Minnie	Lowe, Eldora - Newman, Laverne	Mc Daniel, Rula - Vineyard, Pauline	Cornoll, Cindy & Toddy		Pleasant Grove
Howard, William Randall	Sep 26, 1996	36	U.T.H.	Jeff Folly	Aug 24, 1960	Howard, William R.	Bateman, Patricia	Hopson, Michelle		Cornoll, Cindy & Toddy	Willie		J.M.G.
Howell, Bernice	Nov 30, 1990	45	U.T.H.	New Market	Aug 17, 1945	Mc Campbell, Elmer	Brewer, Doralee	Howell, Lawrence	Crespo, Donna - Taft, Ilene	Chris-Mark-Brian	Frances	Husband - [Phil] Ferrow, Bob - ... Diarrell - Jay	Deep Springs
Howell, Charles Thomas	Apr 25, 1986	63	Care Inn	Jeff Co	Mar 2, 1923	Howard, Clarence	Finley, Flora	Smith, Mattie Pearl	Charles Jr.	Michael & Connie - Deweyann [G]	James-Bob-Lawrence	[1/2] Charles [D]-Lawrence & Betty-Bob & Barbara	Friends Station
Howell, James Edward	Sep 12, 1996	60	Rutledge, Tn	Knox Co	May 22, 1936	Howard, Clarence C.	Whitaker, Mary Voiles	Foster, Betty Jo	Cameron, Eula Mae - Farr, Beatrice - Morgan, Maudie & Charles - Farrow, Bernice & Bobbie - [1/2] Cameron, Eula Mae	Beckett, Regina & Bery [OR] - Murray, Morgan, Maudie - Charles - Farrow, Bernice & Bobbie		Son [Phil] Elmore, Randy-Howell, Chris-...	Wesleys Chapel
Howell, Mattie Pearl	Sep 18, 1992	70	S.M.H.	New Market	Aug 22, 1922	Smith, Robert	Lowrey, Sarah	W	Elmore, Lamon - Johnny Bill-H.L.	Elmore, Lamon - Brown, Jeanette	Smith, Ralph-Jerry		Wesleys Chapel
Howell, Robert C Sr.	Nov 26, 1977	55	Oak Ridge, Tn	Tn	Jun 19, 1922	Howard, Charlie	Smith, Mrs. Bessie Beller	Carden, [Gla] - [2nd] [1st ?]	Patsy-Robbin Sue - Spencer, Barbara [Calif]	Robert C. Jr			Flat Gap

Fielden Funeral Home
New Market, Jefferson County Tennessee

Name	Date	Age		Place	Date	Father	Mother		Frances	Carl	Son	Cemetery
Hubbard, Bessie	Oct 5, 1989	96	J.M.H.	Campbell Co., Tn	Jul 2, 1893	Hannon, Hiram	Pratton, Frances	Hubbard, Abe M. [D-1922]			Wife - [Pals] Solomon, Tom - Collins, Floyd - Anthony	West View
Hubbard, Charles Hubert	Mar 29, 1991		Bn	Jeff Co	May 12, 1911	Hubbard, William Merlin	Rhiea, Ona			Paul-Leon	Son - [Pals] Hubbard, Terry - Dukes, Anthony - Breeden, Jeff	East View
Hubbard, Edith Ariena	Jul 23, 1995	79	J.M.H.	Jeff Co	Aug 3, 1915	Northern, Jasper R.	Davis, Susan Ariena	Hubbard, Hubert [D]	Edmonds, Peggy/ Dukes, Brenda	David-Richard-Ed	Wife - [Pals] Hubbard, Terry - Collins, Floyd - Hensley, Anthony - Dreier, Rob-B.J. - Hayes, Preston - Breeden, Jeff-Dan - Quinn, Jim	East View
Hubbard, Frances Elizabeth	Feb 22, 2000	80	J.M.H.			Hubbard, Abe	S			Jones, Ruth [D] - Billiert, Louise [D]	Richard [D]-Carl - [In-Law] Jones, Walter [D]	West View
Hubbard, Frank Alvin	Apr 23, 1973	54	J.M.H.	Tn	May 29, 1918	Hubbard, Edward	Hubbard, Lillie Mae	Whitaker, Elizabeth	Murry, Lorene & Elmer - Satterfield, Jesse & William [Sq] - Farrow, Bernice & Bobby	Howell, Lawrence - James [Sq]- Bobby	Williams, James Jr. - Whitaker, George - Townsend, Johnny - Murry, Will	Friends Station
Hubbard, James	May 18, 1979	70	Fort Wayne, Ind								Hubbard, Marion	
Hubbard, James Arthur	Jul 25, 1999	57	New Market	Strawberry Plains	Sep 5, 1935	Hubbard, Thomas	Dockery, Lillie		Key, Mrs. Frances - Ford, Dorothy	Williams, James-Bill- Charles	Wife - [Pals] Print, Ron - Rice, Rick - West, Fred Jones, Curtis - Woody, Samuel - Waters, Tom - Evans, Elton - Reece, Ed	Friends Station
Hubbard, Lillie D.	Jul 18, 1994	84	J.M.H.	Jeff Co	Mar 28, 1910	Dockery, Mitchell	Baker, Florence	Hubbard, Thomas [D]	Breeden, Darlene	David	Son - [G-Children] Hubbard, David- Lance- Tommy - Breeden, Darlene	Beaver Creek
Hubbard, Mary Miker	Jan 14, 1997	71	F.S.H.	Sneedville, Tn	Nov 6, 1925	Miker, Robert	Mullins, Sarah	Hubbard, Carl F.		Jeffrey-Dale	Claude Eugene & Frances	West View
Hubbard, Minnie M.	Dec 10, 1982	72	Marion Gen. Hosp.	Jeff Co	Sep 8, 1910	Poore, Dan	Bailey, Anna	Hubbard, James [D]		Artis	Husband - [Pals] Byrd, Greg-Scott - Dawson, Don - Kelly, Dustin - Cornwell, J.C. - Cox, Roscoe	Beaver Creek
Hubbard, Ona Rhinee	Apr 24, 1985	90	J.M.H.	Jeff Co	Aug 6, 1982	Rhines, George	Patton, Mary Lisa	Hubbard, William [D]		Hubbert-Paul-Leon-Sam	[Pals] Bryant, Marvin-Miker-Eddie - Clanton - Hubbard, Mark-Walter- Steve - James - Bill	Beaver Creek
											[Pals] Hubbard, David-Danny-Bob - Marion-Buddy - Humbard, Wayne	Beaver Creek

Name	Date	Age		Place	Birth	Father	Mother			Mil.						Cemetery
Hubbard, William Martin	Dec 6, 1975	89			Aug 16, 1886	Hubbard, Jim	Smith, Cordas		One	unk	Hubbard, Mary/ Rhines, Paulina	Jim [led]+Robert+ Sam+Henry+Paul+ Leon	Townsend, Dora Bell			Beaver Creek
Hobbs, Newell Franklin [Rusty]	May 23, 1992	68		Knoxville, Tn	May 27, 1923	Hobbs, Frank	Mc Millian, Dorus				Smokless, Violet & Don	Floyd & Charlotte - Nellie-Genevieve & Linda-Dwight & Connie	Stipe, Edie - Walker-, Mary-Nell - Bailey, Junior		[Pale] Hobbs, Ken - Stipes, Lindsey - Murphy, Pam/Kate-, Deeds, Dennis - Bailey, Joe-Steve	Roseberry
Huckleby, Walter Roosevelt	Oct 28, 199?	64	New Market	Knoxville, Tn	May 7, 1935	Huckleby, Walter	Walker, Leola	Colliter, Gladys Ruth			Batey, Leola- Kriegle		Taylor, Richard			Beech Springs
Huff, Annie	Aug 29, 199?	74	Jeff City	Tn	Aug 21, 1895	Huff, Will M.	Link	S				Walter-Robert	Lucy C. [Cleveland, Ohio]			Youngs Memorial
Huff, Marshall [Cief]	May 12, 1984	95	Jeff Co	Tn	Feb 12, 1873	Huff, William Henry	Link	Ella Mae			Lyndon-Graham-Henry-Charlie-Minnie			Packer, Willie Lee [Mich.]		Youngs Memorial
Huffaker, Marcia Bell	Dec 12, 1989	79	J.M.H.	Dumplin, Tn	Feb 28, 1910	Underwood, James H.	Hickman, Sarah Cathreen	Huffaker, William R. [D]			Eldridge, Vola	Gann, Ray			Gann, Ray	Beech Springs - Kodak, Tn
Huffaker, Marvin Wilson	Aug 2, 2000	59	Jeff City	Sevier Co	Nov 2, 1940	Huffaker, Lee	Pollard, Iva				Prellitz, Joyce Diana Wattson	Kimberly- [Step] Carpenter, Annette & Eric	Gonzales, Eldridge - Etherton, Iva Lynn - Lewis, Marcia [Pat]		Bill-Michael-Jerry-Jack-Carl [Ca]	Beech Springs
Huffaker, Michael Hall	Feb 16, 1984	43	Knoxville, Tn	Jeff City	Jun 13, 1950	Huffaker, Hal R.	O' Dell, Susan					Cory-Dana	Mc Blex, Amy & Darrell		Write	East View
Huffaker, Shelia Lucille	Jan 17, 1987	84	New Market	Boone Co, Ky	Aug 26, 1912	Huffaker, James	Webster, Luda				Huffaker, John C. Sr. [D]	Vanderzyill, Anna [Sis]- Bates, Alice - Taylor, Cleo & Junior	John C. Jr.	3		Write	J.M.G.
Huffaker, William Ray	Jan 21, 1990	66	F.S.H.	Sevier Co	Mar 15, 1911	Huffaker, Charles	Johnson, Melinda		army		Underwood, Marcis	[Step] Eldridge, Viola	[Step] Gann, Ray	Russell, Nina - Bryant, Hazel - Love, Josie- Buchanan, Nell		J.M.G.
Hughes, Charles Edward Jr.	Sep 26, 1997	29	Jeff City	Hialeah, Fla	Sep 14, 1968	Huffaker, Charles	Templeton, Barbara E.		Div		Hughes, Harold	Charles A & Brenda	Deanna Sue - Caldwell, Deborah	Charles Edward	Beech Springs - Sevier Co	Cromated
Hughes, Mary Elizabeth	Aug 12, 1997	69	Jeff City	Fulton, Ky	Jul 23, 1906	Brady, Theodore	Gates, Ella		Div		Hughes, Harold					J.M.G.
Hughes, Allison	Jul 25, 1996	95	New Market	New Market Thorn Hill, Tn	May 23, 1913	Humbard, Samuel	Elmore, Lillie		Army		Cain, Dorothy- Humbard, Thomas	Faye		Floyd Jr. - Gene	Floyd Jr. - Walker-Judd	Friends Station
Humbard, Anna Belle Isphene	Jan 22, 1992	83	B.H.	Tn	Mar 22, 1938	Atkins, Floyd Sr.	Oliver, Nellie		Army		Jeff, Cathry	Thomas Randle Thomas	Carl-Dan-Bill-Herman	Hardwick, Ernestine	Husband	Friends Station
Humbard, Bertha Isphene	Sep 30, 1996	80	Jeff Co	Tn	Nov 1, 1865	Day, Thad	Day, Kate				Humbard, Charlie				Vance, Mrs. Sam [Daug]	Friends Station
Humbard, Carl	Oct 30, 1994	74	B.H.	New Market	Jan 19, 1920	Baxter, Charles	Elmore, Bertha		Army		Foster, Rene	Humbard, Carllette	Humbard, Bill	Humbard, Charles - Humbard, Chester-Todd - Cochran, Bill - Vance - Roger-	Wife - [Pale] Foster, Larry - Humbard, Charles - Donald - Bobie- Doctor-Todd - Cochran, Bill - Vance - Roger-	Friends Station
Humbard, Donald	Sep 17, 1972	57	Knox Co	Tn	Apr 28, 1915			Mills, Marjorie	army		Donna Leonie- Ginger Lynn		Vance, Pauline	Herman-Carl- Bureau	Wife - Oscar [Father-in-Law] Polk-Nephews]	Friends Station
Humbard, Florence Elizabeth	Jan 13, 1973		Knox Co	Tn	Aug 26, 1888		Green, Isa		W			Ralph-Lawrence- Floyd [Clev., Oh]			W.D. [Alla.]	Friends Station
Humbard, Floyd Anderson	May 22, 1989	67	B.H.	Jeff Co	May 26, 1921	Humbard, Thomas M.		Green, Florence	Div	WW 2	Cain, Connie - Humbard, Judy	Ronnie	Maples, Helen - Hurley, Dorothy- Breeden, Falory	Ralph-Lawrence	Doug- [Pale] Breeden, Harrison - Humbard, James-Tom-Bob- Jerry-Foster, Terry Wayne	Friends Station

Name	Date	Age	Place	Place 2	Date (birth)	Father	Mother	Spouse	War	Misc	Misc 2	Misc 3	Writs	Cemetery
Humbard, Henry Donald	May 25, 1968	59	Knox Co	Tn	Apr 16, 1909	Humbard, Thomas M.	Green, Florence	Lauderdale, Pauline		Atkins, Betty	Thomas-Jerry James-Bobby	Hundley, Dorothy - Maples, Helen - Bredden, Fairy	Ralph-Floyd [Ohio]	Friends Station
Humbard, Herman	Dec 7, 1979	73	J.M.H.	New Market	Feb 3, 1907	Humbard, Charlie	Elmore, Bertha	S				Vance, Pauline	Carl-Bruce	[Polly] Vance, Roger-Charles - Humbard, Charlie - Dardis, Albert - Jerry	Friends Station
Humbard, Karen Denise	Mar 29, 1964		Jeff City	Tn	Jan 8, 1964	Humbard, William S.	Maler, Dorothy A.					Jackie-Kathy	Father - Mitch, Sherman - Husband, Ralph [G-Father]	Friends Station
Humbard, Karen Denise	Mar 29, 1964		Jeff City	Tn	Jan 8, 1964	Humbard, William	Maler, Dorothy Heleen					Stephen	Father - Midx, Sherman - Husband, Ralph [G-Father]	Friends Station
Humbard, Marjorie Ann	Jan 23, 1994	59	J.M.H.	Maeool, Tn	Jul 16, 1934	Mills, Oscar	Bates, Caroline	Humbard, Donald [D]				Clavanger, Myrtle - Milligan, Betty - Murray, Marion	Doug [Phil] Mills, Wilborne - Sill Edd - Milligan, Jim - Murray, Robert	Friends Station
Humbard, Nellie N.	Jan 13, 1983	51		Tn	Sep 28, 1911	Coley, Dan	Lawrence, Mahalay	Humbard, Henry [late]		Thomas-Bobby-Jerry-James	Douglas, Louise - Fred - Buster - Coley, Henry	FLawrence, Fred - Coley, Henry	Husband	Friends Station
Humbard, Ollie L.	Feb 25, 1988	81	New Market	Grainger Co	Nov 15, 1916	Noe, William	Livingston, Lola	Humbard, William Howard [D]					Ken-Mills	Lynnhurst
Humbard, Ralph	Dec 13, 1984	81	J.M.H.	J.M.H.	Dec 13, 1984	Humbard, Ralph	Humbard, Mary						Father - Hubbard, Mary [Father]	Friends Station
Humbard, Ralph	Mar 9, 1999	78	J.M.H.	Jeff Co	Dec 9, 1910	Humbard, Samuel	Elmore, Lillie	Mary N.					Father - Hubbard, Bill [G-Father] Mary - [Father] - Whitehead, Don - McHall, Terry - Humbard, Dilby - Stanton, Bobby - Turner, Jeff	Friends Station
Humbard, Colley Lucille	Mar 19, 1990	56	J.M.H.	Tn	Nov 7, 1923	Morgan, James	Turner, Ethel	Hurst, Reuben					J.M.G.	J.M.G.
Hurst, Helen Elizabeth	Apr 6, 2000	81	Morristown, Tn	New Market	Nov 24, 1918	Howard, Richard T.	Ayers, Ruby	Hurst, Rutherford [D]				Fielden, Ruth H. - James, Evelyn H.	Tate, Vera Lee [Niece]	Mill Springs
Hurst, Jesse Faye	Aug 30, 1987	76	J.M.H.	Cocke Co, Tn	Sep 23, 1910	Hurst, Sam H.	Ward, Corey	Hurst, Roy [D]					Henry [Phil] Hurst, Brian - Dockery, James - Griffin, Gene - Ward, Barry	Macedonia
Hurst, Pauline	Jul 13, 1987	74	Colorado Springs, Co	Jeff Co	Dec 4, 1912	Grubb, Caswell Newton	Finley, Lilly Cordelia	Hurst, Thatcher				Robert-David	Dale-Fred - Dockery, James - Griffin, Gene - Ward, Barry	West View
Hurst, Rendow [M]	Sep 15, 1987	71	Jeff City	Sevier Co	Nov 21, 1915	Hurst, Avery	Williams, Docia Jane	Morgan, Lucille [D]	unk	Hurst, Mills		Roberts, Shiela Mae	Thatcher - Lugton - J.S. - Thatcher - Dillon - R.V. - Everett	J.M.G.
Hurst, Thatcher	Jan 4, 1983	81	J.M.H.	Sevier Co	Jan 26, 1911	Hurst, Avery	Williams, Delcie	Hurst, Thelma					J.W. - Luther - Everett - [Phil] - R.V. [Phil]	
Hurst, Thelma	Jun 20, 1990	76	Westlake, Ohio	Pigeon Forge, Tn	Sep 19, 1913	Hurst, Avery	Williams, Dixie	Williams, Hazel		Sisner, Betty		Rogers, Shiela	J.W. - Thatcher - Luther - Everett - [Me] - Dillon [Me] - R.V. [Phil] - Mitch	West View
Huskey, Nova Pearl	Dec 14, 1999	72	Jeff Cith	Knoxville, Tn	Apr 20, 1927	Cate, Luther	Underwood, Nora	Huskey, Clarence [De]		Henley, Jan - Bryant, Ann	Dean [Me]-Ed-Gary-Jim	[In-Law] Lissie - Agnes - Cate, Reba	J.W. - Thatcher - Lufton - Everett - [Me] - Dillon [Me] - [Phil] - Rick, Ken - Beeler, Roger - French, Fred - Brooks, Mark-Mike	Piedmont

Name	Date	Age	Place	Birthplace	Birth Date	Father	Mother	Spouse						Burial
Huskey, Velma Louise	Jul 22, 1995	72	J.M.H.	Sullivan Co., Tn	Jul 17, 1913	Combs, Elmer C. [2]	Elizabeth	Huskey, Elmer C. [2]	Tolliver, Sandra	Haworth, Camille - Newman, Blanche - Talley Mae	[Pals] Mc Daniel, Charles - Cooley, Michael-James - Stamples, Charles - Cochran, Jim - Glenn, Frank			West View
Huff, Donna Kay	Aug 30, 2000	56	J.M.H.	Camille, Ill	Jul 27, 1944	Coffman, Bill	Bibot, Wilma	Huff, David Lee [2]	Barrera, Barbara [Pal]	David B.	Porter, Ruby			Cremated
Huff, Leona	Jun 8, 1961	57	U.T.H.	Camille, Ill	Mar 26, 1904	Hodges, B.R.	Mollie	Hux, Ross B.				Frank-Harry-Vaughn	Husband	New Market
Hux, Ross Boynton	Nov 30, 1964	59	J.M.H.	Tn	May 22, 1906	Hux, J.F.	Trula			[Step] Hollway, Weldon-Ray-Charlie-Gary	[Foster] Haworth, Mrs. D.L.		Wife	New Market
Hux, Trule	Oct 28, 1957	72	New Market	Tn	May 6, 1885			Dottie	1944	[Step] Hollway, Joyce	Heckendlbov, Hassie		Hux, Ross B.	New Market
Hydell, Vincent	May 19, 1995	71	J.M.H.	Brooklyn, Ny	Sep 8, 1923		Anna	W			Gillen, Dorothy		Sister	Cremated - Florida
Ingle, Francis Inrohjen [M]	Mar 24, 1965	53	Jeff City	Florida	Jan 6, 1912	Ingle, Oxley Patton		Viola Mae					Wife	Write
Ingle, Wiley Patton	Jun 14, 1970	80	Jeff Co	Nc	Nov 19, 1879	Ingle, Erwin	Wilson, Elizabeth	W		Ray [W, Va]	Yesry, Mrs. Opal [G-Daughter]	Roy		Friends Station
Isbell, Helen Irene	Apr 18, 1993	70	J.M.H.	New Market	Sep 15, 1922	Horace R.	Jenkins, Lettie	Isbell, W.H. Jr.		Ronald-Bob	Seals, Nina - Mc Nabb, Hazel - Nabb, Horace-Johnny Margie	[1/2] Sams, Maranna - Tipton, Daisy - Watts, Lizzie		Greenwood
Isley, Everet	May 7, 1990	75	J.M.H.	Elizabeth, N.J.	Jan 7, 1905	William Guy	De Prez, Hannah	unk		Douglas - [Step] William-David		Son- [Pals] Berry, David - Maugin, Charles - Blake,Roy - Worthbrough, Roy - Hobbs, Robert - Alley, Bob		Strawberry Plains
Ivy, Benjamin Lee	Dec 20, 1967		J.M.H.									Mitchell, Ted - Denton, Virgil - Moody, Lawrence - Rouch, Noah - Holloway, Gary - Lawrence, Steve		New Market
Ivy, Herman Lee	Sep 1, 1989	91	J.M.H.	Morristown, Tn	Sep 9, 1897	Ivy, Benjamin	Ridly, Mollie	Bunch, Nettie L.		Patterson, Pearl		Sister- [Pals] Mitchell, Ted - Cochran, James - Hodge, Bob - Holloway, Gary - Fountain, B.A.?, Miller, Robert - Wallace, Ed - Lane, Terrell		New Market
Ivy, Nettie	Nov 5, 1955	70	M.C.		Sep 19, 1895	Bunch, William H.	Stallings, Amanda	Ivy, Herman L.		Patterson, Pearl [Idaho]		Walker-Edward		New Market
Jackson, Quincy Vernon	Nov 27, 1985	59	U.T.H.	Coffee Co., Alabama	Nov 25, 1925	Jackson, Bud	Unk	Brock, Georgia Elizabeth		Mellie-Trude	Sue-Dorothy		D.L.	[Pals] Workman, Buddy, Blan - Mills, Ronnie - Long, Annis - Brock, Franklin-Junior / Pleasant Grove Haworth
James, Gwendolyn Faye	Aug 7, 1991	42	New Market	New Market	Jul 27, 1949	Whitaker, Frank	Wilson, Ruby	James, Robert Glen						Valley View

Name	Death Date	Age	Place of Death	Residence	Birth Date	Father	Mother	Spouse	War	Children / Family	Burial
James, John C.	Jun 8, 1988	87	Sevierville, Tn	Tn	May 30, 1901	James, William M.	Single, Hannah L.	Ellis Sue [D]		Charles [CH] - Gentry, Janet	Nances Grove
James, John William	Mar 4, 1971	47	V.A. Hosp.	Tn	Aug 31, 1923	James, Lee	Wilson, Lula	Pierce, Mary E.	WW 2	Dixon - [12] James, Lyett - Bill Steve	Piney
James, Roy David	Oct 20, 1997	62	Talbott, Tn	Jeff City	Nov 10, 1934	James, Elbert T.	Reed, Betty Lou			Myra Darlene — Danny-Dan-Daniel-Mark — Richard-David — Wanda, Elizabeth Ann - [1/2] James, Brenda — Dixie - [1/2] James, Lyett-Bill Steve	Beaver Creek
James, Sue Ella	Feb 2, 1981		J.M.H.	Granger Co	Nov 6, 1914	Spencer, Crawley	Webb, Iva Belle	James, John		Bobby-Edgar — Jim	(blank)
James, Wesley Edd	Mar 1, 1999	74	Morristown, Tn	Hamblen Co	Apr 23, 1914	James, John J.	Cockrum, Virginia	Howard, Evelyn		Eddie — Henderson, Martha — Jim	Mill Springs
James, Dixie Lee	Aug 17, 1999	35	Oak Ridge, Tn	Jeff City	Nov 24, 1963	Janeway, Dixon C.	Smith, Mary Lea	S		Janeway, Jacqueline — Maudon, Jenis — Hawkins, Monica & Carla & Brian — Kenny - Mc Coy, Troy & Ginny	Valley View
Janeway, Lockie David	Jan 18, 1975		J.M.H.	Sevier Co	Dec 8, 1899	Janeway, Dudley	Emon??, Julia	W		Shatterly, Pearl - Sharp, Edith — Keller, Jannie - Janeway, Y.J.-Dixon — Carmichael, Laura [Mich] - Parker, Estelle — Denton, Hal-Linda	Strawberry Plains
Janeway, Y.J.	Nov 17, 1985	69	Jeff City	Strawberry Plains	Jun 5, 1926	Janeway, John	Denton, Lockie	Seabolt, Delia		Hall, Darlene — Y.J. Jr.-Philip — Sharp, Edith — Janeway, Dixie - Keller, James — Willie	Strawberry Plains
Jarnigan, Jessie Lee	Jan 8, 1997	69	Morristown, Tn	Rutledge, Tn	Aug 18, 1927	Jarnigan, Lee	Moody, Mollie	Kitts, Anna		Maynor, Frances & Jim — Charles & Julia — Whitley, Louise - Mills, Katherine - Moody, Ruth — Moody, Isaac - Jarnigan, James - Robert	Narrow Valley
Jarnigan, Lela Mae	Sep 6, 1992	79	White Pine, Tn	White Pine, Tn	Apr 8, 1903	Kimbro, Henry	Reed, Lou	Jarnigan, Sam [D]		Patterson, Viola — Bob — Mc Craig, Lillie — White, Marilou	Deep Springs
Jarnigan, Milford Holbert	Jul 7, 1983	80	S.M.H.	Jeff Co	Apr 8, 1903	Jarnigan, John	Johnson, Maude	Irwin, Blanche		Jimmy — Fain, Odessa - Johnson, Louise - Anderson, Nola - Johnson, Louise — Milford	Oakley Chapel - Rutledge, Tn
Jarnigan, Robert Eugene	Dec 25, 1959	53	U.T.H.	Tn	Apr 16, 1906	Jarnigan, John	Johnson, Maude	Irwin, Blanche	Tn	Stone, Imogene — Charlie-Jack-Bobby — Anderson, Nola - Johnson, Louise — Fain, Odessa [Sister] — Jarnigan, Bill [Son]	Tampico - Granger Co
Jarnigan, Sam	Jan 31, 1953	72		Jeff Co	Jan 10, 1881	Janeway, John				Moore, Mrs Bill	Deep Springs
Jarvis, Dannie Jean	Dec 31, 1996	54	Sneedville, Tn	Sneedville, Tn	Jun 3, 1942	Rowe, Hobert	Smith, Myrtle	Jarvis, Thurman		Diane — Larry [D] - Foster, Daniel-Tindell, Chad — Bible, Hettie - Alley, Dollie - Swooney, Opal - Dennis, Edith - Oops, Evelyn - England, Glenda — Husband	J.M.G.
Jarvis, Diane Gail	Nov 4, 1999	35	Tazewell, Tn	Tn	Feb 2, 1964	Jarvis, Thurman C.	Rowe, Dancie	Div		Foster, Daniel - Tindell, Chad — Larry [Tn]	West View
Jeffers, Lena Viola	Dec 5, 1969	87	Knox Co	Tn		Peck, Joe	Caldwell, Mary	W		Henry L.	J.M.G.
Jeffers, William Andrew	Sep 29, 1985	80	J.M.H.	Greene Co	Apr 7, 1905	Jeffers, George	Benner Easter	Turnell, Cossie		Howard-Jim-George-John — Ruthorford, Jance - Celn, Syivis - Carter, Billie — Hilda - Pridemore, Grace	Robberteen Church - Hawkins Co, Tn

Name	Death Date	Age	Place of Death	County	Birth Date	Father	Mother	Spouse	War	Relations	Relations	Relations	Cemetery
Jenkins, Conley Chester	Sep 24, 1997	66	Talbott, Tn	Sevier Co	Jul 21, 1931	Jenkins, Voellin	Gann, Ina		Brown, Debra - Jenkins, Annette	Terry & Pam- Gary & Darlene- Barry & Brenda	Theodore [D]- Coolidge [D]- Kenneth		J.M.G.
Jett, Bertha Alice	Nov 23, 2000	79	F.S.H	Rutledge, Tn	Mar 1, 1921	Hodge, Harrison	Myratt, Cora	Jett, Lennis E. [D]		Lowndey, Rose	Terry-Barry-Gary & Darlene- Barry & Brenda	Wills- [Pals] Hodge, B.H.-Steve- Ken - Sindis, Albert - Bacom, Buddy	J.M.G.
Jett, Lennis Eugene	Apr 2, 1994	77	U.T.H.	Talbott, Tn	Jul 20, 1916	Jett, Horace	Mc Murray, Cora	Bertha A.	WW 2	[Step] Lowndey, Rose	Terry-Barry-Gary	Lockhart, Martha	J.M.G.
Jett, Leora	Dec 24, 1995	84	Dandridge, Tn	Hawkins Co	May 7, 1911	Underwood, E.E.	Combs, Gilray Ann	Mc Grew, Bernice- Lowndey, Wilma		Hollis L.	Carter, Mary Ruth	Jim	J.M.G.
Jett, Wiley Clifford	Feb 8, 1992	77	Jeff City	Jeff Co	Jun 18, 1914	Jett, Horace E.	Mc Murray, Cora	Fine, Alma Pauline	unk	Jett, Carl [D]	Lockhart, Martha	Jett, Hollis [Nephew]	West View
Johnson, Addie	Apr 28, 1972	83	J.M.H.					Johnson, Eli [D]		Katherine- Moore, Mildred- Harris, Eula - Shelton, Edith - Lenoir, Sedalia- Thomas, Leetha	Eugene-William [Mich]	Lennis	Felden Chapel
Johnson, Alfred R.	Jul 24, 1985	57	Pontiac, Michigan	Knox Co	Mar 25, 1928	Johnson, Alfred H.	Burnett, Anna Mae	Hankins, Leona	WW 2	Janice [Mich]- Welty, Connie Lee [Pa]	Downey, Viola [Ky]- Cook, Ada, David	Galland-Fritz- Wilbur-Ross- Raymond	New Hopewell- Knox Co
Johnson, Carroll William	Apr 8, 1999	66	Sevierville, Tn	Sevier Co	Feb 14, 1933	Johnson, Robert	Cate, Hazel	Francis, Bonnie		Marlow, Tammy [Pal]- Welty, Connie Lee [Pal]	Dewey & Pamela- Jeff & Sue		East View
Johnson, Charles Edward	Nov 24, 1986	47	Knoxville, Tn	Knoxville, Tn	Nov 18, 1939	Unk	Johnson, Elizabeth	Preston, Kathern		Tosha	Eddie-Ray-Daryl	Earnest-Jimmy	West View
Johnson, Debbie Jane	Nov 20, 2000	93	J.M.H.	New Market	Feb 19, 1907	Snyder, Tom	Branum, Maude	Johnson, Ramsey		Fred E. & Marie [Rev] - Lenny & Lois-Ralph	Patterson, Viola		West View
Johnson, Donald	May 1, 1991	69	F.S.H.	Madison Co, Nc	Jul 31, 1921	Bruce, Hezikah [Step]	Southerland, Maggie	S			Patterson, Viola	Bruce, Hess - Morgan, Hester	White Pine
Johnson, Donald O' Dell	Nov 12, 1984	49	Knoxville, Tn	New Market	May 5, 1935	Unk	Johnson, Dessi Mattie	Div	Korea	Mildred - Lenoir, Sedalia- Shelton, Harris, Eula - Thomas, Leetha - Phipps, Catharine	Nash, Penny - Long, Jo Ann - Collins, Elizabeth - Davis, Jamie - Turner, Bertha Mae - Whited, Annie	Howard	West View
Johnson, Eli [Dot]	May 24, 1957	71-1-19	New Market	Charlotte, Nc	Apr 5, 1886			Johnson, Alfred				Johnson, Addie [Wife]	St. Lukes Presbyterian
Johnson, Ella Leona	Dec 21, 1995	58	Humana Hosp. Florida	Jeff Co	Mar 20, 1928	Hawkins, Mc Kinley	Noel, Lillie	Johnson, Alfred R.		Welty, Corrie Lee [Pa]- Jantac [Pa] - Phil	Ballinger, Frances- Jessica & Joshua	Donald	New Hopewell

Name	Date	Age	Place	County	Birth	Father	Mother	Spouse	Military	Children / Relatives	Cemetery
Johnson, Fanny Bea	Sep 9, 1988	94	Humana Hosp. Morristown	Tn	Jan 2, 1894	Jenkins, Andrew Curtis	Batter, Ellen	Johnson, Walter J. [D]		Carr, Violet & Ezra; Ralph [Ind]; Bruce; Doug - [Pas] Groce, John - Johnson, C.W. - Mullins, Shelton - [Dot] - Lamence, John - Kym, Corient; [Pas] Fielden, Harold - Johnson, Jeff - Downey-Carl - Marlow, Jeff - Smith, Roger	Piedmont
Johnson, Hazel Mae	Dec 16, 1992	75	F.S.H.	Sevier Co	Jan 21, 1917	Cate, Henry	Merritt, Mary Jane	Johnson, Robert		Carr; Carroll; Howard; Willie; Pallotts - Sevier Co	Piedmont
Johnson, Howard Wayburn	Aug 15, 1989	57	Morristown, Tn	New Market, Tn	Mar 26, 1932	Unk	Johnson, Deso			[Step] Dalton, Sherry Ann - Martha Faye; [Step] Dalton, Ronald-Norman; Willie; Nash, Penny - Collins, Eliza - Turner, Bertha - Whitlock, Marie - Long, Jo Ann - Davis, Jamie	West View
Johnson, Job Edward	Jul 5, 1981	55	Sevier Co	Knoxville, Tn	Jan 31, 1926	Johnson, Jack		Cook, Gracie	Air Force	Danny; Keener, Brenda; Bobby-Jimmy-Joey-Tom; Willie	Pleasant Grove
Johnson, Juanita F. Kerr	Dec -, 1968	39	Detroit, Mich.	Jeff Co		Kerr, N.A.	Kerr, Carrie	Johnson, Clyde H.		[Step] Woods, Brenda; [Step] Dalton, Jerry H.; Donald; R.O.G.R. F.H. [Detroit, Mich]	Piedmont
Johnson, Maude	Apr 24, 1985	95	J.M.H.	Cummings, Ga	Nov 5, 1889	Crane, Charlie	Sarah Lou	Johnson, Thomas Howard [D]		[G] Adams, Thomas H. - Blaumight, James W.; G-Sons	Crestlawn - Atlanta, Ga
Johnson, Ray Lenold	Jun 5, 1984	57	Jeff City	Marion, Nc	Dec 20, 1936	Johnson, Walter P.	Lewis, Amelia	Wilma C.	Army	Stampage, Diane - Roach, Kathy - Blair, Tammy; Wade; Price, Diane; Willie - [Pas] Denton, David - Smith, Ron - Lance, Norman - Guinn, Jim - Hutcheson, Donald - Hot, Ronald - Fessler, John - Wellers, Bill	Oakland
Johnson, Robert	Aug 31, 1983	69	F.S.H.	Kodak, Tn	Mar 31, 1904	Johnson, Arthur	Brock, Melissa	Hazel		Carroll; Beecher; Johnson, Dewey - Jeff - Marion, Jeff - Denton, Donald - Clifton, Vergil - Dickerson, Raymond - Hopper, William - Nelson	Oakland
Johnson, Vidal Lynn	Feb 23, 1994	45	U.T.H.	Knoxville, Tn	Jul 2, 1948	Willhite, Carl R.	Hill, Florence	Johnson, Ralph		Jerry-Jaime; Herb-Daryl; Willie - [Pas] Puckett, Chuck - Carr, John - Turkey, Andy - Norther, Stanley - Hopper, William - Nelson	J.M.G.
Johnson, Walter J.	Dec 21, 1974	85	J.M.H.					Jenkins, Fanny		Carr, Violet & Ezra; Ralph E. [Ind]	Piedmont
Jolley, Samuel Dwayne	Oct 22, 1994	56	J.M.H.	Talbott, Tn	Jul 27, 1938	Jolley, James A.	Burnett, Aileen	s		Hill, Carolyn J.; Sister	Mt. Pleasant
Jolley, Palmer	Jun 11, 1981	72	V.A. - Mt. Home		Mar 5, 1909	Patton		Thomas, Mary Gladys	WW 2		Highland Memorial East
Jones, Beulah Ann	Oct 2, 1998	45	Straw Plains	Knoxville, Tn	Jan 18, 1953	Jones, Allen	Leuderdale, Nellie	s		Strand, Nellie [Mother]	Leuderdale
Jones, Carlyn Sue	Jun 3, 1953	1	New Market	Jeff Co	May 12, 1952	Jones, Douglas	Jarnigan, Viola	Tn		Tn; Jones, Mrs Viola	Deep Springs
Jones, Charles E.	Mar 11, 1998	63	Rutledge, Tn	Rutledge, Tn	Jan 8, 1934	Jones, Jack	Trenton, Charity	Div		Ronald-Eddie/Carl-Timmy & Diane; Satterfield, Eula-Roach, Virginia; Audrey; Jones, Mrs Viola	New Blackwell

Name	Date	Age	Place	Origin	Date	Father	Mother	Spouse/Status	War	Family	Relatives	Spouse/Husband	Cemetery
Jones, Charlotte	Jan 20, 1984	76	Greeneville, Tn	Greene Co.	Oct 3, 2007	Neal, Roy	Willis, Pearl	Jones, Joseph Walter	S		Chandler, Lizzie-Sapp, Mattie		Wesleys Chapel
Jones, Claudia L.	Feb 23, 1993	77	J.M.H.	Decatur, Ala.	Jun 8, 1915	Jones, Will	Taylor, Lizzie	S					West View
Jones, D.J.	Feb 5, 1991	70	B.H.	Grainger Co.	Oct 10, 1920	Byrd, Cora E.		Rose Marie [DH]		Wood, Carolyn		Doug-[Pals]-Ethel, Tom-Helen, Harley-Ben-Carter, Donald-Brown, J.M.-Wood, C.L.-Mc-Nish, James	Pleasant View
Jones, Frank Lon	Mar 4, 1981	69	Jeff City	Grainger Co.	Oct 7, 1911	Byrd, Cora Ethel	Jones, Derdrick	S				D.J.	Pleasant View
Jones, Gladys Inlar	Jan 25, 1981	96	J.M.H.	Texas	Aug 21, 1904	Jones, Jerome	Wigs, Laura E.	Jones, Jess	S		Willis, Arlene	Clyde	J.M.G.
Jones, Harold Ray	Jun 27, 1990	34	U.T.H.	Jeff City	Mar 8, 1956	Jones, Floyd	Poore, Mildred	Div			Jeff Billy Jack-Brian	Roger	Pollard's-Kodak, Tn
Jones, Jack James	May 31, 1990	45	U.T.H.	Jeff Co	Oct 1, 1944	Jones, Jake	Lee, Venee	Div		Jessica	Floyd-Anny	Mother	Mc Campbells Chapel
Jones, Jake	Nov 7, 1993	80	Jeff City	Kodak, Tn	Mar 29, 1913	Jones, George	Owens, Ida Mae				Floyd-Dan	Mother	Mc Campbells Chapel
Jones, Jasper Carmichael	Oct 7, 1992	77	J.M.H.	Dandridge, Tn	Apr 7, 1915	Jones, Sam	Hodge, Golda					Willie	Willie
Jones, Jess	Jan 15, 1996	97	J.M.H.	Taney Co, Mo	Jan 25, 1898	Jones, Sam	Youngblood, Arlene	Cary, Gladys			Willis, Arlene	Clyde	J.M.G.
Jones, John F.	Oct 11, 1999	44	Newport, Tn	Sevier Co.	Sep 9, 1955	Unk	Jones, Ruby	S			Jones, Gary L. [G-Son]	Williamson, Shelby [Friend]	West View
Jones, John Henry	Nov 26, 1997	96	Jeff Co.	Jeff Co.	Sep 30, 1911	Jones, J.H.	Summers, Myrtle	W	WW 2		Nezbit, Emily		Greenwood-Sunderland-Talbott, Tn
Jones, Joaquin Walter	Jul 26, 1994	92	Greeneville, Tn	Sevier Co.	Apr 2, 1902	Jones, Jack James	Bailey, Sarah	W			Ivan [Pa]	Harrell, Guy [Ex.]-Loveday, Cretia-France, Nannie [G Mother]	
Jones, Kimberly Renee	May 22, 1976	34	U.T.H	B.H.	May 21, 1976	Jones, Jack James	France, Billie					Billie Jack	Strawberry Plains
Jones, Lucy E.	Jul 11, 1984	73	M.C.	Tn	Jun 1, 1891	Young, Billy	Pruitt, Mettie			Cochrane, Gladys-French, Eula-Foster, Dorcus	Douglas	Perkins, Maggie-Barrows, Blanche-Ballinger, Leia	Mill Springs
Jones, Minnie	Mar 7, 1969		Jeff City	Tn	Feb 20, 1895	French, Jane	French, Minnie	Jones, Sam		Hunt, Mrs. Edd-Sharpe, Mrs. Raymond [In-Law]-Jones, Mrs. Kenneth	Jasper	Howard, Mrs. Sherrills-Howard, Mrs. Georgia	J.M.G.
Jones, Myrtle Sylvia	Aug 9, 2000	88	New Market	Buckhorn, Nc	Mar 30, 1912	Wilson, Minnie	Summers, Eugene	Jones, John Henry [2]	W	Sharp, Golda-Herd, Florence & Edward	Jasper	Howard, Mrs. Georgia	Greenwood
Jones, Sam F.	Nov 2, 1973	83	Dandridge, Tn	Tn	May 20, 1890	Jones, Jim	Jones, Jim	W			Jasper	Clarence	J.M.G.
Jones, Shelby Jean	May 16, 1997	58	Rutledge, Tn	Rutledge, Tn	Sep 19, 1938	Hodge, Vesta	Jones, Charles E.			Ronnie-Tammy & Diane	Sandra	Foster, Dorcus-French, Eula / Barbee, Dora-Nelson, Addie	New Blackwell
Jones, Thomas Edward	Mar 24, 1968	92	M.C.			Jones, Edward						Lakins, Marie [D]-[In-Law] Tuckey, Marlene / Derrick-Kenneth-Wayne-Dean	Jones, Douglas [Son]-Cochran, Gladys
Jones, William Douglas	Nov 6, 1988	76	Jeff City	Jeff Co	Jun 6, 1912	Young, Lucy	Northern, Elaine M.	Morrison, Sandra	WW 2	[G] Keith-Chris		Walter	[Pals] Steven, Clifford-David-Ronald-Morrison, Chris-Keith-Jodie-Umbarger, Carlisle-I. Mc Daniel, James
Jordan, Ethel E.	Jan 15, 1998	82	Morristown, Tn	Jeff City	Sep 3, 1915	Nance, Richard	Glichrist, Nellie	Jordan, Wilko	WW 1				J.M.G.
Justice, Lee L.	Jul 18, 1994	89	Wartburg, Tn	Jeff City	Sep 29, 1894	Justice, William	Abner, Nancy Jane	Ann			Pritts, Rose Ellis [W. Val]-Pritts, Mary Ellis	Smallman, Jean [Niece]	J.M.G.

Name	Date	Age	Place	Place 2	Date	Father	Mother		War				Relatives	Cemetery
Justice, Charles Everett	Apr 19, 1981	83	Knoxville, Tn	W. Va	Oct 19, 1897	Justice, John Isaac	Day, Amanda		WW 1		Charles-Clarence E.-Lowell	Atkins, Eva	[Pals] Romaine, Bob-Steve - Justify - Atkins, Mason - Lucas, Gregson	Hillmell - Dandridge
Kolp, Lois	Feb 7, 1999	90	Straw Plains	Michigan	May 20, 1908	Stevenson, George	Mackenzie, Sarah	Kolp, Charles W. [9]	WW 1	Dwenesarz, Jane	Edward L.		Simmons, W.R. - Frank Kitchen - F.H. [Chicago, Ill]	City - Lewisburg, Pa
Karl, Josephine M.	Jun 23, 1959	95	Sulfenburger Hosp.	Clinton, Iowa	Aug 25, 1862							Charles	Son	New Market
Kearney, Carrie	Aug 6, 1993	91	J.M.H.	Maxxot, Tn	Nov 6, 1901	Norton, John	Bozeman, Marie	Kearney, Hal	WW 2	Greene, Deborah Ann	Bill R.	Billy & Richard	Son - [Pals] Kearney	New Market
Kearney, Hal C.	Feb 23, 1994	91	New Market	Jonestown - Sullivan Co	Jul 26, 1902	Kearney, John Clark	Norton, Carrie			Greene, Ann & Dan			Son - [Pals] Kearney, Dan- Michael - Stephen-Michael - Randy - Carter, David - Adams, Bill	New Market
Kearney, Hal Lloyd	Jun 11, 1920	10	New Market, Tn	Tn	Sep 18, 1939	Kearney, Hal	Norton, Carrie	Tn					Kearney, Hal - Norton, Carrie [P] - Michael	New Market
Kearney, Johnny Darrell	Feb 21, 1989	40	F.S.H.	Sevierville, Tn	Mar 25, 1949	Kearney, Hal	Norton, Carrie		vietnam	Sheldon, Debra Gail	Sharon	John-Darrell	William	[Pals] Kearney, Danny - Sturgill, Michael - Starling, Glenn	Rocky Valley
Kearney, Trista Fay	Feb 23, 1990	94	J.M.H.	Kingsport, Tn	Oct 1, 1895	Kearney, John	Clark, Alice	S					Hall & Richard J.	Rocky Valley
Keck, Dexter Divine	Sep 2, 1983	64	J.M.H.	Claiborne Co	Jun 27, 1919	Keck, Benjamin Lafayette	Berry, Sarah Louisa			Warren, Leona	Hayes, Linda - Scott, Lula [Cari]	Ada - Layman, Dora - Medley, Edith - Bethea, Dialta	Beale-Arice-Sheppard, Carrie Jean - Tex-Jones, Curtis - Carr, Frank	J.M.G.
Keck, Leona Warren	Dec 25, 1983	67	White Pine, Tn	Jeff Co	Feb 3, 1916	Warren, John	Smith, Ethel			Hayes, Linda - Scott, Lula		Beele, Arice - Sheppard, Carrie Jean	Holmes - Manford-Coy- R.L.	Calvary Baptist
Keck, Zettie L.	Sep 3, 1974	77	J.M.H.	Long, James	Sep 28, 1896	Daniel, Meley		Keck, Charles H.		Keck, Charles H. [D]		Rose, Mrs. Tom	Herring, Beatrice [Nece] Clarence	Alexander - Rutledge, Tn
Keck, Idona	Nov 16, 1973	58	Tn		Feb 17, 1915	Keck, John Calvin	Talley, Ardell	S					Keck, John [Pap] - Michael - Talley, Bertha [Aunt]	Buffalo Baptist
Ken, John Calvin	Mar 10, 1981	91	J.M.H.	Grainger Co	Sep 17, 1889	Ken, Ellis	McClain, Louisa			Henderson, Myrtle			Greene, Delta Arlene	Keck, John [Pap] - Sutledge, Allred - Jimmy- Jennings- Jack - Boteman, Herman	Buffalo
Keeler, Harriette J.	Nov 22, 2000	58	B.H.	Harriman - Roane Co	Jun 20, 1942	Trenthan, Andrew	Green, Ruby				Puch, Debbie & Ken	James Jr. & Kim	Mike & Kim	James Jr. & Harriette-Charles F.	Shelterly, Pearl - Sharp, Edith	Valley View
Keeler, James Oscar Sr.	Jun 30, 1997	81	New Market	Dandridge, Tn	Apr 16, 1916	Keeler, Samuel Oscar	Denton, Lockie Janeway	Wilson, Christine Russie			Keeler, James O. Jr.			Elroy & Evelyn- James & Louise	Janeway, Dean C.	Valley View

Name	Death Date	Age	Place	County/State	Birth Date	Father	Mother	Spouse				Cemetery
Kelley, Billie Faye	Sep 7, 1990	68	J.M.H.	Sevier Co	Feb 15, 1922	Metcalf, John	Moore, Mary	Kelly, L.F. [Div]	Condry, Sharon	Spoone, Tina - Kelly, Mattie - Dwyer, Ruby	Doug - Green, Susan - Gray, Sherry [3-Daug] [Paij] Humbard, Al - Green, Jack - Farrar, Taylor - Clevenger, Don - Witt, Danny - Noe, Herbert	J.M.G.
Kelley, John H.	Jun 29, 1987	78	J.M.H.	Grainger Co	Jun 15, 1909	Kelley, William	Noe, Jennie		Rex Steelman	Lurt, Irene	Brooks, Tammy [3-Daug] Steelman, Rex - [Paij] Brooks, Don - Jones, Tim - Farrar, Taylor - Delmas - Munsey, Dean	Cremated
Kelley, Lily Mae	Jan 20, 1993		J.M.H.	Anderson Co	Feb 12, 1926	Hooks, Virgil H.	Webb, Mazzie	Kelley, James Alldus				Crinated
Kelley, Mattie Lee	Jan 7, 1991	73	S.M.H.	Sevier Co	Dec 26, 1918	Metcalf, John	Moore, Mary	Kelley, John Howard [D]				Oakland
Kelly, Eula Mae	Dec 9, 1975	52	Jeff City	Jeff City	Jan 27, 1923	Cochran, Bruce	Carroll, Sallie	Kelly, Walter	J. Harold Walter Thurman	Beecher	[Pals] Kelley, Ben - Corwith, J.C. - Kimbrough, Paul - Parker, Clarence - Moody, Carl	Mill Springs
Kenadore, Timothy Dayne	Dec 3, 1967	2m		Usa			Nance, Peggy Ann				Mother - Phipps, Mrs. Raymond A - Campbell, Bessie [G-Mothers]	West View
Kennedy, Cecil J.	Sep 2, 1998	82	Jeff City	Knox Co	Aug 1, 1916	Kennedy, Albert	Terbeville, Annie ?	Frills, Violes	Army	[Step] Kidd, Barbara [T-4] Mitchell, Wanda	[Step] Potter, Ed [Paij-John [Gda] - Swann, John R.[Cota]	Sherwood Memorial Alcoa, Tn
Kenney, Minnie P.	Mar 29, 1980	70	J.M.H.	Ky	Nov 1, 1909	Kennedy, Albert	Abner, Nancy	Kenton, Cartney				Paris, Ky
Kenney, Anette Lynn	Apr 12, 1971					Justice, William						
Kerr, Ada J.	Dec 27, 1989	96	Dandridge, Tn	Bandtown, Va	Jan 18, 1893	Jordan, John	Skeen, Mary	Kerr, H.W. Sr. [D]	H.W. Jr. [T-4] Bronce	Lane, Mabel	Sutherland, Ruth - Colyer, Hattie - Bivens, Emma - Johnson, Lucille [Vie]	West View
Kerr, Anny Jane Myrtle	Nov 1, 1987	86	J.M.H.	Jeff Co	Nov 13, 1900	French, Leonard Hugh	Snyder, Minnie	Kerr, William Andrew	Darrell-Alger-Jim	Colbuck, Louise	Elder, Hazel - Hoskins, Bonnie	Piedmont
Kerr, Dorthula	Mar 14, 1959	73	Blaine, Tn	Jeff Co		Rick, William		Kerr, W.P.		[1/2] Rick, Loyd	Spoon, Herbert	New Market
Kerr, H.W.	Sep -, 1966	78							Jordan, Ada	Bruce-Roy-H.A. Jr.	Michael	West View
Kerr, Hazel	Apr 5, 1981	67	J.M.H.	Texas	Mar 22, 1914	Vineyard, Elmer	Spooner, Nettie	Kerr, Raymond [D]	Scarlett, Mrs. - Donaldson, Mrs. J.T. - Lance, Mrs. Terrell	Michael	Bissell, Loretta	New Market

Name	Death Date	Age	Place	Birth Place	Birth Date	Father		Mother	Spouse	War	Relations / Family	Cemetery
Kerr, Nelson Alvin	Jun 4, 1966	76	New Market, Tn		Jun 7, 1889	Kerr, Crockett		Arrup, Mary Elizabeth	Carrie Lou			Piedmont
Kerr, W.P.	March 27, 19	78	Virginia	Tn	Jan 16, 1880	Kerr, Henry C.	Tn	Unk				
Kerr, William Darnell	Jun 5, 1991	64	New Market, Tn	New Market	Nov 15, 1926	Kerr, William		French, Myrtle	Haworth, Conda Fae	WW 2	Sellers, Nancy - Wollard, Helen; William Bruce & Sheila - Darrell Driskell; Collioch, Louise; Alger & Louise Jim	Nances Grove
Kelner, Buddy	Mar 18, 1990	81	J.M.H.	Dandridge, Tn	Aug 4, 1908	Kelner, Thomas		Moore, Margaret	Alley, Raye		Mary; Ray; Mother	Mc Campbells Chapel
Kelner, Cody Lee	Oct 19, 1994		U.T.H.	Knoxville, Tn	Oct 19, 1994	Kelner, Tommy L.		Hubbell, Amy			Willis; Willie	New Market
Kettle, Helen Lucille Elaine	Nov 21, 1978	67		Knox Co	Oct 10, 1911	Arthur		Scanlon, Annie	Paul [3]		Sister	Case
Kidd, Alva T.	Dec 8, 1994	85	Jeff City	Bryson, Nc	Jul 4, 1909	Tipton, John T.		Crist, Laura	Kidd, Horace		Valentine, Elsie - Gretts, Letha - Frances - Faliner, Lillie [Va - D]; Case	Case
Kessler, Charles David	Aug 15, 1994	90	J.M.H.	Newport, Tn	Sep 26, 1943	Kessler, Guy		Russell, Polly	Norton, Sheila L.		Hardin, Tina; Michael Wes - Jason; Howard, Paulette - Underwood, Betty; James; Hinton, Floyd - Gretts, Joe - Bialer, Robert	Strawberry Plains
Kessler, John Barnett	Jan 12, 1976	28	Newport, Tn	Cocke Co, Tn	Aug 13, 1947	Kessler, Guy		Russell, Polly	Becky	WW 2	Tammy Jo Ann; John; James, Paulette - Underwood, Betty - Proffit, Amanda - Killis, Viola; Charles - James L.	Strawberry Plains
Kimbrough, Claude Wilbur	Apr 22, 1981	64	New Market, Tn	New Market, Tn	Sep 24, 1916	Kimbrough, Arthur		Gladys	Kimbrough, Claude [3]	WW 2	Children	Ebenezer
Kimbrough, Gladys	Feb 11, 1991	75	Bean Station, Tn	Bean Station, Tn	Oct 3, 1915	Murphy, Arthur		Collins, Mary Jane Lisa	Kimbrough, Claude [3]			Ebenezer
Kinder, April Darlene	Dec 2, 1967	4m				Kinder, Twin			Kinder, Teilo			Ebenezer
Kinder, Charles Luther	Sep 25, 1990	83	J.M.H.	Jeff Co	Feb 3, 1907	Kinder, Luther		Kinder, Ellen	Tate, Mary [3]		Hubbard, Sarah Ellen; Charles Tate; Kerr, Georgia; Charles; Everette - Herman - Kyle - Hubbard, David - Bunch, Loren - Charles; Kinder, S.I. - Bill - Frank - Kerr - Curt ...	Shiloh
Kinder, Earl	Jul 7, 1979	66	J.M.H.	Grainger Co	Dec 15, 1912	Luther		Kinder, Ellen	Ballinger, Della Rae		Conner, Barbara Long, Judy; William; Kerr, Georgia; Charles	New Market

Name	Death Date	Age	Place	County	Birth Date	Father		Mother		Spouse / Informant	Relatives	Will	Cemetery
Kinder, Mary Victoria	Sep 12, 1989	81	Morristown, Tn	Grainger Co., Tn	Jun 9, 1908	Tate, William Andrew	Tn	Lambden, Sarah Frances	Tn	Kinder, Charles L.	Hubbard, Sarah Ellen — Charles Tate	Doug - [Pela] Hubbard, David - Homer, Charles - Ernest-David Jr. - Clevenger, Donald - Mc Nish, Howard - Ferral, Taylor	Shiloh - Grainger Co
King, Cheryl Elaine	May 20, 1994	38	Strawberry Plains	Knoxville, Tn	Mar 7, 1956	King, Clyde William Jr.		Bales, Greta Angelynn Waggoner	S			Mother - [Pela] Wolhfahranger, Wayne - Wellingham...	Oakland
King, Ethel Mae	Jun 21, 1993	62	Rutledge, Tn	Knox Co	Jun 14, 1931	Lowery, Arlie	Tn	Richards, Bertie	Tn	King, Carl E.	Stallings, Teresa D. - Warren, Jerry F. - Spence, Donna L. - Gray, Cheryl Denice	Jeffery A. - Michael A.	Jess	Thorn Grove
King, Lula Mae	Feb 15, 2000	87	J.M.H.	Jeff Co	May 30, 1912	French, Gus		Owens, Minnie		King, Albert [D]	Hawks, Betty - Brewer, Jessie [D] - Jones, [D] - Barbara [D] - Jones, Anny & Don	Bruce [D] - Earnest [D] - Albert Jr. [D] - Oliver-Wayne- Chandar-Roland- Allen-Stanley	Russell, Willie - King, Hazel	Thorngrove
King, Roy Robert [Purkis]	May 18, 1997	75	S.M.H.	Thorn Grove	Jun 9, 1921	King, John	Div	Huffaker, Hattie				Scarbrough, Dorothy & John - Shanda, Mary Pruitt & Jack - Mc Garrels, Frances & Paul	John Jr. & Elizabeth-Carl & Catherine	Thorn Grove - Knox Co
Kingston, Ann Marie	Dec 2, 1998	62	Worcester, Ma	Worcester, Ma	Jun 27, 1936	Combs[k], Stanley		Merlin, Mary	Kingston, Robert F.	Leon, Susan M. [Cal] - O'Brian, Kathleen [Ma] - Taylor, Lauri [Tn] - Lanigan, Ann Marie [Ma]	Kevin [Rh]-James M [Ma]-Robert S. [Cal]	Peck, Justin [Ma]	Robert [Col]	Miller, Edith [Friend]	Sevierville - Menton, Ma
Kirkland, Burley William	Jan 18, 1985	29	J.M.H.	Tn	Nov 21, 1935	Kirkland, Earl Johns		Foster, Lola	Wanda L.			Write	Oakland - Grainger Co
Kirkland, Earl Johnson	Jul 13, 1992	89	New Market	Hawkins Co	Mar 19, 1903	Kirkland, John Wesley		Stewart, Ona Ferris	Foster, Lola [D]	Woods, Jean - Pruitt, Iva Sue	Haggard, Mildred - Kate	Paul	Rene - [Pela] Kirkland, Justin - Steve-Mark- Bradley - Woods, Mike - Dyer, Mathew - Moore,	Mill Springs
Kirkland, John Thomas	Mar 31, 1984	73	F.S.H.	Hawkins Co	Jan 14, 1911	Kirkland, John W.		Ferris, Ona	Trent, Arlie	Chambers, Elizabeth - Morgan, Maxine	Haggard, Mildred - Savidge, Kate	Earl-Worley-Paul	[Pela] Everhart, R.H. - Garland, Charles - Walinga, Con - Gunling, Eddie - Kirkland, Wayne-Frank	J.M.G.
Kirkland, John W.	Aug 18, 1954	83	New Market	Tn	Oct 13, 1870	Kirkland, William		Haggard, Frances	Sandridge, Mrs. W.D. - Haggard, Mrs. James	Roger-Earl-Paul-Worley-John		Kirkland, Earl	Mill Springs

Name	Date	Age	Place	County	Birth	Father	Mother	Spouse	Children					
Kirkwood, Lola Dosha	Mar 29, 1990	78	J.M.H.	Jeff Co	Nov 1, 1911	Foster, Frank	Hardin, Rushia M.	Kirkwood, Earl	Woods, Ivan & Harold - Proffitt, Ira Sue & John W.	Frank	Ballinger, Ruby [Wife] - French, Naomi	Wayne [Ind]	Huntsman - [Pals] Foster, John - Woods, Mike - Dyer, Matthew - Erwin, Jack	Mill Springs
Kinsler, Fannie N.	Dec 2, 1982	96	J.M.H.	Hancock Co	Feb 2, 1896	Lawson, Warren	Sizemore, Sarah	Kinsler, Isaac [D]	Richard, Hazel - Southern, Edna - Livesay, Sybil - Livesay, Sarah - Johnson, Myrtle - Weston, Mary	Edgar-Ellis-J.T.		Ten ?	[Pals] Livesay, Doborn - Kinsler, Earl - Johnson, Jan - Wayne - Richard, Chris	J.M.G.
Kinsler, Mary	Apr 10, 1999	71	Morristown, Tn	Hancock Co	Sep 25, 1927	Livesay, Elmer	Testerman, Willie	Kinsler, Edgar D.						J.M.G.
Kivett, Alice	Jun 24, 1983	79	F.S.H.	Union Co	Aug 29, 1903	Clouse, Wheeler	Brewer, Nancy	Kivett, Conley [D]	Thomas, Bernice - Grant, Lorene	LeeGene - Marshall-Edgar- Talbert - Clouse, Harley	Thomas, Trials - Brunell, Frances - Fanis, Liza	Kermit & Wilma-Ray & Sarah	[Pals] Kivett, Harold-Tony-Sam- Leon-Melvin - Clouse, Gerald-Vernon - Grant, Bill	New Market Presley,
Kivett, Carl Jr.	Nov 19, 1970	34	S.M.H.	Tn	Nov 25, 1936	Kivett, Conley	Clouse, Alice	Div	Tammy Sue		Thomas, Bernice Eugene [1/2] Grant, Lorene	Talbott-Lee-Eugene [1/2]-Marshall-Edgar-Harley	[Pals] Kivett, Sam-Harold-Tony-Leon-Melvin - Clouse, Bill-Vernon - Grant, Bill	New Market
Kivett, Conley L.	Dec 13, 1982	83	F.S.H.	Union Co	Mar 2, 1899	Kivett, Eli	Clouse, Alice		Div		Lee-Gene-Marshall-Edgar-Harley	Rose - Tarbot, Mrs. S.F. - James, Pearl		New Market
Kivett, Corrie D. [F]	Jan 19, 1964	87	M.C.	Tn	Jun 2, 1876	Merdic, Eli	Oxford, Margrit Spangler	Kivett, Eli Merdic	Tarbett, Mrs. Mrs. S.F.- Moyers, Mrs. U.S.- Iarms, Pearl	Anderson, Mrs. Henry	Conley-Elbert		Kivett, Rose [Doug]	New Market
Kivett, Edward Marshall	Feb 23, 1984	62	New Market	Sharp Chapel, Tn	Feb 26, 1931	Kivett, Conley L.	Miller, Ovis		Mc Mahan, Marsha	Grant, Lorene - Thomas, Bernice - Hughes, Unis	Lee-Eugene-Talbert	Wills	New Market
Kivett, Elbert W.	Aug 6, 1979	66	J.M.H.	Union Co	Jul 29, 1913	Oxford, Carrie	Bailey, Nellie		Bailey, Nellie	Jay-Danny	Donald Lee	[Pal] Kenny	New Market
Kivett, Henderson Cornelius	Jan 3, 1964	68	Tn		Apr 16, 1895	Evans, Elizabeth	Berry, Dorothy	Capp, Dessie Mae	WW 1	Ashley, Ruby	Loyd G.-Pat A.	H.G.-John-Milton-S.W.		New Market
Kivett, Rhee Bell	Apr 13, 1983		F.S.H.	Sharpe Chapel, Tn	Dec 10, 1896	Kivett, Eli	Oxford, Connie	S		Tarbett, Waltsie	Talbert, Monroe		New Market
Kivett, Ricky Jane	Dec 17, 2000	51	New Market	New Market	Jan 19, 1949	Kelley	Wilson, Lillie Mae	Kivett, Eugene	Hulbert, Kim - Kivett, Jina	Buckner, Debbie & Bobby	Bailey, Sam-Donald-Eddidie- & Billie-Rick	Kivett, Eugene [Nephew]	New Market	J.M.G.
Kivett, Tonya Lynn	Dec 4, 1975				Nov 7, 1975	Kivett, Lawrence Lee	White, Juanita J.				Harold-Tony	Kivett, Conley [G-Parents] - [Pals] Sesle, Jimmy - Randy - Dale-Terry - Day, Dale- Morgan, Ricky	Flat Gap
Kivette, Albert Edward	Apr 29, 1954		Jeff Co		Feb 20, 1954	Kivette, Marshall	Franklin, Nancy			Gerwittw, Marsha		Father	New Market
Klepper, Quinnie M.	Dec 23, 1981	90		Hawkins Co	Mar 27, 1891	Maddox, M.W.	Coller, Edith K.		Klepper, James K. [D]			Arthur	Buffalo Grove
Knight, Grace Pauline	Jan 1, 1995	81	Morristown, Tn	Jeff Co	Sep 25, 1913	Baker, Lawson	Brown, James	Knight, Lloyd [D]		Reeve, Bonnie Louise - Spoone, Magbe		Son	J.M.G.
Knight, Harold	Dec 25, 1995	60	Morristown, Tn	Hamblen Co	Nov 11, 1935	Knight, Lloyd	Baker, Grace	Div	Daniel Lawson-Russ	Harold		Knight, Joey [Nephew]	J.M.G.

Name	Death Date	Age	Location	Birthplace	Birth Date	Father	Mother	Spouse	War	Daughters	Sons	Sisters	Brothers	Relatives / Relationship	Cemetery
Knox, Mary Jane Clark	Jan 28, 1966	78	J.M.H.	Tn	1889			Knox, Olen		[Step] Peddington, Emma	[Step] Knox, Roy [D]			Husband - [Pat:] Holloway, Garry - Taylor, Jim - Lawrence - Heworth, Bill	New Market
Kooch, Fred Albert	Feb 2, 1965	86	New Market	Tn	Mar 1, 1878	Unk		Solomon, Mel Kooch		Knox	Wright, Ma., Luther - Porter, Mrs., Frank - Ellis, Mrs. - William -	William-Ben C.-Thomas-Frank-Kenneth-Jimmy	1/2] Adams, Litha	Charlie-Claude-Johnson	Wife - [Pat:] Deck, Carl - Blake, Ed - Lowe, Don - Mc Cullin, Lloyd - Kelling, Bob - Hayes, Reba	New Market
Kooch, William Fred	Oct 11, 1965	72	Rutledge, Tn	Mascot, Tn	Aug 16, 1923	Kooch, Fred	Nox, Edna	Nox, Mary Edna	Navy	[Step] Johnson, Bobbie		Porter, Elizabeth - Davis, Mary Nellie - Widener, Addie	Thomas - Benny - Kenneth-Jim	Wife - [Pat:] Alte, Bobby - Messengall, Cille - Lawrence - Miller, Fred - Hicks, Did - Jernigan, Harold	J.M.G.
Kowalewski, Adolf	May 4, 1979	72	J.M.H.	Wachtewn, Poland	Dec 22, 1906	Lowalewski, Joseph	Riess, Luise Nec	Splinter, Ursula	WW 2	Hedwig-Erna- W.Germany (-Reni Hilda [H2]- Renate [H])	Simon-Daniel- Roman [A6-W. Germany] (-Steve-Norbert)				West View
Kyle, King Walton	Oct 23, 1985	69	Strawberry Plains	Monroe Co., Tn	Jan 8, 1916	Kyle, Brunar C.	Pearl W.	Kate N.	WW 2			Blazicek, Gladys - Bracket, Bilenn	Kenneth	Wife - [Pat:] Nichols, Charles - Pollard, Annell - J.C. - Elmore, Fred - Sims, Scott - Charles	Blue Springs
Lackey, James Dwayne	Jul 22, 1978	20	J.M.H.	Pa	Apr 10, 1958	Lackey, James H.	Grace	S		Jo Ann- Tammy - Lynn-Lisa - Jammes - Barbara Ann - Gloria Gene - Johnny Mae - Teresa		Lackey, Tammy- Lisa [1/2] Marks, Tina - Danni-Julanna - Dalton-Joanna - Cody-Brenda - Gibson, Johnnie - Deab, Teresa - [Step] Mullins, Beverly	[1/2] Marks, Tim [Step] Marks, W.L.	Wife - [Pat:] Marks, Grace & W.E. Jr. (Mother & Step-Father) - Brock, Nettie - Foe, Leonard [G- Parents]	J.M.G.
Lackey, John Harrison	Nov 29, 1964	32	U.T.H.	Nc	Dec 21, 1931	Lackey, Harrison		Grace			James Dewayne	Barrett, Anna Mae - Collins, Elizabeth	Earl Othey-Robert	Wife	Gregps Chapel/ Goose Co.
Ladd, Glenn Ronald	Mar 19, 1991	51	J.M.H.	Nc	May 20, 1939	Ladd, Tom	Beaver, Elizabeth	Owens, Margie			Chad	Barrett, Anna Mae - Collins, Elizabeth	Ed-Roy	Wife	J.M.G.
Ladd, Glenn Thomas	Nov 6, 1994	32	Jeff City	Jeff City	May 20, 1962	Ladd, Glenn Ronald	Owens, Margie	Carter, Tonya		Brandi	Glenn & Tonya	Lowe, Mary Ellen	Ronnie-Terry	Wife	West View
Ladd, James Eddie	Feb 5, 1995	48	Marble, Nc	Marble, Nc	Jan 20, 1947	Ladd, Thomas W.	Beaver, Elizabeth	Div		Tracy - Mc Leary, Robin	Mark	Lowe, Mary Ellen & Tom	Roy	Brother	Cremated
Lamb, Effie L.	Dec 2, 1961	63	New Market	Tn	Mar 11, 1898	Keaton, Joseph	Tn	O'Dell, Deisha	Tn	Lamb, M.C.	Maunger, Glledge - Bowser, Iva Lee - Johnson, Opal Lee	Willie-Allen	Seals, Mary - Perry, Cordia	Thomas	Husband	J.M.G.

Name	Death Date	Age	Place	Location	Birth Date	Father	Mother	Spouse		Military	See / Relatives				Cemetery
Lamb, M.C.	Jul 30, 1982	65	Holston Valley Hosp.	Tn	Sep 14, 1896	Lamb, Dos	Tn	Myers, Mary	Tn	Koston, Effie [D]	See Lamb, Effie [R]- [Step] Rogers, Trina & Deering, Debbie [Step]				J.M.G.
Lambert, James Buford	May 27, 1997	65	S.M.H.	Kingsport, Tn	Jun 5, 1931	Lambert, Henry		Blanchard, Maude Irene		Johnson, Martina	Air Force	Hines, Christine [R]- [Step] Henry [R] [Rabid]	Jimmy & Shirley [R]	Hunley, Bettye	Joseph B. & Irene [R]-James H. & Donna [Rev]	New Market
Landrum, Calvin Ocile	Apr 30, 1983	72	V.A. Murrfreesboro, Tn	Dry Ridge, Ky	Dec 28, 1920	Landrum, Merle O.		Baker, Gurkie		Potts, Waden		Keller, Kathleen L.		Williams, Elizabeth	Willie	Cremated - Lexington Memorial
Lane, Agnes	Nov 11, 1969		Tn		Oct 15, 1900	Coggtt, James		Ray, Della		Lane, Mack [D]		Griffin, Pauline - Pruitt, Hattie - Shaffer, Mae	Ray-James	Mason, Ellie - Showmate, Hazel [Rd] - Pruitt, Leora	Nicholas-James-Tony	French Broad Brethren
Lane, Amy Shyann	Dec 13, 1983		New Market	Tn	Feb 23, 1983	Lane, James Lynn		Pruitt, Tonia Gay				Merram, Freddie - Hubbard, Jessie		Courtney, Catherine	Reuben-Edward-Roy [Ch]-Paul [Ch]-Robert [Fa.]	Hillcrest
Lane, Fred G.	Feb, 1967	56						Hazel							Bethel Baptist
Lane, Herbert Terrell Jr.	Apr 14, 2000	84	U.T.H.	Morristown, Tn	Dec 2, 1915	Lane, Herbert Terrell		Haun, Ethel		Kerr, Mabel		Michalski & Karen		Smith, Mary [D]-Carey, Norma Jean	J.W. [D]-Howard	J.M.G.
Lane, Isa Inez	Nov 10, 1998	86	F.S.H.	Cocke Co	Feb 21, 1912	Stuart, Fred		Watts, Polly		Lane, Lee [D]		Hickey, Grace-Brown, Shirley [D] - Allen, Jean-Greenlee, Maude - Young, Mary	Joe [D]-Buddy-Fred-James	Worley, Ellie - Allen, Forrest-Lester-Anna-Onie-Griffin, Oatey	Haskell-Forrest-Lester-Lester-Forrest-Jr-Zane-Worley, J.B.	Rays Chapel
Lane, James B. (Boots)	Feb 28, 1996	68	J.M.H.	Jeff Co	Oct 17, 1927	Lane, Mack		Coggtt, Agnes		S	Army			Griffin, Pauline		French Broad Brethren
Lane, Justin Landry	Dec 13, 1983	23m	New Market	Morristown, Tn	Jan 17, 1983	Lane, James Lynn		Pruitt, Tonia Gay							Lane, Ray Allen [Nephew]	French Broad Brethren
Lane, Lee B.	Jun 20, 1998	78	J.M.H.	Jeff Co	Mar 24 1910	Lane, William		Reece, Sallie		Stuart, Iva	Army	May, Eva Jean-Gertrude-Crowe, Shirley-Hickey, Grace-Young, Mary	Joe-Fred-James-McGordon-Jim-Gordon-Terry	McKinley, Hattie-McColg, Ethel-Lewis, Maude	Haskell-Fred-Asbury-Lester-Forrest-Jr-Zane - Worley, J.B.	Rays Chapel-Newport, Tn
Lane, Robert Edgar	Apr 18, 1999	68	Straw Plains	Knoxville, Tn	Aug 14, 1930	Lane, Millas M.		Allen, Jessie		Smith, Emma L.	Iunea	Smith, Janettie & Roger	Robert C. & Janet	Hickman, Dorothy	Bill-Ronnie-Andy	Pollards-Snider Co
Lane, Winifred Ray	Sep 23, 1981	45	F.S.H.	White Pine, Tn	Mar 31, 1936	Lane, Mack		Coggtt, Agnes		Benny, - [Div]		Betty	Ray Allen	Griffin, Pauline - Shaffer, Mae	J.B.	French Broad Brethren
Langston, Earl Monroe	Oct 15, 1989	49	Knoxville, Tn	New Market	Aug 15, 1940	Langston, Robert C.		Eslinger, Eula		Div	nat. guard	Rhonda-French, Sherry	Gary-Travis	Sherrod, Mabel-Nelson, Diane	Conard	Piney
Langston, Eula Elizabeth	Dec 27, 1989	78	B.H.	New Market	Apr 3, 1921	Eslinger, James		Denton, Collie Victoria		Langston, Robert Chester [D]		Sherrod, Mabel-Nelson, Fred	Earl [D]-Conrad	Hilliard, Mary - Polk, Nadine - Patterson, Pearl	Lowery	Piney
Langston, John Mazie	Nov 15, 1994	84	Sevierville, Tn	Strawberry Plains	Sep 19, 1910	Langston, Marshall		Hickman, Julie		Thrasher, Addie Elizabeth		Ingram, Mary & Jack			Willie	Piney

Name	Death Date	Age	Death Place	Location	Birth Date	Father		Mother		Spouse	Mil.	Relatives					Burial
Langston, Robert Chester	Mar 25, 1991	83	Strawberry Plains	Jeff Co	Aug 2, 1917	Langston, Marshall		Hickman, Julia		Esllinger, Eula		Sherrod, Mabel-Nelson, Diane	Earl-Conrad	Petts, Nadine-Hilliard, Mary-Patterson, Pearl	John-Lowry	[Petts] Long, G.W. Jr.-Mayble, Fred-Brady, Caro-Turner, Charles-Martin, Cecil	Strawberry Plains
Langston, Robert Lynn	Feb 4, 1984	20	New Market	New Market, Tn	Jul 6, 1963	Langston, David		Whisley, Leona		S						Dotson, Bill-Taylor, Steve-Mike-Steel, Michael-Clark, Vernon-Ray, Joey	New Market
Large, D.F.	Oct 20, 1969	63	Jeff Co	Tn	Sep 1, 1906	Large, Frank		Hinchey, Lillie		Pansy		Phillpot, Louise-Hammer, Patsy-Shepard, Katherine		Trott, Annie-Kelton, Augusta-Zibrie, Iona	Harry	Wills	Lebanon
Large, Paralee	Feb 14, 1985	93	Sevier Co	Sevier Co	Jun 6, 1891	Snyder, James A.		Smith, Marie		Large, John S. [D]			James S.				Piney
Langston, Horace Robert	Jun 1, 1963	75	M.C.	Tn	Apr 10, 1888	Langston, James H.		Atchley, Julia		Lettie J.		Seals, Nina-Langston, Mrs. Hazel-Isbell, Mrs. Helen-Nash, Margie	Raymond-Horace Jr.-John	Hodge, Mrs. Luie [1/2] Vaschun, May	Fred H. [1/2] Langston, Roy Jack-Oscar	Langston, Raymond & Jack	Piedmont
Larrance, James Oscar	Aug 25, 1989	73	U.T.H.	Piedmont, Tn	Sep 15, 1915	Larrance, James Henry		Carmichael, Oumma G.		Williard, Einor Cleo	WW 2	Nash, Margie [Ch]-Isbell, Helen-Loy, Hazel-Seals, Nena	James	Hodge, Mae-Ross, Sallie	Ollie-Bruce-Paul	Larrance, John-Horace-John-Don-Howell, Bobby-Hodge, Kenneth	J.M.G.
Larrance, Lula Gidette	Apr 14, 1971	81	J.M.H.	Tn	Jan 20, 1890	Jenkins, A.C.		Butler, Ellen		Ng			Johnny-Horace-Raymond	Shell, Dixie-Johnson, Fannie			Piedmont
Larrance, Maggie Lou	Sep 7, 1997	64	New Market	Knoxville, Tn	Feb 23, 1933	Lloyd, Porter		Denton, Ruby		Div			Larry-Danny & Molly				New Market
Larrance, Raymond Robert	Jun 19, 1981	56	U.T.H.	New Market, Tn	Jun 15, 1925	Larrance, Horace Robert		Jenkins, Gelette			WW 2	Welirs, Wanda Jean	Steve-Richard	Seals, Nana-Loy, Nash, Naiphe [Ch]	Horace-Johnny		J.M.G.
Lauderdale, Clyde	Apr 7, 1995	79	J.M.H.	Strawberry Plains	Aug 19, 1915	Lauderdale, Isaac		Parker, Mary L.		Lindsey, Evelyn							Strawberry Plains
Lauderdale, Daniel	Jun 4, 1977	0	Jeff City	Jeff City	Jun 4, 1977	Lauderdale, Frank [Age 36]	Tn	Barrett, Debbie [Age 21]	Tn					Ginger		Wallace, Agnes [Niece]-[Pete] Wallace, Fred-Lauderdale, Ed-Burns, Jr.-0 Swagerty, Glen-Cannon, Harold-Wickman, Bryan. Parents- Lauderdale, James-Barrett, Ed [Gr-Parents]-Reno, Florence [Gr-Mother]	Lauderdale-Straw Plains

Name	Date	Age	Place	Location	Birth	Father	Mother		Status	Notes				Burial
Lauderdale, Ellie Elizabeth	Aug 1, 1970	72	Knoxville, Tn	Tn	Sep 8, 1897	Compton, Sam	Gilbert, Adds			Lauderdale, Wilmer	Ruby - Votes, Pauline - Crow, Walker, Kay - Gentry, Blanche	William-Johnnie-Freddie	Husband	Beaver Creek
Lauderdale, Faye	Feb 9, 1995	55	B.H.	Corby, Tn	Apr 5, 1939	Barnes, Raymond	Jenkins, Vona	Lauderdale, David			Burns, Genevieve - Payne, Geneva - Snoter, Dolly		David	Lauderdale, Strawberry Plains
Lauderdale, James Sexter	Dec 22, 1983	78	S.M.H.	Jeff Co	May 11, 1905	Lauderdale, Isaac	Lauderdale, Mary				Agnes-Alene- Nelle-Mildred- Beulah	John-David-Frank	Clyde	Lauderdale, Strawberry Plains
Lauderdale, Mary	May 5, 1984	78	Strawberry Plains	Jeff Co	Jun 6, 1907	Lauderdale, James	Emely Lea L.				Walace, Agnes - Strand, Nellie - McCurry, Mildred - Dugger, Beulah	[1/2] Collins, Alton - Douglas, Louise	[1/2] Lawrence, Fred	Thorne Grove
Lauderdale, Maude Jane	Feb 2, 1972	73	J.M.H.	Knox Co	Jun 21, 1898	Wigglstston, John F.	Cannon, Nora	Lauderdale, Nathan	S		Neal, Mary & Robert - McElry, Rubie & Tom - Rucker, Barbara & Hubert	Bruce-Earl	Plant, John- Bill	Husband	Thorne Grove
Lauderdale, Nathan N.	May 29, 1973			Tn	Jun 4, 1903	Lauderdale, Ike	Parker, Mary		Div	Rucker, Barbara & Herbert - McElroy, Ida Mae & Earl - Neal, Mary & Robert				Thorn Grove
Lauderdale, Ruby Evelyn	Nov 4, 1976	40	J.M.H.	Jeff Co	Jun 5, 1936	Lauderdale, Wilmer	Compton, Ella E.	Div			Carter, Mary Elizabeth - Nares, Melvina	James, Mary Elizabeth	Robert-Fred [Fla]-Joe- Buford [Fla]	Mc Curry Mortuary [Knoxville, Tn] - Murphy, Clara [Bud]	Beaver Creek
Lauderdale, Sadie Pearl	Oct 25, 1978	69	S.M.H.	Tn	Dec 15, 1908	Pierce, William	Smith, Susie	W				Walker, Kate - Gentry, Blanche	Bill-Fred-John L	Father - [Fla] Crown, Ralph - William - Foxz, Gentry, Kenny - Lauderdale, Jerry	Strawberry Plains
Lauderdale, William Benice [Bud]	Dec 21, 1994	70	New Market	Strawberry Plains	Jan 15, 1924	Lauderdale, Wilmer	Compton, Ella E.	Navy			Volis, Pauline - Crow, Arlana - Walker, Kay - Gentry, Blanche	William-Johnny- Fred	Fred-John	James-Clyde	J.M.G.
Lauderdale, Wilmer Garfield	Dec 31, 1977	85	J.M.H.	Greene Co	Apr 29, 1892	Lauderdale, Zak ?	Parker, Mary	W					James-Clyde	Willie	Beaver Creek
Lawless, William Alfred	Sep 28, 1991	60	Jeff City	Wheeling, W. Va	Nov 13, 1930	Lawless, William	Moser, Bessie	Prince, Flora			Mauldin, Terecca [Ga]	William Wayne	Peters, Mary - Lilly, Pearl [W. Va]	Tommie [Willie]	J.M.G.
Lawrence, Billy Ray	Dec 6, 1949	0-9-18	Jeff City	Tn	Feb 18, 1949	Lawrence, Houston	Brock, Georgia E.	Tn				Houston	Robert	Tommie, Houston	Piney Grove
Lawrence, Elizabeth	Apr 20, 1983	55	Knoxville, Tn	Tn	May 11, 1889	Cooper, Sam	Lucas, Eliza	Tn			Cline, Mrs. David - Campbell, Mrs. Harvey - Foster, Mrs. Robert E. [Ohio]	Houston	Thompson, Mrs. J.C.	Andrew	Lawrence, Monroe [Husband]	Bell Camp Ground
Lawrence, Elna Margaret	Apr 8, 1999	88	Jeff City	Ny, Ny	Jan 13, 1911	Carlson, Gunter	Addison, Hilda			Lawrence, James Bryson Sr. [D]		James B. Jr.		City - Flushing, Ny

Name	Death Date	Age	Hospital	Place	Birth Date	Father	Mother							Cemetery
Lawrence, James Russell	Feb 25, 1997	58	J.M.H.	New Market	May 19, 1938	Lawrence, Roy	Smith, Mary	Lynn, Barbara	Kim [Gay]	Osteen, Christine [D]- Collins, Sandra [D]- Whaley, Betty - Murray, Jewell - Sliwon, Jane - Roach, Brenda - Lawrence, Shirley	Bill-Dan	Willie		J.M.G.
Lawrence, Mary T.	Nov 6, 1979	65	J.M.H.	Knox Co.	Oct 12, 1914	Smith, Samuel Houston	Bailey, Florance							J.M.G.
Lawrence, Ray A.	Jun 16, 2000	59	J.M.H.	New Market	Sep 16, 1940	Lawrence, Andrew Porter	Alley, Ruby A.	S			Jack P.			J.M.G.
Lawrence, Roy Russell	Jan 7, 1969			Jeff Co	Feb 7, 1911	Lawrence, James	Chambers, Cuma	Mary		Sardis-Shirley- Whaley, Betty- Murray, Jewell- Slivon, June [1½]- Oaks, Christine	Bill-Jim [Ky]- Donald	Willie		
Lawrence, Ruby Aileen	Feb 20, 1994	75	B.H.	Jeff Co	Jun 12, 1918	Alley, Arnold	Newman, Laura	Ray [D]	Lawrence, Andrew P. [Jack]	Hammer, Judy & Dallas- Calloway, Wanda & Robert- Gene, Wilma & Earl	Ray Allen-Jackie	Elmore, Beulah	Robert-Curtis	J.M.G.
Lawrence, Charlie Hubert	Jan 7, 1995	83	Knoxville, Tn	Luttrell, Tn	Jun 8, 1911	Lawrence, Luther	Norris, Bettie	Clevenger, Mamie [D]	Amy	Cavallaro, Jo Ann - Elkins, Betty- Cavallaro, Genevieve [Dragon]- Dembery, Carolyn & Charles	Chambers, Trutia	Robert-Curtis		J.M.G.
Lawson, Darrell Lynn	Dec 3, 1995	38	U.T.H.	Knoxville, Tn	Dec 10, 1956	Mc Ghee, J. Everett	Lundy, Lillie Walker	S		Heck, Debra	Lawson, Darrell [D]-named [Ny]- Kevin	Heck, Debra	James Mc Ghee Charles [Va]- Walker, Mae- Larry	East View
Lawson, Frances Lee	Feb 3, 1989	62	S.M.H.	Knox Co.	Apr 21, 1926	Lawson, Billy	Mc Alen, Frances	Lawson, Bill [De]		Heck, Debra	Lawson, Darrell [D]-named [Ny]- Kevin	Davenport, Wanda [Ky]	Mc Ghee, Charles [Va]- Walker, Mae- Larry	J.M.G.
Lawson, Mamie Allene	Nov 5, 1992	72	Jeff City	Knoxville, Tn	May 1, 1920	Clevenger, Donald	Harvey, Ora	Lawson, Charles		Cavallaro, Jo Ann [Ab]- Elkins, Betty- Lawson, Mrs. Genevieve [Dragon]- Dembery, Carolyn & Charles	Largo, Vance & Robert - Lawson, Mildred [D]	Tom-Robert- Elijah-Grover [0]	Doug - Carl	J.M.G.
Layman, Raymond Cleo	Mar 30, 1990	75	J.M.H.	Sevier Co	Feb 24, 1915	Layman, Mitchell	Fish, Catheren	Kick, Dora L.		Beasley, Sarah Arietta - Hunt, Anita		Edward-David- Howard Curtis	Teague, Lillie- Glenn, Ruth	New Market
Le Roy, Lorena Mae	Oct 10, 1991	60	F.S.H.	Anderson, Indiana	Mar 25, 1931	Maddux, George E.	Johnson, Rosella	Le Roy, Guy C.		Maddux, Audrey- Crom, Pamela Rose	Crom, Richard Blain	Shock, Anna Lee [nc]		J.M.G.
Lee, Charles Albert	Sep 30, 1989	76	Sevier Co. Hosp.	Dandridge, Tn	Apr 2, 1913	Lee, Henry	Hawkins, Maude	Martha [D]			Sherman	Jones, Mrs. Jake	Frank-Edd- Don	Audrey	Piney

Name	Death Date	Age	Place of Death	Place of Birth	Date of Birth	Father	Mother	Spouse	Notes / Children / Relatives	Cemetery
Lee, Georgia Belle	Jan 5, 1995	86	J.M.H.	Cocke Co., Tn	Dec 27, 1908	Besser, William	Mooneyham, Polly	Lee, Willie Thomas	Dalton, Margaret Lois - Snyder, Imogene / Robert Dale / Elbert / Son - [Pals] Shaffer, Dennis- Gary-Eugene- Gary & Robert- Downry, Tim - Snyder, Gary - Lowery, Curtis	Shiloh
Lee, James Donald	Jul 14, 1995	72	Morristown, Tn	Knoxville, Tn	Nov 22, 1922	Lee, John Henry	Hardin, Maudine	Solomon, Grace [D]	Army / Wayne & Betty- Ray & Michelle- Dan & Leanne- Jim & Becky- Lawrence & Sandy-Bob / Jones, Venice / [Pals] Lee, Cecil- Darrell - Large, David - Salling, J. Roy - Rood, David. Dammewood, James	Pullams - Sevier Co.
Lee, Martha Edith	May 10, 1985		U.T.H.	Jeff Co.	Aug 21, 1915	Large, John S.	Snyder, Paralee	Lee, Charles A.	Sherman H. / Reagan, Tommie- Clute, Hazel - Sallings, Estraline- Hardewood, Kathleen / James S. / Harlows, Nevella- Faye [Nilsor] Sister - [Pals] Reeam, Nellie- Fox, Brian- Household, Henry-Bil- Adams, Steve	Piney
Lee, Teddy	Aug 10, 1985	94	Rockwood - Roane Co., Tn	Carroll Co	May 25, 1901	Lee, William P.	Sullivan, Joanne	S	Householder, Juanita / Bobby Gene [N]- Terry Wayne [N]	Eron - Mc Kendis, Tn
Lefever, Revina Rae	Jul 18, 1994	59	New Market	Cary, Ky	Sep 3, 1934	Lefever, Loyd	Jones, Mary	Div		Hillcrest
Leimbacher, Gerald Leon	Dec 19, 1994	47	Hollywood, Florida	Hollywood, Florida	Mar 26, 1947	Leimbacher, George A.	Denhart, Lucille	Graves, Barbara	Dawn-Kari / Don-Russ	Valley View
Leonard, Angela Marie	Nov 18, 1994		F.S.H.	Knoxville, Tn	Oct 6, 1989	Mize, Edward Marshall	Northern, Imogene	Leonard, Danny	Ashley / Davis, Connie- Becky-Debbie / James-Bobby- Justin / Husband	Indian Ridge
Leonard, Bobby Darell	Mar 15, 1970	1d	Knoxville, Tn	Knoxville, Tn	Mar 14, 1970	Leonard, Thurman K.	Burchett, Hazel		Debra-Linda / Dannie-William- Charles / Father - Burchett, Lee - Leonard, M.F. [G-Parents]	Oak Grove- Dandridge, Tn
Leonard, Frieda Carolyn	Mar 13, 1983	1d	Jeff City	Jeff City	Mar 13, 1983	Leonard, Fred M.	Solomon, Bertha		Father	French Broad
Leonard, Hazel Lee	Jul 2, 1967	63	Jeff City	Rutledge, Tn	May 2, 1934	Burchett, Henry Lee	Mc Daniel, Mary Lou		Leonard, Thurman K. / Mc Tilney, Betty- Carr, Beatrice- Elmore, Virginia / Father	Sunderland
Leonard, Jo Anne	Jul 29, 2000	63	F.S.H.	Morristown, Tn	May 2, 1937	Whitaker, Frank	Miller, Ruth		Leonard, Claude C. / Frew, Luci & Jeff / Claude Gordon & Luca- Jim & Edward- Ken & Denise- Shawn & Lina	J.M.G.
Leonard, Marion Franklin	Sep 1, 1986	86	Hawkins Co	Hawkins Co	Jul 6, 1900	Unk	Unk	Unk	Down, Leona [D] / Cain, Betty- Glenn, Mary- Poe, Ann / Clarence-Bill- Sheltn, Ron- Thurman-Dexter- Fred	French Broad- Dandridge, Tn
Leonard, Martha	Jul 22, 1975	72	Hancock Co., Tn	Hancock Co., Tn	May 15, 1903	Adams, John	Traille/Praille, Adaline	Leonard, Sam	Julia - Carroll, Minnie & Lynn - Webber, Betty & Ronald - English, Mary & Gary / Paul-Claude-Jay- Joe-Kyle / Husband - [Pals] Leonard, Austin- Clay-Joe- Adams, Jack - Cook, Ronald - Wright, Harry	New Market
Leonard, Paul Edgar Jr.	Oct 24, 1959		Jeff Co	Jeff Co	Oct 23, 1959	Leonard, Paul Edgar	Tn / Kinstler, Una	Tn	w / Bill [ON] / Father	Father
Leonard, Sam B.	Mar 9, 1982	76	Morristown, Tn	Jancock Co	Jul 5, 1905	Leonard, Will	Allen, Susie		Carroll, Minnie- Leonard, Paul- Claude-Jay-Kyle- English, Gary E.- Webber, Betsy	

Name	Death Date	Age	Place	Location	Birth Date										Cemetery
Lewis, Bonnie Rivers	Aug 2, 1977		Morristown, Tn	Tn	Sep 29, 1907	Elmore, W.W.		Div	Walking, Ruth - Holloway, Edna - Price, Josie - Campbell, Betty	Clyde	Cate, Ollie				Pleasant Grove
Lewis, Clifford Alvin	May 30, 1979	72	Knox Co		Mar 12, 1907	Lewis, David		Elmore, Bonnie [2]		Clyde			Wills		Nances Grove
Lewis, Clyde Randall	Sep 21, 1992	80	New Market	Tn	Sep 24, 1931	Lewis, Clifford Alvin	Army	Morgan, Lillian Anne	Mardin, Susan - Colwell, Aleda Dawn - Nichole	Dale			Wills		Cremated - Pleasant Grove
Lewis, David	Jun 15, 1953		New Market	Tn				Douglas, Minnie	Rettif, Flora	Clifford			Lewis, Minnie		Piedmont
Lewis, Edith Lorene	Jul 5, 1994	71	J.M.H.	New Market	May 4, 1923	McClain, Bert		Davis, Sallie	Lewis, Robert			Britton, Lula		Son - [Pala] Carter, Carroll - John - Phipps, William - Mills, Olaf - Davis, Gerald-James - Ledford, Tom	Nances Grove
Lewis, Frances Lynell	Apr 21, 1973		Bean Station, Tn	Tn	Nov 27, 1973	Lewis, Henry		Hampton, Frances B.		Kenneth			Faith - Wright - Lonnie - Lewis, F.W. [G-Parents]		J.M.G.
Lewis, Francis Willard	Jun 2, 1983	71	Sequatchie Valley, Tn	Tn	Mar 16, 1912	Lewis, E.R.	Johnson, Lula		Peck, Virginia		Dyer, Marilyn L.	Henry-Eugene		Ralph	J.M.G.
Lewis, Harry Peck	Jul 30, 1972	2	Bean Station, Tn	Tn	Sep 26, 1969	Lewis, Henry E.		Frances					Kenneth	Nanos, Harold - L.C. Jeff - Lewis, Steve - Berry, Harry - Parents] - Lewis, David - Husband, Bobby	J.M.G.
Lewis, Henry V.	Feb 2, 1979	89	J.M.H.	Jeff Co	Jun 1, 1889	Lewis, Eli		Kerr, Della		w			Berry, Daisy - Arthur, Gladys - Bradley, Helen	Morgan, Jimmy - Lewis, Robert	Cline, Daisy [No]	Will Edgar	Nances Grove
Lewis, James Robert	Dec 7, 1998	73	J.M.H.	New Market	Nov 1, 1925	Lewis, Henry	Tn	Watson, Minnie	Edith Lorene			Mitchell, Shirley - King, Sue - Murray, Debbie	J.R.-Steve R.- James Darryl	Arthur, Gladys - Bradley, Helen	Jim	Nances Grove
Lewis, Minnie	Aug 2, 1962	72	Tn	Tn	Oct 15, 1889	Douglas, G.W.	Tn	Priette, Elizabeth		Edith Lorene						Piedmont
Lewis, Margaret Ann	Feb 13, 1998	79	Washington Co, Va		May 4, 1908	Shaffer, George		Shaffer, Adeline		Lewis, Will	Faulkner, Hazel		Bradley, Helen - Arthur, Gladys - Berry, Daisy	Will R.	Leonard, Susie	Clark, Eva Nell [Neice]	Richmond - Blaine, Tn
Lewis, Minnie Watson	Dec -, 1998	76				Lewis, Henry				Lewis, Henry			Archly, Irene	Robert-Jimmy	Atchly, Irene	Guy-Edd	Husband
Lewis, Robert [Black]	May 1, 1993	65	J.M.H.	New Market	Jun 7, 1927	Hodge, John Jordan		Cunningham, Mary		Lewis, Cora Agnes			Arnot, Frances	Lewis, Robert	Britton, Lula	Lewis, George D.	Lewis, George Carter, Carroll - John - Phipps, William - Mills, Olaf - Davis, Gerald-James - Ledford, Tom	Youngs Memorial
Lewis, Rufus Daniel	Jul 14, 1971	84	Blaine, Tn	Tn	Mar -, 1887	Lewis, Eli		Kerr, Della		S					Henry-William- Edgar	New Market
Lewis, William Robert	Nov 30, 1991	92	Morristown, Tn	Jeff Co	Jun 14, 1899	Lewis, Eli		Kerr, Della		Shaffer, Margaret Ann	Anderson, Carolyn		Cline, Daisy [No]	Robert	Anderson, Carolyn	Lewis, Henry [Police] - Vineyard, Johnny	Bradley, Helen [Police] - Vineyard, Johnny	Richland - Blaine, Tn

Name	Death Date	Age	Init.	Place of Death	Birth Date	Father	Mother		Mil.	WW2			Names	Relations	Burial
Linares, Ramon Vera (Mexican Male)	Jan 30, 1994	18	New Market	Vera Cruz, Mexico	Aug 24, 1975	Rodriguez, Jacono Vera	Linares, Teodula	S				Vera, Martin-Julie-Griselda - [Is- Lee] Linares, Tina Vera	Cruz, Lissette - Rainwater, Flora Mae	Clyde	Willis - [Pris] Helen - Cruz, Nida - Lindsey, Mark-Jeff-Tim - Rainwater, John	Mexico
Lindsay, Carl Mayford	Jan 28, 194	74	B.H.	New Market	Mar 30, 1920	Lindsay, James Albert	Bailey, Mary Magnolia	S			Louis Mack-Ronald L.	Cato, Lavella - Rainwater, Flora Mae	Clyde	Willis - [Pris] Helen - Lindsay, Nida - Mark-Jeff-Tim - Rainwater, John	J.M.G.
Lindsay, Jesse	May 23, 1979	74	New Market	Sevier Co.	Sep 23, 1904	Lindsay, --			WW 2		Ross-Ted	Ogle, Bertie - Hey, George	Robert-Johnny-George	J.M.G.
Lindsay, Johnny Washington	Mar 15, 1999	85	J.M.H.	Sevier Co.	Sep 21, 1913	Lindsay, Melvin	Stamons, Ida		WW 2		Clayton & Dorothy-David L.	Arnott, Gincy	George	J.M.G.
Lindsay, Lillie Ida	Jan 9, 1978	94	Hall Mark Rest Home	Carter Co.	Jan 18, 1883	Pell, Rodohia	Stamons, George				Lindsay, Jesse Melium (D-1925)	Hey, Grace		Wesley Chapel
Lindsay, Ollie Allie	Mar 29, 1988	78	J.M.H.	Madison, Co. Nc.	Jul 4, 1911	Willett, William	Clemmons, Lura Ann				Lindsay, Jesse (D)	Churchman, Dorcities (Dot)	Ross-Ted	Son	J.M.G.
Lindsay, Pearlie Jane	Jan 20, 1994	98	J.M.H.	Morristown, Tn.	Mar 24, 1907	Wright, John	Becker, Willie				Lindsay, Johnny W.	Baz, Darlene	Clayton-David L.	Isaac	Son - [Pris] Baz, Chris-Eric - Lawrence - Lindsay, Shawn-Jarred - Lawrence - James	J.M.G.
Lindsay, Howard Hale	May 28, 1966	22	Jeff City	Tn.	Jun 20, 1944	Lindsay, James Earnest	Whitaker, Mary E.				Roady, Victoria			Potter, Patricia [1/2] Mc Nabb, Brenda Gail	James Lee [1/2] Lindsay, Gerry Lynn	Lawrence-Chrissy- Willie [Adeila, Ala.] - Father & Stepmother - Whitaker, L.K. - Lindsay, Jess [G- Parents]	Hamblen Memorial
Lips, Daniel Curtis	Oct 20, 1986	28	F.S.H.	Indiana	Apr 3, 1958	Lips, Marion Eugene	Mc Lean, Charlotte Ann		S				David & Bobbie	James Lee [1/2] Lindsay, Gerry Lynn	Highland Memorial - Rogersville, Tn
Lippincott, Russell N.	Nov 4, 1980	84	J.M.H.	New Jersey	Oct 14, 1896				S				Edward H.[B.2714/1874 J-Evert [B.787]- Samuel [B. 3/5/91]-Russell N. [B.10/14/96]	George J.- James H. - [1/2] Liveray, James [B]	New Market
Liveray, Benjamin Douglas	Feb 21, 1999	47	Knoxville, Tn	Middlesboro, Ky	Sep 2, 1951	Liveray, Ralph A.	Cox, Barbara		S			[1/2] Ritz, Alma [FR]		George J.- James H. - [1/2] Liveray, James [B]	Brother	Cremated
Livingston, George Robert	Sep 16, 1993	73	Jeff City	Bath, Ill.	Dec 29, 1919	Livingston, William	Shetler, Alva		S			Michelle-George- Jeffrey		Brother	West View
Livingston, Peggy	Dec 26, 1998	51	J.M.H.	Jeff City	Sep 8, 1937	Bateman, Theo	Williamson, Ruby				Bateman, Peggy [D]	Bowen, Debbie	Livingston, Jeffery - Robthen, Michael	Malone, Arilene - Rhymer, Helen	Bateman, David	Husband - [Pals] Garrham, Adah - Robben, Jeffery-Robert, Mannery, James - Lindylter, Glenn	West View
Lloyd, Ruby Denton	Jul 21, 1973	60	J.M.H.	Tn.	Aug 9, 1917	Denton, J.H.	Williams, Lula		W					Hill, Elizabeth Denton - Chambers, Mannette Ginny	Virgil-Willie	Lemmons, Maggie L. [Doug]	New Market

Name	Date	Age	Place	Origin	Date	Father	Mother	Mil.	Daughters	Sons	Sisters	Brothers	Burial
Lockhart, Cameron Mason Sr.	Sep 14, 1975	68	New Market, Tn	W. Sulfer Springs, V	Aug 20, 1908	Lockhart, Walker	Warren, Ollin		Norma Gay [W. Va] - Denton, Diane - Cannon, Mary Jane - Wurmer, Opal [Va] Frank, Martha [Va], Smith, Betty [W. Va]	Jerry-John [W. Va] - Denton, Wesley-Cameron Jr. [W. Va]- Dennis [Va]- Jaimes' Kenneth [OK]		Wife - Musick, Mrs. Glenna [Niece - Washington D.C.]	Strawberry Plains
Lockhart, Cecil Everett	Nov 16, 1997	82	Jeff City	New Market	Apr 7, 1915	Lockhart, Benjamin Martin	Edwards, Collie Geneva	Navy	Seals, Sally & Bart	Jim [D]-Don & Kathleen	Cochran, Ellie- Bates, Opal	Doug [Pials] Lockhart, Don- Cochran, Ron - Seals, Bart - Brooks, Joe - Fenimore, Austin	Flat Gap
Lockhart, Clare Mae	Feb 22, 1996	88	J.M.H.	Optima, OK	Mar 5, 1909	Whaley, Samuel	Sims, Myrtle		Lockhart, J.A. [D]	Cowen, Cpotee			Mill Springs
Lockhart, Ella Louise	May 3, 1997	74	B.H.	White Sulphur Springs, W. Va	Apr 5, 1923	Buckland, Norman	Cox, Jane		Lockhart, Cameron M. Sr.	Drenton, Diane & Clark - Cannon, Mary Jane & Bill	Finch, Edith [Oh] - Cannon, Lillian [W.Va.]		Strawberry Plains
Lockhart, Jerry Eugene	Oct 31, 1994	55	V.A.-Mt. Home	Jeff City	Nov 6, 1938	Lockhart, Wayne	Jett, Martha	unk	Clevenger, Wilma [Div]	Roach, Kathy- Blair, Tammy	Seals, Barbara- Wright, Dorothy	Sister	Mt. View
Lockhart, Leslie Glenn	Nov 15, 1994	45	Houston, Texas	Knoxville, Tn	Jan 11, 1949	Lockhart, Elbert B.	Cochran, Berta Lee	Army	Todd, Virginia	Jeff [D]-Jim-Larry Ronnie	Clarence	Wills	E. Tn Vets Knoxville, Tn
Lockhart, Martha Emily	Jul 8, 1998	79	Morristown, Tn	Jeff Co	Sep 16, 1918	Jett, Horace	Mc Mary, Cora		Div	Seals, Barbara & Albert - Wright, Dorothy	Richard- Bobby- Doug-David	Clarence	Mt. View
Lockhart, Rugal Archie	Sep 15, 1999	66	S.M.H.	New Market	Aug 3, 1933	Lockhart, Joe Henry	Silver, Mary		Knott, Verna Bernice	[Step] Brooks, Dusti - Bowling, Rose [Orl]	Richard Bobby- Adams, Roxie	Roger	Flat Gap
Lockhart, Alonzo Samuel	Mar 9, 1984	71	J.M.H.	Hawkins Co	Sep 19, 1912	Long, Frank	Ward, Nora		Desa [D]	Long, Jo Ann- Whitlock, Marie- Davis, Janice- Turner, Bernha- Collins, Elizabeth-n - Nash, Pansy	Johnson, Harold- O' Dell	Vineyard, Ella- Jarnigan, Gladys	J.C.	West View
Long, Deso Mattie	Jul 18, 1978	65	Jeff Co	Tn	Sep 13, 1912	Johnson, William Frank	Jernigan, Thenia		Long, Lonzo	Jo Ann - Nash, Pansy- Elizabeth- Turner, [Sr]- Davis, Jemicco [Sr] - Whitlock, Marie Minnie - Collins, Rose- Clevenger, Bonnie - Baller, Nora	Johnson, Howard- Donald	Clewers, Lizzy- Glass, Helen	West View
Long, Fannie C	Oct 21, 1988	74	Knoxville, Tn	Virginia	Sep 8, 1984	Campbell, Will	Roach, Jane	Via	Long, Arthur		Dan E.-Fred	Husband	New Market
Long, Helen	Dec., 1966						Brooks, Lela	WW 2	Nina B.	William Mike		[Pials] Curr, Clay- Ripley, Robert- Zachary, Sam- Anderson, Hugh- Cook, Ray- Newman, Allen	Strawberry Plains
Long, William Coy	Nov 25, 1983	61	Hawkins Co		Oct 15, 1922	Long, Lige							New Market

Name	Death Date	Age	Place	County	Birth Date	Father	Mother	Spouse						Burial
Longmire, Minnie J.	Nov 4, 1973	67	J.M.H.	Tn	Mar 6, 1906	Homer, Charlie	Taylor, Cornilla F.	Longmire, Ray		Blanard, Jesse [Ca]	Ray Jr. [Med]-Charles [Med]	Elliot, Mary Ruth [Mich]-Hedrick, Cora - Palmer, Juanita - Clan, Wm - Lee, Rhea Kate - Brooks, Hazel	Husband - [Pals] Longmire, Earl-Consonie-Wendell - Wife - Anderson, Bobby - Greenlee, Shields	Mill Springs
Longmire, Ray C.	Jan 17, 1979	75	U.T.H.	New Market	Nov 18, 1903					Blanard, Irene [Ca]	Charles F.R.C. [Mich]	Kidgen, Ophelia [Ok]	Abbie Edd-Hedden-T.J.	J.M.G.
Longmire, Roy Dale	Jan 17, 1979		U.T.H.	Lafollette, Tn	Nov 18, 1903	Longmire, James	Homer, Minnie	Minnie	army				[Pals] Longmire, Lee-Lewis-Jaymen-Douglas, Donald - Martin, Bill	
Longmire, Gary Wayne	Jun 12, 1984	21	J.M.H.	New Market	Oct 18, 1962	Looney, Robert	Smith, Alla	S				Eslinger, Earlene	Bobby-Frankie	
Looney, George Washington	Sep 29, 1989	65	S.M.H.	Hawkins Co	Feb 22, 1924	Looney, Edgar	Hensley, Christine			Campbell, Dollie Lorena	Jeff		Son - [Pals] Looney, Jeff-Allan-Bob - Framz, Lenny	Indian Ridge-Rutledge, Tn
Looney, Mary H.	Feb 28, 1990	92	Rutledge, Tn	Hawkins Co	Dec 18, 1897	Hensley, Phillip	Shingolere, Hulda	Looney, Ongier ?		Tipton, Margaret & Ralph	Clyde-Robert	Crowe, Hassie - Bull, Esther - White, Ethel - Salloten, Ann	James	Mill Springs
Looney, Oncie	Jun 6, 1975	78	Jeff Co		Jul 27, 1896					Farrow, Earlene & Lennie - [Pr-Law] Looney, Sharon	Gary W. [D]-Bobby & Pally	Tipton, Margaret	Clyde	Mill Springs
Looney, Robert Kyle	Jan 5, 1997	77	New Market	Hawkins Co	Aug 14, 1919	Looney, Oncie	Hensley, Mary	Smith, Alta P.		Connie-Elizabeth Ann	Frank [D]-Bobby & Tonia	Booth, Elizabeth - Denton, Florence - Lovell, Shirley [pals] - Broyles, Geraldine	John [pals]-George-Wayne-Tommy	Valley View
Love, Artie Jr.	Feb 22, 2000	67	New Market	Jeff Co	May 28, 1932	Love, Artie Sr.	Dilis, Geneva	Love, Helen [D]				Waldron, Frances-Wood, Dorothy-Southerland, Katharine - Cochran, Juanita - Ramsey, Carolyn - Carroll, Sue	Frank-Bill-Joe	Valley View
Love, Bobby Gene	Feb 5, 1996	55	Hill Haven	Jeff Co	Jun 15, 1940	Love, Marshall	Huffaker, Janie	S					Brother	Beech Springs-Sevier Co
Love, Franklin Arlie	May 7, 1997	37	Jeff City	Jeff Co	Jul 8, 1959	Love, Artie Jr.	Crowe, Helen E.	Horton, Brenda		[Step] Burchfield, Angela-Ashley Martha	Connie-Elizabeth		Bobby Hodge	Valley View
Love, Helen Elizabeth	Sep 18, 1996	58	J.M.H.	New Market	Sep 22, 1938	Crowe, Hodge	Myers, Jennie Pitts	Love, Artie Jr.		Connie-Elizabeth Ann	Crowe, Bobby & Frank, [D]	Hurst, Ruth - Barry, Ann - [Step] James, Juanita - Redding, Elizabeth	Carl-Steve-Bobby [Step] Pitts, Cecil [Pa]	Valley View
Lowdep, Bertha Ellen	Oct 31, 2000	81	F.S.H.	Jeff Co	Oct 17, 1919	Walls, Joseph A.	Burchfield, Martha	Lowdep, Charlie		Mc Carter, Carolyn & Jack-Spoon, Jean & Don	Cory-Lee & Vicky [Mc]-Rose	Findrum, Bessie A.	Roy-Boyd	J.M.G.
Lowdep, Cretis Lou	Jun 5, 1990	82	U.T.H.	Sevier Co	Apr 4, 1908	Guilimore, Andrew	Mc Carter, Eliza Jane	Francis, Eurea		Lowdep, Lawrence [D]		Lowdep, Estelle - Elmore, Myrtle - Carr, Madeline - Lowdep, Ola	Francis, Eugene [G-Son]	Strawberry Plains

Name	Date	Age	Place	Location	Date											
Lowrey, Daniel Lowrance	Dec 9, 1981	63	Strawberry Plains	Sevier Co.	Oct 24, 1918	Lowday, Arthur		Sneed, Bertie		Guillume, Crelite	[Step] Francis, Euras		Moore, Luselle	Green, Lee	[Pet] Stansberry, J.W. - Smith, Jack, Tammy - Trent, Sonny - Hawkins, Raiston - Triplin, Randall - Ballard, Fred	Strawberry Plains
Lowday, Wilma Carline	Apr 23, 1996	60	New Market	Jeff City	May 24, 1935	Jett, Carl L.		Underwood, Leora		Lowday, Troy			Boby D.	Mc Ghee, Bernice	Hillis	Husband	J.M.G.
Lovin, Hazel Mae	Oct 5, 1979	55	F.S.H.	Grainger Co.	Sep 16, 1924	Carpenter, Will		Underwood, Martha	W	Bell, Brenda		Bobby D.	Mc Ghee, Bernice	Herbert-Hubert-Odell-Ralph-Carson-Kyle-Major	[Pet] Short, Billy-Jim-Joe-Max.-Sis-John-Gregg, Danny-Yount, Tommy	Lovin - Moorresburg, Tn
Lowe, Dorothy Evelyn	Jan 17, 2000	77	S.M.H.	New Market	Mar 21, 1923	Finchum, Jesse		Underwood, Daisy Hope		Lowe, Kenneth	Lowrey, Virginia [Step] Smith La Donna [Step] Openinger, Christine - Bamhouse, Gail [Ch]	James, Jesse Earl [D]-Lowe, William Jack [D]- [Step] Lowe, Danny-Fain [Ch]	Hairmaker, Mary	Harold [D]- Flood-Lurance	[Pet] Lowday, Irene [Active]	J.M.G.
Lowrey, Callie	Jun 11, 1950	69	New Market, Tn	Tn	Feb 17, 1881	Lowrey, Arlie	Tn	Hodge, Mary	Tn			Petty, Floyd L.- Lowrey, Cecil F.- James S.		Lowrey, Henry	Friends
Lowrey, Cecil Franklin	Mar 5, 1966	77	Knoxville, Tn	Jeff Co	Apr 8, 1908	Lowrey, Henry		Glenn, Callie				Todd, Iris C.- Phillips, Eloise			Ralph-Leon	Friends Station
Lowrey, Charles J. Sr.	Jul 11, 1998	53	New Market	New Market	Dec 19, 1944	Lowrey, Raymond		Smith, Elizabeth Irene	Dir	Solburg, Karen [B] - Miller, Sharon - Lowrey, Amanda	Charles Jr.-Ron	Bob-Gary D.- Darrell Lynn - James - Gregory			Flat Gap
Lowrey, Christopher Columbus	Jun 26, 1985	68	B.H.	Knox Co	Feb 22, 1917	Lowrey, Arlie		Richard, Bertie		Brown, Mary E.	Willard, Virginia	George Robert- John Wesley	King, Ruby-Elizabeth Ethel - Patterson, Mary - Lovin, Maggie - Browning, Imogene - Pratt, Beulah-Betty	Jess-James	[Pet] Phillips, Walter - Misty, Ron Waller, Steve - Patton, Steve - Warren, Coy - Cole, Ken- Osborne, James - Stifery, James - King, Jerry	J.M.G.
Lowrey, Clifford Leon	Feb 14, 1987		V.A.-Chattanooga, Tn	New Market	Sep 4, 1917	Lowrey, Henry		Smith, Dorothy		Smith, Dorothy	Greenbury, Kathy	Steve-Fred [Step] Daniels, Paul-Raymond-Lewis		Ralph	Cremated - Friends Station
Lowrey, Cordia Delia	Mar 24, 1976	95	J.M.H.	Jeff Co	Dec 11, 1879	Newman, John		Sharps, Sallie ?				Bailey, Trula	Earl	Taylor	[Pet] Lowrey, Earnest-Franklin- Day, Derwein - Mc Daniel, Jerry - Courtney, Charles	Friends Station
Lowrey, Doris June	Jun 28, 1977	27	Strawberry Plains	Jeff Co	Feb 28, 1950	Wells, James	New	Pollard, Lutllian		Lowrey, Charles			Kenneth Rives [D]	Emmie & Ester	Husband	Highland Memorial
Lowrey, Earl Henry	May 29, 1999	89	J.M.H.	New Market	Sep 14, 1909	Lowrey, George		Newman, Cordia		Sellers, Rozella [0]	Lowrey, Cecil	Lowrey, Cecil Jr.-, Petty, Floyd Jr.	Trula [D] - [In-Law] Elizabeth, Catherine	Rahm, Ball - Miller, Ellen - Russell, Flora - Howell, Maude - Baldwin, Barnola	Highland Memorial
Lowrey, Edna	May 14, 1985	89	Knoxville, Tn	Blount Co., Tn	Nov 20, 1915	Keeble, Sam		Williams, Martha		Lowrey, Cecil				W.T.-Bob-Carl-Edgar		Friends Station
Lowrey, Elda	Jul 6, 1971		Tn	Tn	Jul 4, 1912	Bates, Charles		Henry, Miranda		Lowrey, Ralph			Lynn-R.G.	Mc Henry, Mrs. Earnest [Vs]		Friends Station

Name	Date	Age	Place	Place	Date										Cemetery
Lowery, Floyd Allen	Dec 30, 1974	32	Knoxville, Tn		Jul 6, 1942		Smith, Irene		Brenda Lee	Raymond Mark-Charles Daniel-Tommy	Charles Jr-Bobby Ray-Gary Dean-Paul Randle-Darrell-James Gordy	Smith, Robert & Sarah [G-Parents]	Flat Gap
Lowery, George Washington	Apr - , 1966	85									1/2) Sullens, Tom		J.M.G.
Lowery, Gladys Marie	Mar 16, 1990	67	F.S.H.	Jeff City	Apr 15, 1922	Edmonds, William Anderson	Kilgore, Julia Adle		Cordie	Earney-Earl	Jimmy Douglas		J.M.G.
Lowery, J. Henry	Apr 21, 1976	93	Care Inn	Jeff Co.	Oct 22, 1882	Pierce, Tom		W	Lowery, Harold W. [D]	Ralph-Leon [Toledo, Oh]	[Pals - G-Children] Lowery, R.G.-Lynn-James-James-Fred-Pitner, Rick-Petty, Loyd	Friends Station
Lowery, John Wesley	Oct 8, 1994	16	J.M.H.	Knoxville, Tn	Jun 16, 1978	Lowery, John Sr.		S			Gerald	Father	J.M.G.
Lowery, Lillie B.	Dec 6, 1968	70	Jeff Co	Tn	Nov 22, 1898	Baker, James	Gladis, Lizzie	W		Nathan D.	Ray	Gilbert, Doran	Lowery, Nathan	Flat Gap
Lowery, Mark Richard	Nov 25, 1957	4	Jeff Co	Tn	Mar 4, 1953	Lowery, Nathan		Tn			Mary Lou	Wayne-James Edward-Nathan Jr.	Lowery, Nathan	Flat Gap
Lowery, Michael Allen	May 8, 2000	1	U.T.H.	Morristown, Tn	Sep 30, 1998	Lowery, Randall Allen	Snyder, Tina				Christina	Cody-Damian	[Snyder, J.A. & Wilma-Barlow, Mary Ruth-Lowery, Carlie Irene [G-Parents]	Snyder Family-Sevier Co.
Lowery, Ralph Glenn	Apr 10, 1989	79	New Market, Tn	New Market, Tn	Nov 9, 1909	Lowery, Henry	Glenn, Callie		Frazier, Ruth		Lynn-R.G. Jr. [Chip]	Wife - [Pals] Lowery, Carlie Irene [G-Parents]-Mamooth, David	J.M.G.
Lowery, Raymond Lee	Mar 20, 1965	44	Tn	Tn	Sep 7, 1920	Lowery, Charles Arthur	Lillie		Smith, Irene	Marriooth, Betty Rose - Turner, Faye	Floyd-Charles-Bobby-Gary-Paul-Darrell-James	Haworth, Mrs. J.O. - Horner, Mrs. James W.	N.O.	Flat Gap
Loy, Annie Lee	Mar 1 1976	86	Wythe, Va	Jeff Co	Nov 21, 1889	Repass, James W.	Holbrook, Elizabeth C.		Loy, G.W. Jr.	McLane, Carolyn Malone & Steve	Loy, Bill & Sharron	Bates, Elizabeth - Foster, Helen	Wilson, Woodrow	New Market
Loy, Annie Frances	Jun 14, 1966	78	New Market	Tn	Apr 11, 1920	Wilson, John L.	Doane, Mary E.		Smith, Irene				Friends Station
Loy, Bertha	Aug 7, 1955	72	Knoxville, Tn	New Market	Sep 12, 1882	Long, G.W.	Unk		Loy, James N.	Walters, Mrs. Ed	James N. Jr.	Taylor, Mrs. Paul	New Market
Loy, Edna	Mar 14, 1956				Oct 23, --10	New Market			Loy, Mack [D]			De Groat, Mrs. W.A. - West, Mrs. Fred-Malcolm, Helen L.	Brown, John B. [Son-in-Law]	West View
													Loy, Leon - Julian, Michael V. - [Pals] Mosley, Joe - Fountain, L.A. - Davis, Richard - Harper, Jerry - Miller, Harper - Wallace - Stricklin, Neal - Stines	
Loy, Elmert Rudolph	Nov 22, 1983	72	Care Inn	Union Co.	Jan 22, 1911	Loy, John Carr			Walters, Ruth	Marilyn	Robert		Edward	J.M.G.
Loy, Eugene	Mar 25, 1996	62	Knox Co	Anderson Co.	Apr 23, 1935	Loy, Ulysses	Brantley, Bessie		Huxley, Grace	Preston, Darlene - Jones, Denise	Rick & Tammy		J.R.	East View
Loy, George Wooten Sr.	Feb 25, 1975	84	Dandridge, Tn	Jeff Co.	Apr 28, 1890	Loy, George Patrick	Hodge, Ellen Ann		Jones, Mary Ruth		G.W. Jr.			Friends Station

Name	Date	Age	Place	City	Date 2												
Loy, J. Marvel	Feb -, 1967	83	S.M.H.									Williams, Mrs. Edd		James M.		G.W.	Friends Station
Loy, James H.	Mar 30, 1976																
Loy, Leon	Jun 12, 1959	91	Knox Co	Jeff City	Jul 19, 1987	Loy, Bruce		Thomas, Nina		Bartow, Edna						Harold John J. Marvel - Mehan, Joe	West View
Loy, Mack	Mar 23, 1960	79	Hamblen Co	Jeff Co	Jun 26, 1880	Loy, George P.	Tn	Hodge, Margret	Tn	Rapass, Annie		Pierce, Ann				John J. Marvel [Niece] Witts	New Market
Loy, Mary Ruth	Mar 12, 1999	94	Jeff City	Dandridge, Tn	Mar 27, 1904	Jones, Sam R.		Frye, Alice				[Step] Loy, G.W. Jr.			Loy, Rubie K.	Friends Station
Loy, Mayne N.	Oct 27, 1957	51	M.C.	Tn	Oct 15, 1906	Unk	Tn	Stockberry, Arrie	Tn	Loy, G.W. Sr. [D]		Peck, Mrs. Harry [D] Welch, Mrs. John [D]	4	George M. [D]	Loy, Rubie K.	New Market
Loy, Rubie K.	Jan 18, 1976	69	Knoxville, Tn	Union Co, Tn	Jul 26, 1906	Loy, John Carr		Onks, Ada Maude		Lammons, Hazel		Harold		Emert-Fred D.- Edward		New Market
Lusk, James Harrell	Jul 21, 1987	58	New Market, Tn	Knox Co	Sep 2, 1928	Lusk, T.M.		Roach, Ona		Snyder, Lucille		Ronald		Knight, Deborah	Duke, Mary - Wells, Betty - Underwood, Beecher-J.W.- Borelle - Tennelce, Tom-Robert Dorothy	Witts - [Pals] Lawson, Robert - Underwood, Roy- Ray - Cook, Ray - Bailey, J. Thomas - - Wisconover, Raymond	Highland Memorial East
Luttrell, Raymond L.	May 28, 1983	74	U.T.H.	Grainger Co	May 2, 1909	Luttrell, Frank		Stout, Rina		Cook, Dora		Franklin		Bates, Zella - Newman, Helen	Hamblen, Betty - Rapass, Vera - Griffin, May Bell	[Pals-G-Sons] Bates, Ray-Tim- John A. - Hart-Charles-Allen - Wagoner, L.E.	Strawberry Plains
Luttrell, Raymond W.	Jun 16, 1990	49	Strawberry Plains	Jeff Co	Mar 25, 1931	Luttrell, Raymond		Cook, Donna	korea	Lee, Wanda [Bonnie]		Jr.-Tom		Melissa-Craig- Nipper, Mrs. Charles - Branch, Faye	Bates, Zella - Newman, Helen	[Pals] Edmonds, Dewey-Cook, H.C. Jr. - Hart, Allen - Lawson, Ralph-Harold - Cook, Roy	Strawberry Plains
Lyle, Tammy Renee	Jan 15, 1982	19	New Market	Talpei, Taiwan	Dec 7, 1972	Lyle, Gary Lee		Boldy, Mary Ann	S			Ronald		Ryan		[Pals] Edmonds, Dewey-Cook, H.C. Jr. - Hart, Allen - Bailey, Jack & Kathleen - Hensley, Mary Louise [G-Parents] - [Pals] Perene - [Pals] Lyle, Tom - Boldy, Steve-Jerry-Jackie-Mike	J.M.G.
Mabe, Norman Harold	Sep 14, 1983	63	F.S.H.	Stonega, Va	Nov 2, 1919	Mabe, Thurman		Sizemore, Neelia	S					Collins, Edith - Lowe, Inez - Humbard, Dorothy	Earnest-Ralph- Robert	Mott, Dorothy	Friends Station
Mabe, Sherman Britton	Apr 12, 1971	60	Tn	Va	Aug 9, 1890	Mabe, Sam		McCullee, Elizabeth	W					Humbard, Dorothy - Collins, Edith - Lowe, Inez [Pal]	Robert-Norman- Ralph-Ernest [Val]	Scruggs, Hester - Thompson, Lillie	Friends Station
Mack, Millie [Col]	Aug 24, 1958	72	Jeff Co	Clifflside, Nc	Jul 24, 1886					Mack, Robert		Van-Claude			[1/2] Scruggs, William	Stover, Claude [Nd]-Bruce [W. Val]	Methodist Church
Mack, Robert	Mar -, 1967	67													[1/2] James Gilmer	Mack, Albert & Vance	Youngs Memorial
Mackey, Harold Raginald [Negro]	Jun 25, 1977	21	Canton, Ohio	Canton, Ohio	Oct 1, 1955	Mackey, William		George, Sue	Div	72-75	Tracy-Ivy [Springfield, Oh]	George, Chris, Lizz			George, Pat- Steve - [Uncle] Pruitt, Thaddeus	Jernigan, Sue & James R. [Mother & Step-Father] [Pals] Mills, Carl - Moore, Paul - Carter, Lawrence - Shevis, Tommy- Wayne	West View

Name	Date	Age	Place	Place 2	Birth	Father	Mother	Spouse	Children				Cemetery
Maples, Danielle Suzanne	Jul 1, 1987	2	Birmingham, Alabama	San Antonio, Tx	Apr 24, 1985			Maples, Susan E. [Amy]					Cremated
Maples, Perlin Jr.	May 3, 1998	68	Rutledge, Tn	Washburn - Granger Co	Mar 5, 1930	Maples, Samuel	Bullen, Winnie	Maples, Helen		Roger & Tammy	Watson, Ethel & Junior - Milton, - Hendersight, - Wanda & Sam - Watch, Cleo - [br-Law] Maples, Len - Wanda		Oakland
Maples, Winnie Mae	Aug 22, 1994	93	Rutledge, Tn	Granger Co	Mar 6, 1901	Bullen, William	Brooks, Angie	Maples, Samuel [D]		Perlin-Frank		Doug - [Pink] Hendersight, Jeff - Maples, Roger - Watson, Doly - Wright, Barry - Collier, Mike - Vanderagrift, Martin	Oakland
Melton, Marion Albere	Sep 22, 1999	70	Jeff City	Jeff City	Aug 17, 1929	Williamson, Ruby Spencer	Melton, Jack S. [Quinn, Fermin M. [D]]		Abbott, Brenda & John - Waldrop, Judy & Dick	James & Kathy	Rhymes, Helen & Joe	David Earl & Nancy Sue	West View
Merlin, Lindsay Nichole Jones	Feb 19, 1995	0	S.M.H.	S.M.H.	Feb 19, 1995	Merlin, Aaron	Griffin, Charlene					Griffin, Anna [G-Michael]	Blue Springs
Manley, Nellie Kate	Aug 27, 1975	81	Morristown, Tn	Granger Co	Nov 6, 1893	Gobble, Daniel	Tate, Mary	W	Goodman, Anna Mae & Jake [Ind]	Ralph-J.D. [Ind]- Raymond [and]- Gene	Dances, Bessie	Amos	[Pink] Helm, Fifty - Curt, H.B. - Deals, Johnny-Frank - Ramsey, Luther - Combs, T. - Ralph -	Shiloh
Manley, W.M.	May 31, 1975	84	Wabash, Indiana	Rutledge, Tn	Nov 17, 1890	Manley, James William		Goodin, Nellie	Goodman, Anna Mae & Jake	Ralph-J.D. [Ind]- Raymond [and]- Gene		Willie	Shiloh
Mann, John Charles	Nov 3, 1989	83	Jacksonville, Fla	Granger Co	Apr 19, 1906	Mann, Joseph	Mays, Martha	Mann, Pearl [D]	Route, Helen	Gary	Underwood, Susie	[1/2] Bradshaw, Clifford [D]	Flat Gap
Mantooth, Charles Patrick	Nov 14, 1982	65	F.S.H.	Knoxville, Tn	Jun 9, 1927	Mantooth, Joe	Stevens, Minnie		Gross, Jamie - Hamilton, Linda	David	Conrad, Hazel	Write - [Pink] Conrad, Jimmy - Mantooth, Eddie - Lowery, Mark- Aaron - Halt, Lee - Bates, Darrell [Kinfolks]	Powder Springs
Maples, Alice S.	1970	82	Knoxville, Tn					Maples, Walter R. [D]	unk		Witt, Bertha M.		Beaver Creek
Maples, Arlie Lee	Oct 1, 1998	87	Jeff City	New, Market	Nov 29, 1910	Carter, Dan	Diel, Ethel	Maples, Tom [D]	Tolliver, Mary - Rutledge - Lundy, Alice- Blair, Shirley- Williamson, Betty- Cobble, Paula- Smith, Myrna - [in-Law] Maples, Ruby	Murl [D]-Fred-Joe Wayne			Pleasant Grove
Maples, Jack	Nov 23, 1999	81	Jeff Grth	Blaine, Tn	Oct 16, 1918	Maples, Lon	Northern, Laura Ellen	Maples, Virgie	Lee, Virgie	Curtis-Gene		Roy	J.M.E.
Maples, Samuel Crockett	Dec 4, 1987	82	Knox Co	Sevier Co, Tn	Jun 18, 1905	Maples, George	Haggard, Lorettin	Maples, Veda R.	Henderson, Dora - Snyder, Blanche	Jamteh-Vaughn- Kenneth-Clifford	Myrtle - Woodley, Maude - Conner, Nora	Hollie-Claude- Herbert	Thorn Grove - Knox Co
Maples, Sylvester	May 2, 1962		Cave Inn	Claibourn Co	1898	Maples, George							New Market

Name	Death Date	Age	Place of Death	Origin	Birth Date	Father	Mother	Spouse	War	Children	Relatives	Relatives 2	Cemetery
Maples, Virgie Lee	Aug 4, 1957	69	B.H.	Tazewell, Tn	Jun 7, 1928	Day, I.A.	Walker, Mary	Maples, Jack		Curtis-Gene	James-Earl-Don-Leroy		J.M.G.
Maples, Walter R.	May 20, 1963		J.M.H.	Grainger Co	Jul 27, 1882	Maples, William	Phillips, Elsie			James A.	Willie		Beaver Creek
Martin, David Edward	Feb -, 1967	25		Tn	Mar 4, 1941	Maples, Clarence Albert	Bettis, Annette	Owens, Glenda Sue	icebox	Michael Allen-Troy-David Jr.	Hickey, Bessie - Richards, Mary	Willie - V.A.	J.M.G.
Martin, Myrtle	Jul 14, 1992	73	J.M.H.	Sevier Co	Aug 26, 1918	Gann, John	Walker, Ethel	Martin, Calvin R. [D]		Keck, Saundra M.	Purley, Elizabeth - Smith, Mary	Doug	J.M.G.
Martin, William E. Jr.	Oct 21, 1990	67	J.M.H.	Jeff Co	Aug 14, 1923	Martin, W.E. Sr.	Underwood, Patsy Alice	Grace	WW 2			Willis	J.M.G.
Marshall, Henrietta [Col]	Aug 21, 1978	54	Jeff Co		Apr 24, 1923	Reed, Powell	Miller, Eva	Marshall, Jessie Sr. [D]		[Step] Write, Betty [Sis]	[Step] Marshall, Jessie Jr. [Ch]		Youngs Memorial
Martin, Cecil [M]	Jun 11, 1984	67	Tn	V.A.-Columbia, Sc.	Feb 3, 1917	Martin, Hall	Colbaugh, Sally		WW 2	Me Ginnis, Mrs. Wesley - Turpin, Jayne	Martin, Tony-Woods, Earl - Martin, Larry	[Pals] Solomon, Lloyd - Martin, Brazelton, Mary [Aunts] Miller, Albert [Uncles]	Pleasant Grove
Martin, Gladys Genevieve	Apr 22, 1987	87	New Market	Jeff Co	Sep 6, 1909	Riley, Arthur	Benson, Etta	Martin, Mack Preston [D]		Crawford, Sue	J.C.	Frye, Laura	Hillcrest
Martin, Harold Tony	Aug 27, 1982	39	New Market, Tn	Tn	Feb 13, 1943	Martin, Mack	Riley, Genevie			Tony	Carman, Pat & Harold	Riley, Ernest	Hillcrest
Martin, Mack Preston	Sep 9, 1973	66	Knox Co	Tn	Jun 11, 1912	Martin, Lawson	Hall, Bertie	Genevie		Carman, Patsy & Harold	Tony-Larry - [Step] Woods, Earl	Martin, Larry-Woods, Earl - French, Ronnie - Murray, Robert	Hillcrest
Messengill, Elsie Elizabeth	Feb 8, 1988	89	J.M.H.	Grainger Co	Apr 2, 1906	Cameron, James William	Cox, Bettie	Messengill, William C.		Lane, Lorene	George W.-James Walter-Bob	Gibbons, Marcella - Bishop, Virginia		J.M.G.
Messengill, James Walter	Mar 9, 1988	89	B.H.	Jeff Co	Dec 28, 1906	Messengill, William Carroll	Cameron, Elsie E.			Bailey, Audrey	Doris - Ebryck- Donnie - Keasling - Rhonda - James Barnett	Robbie-Larry [M]-Eddie-Kenny-James Barnett	Billy-Bob	J.M.G.
Messengill, William Carroll	Jul 2, 1996	89	Morristown, Tn	Jeff Co	Dec 28, 1906	Messengill, George W.	Cameron, Elsie			Lane, Lorene	George W. & Opal - James Walter & Sue - Robert & Faye	Burchfield, Yvonne [Gal]	Earl-W.B. [Lena, Orl]-Ben Nolin-Lon	J.M.G.
Metts, Jerry David	Jan 29, 1995	39	U.T.H.	Anderson, Ind	Apr 27, 1956	Metts, Gilbert	Carter, Cindy			Paula D.-Ashley M.	Michael D.- Marcus Lee	Keller, Carolyn S. - Smith, Charles W.		J.M.G.
Mathews, Esma [Col]	Dec 28, 1969	89	Knox Co	Tn	Oct 22, 1880		Key, Alice	W		[In-Law] Smith, Lillian		Carter, Minnie	Youngs Memorial
Mathews, Nida	Dec 22, 1979	94	Morristown, Tn	Claiborne Co	Mar 16, 1885	Owsley, George	Edmonds, Ann	Mathews, Arthur [D]		Edith-Rita Rose		[Pals] Owsley, Steve-Tim - Whaley, Bernard - Clark, Raymond	Youngs Memorial
Mathis, Frank	Feb 10, 1950	90	New Market, Tn	Tn	Aug 31, 1870	Owsley, George		Martha			Barnard, Ellen - Cartwell, Nola	Mathis, Freeman [Son]	Indian Ridge - Rutledge, Tn
Metts, Lucy	Apr 14, 1992	82	New Market	Sweedville, Tn	Jun 18, 1869	Rhea, Sterling					Barnard, Ellen - Cartwell, Nola	Sterling [Ind.]	Burke - Swedville
Mathis, Martha			New Market	Sweetville, Tn		Rhea, Sterling	Mc Mills ?, Samantha	Tn	Martha			Burke, Lucy - Jourdan, Polly	Burke-Swedville

Name	Death Date	Age	Place	Residence	Birth Date	Father	Mother	Spouse	Children					Burial
Matthews, Coburn	Oct 20, 1996	66	Sevier Co		Nov 17, 1929	Matthews, Albie	Morgan, Ruth	Lyle, Gladys	Moeser, Connie- Rhodes, Carl & Rita & Joel	Robert & Deborah	Gibson, Pauline - Mc Gill, Joyce- Walker, Elaine	Chon-Lester- Harrell-Jerry	Willie	Fair- Dandridge, Tn
Matthews, Edgar Louis	Feb 1, 1990	89	Hill Haven	Tazewell, Tn	Apr 14, 1900	Matthews, Henry	Neil, Lizzie	Matthews, Lora Bell						J.M.G.
Matthews, Lora Bell	Nov 17, 1990	77	J.M.H.	Goins, Tn	Nov 20, 1912	Shelton, Alfred Jacob	Keck, Vina Isabell	Matthews, Edgar L. [D]		Collins, George- Bandie, Louis- Pistelton, Norma- Massee, Lurene- Caruso, Vern	Wayne-Roy- Wally-Calf- Willie		Son	J.M.G.
Matthews, Pantrenia	Apr 25, 2000	89	F.S.H.	New Market	Jun 22, 1930	Mc Campbell, John Wallace	Underwood, Julia	Matthews, Frank	Hayes, Wilma K. & Jerry [Gal] - Walker, Judy & Mack	Robert & Deborah	Cable, Venice- Matthews, Vineyard	James [P]- L.C.-Paul- David	Fair	Fair
Mattox, Anna Rosalie	Jan 28, 1982	89	J.M.H.	Anderson, Ind	Aug 2, 1892	Johnson, J.E.	Urik	Mattox, George E.	Audrey - Shock, Anna Lee	John				J.M.G.
Mattox, Audrey Alberta	Feb 25, 1999	49	B.H.	Anderson, Ind	Oct 29, 1949	Div	Div	Div	Ballinger, Tamara & Greg	Collins, Dale & Christine- Talley,Gary R.	Shock, Anna Lee	Mattox, John [Com]- Comn, Richard B.	Son	Mill Springs
May, Dorothy Elizabeth	Jan 15, 1991	81	U.T.H.	Knox Co	Feb 4, 1910	Cable, Robert	Wootton, Lora	May, Lloyd E. [D]	Smith, Lloyd M.	Stephen D.			Son	J.M.G.
Mayes, Hubert Preston Jr.	Jan 13, 1997	68	New Market	Granger Co	Sep 5, 1928	Mayes, Hubert P.	Mc Daniel, Grace B.	Duckles, Gladys	Trent, Brenda- Carnahan, Gail & Sam- Gibbons, Donna & John - Scarlett, Lisa & Danny	David-Rick	Morgan, Mary- Hanna, Estill- Homer, Bafish	Christie- Simmah-James- Robert-Gene Roger	Husband	J.M.G.
Mayes, Robert Wayne	Mar 30, 1987	46	Jeff City	Verda, Ky	Apr 29, 1940	Mayes, Glenn B.	Greer, Hazel	Adkins, Mary Ann	Navy	Johnson, Ladonna - Mayes, Micky- Hendley, Vonna- Wiles, Carmeletta	Michael	Linda	Glenn Jr.-Jerry	Willis	U.T. Medical- Memphis, Tn
Maynard, Mary Acuff	Jan 24, 1990	90	Jeff City	Tn	Jan 26, 1899	Calvin	O'Dell, Emma Lee	Maynard, R.B.	Spradlin, Mrs. Buford - Whittle, Mrs. D.E.- Ellison, Mrs.- Carroll- Whitlock, Mrs. Paul	Clark, Condon C.			Husband	J.M.G.
Mc Bee, Betty Ray	Oct 25, 1989	55	Jeff City	Rutledge, Tn	Jun 3, 1934	Wright, Alfred	Rinehart, Katie	Maynard, R.B.	Vandergriff, Linda	Robert-Bobby- Barry	Glenn Jr.-Jerry	Willis		
Mc Bee, Jake Andrew	Jan 31, 1997	60	Rutledge, Tn	Granger Co	May 3, 1936	Mc Bee, Thomas	Daniels, Leroy	Brooks, Leona	Mc Bee, Robert E. [D]	Hill, Bertha	Earnest-Leroy	Son - [Field] Morgan, Bob- Darron, Frances- Blackwell, Shirley- Pinkston, Sylvia- Buchannon, Faye		Narrow Valley

Name	Date	Age	Place	Location	Birth	Father		Mother		Spouse	War							Chapel
McBee, Robert Armon	Aug 6, 1984	63	B.H.	Granger Co	Jun 26, 1921	McBee, Thomas		Daniel, Lexie		Wright, Betty Ray	WW 2	Vandergriff, Linda	Robert E.-Bobby Lee-Bennie	Crowe, Cora - Lowe, Dorothy - Hill, Bertha	Ernest-Bill-Leroy-Jake-Kyle-Smith, Onzie-Sonny-Jimmy	Willie - [Pix] Vandergriff, Bill - McK - Geffrey, Bill - Jess - Debb, Roger - Leonard, Kyle - Smith, Onzie	Norma Valley - Rutledge, Tn
McBride, J. Frank	Jul 21, 1990	77	New Market	Kansas	Mar 31, 1883	McBride, Drucilla											Piedmont
McBride, Jess C.	Sep 13, 1976	77	J.M.H.	Stillwater, Okla.	Jun 1, 1899	Tryon, Emma				Whittaker, Maude		Moore, Mrs. John	Dickinson, Mary Margaret [Sis] - Stephens, Sue & Hugh [Pix]	Bradley, Mrs. Grady	J.C.	McBride, Stella [Wife]	J.M.G.
McBride, Lois May	Mar 9, 1977		Athens Com. Hosp/ Knoxville, Tn		Jul 19, 189	McBride, John		Sarah				[In-Law] McBride, Margaret		Lane, Mrs. Robert		Pollards
McBride, Maude W.	Jan 7, 1998	89	J.M.H.	New Market	Sep 3, 1908	Whittaker, C.C.		Diel, Sallie		McBride, Jess [D]		Moore, Sally & John					J.M.G.
McBride, Stella J.	Feb 21, 1972	67	Knoxville, Tn		Oct 1, 1904	Whittaker, C.C.		Diel, Sally B.				McBride, Mrs. J.C. - Kerr, Mrs. Clarence		Frank		[Pals] Loy, G.W. Jr. - Pratt, John - Chandler, Gene	Piedmont
McCall, John Clarence	Jul 27, 1987	68	J.M.H.	Sevier Co	Feb 22, 1919	McCall, Frank D.		Snyder, Hattie L.		Scott, Imogene	WW 2					Husband - [Pals] Hafner, Odo-A.S. - Chase - Petty, Wayne-John - Edwards, David	Strawberry Plains
McCampbell, Beulah Pearl	Jan 30, 1994	57	J.M.H.	Jeff Co	Jan 8, 1936	Sharp, Saba		McCampbell, Della		McCampbell, Neil Edward		Cochran, Sheila - Cochran, Veronica	Neil		Frank-Charles	McCampbells	McCampbells
McCampbell, Carl Sanford	Nov 12, 1998	63	Jeff City	New Market	Jul 9, 1935	McCampbell, Robert J.		Underwood, Mae		Hubbard, Mary L.			Charles & Rosalee	Breeden, Rosalee - Borden, Ruth	Ray-Robert	Don - [Pals] Denton, Jim-Dan - Scott, Mike-Billy-Brian	Valley View
McCampbell, Cecil Richard	Jul 7, 1987	56	F.S.H.	New Market	Jun 27, 1941	McCampbell, Elmer		Brewer, Dove Lee		Danton, Margaret Mae		Loretta - Edmonson, Susan	Richard	Cox, Martha - Glenn, Margie - Hayes, Loraine	Paul-Elmer Jr. - David-Charles - Donald	Brother - [Pals] Garman, Randal-Dan - Mc-Campbell, Greg-Bryan - Cheonk, Mike-Marc	McCampbells Chapel
McCampbell, Curtis Eugene	Oct 15, 1987	59	Jeff Co	New Market	Feb 21, 1929	McCampbell, Walter B.		Fries, Ollie		S				Garman, Trula - Shultu, Beulah - McHunt, Indiana	Walter Jr. - [Pals] Mehiss	Campbell, Randal-Dan - Mc-Campbell, Greg	McCampbells Chapel
McCampbell, Donald Lee	Mar 2, 1999	63	Jeff City	Jeff Co	May 21, 1935	McCampbell, Elmer		Brewer, Dovie		S				Murray, Juanita - Collins, Jeanette - Haynes, Loraine - Cox, Martha - Glenn, Margie	Elmer Jr. - Paul - Charlie-David	McCampbells Chapel
McCampbell, Donatos Lee	Aug 28, 1996	71	U.T.H.	Knoxville, Tn	Jul 8, 1915	Grewer, Frank		Owens, Maggie		McCampbell, Elmer [D]		Donald-Elmer Jr. - Paul-Cecil - Charlie-David		Murray, Juanita - Collins, Jeanette - Haynes, Loraine - Cox, Martha - Glenn, Margie	Victory, Lorene - Brewer, Ricky	Benny	McCampbells Chapel
McCampbell, Elmer Lee	Feb 19, 1973	61	Jeff Co	Tn	May 17, 1911	McCampbell, John		Martha		Brewer, Donna Lee		Martha-Magrie - Lorane-Jeannette - Howell, Mrs. - Larronos - Murry, Mrs. Hood		David-Paul-Elmer Jr.-Donald	Bob	Willie	McCampbell Chapel

Name	Date	Age	Col4	Col5	Date2	Father	Mother	Spouse	Col10	Col11	Col12	Children/Notes	Burial
Mc Campbell, James	May 1, 1977	68	Sevier Co.	Jeff Co.	Nov 11, 1908	Mc Campbell, John	Martha	w	Scarlett, Louise - Borden, Ruth - Bowdon, Rose				Mc Campbells Chapel
Mc Campbell, Raye Elizabeth	Oct 13, 2000	60		Maricol, Tn	Oct 19, 1939	Runion, Raymond M.	Wyrick, Edith Mae	Mc Campbell, Lee Donald [D]	Hensley, Tammy		Joseph		Mc Campbells Chapel
Mc Campbell, Warren Keith	Aug 31, 1993	85	S.M.H.	New Market	Sep 1, 1907	Mc Campbell, Joe	Moreland, Ellis	S			Shultz, Beulah		Mc Campbells Chapel
Mc Carter, Betty G.	Jan 29, 1990	57	J.M.H.	New Market	Mar 21, 1932	Nox, Mack	Martin, Pauline	Mc Carter, E.J.			Watehous, Therita L. - Mayers, Grace? - Horton, Martha - Mc Glannery, Mary Ellen	Husband - [Pals] Brown, Hugh - Hodge, Harold - Whitaker, Jim - Miller, Rod - Davis, Dave - Kearney, Bob - Collins, Tom (Em)	New Market
Mc Carter, E.J.	Apr 23, 1991	66	J.M.H.	Knoxville, Tn	Jul 3, 1924	Mc Carter, Ellis J.	Frazier, Lona	Nox, Betty		Viola	Jack-Glenn	Wife - [Pals] Collins, Tom (Em)	New Market
Mc Clain, Albert Eugene	Mar 15, 1991	62	New Market	New Market	Nov 15, 1928	Mc Clain, Bert	Davis, Sallie	Miller, Ann		Denny-Steve-Joe-Tom	Lewis, Lorene	Willis	J.M.G.
Mc Clain, Burt	Nov 23, 1974	79	New Market		Jul 24, 1895			Sallie	Randies, Lorene	Eugene-Willis		Jack-Glenn	Nances Grove
Mc Clain, Sally E.	Aug 9, 1992	90	J.M.H.	Blaine, Tn	Mar 30, 1902	Davis, William Nelson	Renfro, Solome	Mc Clain, Bert [D]	Lewis, Lorene	Willis	Curtis	Son - [Pals] Elmore, Wayne - Miller, George - Hubbard, Bobby - Thompson, Ernie - Hood, Chuck - Howard, Larry - Minton, Ira - Harper, John	Nances Grove
Mc Coig, Mollie	May 28, 1977	81	J.M.H.	Jeff Co	Feb 28, 1896	Henry, William	Burchfield, Jane	w		Jack		[Pals] Hubbard, Bobby-Ed - Nance, Harold - Minton, Ira B. - Renfro, Harold - Howard, Edwin	Hills Union
Mc Coig, Nellie H.	Jun 13, 1982	84	J.M.H.	Jeff Co	Feb 4, 1898	Henry, William	Burchfield, Jane	Mc Coig, Otha				[Pals] Hammond, Gary-Danny- Richard - Chambers, Steven - Shrader, Miller - Chism, Bryan	Hills Union
Mc Coig, Otha William Cleveland	Oct 11, 1965	72	White Pine, Tn	No	Sep 19, 1913	Mc Coig, Dan M.	Messer, Nancy E.	Mc Coig, Otha					Hills Union
Mc Coig, John Cleveland	Nov 15, 1965	74	B.H.	Birmingham, Ala	Nov 17, 1920	Mc Coig, Julius H.	Hathcoat, Myrtle	Lauderdale, Mildred [D]	Spraig, Carolyn		Betty [Ale] - Smith, M.H. [Ale]	James [Ale]	Doug	Lauderdale - Straw Plains
Mc Crary, Mildred	Apr 29, 1994	64	Strawberry Plains	Strawberry Plains	Mar 14, 1930	Lauderdale, James	Lawrence, Mary	Mc Crary, John	Spraig, Carolyn		Wife	Husband - [Pals] Dugger, Delbert- Tan-Anthony - Mckelvey, Robt - Wallace, Fred - Lauderdale, Edd	Lauderdale - Straw Plains

Name	Death Date	Age	Place	Location	Birth Date	Father	Mother		Spouse	Service	Relatives / Children			Pallbearers	Burial
Mc Cubbins, James [Bud]	Jul 23, 1975	55		Jeff Co	Dec 26, 1919	Mc Cubbins, Charles	Koontz, Jessee		Beals, Jamie	army	Trent, Mrs. Jerry	Bruce Edward	Wilson, Mrs. Charles - Brown, Mrs. Harvey - Miller, Mrs. J.T. [Ar]	[Pals] Jones, Leland - Koster, James - Zirkle, Charles - Zirkle, Carroll - Hodges, Bill - Blazer, Wagnes	Friends Station
Mc Cubbins, Nellie O.	Jan 3, 1995	86	Hill Haven	W. Va	Sep 23, 1908	Pritchard, Frank	Clayton, Maude							Husband	Cremated - West View
Mc Cubbins, Addie Edith	Nov 11, 1972	63	U.T.H.	Tn	May 14, 1909	Ballinger, John	Lena		Mc Cubbins, Roy S.				J.W.-Bud-Tren-Charles	Husband	New Market
Mc Curry, Dora Ellen	1966	87			Dec 7, 1878	Cogdill, —									
Mc Curry, George Neal	May 1,1 1981	78		Cocke Co, Tn	Jul 27, 1904	Mc Curry, William Lee	Cogdill, Dora		Ballinger, Edith				Tom-Clarence-[Calif]-Bill-Curtis-George Sr.	[Pals] G-Sons	New Market
Mc Curry, Paul	Mar 19, 1976	73	U.T.H.	Cocke Co, Tn	June 3, 1902	Mc Murry, Will	Cogdill, Sara		Vola C.			J.O.-David Earl-Tyler, Thelma [Mont]-Paul Jr.-Daniel H.-King, Mrs. [Mont]-Step Springer, Charles	Ballinger, Julia-Bury [Calif]-Tyler, Mrs. Beryl-Hannigan, Mrs. Rea [Calif]	[Pals] Mc Curry, George Neal-Thomas-Ronnie-David-James D-Robert	Flat Gap
Mc Daniel, Carroll Eugene	Oct 21, 1993	96	Greenville, Ga	Knox Co	May 11, 1937	Mc Daniel, Albert	Trent, Etta		Dockery, Bonnie N.	Navy	Rhonda-Vickie-Taylor, Melba	Doyle-Doug	Allen-Jerry	Neil	Write	Valley View
Mc Daniel, Etta L.	Feb 2, 1999	95	Sneedville, Tn		Apr 19, 1913	Trent, Fred	Odom, Lara		Mc Daniel, Albert						Write	J.M.G.
Mc Daniel, James Paul	Jul 21, 1995	63	U.T.H.	Rutledge, Tn	Apr 25, 1932	Mc Daniel, William	Bates, Beulah B.		Rice, Mary Louise			Greene, Patrick-Greene, Michael	Kitts, Anna Lou-Hixon, Estelle-Faye-Maples, Barbara	Roy Cotton-Eugene-David	Mitchell Springs-Rutledge, Tn
Mc Daniel, James Phillip	Oct 8, 1992	52	Morristown, Tn	Jeff City	Jul 17, 1940	Mc Daniel, Lawrence	Williamson, Bess		Div	Marines	Oliver, Debbie-[Ind]-Owens, Donna		[1/2] Holloway, Vickie- Sands, Betsy [D]-[La]	[1/2] Mc Daniel, Billy [La]	Debbie - [Pals] Whitaker, Jim-Wells, Ron-Alley, Denver-Johnson, Nick-Carmichael, Bill-Cox, Dale	West View
Mc Daniel, Marjorie Le Anne	Aug 27, 1982		U.T.H.	Tn	Jul 1, 1982	Mc Daniel, C.E.	Dockery, Bonnie	Tn			Tn		Rhonda		Mc Daniel, C.E. [Sons]	Valley View
Mc Daniel, Percey Mae Large	Mar 10, 1999	87	Knoxville, Tn	New Market	May 24, 1911	Willings, Coy	Riggs, Ollie		Mc Daniel, Aaron [D]-Large, D.F. [D]		Glaydon, Louise Large & Darrell-Mouron, Katherine & Lois-Patterson, Patsy & Jim	James & Louise-Roy-Eugene-David	[In-Law] Willings, Effie	Acuff, Virgie - Mays, Hazel	Lebanon Cumberland Presby.
Mc Daniels, Beulah B.	Sep 8, 1980	73	Jeff City	Union Co	Mar 5, 1907	Bates, Joe	Merritt, Lola		Mc Daniels, George William [D]		Hixon, Faye-Estelle-Kitts, Anna Lo-Kay, Evelyn-Maples, Barbara			Earl-Lonnie-Vergil-Reuben	[Pals] Green, Pat-Kitts, Thomas-Steve-Donnie-Kay, William-Davis, Clifford	Mitchell Springs

Name	Date	Age	Place of Death	Town/County	Birth Date	Father	Mother	Spouse	In-Laws / Parents	Children	Siblings / Relatives	Pallbearers	Cemetery
Mc Daniels, Roy M.	Feb 3, 1982	70	J.M.H.	Grainger Co	Mar 10, 1911	Mc Daniel, Eli	Byrd, Nancy	Pasteull, Louise		James Everett	Rauch, Mae	[Pals] Kim, Floyd- Daniel, Eugene- Williams, Donnie- Willie	Mc Daniels- Rutledge, Tn
Mc Farland, William [Black]	Jan 12, 1992	71	J.M.H.	New Market	Oct 18, 1920	Mc Farland, Will	Massengill, Nan					Willie	J.M.G.
Mc Farland, Anna Belle [Black]	Feb 20, 1995	74	U.T.H.	New Market	Jan 21, 1921	Turk, Gorham	Fults, Ina	Mc Farland, William Jr. [D]				Chambers, Robert- Colkin [Nephew]	J.M.G.
Mc Gaha, Howard C.	Jul 19, 1988	87	J.M.H.	Cocke Co, Tn	Apr 22, 1901	Gaddis, Anderson		Gaddis, Ross Mae [D]	Kerr, Katharine	Jim-Norman			New Market
Mc Gaha, Mattie	Oct 19, 1949	81	New Market, Tn	Cosby, Tn	Dec 10, 1857	Dennis, Joel	Tn	Link	Cora - Parrott, Rexca, Dessie	Howard-Roy [Ind.]		Mc Gaha, Howard	Hillis Chapel
Mc Gaha, Ross Mae	Jan 13, 1974	69	Hamblen Co	Tn	May 8, 1904	Vineyard, --		Mc Gaha, Howard	Kerr, Katherine & Bronce	James [Cal]- Norman		Husband	New Market
Mc George, Johnny	Dec 28, 1983	59	Humana Hosp. Tazewell, Tn		Jul 25, 1925	Mc George, Joe	Shelton, Nina	Hensley, Dorcus	Dunkno, Brenda	Steve	Russell, Hazel	Bowman, Mrs. Raymond [Sis]	J.M.G.
Mc George, Nina	Oct 22, 1980	66	Jeff Co.	Tn	Aug 20, 1892	Shelton, Bill	W	Hensley, Nancy		Robert		[Pals] Foster, Charles - Vineyard, Robert- Hensley, Kenneth- Dale, Ezra- Allsup, Don	West View
Mc Ghee, Cecil Clifford	Oct 17, 1988		M.C.	Tn	Apr 24, 1905	Mc Ghee, Lenord	Mc Nish, Carrie	W	Russell, Hazel - Pierce, Bertha Boling, Louise- Francis-	James	Sharp, Ida - Tolliver, Mary	Jake-Russ- Walter	Pleasant Grove
Mc Ghee, Garrett Monford	Feb 5, 1996	71	Rutledge, Tn	Rutledge, Tn	Mar 25, 1924	Mc Ghee, Hubert	Mitchell, Lila	Vineyard, Pauline	White, Wanda	Donald	Nina	Willie	Grainger Memorial
Mc Ghee, James Edward	Aug 9, 1972	44	J.M.H.					Mae	Pearl B.	Clyde	Hubert, Jr.	W.R.- Carter, Bill Howard, Ludford- Gene, Ken-Hot- Howard, Ludford	Pleasant Grove
Mc Ghee, Mae Grace	May 31, 1989	82	Jeff City	Hawkins Co	Oct 13, 1906			Mc Ghee, Cecil [D]	Watson, Edna - Crowe, Hassie Lee- Carl, Frances	James	Norton, Barbara- Jean	Doug - [Pals] Carr, Mike-David- Gen, Mike - Mc Ghee, Mike- Warwick	Pleasant Grove [Haworth]
Mc Ghee, Mary Ann	Dec 9, 1989	45	F.S.H.	New Market, Tn	Jul 19, 1944			Mc Ghee, Paul Ray Sr.	Shallend, Mary	Mc Ghee, Raymond Jerry	Timothy Ray- Death Deverger- Raymond Gregory-Mark- Anthony	Paul Ray- George Franklin	Husband - [Pals] Clark, Miller- Mc Ghee, Chris- Brandon, Fred- Lawson, Richard- Brewer, Jim	J.M.G.
Mc Ghee, Pearl Irene	Dec 17, 1997	68	Jeff City	Rutledge, Tn	Mar 14, 1929	Burchell, John	Mc Gill, Jessie E.	Mc Ghee, James [D]	Arnold, Evelyn & H.G.	Clyde & Brenda	Ray	Pleasant Grove/Haworth- New Market	Pleasant
Mc Ginnis, Clara Zelma	Jun 10, 1999	80	Jeff City	Knox Co.	Aug 9, 1916	Mc Ginnis, Oral B.	Bingahm, Maynee	Div	Clayton- T.J.				East View
Mc Ginnis, Herman Chester	Jun 25, 1999	82	Jeff City	Thorn Hill, Tn	Nov 22, 1918	Mc Ginnis, Oral B.	Farmer, Martha E.	West, Dena V.	Army	Alexander, Darlene & Tom	Curt, Jessie [D]- Suffrage, Pauline	Clarence E. [D]-Wiley- William-Earl Herman [D]- Clarence	Shiloh
Mc Ginnis, Wiley Edward	Dec 10, 2000	78	Jeff City	Thorn Hill, Tn	Jul 25, 1922	Mc Ginnis, Oral	Farmer, Elizabeth	Mc Mahan, Betty	Spencer, Rebecca		Curt, Jessie [D]	Ethel [D]-Earl-William	West View

Name	Date	Age	Place	Place 2	Date 2	Father	Mother							
Mc Glamery, Charles	Jan 15, 1991	63	J.M.H.	New Market	Jun 30, 1927	Mc Glamery, Clifford	Bates, Edith	Nox, Mary Ellen		Charles W. - Mackie A.	Green, Blanche - Stapleton, Wells, Frances - Parrott, Phillis		Wills - [Pals] Bates, Carroll - L. N.	J.M.G.
Mc Glamery, Clifford R.	Sep 29, 1976			New Market, Tn	Dec 8, 1902	Mc Glamery, Andrew B.	Glenn, Blanche	Edith		Green, Blanche & Fiance - Stapleton - Marjorie & Kyle - Wells, Frances & Boyd - Parrott, Phillis	Charles [Gal] - Brice [Nd]	Bates, Mary	Hood	J.M.G.
Mc Glamery, Edith L.	Jan 3, 1992	89	J.M.H.	Jeff Co	Apr 20, 1902	Bates, W.T.	Arnd, Angle	Mc Glamery, Clifford [?]		Stapleton, Marjorie - Greene, Blanche - Wells, Frances	Brice			J.M.G.
Mc Glamery, Hood Franklin	Oct 7, 1996	91	J.M.H.	Jeff City	Mar 15, 1905		Glenn, Blanche	Edgar, Kathleen		[Niece] Stapleton, Marjorie & Kyle - Green, Blanche & Fiance & Wells, Frances & Boyd - Parrott, Phillis - Mc Glamery, Mary Ellen	[Nephew] Marjorie, Brice & Shirley	[In-Law] Edgar, Lucille		West View
Mc Gregor, Nellie Young	Apr 13, 1954	82	New Market	Hawkins Co, Tn	Oct 30, 1892					Wilson, Mrs. Wallace	Jones, Harry [Fl]	Knetsburg, Laura - Fields, Mattie - Estes, Mrs. Charles	Young, James - Andrew-Isaac	Wilson, Wallace - Jones, H.C.	
Mc Koon, James Edward	Aug 1, 1991	48	F.S.H.	Syracuse, Ny	Dec 19, 1942	Mc Koon, Francis D.	Munsford, Marina	Navy		Marina-Shannon	Timothy-Daniel	Hodge, Marilyn	Robert-John [1/2] Thomas-Brian	Wills - [Pals] Greer, Dennis - Hodge, Ron - Semno, Mike - Cooper, Ron - Walker, Mike - Solomon, Trank	J.M.G.
Mc Kinney, Royce Gene	Mar 4, 1980		Morristown, Tn	Morristown, Tn	Mar 4, 1980	Mc Kinney, Royce Gene	Smith, Alma June					Dustie Marie		Smith, Cecil Jr. & Kate [G-Parents]	J.M.G.
Mc Neer, Albert Seldon [Rev-Fla]	Apr 8, 1989	72	Jeff Felty	W. Va	Mar 19, 1920	Mc Neer, Eldridge	Fisher, Effie	O' Dell, Julia [Fla]	Army					
Mc Neer, Beatrice Pauline	Apr 30, 1990	78	J.M.H.	Beckley, W. Va	Aug 3, 1911	Bibb, Pearl	Bessie	Mc Neil, George A. Sr. [X]		Mc Neil, Mary Catherine - Stanbro, Linda Mae - Slym, Tress Ann ?	Dennis, Orlo - Ronald Eugene - Knight, Robert - David	Peters, Mary E.	Lawless, Bill	Dennis, Ronald - Mathes, Rex - A. [Pals] Glenna - Ricky-Wood, Oscar - Peters, Larry	Pleasant Ridge Talbott, Tn
Mc Neil, George Alexander	Apr 8, 1987	72	Elizabethton, Tn	Tn	Oct 1, 1914	Mc Neil, William Ray	Campbell, Sarah Elizabeth	Bibb, Pauline			[Step] Knight, Robert A.			Wills - Wood, Carolyn S. - [Pals] Hardin, Roger - Barlow, Jack - Crow, Jerry - Shortley, James - Torless, Gary - Mc Neal, George Jr.	West View
Mc Neil, James Harris	Oct 1, 1994	76	New Market, Tn	Morristown, Tn	May 2, 1918	Mc Neil, William R.	Campbell, Sarah E.	Dennis, Mary Catherine		Spencer, Vickie Lynn - Agnostus, Bernice		Kidwell, Jessie	Howard	Wills	West View
Mc Neil, Junior Dwayne		28d	New Market, Tn	Jeff City	July 28, 197?	Maples, James R.	Mc Neil, Emma Jane							Mc Neil, Richard [G-Father]	Pleasant Grove

Name	Death Date	Age	Place	Birth Location	Birth Date	Father	Mother							Burial
Mc Nish, Richard Earl	Feb 9, 1988	87	B.H.	Jeff Co	Feb 10, 1900	Mc Nish, Edward	Park, Rosann	Div			[1/2] Mc Gill, Emma		Diag.	Pleasant Grove
Mc Pherson, Donald Vaughn	Mar 10, 1997	72	U.T.H.	Cass City, Michigan	Sep 3, 1924	Mc Pherson, Alfred	Jones, Elma	Logan, Gloria May	Marines		Daniel M.	Alfred [Mich]	Willie	Cremated
Medlock, Frances	Nov 11, 1988	88	J.M.H.	Grainger Co.	Jan 7, 1908	Medlock, Charles N.	Morgan, Frances	Div			Carroll, Novella & John E.		Slater	Oakland
Medburg, Ruth Russell	Oct -, 1965	55				Medburg, Jess H.				[1/2] Patterson, Mary Lou [Nd] - Newe, Elizabeth [Chattanooga, Tn]		Husband [Sheldon, Nd] - Russell, Junior - Eddie - Stange, Clyde - Ecco, Bentley		New Market
Melton, Mary Ann	Jul 31, 1997	57		Rogersville, Tn	Oct 1, 1909	Cannon, Frank Riley Sr.	Kennedy, B. Roberta			Kelley, Beth Ann [Calif] - Parrish, Alyssa & Andy [Va]	Pugh, Betty Jo	Frank R. Jr.		Strawberry Plains
Metcalf, Jessie Louise	Sep 27, 1999	72	Jeff City	Sevier Co.	Apr 1, 1927	Hodges, Charles	Newman, Cleo		Metcalf, John Sr. [3]	Watson, Joy Yvonne - Harmer, Kathy Carroll				Mitchell Springs
Metcalf, Johnny Allen	Apr 10, 1996	50	S.M.H.	Turkdge, Tn	Jul 27, 1945	Metcalf, John Sr.	Hodges, Jessie	Walliver, Debbie		Leah	Watson, Joy - Harmer, Cathy	Wayne-Doyle	Willie	Mitchell Springs
Metcalfe, Clark David	May 18, 1990	26	Sevier Co	Grainger Co	Jul 13, 1963	Metcalfe, Johnny	Hodges, Jessie		S		Watson, Joy Evan - Carroll, Kathy	Johnny Jr. - Doyle-Wayne - Proffitt, Eddie - Ruth, Luther		Mc Danicks - Mitchell Springs, Tn
Metcalfe, Johnnie	Jan 29, 1978	55	F.S.H.	Tn	Feb 15, 1922	Metcalfe, John	Moore, Mary		WW 2	John Jr.-Doyle-Wayne-David	Kelly, Billy-Mattie - Spoon, Mrs. - Reach, Alan	Swann, Grace - Dyer, Ruby	Jim	Mc Danicks - Mitchell Springs, Tn
Miles, Anna Lou	Jul 2, 1998	89	J.M.H.	Jeff Co	Jul 18, 1908	Young, James A.	Workman, Cora		Hodges, Jessie			Miles, Joe [3]	Willie	J.M.G.
Miles, Bruce Harold	Jul 23, 1991	72	New Market	Jeff City	Mar 6, 1919	Miles, Jim	Peck, Georgia	Gray, Myrtle [3]	Harold	Morrison, Darlene	Harold	Wars, Pauline-Walker, Ruth	Haskell	Oakland
Miles, Joseph Ashley	Sep 17, 1990	80	J.M.H.	Jeff City	Jul 27, 1910	Miles, Jim	Peck, Georgia	Young, Ann				Walker, Ruth - Wars, Pauline	Bruce-Haskell	J.M.G.
Miles, Myrtle Isbell	Feb 17, 1987	65	J.M.H.	Sevier Co.	Jan 17, 1922	Gray, Henry	Ogle, Sarah		Miles, Bruce H.		Morrison, Darlene	Harold	Avis	Oakland

Name	Date	Age	Place	Birth Date	Birth Place	Father	Mother	Spouse	Children / Relations		Cemetery
Miller, Arlie Amanda	Nov 28, 1984	81	New Castle, Ind.	Feb 18, 1903		Brickson, Bertie	S			Sister - [Pink] Petit, Doyle - Miller, Alex - Crain, Roy - Shelton, Paul - Bates, James	Hopewell
Miller, Clayton William Lloyd	Feb 12, 1987		U.T.H.	Feb 12, 1199		Miller, Clayton Jasper	Sweigo, Shannon		Smith, Gertrude - Anderson, Clara - Bates, Kathleen - Shelton, Nellie - Whitlock, Naomi	William T. - George	Slater - [Pink] Petit, Doyle - Miller, Alex - Crain, Roy - Anderson, Paul - Bates, James	Nances Grove
Miller, Dorthy E.	Jul 1, 1984	35	Morristown, Tn	Jan 14, 1949	Strawberry Plains	Trent, Charles Otto	Bailey, Ollie Maude	Miller, Lee Roy	Charles Leroy	Smith, Carolyn - Patterson, Shirley	David	[Pink] Miller, Alex - Batch - Smith, Roger - Shoun, Ronald - Rogers, Glenn	Strawberry Plains
Miller, Edna	Sep 28, 1989	83	Shenandoah, N.H.	Dec 8, 1905	Jeff Co	Randles, Arthur	Hayden, Anna Belle	Miller, Robert Abe	Bolin, Leota	W. E. Tony	Brother	Mc Crain, Willis	Nances Grove
Miller, Emil [Bill]	Oct 25, 1981	66	J.M.H.	Sep 28, 1915	Jeff Co	Miller, James	Reposes, Maude	Griffey, Mary Virginia	Jimmy		New Market
Miller, Emil Mayfield	Feb 19, 1995	88	Morristown, Tn	Sep 8, 1906	Jeff City	Miller, Dave	White, Maude	Grubb, Ollie Jewell	Gorman, Peggy - Gorman, Shirley	James F.	Shaver, Bobbie	Carl	[Pink] Shaver, Fred-Ed - Miller, Gene - Gibbon-Bill - Rush, Mike	J.M.G.
Miller, Everet Earl	Apr 14, 1981	56	Indiana	Jul 19, 1924		Miller, David	White, Maude		Kerr, Debora	Fielder, Donna	Ronald	Davis, Stella - Shaver, Bobbie	Emmet-Carl	[Pink] Russell, Perry - Cochran, Fred - Massengill, Miller, Donnie - Whitlock, L.M. - Arnold, Paul	J.M.G.
Miller, George A.	Aug 5, 1954	82	New Market	May 22, 1872	Tn	Miller, George Alexander	Gibbon, Jo	Tn	S	Howard, Rosie - Anderson, Clara - Black, Kathleen - Smith, Gertrude - Shelton, Nellie - Whitlock, Naomi	Ben-Enone-S.C.-William-Affie-George Jr.	Ben	Children	Nances Grove
Miller, Mary Lajuana	Dec 21, 1983	9-0-11	Tn	Dec 10, 1954	Tn	Miller, George Alexander	Rusmasor, Rosalie ?	Tn	S		Carol Elaine	George A. Jr. - Andrew Carter	Father	Nances Grove
Miller, Mary Ruth	Nov 29, 1980	55	S.M.H.	Apr 8, 1925	Tn	Thomas, Floyd	Tipton, Della		Forster, Donna	Ronald	Thomas, Helen - Betty - Ellison, Louise	Thomas, Helen	J.M.G.
Miller, Mary Virginia [Doll]	Jan 11, 1993	72	J.M.H.	Jul 10, 1920	Kodak, Tn	Griffey, Sam	Blair, Maude	Miller, Bill [D]	Mc Clain, Ann	James Sr.	Mashburn, Ella	Sam	Son [Pink] - G- Sons & Juroy Shalld]	New Market
Miller, Maude C.	Dec 23, 1995	83	Wyth Co, Va	Apr 9, 1882		Reposes, James Winton	Holbrook, Cordia	Miller, James H.		Davis, Mrs. George - Loy, Mrs. Mack - Taylor, Mrs. Paul	Miller, Mrs. Bill	New Market
Miller, Nathan A.	Jan 1, 1985	70	Miami, Fla.	May 24, 1914		Miller, T.N.	Davis, Laudista	Reed, Alfreda	Emil [Bill]	Tom	Davis, Mrs. George - Loy, Mrs. Mack - Howard, Ann - Margaret - Lee, Cordance	Frank	West View
Miller, Nora Lee	Jun 2, 1997	76	Jeff Crih	Nov 16, 1920	Bluff City, Tn	Hicks, Toy	Morrell, Annie	Miller, Tinsley [D]	Spencer, Bucky - Walker, Betty	Tom	[1/2] Dixon, Dorothy - Spencer, Bucky - Walker, Betty	[1/2] Hicks, Toy Lewis	West View
Miller, Ossie Jewell	Sep 2, 1997	89	Morristown, Tn	Jul 21, 1908	Baine, Tn	Grubb, Rex	Burchell, Maude	Miller, Emil [D]	Gorman, Peggy - Gorman, Shirley	James F.	[1/2] Baine, Emma [D] - Jackson, Reva - Rush, Betty - Rott, Mary - Shaver, J.B.	Plas Jr. [D]	Shirley	J.M.G.
Miller, Robert Abe	Aug 10, 1980	79	Knoxville, Tn	Jun 16, 1901	Sullivan Co, Tn	Miller, P.H.	Buckingham, Martha	Randles, Edna			Morning View - Sullivan Co, Tn

Name	Death Date	Age	Place	County	Birth Date	Father	Mother	Spouse	Military	Survivors / Relatives / Pallbearers	Cemetery
Miller, Ronald Earl	Jul 15, 1988	38	U.T.H.	Jeff City	Oct 18, 1949	Miller, Earl	Thomas, Mary Ruth	Jarnagin, Cecilia Darlene	Army	Stephanie-Amberly; Fielder, Donna E.; Wife - [Pals] Crawford, Jack - Collins, Floyd - Jarnagin, Rick - Wilson, Don - Delk, Glen - Harris, David - Miller, Donnie	J.M.G.
Miller, Vera Scheenla	Nov 7, 1989	97	J.M.H.	Rutledge, Tn	Mar 6, 1892	Dodd, Frank	Kinder, Lucy	Miller, Zack G.		Wallace	New Market
Miller, William T.	Dec 13, 1985	67	Mt. Home, Tn	New Market	Oct 26, 1918	Miller, George A.	Carter, Mora	Mc Nabb, Violet [Div]	WW 2	Shelton, Nelle, Whitlock, Anderson, Clara - Bates, Kathleen; George; Brother - [Pals] Anderson, Paul - Franklin-John - Daniels, James - Cain, Roy - Miller, Alex	Nances Grove
Milligan, Henderson Day	Nov 23, 1985	88	S.M.H.	Sevier Co	Sep 4, 1897	Milligan, Leslie N.	Bates, Sarah	Susan [D]		Frank, L.; [Pals] Green, Gene - Manley, Neal - Hassen, Winter - Armstrong, Jeff - Dalton, Norman - Sharp, Clayton	West View
Milligan, Susan	Nov 14, 1978	80	New Market		Oct 20, 1898			Milligan, Henderson		Milligan, Henderson; Husband	West View
Milligan, Susan Augusta Davis	Nov 14, 1978	80	New Market, Tn	Grainger Co	Oct 20, 1898	Davis, Judson	Maples, Sarah Jane	Milligan, Henderson		Mrs. Eugene Nelle - Mrs. Louise; Marion - Humbard, Marjorie - Milligan, Betty Jo - Cloninger, Myrtle; Shirley, Grace; Husband	West View
Mills, Caroline Elizabeth	Feb 12, 1988	63	Jeff Co	Tn	Aug 21, 1924	Bates, David M.	Simons, Dela	Mills, Oscar		Matthews, Louise [Ark] - Mc Nabb, Edith - Mc Nabb, Louise; Wilson, Bertie - Collins, Pauline - Mills, Flora; Bates, Stan - Frank-Bruce-Claude; Husband	Frances Station
Mills, Claude William Sr.	Jul 19, 1983	61	F.S.H.	Mascot, Tn	Apr 18, 1932	Mills, Oscar	Bates, Callie	Cox, Frances		Fields, Claudia - Large, Debbie - Sherrill, Tonya; Billy Jr - Eddie; Cloninger, Myrtle - Milligan, Betty - Humbard, Marjorie - Murray, Marion; Herbert; Wife - Holly Hills - Knoxville, Tn	Piney
Mills, G.A.	Oct 24, 1950	70	Knoxville, Tn							Brewer F.H. [Knoxville, Tn] Hickman, T.A. - E.H.; Wife	
Mills, James Alfred Monroe	Jul 27, 1982	74	Mascot, Tn	Knox Co	Oct 4, 1907	Mills, John David	Roberts, Edna	Tarbundil, Dorothy		Wanda-Evelyn-Joyce; Johnny-Bobby-Railey, Ed; Adams, Mrs. Jack- Railey, Clyde; Johnny	Trentville - Strawberry Plains
Mills, James Nichole	Jun 5, 1996	13	Jeff City	Jeff City	Jan 10, 1983	Mills, Ronnie L.	Light, Susan			Suzanne; Jason; James, Elizabeth [G-Mother] Childers - [Pals] Morton - Mills, Billy-Joe-Bud- Robert-Brad	East View
Mills, Juanita	Apr 11, 1976	44	Knoxville, Tn	Jeff Co	Oct 28, 1931	Brooks, Arthur Eugene Sr.	Gilbert, Bertie L.	Mills, Curtis		Hoover, Sandra- Susan- Coleman, Mrs. Deborah H.; Wilson, Merle Jr & James - Rockdeck, Mabel & William - Welch, Betty Jo & Clifford; Mc Millan, Mary Ruth & James- Rockdeck, Mabel & William- Welch, Betty Jo & Clifford; Arthur Jr. [Pal] Ralph Donald; Gladys - James E. Morton - [Pals] Curll, Marion - Mills, Billy-Joe-Bud- Robert-Brad- Herbert	Blue Springs
Mills, Manley Edwin	Nov 17, 1972	47	Jeff Co	Tn	Oct 3, 1925	Mills, Oscar [NV]	Norvell, Vivian	Mills, Charlotte		Willson, Elizabeth M.; Miller, Robert E. - Mills, Michael; Raymond [NV]; James, Elizabeth [G-Mother] Childers	Frances Station
Mills, Marie Elizabeth	Oct 2, 1995		Jeff City	Ky	Jul 15, 1924	France, Oscar [NV]				Mills, Herbert [D]; Mills, Michael; Kendall, Curtis - Tri-City F.H. [Benham, Ky]	[Benham, Ky]

Name	Date	Age			Date	Father	Mother	Spouse					Cemetery
Mills, Oscar	May 9, 1978	75	Jeff Co	Knox Co, Tn	Jul 14, 1902	Mills, James	Beal, Ann	Blaine, Callie [D]	Humbard, Marjorie - Milligan, Betty Jo - Clevinger, Myrtle	Roy [D]-Mealey [D]-Herbart-Bill	Williams, Lucy	[Pate] Mills, Dewya-Gregory-Blaine-Edith-House - Milligan, Jimmy	Friends Station
Mills, Samatha Jean	Feb 15, 1979	2m	Talbott, Tn	Hamblen Co	Dec 10, 1978	Morgan, Sammy	Light, Barbara						Strawberry Plains
Mills, Wanda Sue	Oct 26, 1994	47	B.H.	Jeff City	Oct 10, 1947	Massey, Claude H.	Griffin, Nan	Mills, Lloyd A. [DIv]	John-Dewayne-Gary	King, Bobbie	Bill Stew-Larry-Harvey-Kyle-Farris-Jim	Vance, Johnny	Vance - New Market
Mills, Blanche	Oct 13, 1954		E.T.H.	Tn		Rush, Henry	Unk					Minnis, W.E. [Husband]	New Market
Minnis, Ethel B.	Aug 30, 1965	86	J.M.H.	Tn	Jun 10, 1879	Minnis, William B.	Pierce, Augusta	S				Campbell, Helen [Husband]	New Market
Minnis, India M.	Jun 28, 1959		M.C.	Tn		Minnis, W.B.	Pierce, Augusta	Tn		Ethel B.		Minnis, Sam P. [Brother]	New Market
Minnis, Samuel Pierce	Aug 5, 1983	90	F.S.H.	Tn	Mar 5, 1893	Minnis, William B.	Pierce, Augusta		Caldwell, Bess Mae			Minnis, Ethel [Sister] - Minnis, Helen [Sister] - Newman, Ruth [P.L.] - Stremli, S.W [Nic] - Mc-Connell, Andrew [N]	New Market
Minnis, William Edwin	May 9, 1956	85	M.C.	Tn	Aug 10, 1870	Minnis, W.B.	Pierce, Augusta	Tn	Ruth, Blanche [D]	Ethel-India	Sam P.	Ballinger, Mrs. N.G. - Minnis, Mrs. Roy [G-Mother]	New Market
Minton, Phillip Edward	Feb 18, 1980		Vietnam	Knoxville, Tn	Oct 21, 1969	Minton, T.C.		vietnam		Ethel-India	Gerald W.		Oak Ridge Memorial
Minton, Toby H.	Jul 31, 1972		U.T.H.	Tn	Jul 28, 1972	Minton, Roy	Dustin, Debbie					Father	Mt. View
Miser, James Talmadge	Feb 10, 1998	70	B.H.	Sweetville, Tn	Apr 21, 1928	Miser, Robert	Mullins, Sarah	Byers, Daisy			Bruce [D]-Lewis [D]	Hubbard, Jeffrey [Nephew]	W'stview
Mitchell, Charles Arthur	Jul 9, 1966	21	Germany	Tn	Dec 10, 1944	Mitchell, Herbert	Williams, Alice	S	army	[1/2] Amerine, Lucille?	[1/2] Mitchell, James	Father & Stepmother - Johnson, Mrs. Alice [Mother] - Universal Mortuary Inc. [New York]	Holston View
Mitchell, Edith C.	Feb 16, 1994	81	J.M.H.	Jeff City	Dec 11, 1912	Mitchell, Tom	Murdock, Ella Caroline	Mitchell, James William [D]	Bartley, Mary Ruth	Cox, Alice	Doug		Flat Gap
Mitchell, Herbert J.	Jul 23, 1975	76						Lula	[Step] Amerine, Lucille	James	Roy	[Pate] Erroz, Richard - Curt, David - Provitroo, William - Cobb, Mack - Keuster, James	Holston
Mitchell, Hubert Walter	Dec 16, 1975	82	Granger Co., Tn		Feb 25, 1893	Mitchell, Greenbury				Waldrop, Lula M. / Acuff, Lucille - [in Lang Vineyard, Thelma			Richland
Mitchell, Lula Mae	Feb 25, 2000	89	Jeff City	Blaine, Tn	Aug 5, 1910	Davis, Amy		Mitchell, Herbert [D]			H. Jr.		Strawberry Plains
Mitchell, Marie	Sep 1, 1984	84	Knoxville, Tn	Knox Co	Mar 11, 1900	Seymour, Jack	Mitchell, Miranda	S		Ruth [Cousin] - Webb, Wallace - Carr, Clay - Mc-Carl, Charlie - Trent, Tim - Sliburt, Jim - Witt, Clarence			Strawberry Plains Baptist

Name	Date	Age	Place		Birth											
Mitchell, Ona	Oct 30, 1961	75	S.M.H.	Tn	Aug 25, 1886	Vineyard, W.A.	Tn	Murph, Fannie	Tn	Mitchell, W.T.			John-W.T. Jr.- Ted			Richard
Mitchell, Ray W.	Nov 14, 1977	61	B.H.	Tn	Mar 16, 1926	Collins, James		Grover, Rachel		Mitchell, Ray [D]	WW 2	Greer, Rachel	Mike [D]/Dale- Billy	Stallings, Louella	Wife	Mill Springs
Mitchell, Ruth Virginia	Nov 30, 2000	75	Riverside, Ca	Jeff Co	Jul 19, 1925	Foster, Florence		Nora		Mitchell, Ray [D]		Greer, Rachel				Mill Springs
Monday, Andrew Houston	Jun 20, 1964	83	Knox Co	Tn	Oct 12, 1880	Monday, J.B.		Hines, Martha								New Market
Monday, Larry Dale	Apr 20, 2000	48	Jeff City	Knoxville, Tn	Mar 3, 1952	Monday, Grlf Wallace		Brady, Gladys Daniel		Bailey, Jamie	unk	Sarah Jo	James Larry Dale			Strawberry Plains
Monday, Minnie Nora	Mar 17, 1984	95	J.M.H.	Grainger Co	Apr 11, 1898	Phillips, Jim		Bateman, Lizza		Monday, A.H. [D]		Gilbert, Agnes - Garris, Edith	Spencer, Fred- Charlie		Bill	J.M.G.
Moody, Doris Louise	Feb 25, 1999	98	Morristown, Tn	Lynch, Ky	Aug 27, 1930	Smith, John Henry		Love, Miss Cleo		Moody, Wayne [D]					Marshall & Evelyn-Stanley & Sally - [1/2] Lawrence [Fa]	J.M.G.
Moody, Donald, Lee	Jul 24, 1973	45	New Market, Tn	Tn	Aug 13, 1927	Moody, Glenn J.		Kinzdel, Katherine		Arlene T.	43-45	Gregory-Roger- Dean-James			Paul-S.T.	Mill Springs
Moody, Florence	Apr 9, 1983	87	J.M.H.	Grainger Co	Nov 14, 1895	Farrar, Samuel G.		Roach, Sarah E.		Moody, Hugh F. [D]		Gray, Dorsie	Henry	Gray, Dorsie	Tip	Shiloh Grainger Co
Moody, Hattie Leroy	Mar 1, 1997	98	Calhoun, Mo Minn Co, Tn	Hancock Co, Tn	Feb 21, 1899	Ramsey, James H.		Hobbs, Mary Elizabeth		Moody, Laurence H. [D]-Rice, Edward [D]		Davis, Gladys & Ray		Peebles, Lillian & Joe	[Feb-G-G-Sis- See Obit]	J.M.G.
Moody, Henry O'Dell	May 31, 1990	66	J.M.H.	Grainger Co	Mar 20, 1924	Moody, Hugh		Farrar, Florence		Moody, Mamie		Layman, Melissa	Hugh-Darrell	Gray, Dorsie		Shiloh
Moody, Isaac Eugene	Feb 6, 1972	62	New Market, Tn	Tn	Aug 30, 1909	Moody, --		Moody, Mary D.		Ruth J.		Delors - Landon, Louise & Stew-Hodge, Pauline & Wann, Mrs. Burl	Sammy-Dean- Lester-Wayne	Wheatley, Mrs. Earnest - [Slee] Mills, Mrs. Charlie- White, Mrs. Glen	Jernigan, J.L.- Robert	J.M.G.
Moody, Joe Clyde	Jul 21, 1989	68	Ridge View - Rutledge	Jeff Co	Apr 14, 1921	Moody, James Dedrick		Gilmore, Georgia	S					Miller, Null - Mc Bee, Florence	John	Shiloh

Name	Death Date	Age	Place	County	Birth Date	Father		Mother		Spouse	Mil.					Cemetery
Moody, Laurence Horace	Jun 6, 1966	75	New Market, Tn	Grainger Co	Feb 22, 1911	Moody, Horace Clay		Cameron, Harriet		Ramsey, Hattie				Callaway, Jewell	Jim-Horace [J.R.]	Wife - [Pele] Mitchell, Ted - Alley, A.R. - Cochran, James - Mooney, Floyd - Lane, Terry - Young, Walter · J.M.G.
Moody, Lillian Ruth	Nov 9, 1967	81	J.M.H.	Grainger Co	Mar 20, 1916	Jarnigan, Robert L.		Creech, Claudia		Moody, Isaac		Wayne A. [D]- Hilliard, Elsie - Hodge, Pauline- Moody, Delois	Mills, Katherin - White, Kathryn - Whaley, Louise	Robert [D]- Jesse Lee [D]		J.M.G.
Moody, Samuel George	Nov 1, 1969	43	F.S.H.	Tn	Mar 25, 1926	Moody, Hugh F.		Ferrier, Florence		Murry, Irene		Lynn, Kathy	Samuel-Richard	Gray, Mrs.	[Pele] Carr, Frank - Phillips, Walter - Kerr, Herman - Smith, Buford - Helmer, A.J.	New Market
Moody, Stella Irene	Dec 22, 1977	49	J.M.H.		Jun 13, 1928	Murry, Charlie		Mr. Sween, Eliza		W		Kathy	Samuel	Henry	Foster, Lavilla	New Market
Moody, Wayen Allen	Apr 15, 1996	59	U.T.H.	Grainger Co	Aug 9, 1936	Moody, Isaac E.		Jarnigan, Lillian Ruth		Smith, Doris		Chandler, Louise - Hilliard, Elsie - Hodge, Pauline- Chandler, Louise - Moody, Delois	Lester-George- Fain-Sam B.	Wife	Moore, Robert	J.M.G.
Moore, Barbara Sue	Oct 5, 1959	72	Jeff Co	Jeff Co	Oct 5, 1959	Moody, Robert	Tn	Whaley, Grace	Tn	Bailey, Ollie Maude		[Step] Smith, Carolyn	Connor, Gaynell		Moore, Robert	Cremated
Moore, Fred	Apr 30, 1997	72	Jeff City	Jeff Co	Jun 15, 1924	Moody, Robert	Tn	Whaley, Grace	Tn	Unk	Tn	Unk				New Market
Moore, Ira Mae	Oct 24, 1982	83	S.M.H.	Grainger Co	Nov 25, 1898	Jarnigan, Sam		Burchell, Carrie		Moore, John W. [J]		Morgan, Leona - Gunn, Wilma	White, Walter - Collins, Jr. - Moore, Robert-Philip	Charlie-Bob	[Pele] Gunn, Tim - Bill - Collins, Tommy-Gary - Woods, Tom - Langston, Robert- Foster, Howard - Franklin, Larry	West View
Moore, Jamie Lee	Dec 21, 1981	52	S.M.H.	Lee Co, Va	May 13, 1929	Moore, Hubert	Va	Denny, Grace	Va	Moore, Martha Jo		Maples, Deborah - Garrity, Norma - ?- Maples, Tressa - Moore, Jeana	Lenhon, Joe - Richard-Danny		Moore, Ira Mae [Wife]	Indian Ridge
Moore, John Arthur	Apr 24, 1976	88	Knoxville, Tn	Grainger Co	Jan 9, 1888	Moore, Joseph		Tucker, Racheal E.		W		Suite - Gunn, Wilma [Step] Morgan, Leona - Webb, Ann	Robert-Phillip [Step] Collins, Junior-White, Walter	Arnold, Nora - Vineyard, Sallie	Moore, Ira Mae [Wife]	West View
Moore, John W.	Oct 6, 1958	60	Tn	Tn	Jun 3, 1896	Devis, Dave		Thompson, Eliza		W		Ruth [D]-Dorothy [D] - Wilson, Grace - Smith, Caroline- Patterson, Shirley [Step-See Dad]	Woods, Verley K. [D]- Wilson, Jimmy R. [TA]- Trent, David	Barnes, Bertha - Tipton, Zora - Ballinger, Mary - Phipps, Betsy [Miss]		Methodist - New Market
Moore, Mary Sallie [Cal]	Aug 30, 1948		Knoxville, Tn	Tn		Devis, Dave		Thompson, Eliza		W					Cunningham, Willis	West View
Moore, Ollie Maude	Nov 9, 1997	90	Jeff City	Strawberry Plains	Oct 6, 1917	Bailey, Sam		Blacklow, Shine		Moore, Fred [D]- Trent, Otto [D]	Navy	Helms, Connie- Coffey, Vickie	Woods, Verley K. [D]- Wilson, Jimmy R. [TA]- Trent, David	Barnes, Eva - Bowling, Opal - Reagan, Martha - Underwood, Essie	Strawberry Plains
Moore, Phillip Von	Dec 7, 1996	58	S.M.H.	Jeff City	Sep 25, 1938	Moore, John William		Jarnigan, Ira Mae		Moore, Geraldine	Army	Helms, Connie- Coffey, Vickie	Robert	Wife	J.M.G.
Moore, Victor Henderson	Feb 1, 1993	59	New Market	Sevier Co	Aug 18, 1933	Moore, Joe E.		Stevrn, Naomi Ruth		Rickard, Mary Louise	Army	Gerald Lynn- Ronald Dean	Baker, Eva - Bowling, Opal - Chandler, Martha - Underwood, Essie		Wife - [Pele] Jones, Steve-Gary - West, Bill - Rickard, James - Moore, John Jr.- Shirkey, Sam	Hillcrest

Name	Death Date	Age	Place of Death	Birthplace	Birth Date	Father	Mother	Spouse	Survivors / Notes	Cemetery
Moore, Wayne Perry	Oct 4, 1992	83	Lansing, Mich.		Jun 1, 1929	Moore, Ellsworth	Martin, Ethel	Hopson, Martha	Leff??, Teresa [Mich]- Michelle?- Hayes, Pamela [Ohio]- Herscher, J. Diane [Mich]- [Step] Carroll, Nancy & Charles- Laquinn, Connie & Raymond; Wayne E. [Mich]- Robert; Moore, Robert	Sunderland
Moore, William Robert	Jan 13, 1955		S.M.H.		Jan 11, 1955	Moore, Robert		Tn		New Market
Moore, Wilma Juanita	Apr 19, 1998	75	Jeff Co.	Jeff Co	May 26, 1922	Swanner, John	Whaley, Grace	Tn	Moore, Paul W.	East View
Moreland, Harold E.	Dec 20, 1971	68	J.M.H.	Knox Co. Tn	Apr 15, 1909	Moreland, Edward	Chrisman, Minnie	Bess (WW 2)	Holloway, Vicky & Gary [Step]; Johnson, Betty; Sally- King, Gladys; Thelan, Mrs. Frank; Robert-Lee [Oh]	West View
Morgan, Angel	Apr 25, 1996	88	F.S.H.	Hancock Co. Tn	Nov 13, 1927	Morgan, Thomas	Livesay, Rachel	S	Sharp, Helen- Linsey, Delay; Angel [Ol]- Marphite [Ol]; Luther-Clifford-George; Brother	Piedmont
Morgan, Clifford Kyle	Jun 11, 2000	64	Dandridge, Tn	Sneedville, Tn	Sep 15, 1935	Morgan, T.M.	Livesay, Rachel	Dean & Brenda	Thelbert-Bill-Clarence-Lewis-Buford; Luther-George	Cremated
Morgan, Clifford Otis	Mar 19, 1970	53	V.A. Mt. Home	Tn	Mar 3, 1917	Morgan, Eli	Garliede	W	Elmore, Pearl- O' Dell, Florence; Morgan, William	New Market
Morgan, Earl Fain	Nov 25, 1995	59	Rutledge, Tn	Rutledge, Tn	Aug 15, 1937	Moran, Henry	Phillips, Pearl		Wright, Carolyn; Jones, Lena Mae; Doug	Shiloh
Morgan, Ethel	Oct 23, 1972	78	J.M.H.					unk	Chambers, Lisa- Morgan, Carol-Rita; Raylord-Vaughan	Shiloh
Morgan, Fred James	Nov 9, 1990	63	F.S.H.	Rutledge, Tn	Feb 5, 1927	Morgan, James W.	Turner, Ethel	WW 2	Ronald; Light, Novella; Spoone, Paul	Shiloh
Morgan, George	Jan 25, 1978		Knoxville, Tn						Morgan, James; Robert-Wayne-Fred; Turner, Dewey	Granger Co.
Morgan, Hazel Alice	May 16, 1989	72	Morristown, Tn	Granger Co	Jan 7, 1918	Byrd, James L.	Phillips, Hattie	Morgan, W.H. Sr. [Ol]	Taylor, Thelma & Dale- Williams, Sarah & Colbert; W.H. Jr-Donald; Hurst, Lucille; Lester	McClanahan - Rutledge, Tn
Morgan, Hugh	Jan 12, 1971	54	Talbott, Tn			Morgan, Jim			Hurst, Lucille; Robert-Wayne	
Morgan, James Wesley	Jan 24, 1975	83	Talbott, Tn	Tn	Aug 2, 1890	Morgan, Wesley	Martha		Hurst, Lucille [Ni]- Light, Novella [Pa]; Robert-Fred-Wayne; Turner, Dewey; [Pals] Mayes, H.P. Jr.- David-Samuel- Scarlett, Pete- Buchanan, Randy- Love, Tommy	Shiloh
Morgan, John E.	Sep 2, 1956	56	E.S.H.	Ball Co. Ky	Jan 29, 1900	Morgan, J.P.	Parton, Susan	Ky	Morgan, Lora Smith	West View
Morgan, John Olt	May 10, 1989	70	Rutledge, Tn	Rutledge, Tn	Sep 28, 1918	Morgan, Claude	Spoone, Bessie Stratton		Greenlee, Nadine; Willis	Central Point - Rutledge, Tn
Morgan, Lelia Mae	Feb 16, 1980	75	Knoxville, Tn	Tn	Mar 8, 1904	Epps, Thomas	Carver, Della		Eppe, Hubert- Barnett, Pauline	Central Point - Rutledge, Tn
Morgan, Lillie Gertrude	Oct 12, 1966	79	Jeff City	Tn	Dec 28, 1895	Mays, Johnny	Long, Maggie	O' Dell, Florence - Elmore, Pearl	Morgan, Eli; Clarence [Ind.]- Bill-Lewis-Clifford-Thelbert; Byrd, Kate - Morgan, Bulah; Husband	New Market

Name	Date	Age	Place	Loc.	Date								Husband	Cremated
Morgan, Lois Helen	May 4, 1995	57	Jeff City	Pa	Dec 2, 1937	Unk		Morgan, Clifford K.					Turner-Jim-Elmer	New Market
Morgan, Lucille Shelby	Nov 1, 1984	38	B.H.	Tn	Feb 27, 1926	Betts, Mack H.	Owens, Hattie	Morgan, Clifford O.	Carolyn			Dixon, Homer		New Market
Morgan, Minnie Marie	Nov 12, 1988	80	Grainger Co		Mar 9, 1908	Dixon, Edward		Begenger, Elmer [D]	Begenger, Wanda Sue			[Pals] Scarlet, Pete - Carlham, Sam - Bettis, Norris - Myers, Stan - Charlie Jr. -	Daug	J.M.G.
Morgan, Robert Hodge	Jul 16, 1982	69	J.M.H.		Jul 25, 1912	Morgan, Jim	Turner, Ethel	Mayes, Mary				Willie - Byrd, Lester & Pauline [Judge Parents] - [Pals] Byrd, Jimmy - Dale, Dwayne - Wynn, Scott - Morgan, Dan-Randy-Daniel, Jeff Shirley, Carol [Legal Guardians] - Mitchell, Gregory J. [Exe.]	Daug	Central Point
Morgan, Sarah Nadine	Jan 23, 2000	78	Rutledge, Tn	Grainger Co	Jun 21, 1921	Greenlee, Ien	Nelson, Betty	Morgan, John O. [D]					J.C. - Howard - [In-Law] Byrd, Tish-Ron-Doug-Mike	
Morgan, Roy Edward	Nov 4, 1995	56	Rutledge, Tn	Grainger Co	Feb 9, 1940	Morgan, William Bruce	Cameron, Lillie	Byrd, Judy Ann				Daniel, Cora Mae		J.M.G.
Morgan, William A.	Feb 18, 1979	54	Knoxville, Tn	Jeff Co	Oct 4, 1924	Morgan, Eli	Mays, --		Grainger Co	Beaulah				New Market
Morgan, Willie Herbert	May 19, 1998	75	Morristown, Tn	Grainger Co	Sep 23, 1912	Morgan, Joe H.		Satterfield, Thursie	Byrd, Hazel Alice	Taylor, Thelma & Dale - Williams, Sarah & Colbert, Shelton, Shirley & Ray	W.H. Jr.-Donald	Walker, Mossie	James H.	Mc Daniel - Rutledge, Tn
Morgan, Willie Mae	May 28, 1987	80	Jacksonville, Ill	Tn	May 9, 1907	Bateman, Marion	James, Carrie	Morgan, Joe [D]		Bowman, Dixie	James		Bateman, Joyce O. & Clarence E. - Morgan, James E. [Springfield, Ill]	West View
Morrison, Michael Stacy	May 7, 1988	19	New Market	Hamblen Co	Oct 30, 1969	Morrison, Jack	Mills, Darlene	S		Bowman, Dixie			Parents	Oakland
Morrow, Finley David	Sep 14, 1995	87	B.H.	Murphy, Nc	May 31, 1909	Morrow, G.W.	Mc William, Alice	Mc Clain, Edith Anna Belle		Gaut, Ella & Charles E.	Finley D. Jr. [N] - Robert-Goldie - Billy-Marvin - Eugene [D] - Gracly [D]	Hunt, Lydia [M] - Dewane, Mollie [Alesto]	Willie	West View
Mozen, Lula	1979	72	Hillcrest N.H.	Grainger Co	1907	Roach, Ben	Mapton, Beatrice			Gaut, Ella D.		Stansberry, Mrs. Lilburn R. - Calhoun, Mrs. Fred		Strawberry Plains
Mozen, Lula	Oct 30, 1979	72	Jeff City	Packard, Ky	Mar 15, 1907	Smith, Sherman	Mapton, Beatrice	Mozen, Albert [D]				Stansberr, Ellie - Dalton, Thelma	Curtis	Strawberry Plains
Mullins, Bertha	Dec 13, 1983	93	Jeff City	Packard, Ky	May 8, 1900		Anna Mee [Unk]	Mullins, W.M. [D]						West View
Mullins, Delores Deanna [Granny Dee]	Nov 15, 1988	44	New Market	Deer Lodge, Morgan Co	Jul 11, 1944	Fowler, Charlie Edgar	Scott, Ella	Mullins, William K.				Brown, Alice - Bennetta	Luther-Tom Leon-Bud	Husband - [Pals] Thompson, Sam - Mullins, Bud - Dugan, Jeff - Fowler, Dan-Rich - Jones, David - Hill, John L. - Satterfield, Michelle	J.M.G.

Name	Death Date	Age	Place of Death	Place of Birth	Birth Date	Father	Mother	Spouse	Family / Relatives	Cemetery
Mullins, Shelton [Don]	Oct 25, 1999	74	Morristown, Tn	Hejra, Va	Feb 8, 1925	Mullins, Silas	Potter, Chrissie	Kyle, Ruby Jane	WW 2	J.M.G.
Munsey, Claude	Nov 8, 1982	69	S.M.H.	Claiborne Co.	May 18, 1913	Munsey, Richie	Griffin, Nan		King, Bobbie - Savage, Shirley - Vance, Wanda / [Pals] Stevens, Michael - Munsey, Michale - Ven - Collins, Buddy - Vance, Gary - Dennis / Greg & Pam [Pal] / Rawlff, Naomi [Ch] - Counts, Gleorbia [Ch] / Marvin [Ch]	New Market
Munsey, Donnie Ray	May 25, 1997	43	Morristown, Tn	New Market		Munsey, Claude H.	Griffin, Nan	Div		New Market
Munsey, Hayley Michelle	Jun 28, 1997	1hr	Knoxville, Tn	Knoxville, Tn	Jun 28, 1997	Munsey, Jackson Claude	Jones, Tonya Michelle		Jones, Larry & Vivanna - Munsey, Peggy - Munsey, Ferris [G-Parents]	Oakland
Munsey, Nan G.	Jan 8, 1991	68	LaFollette, Tn	Tazewell, Tn	Jul 24, 1922	Griffin, Earnie	West, Effie	Munsey, Claude H. Sr.	[In-Law] Munsey, Thelma / Thelma - [Pals] Vance, John - Munsey, Roger - Bean - Vance, Peggy - Richer, James - Bell, Albert	New Market
Munsey, Steve Randall [M]	Dec 1, 1996	37	New Market	Charleston, W. Va	May 31, 1959	Munsey, Claude H.	Griffin, Nan	Ballinger, Connie	Gwen K. / Steve Randall Jr., Joshua / 1 / 2 / Willie	New Market
Murat, Rene [M]	Feb 9, 1992	34	Jeff Co	Sevier Co	Nov 20, 1927	Murat, Armand G.	Mary	S	S / Murat, Armand G. [S. Bend, Ind.]	New Market
Muray, Ollie B.	Mar 18, 1997	74	J.M.H.	Reliance - Polk Co	Mar 11, 1923	Davenport, Bess	Hall, Ida	Murray, Isaac [D]	James - Vic - Benny - Anna [W] - Stranph, Savannah / James - Vic - Benny - Eddie / Wiseman, Anna Mae - Goforth, Easter Ruth / Warren - Ed - Vance	New Market
Murphy, Aileen Elizabeth	Sep 21, 1983	63	Dandridge, Tn	Dandridge, Tn	Dec 9, 1929	Patterson, John	Loveday, Ada	Murphy, Jake	Murphy, Kathleen - Smith, Bonnie - Murray, Ruth - Kathleen / Ray - [Step] Frank / Kyle - Ray / Sibly, Minnie - Wells, Ruth - Daltis, Lucile - Scarlett, Wanda	Deep Springs
Murr, Ronnie Lee	Sep 6, 1978	75	Morristown, Tn		Mar 15, 1903	Russell, -	Russell, —	Murr, J.W. [D]	Griffin, Deborah - Wheatley, Mary & George / Taylor, Mary / Carl Dean / Wheatley, Mary - Russell	New Market
Murr, Harold Leon	Jul 31, 1976	36	B.H.	New Castle, Ind.	Jan 7, 1946	Murr, Oscar	Plitts, Pauline	Flenioes, Marie	Jim / Bonnie [Step-G-Mother]	Buffalo Baptist
Murray, Charles T. [Bill]	Oct 27, 1981	30	New Market	Tn	May 3, 1931	Murray, Charlie (Tn)	Mc Swain, Eliza (Tn)		Irene - Millis, Gladys - Ghootoe, Juanita - Foster, Lorrita / Murray, Mrs. Eliza	New Market
Murray, Charlie	Jul 21, 1953	69	New Market	Tn		Murray, Mark (Tn)	Cross, Nancy (Tn)			New Market
Murray, Eliza Savannah	Aug 20, 1999	96	Asheville, Nc		Apr 1, 1903	Mc Swain, John Franklin	Guinn, Nancy	Murray, Charlie	Mills, Gladys - Foster, Lorrita [2-D] / [3-D] / Eliza [Mother] / Murray, Mrs. Eliza	New Market
Murray, Fred Daniel	May 13, 1990	71	J.M.H.	New Market	Jul 17, 1918	Murray, Andy	Mc Swain, Dora	Kerr, Mamie	Kerr, Ronnie - Murray, Bill - Tom / Willie [Pals] Franklin, Frank - Shaffer, Buford - Oakes, Jack - Oakes, Elmer	New Market

Name	Date	Age	Place	Location	Date 2								Burial
Murray, Harley	May 24, 1986	80	J.M.H.	Jeff Co	Feb 14, 1906	Murray, Martin	Cross, Mercy	Smith, Lena Mae [D]			[Pat] Murray, Robert-Ralph - George - Miller - E.L. - Phillips, Dianne- Stalans, Buck		New Market
Murray, Hood H.	Nov 1, 1995	61	New Market	New Market	Jul 18, 1935	Murray, Harley	Smith, Lena	Mc Campbell, Juanita [D]	Tolliver, Robin - Jones, Ada Sue	Looy	Bud Edd- Junior-Doug	Wills	New Market
Murray, Isaac Martin	Mar 30, 1981	56	New Market	New Market	Nov 30, 1924	Murray, Charlie	Davenport, Ollie						New Market
Murray, Jackie Elmer	May 7, 1957		Jeff Co	Jeff Co	May 6, 1957	Murray, Elmer	Howell, Lorene		Tn			Murray, Elmer	Francis Station
Murray, Jim Jr.	Jan 25, 1990	0	Morristown, Tn	Morristown, Tn	Jan 25, 1990	Murray, James Allen	France, Christine	Tn					New Market
Murray, John F.	Oct 19, 1945		Germany	New Market, Tn	Dec 24, 1920	Murray, Charley	Newport, Tn	Nc	Army		Gladys-Irene-Juanita-Loni	Father	Francis Station
Murray, Lena Mae	Apr 9, 1983	79	Morristown, Tn	White Pine, Tn	Nov 26, 1903	Smith, Steve	Reed, Mary Frances	Murray, William Harley	Leonard, Hazel - Mc Campbell, Lois - Campbell, Leslie - Whitaker, Bonnie	Edd-Elmer-Hood-Junior-Douglas	Baker, Bessie - Fox, Mary	[Pat] Murray, Robert - Elmore, Billy - Miller, F.L. - Schaffer, Troy - Phillips, Dennis - Howell, Christine - Tom - [Pat] Kerr, Brent-Bryan-...	New Market
Murray, Minnie N.	Apr 17, 1995	78	J.M.H.	Jeff City	May 26, 1916	Kerr, Adrew	Oulsenberry, Lonie	Murray, Fred [D]		Kerr, Ronald - Murray, Bill-Tom	Greenlee, Dora	New Market
Murray, Ricky Lynn	Dec 5, 1975	19	S.M.H.	Tn	Sep 22, 1956		Murray, Juanita	S		Greenlee, Wesley - [Step-father] - Murray, Elbut [D-Mother]	Greenlee, David	Rocky Valley
Murray, Willis James	Nov 27, 1998	67	J.M.H.	New Market	Jul 19, 1931	Murray, Buford	Beck, Etta	Dix	Nancy [Fin] - Hooks, Pat	Purkey, Dorothy - Franklin, Reene - Patterson, Shirley	Arvin-Ralph-George-Robert	Sunderland
Massar, Howard H.	Jul 28, 1997	80	Talbott, Tn	Talbott, Tn	Jun 10, 1917	Massar, John W.	Treece, Maggie	Shelton, Lenoir	Loper, Stephanie Ann	Willis Jr.	Greenlee, George-Robert	Ft. Lauderdale Memorial - Fla
Myers, Carolyn	Jan 2, 1986	67	J.M.H.	Idaho	Nov 15, 1921	Miller, Earl Martin	Farrow, Laura	Mullins, Lewis M.	Mullins, B.U.	Stephen Howard		Daug. - Fairchild - F.H. [P], Lauderdale, Fla]	Flat Gap
Myers, Doxie Iona Whaley	May 9, 1983	78	J.M.H.	Idaho	May 6, 1905	Lamar, Samuel	Whaley, Myrtle E. - Simms	Myers, George			Lockhart, Clara - Cochran, Elsie - Taddington, Leslie - Baker, Opal	[Pat] Cochran, Pat-Ronnie-Tim - Grout, Mark - Brooks, Joe-David	Flat Gap
Myers, George Jacob	Dec 23, 1976	75		Pa	Feb 6, 1901	Murray, Buford		Whaley, Doxie	Wheeler, Lillian [Md] Telmanoskie, Nadine	Robert [Pat]- Kenneth [Md]- Frank [Md]	Harvey	[Pat] Cochran, Roger - Wicks, David - Lockhart, Jim - Baker, Danny - Stalls, Bert - Kenefit, Lee ?	Flat Gap
Myers, John L.	May 18, 1969	70	Knoxville, Tn		Jun 6, 1916							Pitts, Jennie - Smith, Mollie	
Myers, Mabel L.	Apr 1, 1988	70	S.M.H.	Ducktown, Tn	May 7, 1917	Hughes, John G.	Sandlin, Minnie	Myers, Craton Jr.	Connor, Kay	Hughes, Beckwith - Huffaker, Billie	B.T.	Husband - [Pat] Kerner, Eugene - A.J. - Huffaker, Mike-Ray - Dugan, Paul	J.M.G.

Name	Date	Age	Place	County	Birth Date	Father	Mother			Relations	Relations	Cemetery
Myers, Margaret (Elizabeth)	Dec 4, 1982	94	Jeff City	Jeff Co	Jun 26, 1888	Mc Crary, Joseph N.	Nos, Eve Kate				Son - (Pele) Wilder, Bacon - Campbell, Bud - Glenn - Gipson - Gentry, J.C. -	J.M.G.
Myers, Richard Crowson	Aug 16, 1989	70	Jeff City	Sevier Co	Nov 2, 1918	Myers, Luther	Crowson, Susan	Greene, Frances [D]		Carr, Lillie & John - Golden, Nell [W] - Flynn, Zora [W]	Myers, Carl - Myers, Randy - Collie, Daniel - David Larry	Mt. View
Myers, William Frost	Feb 8, 1981	85	Collin Co, Ga	Greene Co, Tn	Oct 6, 1895	Myers, John	Day, Ellen	Mc Crary, Margaret	WW 1	Collins, Lois [Nis]	Charles [Kv]	J.M.G.
Myratt, Alice	Nov 8, 1966	78	Knox Co	Tn	Oct 1, 1888	Myratt, Sam [D]	Senter, Fanny	Myratt, Sam [D]		Jackson, Lue - Ella - Myratt, Ruby	Ernest-Eugene-Thurman-Carl - Birk, Ada	Bethlehem
Myratt, Annie	May 19, 1959	80	Jeff Co	Tn	Nov -, 1877	Linkus, John	Simpson, Julia			Lewis, Patsy - Taylor, Tewanda	Brewer, Mary [Neice]	Friends Station
Myratt, Carl Spencer [Black]	Jun 23, 1989	75	New Market	Knox Co, Tn	Oct 8, 1913	Myratt, Samule	Alice	Ruby B.	WW 2	Cameron, Mrs. William L.	Guynn, Luwella	Younge Memorials
Nance, Alice Suthridge	May 5, 1957	63	Blaine, Tn	Union Co, Tn	Nov 30, 1903		Norris, Margarete	Nance, Glenn			Burnett, Mrs. Jack - Botin, Mrs. Roy	Nance - Blaine, Tn
Nance, Bert C.	Jul 9, 1958	73	M.C.	Tn	Dec 14, 1874	Nance, Jeff			Tn		Loy, Georgia	Nance Farm
Nance, Bertha	May 23, 1955	72	Knoxville, Tn	Tn	May 6, 1883	Norris, James	Crippen, Betty		Tn		Wilson-Robert-Lon Wilson-Lon-Robert	Suthridge, Claude - Family
Nance, Beulah Bessie	Oct 9, 1957	84	S.M.H.	Union Co	Sep 28, 1913	Kidwell, Rector	Loy, Vandslee	Nance, Rupert T. [D]		Jerry [D]	Frazier, Adat - Goln, Edna	Nance Family
Nance, Charles Wesley	Jan -, 1957	65	Blaine, Tn	Tn	Jul 1, 1901	Nance, L.W.	Murph, Nettie	S		Shipe, Mrs. Sanford - Hammond, Mrs. Donald	Hammond, Carolyn & Charles [Niece & Nephew] - Glen	Hammond
Nance, Cora Jane	Sep 19, 1957	85	Tn	Tn	Sep 18, 1882	Anderson, John William	Rodgers, Allie	Nance, Hugh M.			Korsdie, Irene - Floyd-Austin - Daniel, Merle [Neice]	Nances Grove
Nance, Dan	Mar 12, 1952	69	New Market	Tn	Sep 12, 1882	Nance, Newton	Vineyard, Selby		Tn		Albert-T.W.-Clarence - Nance, Laura [Wife]	Nances Grove
Nance, George Luther	May 5, 1954	94	J.M.H.	Tn	Jan 7, 1870	Nance, Hamilton	Galleher, Sara	Beulah			Atkins, Mrs. Ed [Jennie M. - Sister]	West View
Nance, Glen Marph	Jan 14, 1970				Mar 8, 1897		W			Shipe, Mrs. Sanford - Hammond, Mrs. Don	Glen	Nances
Nance, Herbert L.	Aug 27, 1957	55	New Market	Tn	May 9, 1902	Nance, Robert	Loy, Mattie			Elizabeth Ann	Zickle, Mrs. Elmer - Colle, Mrs. John - Nance, Gertrude	New Market
Nance, Jerry Joe	Nov 17, 1958	29	Knoxville, Tn	Tn	Aug 13, 1999	Nance, Robert	Kidwell, Beluh	S	Tn		Kidwell, Beluh	Nances
Nance, Michael Brian	Aug 24, 1997	31	J.M.H.	Jeff City	May 25, 1960	Nance, James Harold	Smith, Georgia Ruth	S			[In-Law] Nance, Lisa - Nance, Lun & Helen - Smith, Brody - Edna [Gr-Parents]	Nance Family

Name	Death Date	Age	Place A	Place B	Birth Date	Father	Mother	Spouse	Notes	Relatives					Cemetery
Nance, Mildred Cleo	Feb 9, 1993	72	Jeff City	Rutledge, Tn	Jun 22d, 192_	Nance, Mac	Spoon, Martha		S			Williams, Lucille - Foster, Pauline - Puckett, Ruth [D]	Roy [D]	Milsap, Teresa [Niece] - [Pals] Reagan, Leon - Morgan, Leon - Spoon, Leon - Jack - Whatley, Leon - Nance, Don - Whitt, Henry	Central Point
Nance, Quincy Rimona [Black]	Sep 9, 1982		Morristown, Tn		Sep 9, 1982	Nance, Richard Henderson	Dirt, Nellie							Sister	West View
Nance, Raymond R. [Black]	Jun 26, 1982	74	Morristown, Tn	Jeff City	Jul 1, 1917	Vineyard, Sterling	Dirt, Nellie	Mary Ella [DM]		Harris, Dorothy - Simon, Emma J. - Mitchell, Polly C. - Frison, Peggy A.	Jerry Joe	Fritts, Rosetta - Jordan, Ethel - Pitts, Mary Ellen - Keese, Nadine	Lon-Wilson	Whitlock, S.H. [Pals] Jenness, Y.T. - Roberts, H.B. - Anderson, Paul-Willis-Franklin - Shelton	Nances Grove
Nance, Robert T. [Rubel]	Jan 13, 1983	49	F.S.H.	Tn	Aug 4, 1913	Nance, Bert	Norris, Bertha	W		Kidwell, Beulah		Rumee, Dorothy - Casksey, Betty - Smith, Cecile - [1/2] Johnson, Ann [Mich]	Lon	Nances	Nances
Nance, Susie	May 10, 1949	96	Jeff City	Tn	Jun 10, 1852	Nance, Bert	Unk	W						Nances	Nances
Nance, Velma	Jun 20, 1985	67	J.M.H.	Tn	Oct 6, 1917	Smith, Preston	Stansberry, Flora	Nance, Wilson	Army	Stansberry, Flora		Nance, Wilson	Vinyard	Nances	Nances
Nance, Wilson James	May 20, 1995	66	V.A.-Mt. Home	New Market	Jul 2, 1906	Nance, Bert C.	Norris, Bertha	Smith, Velma	Army	Smith, Velma			Lon	Nance, Harold [Nephew]	Nances
Nash, Cora E.	Sep 5, 1983	83	J.M.H.	Grainger Co.	Feb 1, 1900	Roach, Wesley		W				Miles, Pearl	Raymond-Troy-Johnny	Miles, Pearl	West View
Nash, John	Oct 29, 1997	76	J.M.H.	Strawberry Plains	Apr 11, 1921	Nash, Houston	Villstone, Mae			Lamarco, Marjorie		Megaw, Peggy & Bill [Ch]	Raymond-Troy-Johnny	Purkey, Sherry	J.M.G.
Nash, Johnny Ray	Apr 11, 1990	38	J.M.H.	Jeff City	Feb 20, 1952	Nash, Jonny	Alltop, Genevieve	Barnard, Liza	Vietnam			Renee Dawn	Fred Ray	Purkey, Sherry - Tim	Pleasant Grove
Nash, Lorraine Ethel	Jun 28, 2000	66	J.M.H.	Cliffield, Va.	Jul 4, 1931	Archer, Clifford	Lawson, Lucy Irene Cochran	Nash, Johnny - Hoskins, Will Ed [D]		See Obit		Hoskins, Mack [D]	Payne, Alma	Troy-John	Blue Springs
Nash, Mary Faye	May 28, 1990	63	Mascot, Tn	Mascot, Tn	Sep 20, 1926	Russell, Clay	Rivers, Ada	Nash, Raymond [D]		Nash, Raymond [D]				Howard	West View
Nash, Myrtie Ann	Nov 27, 1977	81	B.H.	Grainger Co.	Oct 27, 1896	Nash, Stoke	Smith, Josephine			Nash, Hugh C. [D]		Clayton, Mrs. Bell [Nc] - [In-Law] Greenlee, Louise - Mary Ann		Howard	New Blackwell
Nash, Raymond Franklin	Feb 2, 1990	66	S.M.H.	Jeff City	Apr 19, 1921	Nash, Stoke	Roach, Cora	Russell, Mary F.	WW 2				Miles, Pearly	Troy-John	West View
Nash, Troy Sr.	Apr 10, 1991	68	Jeff City	Jeff City	Feb 17, 1923	Nash, Stoke	Roach, Cora	Johnson, Penny		Warren, Carolyn - Coffee, Diane - Whitaker, Lois - Odom, Linda	Frank-Stokely	Miles, John	John	Willie	West View

Name	Death Date	Age	Place of Death	Residence	Birth Date	Father	Mother	Spouse / Status	War	Cemetery
Neal, Troy W. Jr. [Cricket]	Nov 22, 1989	29	V.A. Mt. Home	Grainger Co	Jul 15, 1966	Neal, Troy	Johnson, Pansy			West View
Neal, Bertha Zula	Nov 25, 1976	73	J.M.H.	Jeff City	Sep 11, 1902	Bull, George	Ladkins, Mary	W		Nances Grove
Neal, Cecil P.	Oct 30, 1982	71	New Market	New Market	Dec 4, 1910	Neal, Frank	Tuggins, Flora	Div	WW 2	New Market
Neal, Earl Andrew	Oct 25, 1957	73	M.C.	Jeff Co	Aug 24, 1957	Neal, Ralph A.	Northern, Shirley			Nances Grove
Neal, Flora	Sep 17, 1982	75	New Market, Tn	Tn	Aug 13, 1887	Neal, Frank				New Market
Neal, Frank	Sep 13, 1971	84	Tn	Tn	Jun 1, 1887	Neal, Thomas	Green, Nannie	W		New Market
Neal, George W.	Sep 3, 1980	55	New Market, Tn	New Market, Tn	Aug 21, 1925	Neal, Raymond	Bull, Bertha	Div	WW 2	Nances Grove
Neal, James	Dec 27, 1983	72	U.T.H.	Tn	Jan 17, 1891	Neal, Thomas	Green, Nannie	WW 1		West View
Neal, Mack A.	Sept 22, 196_	72	Talbott, Tn	Tn	Jul 29, 1894	Neal, Thomas	Green, Nannie			New Market
Neal, Raymond	Jan 18, 1971	77	E.S.H.	Jeff Co	May 3, 1906	Neal, William	Green, Nancy			Nances Grove
Nelson, Addie Bell	Aug 14, 1969	64	Jeff Co	Tn	Jul 23, 1881	Neal, Thomas	Bradshaw, Rosa			Nances Grove
Nelson, Mary Kathryn	May 8, 2000	88	Jeff City	Tn	Mar 1, 1928	Jones, Thomas	Bailey, Sara			Mill Springs
Nelson, Robert Lee	Apr 20, 1988	72	J.M.H.	Jeff City	Apr 17, 1922	Peck, George	Moore, Willie		WW 2	J.M.G.
Nelson, Bertha M.	Mar 23, 1976	66	J.M.H.	Kansas	Sep 24, 1908	Nelson, Francis D.	Elmore, Blanche			Cremated
Newman, Buford	Apr 14, 1973	67		New Market	Dec 19, 1898	Elmore, Fred	Withrow, Lula			Friends Station
Newman, Charlene M.	Apr 30, 1983	39	F.S.H.	Rutledge, Tn	Jan 22, 1944	Beckham, Otis	Graves, Fannie	Donna		Church
Newman, Ethel C.	Jul 22, 1978	87	Johnson City, Tn			Newman, Curtis				J.M.G.
Newman, James Eddie	Dec 13, 1994	60	Plantation, Florida	Strawberry Plains	Sep 9, 1934	Hodgin, Owenna S.	Luttrell, Helen	Black, Shella - Sweed, Tina [Fla]		New Market
Newman, James Lee	Jul 13, 1966	74	Rutledge, Tn	Rutledge, Tn	Mar 19, 1892	Newman, John	Nellie Mae	Norma - (G) Newman, Dona		East View
Newman, John J.	Nov 25, 1994	88	Jeff City	White Pine, Tn	Apr 20, 1906	Newman, Luther	Sellers, Luzille	Watkins, Kathleen - Nichols, Dorothy		New Market
Newman, Mary Lucille	Feb 18, 1998	86	Jeff City	Jeff City	Jun 11, 1911	Sellers, Charlie	Newman, Luther	Newman, John J. [D] Watkins, Kathleen - Nichols, Dorothy		Mt. View

Name	Date	Age	Place	Place	Date	Father	Mother					Cemetery
Newman, Michelle Ray	Sep 21, 1973	4		J.M.H.	Tn	Jan 30, 1989	Newman, Johnny Ray	Murray, Sybil		Norma - Bailey, Mary & Larry	Father - Murray, Ike [G-Father] - Murray, Eliza [G-G-Mothers]	New Market
Newman, Nellie Mae	Nov 27, 1976	74	U.T.H.	Tn	Oct 4, 1902	Byrd, John	Langdon, Leona	W		Frank	Kenneth [Jr6]-Luther-Frank	West View
Newman, Ralph Harold	Apr 14, 1999	67	S.M.H.	Hamblen Co., Tn	Feb 23, 1932	Newman, George	Reese, Dorothy	Army	Wayne & Cindy [Ch]-Rick & Gail [Ch]-Steve [Ch]	Howard [D]-Bill [Ind]		J.M.G.
Newman, Samuel Aaron	Jul 25, 1999	79		Jeff Co.	Sep -, 1889		W	Army	Shirley -[Step] Owens, Irene - Cameron, Mary - Davis, S.W.	[Step] Davis, S.W.	Newman, Johnny [Son]	New Market
Newman, T. Taylor Roscoe	Apr 5, 1965	99	New Market	Tn	Jun 26, 1865	Newman, Luther	Newman, Sally [D]	Army			Doug	New Market
Newman, William Curtis	Nov 15, 1959	74	New Market	Tn	Nov 17, 1881	Newman, R.B.	Green, Melissa	Tn		Hubbard, Alberta	William Joseph	Newman, Ethel [Wife]	New Market
Nicely, Juanita	Jan 9, 1998	73	Straw Plains	Powell, Tn	Apr 14, 1924	Smith, Roy C.	Minton, Lena		Nicely, Elmer	Pollard, Shelia & Jack	Tony	Lloyd	Toy-Lynn	Elsil View
Nichols, Charles D.	Mar 31, 1997	68	F.S.H.	Strawberry Plains	May 1, 1928	Nichols, John B.	Lyle, Maggie		Dodson, Chris [Pappy] A.	Charles [All] - [Step] Galbraith, Chester E. & Judy	Pollard, Pauline - Haggard, Kate - Chine, Anna Maude	Floyd-James	Blue Springs
Nichols, Della Sarah	Feb 21, 2000	92	Jeff City	Straw Plains	Apr 7, 1907	Hicks, Dowell	Foster, Emilee S.		Nichols, Carl D.	Kenneth S. [Abe] Carl Luther-David D.		Tom	Pleasant Grove
Nichols, Johnnie Margaret	Sep 10, 1993	62	Nashville, Tn	Strawberry Plains	Oct 30, 1930	Nichols, Carl D.	Hicks, Della	S		Shockley, Danny	Dunn, Emma Lou	Abe-Carl-David	Son	Strawberry Plains
Nippor, Prez Mc Chung	Jul 23, 1974	78	Jeff City	Tn	Jan 2, 1896	Nippor, Frank	Greers, Iowa	WW I	Templin, Pauline E.		Dunn, Emma Lou	J.W. [Columbus, OH]	New Market
Noe, Frank	Oct 7, 1959	81	New Market	Tn	Aug 20, 1878	Noe, Thomas	Rich, Sarah	Tn	W	Kooch, Mrs. Fred - Claude F.	Mack-Ernest-Odell	Cameron, Mellie	Willis	New Market
Noe, George Calvin	Mar 6-1968					Moody, H.T.			Moody, Gladys [D]	Williams, Mrs. Claude F.	James E. [Tn]-Fred T. [Pa] See Obit		Noe, M.T.	Shiloh
Noe, Gladys Moody	Aug/Sep, 1965								Noe, George C.			Husband	
Noe, Pauline	Aug 20, 1985	74	Jeff City	Union Co	Sep 22, 1910	Martin, Thomas	Key, Lula		Noe, M.T.	Waterhouse, Thenia - Mc Carter, Betty - Cox, Grace - Horton, Pat - Mc Ghmmery, Mary E.	Thomas		Noe, M.T.	New Market
Noe, Sadie Emmaline	Aug 7, 1991	94	Dandridge, Tn	Mascot, Tn	Jan 1, 1897	Luttrell, R. French	Adams, Harriet		Noe, Odeel [D]	Bundine, Mildred - Cochran, Catherine	Hugh [Pa]- George [Cal]- Kenneth-Earnest- James[Gal]-John D.		Milford - [Pa's] Noe, Sonny-Jim- Hugh-Ken-Fred- John - Cochran, Jr.	J.M.G.
Noe, Thenia	Jul 25, 1949			Grainger Co		Roach, Will	Lacey, Mary J.	Tn	Noe, Frank		Ernest-Mack		Noe, Frank	Presbyterian - New Market
Norris, David C.	Dec 17, 1938	79	New Market, Tn	Chilton Co., Ala	Aug 1, 1901	Norris, Eastman	Robinson, Caltie		Drinnon, Minnie	Jean		Jones, Vallie		Bethsaida - Morristown, Tn
Norris, Kione Michelle	Oct 31, 1994	1m	J.M.H.	Knoxville, Tn	Sep 4, 1994	Phipps, Alex A.	Norris, Connie	N					Mother	J.M.G.

Name	Death Date	Age	Place of Death	County	Birth Date	Father	Mother	Spouse	Svc	Relatives	Relatives	Relatives	Pallbearers / Relatives	Cemetery
Norris, Lucille	Jan 25, 1994	81	S.M.H.	Cocke Co., Tn	Nov 8, 1912	Sexton, Nicholas N.	Greene, Mollie E.	Norris, Tom [D]		Griffin, Jo - Wagner, Jean	Fowler, Kathleen - Underwood, Helen	Ed	Doug - [Pals] Wagner, Randy - Devine, Don - Griffin, Trudi - Campbell, Daniel - Singleton, Nick - Glenn, Stephen	Piney
Northern, Clifford	Nov 21, 1987	71	J.M.H.	Jeff Co	Mar 31, 1916	Northern, Henry	Dye, Myrtle	Rice, Sallie [D]			Puckett, Delta		Sister - [Pals] Kidwell, Leon - Kidwell, Louis - Puckett, Charlie - Charlie-Wagner - Northern, Kenneth Paul-Jim - Register, David ?	Logston - Maynardville, Union Co
Northern, Edward M. Sr.	Jan 3, 1995	98	S.M.H.	New Market	Jul 28, 1896	Northern, Adam	Talley, Anna	Foster, Maude	WW 1	Jones, Elaine	Hollis [Step] Crawford, Carl	Edward Jr.-John	Austin / Son	Mill Springs
Northern, Harrison	1970	64	J.M.H.	Tn			Nancy Ellen	Northern, Beecher [D]		Elmore, Shirley - Tolliver, Wanda - [Step] Payne, Mrs. Darrell	Hollis [Step] Crawford, Carl	Dauarier, Blanche	Harrison [Son]	Mill Springs
Northern, James Thomas	May 14, 1949	71	Rock Island, Tn	Tn	Oct 24, 1877	Unk	Unk	Mabel						Mill Springs
Northern, Mable M.	Jan 4, 1951	66	New Market, Tn	Tn			Mabel	Hudson, Blanche [Ind.]			Harrison [Son] - Goodwin Bros. F.H. [Ind.]	Hudson, Blanche [Ind.]	Harrison [Son] - Goodwin Bros. F.H. [Ind.]	Mill Springs
Northern, Maude Beatrice	Oct 9, 1997	97	Frankfort, Ind.		Dec 5, 1899	Foster, John	Ballinger, Mamie	Northern, Edward M. Sr.		Jones, Elaine	Ballinger, Mrs. Raymond - Fielden, Mrs. Carl	Hodge, Grace [Niece]	Northern, [Son] - Harrison [Son] - F.H. [Ind.]	Mill Springs
Northern, Nannie Carol	Jun 28, 1957	96	New Market	Tn	Sep 29, 1870	Carrol, Thomas (Tn)	Tunnell, Mary (Tn)	Northern, Sam [D]		Northern, Raymond, Mrs. - Fielden, Mrs. Carl	Clarence	Dauarier, Blanche	Carol, Mack [Son]	Mill Springs
Northern, Russia A.	Feb 1, 1954	98	New Market	Tn	Jul 28, 1863	Atchley, Rush	Franklin, Nancy			Northern, Beecher [D]		Clarence		Pleasant Grove
Northern, William Hollis	Jun 25, 1990	63	J.M.H.	New Market	Apr 18, 1927	Northern, Harrison	Smith, Helen	Jo Ann-Cindy	WW 2	Gary-Danny-Barry	Neal B.	Tolliver, Wanda - Elmore, Shirley	Northern, Neal B. [B.] Willie - [Pals] Tolliver, Billy - Stoner-Ronnie-Tim - Nalany, Marshall - Lowe, Wesley	New Market
Norton, Barbara Jean	Mar 10, 1999	60	New Market	New Market	May 23, 1938	Brewer, Paul	Stallard, Mary	Norton, James Thomas		Northern, James Thomas	Mc Ghee, Mary Ann [D]	Paul Ray [D]- George - Franklin	Husband - [Pals] Ray, Charles - Young, Curtis - Harris, Richie - Hufaker, Charlie - Poors, Bill	J.M.G.
Norton, Cecile Mae	Mar 29, 1998	70	S.M.H.	Union Co, Tn	Apr 10, 1917	Walton, John Elvin	Purkey, Viola	Norton, J. Clay		Gurkel, Joyce	Jimmy	Fain, Ada Beeler		J.M.G.
Norton, Dixie Mae	Nov 24, 1987	67	S.M.H.	Tn	Jun 10, 1920	Stippling, Robert	Fritts, Maggie	Norton, James A.		Solomon, Shirley		Wilson, Annie	Fritts, John	Highland Memorial - Straw Plains
Norton, Floyd	Jul 27, 1998	65	J.M.H.	Mascot, Tn	Aug 18, 1932	Norton, Floyd Sr.	Rimpon, Mary Belle	Norton, Margie		Morton, Margie [D]	Joey Lynn [D]- Tracy	Cain, Mattie	Paul - L.C.	Shiloh
Norton, Henry Clay	Aug 8, 1995	80	Union Co	Knox Co	Sep 25, 1914	Norton, John	Ellison, Margaret Anne	Walton, Cecil [D]	Korea	Morton, Margie	Walton, Cecil [D]	Div		J.M.G.
Norton, Joey Lynn	Feb 26, 1999	35	Jeff City	Jeff City	Aug 15, 1963	Norton, Floyd Jr.	Morton, Margie L.			Joey Lynn [D]- Tracy	Jim	Cain, Mattie	Joyce	East View
Norton, Joseph Donald	Nov 22, 1999	63	Straw Plains	Straw Plains	Aug 15, 1936	Norton, Edward F.	Curnutt, Geneva	Evans, Sena		Ronald & Sandra- Kevin-John & Darlene	Daryl-Joseph & Dana	Cox, Shirley & Tom	Clarence- Kenneth	East View
Norton, Martha	Feb 16, 1979	61	Knoxville, Tn	Nc	May 16, 1917	Rice, Zebdee	Norton, Betty	Norton, Earl		Norton, Betty	Norton, Earl	Carolyn- Whitt, Ann	Norton, Bernard - St. & Jr. - Ronald Sr. & Jr. - Parris, B.	St. Josephs - Greeneville, Tn

Name	Date	Age	Place	County	Date									
O'Dell, Charles Edward	Jul 6, 1997	64	New Market	Jeff City	Feb 14, 1933	O'Dell, James Marion	Williams, Flossie		Morgan, Florence	Army	Fox, Joyce	Irene [D] - Hulling, Juanita [D] - Dolly, Marsha - Kiki & Ruth	James Jr.	J.M.G.
O'Dell, Florence	May 26, 2000	72	S.M.H.	Knox Co	Jul 19, 1927	Morgan, Ell	Mays, Gertrude		O'Dell, Charles [D]			Burkhart, Pearl	Lewis- Terry Buford [br]	J.M.G.
Oakes, Christian L	Apr 26, 1981	38	F.S.H.	New Market, Tn	Oct 30, 1942	Roy	Smith, Mary		Oakes, Jack					J.M.G.
Oakes, Edna Leona	Sep 3, 1995	85	Dandridge, Tn	Grainger Co	Mar 14, 1910	Moore, Lute			Oakes, Wallace R. [p]		Luther-Robert	Butler, Tittie - Morgan, Johnnie - Greenhawe, Mary - Roberts, Myrtle Allen - Bales, Frankie	[Pals] Oaks, Robert B.- Nick-Bynn- Hobb, Earnest- Eslinger, Gene	Piney
Oakes, Kenneth Leroy	Oct 14, 1999	76	Jeff City	Knox Co	Feb 16, 1923	Oakes, Mc Kinley	Clark, Elizabeth E.		Div	U.S.A.F.		Kimball	Howard [D]	Pleasant Grove
Oakes, Robert Willis	Nov 16, 1996	54	Morristown, Tn	Jeff City	May 14, 1942	Shaver, Edna Leona			Cooper, Joyce		Robin - [G] Taylor		Luther	J.M.G.
Oakes, Seba (Buddy)	Nov 6, 1985	66	F.S.H.	Union Co	May 10, 1917	Oakes, Gipson	Kidwell, Beatrice		Oaks, Mona Dukes	WW 2		Evans, Nancy	West View	
Ogle, Bertie Lindsey	Jul 2, 1982	67	J.M.H.	Sevier Co	Jun 29, 1895	Jessie M.	Rector, Laura		W				Lindsey, [Sister-in- Law] - [Pals] Lowdlos, Ted- Ross-Jack-Greg- Carl - Charshman, Bruce	
Ogle, Grace Marie	Mar 1, 1998	85	F.S.H.	Hardy, Ark	Jul 28, 1912	Spicer, John W.	Fisher, Eva Mae		Ogle, Glenn [D]					
Oliver, John Harrell	Dec 9, 2000	59	S.M.H.	Knox Co	May 31, 1942	Oliver, Harry G.	Sing, Ellen		Webster, Doris Marie		Westervelt, Doris Jean	Elsie, William- Jerry-Daniel	Robert-Bill- [Step] Dockins, Clarence	Greenwood
Osborne, Benjamin	Jun 18, 1995	77	B.H.	Knoxville, Tn	Aug 2, 1917	Osborne, C.C.	Brock, Dicie		Henry, Louise		Francis, Carolyn & Charles - Ellen & Bill [Cal]- Barns, Kathy & Ronald	Osborne, John Bonnie & Shirley- Henry, Gerald & Marian [Da]	C.C.	Rocky Valley
Osborne, Yancy	May 26, 1992	31	J.M.H.	Knoxville, Tn	Sep 10, 1960	Osborne, Presley	Hobbert, Ruby		Mc Croskey, Mary Jane		Dale Johnson- Johnny Martin	Smith, Barbara- Lennon, Bonnie- Templeton, Bonnita- Hall, Ruby- Dockins, Wanda	Clarence- Junior-Billy- John-Homer- Presley	Mill Springs
Ostrander, Frieda	Aug 6, 1990	98	Texas								Caldwell, Hope & Harold - Virginia & Edgar [Va]	Ronal J. & Nadine	Davis, Bonnie	Metcalf F.H. [Conroe, Texas]	Cremated - Strawberry Plains
Owen, Inez	Mar 4, 1997	98	Powell, Tn	St. Louis, Mo	May 11, 1898	Law, George	Camp, Elizabeth		Owen, John Carol [p]				Hope- [Pals] Stashnom, Donald - Maude, Ackley- Jones, Bill - Me - Dougal, Sam - Moore, George - Amanos, Dan	J.M.G.

Name	Date	Age	Place	Birthplace	Birth Date	Father	Mother	Spouse	Mil.						Cem.
Owen, John Carol	Nov 27, 1983	88	V.A. Mt. Home	Ft. Blackmore, Va	Sep 7, 1895	Owen, Phillip	Gatewater, Ann	Lex, Inez	ww I	Bingham, Virginia [Wd] - Caldwell, Hope	Reed [Mch] - John Carol [D]			Satterfield, Bob - Roy & Ricky - Tolley, Vernon [B-Parents] - Meyard, Howard - Hemsley, Waco - Thornton, Lois [C-G-Parent]	Satterfield, Bob - Holsclaw, James - Shelton, Howard - Bass, William - Cate, Ezra	J.G.
Owens, Kelly Denise	Sep 14, 1977	0	J.M.H.	J.M.H.	Sep 14, 1977	Owens, James Graton [Age-23]	Talley, Glenda Faye [Age-23]	Kingsport, Tn							Son	Piney
Owensby, Mary Louise	Nov 5, 1988	87	Hill Haven, Tn	Rising Fawn, Ga	Aug 27, 1901	Smith, Thomas	Pennington, Nancy	Owensby, L.V. [D]		Holcomb, James E.				Piney	J.M.G.
Ownby, James Earl	Oct 22, 1998	76	New Market	Knoxville, Tn	May 7, 1922	Ownby, James Mother	Frazier, Mollie	Black, Reba	Army	Shelton, Shirley & George - Williams, Melba & Dennis - Cutshaw, Gail & Allen	Dale & Sylvia	Lucille [D]-Gene [D] Brannon, Lillie [D]- McMahan, Margaret [D] - Conner, Edith [D] - Conner, Dorothy [D]			Valley View
Palladino, Norma	Dec 30, 1997	82	Portland-Sumner Co	Claiborne Co	Nov 6, 1915	Shelton, A.I.	Kick, Isabell	Palladino, John [Dia]-Kirpetz, Alex J[D]		Childress, Christina		Bender, Louis- Maxwell, Lucille - Carson, Vern [N] - Collins, Georgia - Simpson, Vesta	Otey-W.W.- Carl Wayne- Roy		J.M.G.
Paramore, Austin V.	Jan 28, 2000	85	Jeff City	Foothom, Tn	Aug 19, 1914	Paramore, William W.	Lisonby, Ida June	Paramore, William A. [D]				Simpson, Charles			J.M.G.
Paramore, William Abner	Mar 14, 1982	69	Talbott, Tn	Green Pit Co, Nc	Feb 13, 1913	Paramore, Hall	Bixler, Hattie Mae	Easley, -	navy	4	1	Bunsworth, P.G.- Simpson, Charles- Ray, Cauln, Green, Darrell		[Pall] Griffey, Eddie - Collins, John - Hillard, Charles - Parker, James - Kerr - Thomas, David-Eric	Mill Springs
Parker, Clarence Edgar	May 31, 1995	95	S.M.H.	New Market	Sep 28, 1909	Parker, Decatur	Shopkins, Eva Mae	Carroll, Mary Lou		Thomas, Carolyn	Bill-Don-Bob			Wife - [Pall] Cochran, Beecher - Hillard, Charles - Parker, James - Kerr - Thomas, David-Eric	J.M.G.
Parker, Lillie Mae	Mar 16, 1998	92	Straw Plains	Knox Co	Apr 26, 1905	Wrada, John	Simpkins, Mae	Parker, Clarence L. [D]		Jarnigan, Helen - Blair, Estelle	Clarence Jr. [D] - Imbert [D]-Bobby			[Pall] Thomas, Jason-David-Eric - Hibbard, Charles - Pebley, Kiran	Trentville
Parker, Mary Lou	Oct 28, 1996	80	Jeff Co		Jun 10, 1916	Carroll, Dudley	Simpkins, Ida	Parker, Clarence E. [D]		Thomas, Carolyn	Don-Bill-Bob			Moore, Mrs. Robert [3-G-Dead]	Mill Springs
Parton, Bill	Dec 20, 1967	78	J.M.H.	Jim	Mar 19, —			S							New Market
Peabwill, Kate	Apr 22, 1977	85	J.M.H.	Grainger Co	Jan 30, 1891	McDaniel, Isaac G.	Grant, Mary			[Step] Carter, Lucy - McDaniel, Louise	[Step] Carter, Lucy - McDaniel, Victor			[Pall] Hicks, Tom - Carter, Johnny - McDaniel, Rea - James-Gilbert - Bridgewater, Curt	Mitchell Springs Baptist

Name	Death Date	Age	Place	Co/State	Birth Date	Father	St	Mother/Spouse	Status	War	Relatives	Elbert [D]- Thomas [D]	Relatives	Cemetery
Pate, Carl Edward [Black]	Nov 18, 2000	67	Mt. Home	New Market	Dec 31, 1932	Pate, Carl S.		Bewley, Roberta S.	Div		Brazelton, Louise - Gilbert - Davis, Ethel - Cortner, Barbara - Wilson - Rice, Dorothy			Younge Memorial
Pate, Carl William [Col]	Jan 5, 1965	59	Jeff Co	Jeff Co	Jan 5, 1965	Pate, Thomas A. [Age-27]		Patton, Katherin L.				Father - Patton - Pate, Anella - Pate, Roberta [6-Mothers]		Younge Memorial
Pate, Hattie E.	Oct 16, 1962	85	New Market	Tn	Mar 3, 1877	Shannon, Warner	Tn	Unk	Pate, Preston [D]		Taylor, Bonnie - Scott, Sarah - [In-Law] Pate, Roberta	Hugh-Pez	Ray, Razr & Jim [Doug]	West View
Pate, Mary Frances	Jan 2, 1969							Alexander, Mattie S.	Pate, Pleas		Taylor, Theola [Ny] - Cobb, Betty Mc Custer, Dennie - Young, Clara - Marshall, Mellisa [Ny]	Alexander, Charles	Scott, Sarah [Sister] Alexander, Mattie [Mother-In-Law - No]	
Pate, Pleas M. [Negro]	Feb 16, 1970	58	Kodak, Tn	Tn				Shannon, Hattie	W	unk	Loy, Ruby - Taylor, Bonny [Ny] - [In-Law] Pate, Roberta	Hugh	Youngs Memorial	Younge Memorial
Pate, Roberta Savanah [Black]	Jun 10, 1991	86	J.M.H.	New Market	May 3, 1905	Bewley, Tom Ell		Young, Amanda	Div	korea	Brazelton, Louise - Davis, Ethel - Cortner, Hattie - Pauley, Barbara - Langston, Margaret - Rice, Dorothy		Son	Younge Memorial
Pate, Thomas Arthur Sr. [Black]	Nov 18, 1989	82	S.M.H.	New Market	Feb 9, 1927	Pate, Carl		Bewley, Roberta	Div		Thomas A. Jr.	Davis, Ethel - Brazelton, Louise - Cortner, Hattie - Langston, Margaret - Rice, Dorothy - Daley, Barbara		Youngs Memorial
Pate, Walter Shiner [Col]	Jan 5, 1965		Jeff Co	Jeff Co	Jan 5, 1965	Pate, Thomas A.		Patton, Katherin L.				Elbert-Carl-Hugh	Father	Youngs Memorial
Patterson, Barbara	Jun 25, 1959	67	Jeff City	Sevier Co. Tn	Aug 12, 1892	Hurst, William	Sevier Co	Williams, Mary			Garfield-Jeff. Lofurd-Theodore - Constable, Mrs. Nelbert	Elbert Ed- Hugh	Newman, Ruby [Doug]	Perrotts
Patterson, Essie Lee	Sep 12, 2000	90	Jeff City	Sevier Co	May 13, 1910	Shultz, Charles		Perrott, Elizabeth	Patterson, Jess [D]		Banks, Damarus Parrott, Kathryne & Thomas		Perrotts	Hills Union
Patterson, James G.	Mar 5, 1965	81	J.M.H.	Sevier Co	Jan 30, 1912	Patterson, Fred E.		Hurst, Barbra J.	Ruth		Jarnigan, Linda- Manning, Dorothy	Bill-Dennis-David- Gerald	Son - [Pate] Jarnigan, Jason - Lee - Patterson, Tony - Hickaman, Jimmy - Manning, Tony	J.M.G.
Patterson, Jeffery Kyle	Oct 14, 1978	19	J.M.H.	Florida	Feb 20, 1959	Patterson, Raymond K.		Griffey, Lois				Curtis-L.P.	Keith	Deep Springs
Patterson, John Wesley	Nov 15, 1982	92	M.C.	Jeff Co	Apr 26, 1870	Patterson, George	Tn	Unk	Mary [D]			R.L.	Jim	New Market

Name	Death Date	Age	Place	Birthplace	Birth Date	Father	Mother		Note				Cemetery
Patterson, Lewis Grayson	Mar 22, 1997	82	F.S.H.				Rhea, Lillie [D+] Henley, Ethel [D]	Army	Rhea, Mildred - Parks, Bonnie - Hammer, Inez [D] - Park, Bonnie	Tom [D]-Hall [D]	Hall, Jack [1st Cousin]- J.M.G.		U.T. Memphis- Cremate- J.M.G.
Patterson, Ola Pearl	Jan 25, 1993	96	J.M.H.	Jeff Co	Mar 2, 1895	Patterson, John W.	Mount, Mary	S				Taylor, Stara [Friend]	New Market
Patterson, Paul E.	Jan 14, 1996	95	J.M.H.	Morristown, Tn	Sep 18, 1900	Ivy, Ben	Ivy, Molly					Fielden, Gene	New Market
Patterson, Raymond Kyle	Feb 15, 1997	57	J.M.H.	Dandridge, Tn	Aug 21, 1939	Patterson, John	Lovelay, Ada Lee	Div		Seefe, Janell - Simmons, Lorraine [Ar]- Brooks, Lisa	Seay, Mamie- Webb, Ruth- Dalton, Lucille- Scarlett, Wanda	Roy	Deep Springs
Patterson, Robert Gray	Mar 8, 1989	85		Hawkins Co, Tn	Jul 28, 1903	Patterson, Clyde	Brashaw, Elsie	Ivy, Pearl				Wife	New Market
Patterson, Sulean [Pat]	Nov 13, 1997	75	Hamplill, W. Va.		Mar 23, 1922	Patterson, William	Carrington, Ethel	Jones, Margaret	WW 2	Sherrod, Patricia & John	Jordan, Sylie [Pat]	Richard & Gladys [Pa]- Virginia [Pa]- Everett [Pa]	Garfield Memorial
Patterson, Tony Scott	Dec 25, 1982	15	Jeff City		Aug 7, 1967	Chapman, Lena Lucille		S			Kathy-Sheila-Angela	[Pa]- Patterson, Chassius- Rickey- Roland, Tony- Randy- Green- Rance- Borders, Paul	Deep Springs
Patterson, Viola Ann	Feb 13, 1992	65	J.M.H.	White Pine, Tn	Jun 5, 1926	Jernigan, Sam	Patterson, Ray					Husband	Deep Springs
Petty, Beulah K.	May 31, 1981		Knox Co. Tn		Feb 1, 1898	Patton, W.C.	Louisa Virginia	Greene Co	S			Edwards, E.R. Jr. [Ex - Nephew]	West View
Petty, Claude Raymond Sr.	Oct 28, 1994	82	J.M.H.	Mascot, Tn	Mar 12, 1912	Patterson, James Anthony	Clifton, Cora	Cassidy, Hester [D]		Ford, Sylvia		Ralph	East View
Payne, Eva	Dec 11, 1987				Nov 9, 1112							Loy, Leon - Julian, Michele V. - Greenwood Cemetery To	West View
Payne, Jennie H.	Oct 13, 1973	88	New Market, Tn		Mar 3, 1885	Hall, Henry		W		Finchum, Mamie - Clendon, Evelyn Brown [Pa]- Deathridge, Mary	Sewell, Annie [Pa]- Skinner, Elsie [Coll]	Fred	West View
Payne, Luther H.	Feb 20, 1959	76	M.C.	Georgia	Nov 18, 1882	Payne, Joseph F.	Ga	Tn		William T.- Norman R.-Don- Joe		Payne, Jennie- Loy, Leon - Julian, Michael V.- Greenwood Cemetery To	West View
Payne, Norman	Jan 18, 1978				May 16, --12	Payne, Joseph F.	Bryant, Martha					Michael V.- Greenwood Cemetery To	West View
Peck, Harry	Dec 3, 1978	66	J.M.H.			Peck, Joseph W.	Mary	W		Finchum, Eiden Lewis & Eugene- Lewis, Virginia & F. Willard - Berhleanship, Alta Ruth & Max		Miller, Mary Alice [Daug]	West View
Peck, Harry Lee [Coll]	Dec 3, 1978	86	J.M.H.	Jeff Co	Jun 4, 1882	Peck, Joseph W.	Caldwell, Mary	Jeff Co					West View
Peck, James Rubin [Coll]	Jul 25, 1962	56	New Market	Mar 28, 1906	Reed, Powell	Hodge, Ellen	Unk			Easley, Billy Ray [Step] Scruggs, Calvin	Inglis, Claudine [D]- Gaul, Maris	Wilma [Wife]	West View
Peck, Wilma [Black]	Apr 13, 1982	72	New Market	Sep 7, 1909	Reed, Powell	Hodge, Ellen				Scruggs, Calvin	Brazelton, Mary	Young Memorial
Perry, Mary Louise	Sep 17, 2000	68	Blaine, Tn	Lee Springs, Tn	Oct 26, 1931	Mitchell, Reese	Collins, Dora	Perry, James Alfred Sr.		James Jr. & Darlene	Inglis, Claudine [D]- Gaul, Maris	Paul [D]- William A.	Indian Ridge

Name	Death Date	Age	Place	County	Birth Date	Father	Mother	Spouse	Relations	Relations	Relations	Relations	Cemetery
Petree, Amanda	Jan 8, 1987	72	Appalachian Hosp.	Jeff Co	Sep 23, 1924	Pitts, Charlie	Murray, Martha C.	Petree, Winton B. [D]+Hill, James B. [D]	Howell, Barbara & Bob - Bullock, Wanda & David	Hill, James B. Jr. - Murr, Pauline & Matthews, John D. [Sd] - Campbell, Beulah [D] - Herron, Mary Kate [D] - Pitts, Glenna [D]	Rimmer, Ruth & Earl - Murr, Pauline & [Oscar-D] - Campbell, Beulah [D] - Herron, Mary Kate [D] - Pitts, Glenna [D]	Shelter, Ernest - Pitts, Frank [D] - Pitts, Hubert [D]	James Hill [Son]	Mt. Pleasant
Petty, Clyde Marion	Jan 7, 1993	82	S.M.H.	Kodak, Tn	Jun 10, 1910	Petty, George Henry	Campbell, Emma	Virgie	Lea, Marine & Sherman - Chesney, Wilma & Leon - Russell, Marie	Underwood, Max - Russell, Anabe - Newman, Ruth	Samuel Barton	Daug - [Pits] ... - Strawberry Plains	Paw Paw - Kodak, Tn
Petty, Olaf	Jun 8, 1993	78	Sevierville, Tn	Kodak, Tn	Oct 24, 1914	Petty, Ed	Hardin, Ruby Edna	Yarber, Geraldine - Duncan, Nadine	Doyle - Jay Harold	Childress, Charlie - Lou - Underwood, Jessie	Edd	Son - [Pits] Glenn - Harold-Doyle-Jay - Underwood, Ray	Paw Paw - Kodak, Tn
Petty, Ronald Wayne	Sep 22, 1993	22	Kodak, Tn	Knoxville, Tn	Dec 19, 1960	Petty, Doyle Leon	S					Wayne - [Pits] Glenn	Paw Paw - Kodak, Tn
Petty, Ruby Edna	Sep 15, 1991	69	B.H.	Sevier Co	Dec 19, 1921	Hardin, Elbert	Petty, Olaf		Geraldine - Nadine	Doyle, Jay Harold	Reed, Edith	Ray	Husband - Petty, Olaf - Yarber, Geraldine - Doyle - J. Harold - Jay-Olaf	Paw Paw
Petty, Virgie	May 2, 1992	79	S.M.H.	Sevier Co	Sep 11, 1913	Lea, Charlie	Underwood, Carcie	Petty, Clyde	Chesney, Wilma - Lea, Marine - Russell, Marie	Bailey, Lucy	Auckley, Eldridge	Husband - [Pits] - Anderson, Hugh - Jeff - Halbrook, Bill - Glenn, Andrew-Wayne	Paw Paw - Kodak, Tn
Phillips, John Warner	May 13, 1990	69	F.S.H.	Rutledge, Tn	Feb 21, 1919	Phillips, William E.	Rosen, Eliza	Boston, Marian Lois	U.S.A.F.	John L. & Kim	Simms, Mary [Sd] - [H-Law] Jernigan, Elaine	Grady [D]-Son - Holton, Ronnie - Holt, Mark - Boston, Samuel - 3rd - Thomas, Roy-Burl	Oakland
Phillips, Shirley Louise	Feb 21, 1993	42	J.M.H.	Tazewell, Tn	Oct 8, 1950	Murray, Claude	Griffin, Nan	Phillips, Ferre [D]	Bishop, Tina	James-Scott, Edward	Mills, Wanda Vance - King, Barbara	Murray, Ferrie - Don-Steve - Kyle-Caleb - Jr. - Larry - Griffin, Jim	Oakland
Phillips, Eleanor Maggie	Sep 21, 1995	66	Rutledge, Tn	Dandridge, Tn	Nov 18, 1928	Denton, Mel M.	Hicks, Frances	Phillips, Samuel L.	Renfro, Judy - Caldwell, Jane	Terry	Alley, Louise - Myers, Swannie - Hubert, Dean	Jim [D] - Bill [D] - Shields-Roger	Oakland
Phillips, Gene Turney	Sep 1, 1989	56	B.H.	Grainger Co	Mar 27, 1933	Phillips, Earnest	Mitcaill, Rose	Murray, Shirley		Terry	Warren, Betty	Jack-Bill	Oakland
Phipps, Alex Allen [Black]	Jun 29, 1997		F.S.H.	Sevier Co	Jun 29, 1997	Phipps, Alex Allen Jr.	Bentley, Elizabeth					Phipps, Alex & Connie - Hellmuth, Sharon [D - Perennial] Phipps, Harry J. & Mary - Shoals, Gertrude [G-G-Parents]	Youngs Memorial
Phipps, Barnez [Black]	Nov 13, 1995	79	Hill Haven	New Market	Aug 28, 1916	Phipps, Raymond	Braselton, Laura	S			Scruggs, Lorena	Augustine-William Taylor	Sister - Youngs Memorial

Name	Date	Age	Place	St	Birth/Marr.	Father	Mother	Family / Notes	Cemetery
Phipps, Eula Mae	Feb 1/2, 1982	37	U.T.H.	Tn	Jun 2, 1924	Phipps, Harry C.		WW 1; Celia-Wincie-Barbara Ann-Margaret; Ledford, Betty - Moore, Naomi; [Ind] - Brown, Thelma - Nannie, Stokes, Margaret; Raymond Leon; Moore, Mrs. Ronald E. - Brown, Thelma - Ledford, Betty; Harry, Jr. [1/2], Bryant, Charles; Phipps, Harry	Methodist
Phipps, Harry C. Sr.	Sep 2, 1973		New Market, Tn		1896			Wife	Younge Memorial
Phipps, Lillian Helen [Negro]	Dec 2, 1968	73	Jeff City	Tn	Nov 16, 1895	Brazelton, Edgar	Martin, Laura	Annie; Raymond A. - Duffy, Dorthy - Fitzgerald, William [N]; Miles, Modest - Mc Duffy, Dorthy - Fitzgerald, William [N]; Lionel-Ross-Hoyle; Brazelton, Lionel D.	Younge Memorial
Phipps, Michelle Todd [Black]	Dec 7, 1986	25	Morristown, Tn	Tn	Aug 22, 1970	Phipps, Leroy		W; Phipps, Harry Jr. [Ind] - Leroy-Raymond - Bryant, Charles; Phipps, Mrs. Lillian (Mothers); Phipps, Ms. Lillian; H.W. [Aunt] - Doorn, J.N.; Humphreys, Beulah	Trentville
Phipps, Raymond H. [Col]	Mar 28, 1983	69	New Market	Tn	Jan 23, 1894	Phipps, Aleck	Davis, Jenny	Father - Moore, Naomi [Ind] - Phipps, Annie [G-Mothers]; Phipps, Ms. Lillian; H.W. [Aunt] - Doorn, J.N. [Nephew]	Younge Memorial
Pickens, Troy Otho	1970	74	Knox Co			Walker, William B.	Huff, Molly		Trentville
Pierce, Belle Vadna	Nov 17, 1983	69	Granger Co		Sep 9, 1894	Pierce, Tate [B]	James, Elizabeth	Faddis, Beth - Nan Elizabeth; Rutledge, Katherine - Pierce, Jennie; Rutledge, Katherine; [Pse] Pierce, Edd-Albert-Michael-Shaun-Keith - Faddis, Jeff-Mark	Pleasant View
Pierce, Robert	Dec 16, 1984	71	V.A.-Mt. Home		Jan 31, 1923	Pierce, William	Smith, Susie	Duckworth, Lula; Army; Brickey, Bobbie - Anderson, Mary Sue - [Step] Sipe, Pat; Tate-Mack [Pa]- Franklin Brewer- Bill; Dennie, Nellie - Hodges, Maude; James, Mary Elizabeth; Fred [Pa]	East View
Pierce, Buford P.	Nov 22, 1988	80	S.M.H.	Jeff Co	Dec 28, 1901	Walkers, W.B.	Smith, Susie	Smith, Susie; Stacy, Shirley - Lawrence, Linda; Audrey; Fred-Robert-Joe; Smith, Jessie [Sister-in-Law]	Piney
Pierce, Jennie Elizabeth	Jan 4, 1995	83	S.M.H.	Granger Co	May 15, 1908	Pierce, Will P.	James, Elizabeth	Vance, Drifnea; Pierce, Elizabeth; Rutledge, Katherine; William T.-Dean H.; Rutledge, Katherine	East View
Pierce, Tate	Jun 13, 1990	83	J.M.H.	Hamblen Co	Aug 22, 1897	Pierce, Franklin	Medows, Nannie	Watkins, Belle; Faddis, Tabitha & John; Dennie, Nellie - Hodges, Maude; [Pa] Pierce, Eddie-Shawn-Keith-Albert-Mike-Bill - Faddis, Jeff-Mark; Wheeler, Andrew-Weston, Bobby-Events, Dwight	Pleasant View
Pike, Patricia Ann	Jul 3, 1999	48	Knoxville, Th	Harlan, Ky	Dec 14, 1950	Campbell, William	Drew, Billie Ball	Pikes, William Curtis; Hedrick, Tabitha & John; Tate-Mack [Pa]- Franklin Brewer- Bill	West View
Pilgrim, Raymond Richard [Jack]	May 30, 1992	72	J.M.H.	Mascot, Tn	Sep 7, 1919	Pilgrim, John	Roper, Orie	Welch, Nola; Navy; Kerr, Jackie	East View
Pittman, James Arthur	Aug 30, 1998	92	Copper Hill, Tn		Jan 31, 1896	Pittman, S.R.	Corbin, Caroline	Clevenger, Ellie; John-Claude-Clifford; [Pse] Pittman, Mack - Clevenger, Richard-G.H.-Steve - Beam, Gerald - Farmer, Curtis - Brown, Darrell	West View

Name	Date	Age	Place	Birthplace	Birth Date	Father	Mother	Spouse		Children / Relatives				Burial
Pittman, Lottie Ethel	Apr 1, 1997	88	Maryville, Tn	Tazewell, Tn	Jan 6, 1909	Seals, Grant	Ferguson, Catherine	Pittman, James Arthur		Clevenger, Ellis	Joe-Claude-Clifford (Fla)-Donie-[Step] Pittman, Johnny	Whitaker, Helen [M]		West View
Pittman, Patricia Anne	Oct 25, 1994	48	U.T.H.	Blaine, Tn	Oct 9, 1946	Wade, John R.	Wolfenberger, Mae	Pittman, Claude		James	Mc Elheney, Shirley	Dodge-Jackie-Davd-Joe-Claude-Donnie-Johnnie	Husband	Red House-Rutledge, Tn
Pittman, Robert Blain	Dec 21, 1994	38	Ft. Myers, Fla	Tazewell, Tn	May 24, 1945	Pittman, James Arthur	Seals, Lottie	S			Clevenger, Ellis	Clifford-Donnie-Johnnie		West View
Pitts, Frank Taylor	Oct 31, 1981	44	V.A.-Johnson City, Tn	Tn		Pitts, Charlie	Murray, Mattie		WW 2		Harrison, Mary Kate-Herron, Amanda-Rismer, Ruth	Pitts, Hubert-[Sister]-Shaffer, Ernest-Jas [Step-Father]	Matt, Pauline	Flat Gap
Pitts, Hubert C.	Dec 30, 1981	78	Jeff City	New Market	Apr 9, 1913	Pitts, Charlie	Murray, Mattie	Myers, Jennie		Radding, Elizabeth-Jones, Juanita	Cecil	Rismer, Ruth-Murr, Pauline-Pralee, Amanda	Shaffer, Earnest	J.M.G.
Plough, Leona M.	Jun 20, 1950	87	Meadville, Pa	New Market	Nov 12, 1907	Mohler, Clifford L.	Hensley, Maude			Plough, Henry L. [2]	James G.	Warrenberger, Thelma [Fla]	Claude H. [Oh] Son	Cremated-Salamanca, Ny
Pollard, Estel Sidney [M]	Jan 5, 1985	57	S.M.H.	New Market	Jul 17, 1927	Pierce, Buford	Pierce, Gladys	Beatrice		Case, Pat-Mueller, Lula-Pollard, Debbie	Pollard, Jackie	Mueller, Lola [Fla]-Kimbrough, Sue-Case, Pat-Lindsey, Donie-Pollard, Debbie		Piner
Pollard, Jaticoe Wayne	Sep 3, 1999	92	Jeff Co	Jeff City	Dec 23, 1946	Pollard, Estel	Fritz, Ellie	Nicely, Sheila	Army		David			East View
Pollard, Ruth Ann	Sep 2, 1998	43	Jeff Co	Harrisburg, Ill	Oct 18, 1954	Lagostin, Robert	Clemens, Mary M.-Ramirez [M]	Pollard, Edward			Shayne [M]			J.M.G.
Poole, Albert E.	Mar 27, 1998	81	Jeff City	Harrisburg, Pa	Apr 16, 1894	Poole, Andy								New Market
Poore, Charlie James	Jul 22, 1996	57	Morristown, Tn	Jeff Co	Jan 19, 1929	Poore, James	Rodrick, Mary Ellen	Cain, Betty		Berry, Kay-Jett, Pam	Bill	Churchman, Genova-Mae-Hensley, Anna Mae-Hicks, Rozella-Poore, Mary-Breeden, Juanita	Raymond-Edgar-Earl	Seals, Beulah Willis-Tom	J.M.G.
Poore, James Bruce	Mar 5, 1987	81	New Market, Tn	Jeff Co	Apr 5, 1905	Poore, Daniel	Bailey, Annie			Hensley, Marie		Churchman, Genova-Mae-Hensley, Anna Mae-Hicks, Rozella-Poore, Mary-Breeden, Juanita	Lippencott, Russell [Friend]-Willis [Friend]-Cochran, James-Harrell, Jim-Cameron, Ellis-Shrader, Robert-Poore, Mary-Ernest - Mc Clain, Eugene	Pangup Hollow - Kodak, Tn

Name	Death Date	Age	Place	County/Place	Birth Date	Father		Mother		Spouse	
Poore, Marie Katherine	Mar 9, 1995	65	J.M.H.	Mascot, Tn	Nov 2, 1929	Hensley, Albert		Taylor, Vinney		Poore, James B.	
Poore, Mike Mac	Jan 10, 1987	63	Mascot, Tn	Hancock Co	Apr 28, 1923	Barnard, James Perry [D-1971]		Nancy		Poore, John T.	Brock, Judy
Porter, Joseph Jr. [Black]	Jan 14, 1990	23	V.A. - Mt. Home	Morristown, Tn	Jan 6, 1967	Porter, Joseph Sr.		Hodge, Mildred			
Porter, Ronda Jean [Black]	Oct 11, 1998	35	Morristown, Tn	Jeff City	Jan 11, 1963	Nance, Robert Donald		Stokes, Barbara Ann Kyle		Porter, Joseph Jr. [D]	
Potter, Elmer Lee	Nov 6, 1994	57	Knoxville, Tn	Eaton, Ohio	Nov 19, 1936	Potter, Wilbur		Hampton, Cynthia		Mitchell, Wanda	Army
Potter, Cordie E.	Jun 28, 1954	57	New Market	Tn	Jan 21, 1897	Potter, W. Henry	Tn	Hatmaker, Elizabeth	Tn	S	
Prater, Willie Lee	May 29, 1954	63	New Market	Tn	May 10, 1891	Prater, Henry	Tn	Hatmaker, Lillie	Tn		
Pratt, David Lee	Apr 26, 1973	8d	Knox Co		Apr 18, 1973	Pratt, Ronnie		West, Betty			
Pratt, Della Bibbins	Dec 26, 1998		Knox Co	Grainger Co	Jul 5, 1895	Pratt, Robert		Picton, Cordia		W	
Pratt, Gene Wesley	Jan 27, 1990	55	U.T.H.	Knox Co	May 6, 1934	Pratt, Edith		Hornback, Elva Premier	Iuone	Barnard, Christine Hickey	
Pratt, Hattie	Dec 3, 1979	59	J.M.H.	Dandridge, Tn	May 21, 1920	Lane, Mack	Cocke Co			Pratt, Walter Sam [D]	
Pratt, John William	Jun 6, 1963	84	Strawberry Plains	Tn	Sep 11, 1879	Pratt, Albert		Williams, Tammer		Bibbins, Della	
Pratt, John William Jr.	Jan 29, 1996	70	Bay City, Texas		Aug 4, 1925	Pratt, John William Sr.		Bibbins, Della		Kornuth, Betty	
Pritchell, L.E.	May 12, 1951										
Prince, Bonnie Belle	Oct 11, 1993	90	Knox Co		Mar 4, 1903	Glover, George R.		Hodge, Delilah		Prince, George Sr. [D]	

Name	Date	Age	Place	County	Date	Father		Mother		Spouse		Children/Relatives	Cemetery
Prince, George Clarence	Nov 13, 1999		Dandridge, Tn	Cherokee Co, Nc	May 26, 1905	Prince, J.W.		Craig, Susin B.	Bonnie	Upclose, Faye - Tommie - Finley, Oline	George Jr. [Son]	Dora	George Jr. [Son] — [Pals] Trent, Wayne - Byrd, Gene - Colins, Bobby - Dexter, Bob - Phillips, Ronnie - Proffitt, Chris	J.M.G.
Proffit, Jacky Allen	Feb 23, 1982	24	New Market, Tn	Jeff City	Jun 29, 1957	Proffit, Arnold		Byrd, Velma	S			Randell	Wife - [Pals] Aaron-Henry - Donald-Jimmy - Ralph-Dave	Ebenezer
Proffitt, John Mack	Dec 22, 1984	70	J.M.H.	Sevier Co.	Jan 22, 1914	Proffitt, Jim		Clabo, Katherine	Betty Ann	Keith	Berry-Ruth	Aaron-Henry - Donald-Jimmy - Ralph-Dave	Son - [Pals] Cedile, Mike - Swann, Son - Johnny-Junior- Sellers, Jony - Hill, Stacy - Colley, Mike	Ebenezer
Proffit, Amanda Mae	Oct 9, 1986	65	J.M.H.	Jeff Co	May 20, 1921	Kimbrough, Author		Walker, Lettie Ann	Proffit, John [D]	Keith G.		Kimbrough, Amanda Mae	Son - [Pals] Cedile, John - Swann, Junior-Jr. - Sammy - Sellers, Jay - Hill, Stacy	Ebenezer
Province, Annie Myrtle	Nov 3, 1990	97	Hill Haven	Knoxville, Tn	Sep 5, 1893	Pedigo, Henry Clay		Smith, Martha Josephine [Josie]	Ng		Hancock, Ada	Province, Charles A. [D]	Moore, Paul (Nephew)	Trevelile
Pruitt, Boyd	Jul 17, 1978	68	Jeff Co		Jun 13, 1910			Reneau, Lockie	W	Sandra	Kenneth [Fia]- Harold-Hugh- Leland	Davis, Ruth - Halley, Erna	Edmonds, Paul [Sons] — Prince, Leland E. - Hickman, Edde - Dennison, Lowell - Luttrell, Frank - West, Kyle - [Pals] Profitt, Paul	Strawberry Plains
Pruitt, Mary Alice	Nov 8, 1991	68	Strawberry Plains	Jeff Co	Feb 12, 1923	Dennison, Hugh		Rudder, Jessie	W	Dennison, Mary Alice	Kenneth [Cal]- Harold [Ted]- Hugh-Bud	West, Mrs. Kyle	Orville-Lowell- Ronnie — Bill - Dale, Martin - Murray, George - Luttrell, Frank - West, Kyle	Hillcrest
Pruitt, Mary Elizabeth	Apr 8, 1951	81	New Market, Tn	Tn	Jul 30, 1869	Reneau, Perry	Tn	Unk	Ng			Pruitt, James	Jernigan, Sue [Niece] - Stephton & Son F.K. [Canton, Ohio]	Hillcrest
Pruitt, Thaddeus [Black]	Aug 22, 1984	82	J.M.H.	Arkansas		Pruitt, James		Rice, Mary	W			Puckett, James [Canton, Ohio]	Wife - [Pals] Hunsdard, Jim - Puckett, James - Huxley, Clarence - Dial, Ransell - Morgan, Donald - Neal, Frenly	Canton, Ohio
Puckett, Bobby D.	Dec 5, 1984	50	Dandridge, Tn	Jeff Co	Dec 2, 1934	Puckett, Howard		Dilo, Nancy	Neal, Velma		Morgan, Bonnie	Dilo, Howard	[Pals] Hunsdard, Jim - Puckett, James - Puckett, Clarence - Dial, Ransell - Morgan, Donald - Neal, Frenly	Piedmont
Puckett, Howard Nelson	Mar 10, 1997	84	Jeff City	Sevier Co.	Oct 6, 1912	Puckett, Arthur		Betts, Minnie	Dilo, Nancy Velma		Morgan, Bonnie	Brown, Gladys	Puckett, Arthur — [Pals] Kidwell, Leon - Dilo, Ransell - Morgan, Puckett, Derwyne - Henderson, Tom - Hardin, Cerrol - Petree, Herbert	Piedmont

Name	Date	Age	Place	Place	Date										Cemetery
Purkey, Bonnie Catherine	Apr 6, 1983	69	F.S.H.	Jeff Co	May 10, 1913	Barber, William T.	Jones, Dora	Purkey, Robert	Parker, Barbara & Hugh			Curtis-Winford	[Pals] Newman, Bill - Nugum, W.K. - Lindsey, Ben - Kinder, Robert - Ewing, Joe - Lindsey, Ted - Howard, Carroll		J.M.G.
Purkey, Ethel Viola	Sep 25, 1981	81	Tn	Grainger Co.	Mar 2, 1900	Solomon, Jim	Jernigan, Nancy	W	Solomon, Lucille Sherrod, Mary Ruth - Winn, Pauline - Barbara - Lane, Alene		Bailey, James - Henry	McDaniel, Ada	James [Nil] Henry	[Pals] Moody, Lucile - Bailey, Timmy-Johnny - Winn, Johnny - Solomon, Morris	New Market
Purkey, James Harvey	Feb 6, 1985	81	J.M.H.	Tn	Dec 28, 1885	Pirkey, John Thomas	Lockhart, Mary Belle	W	Lee, Mrs. Dean - Moneymaker, Anna Belle - Meston, Mrs. Charles		R.P.-Clarence	Cundiff, Mrs. W.W.	Willie		New Market
Purkey, James Robert	Aug 14, 1983	80	Jeff City	Jeff City	Nov 24, 1912	Purkey, George A.	Quisenberry, Rachael	Barber, Catherine [D]	Parker, Barbara		H.B.-Geraldine & [Dal] Roy	Jack	Doug		J.M.G.
Purkey, Ollie Josephine	Nov 7, 1972	80	Hamilton Co	Tn	Jun 12, 1894	Ballinger, John E.	McCurry, Julia	Purkey, Don	Debra Kay-Penny Jo-Minton, Rebecca Ann		Cass, Doris		Charles Adam-Anderson, Eugene-Jerry Michael-Johnny Dwaine	Husband - [Pals] Denton, Jack - Anderson, Eugene - Purkey, Joe - Johnny - Webb, Earnest - Durreh, George	West View
Purkey, Rebecca J.	Sep 7, 1997	39	J.M.H.	Jeff City	Dec 20, 1957	Shelton, Jerry	Ellison, Jewell	Purkey, Bobby Don	Kara - Brown, Michelle				Ellison, Bess - Collins, Edith [E-McDoch]		J.M.G.
Purvis, Margie Lorjean	Jan 12, 1996	59	McDowell Co. W. Va.	Knoxville, Tn	May 8, 1937	McClain, Bill	Ward, Bessie	Purvis, Robert [D]	Valentine, Anna Mae & Willie Lee				Dellmar & Minnie [Nil]	Stephen F.H. [Cedar Bluff, Va]	Osborne - Buchanan, Va
Quarles, Nancy Ellen	Jan 2, 1994	92	Jeff City	Knoxville, Tn	Jan 24, 1901	Line, James A.	White, Lou	Quarles, Brown [D]	Morgan, Joyce		Larson, Dixie-Gene-Royce-Fred		Maurice		J.M.G.
Queen, Ola Curtis	Feb 22, 1985	78	Cleveland, Tn	McCoyville, Ga	Mar 1, 1906	Curtis, Robert A.	King, Laura	Queen, Charles Baker	[Hr-Law] White, Frannie		[Hr-Law] White, Bob		White, Chris-Robin-Dejana & Clifford		Hopewell
Quillams, Garland	Feb 12, 1990	69	Mt. Home	Sevier Co	Sep 20, 1920	Quillams, Andy	McCarter, Lisa	Lucille [Separated]	Mc Null, Charlotte	WW 2	Dwayne-Danny	Lonsley, Orelle-Estelle-Ola-Elmore, Myrtle-Carr, Malathon	Carr, Clay [Nephew]		Strawberry Plains
Quinton, Walter P.	Feb 15, 1990	72	M.C.	Tn	Jun 1, 1887					Navy			Harris, Eva-Romines, Emma	Sam-Roy-Perry-Otha	West View
Quinton, Alice	Jan 30, 1987	83	New Market	Jeff City	Jan 10, 1914	Vessoir, Walter	Jones, Hattie		[Step] Grubb, Hansel-Ples				Norris, Mary - Lamplin, Lois	Quinton, Maude B. [Wife]	New Market
Quisenberry, Elizabeth	Oct 24, 1972	89	J.M.H.	Cocke Co.	Aug 24, 1918	Samples, Charles O.	Denton, Mell	Quisenberry, W.A. [D]	[Step] Miller, Mrs. Emmit - Bales, Mrs. E.O.-Jackson, Mrs. Arthur - Ferguson, Mary - Noe, Ruby & Kenneth - Fielden, Aileen [D]		Bill		Norris, Mrs. Albert	Robert-J.P.-Charles-Freeman	Husband	J.M.G.
Quisenberry, Phillippa E. (Pie-F)	Mar 28, 2000	89	Jeff City	Greeneville, Tn	Nov 12, 1910	Ellis, Harry D.	Smith, Mary F.	Sanford [D]	Navy	[Step] Brewers, Mary Ann	Busise, Mrs. Mary ?	Smith, Sue Booher		Pleasant Grove	WoodTown

Name	Date	Age	Place	Location	Birth	Father	Mother	Spouse	Other	Relations	Relations	Relations	Cemetery
Quisenberry, Sanford Franklin [Jack]	Apr 10, 1982	77	J.M.H.	Jeff Co	Aug 16, 1904	Quisenberry, George	Price, Mollie	Quisenberry, Phillippe E.	unk	[Step] Bivens, Mary Ann & Max	[Pals] Fielden, James - Hansel, Jim - Cline, Doyle - Cox, Bill - Downing, Fred - Walston, Fred	[Pals] Fielden,…	Pleasant Grove
Rader, John Porter	Dec 21, 1991	87	Houston, Texas	Bulls Gap, Tn	Nov 17, 1904	Rader, Dailey	Barr, Tinersey ?	Reynolds, Ruth		Day, Jaclsye Ann		Doug	New Market
Rader, Ruth Ann	Jan 3, 1994	82	Houston, Texas	Mt Milton Co, Tn	Jan 14, 1911	Reynolds, C.C.	Green, Prestha	Rader, John Porter [D]		Day, Jaclsye Ann	Reynolds, Grace - Reems, Mary	Doug	New Market
Rader, Tinersey Berry	Apr 14, 1967	82			Sep 22, 1885		Gulley, Sarah	Rader, Dailey [D]					
Rainwater, Dana Thoe [M]	Jan 6, 1981	57	New Market, Tn	Tn	Sep 24, 1923	Rainwater, Oscar	Carter, Nancy	Lindsey, Flora Mae		Horner, Jean	Mc Daniel, Mary Helen - Hill, Alma - Greene, Judy - Walton, Eddie - Wittman, Jean	Junior - Billy Greene, Judy - Joe - Tommy	Pollards - Sevier Co
Rainwater, Flora Mae	Nov 12, 1995	71	S.M.H.	New Market	Oct 15, 1924	Lindsey, Albert	Bailey, Molly	Rainwater, Dana [D]		Horner, Jean	Cake, Lissie	Clyde	Pollards - Sevier Co
Ramsey, Carl William	Aug 19, 1997	67	B.H.	Claiborne Co, Tn	Oct 20, 1929	Ramsey, Jessee	Massey, Viola	Div		Smith, Tiffany	Ramsey, Hazel [CH] - Mitchell, Nancy - Emma Ruth [Pa]	Son	Cremated
Ramsey, Cirta Garfield	Nov 9, 2000	59	Morristown, Tn	Buncombe Co, Nc	Mar 27, 1941	Ramsey, Luther	Mc Glothe, Harriet	Collins, Helen	Air Force	Kinsler, Lisa & Scott - Fritts, Regina & Marion	Slabworth, Joan - Long, Ann - Williams, Bobbie - Walton, Peggy	Luther Z.	J.M.G.
Randles, Arthur Lynn	Sep 2, 1974	63	E.S.H.	Tn	May 18, 1911	Randles, Arthur Eugene	Hankins, Anabell	Mc Clain, Lorene		Miller, Edna - Bolin, Lucile	Gary [Calif]	Lynn - W. E. [Tony] G.S.	Nances Grove
Randles, Annabelle H.	Feb 28, 1973	89	Knoxville, Tn	Tn	Jan 15, 1883	Hankins, John	Rey, Mary E.	W		Miller, Elva & R.A. - Bolin, Mrs. George - Anderson, Brenda - Burchfield, Dorothy		Randles, John W. E.	Nances Grove
Randles, Arthur Eugene	Jan 21, 1970	90	Knoxville, Tn	Tn	Dec 29, 1879	Randles, Anderson	Lewis, Frances	Anna Belle		Miller, Edna - Bolin, Lucile	Lynn - W. E. [Tony]	Randles, W.E.	Nances Grove
Randles, Eva Mae	Jan 31, 1981	78	J.M.H.	Green Co, Tn	Oct 20, 1912	Massey, Dudger	Sims, Julia	Randles, Paul [D]		Mettler, Nancy	Miller, Edna - Bolin, Lucile	Kermit	Nances Grove
Randles, Paul Allison	Jan -, 1967	57	New Market	Tn	Apr 16, 1909	Randles, Arthur Eugene	Hankins, Anabell	Eva		Randles, Paul [D]	Miller, Edna - Bolin, Lucile	Willo	New Market
Rankin, Thelma M.	Mar 26, 1996	79	J.M.H.	Dandridge, Tn	Jan 13, 1916	Merrie, Grant	Moore, Martha	Rankin, Samuel Lyle			Sammy & Julie	Moore, Reoline - Moore, Pauline	Husband	Hill Crest
Raper, Danny Michael	Jun 15, 1999	44	U.T.H.	Mc Keynville, Ga	Jul 6, 1953	Raper, Everett J. Tn	Robinson, Joan Tn	Shelton, Carolyn		Amantle - Michelle - Purkey, Crissy - Stroul, Dorothy - Elmore, Eva	Michael	Bobby - Spencer - Tommy	Bassmiddson, Myrtie	Dennis - David	Robinson, Clara [G-Mother]	J.M.G.
Raport, Lillie Lee	May 3, 1969		Knox Co	Tn	Feb 7, 1905	Higdahn, Arch	De Vault, Eva Etta	W		Div			Community Chapel
Rasnick, Herbert J.	Jan 8, 1992	62	J.M.H.	Clinchfield, Va	May 3, 1929	Rasnick, George	Martha				Lawrence - Charles - William [Fa]	Brother	Cremated
Ray, Dockey Thomas	Jul 3, 1971		Knoxville, Tn	Tn	Dec 20, 1915	Ray, Luther	Swann, Julia	S	U.S.A.F.	Div	Moore, Lucille	Hershel - Hugh	Presbyterian

Name	Date	Age	Place	Location	Birth Date	Father	Mother	Spouse	Children / Relatives	Notes	Siblings	Burial
Ray, Frances Elizabeth	Aug 14, 1994	75	J.M.H.	Jeff City	May 28, 1919	Collins, John D	Clark, Emma	Ray, Robert W. [D]	Boyle, Gladys - Quinn, Kathy - Ray, Marie	Calvin	Lowe, Emma Lou - Shrayer, Jean	J.D.-Carroll / Doug / Oakland
Ray, Hugh	Apr 28, 1972	58		Knoxville, Tn								Presbyterian
Ray, James William	Feb 25, 1989	79	Hill Haven	New Market	May 1, 1909	Ray, Luther	Swann, Julia	Ray, Ruby	Stephenson, Ruth - King, Lucille - Ray, Anna Lee	Herman - James	Nicholson, Arlene [Pals] Nephews	St. Lukes - New Market, Tn
Ray, Luther B. [Col]	Nov 4, 1985	65	Knoxville, Tn	Tn	Mar 15, 1890	Ray, Joe	Unk			Ray, James		St. Luke Presbyterian
Ray, Mildred Louise	May 26, 1993	68	Winter Park, Florida	New Market	Mar 22, 1925	Strawberry, Lilburn	Roach, Effie	Ray, Clifford [D]	Bob	Richard, Katherine - Cain, Betty - Swann, Sue - Trent, Barbara - Lewis, Leona - Hogan, Judy	Herman-Fred-Ed-Joe-L.R. Jr.	Brother - [Pals-Nephews] / Strawberry Plains
Ray, Robert William	Feb 28, 1978	60	F.S.H.	Ky	May 12, 1917	Ray, John D.	Frances		Marie - Boyle, Gladys R.- Quinn, Kathy	Sweeten, Jan [A/N]	Willie	Oaksland - Granger Co
Ray, Ruby Joe [Black]	Dec 3, 1980	90	Morristown, Tn		Dec 26, 1902	Leabough, Green	Shannon, Hattie	Ray, James [D]	S	Quinn, Kathy - Ray, Marie	Scott, Sarah / Calvin	Sister / St. Lukes
Ray, Stanley William	Feb 16, 1988	47	J.M.H.	Tn	Nov 27, 1940	Ray, Robert	Ray, Frances	S	84-66	Quinn, Kathy - Boyle, Gladys - Ray, Marie	Calvin / Mother	J.M.G.
Ray, Vernon R.	Mar 7, 1976	33	F.S.H.	Sweetwater, Tn	May 21, 1943	Ray, Robert W.	Betty		Marie - Boyle, Gladys - Quinn, Kathy	Joey-Ricky	Stanley-Calvin / Mother	J.M.G.
Reagan, Wanda Faye	Aug 15, 1996	53	S.M.H.	Sevier Co	Jun 2, 1943	Matthews, William	Price, Mable	Reagan, Jack	Miley, Angela & Wayne	Ron	Holland, Gaynell & Bill - Hewett, Darleene [H-Lee] Matthews, Helen [Ind]	Husband / J.M.G.
Rector, Ollie Bell	Sep 9, 1979	74	J.M.H.	Tn	Aug 10, 1903	Climes, -	Bell, Mattie	Rector, Charlie S. [D]			Owens, Barrie	Jim & Betty / Husband
Reece, Annie Mae	Sep 2, 1987	73	F.S.H.	Claiborne Co	Oct 9, 1913	Harrell, Calvin	Ferguson, Louenia	Reece, Charlie [2]	Lynn			Son / Cave Springs - Tazewell, Tn
Reed, Calvin C.	Dec 13, 1967	59		Tn		Reed, Robert		[Nieces]- Marshall, Henrietta [Sci]- Arnold, Rina - Sherman [Ky]	Peck, Mrs. Wilma - Brazelton, Mrs. Leonell	Chapman, Sallie [G-Aunt]		Young- Memorial
Reed, Robert T.	Sep 1, 1957	68		Tn		Reed, Robert	Unk					Reed, Cordie
Reed, William Richard	Apr 14, 1990	69	J.M.H.	Knox Co	Nov 4 1930	Reed, John W.	Oglesby, Nina	Long, Imogene	Terry, Mary - Widener, Terisa - Vickers, Sharon - Hampton, Debbie - Matthews, Vickie - Turner, Cynthia	Billy - [Foster] James, Danny	Bell, Roberta - James, Betty - Glen, Elsie	Frank-Gene-Allen / Willie / Piney
Reedy, Dorthy	Feb 25, 1978	27	Jeff City	Ky	Feb 2, 1951	Brock, Monroe	Caldwell, Nettie	Reedy, Charles	Rita Faye	Tony Lee	Marks, Grace - Shaw, Mollie - Massey, Sue - Hammer, Faye	Walker [Ky]- Charles [Gar]- Elmer [Calif]- David / Shaw, Mollie - Brock, Gill - Caldwell, Millie & David [Late] J.C. [G-Parents - Ky] / J.M.G.
Reese, Ruth	Jul 11, 1989	56	F.S.H.	New Market	Sep 21, 1932	Dukes, M.M.	Dornbush, Bessie	Reese, Conley [Dx]	Conley Seba		Coletan, Bonnie - Kidwell, Zollie - Oakes, Mona	Paul Haskell - James / Son / Nances Grove

Name	Death Date	Age	Place	Birth Place	Birth Date	Father	Mother	Spouse	Children / Relatives	Cemetery
Redfern, Tommie E.	Nov 13, 1975	62	Talbott, Tn	Texas	Nov 14, 1913	Redfern, Andrew Thomas	Luman, Lillie May	Woodbury, Aileen	WW 2; Betsy; Timothy; Long, J.O. - Redfern, Troy [Calif]	J.M.G.
Repass, Armicia T.	Sep 26, 1991	91	J.M.H.	New Market	Feb 18, 1900	Elmore, Elbert S.	Hall, Ellen H.	Repass, Paul H. [D]	Cochran, Jean R.; Dug	New Market
Repass, Carl H.	Nov 28, 1976	84	J.M.H.	Va	Sep 6, 1892	Repass, Emery S.		W	WW 1; Watson, Mrs. Fred [No]; Dugins, Mrs. Harve; E.G.[Fla] Traylor, Wheatley, George - Hodge, Edward - Scarlet, Sam - Deaton, Tom - ??, Frank	New Market
Repass, Paul H.	Nov 11, 1972	72	Jeff Co	Va	Feb 20, 1900	Emery S.	Sutton, Lucy	W	Cochran, Jean; Vernon; William N. - [b-Law] Schaffer, Charles [Net]; Dugins, Ruth; Carl-Garland [Fla]	New Market
Repass, Rillie Elizabeth	Sep 22, 1972	73	J.M.H.	Tn	Oct 10, 1898	Elmore, Elbert S.	Hall, Ellen	Repass, Carl Heber	Watson, Mrs. Fred [No]; Repass, Minnie & Paul H.; J.W.	New Market
Reynolds, Jess E.	Jan 19, 2000	90	Knox Co.	Grand Rapids, Mich.	Sep 26, 1909	Johnson, Frieda Ann [D]	Link	Jessie D.	Randy-Anthony; Hobe	East View
Rice, Ida Belle	Mar 19, 1995	83	Jeff City	Midway-Green Co	Mar 5, 1912	Peck, Tom	Methwood, Letie	W	Whitt, Ann - Henry, Carolyn; Gordon-Kenneth-Clarence; Lacy	St. Joseph Chapel - Midway, Tn
Rice, Vivian Leoena	Apr 5, 2000	70	Claiborne Co.		May 5, 1929	Snoder, Gilbert	Wilson, Verna	Rice, Hobert William [D]	Stivenston, Angela Kay [M] - Lawson, Mavia - Ramona & Mark; Hebert L. & Bonie; Dodds, Pauline [D] - Ragan, Doris [D] - Sawyer, Joyce [Va] - Mauk, Arlene [Va] - Snoder, Eleanor; Ruddph [D] - Robert [D] - Jack, [D]	Hillcrest
Rice, Zelotes [Zeke]	1970		Durham, Nc						Whitt, Ann - Henry, Caroline - Norton, Martha; Clarence-Kenneth-Gordon; Bodine, Laurie B. [G-Daug]	St. Josephs - Green Co
Richardson, Dorothy Mae	Feb 16, 1996	90	New Market	Decatur, Ill	Sep 4, 1905	Stester, Charles	Josleph, Paulina	Richardson, Buford [D]	Booker, Pauline - Doniell, Hazel - [Step-See Obit]; Hall [D]-Sherman & Katherine; Moore, Ellen - Collier, Cora; Half-Wynn F.H. [Durham, Nc]	Cremated
Rickard, Daniel Emett	Sep 17, 1998	95	New Market	Talbott, Tn	Nov 6, 1902	Rickard, Porter	Ryans, Mary	W	WW 2; Lee, Minnie - ?, Margaret [D]; Blaine	Strawberry Plains
Rickard, Michele Wayne	Oct 15, 2000	48	U.T.H.	Jeff Co	Mar 20, 1952	Rickard, Sherman	Strawberry, Katherin	Hobby, April	Chris [D]-Bryan; Ballard, Brenda - Mc Carter, Sharon	Strawberry Plains
Ricker, Arthur R.	Mar 2, 1997	77	J.M.H.	Greeneville, Tn	Mar 18, 1919	Ricker, Harvey Erskin	S	Div	Kelly, Larry [Guardian ?]	Tn Vets - Knoxville, Tn
Riddle, Ada	Jun 29, 1994	87	Jeff Co	Kodak, Tn	Dec 9, 1906	Johnson, Arthur	Brock, Melissa	Riddle, James Grady [D]	Hubort-Paul; Don	New Market
Riddle, James Grady	Jun 14, 1993	85	J.M.H.	Jeff Co	Apr 14, 1908	Riddle, James Alfred	Alpha	Johnson, Ada	Rudder, Thelma - Juanita - Tipton, Bernice - Ingram, Lorene; Hubort-Paul; Rudder, [Pals]-G-Soria] Rudder, Ed-Fred - Rick - Loy, Tom - Mc Cottier, Lorene; Charles	Piney
Riddle, Nancy Evelyn	Jan 19, 1994	45	Jeff Co	Knoxville, Tn	Apr 10, 1948	Ward, Eldridge E.	Smith, Glassie Lou	Smith, Sadie Lou	Smith, Louise - Longmire, Avon - Jones, Helen - Boheman, Ann; Harrol, C.-James A.; Nichols, Patty - Mc Ghee, Brenda; Grady-Donald	Strawberry Plains
Riddle, Robert C.	Nov 28, 1987	73	New Market, Tn	New Market, Tn	Apr 12, 1914	Riddle, James Alfred	Childress, Cordelia	Riddle, Herma	Riddle, James C.; Wayne; Lowe, Leala; Wills - Smith, Roger - Phil - Lee, Roger - Riddle, Frank-David - Mink, Robert	Piney

Name	Date	Age	Place	Birth													Cemetery
Riley, Earnest	May 9, 1980	68	New Market, Tn	Jun 19, 1911	Riley, Arthur		Benson, Elise	Hickman, News			Mc Coil, Brenda	James A.-Donald A.-Ronald A.	Martin, Geneva-Frye, Laura		[Pele] Martin, Tony-Larry - Hamilton, Howard - Clifford - Woods, Jim - Whitley, Chas		Piedmont
Riley, Ella	Jul 2, 1972	85	Jeff Co	Nov 27, 1886	Benson, Neal	Alley, Sarah		W			Martin, Genevieve - Frye, Laura	Ernest		Ross			Piedmont
Riner, Barbara A.	Dec 19, 1990	51	J.M.H.	Oct 10, 1939	Anderson, Kenneth B.	Lamon, Stella		Riner, Bobby G.			Chambers, Jamie	Gary	Haynes, Jo				Piedmont
Riner, Minnie Belle	Mar 26, 1998	82	Dandridge, Tn	Nov 26, 1905	Horton, Mack	Davis, Catherine		Riner, William Mc Kinley	WW 1		Carmichael, Nadine & R.C.	Bob-Bill-Jimmy-Kenneth-Dennis Ray	Bacon, Elizabeth	John-Carkin	Son		East View - Strawberry Plains
Riner, William Mc Kinley	Aug 5, 1978	82	Wise Co, Va	Apr 21, 1896	Riner, George	Honeycutt, Jicey	Horton, Minnie Belle	WW 1		Carmichael, Nadine & R.C.	Bill-Bob-Jerry-Kenneth-Jimmy	Riner, Daniel E.	Charlie-King	Aug 5, 1978			Strawberry Plains
Rines, Clifford Lee	Dec 25, 1994	82	V.A. Mc Home	Feb 14, 1922	Rines, Emmet	Lane, Ida			WW 2	Williams, Kathy	Clifford Jr.-Danny-Mickey	Rines, Margaret - Smith, Rachel - Mathews, John - Watts, Mae	East-Carl-Ebony	Rines, Daniel E. [Snr] - [Pele] Rines, W. E. - Foster, J.R.	White Pine		White Pine
Rines, Irene	Nov 1, 1957	30	New Market	Mar 1, 1927	Sawyers, Art	Rines, Clifford	Sawyers, Irene [2]			Kathy	Clifford-Danny-Mikel	Peoples, Lori - Chas, Henderson - Ada-Gray, Cecil	3		U. Brethern - White Pine, Tn		
Rines, John Albert	Aug 5, 1987	59	Jeff City	Mar 8, 1938	Rines, Jackie	Knight, Lillie Mae	Louise [Div]	Emily R. Reva		[Step] Long, Frank		J.T. [B] - Sanford			Friendship Missionary Baptist		
Ripley, Herman Stratton	Jan 7, 1998	77	Morristown, Tn Mc Graw, Ky	Jan 18, 1920	Ripley, Thomas	Medlin, Leah	Fulton, Thelma	Dennis, Anna May		Phillips, Ann [M] - Drake, Terry - Ripley, Sheila	Timothy [M] - Gary [M]	Stansbury, Effie - Dalton, Thelma			Littlebrook - Maryville, Tn		
Roach, Curtis	Feb 15, 1981	71	Grainger Co	Jan 17, 1909	Roach, Ben	Maples, Beatrice		Medlin, Leah							Highland Memorial East		Highland Memorial East
Roach, Lawrence Martin	Sep 22, 1987	54	Grainger Co	Sep 3, 1933	Roach, Marion	Roberts, Minnie	Taylor, Lorene		Ng	Turley, Mariane-Darlene	Clevenger, Helen - Williams, Irene	Howard-Halliner-Harrell	[Pele-Nephews] Williams, Tom-Rick - Spears, Ron - Wright, Ron - Leon - Shirea, Max	Oakland			Oakland
Roach, Neal R.	Apr 13, 1982	76	U.T.H.	Apr 15, 1906	Roach, R.	Wynick, Kathy							[Pele] Banks, Carol - Reich, Ralph - Mitchell, Ted - Drummer, James - Taylor, Gene	[Pele] Banks, Carol - Reich, Ralph - Mitchell, Ted - Drummer, Leon - Shirea, Max - Mullins, Bill			

Name	Date	Age	Place	Residence	Birth Date	Father	Mother	Spouse	Military	Family / Survivors	Other	Informant	Cemetery
Roach, Noble Elizabeth	May 17, 1990	91	Powell, Tn	Granger Co	Jan 27, 1899	Roach, Jim Frank	Morgan, Cordelia			Duck, Gladys		Hoback, Alice [Ind]-Herbert-Ballinger, Austin-Ed-Cochran, Chester-Boecher-Satterfield, Donald / [Pals] Duck, Donald-Patrick-Ellis, George-Pitkey, Richard-Womble, Roger	Oakland
Roach, Ruby Mae	Dec 25, 1976	75	J.M.H.	Jeff Co	Apr 10, 1901	Franklin, W.C.	Gant, Suda	W		Roach, Robert-Gay, Raymond-[Ind]-Lester [Calif]		Charles	Ballinger
Roberts, H.B. Sr.	Jun 8, 1984	80	J.M.H.	Hancock Co	Dec 11, 1903	Roberts, James A.	Williams, Roda	Trent, Velena		Hutson, Leoria-Harrison, Elizabeth-Jean-Bowlin, Vivian-Williams, Williams Jo	Roberts, H.B. Jr.-Pope, Irene-David, Leslie	Wife-[Pals] Anderson, Paul-Shelton, Roy-Curt-Jackson, James-Wilder, Buster-Bates, Donnie	J.M.G.
Roberts, Myrtle Lou Brooks	May 15, 1992	88	J.M.H.	Granger Co	May 3, 1904	Kitts, Lorzo	Seymour, Martha	Roberts, Thomas [D]			Brewer, Condon	[Pals] Jernigan, Troy-McCall, Charles-Haggard, Bill-Duck, Donald-Bruner, Egar-Renes, Chris	Strawberry Plains
Robinson, Charles Daniel	Sep 8, 1993	68	V.A.-Mt. Home	Murphy, Nc	Jan 28, 1925	Lewis, Roy L.	Lewis, Mamie	Gann, Dorcas Earleen	Army	Edmonds, Sara	Dan	Military	J.M.G.
Roderick, Alvin [Zack]	Nov 4, 1996	70	S.M.H.	Strawberry Plains	Jul 10, 1918	Roderick, Jim	Thomas, Fannie	Jones, Velma J.	Air Force	Roderick, Arthur Jr. E.	Yoder, Mary Alice-Minton, Deloris	Arnold-Don-David-Rick	Charlie	Valley View
Roderick, Betty Jo	Nov 3, 1997	63	Morristown, Tn	Jeff City	Jul 28, 1934	Pruitt, Victor		unk		Roderick, Arthur Jr. [D]			Piney Grove
Roderick, Edgar J.	Oct 29, 1982	59	Vet Hosp.-Mt. Home	Jeff City	Aug 10, 1878			Unk		Roderick, James	Thomas-Charles-Alvin	D.A.-A.M.	Piney
Roderick, Fannie	Jan 25, 1965	86	Maloneyville	Wales, England		Thomas	Unk	Roderick, James				D.A. A.M.	Roderick, D.A.
Roderick, Leona Joyce	Jan 12, 1990	67	U.T.H.	New Market	Oct 4, 1922	Willard, Earl	Wilson, Frannie	Roderick, Charlie		Moneymaker, Clara	James	Hazel-Denton, Lucy	Welch, Mealy [Doug.]-Ala. / Hatband-[Pals] Roderick, Jerry-Ralph-Charles-Denton, Charles-Lawson, James-Hensley, Dan	Valley View [Rocky Valley]
Roderick, Steve William	May 16, 1998	49	Jeff City	Aug 26, 1948	Roderick, William	Brooks, Mable L.	Dix	Army	Summers, Tina A.	Steve A-Bryan L.-Chabough, Sabrina & Rusi	Heath, Judy & Bud-Chabough, Sabrina & Rusi & Rusi & Charlene	Brooks, Bertie [G-Mother]	Blue Springs
Roderick, Thomas Edward	Jun 19, 1990	80	J.M.H.	Jasper, Alabama	May 20, 1910	Roderick, James	Welch, Fannie	Denton, Mary Frances		Heath, Judy & Bud-Clabough, Sabrina & Rubin		Wife-[Pals] Roderick, Jerry-Gary-Ralph-James-Hensley, Dan-Allsup, Rex	Piney
Roderick, William Alvin	Oct 28, 1998	70	S.M.H.	Shaw Plains	Apr 28, 1928	Roderick, Arthur	Lawson, Annie Lou	Brooks, Mabel			Rhea & Charlene	Everett / [Pals] Smith, Roger-Roderick, Jerry-Gary-Ralph-Cline, Danny-Jack-Berduna, Tony	Blue Springs
Rogers, Flora Gertrude	Sep 22, 1995	93	Jeff City	Oak Grove, Tn	Jan 9, 1902	McCreary, Joseph N.	Nov, Eve Kim	Rogers, Stephen Leslie [D]			Rogers, Stephen Leslie [D]	Myers, Tom [nephew]	Cuibert Memorial - Sheffield, Ala.
Rogers, Natalia	Jan 1, 1971	12				Rogers, Joseph N.	Rogers, Mamie					Theresa-Valarie-Evelyn / Ott-Darrell-Tommy / Riley, Mary-Fretn, Mrs. ?-[G-Mother]	St. Luke Presbyterian

Name	Date	Age	Place	Location	Date	Father	Mother	Spouse	Children / Relations			
Rogers, Rebecca / Rogers, Roger	Dec 27, 1955 / Dec 27, 1955		Jeff City / Jeff City		Dec 27, 1955 / Dec 27, 1955	Rogers, Tom E.	Ga	Ga				Rogers, Tom / Rogers, Tom
Romines, Arvilla Clyde	Aug 28, 1994	95	F.S.H.	Dandridge, Tn	Apr 26, 1899	Romines, James L.	Burchfiel, Elizabeth	Romines, Clyde [D]	Justion, Elizabeth - Thornton, Shelbie	J.C. & Alice		Rogers, Tom Romines, Steve-Bob-Harold- Coleman, Philip- Lynn, Stan - Posey, John	Hillcrest
Romines, Zola Mae	Oct 22, 2000	96	Doylestown, Pa	Mascot, Tn	Jan 14, 1912	Mowery, Arthur	Bailey, Mattie	Romines, Clyde [D]	Mary Frances- Crooks	Walker-Leftwicki	Clyde [D]		Hillcrest
Roper, John [Col]	May 7, 1954	88	New Market	Tn	Aug 18, 1892	Roper, James	Usie	S			Walker	Roper, Walter Herman- Johnson, Ezmel- Scruggs, Caleb- Pate, Edd	St. Lukes Presby, New Market
Roper, Leedy [M - Col]	Oct 28, 1979	45	F.S.H.	Tn	Jul 1, 1934	Roper, John Manuel	Hardine, Lois	S				Walter [Pat] Thomas, Herman - Willis [Pat]	St. Lukes Presbyterian
Ross, Hilliard Robert	Mar 6, 1985	72	J.M.H.	Lone Mt. Claibourne Co	Mar 23, 1912	Ross, Frank	Liford, Maude		Gass, Priscilla & Fred - Clark, Vada & Raymond	Vocial Lee	Hazel		J.M.G.
Ross, Leon	May 9, 1990	80	New Market	New Market	Apr 26, 1900	Ross, Tom	Long, Beulah		Collins, Margaret G.	Carroll, Shirley	Larry	Rucker, Beatrice	Billy
Ross, Lillian Pearl	Dec 23, 1996	33	Jeff City	Tn	Jun 17, —	Ross, John	Young, Lellla	Ross, Vocial Lee	Debbie	Jeffery-Ricky-Jerry	Johnson, Hettie		Mills Springs
Rosenbalm, Birkie Beatrice	Jan 7, 1990	88	Forrest Hills	Greene Co	Jun 10, 1891		Morrisson, Polly	Rosenbalm, James [D]					
Rosenbalm, James M.	Feb 3, 1995	67	J.M.H.	Hamblen Co	Jan 26, 1917	Rosenbalm, James	Gaby, Birkie	Lane, Minnie	Hinchey, Sylvia-Garland, Sandy	James-Earl-Archie-Gary	Shelton, Ora Nan - Hefner, Lily	Earl-Archie-Gary	J.M.G.
Rudder, Creola Bernice	Sep 18, 2000	90	Jeff City	Knox Co	Sep 26, 1919	Reece, Johnnie	Walker, Lula	Rudder, Edgar [D]	Ley, Pet	Joe [D]	Hammstead, Mabel - Ley, Polly	McGhee, Ruth	Roseberry
Rudder, Dorothy	Dec 3, 1993	67	Hill Haven	Knox Co	Feb 27, 1926	Rudder, Fred	Titis, Maude	S		Chris		Allen-Claude	Friends Station
Rupert, Elizabeth Nell	Dec 21, 1998	25	Knox Co	Tn	Jan 21, 1943	Wollenhanger, Carl Verlin	Howard, Virginia Nell	Rupert, William Thomas	Missy	Bobby	Allen-Claude	Sister Husband- Wollenhanger, Walter-Howard, Russ [O-Parents]	Mills Spring
Rupert, Robert James	Dec 6, 1964	65	J.M.H.	Tn	Nov 2, —	Rupert, William M.	Campbell, -	Lillie L.	Miller, Lena Kate - Stroud, Dorothy - Lorine - Elmore, Eva K.	Bobby Spencer-Tommy	Bryant, Marie - Stelle, Sue	William K.	Rupert, Bobby [Son]
Russell, Alice	Sep 21, 1978	65	Knoxville, Tn	Tn	Aug 21, 1918	Rudder, Fred	Titis, Maude	Russell, Clifford L.	Spencer, Brenda - Medbron, Donna L.		Sallee, Lucille - Glove, Ruth - Rudder, Miss Dorothy	Allen, Claude	Friends Station

Name	Death Date	Age	Place	Residence	Birth Date	Father	Spouse/Mother	N.M.	Status	War	Relatives	Mother	Burial
Russell, Angela Michelle	Aug 19, 1994	20	Jeff City	Morristown	Jul 5, 1974	Ray, Arlie	Russell, Glenda		S			Husband - (Rita) Trent, Curtis-Mike-Glenn - Mr. Daniel, Jerry	J.M.G.
Russell, Bertie Edna	Dec 28, 1987	67	F.S.H.	Hancock Co.	Dec 2, 1920	Trent, Fred	Odom, Laura				Lithsey, Evelyn - Shanks, Lois - Tipton, Linda	Griffey, Eddie - Russell, Michael - Patrick-Randy	Kincaid, Arkie - Mc Daniel, Elma	Husband - Pollards - Kodak, Tn
Russell, Clifford Lee	Oct 24, 1999	85	Jeff City	Sevier Co.	Dec 10, 1913	Russell, Harvey	Underwood, Hattie			WW 2	Spencer, Brenda - Lamb, Donna	C.L. - [Step] Mc Nish, Fred	Hazelwood, Willie	Friends Station
Russell, David	Aug 25-1970	14	Jeff Co.	Tn	Oct 22, 1955	Russell, Harvey	Cain, Martha		S			Ross, Jeanie - Lockhart, Mrs. Bert Lee - Nora, Mrs. Micky		Friends Station
Russell, Doris Jean	Sep 18, 1965		Tn	Tn	Mar 19, 1947	Russell, Clifford	Rudder, Alice		S					
Russell, Eva Madaline	Jun 5, 1997	78	J.M.H.	Jeff Co	Sep 30, 1918	Russell, George E.	Kooch, Mary Jane		S				Ray D.	Mc Campbells Chapel
Russell, George Albert	Jun 22, 2000	69	F.S.H.	Sevier Co.	Jun 3, 1931	Russell, Harvey	Underwood, Hattie				Lightsey, Evelyn [Td] - Hill, Bertie Leo Gritty [Td] - Tipton, Linda	Russell, Randy [D] - Griffey, Stan - Russell, Mike-Pat	Williams, Mary [D]	Pollards
Russell, Harriet Ann	Jun 15, 1984	70	Knox Co	Tn	Jun 7, 1894	Turner, Joseph	Williamson, Elizabeth				Clotfelter, Mattie Byrum, Ruby - Myruett, Mrs. Paul	James W. - William Robert - Clifford-Harvey-George	Hill, Easter	Husband
Russell, Harve	Mar 10, 1989	80	Jeff City	Tn	Jul 28, 1888	Russell, Sam	Bates, Ellen				Hattie U.		Frank	Wife
Russell, Harvey Harry	Sep 28, 1973	53	Jeff Co	Tn	Sep 1, 1920	Russell, Harve	Underwood, Hattie		WW 2		Nora, Mrs. Mickey - Ross, Jeanie Lockhart, Bertie Lee	Elnora, Mrs. Willie - Williams, Mary	Clifford-George	Friends Station
Russell, Hattie Paralee Underwood	Jul 16, 1994	89	Sevier Co	Apr 12, 1895	King, George	Underwood, Alice		S		Hazelwood, Willie [D]	Raineater, Mary Jane - Smith, Betty	Harvey, Ethel - Fath, Mrs. Mack	Daughter	Pollards - Kodak, Tn
Russell, Hugh Paul	Dec 23, 1977	70	Hamblen Co	Hawkin Co	May 18, 1907	Russell, Joseph J.	Stubblefield, Mollie				Rooch, Nellie J.	Russell, Harvey [D]	J.D.-John-James - Hollis-Hugh	Harvey, Ethel - Fath, Mrs. Mack	Wife	Sunderland
Russell, J. Frank	Sept 8, 1950	54	New Market, Tn	New Market, Tn	Aug 31, 1896	Russell, J.A.	Bunch, Ellen M.	N.M.	N.M.			Mary - Harder, Mrs. Charles [Nd] - Allny, Mrs. A.R. [Ga]	William-James A.	New Market
Russell, James A.	Aug/Sep, 1966		J.M.H.		Sep 7, 1918		Hazel		Hazel		[Step] Banks, Ruth - Rupert, Mrs. Tommy	Whaley, Mrs. George [W. Va]	Estate	New Market
Russell, James A. 3rd [Cpl.]	May 29, 1968	21	Vietnam	Tn	Mar 30, 1947	Russell, James [D]	Hazel		S	vietnam		Banks, Ruth - Rupert, Mrs. Tommy	Ronnie	[Escort] Sgt. Cole
Russell, Joseph Deadrick	Dec 27, 1992	60	Jeff Co	Jeff Co	Apr 15, 1932	Rooch, Paul	Rooch, Nellie		S	korea	Div	Martin, Linda Sue - Tipton, Nora J.	Smith, Barry - Odom, Mary Jane	Nora	Hebron - Jeff City, Tn
Russell, Nellie Jane	Jan 13, 2000	91	Peoria, Ill	Jun 18, 1908	Byrd, Rachael	Russell, Hugh Paul [D]	Zola	Smith, Betty Lou - Odom, Mary Jane	Michael Joseph	J.D. [D]-Hollis-Hugh T.-John	Russell, Michael-Patrick [1/2] Griffey, Edward	Nora	Sunderland
Russell, Terry Randy	May 7, 1989	23	New Market	Jeff City	May 24, 1966	Russell, George	Trent, Bertie		S			Whaley, Mrs. George [W. Va] - Banks, Ruth - Rupert, Mrs. Tommy	Mann, Mrs. Barrie [Step-Mother]	Russell, Chris - Mills, Greg - Whitehead, Scott - Bates, Jeff - Randy - May, Bobby	New Market
Salyer, Earnest B.	Oct 25, 1977	59	J.M.H.	Va	May 21, 1918	Salyer, Paris	Gibson, Lafkie		S		Dyer, Joe P. - Salyer, Earnest - Betty Lou [Pat] - Butcher, Carolyn	Gardos, Delora [Kit] - Mc Ghee, Betty Lou [Pat] - Lynn-Sam-Lyel [Co]	Dyer, Joe P. - Salyer, Earnest Lynn-Sam-Lyel [Co]	Wife	Friends Station

Name	Death	Age	Loc1	Loc2	Birth	Father	Mother								Burial
Sanders, Edna Marie	Apr 28, 1995	67	B.H.	New Market	Apr 27, 1927	Northern, Hasiow	Blanche		Sanders, George Gordon [D]	Callies, Donnie - Graves, Linda	Title, Earl A. - Smith, Steve	Rickson, Elleene [Ind]	George [Ind]- Jack [Ind]	Debbie - [Pats] Johnson, Rob- Warren - Smith, Jason - Title, Tim - Strucomen, Eric - Graves, Dennis - Grey, Dennis - Odom, Roger	Hamblen Memorial
Sanders, Esther A.	May 13, 1959	82		New Market	Apr 28, 1877	James, Joe	Pierce, Mary	Tn	Sanders, James A.					Husband	Friends, Station
Sanders, George Gordon	Nov 17, 1994	74	Morristown, Tn	Blacksville, Sc	Nov 12, 1920	Sanders, Edmond	Beckly, Daisy		Echa N.	Army	Graves, Linda - Callies, Debbie	Earl Title-Steve Smith	Farrell	Willie - [Pats] Callies, Dwayne - Graves, Brook - Graves, Dennis - Donnie, Pat - Mirachell, James - Kroy, Bob- Bowling, Rick	Hamblen Memorial
Sanders, James Hopkins	Jul 11, 1983	83	J.M.H.	Tn	May 15, 1880	Sanders, Band	Little, Sarah	Tn	Esther Ann	Army		M.F.-Kyle D.	Sanders, Kyle D. [Son] - Maples, Ann [Niece]		Friends Station
Sanders, Kyle Doane	Jul 13, 1994	76	S.M.H.	New Market	Sep 6, 1917	Sanders, Jim	James, Esther	S				Sellers, Addie			Friends Station
Sanders, Millard	Aug 6, 1981	73	U.T.H.	Jeff Co	Aug 17, 1907	Sanders, Jim	James, Esther	Tn	Sellers, Lucy		Kleple, Mrs. Marion - Cunningham, Lola - Miller, Irene - Millington, Mary Ann - White, Barbara - Janice	Barbara-Janice - Dunn, Mrs. Floyd - Miller, Mrs. Jim - Cunningham, Mrs. Fred - Millington, Mrs. Charles	Kyle		New Market
Sanders, Ray Leonard	Aug 28, 1983	32	U.T.H.	Jeff Co	Oct 10, 1931	Sanders, M.F.	Sellers, Lucy	Tn	Poore, Geneva	Virginia Gail	Monte-Ray-Ricky Gary	Holloway, Vickie	Mc Daniels, Phillip		Friends Station
Sands, Betsy Lou	Jul 12, 1983		Knoxville, Tn	Jeff City	May 2, 1935	Smith	Wilkerson, Bess		Sands, Paul				West View		West View
Sartain, Pauline Elizabeth	Mar 28, 1984	76	F.S.H.	Jeff Co	Nov 9, 1907	Templin, Will	Denton, Lena		Sartain, Lewis T.				George	Husband - [Pats] White, Francis - Daughtry, Ron - Carmichale, Don - Denton, Rob- Carkin - Crawford, Cordelle - Fox, Robert	J.M.G.
Satterfield, Horace A.	Mar 29, 1960	82	New Market		Jan 6, 1878	James, Joe	Daniel, Martha	Tn		Jennie - Anderson, Elsie - Combs, Lillian	Wiley-Russell- Harry	Morgan, Pearl	S.G.	[Pals] Guire, John - Denton, Jack - Whitaker, Jim - Helc, Jim - Willis, Donnie-Toby	Nances Grove
Satterfield, Horace Albert Jr.	Mar 21, 1977	71	J.M.H.	Tn	Sep 7, 1905	Satterfield, Horace Albert Sr.	Hodge, Aurilla	Tn					Satterfield, Albert [Son]		Nances Grove
Satterfield, Jennie	Mar 23, 1977	69	U.T.H.		Sep 12, 1907	Satterfield, Albert Sr.	Hodge, Aurilla						Jennie - Combs, Lillian	Willey-Harvey- Russell [Pa]	Nances Grove
Savage, David Franklin	Jan 7, 1997	32	Strawberry Plains	Toledo, Ohio	Sep 26, 1964	Watertoo, Dwaid	Snyder, Rita	S				Whitmill, Kathy & Doyle	Harrison, Danny [Step-Mark]	Harrison, Dan [Step-Father]	Cremated

Name	Death Date	Age	Death Place	Birth Place	Birth Date	Father		Mother		Spouse	Children / Notes	Other	Burial
Scott, Arthur Elinore	Jun 25, 1979	48	Nashville, Tn	Tn	May 29, 1931	Scott, Minter Arthur	Tn	Roach, Eva	Tn	Will, Dorothy	Barbara - Tned, Patricia	[Pals] Mc Call, House, Margaret - Mc Call, Tim - Sheek, Maudie - Dunson, Middie - Hensley, Judy - Lawson, Alma	Strawberry Plains
Scarbrough, Jessie	Jan 6, 1950	68	Jeff City	New Market, Tn	Nov 27, 1881	Taylor, W.H.	Tn	Biddle, Mary C.	Tn	Scarbrough, Sam M.	Patterson, Mrs. R.L. [N] - Neese, Mrs. D.M.	William M.	Scarbrough, Sam	Patterson, Chucky	[Pals] Mc Call, Johnny - Gary - Scott, Billy - Patterson, Chucky	New Market
Scarlett, Bonnie Beatrice	May 21, 1968	72	Paint Rock, Tn		Mar 26, 1916	Jordan, Ada		Scarlett, J.P. [U]			Pem	Pete	Lane, Mabel	Husband	New Market
Scarlett, William Alger	Feb 9, 1982	38	J.M.H.	Tn	Jun 2, 1943	Scarlett, J.P.		Kerr, Bonnie			Sammie Lynn	John	Jack	[Pals] Fox, Robert - Kerr, Jack - Lane, Mike - Holloway, Gary - Scarlett, Sam	New Market
Scarlett, Edna Mae	Oct 29, 1987	82	J.M.H.	Jeff Co	Apr 6, 1905	Scarlett, Thomas Sherman		Williamson, Sarah Ann		Scarlett, William A. [D]	Pete-Bill Billy - [Step] Sammy Lynn - Johnny Bell	Scott, Peggy & Harold [Retired]	[Pals] Halloway, Gary - James, Bobby - Mitchell, Bill - Scarlett, Sam - Robert-John Ned	Deep Springs
Scarlett, John Perry	Jul 3, 1973	60	J.M.H.	Tn	May 18, 1913	Scarlett, C.M.		French, Lula		Kerr, Bonnie			Wills	New Market
Scarlett, Sarah	Aug 8, 1977	30	J.M.H.	Jeff Co	Oct 23, 1946	Ellison, Thomas				Scarlett, Bill	Pem		Husband	New Market
Schrader, Oliver C.	Oct 9, 1951	55	Jeff Co	Tn	Mar 2, 1896	Unk		Unk		Lorene		Jack	Schaffer, Charles G. [brother - Not Dead] Doug - [Pals] Fink, Bill - Schrader, Lloyd - Sam-Mike-Almeda - Justin-Tim - Glenom, Morgan	Sutherland
Schrader, Alger Ray	May 4, 1995	88	Chestnut Hill, Tn		Mar 10, 1907	Shrader, Robert		Finchum, Pearl		Schrader, Maude K. [D]	Robert-Wayne	Radine - Mc Ghee, Ann	Robert-Frank-Oliver	Beaver Creek
Schrader, George Lenora [F]	Oct 15, 1991	87	Cummings, Ga.	Sevier Co	Jun 29, 1904	Lowe, William		Cotter, Lucy		Schrader, John W. [D] Lowe, George Lenora	John Caton	John C.	Son	East View
Schrader, John Wilber	Nov 28, 1972	71	Knox Co	Tn	Mar 13, 1901	Schrader, Palmer		Williams, --					Holston View
Schrader, Maude Lee	Aug 14, 1982	74	Waco, Texas		Mar 4, 1908	Kimbrough, James Hale		Sheen, Mary Lou		Schrader, A. Ray	Radine - Mc Ghee, Beverly Ann	Jones, Ada - Lester, Robert Hale-H. Wayne	[Pals] Shrader, Miller-Stam-Jack-Lester, Ronnie-Patterson, Carl-Jones, Arvin	Beaver Creek
Schrader, Hartense [N,U]	Oct 25, 1983	76	J.M.H.	Jeff Co	Nov 17, 1906	Unk		Henry, Margaret		Schreiber, Harvey William			Finchum, Bill	Cremated
Schroer, Gerald Allen	Oct 31, 1964	1d	E.T.H.	E.T.H.	Oct 30, 1964	Schroer, Kenneth J.		Lamar, Kathleen		S			Father	J.M.G.
Schroer, Steven Scott	Dec 31, 1963	1d	Hamblen Co	Tn	Dec 20, 1963	Schroer, Kenneth J.		Lamar, Kathleen		S			Father	J.M.G.
Scott, Edward [Negro]	Nov 25, 1977	81	Mt. Home	Tn	Jan 12, 1896	John		Callie		Sarah			Appalachian F.H. [Johnson City, Tn]	Holly Hills
Scott, Hubert Glenn	Feb 18, 1981	73	J.M.H.	Jasper Co, Mo	May 17, 1907	Scott, Winfield Fredrick	III	Mc Neamey, Margaret Agnes	Ind	Hackett, Gwendolyn			Scott, Michael	G.A.R. - Miami, Oklahoma
Scott, James	Feb 5, 1974	40	Allegan, Mich	Tn	Feb 21, 1933				S	S	Lucy - Dotson, Julia Fay		Lucy - Dotson, Julia Fay	Nyberg F.H. [Allegan, Mich]	New Market
Scott, Ruby Jean	Oct 2, 1948	6m	New Market, Tn	New Market, Tn	Mar 29, 1948	Brooks, Hubert		Scott, Catherine	Tn	S			Brooks, Hubert	Father	Piedmont

Name	Date	Age	Place	Date	Link							Cemetery
Scruggs, Base [Negro]	Jan 14, 1960	79	New Market	Feb 22, 1882	Scruggs, Henry		S			Scruggs, Roger [Son]; Arnold, Jack L. [Bro, Sis]	Scruggs, Roger [Son]	Methodist / Younge Memorial
Scruggs, Calvin E.	Jul 21, 1997	65	New Market	Sep 16, 1931	Scruggs, Wilmer					Scruggs, Sophia [Aunt]; Taylor, Nickolas [Neph]; Scruggs, Ronald [Nephew - Oh]		Younge Memorial
Scruggs, Harvey [Son]	Apr 6, 1953	40	New Market, Tn	May 5, 1912	Scruggs, Boss							Methodist [Col]
Scruggs, Mathew [Col]			Harris, Nc		Reed, Geneva				Taylor, Nadine	Wilmer		New Market Methodist [Col]
Scruggs, Hester [Negro]	Feb 22, 1960	69	Nc	Jul 21, 1890	Harris, Hester	Nc			Scruggs, Boss	Jessie [1/2]; Thompson, Lillian	Willmer	Father
Scruggs, Infant [Negro]	Nov 11, 1954	sb	Jeff Co	Nov 11, 1954	Phipps, Lorene	Tn					Wilmer-Roger; [1/2] Scruggs, Will	
Scruggs, Wilma R. [Negro]	Sep 5, 1978	66	Forrest City, Nc	Dec 9, 1909						Calvin	Roger	Beaver Creek
Seabolt, Marvin Carlise	Aug 2, 1999	63	Tazewell, Tn	Feb 22, 1936	Seabolt, Silas				S	Cox, Mary Lee		Beaver Creek
Seacrest, David Fitzgerald	May 7, 1996		Jeff City	Apr 28, 1964	Donahue, Nora		Northern, Pauline			Carl Jr. & Robbie-Ray & Lisa	Lawrence-Stanley	Cremated
Seal, Ethel Christine [German]	Apr 1, 1999	73	Decatur, Ga	Feb 18, 1926	Seacrest,William G.			S	Navy	Mayes, Etta	Dennis-Wayne-Timothy S. [Ga]	Slater - Brown, Craig	Beaver Creek
Seals, Barbara Faye	Aug 31, 1990	62	Jeff City	Jun 6, 1937	Burkhart, William C.		Seal, Milborn				Duggan, Mary [Cal]; Graves, Elttie - Hall, Susie	Stanley-Steve [Ky]; R.T. Patterson F.H. [Norcross, Ga]	Beaver Creek
Seals, Beulah Goldie	Jan 1, 1997	84	Mascot, Tn	Sep 2, 1912	Lockhart, Wayne		Seals, Albert J.	WW 2		Reeves, Hazel & Conbey - Faanbush, Christine	Tim-Danny & Danella	Jerry [D]-Jim-Larry-Ronnie	J.M.G.
Seals, Grant Campbell	Jun 16, 1998	84	Hancock Co	Dec 14, 1913	Poore, Dan		Seals, Beulah G.[d]	Navy			Calvin	Seals, Don & Betty - Carroll; Charlie - Atkins; Lena Mae [G-Parents]	Beaver Creek
Seals, Randi Marie	Jun 27, 1984		F.S.H.	Jun 27, 1984	Seals, Randall Jerome		Seals, Grant	unk		Wright, Dorothy	Don-Albert	Collins, Ollie - Atkins, Viola & Gene - Carroll, Earnest	West View
Seals, Alfred	Jan 11, 1994	91	New Market	May 2, 1902	Seals, Neal Sr.		Seals, Neal			Manning, Sharon	Robert-Donald- Albert-Marcel-Ronnie	Smith, Bea- [Step] Turner, Valena	Flat Gap
Seals, Carol Ann	Dec 21, 1984	26	Tn	Oct 22, 1958	Seals, J. Wiley		Roe, Cordie			Jez, Martha	Don-Albert	Harrison-Neal Jr.	New Market
Seals, Clay	Mar 14, 1993	77	Knox Co	May 12, 1915	Seals, Neal		Roe, Cordie			Bailey, Annie	Tim-Danny & Danella	Graham, Martin- Combs, Augusta - Willhoit, Tilda	J.M.G.
Seals, Cordie	Jul 25, 1984	82	New Market	Apr 10, 1882	Rowe, Wiley		Herron, Edith		Clay Alfred	Purkey, Bertha	Smith, Beau-	Mother - Roach, Little - Seals, Neal [G-Parents]; Willis [Paid]; Herron, Junior - Walker Bryon - Murray, Bud - Graham, Jim - Monroe, Collins	Rocky Valley - Jeff Co
Seals, Donald Roger	Jun 19, 1959		Jeff Co	Jun 17, 1959	Seals, Donald	Tn	Collins, Betty	Tn	S		Clay Alfred	Alfred-Harrison-Neal Jr.	Seals, Neal Jr. [Son]	West View

Name	Death Date	Age	Place	County	Birth Date	Father	Mother	Spouse/Relation	Relatives 1	Relatives 2	Relatives 3	Relatives 4	Cemetery
Seals, Harrison John	Jan 12, 1996	84	J.M.H.	Hancock Co.	Nov 15, 1911	Seals, Neal	Rose, Cordia		Allay, Polly & Bob - Denton, Barbara & Roger - Longmire, Joyce & Carl - Bellinger, Sue	Wilts - [Pati] Allay, Joe - Denton, Chris-Jeff-Matt - Longmire, Cole - Bellinger, Curtis - Watson, Brad	Timothy Albert - James Edward	Neal Jr. / Parents	J.M.G.
Seals, Jeffrey Mitchell	Jun 9, 1963	89	J.M.H.	Tn	Jun 8, 1963	Seals, Clay Albert (Tn)	Cook, Lena F. (Tn)	S	Lemmon, Nina				Rocky Valley Baptist
Seals, Neal Sr.	Feb -, 1967	89		Tn				Seals, Alfred			Johnson, Ida - Wilhite, Tida - Graham, Myrtle - Cox, Augusta - Thomas, Bertha [Ill.]	Alfred-Harrison-Clay-Neal Jr. / Robert; Harold; Roger Allen	First Gap
Seals, Ollie Kate	Sep 10, 1993	87	J.M.H.	Jeff City	Aug 20, 1906	Henchey, Robert P.	Clevenger, Birdie	Seals, Alfred	Mason, Margie - Daniels, Mary Lou - Bellinger, Betty	Richard-John-George-Bert-Buddy	Robert	Robert	
Seals, Ray Neal	May 14, 1957	11	Jeff Co	Tn	Nov 14, 1945	Seals, Raymond (Tn)	Clark, Corum (Tn)						
Seals, Raymond Wooten	Nov -, 1966	48	S.M.H.	Tn	Aug 28, 1916	Seals, Neal Sr.	Lowe, Cordia (Tn)	Corum	Infantry		Robert	Robert	New Market
Seals, Roger Allen	May 21, 1964	10	Jeff Co	Tn	Nov 1, 1963	Seals, Raymond	Clark, Corum						New Market
Sellers, Irene	Feb 23, 1963	63	Sevier Co. Hosp.	Jeff Co.	Jun 28, 1919	Gibbons, John Ebb	Cameron, Mary Kate	Sellers, Floyd	Vance, Mae Belle - Blake, Katherine - French, Elizabeth - Bates, Shirley - [Step] Guess, Lorine	Crue, Blanche - Walker, Ollie - Thompson, Bessie - Hubbard, Margaret	Cameron, John - [Step] Sellers, Roy		Deep Springs
Sellers, Amanda Erin	Mar 10, 1986	0	Dandridge, Tn	Dandridge, Tn	Mar 10, 1986	Sellers, Paul	Holbrook, Tina					Sellers, Paul F. Sr. - Hollrook, Sam S. - Reed, Chester [G-Parents]	New Market
Sellers, Beulah Mae	Jan 18, 1990	79	Morristown, Tn	New Market	Jan 16, 1911	Foster, J.S.	Wright, Virra	Sellers, Coy	Mills, Betty [Dolly] - Lathron, Clara Ann - Carmichael, Ivahna Lee - Green, Chris		Howard, Gladys		Piedmont
Sellers, Billie Ruth	Mar 14, 1985	75	Shelbyville, Tn	Knox Co	Jul 31, 1909	Leek, Charlie	Vaughn, Della	Sellers, Paul J. [P]			William F.	Sellers, Sessie E. [Son] - Sellers, J.D.-Dean - Vance, Jessie - Cunningham, Fred	J.M.G.

Name	Date	Age	Place	County	Birth Date	Father	Mother	Spouse	Children / Relatives				Wills	Cemetery
Sellars, Coy Dallas	Sep 27, 1972	63		Tn	Jun 13, 1909	Sellars, Elbert	White, Sarah	Foster, Beulah	Carmichael, Mrs. Bill - Larcco, Mrs. - Mills, Mrs. W.A. - Green, Mrs. Robert				Wills	Piedmont
Sellars, Duane Alexander	Nov 17, 1985	72	J.M.H.	Knox Co	Oct 5, 1985	Sellars, Jesse	Sanders, Mattie	Sellars, Ruth		J.D.-Owen	Vance, Ruth	Tabert		Jarnigan
Sellars, Ellen Lucille	Mar 9, 1982	65	J.M.H.	Tn	May 8, 1911	Rudder, Fred	Tittle, Maude	Ng	Floyd Jr.-Boris [Mich.]	J.D.	Floyd Jr-Boris [Mich.]	Coy		Piedmont
Sellars, Floyd Emerson	Oct 21, 1986	65	Royal Oak, Mich.		Oct 17, 1901	Rudder, Fred				J.D.				Piedmont
Sellars, Jarrell D.	Aug 14, 1984	83	J.M.H.	Davidson Co, Tn	Aug 25, 1920	Dudley, George	Dickson, Jenn	Sellars, Duane						Jarnigan
Sellars, Jessie Alexander	Jan 30, 1984	79	Jeff City	Tn	Oct 14, 1904	Sellars, Alex	Brogdon, Mary	Tn	Matlie L. [D]	Paul-Duane-Robert	Vance, Mrs. Ernest	Sellars, Paul [Bird]	Ed	Piedmont
Sellars, Mattie L.	Nov 3, 1981	77	New Market	Tn	1904	Sanders, Ben	Little, Sarah	Sellars, Jesse		Paul-Duane-Robert	Vance, Ruth	Sellars, Addie	Husband	Friends Station
Sellars, Paul J.	Jun 15, 1978	72	Lawrenceburg, Tn					Ruth	Wagner, Mrs. Floyd - Riley, Mrs. Claude - Stripe, Mrs. Ralph [Fla.] - Foster, Mrs. W.R.	Jese Ed	Vance, Ruth	Duane-Robert	Freeman F.H.	Friends Station
Sellars, Sarah Clementine	Dec 23, 1984	89	Tn		Sep 10, 1875	White, ---	Tiney	Sellars, Albert Emerson			Sellars, Coy D. [Bird] - Sellars, Floyd [Detroit]	Husband		Piedmont
Semer, Hazel Lou	Dec 5, 1995	74	Elkort Co, Tn		May 18, 1921	Hill, George L.	Blount Co	Gibbs, Artie Lou	Semer, Lester A.	O' Mary, Mary Alice - Williams, Naomi Ruth	C.G.-Cecil D.	Husband		City, Louisville, Blount Co, Tn
Seymour, Robert Marion	Feb 4, 1984	87	Bracebill N.H.	Grainger Co	Dec 12, 1896	Seymour, Asa	Mc Million, Mando	S	[Nephews] Bates, Alice Ruth - Collins, Thelma - Wilson, Denise	[Nephews] Mitchell, Marie - Gallant, Hazel-Edna, Claude- Estes, Frank	Nicely, Juanita - Smith, Martha - Anderson, Reba - Miller, Margaret - Harmon, Evelyn			Strawberry Plains
Shackelford, Delores Jean	Jun 10, 1993	60	Strawberry, Tn		Mar 17, 1933	Smith, Roy C. Sr.	Morris, Lena		Lisa			Roy C & Lynn	Doug - [Fifs] Anderson, Juli - Pollard, David - Jack - Lumpkin, Robert-Buddy - Nicely, Tony	Hopewell - Knoxville, Tn
Shackelford, Paul Vaughn	Jan 1, 1993	69	Straw Plains, Tn		Mar 19, 1923	Shackelford, Lee	Murray, Gertrude	Paul, Mary Alma						Piney
Shackelford, Buford Ray [Buck]	Apr 14, 1993	65	U.T.H.	New Market	May 29, 1927	Shaffer, Ray	Childress, Mattie M.	Shackelford, Burt M. [D]		Donald-Eugene Gary-Spencer [Nd]-Roger [Va]	Newman, Louise [Va]	Hoskell-Harold Troy	Shaffer, Donald & Agnes	Flat Gap
Shaffer, Fannie M.	Oct 10, 1979	84	J.M.H.	Va	Apr 15, 1895	Woods, Winfield	Graham, Sarah	Shaffer, Jese [D]		[Step] Shaffer, Dorothy	[Step] Earnest-Jack-Charlie	Ada - Rogers, Lou	[Fifs] Gilbert, Jim - Gardner, David - Webb, Walter - Mc Call, Charlie - Compton, Harold - Cannon, Jim	New Market
Shaffer, James E.									[Adopted] Glenn, Mary - [Step] Baker, Bessie - Murray, Lena	[Step] Ernest- Smith, Robert	Shaffer, Mary F. [Wife]	[1/2] Roach, Sam	Shaffer, Mary F. [Wife]	New Market

Name	Date	Age			Date	Father		Mother		Spouse				Wife	New Market
Shelter, Jess Earnest	Oct 12, 1972		J.M.H.	Tn	Mar 2, 1902	Shelter, Jim		Mollie		Woods, Fannie Mae	[Step] Rimmer, Ruth - Murr, Pauline - Herman, Mary Kate - Petree, Manda [Va]	Earnest-Jack [Pat] - [Step] Pitts, Hubert	Mr Curry, Christine - Herman-David Mc Millan, Clara		
Shelter, Mary Frances	Aug 28, 1984	81	J.M.H.	Tn	Sep 1, 1883	Reed, Robert		Reys, Frances		Shelter, James E.	Smith, Robert [Son]			Smith, Robert [Son]	New Market
Shelter, Ray S.	Sep 2, 1986		J.M.H.	Tn	May 9, 1897			Lois						Shelter, Harold - Buford, Troy - [Pat] Gilmore, Jeff - Sturgeon, Tim - Mc Fells, Jim - Skelly, Hartley - Widner, Dan	Flat Gap
Sharp, Faye	Sep 17, 1990	74	U.T.H.	Jeff Co	Nov 10, 1915	Brooks, Mack Crain		Moris, Nellie Estelle		Sharp, Jasper [D]					Shady
Sharp, Mary Jane	Oct 6, 1996	59	J.M.H.	Strawberry Plains	May 14, 1937	Wilson, James		Bailey, Lucy	Navy	Sharp, Paul [Dw]	[Nephew] Cox, Bill-Dale-Lynn-John - Shedstan			Doug	Lynnhurst
Sharp, Raymond B.	Jun 26, 1994	72	Jeff City	Belle Gap - Hawkins Co	Jul 21, 1921	Sharp, Charles Edward		Darek, Ethel							
Sheldon, Allie Mae	Aug 10, 1986	75	S.M.H.	Jeff Co	Dec 26, 1910	Cox, John		Newman, Melinda		Sheldon, Hugh	Linda Gail	Emery-Herbie-Jim - [Step] Frank	Elmore, Lou Ellen - Griffin, Mrs. Lora [Nc]	Hill, John T. [Nc]	Mt. Horeb
Sheldon, A.J. (Jake)	Apr 22, 1981	70	U.T.H.	Claiborne Co	Jul 12, 1890	Sheldon, William	Tn	Mattox, Nancy E.		See-Sheldon, Isabelle	See-Sheldon, Isabelle	Tubner, Mary - Sharp, Ida	Walter-Ross	West View
Shelton, Cheris Mae	Jun 10, 1967	66								Shelton, J.M.	Hankins, Glenna & Gary - Roach, Margaret - Robinson, Edith [Nc]	Emery-Herbie-Jim - [Step] Frank	Elmore, Lou Ellen - Griffin, Mrs. F.P.		Fodlin
Shelton, Isabell	Jul 1, 1960	73	New Market	Tn	Feb 18, 1887	Keck, F.P.		Sanders, Sarah	Ng			Chap W.W.-Carl-Weyer-Roy	Cox, Mrs. F.P.	Hesketh-Johnny	Shelton, Weyer [Son] / West View
Shelton, Infant	Oct 27, 1951	90	Jeff City	Jeff City	Oct 27, 1951	Shelton, Weyer	Tn	Bunchell, Dema	Tn					Father	West View
Shelton, Jonathan Mc Kinley	Aug 15, 1984	85	Knoxville, Tn	Cocke Co, Tn	Oct 27, 1898	Shelton, Rose		Rimer, Susan		Shelton, Charlie	Roach, Margaret - Robinson, Mary Edith	Frank-Elmory-Jim - R.D.-Herbert		Shelton, Delia - Barnett, Johnny - Cox, Denis - Wilson, Steve	Baltimore - Newport, Tn
Shelton, Rose Daniel	Dec 5, 1993	56	Ft. Lauderdale, Fl	Newport, Tn	Mar 6, 1937	Shelton, Jonathan Mc Kinley		Hill, Clara Faye	Div	Lisa	John-Dan	Roach, Margaret - Robinson, Edith	Frank-Emory-Jim-Herbert	Hunter F.H. - Lash [Pat]	Fodlin - Cocke Co
Shelton, William Omer	Dec 23, 1989	41	New Market	Jeff City	Sep 11, 1958	Shelton, Larry		Green, Irene		Cooke, Barbara		Rumie [Jung] Jim-Herbert	Rumie [Jung] - Gary	[Pals] Massore, Steve - Frazier, Jimmie-Johnny - Ragge - Greene, David - Brown, Kali - Anderson, - Shelton, Bob - Franklin	Fodlin - Nances Grove

Name	Death Date	Age	Place	County	Birth Date	Father	Mother	Spouse	Service	Relatives / Notes	Cemetery
Sherrod, Holly Marie	Nov 7, 1994	14dr	Knoxville, Tn	Knoxville, Tn	Nov 6 1994	Sherrod, John Jr.	Patterson, Patricia	Dorthey		Treece, Sheila - Belts, Mrs. Jean; Ramsey, Hattie - Roberts, Thelma; [Pals] Vineyard, Johnny-Glen - Dutton, Archie - Nance, Roy-Bill - Stone, Marali	Piney
Sheets, James Clifford	Feb 4, 1978	55	B.H.	Tn	Sep 25, 1921	Shields, Fred	Jernigan, Alice	Dorthey		Willis	Russellville
Shipe, Hazel Katherine	Jun 20, 1975	70		Grainger Co	Nov 13, 1904	Nance, Luther	Murph, Nettie	Shipe, Sanford E.		Hammond, Lois & Don	Nance's
Shipley, Effie Mae	Mar 7, 1988	91	J.M.H.	Hawkins Co., Tn	Nov 25, 1896	Long, Walter	Wright, Margaret	Shipley, Joe [D]	Walter	Repass, Betty; Horner, Dora - Fields, Ruth - Shipley, Agnes - Hoosier, Katherine - Heath, Willie; Howard-John; Repass, Betty & Paul V.; [Pals] Dance, Bob - Blatsr, Adrian 3rd - Howell, Allen - Nott, Fred E. - Crespo, Orlando - Boyle, Jim	Bethedere - Morristown, Tn
Shires, Kenneth Michael	May 26, 1992	44	Jeff City	Nc	Aug 13, 1947	Shires, John H.	Lindsey, Geneva	Div	Navy	Click, Shannon; Repass, Betty & Paul V.; John-Stephen	J.M.G.
Shockley, Arthur Robert	Jan 17, 1995	96	Talbott, Tn	Rutledge, Tn	Aug 28, 1908	Shockley, John A.	Morgan, Hattie	Shockley, Dexter C.		Carter, Naomi; Angel, Doris - Hayles, Judy; Robert-Charlie - Gary-Dennis; Brady, Ruth; D.C.-Clifford - Aldridge - Howard-Jack	Miami Memorial - Centerville, Ohio
Shockley, Edna Faye	Jan 27, 1988	83	Jeff City	Jeff City	Jun 25, 1915	Shockley, Joe C.	Solomon, Hattie	Shockley, Dexter C.		Donald [Pa]; Dewey - Bobby[D] - Jackie [D]; Willis - F.H. [Carrollton, OH]	J.M.G.
Shores, Hugh Anderson	Oct 9, 1995	45	F.S.H.	Greene Co	Dec 4, 1949	Shores, Robert Jr.	Easterly, Mable	Div		Kidwell, Carolyn - Alkard, Geraldine - Howard, Martha; Fine, Mildred; Son - [Pals] Fine, Bill - Shrader, Bill - Mike-Robert - Wayne-Lloyd - Ashton	J.M.G.
Shrader, Floyd Rex	Nov 23, 1994	75	New Market	Dandridge, Tn	Apr 6, 1919	Shrader, Robert.	Finchum, Martha	Swann, Gladys [D]	Army	Kidwell, Carolyn - Alkard, Geraldine - Howard, Martha; Samuel-Charles; Fine, Mildred; A. Ray; Willis - [Pals] Hammonds, Ben - Chambers, Mark - McCoig, Lyle - Shrader, Sam - Lloyd-Robert	J.M.G.
Shrader, Frank Lee	Jul 1, 1992	78	F.S.H.	Dandridge, Tn	Oct 10, 1913	Shrader, Robert.	Finchum, Pearl	McCoig, Edith	Army	Chase, Pat; Mike; Fine, Mildred; Rex-A. Ray; Willis - [Pals] Shrader	Hills Union
Shrader, Gladys Ruth	Jan 19, 1993	74	Dandridge, Tn	Dandridge, Tn	Sep 11, 1918	Shrader, Robert	Moore, Liza Ann	Shrader, Rex		Shrader, Rex; Samuel-Charles; Lester-Bill - Calvin-A.B. - D.R.	J.Mg.
Shrader, Martha Pearl	Jan 24, 1975	88	Jeff Co	Tn	Apr 3, 1886	Finchum, Rosen	Patterson, Elizabeth	Shrader, Bill [D]		Finchum, Martha Shrader; Finchum, Arthur - [1/2] Chaney, Eddie - Hill, Maude - Bush, Revie - Thomas, Imogene; Finchum, Arthur - [1/2] Finchum, Heck; Fine - [Pals] Fine, Mildred - Ray-Rosen-Frankie, Rex	Hills Union
Shrader, Robert Frank	Jul 25, 1994	81	New Market	Tn	Sep 20, 1992	Unk	Finchum, Martha Shrader	Martha Pearl		Finchum, Ida - Fine, Mildred; McCoig, Maudie - Hick, Laura - Ellis, Pauline; Wife	New Market
Shultz, Ralph Porter	May 9, 1988	43	J.M.H.	Tn	Feb 8, 1945	Shultz, Lawrence	Trentham, Delfie	Shultz, Mary Ruth Shelton	Army	Brother - [Pals] Jones, John-Bill - Koone, Isbr - Ashby, Tom - Courtney, Jeff - Burns, Robert - Silver, James	Hills Union
Silver, Charles Louie	Feb 14, 1988	49	Jeff City	Rutherford, Nc	Apr 5, 1938	Silver, H.J.	Dalton, Leah	S		Katherine - Burd, Marjorie - Estrada, Louise; Horace S.; Brother - [Pals]	Flat Gap

Silver, Fred Jennings	May 6, 1981	24	F.S.H.	Jeff Co	Jul 21, 1956	Silver, Curtis	Spoon, Thelma			[Pila] Whaley, Dudd-Claude - Elder, Fred - Shellz, Freddie - Beck, Garth	Flat Gap
Silver, Horace Jennings	Aug 22, 1984	86	Newport, Tn	Mc Dowell Co, Nc	Jul 8, 1898	Silver, Stelzoo	Canaway, Rhoda	Nc			Son - Daughter	Flat Gap
Silver, James Curtis [Shorty]	Oct 15, 1976	51	Jeff City	Rutherford Co, Nc	Sep 15, 1925	Silver, H.I.	Spoon, Thelma			Exbraster, Louise Silver, Katherine Byer, Marjorie	Jame-Fred		Flat Gap
Silver, James E.	Nov 10, 1980	83	Dellwyn, Va		Nov 23, 1896	Portland, Staixes	Canaway, Rhoda			Kaye - Lamphier, Marjorie [Va] - Estrada, Louise [Jake]	Lockhart, Mrs. Joe	Silver, Horace T.	Fielden, Mrs. Marion [Nn] - [Pilla] Fields, Maxuif-Bill-Joe	Flat Gap
Silver, Leah Ella	Jun 18, 1973	69	Morristown, Tn	Nc	Apr 6, 1904	Dalton, Lee	Buford, Martha		Silver, H.I.		Lockhart, Hettie [Nc] - Koone, Linnie [Nc] - Conner, Isa [Nc]	Marion [Nn] & Vella Dalton [Nc]	Husband	Flat Gap
Silver, Robert Stanley Jr.	Jun 14, 2000	34	Jeff City	Cincinatti, Ohio	Oct 26, 1965	Silver, Robert S. Sr.	Pollard, Dorothy		Div	Shipe, Brenda - Wollard, Chris - Dilka, Sharon [Ind] - Emming, Donna - [Step] Brown, Amy	Victer [D] - [Step] Brown, Stanley-Ken-Kevin	Silver, Betty [Step-Mother]	Pleasant Ridge
Simon, John H. [Col]	Nov 25, 1992	70	New Market	Tn	Nov 23, 1882	Unk	Unk			Miller, Ruth - Milas, Virginia [Ohio]	John H.		Younga Memorial
Simon, Nona [Negro]	Dec 25, 1969	79	New Market	Tn	Dec 29, 1896	Martin, William	Huff, Ida		W	Miller, Ruth - Milas, Virginia - Jones, Edna [Oh]	Hodge, Mrs. Beecher	Simon, Nona [Wife]	Younga Memorial
Simpson, Bessie	Jun 6, 1972	80	Johnson City, Tn	Tn	Sep 16, 1891	Bailey, William	Williams, Amanda		W	Edward [Sol] - Arnold [Sol]	Floyd-Elvin	Sherrod, Alica & Howell [Daug] - [Pilla] Bowers, Paul - Linekecker, Jerry - Graves, Gary - Church, Paul - Atkins, Charlie	Straw Plains
Sims, Delmer C.	May 6, 1992	65	Dandridge, Tn	Lucac Co, Ohio	Jan 17, 1917	Sims, Irvin	Welland, Cary		Dickson, Leona	Childress, Jewell	Buddy-Martin-Delmer-Leroy-Gary	Graves, Alina & Earl	Carl	Husband [Pila] Cockrum, George - Jim - Sillon, Leon - Henry, Horace- Donnie - Potter, Harold-Tony	New Market
Sitton, Margaret	Jun 11, 1978	90	Jeff Co		Feb 28, 1888	Helm, John H.	Ward, Rodha Cathene		Sitton, Stanley		Cockrum, Nora		Husband [Pilla] Cockrum, George- Jim - Sillon, Leon - Henry, Horace- Donnie - Potter, Harold-Tony	J.M.G
Sitton, Stanley	Nov 29, 1986	83	Rutledge, Tn	Nc	Feb 9, 1903	Sitton, Milton S.	Brindle, Ruth			Rourk, Hester - Morgan, Ruth			J.M.G.
Sizemore, Elsie Pearl	Nov 25, 1991	73	Knoxville, Tn	Hancock Co	Mar 3, 1918	Kinsley, William D.	Johnson, Sara Jane		Sizemore, T.W. [D]	Miller, Juanita	Basil	Kinsler, Ora - Ford, Elizabeth - Russell, May - Hayes, Geneva - Campbell, Bobbie	Basil - [Pila] Sizemore, Walter- Fred - Miller, Jim - Mc Clain, Tom - Conner, Mike	J.M.G.
Sizemore, William Talmadge [Sam]	Feb 5, 1978	24	Knox Co		Jan 6, 1916	Kinsler, Pearl			Kinsler, Pearl	Miller, Juanita - Gilland, Lona - Mae	Basil	Sizemore, Mrs. Elsie - Gibson, Betty Jo - Basher, Odell - Baker, Mary - Brown, - Grecia [Cel]	Albert S.	J.M.G.

Name	Date	Age	Place	Place	Date	Father	Mother	Spouse						Cemetery
Slagle, Blanche Susan	Jan 19, 1989	90	J.M.H.	New Market	May 7, 1898	Haworth, Dillon	Campbell, Lillie	Herman-Dillon-Gordon-Earnest-Vernon		Whitehead, Alma - Reed, Kathleen - Ellis, Elizabeth	Herman-Dillon-Gordon-Earnest-Vernon		Vernon - [Pale] Whitehead, John R.-Dan - Slagle, Gary-Buck-Ben-Chester - Griffin, Phillip, Jr.	Nances Grove
Slagle, Herman. T.	Dec 31, 1989	71	J.M.H.	New Market	Aug 20, 1918	Slagle, Talmadge	Haworth, Blanche	Creech, Mae		Margar, Barbara Morgan, Barbara - Slagle, Wanda	Herman R.-Bush- Roy T.		Wills - [Pale] Slagle, Gary-Ron- Martin-Joe - Whitehead, John- Danny	Nances Grove
Slagle, Mae	Aug 25, 1986	73	J.M.H.	Loyall, Ky	Aug 3, 1897	Creech, Roy	Turner, Margaret	Slagle, Herman T. [x]	WW 2	Slagle, Wanda- Morgan, Barbara & Lawrence	Herman R.& Cathy-Roy T. & Vicki	William D- Lloyd [Cal]- Bobby [III]		Nances Grove
Slagle, Ollie [F]	Dec 13, 1999	72	Knox Co	Tn	Aug 3, 1897	Green, Jerry	Inman, Martha	W						Friends Station
Slagle, Talmadge G.	May 28, 1987	59	M.C.	Tn	Jun 23, 1897	Slagle, James	James, Sarah	Blanch		Whitehead, Alma	Ernest-Wayne- James D.- Gordon	Cynthia - Anderson, Florida	Husband - [Pale] Slagle, Jim-Ron- Maurice-Wilton- George, Wagner, Jr.	Nances Grove
Slagle, Virgie Irene	Apr 22, 1991	69	J.M.H.	Grainger Co	Jul 13, 1921	Whitz, Sears	Mc Cann, Ethel	Slagle, Gordon		Cain, Katherine		Cox, Dorothy - Widner, Alline		Nances Grove
Slagle, Wayne Vernon	Jul 10, 1994	59	F.S.H.	New Market	Jun 28, 1936	Slagle, Talmadge	Haworth, Blanche	Beaver, Geraldine	Army		James-Maurice- Ronald	Whitehead, Alma- Reed, Kathleen- Ellis, Elizabeth	Wills - [Pale] Johnson, Hal - Kirk, Hugh - Mc Ghin, Ellis- Griffin, Bill- Stanley - Donnie, Roger	Nances Grove
Shoun, Allie Cleo	Dec 29, 1999	95	J.M.H.	New Market	May 4, 1904	Carmichael, James C.	Underwood, Georgia Ann	Shoun, Thomas L. [D]				Inglis, Gladys	Dillon-Gordon- Ernest	Nances Grove
Shover, B. O' Dell	Jul 3, 1994	36	Jeff City	Tn	Jul 22, 1915	Shover, Frank	Eledge, Margret	Tn			O' Dell Jr.	Winston, Mrs. Sherman	Love, Claude	Piedmont
Shover, Jessie Brunette	May 20, 1987	86	J.M.H.	Jeff Co	Jan 18, 1901	Talley, J. Wiley	Hopkins, Mattie	Shover, Charles B.		Ballinger, Alleen	Charles	Barker, Dorothy	Hollis	Mill Springs
Shover, Mary Katherine	Feb 5, 1999	33	Morristown, Tn	Grainger Co	Jan 4, 1966	Byrd, James Lawrence	Hamner, Georgia L.	Shover, Terry		Tammy Dawn		Lorena, Steven- Sutton, Brenda	[64-Lonnie-Ben- Roger	J.M.G.
Shover, William Darrell	Jun 2, 1994		U.T.H.	Knox Co	Jun 2, 1964	Shover, William Darrell	Ramsey, Tammy Gail							
Smallman, Bland [Doc]	Feb 21, 1970	61	Knox Co	Tn	Oct 9, 1908	Smallman, John	Underwood, Minnie Lee	Evelyn Idel		Joaca Ann- Brenda - Foster, Patlee & J.K. - Darlene & Grant Ballinger ?	William B.-David	Hazelwood, Lucile- Quarles, Mrs. Charles - Snyder, Mrs. D.P.	Gunner H.- Dewiese- Taylor [Or]	Wife

Name	Death	Age	Place	Birthplace	Birth	Father	St	Mother	St	Spouse	Family	Family	Family	Family	Family	Cemetery
Smith, Abe David	May 24, 1998	59	Springfield, Ohio							Pierce, Elsie		[Step] Ellis, Dorothy - James; Helen - Shelley; Willie Mae [OH] - Inzer, Jean [Cal]; Mc Ghee, Bessie - Castrell, Judy - Northern, Helen	Dillard, Hester - Johnson, Clara [Ohio] - Gibson, Bertha [TX]	George [TX]-	Willie	Strawberry Plains
Smith, Allie Nan	Dec 21, 1996	84	Jeff City		Aug 28, 1912	Stinnett, Fate				Smith, Frank [D]		Mc Campbell, Bertha	Curtis	Alvin		New Salem - Kodak, Tn
Smith, Andrew P.	Apr 14, 1960	85	New Market	Tn	Sep 20, 1874	Smith, Levi	Tn	Reed, Martha	Tn			Brunner, Myrtle - [Step] Brickins, Ella - Parker, Elsie - Hurst, Georgia	[Step] Creswell,bery, Dane		Smith, Josie [Willie]	Methodist
Smith, Aria	Jan 29, 1984	78	Care Inn	Kenton, Nc	May 20, 1907	Burgess, Henry		Kinley, Edna		Smith, George W.		Brown, Pattie & Miss - [In-Laws See Obit]	David-Wayne	James	Son	Holston Memorial East
Smith, Betty Lou	Dec 6, 2000	67	New Market	Mooresburg, Tn	Jul 14, 1933	Russell, Hugh P.		Roach, Nellie Jane		Smith, David Cleveland			Odom, Mary Jane	J.D. [D]-Hollis-John+Hugh		J.M.G.
Smith, Billy Ray	Jun 24, 1988	46	S.M.H.	Knoxville, Tn	Apr 6, 1942	Lauderdale, Mary		Duane, Jessie M.K.					David M. [D]- Brian & Elaine		Willie	Beaver Creek
Smith, Billy Wiley [Stuff]	May 11, 1998	57	Straw Plains	Jeff City	May 5, 1941	Smith, Harley R.		Davis, Martha Crick	Div			Bruner, Mattie & Allen				Strawberry Plains
Smith, Bryan Scott	Sep 6, 1977	0	Jeff City	Jeff City	Sep 6, 1977	Smith, Fredrick [Age-28] Granger Co	Tn	Chambers, Barbara Jane [Age-28]	Tn						Smith, Cecil - Chambers, Walt - [G-Fathers] Carter, James A. - Smith, Cecil [G-G-Fathers]	J.M.G.
Smith, Burl Ray	Jul 29, 1998	59	F.S.H.	Dandridge, Tn	Jan 15, 1939	Smith, Albert		Laguire, Jeunita		Glenn, Mary		Floyd, Sherrie & Ronnie - Williams, Teresa	Burl Allen	Alger		Hillcrest
Smith, Charles William [Black]	Mar 1, 1984	75	Knoxville, Tn	New Market	Oct 9, 1908	Smith, Mark		Mathews, Esma				Summerour, Rose Marie - Satterfield, Betty - Smith, Archabill	Coleman, Howard-Bobby Joe - Mills, Rudolph	Cantrell, Inezetta - Strange, Flora Jane - Norton, Virginia	[Pids] Satterfield, Howard-Hurley - Coleman,n, Howard- Bobby- Summerour, James - Frears, Wagner - Smith, Dwight - Middlebrook, Marshall	Hillcrest
Smith, Charles Winford	Mar 4, 1994	71	Kodak, Tn	Kodak, Tn	Apr 5, 1922	Smith, Isaac L.		Mc Bride, Katherine		Div	WW 2			Lane, Emma Lee	[R-Law] Lanis, Robert E.	Pollards - Kodak, Tn
Smith, David Malcolm	Jan 20, 1995	41	V.A.-Mt. Home	Falmouth, Mass	Apr 25, 1953	Smith, David		Russell, Betty		Tolliver, Rebecca		Jennifer-Kelly		Brown, Patty	Bryan	Willie
Smith, Emma	Oct 23, 1953	72	New Market		Aug 16, 1881	Groves, Robert J.	Tn	Wagner, Mary	Tn			Haynes, Mrs. Burl - Howard, Mrs. T.O.- Nelson, Mrs. H.E.			Haynes, Esther	Mill Springs
Smith, Eunice Elizabeth	Sep 3, 1993	66	Nashville, Tn	Strawberry Plains	Jul 4, 1927	Nichols, Carl D.		Hicks, Della						Dunn, Emma Lou - Nicholas, Margaret	Abe-Carl- David	Robert	Priory
Smith, Gladys F.	Nov 8, 1985	73	Morristown, Tn		Jan 28, 1912	Smith, Sam H. [D]		Smith, Jack					Robert B.		Husband	Priory

Name	Death Date	Age	Place	Location	Birth Date	Father	Mother		Spouse	War	Children/Survivors			Pallbearers		Cemetery
Smith, Harley Roosevelt	Feb 26, 1977	59	V.A. Hosp. Johnson City	Texas	Jun 27, 1917	Smith, Ave	Marlowe, Sadie			WW 2		Billy Ray [Pa]- Harley Wayne- Michael Elmer		Willie [Pals] Gibson, R.C.-Joe- Duggan, Doug- Roberts, Billy John-Johnny- Roger	Willie [Pals] Atkins, Ad- Gibson, Don-Ray- Morgan, Tim- Terry	Beaver Creek
Smith, Harley Wayne	Sep 21, 1991	42	Knoxville, Tn		Mar 27, 1949	Smith, Harley Roosevelt	Lauderdale, Mary E.		Cain, Mildred Evelyn		Debbie-Robin	Daniel Wayne	Gamer, Edith & Louise	Michael	Willie	West View
Smith, James Mayford	Oct 1, 1994	88	Jeff Cith	Monroe Co. Tn	May 25, 1906	Smith, James Sr.	Cunningham, Rosa		Martha D.	WW 2	[Step] Strange, Lena	[Step] Harmon, Michele		Willie	Willie	West View
Smith, James Ronnie	Oct 21, 1992	43	Newport, Tn	Jeff City	Dec 7, 1948	Smith, James William	Miller, Grace		Miller, Othie Renee	unk				Willie- [Pals] Cotter, Lonnie- Robert-Frank- Doyle-Cannon- Ralph- Simon- Eddie		J.M.G.
Smith, James William	Oct 13, 1994	78	F.S.H.	New Market	Jan 28, 1916	Smith, W. Walter	Miller, Nora		Davis, Martha				Billy	Son	Son	Strawberry Plains
Smith, Jerry Michael	Jun 10, 1988	17	U.T.H.	Knoxville, Tn	Jun 4, 1971	Smith, Jerry Jr.	Baysinger, Sarah E.		S				John Jr.	Son	[Pals] Wallace, Ed- Jeffers, Tracy- Carpenter- George- Elmore, Hubbs- Robert- Whitt, James	Weslays Chapel
Smith, John Agie	Feb 28, 1992	85	Knoxville, Tn	Harlan Co. Ky	Feb 17, 1907	Smith, Joseph	Mary		Hazel Lenora Helen					Son	Son	West View
Smith, John W. [Black]	Jul 13, 1998	57	J.M.H.	New Market	Aug 28, 1940	Smith, William	Spiva, Rebecca		S						Youngs Memorial	Youngs Memorial
Smith, Juanita	May 12, 1987	66	J.M.H.	Sevier Co.	Jan 12, 1921	Loquire, Will	Greene, Cora		Smith, Albert Ray [D-1971]		Carnell, Irazelda - Strange, Flora Jane - Norton, Virginia	Buel-Alger	Baysinger, Emaline- Teester, Lillie	[Pals] Lewaine, Raymond- Smith, Kenneth-Harris- Strange, Floyd- Harris, Elmore, Don		Weslays Chapel
Smith, Katy Lee	Jun 19, 1976	92	F.S.H.	Knox Co. Tn	Jan 20, 1883	Mc Bride, John H.	Sarah		W		Lane, Emma Lee & [Step] Smith, Harold & Robert E.	[Charles W. [Step] Smith, Harold		Mc Bride, Lida	[Pals]	Pollards
Smith, Marshall Edward	Apr 22, 2000	87	Ridge Terrace, Nb	Straw Plains	Dec 27, 1912	Mc Bride, John H.	Parker, Linnie		Seal, Beuna	Army			Mike	Witt, Ruby [D]- Cole, Pauline [D]- Stackelford, Jean	Ralph	Beaver Creek
Smith, Martha Delzina	Nov 20, 1998	72	Straw Plains	Straw Plains	Aug 1, 1926	Smith, Charlie	Morton, Lena		W		Strange, Lena & George	Harmon, Michael	Witt, Ruby [D]- Cole, Pauline [D]- Stackelford, Jean [D]- Harmon, Evelyn [D]- Hamon, Alberta [D]- Anderson, Reba- Miller, Margarie	Norman [D]- Ray C.- Jr.- Lynn		West View
Smith, Maude	Aug 5, 1960	78	Tn	Jeff City	Sep 17, 1881	Davis, Charlie	Unk	Tn	W		Erwin, Blanche			Smith, Paul [Paul Mich.]		Mill Springs
Smith, Mildred Evelyn	May 20, 1996	45	U.T.H.	Jeff City	Jun 18, 1950	Cain, John R.	Leonard, Betty		Smith, Wayne [D]		Roberts, Marti			Ken-Daniel- Eddie [1/2]- Banks, Bobby	Brother- [Pals] Lampkins, Buddy- Nicoly, Tony- Snyder, Cecil- Buddy- Pollard, Anderson, Jeff	Strawberry Plains
Smith, Norman Edward	Nov 5, 1987	50	J.M.H.	Strawberry Plains	Nov 28, 1936	Smith, Roy C.	Morton, Lena		Div				Futz, Willie - Haley, Jaunita - Smith, Martha - Harmon, Evelyn - Anderson, Reba - Stackelford, Jean - Miller, Margaret		Roy C. Jr.- Lynn	New Hopewell

Smith, Patrick Eugene Sr.	Jun 21, 2000	71	F.S.H.	Powder Springs, Tn	Feb 25, 1929	Smith, Charlie	Merritt, Ella Mae	Greenlee, Anna Belle - Helen	Army	Eugene-Darrell (Step) Longmire, Steve - Patterson, Eugene	Lucy Mae [D]	Bill & Treassa [Ret]-U.P.-Bob & Betty	Son	Central Point - Granger Co
Smith, Pearl Lou	May 26, 1992	81	F.S.H.	Powder Springs, Tn	Sep 1-0, 1911	Wright, Link	Newman, Maggie	Smith, George [D] [De]					Son	West View
Smith, Robert C.	Oct 15, 1988	68	J.M.H.	Todd Co, Ky	Jul 31, 1920	Smith, Collier L.	Willis, Ines	Ewan, Dorothy [De]		Charles R.	Gann, Kathleen - Coppfin, Roberta - Canner, Jean - Bryce, Betty	[Pals] Elmore, Lapner-John - Bill - H.L. - Smith, Terry - Doug	Joe	J.M.G.
Smith, Sarah Elizabeth	Sep 19, 1982		J.M.H.	Jeff City	Feb 16, 1903	Lowery, Dave	Bodin, Frances	Smith, Robert Lee [D]		Howell, Mattie Pearl - Lowrey, Irene - Colo, Evelyn Nadine - Brown, Jennette	Ralph Earl-Jerry	Richards, Edna		Westhope Chapel
Smith, Scott	Nov 21, 1991	19	Johnson City, Tn	Johnson City, Tn	Nov 21, 1991	Smith, Gregory Scott	Mullins, Sandy Lee	S						Granger Memorial
Smith, Sonja Lynn	Jan 25, 1991	19	Knoxville, Tn	De Kalb Co, Ala	Apr 5, 1971	Smith, Lawrence	Graham, Mary	S				Smith, Leon [G-Father]		J.M.G.
Smith, William Cecil	Apr 22, 1996	84	J.M.H.	Granger Co	Apr 6, 1912	Smith, Will	Duck, Sue	Edith [D]		Cecil Jr.-William Rose	Maple, Agnes - Willson, Greta - Vineyard, Willie Mae - Morgan, Betty Sue - Corum, Faye			Granger Memorial
Smith, William Rose	Nov 19, 1985	70	J.M.H.	Anderson Co	Sep 11, 1925	Smith, Cecil	Taylor, Edith	Trent, Carolyn		Willey, Jane (Step) Foust, Lawonda	Maple, Agnes - Willson, Greta - Vineyard, Willie Mae - Morgan, Betty Sue - Lowrey, Alta - Corum, Faye		Willie	Strawberry Plains
Smith, Wilson [Col]	Oct 13, 1969	63	Jeff Co	Ne	Jan 16, 1906	Smith, John	Robertson, Mary	Spiva, Rebecca		Wooley, Gail Bettie, Nauona	John Wesley - [b-Larry Wooley - Travis - Bettie, Benny	2	1 [Re]	Young Memorial
Snyder, Arthur Alexander	Oct 25, 1989	65	Jeff City	New Market, Tn	Jan 23, 1904	Snyder, Humphrey	Willard, Millie	Cate, Mollie		Dorothy-Trula Bell	Wright, Jennie - Turner, Debbie	Smith, [Pals] Snyder, Paul - Cate, Ray-David-Don-Jerry-Perry	Willie	Mt Campbells Chapel
Snyder, Deborra Jeanette	Jul 27, 2000	68	Straw Plains	Straw Plains	Jan 9, 1932	Esly, Jewell E.	Trent, Arkie Nipper	Snyder, Ralph Rudolph		Karen	Eddie-Robin- Tommy	Son- [Pals] Stroud, John - Terry - Huffner, Calvin-Ed-Bob - Widner, Dan		Cate
Snyder, Dorothy Louise	Jun 2, 1982	55	J.M.H.	New Market	Jan 23, 1937	Snyder, Arthur A.	Cate, Mollie	S			Snyder, Greg	Trula Bell		Mt Campbells Chapel
Snyder, Mollie Louise	Jul 15, 1999	80	New Market	Jeff Co	May 16, 1919	Cate, Perry	Henry, Ida M.	Snyder, Arthur A. [D]		Bell, Trula - Dorothy [D]	Taylor, Martha - Cate, Delia Pearl - Mills, Viola - Cate, Bonnie - Cate, Fern - Palmer, Gertrude [bd]	Ray-Don		Mt Campbells Chapel
Snyder, Robert P.	1963		New Market	Jeff Co		Snyder, Humphrey	Cate, Mollie	Carrie Louise		Martin, Mrs. Earl Prince, Mrs. Clay [Nd] - Johnson, Debbie - Christian, Mrs. Walter	Robert Jr.	Ernett	Doughty-Stevens [Granville]	Piedmont
Snyder, Tom	Apr 19, 1996	87	New Market	Tn	May 6, 1866	Snyder, Bill		Prince, Mrs. Clay [Nd] - Johnson, Debbie			William E.- Robert P.	French, Lillie	Ernett	West View
Snyder, Velma Purdit Jones	Jul 1, 1981	70	J.M.H.	Sevier Co, Tn	Oct 29, 1910	Jones, George	Owens, Ida Mae	Snyder, Bill		Roderick, Betty Jo	Prince, Mrs. Clay [Nd] - Johnson, Debbie	Rowe, Lena - Cates, Martha	Jones, Jake	Blue Springs

Name	Date	Age		Place										
Snyder, William Dedrick	Feb. 7, 1984	66	B.H.	Jeff Co.	Oct. 16, 1897	Unk	Leslie		Pruitt, Velma [D]		Fisher, Billie - Whittaker, Wilma - Lawson, Jesse - Lunch, Lucille	William-Frank-Paul-Ralph		Cates - New Market
Solomon, Joe	Feb. 13, 1984	79	J.M.H.	Spartanburg, Sc	Jul 15, 1904	Solomon, Shade	Solomon, Ida		Bailey, Lucille		Hubbard, Annie S. - Oakes, Marie	Robert-Kerr-Tom-Frank		New Market
Solomon, John James	Sep 3, 1999	75	B.H.	Dandridge, Tn	Oct. 18, 1923	Solomon, George	Brown, Chiney		Miller, Blanche Penny		Long, Peggy & Ray - Brooks, Rose - Lonsert, Bertha	Lee & Jan		Dandridge Memorial
Solomon, Mittie Ann	Mar 1, 1999		Jeff City	Dandridge, Tn	Nov. 19, 1918	Lowery, Alex	Cross, Emily		Solomon, Murphy [D]		Elmore, Betty - [G] Kidwell, Donna	Solomon, Jack		New Market
Solomon, Murphy C.	Sep 24, 1981	66	J.M.H.	Sc	Jan 15, 1915	Solomon, Shade	Ida		Lowery, Mollie		[Step] Strange, Betty	[Step] Guinn, Carl-Jack	Solomon, Joe - Brady, O.T.	New Market
Solomon, Robert Earl	Feb. 21, 1999	66	New Market	Jan 6, 1933	Solomon, Joe	Ida		Trent, Jewell		Korea	Wendy-Ambum, Andrea	Kenny-Dean	Hubbard, Annie - Oakes, Marie	Kennedy-Frank-Tom E.	West View
Solomon, Ruth	Apr 30, 1986	71	S.M.H.	Jeff Co	Apr 28, 1915	Bolin, Samuel	Wayman, Ethel		Solomon, Henry [D]		Whitehouse, Betty Joan	Lloyd	Martin, Geneva - Brooks, Imogene	Roy	Pleasant Grove
Solomon, William Henry	Feb 20, 1973	79	Knox Co	Tn	Feb 18, 1898	Solomon, John	Snider, Ellen/Newnham, Emma		Ruth		WW 2	Whitehouse, Betty-Jean	William Lloyd	Cox, Ida - Meadow, Dona [Cin, Oh]	Write	Piney Baptist
Solomon, Henry Scott	Nov 7, 1995	16	S.M.H.	Knox Co	Nov 18, 1969	Solomon, Lloyd	Frazier, Bonnie		S						Father	Pleasant Grove
Southerland, Essie	Dec. 4, 1985		J.M.H.	Madison Co, Nc	Jul 5, 1896	Southerland, John Wesley	Gentry, Eliza						Brother [Leicester, Nc]			Brother McCampbells Chapel / Highland Memorial
Spencer, Charles	Dec 1, 1999	70	S.M.H.	Jeff City	Dec. 1, 1929	Spencer, George	Lane, Elizabeth		Riddle, Herma Wiles		Roberts, Pam - Thompson, Judy	Patrick-Tom		Roy	
Spencer, Charlie James	Sep 9, 1999	82	Morristown, Tn	Granger Co	Aug 31, 1917	Spencer, Frank	Phillips, Nora Mae		Smith, Stella Mae		Marshall, Mary Millyxelene [D] - Bungin, Shirly & Carroll	Marshall Lee [D]-Eugene & Carolyn	Gilbert, Agnes		West View
Spencer, Earl W.	May 1, 1964	46		Tn		Spencer, Crawley	Watts, Ine Belle		S				Herman	West View
Spencer, Frank N.	Sep 5, 1983	90	Jeff City	Grainger Co.	Oct 12, 1906	Spencer, James	Cook, Sanna		Div		Euline - Gilbert, Agnes - Glenn, Edith	Fred-Charlie			Pleasant Grove
Spencer, Fred William	Sep 19, 1989	66	J.M.H.	Tn	Feb 20, 1923	Spencer, Frank N.	Phillips, Nora M.		Barnett, Margie		Hamby, Dorothy/ Collins, Bonnie/ Williams, Joyce - Hillman, Pat - Lane, Jeanne	Clyde William-Dwight Jeffrey	Guinn, Edith - Gilbert, Agnes	Charlie J.	Jones, Mrs. John [Sister] / Wife- [PxS] Williams, Lewis/ Collins, Michael - Hamby, Stephen - Collins, Darrell - Grainger, Donald - Glenn, Andy	J.M.G.

Name	Death Date	Age	Place	County	Birth Date	Father		Mother						Burial
Spencer, Layman	Feb 7, 1998	73	J.M.H.	Grainger Co	Sep 26, 1924	Spencer, Lilbert		Morgan, Nancy	Rixby B.		Satterfield, Wanda - Bell, Linda	Elkridge, Julie - Lynn, Dollie	Michael-Gary [Bis]	Brown, Debbie [Step-Gt-Daug]	West View
Spencer, Lloyd Taylor Jr.	Feb 16, 1997	73	New Market	Jeff City	Jan 5, 1950	Spencer, L.T. Sr.		Fritts, Georgia	Ezell, Pauline		Myers, Nancy & Mike - Long, Jewell & James - Lewis & Jerry - Talley, Cathy & Douglas	Thomas J.	Carter, Lucca - Myers, Nancy - Talley, Cathy - Long, Jewell K.	Wife	West View
Spencer, Lloyd Taylor Sr.	May 10, 1996	74	New Market	Rutledge, Tn	Apr 2, 1922	Spencer, Lilbert		Morgan, Nancy	Fritts, Georgia		Hamby, Dorothy - Williams, Joyce - Hillman, Pat - Lane, Jeanne	Lloyd Jr. & Pauline-Gary & Jerry - Talley, Kathy Sue - Cathy & Douglas - Michael & Vickie	Clyde William - Dwight Jeffrey	Wife	West View
Spencer, Margie Avella	Dec 25, 1993	59	Jeff City	Knoxville, Tn	Aug 23, 1934	Spencer, Fred William [D]		Stone, Marie	Spencer, Fred William [D]					Layman-Henry	J.M.G.
Spencer, Robert	Jan 18, 1973		Jeff Co	Tn	Jul 26, 1929	Spencer, Frank	Tn	Phillips, Nora	Jennings, Norma					Spencer, Charles	Shiloh
Spencer, Ruby Magdalean Bateman	Dec 2, 1996	84	J.M.H.	Sevier Co	Aug 9, 1912	Williamson, Ralph		Burchfield, Dorothy	Spencer, Layman - Chester Theodore [D]		Rhyner, Helen [Sd] - Malone, Allen - Bateman, Barbara Gail [D] - Livingston, Peggy Bateman [D]	Bateman, David Earl		Husband	West View
Spencer, Sinnie	Feb 18, 1957	93	Knoxville, Tn	Grainger Co	Jun 6, 1863	Cook, David	Tn	Link			Weeks, Lillie - Duncan, Alice - Anderson, Virginia				Shiloh
Spencer, Stella Mae	Dec 22, 1987	68	S.M.H.	Jeff Co	Aug 11, 1919	Smith, George		Brooks, Liza Jane	Spencer, Charlie J. [Dv]		Burgin, Shirley - Sexton, Emileen - Thompson, Maxine	Eugene-Marshall	Elmore, Mary Sue	James	West View
Spiva, Rollin Joseph	Aug 24, 1975					Spiva, W.L.		Smith, Rebecca	Josie		[Step] Southall, Artelia - Wells, Mollie [B] - Bh-Lawj Mills, Nannie	[Step] Mills, Kda. Jr. - Rogers, Honco - Mills, Walter	Smith, Rebecca	Samuel	
Spiva, Samuel	Nov 15, 1996	80	J.M.H.	Jeff Co	Nov 7, 1906	Spiva, Luther		Heyworth, Eliza R.	Chandler, Mary Ruth [Dv]		Lucas, Pauline - Haynes, Mary Kate	Ulyesas Van- Walter E- Clarence	Smith, Rebecca	Son - [Pals] Lequire, Raymond - Henly - Lynn - David-Walter - Gann, Jim	J.M.G.
Spoon, James Jessie	May 20, 1965	89	Rutledge, Tn	Grainger Co	Apr 20, 1896	Spoon, George		Greenlee, Mollie	Div					Spoons, Leon [Gr-Son] - [Pals] Cunningham, Wallace - Greenlee, Tom - Clemmon, Tom - Tony-Teddy - Reach, Ansie	Central Point, Rutledge, Tn

Name	Date	Age	Place	County	Date											
Spoon, John Cleason	Nov 8, 1981	69	J.M.H.	Grainger Co	Jun 14, 1913	Spoon, Clay	Cameron, Neloma		Roach, Lora		Pratt, Evelyn - Gross, Gail - Roderick, Jewell	Buddy-Don	Doris Rodney - Kelley, Ellie - Moody, Beulah	Hands-Horace - O.C.	[Pas] Spoon, Milton-Junior - Hicks, Tom - Bridgewater, Curt - Danielle, Fred - Howell, Willard	Mitchell Springs - Rutledge, Tn
Spoon, Lora Helen	Nov 12, 1988	74	J.M.H.	Grainger Co	Jul 22, 1914	Roach, John W.	Mc Horney, Mary M.		Spoon, Cleason [S]		Pratt, Evelyn - Roderick, Jewell Goss, Gail	Don-Buddy	Morgan, Edith - Haynes, Stella - Hoffner, Teresa	Lee-J.W.	[Pas] Collins, Don - Pratt, Steve - Spoon, Tony-Scott - Bell, Steve - Roderick, Clair - Hayes, Rick - Grress, Brett	Mitchell Springs - Rutledge, Tn
Spoon, Milton	Mar 2, 1991	83	J.M.H.	Rutledge, Tn	Dec 4, 1907	Spoon, Sam	Williams, Armanda		Hodge, Mildred		Whaley, Carolyn - Leon, Mrs.	Don-Buddy	Morgan, Edith - Haynes, Stella - Hoffner, Teresa	Lee-J.W.	[Pas] Bell, Jim - Ragan, Floyd - Mc Donald, Carl - Linden, David - Cameron, Tom Jr.	Lynhurst
Spoon, Doris Jean	Jun 13, 1982	45	J.M.H.	Lee Co, Va	Jun 15, 1936	Ledford, John	Deen, Bertha		Spoon, Carroll		Spoon, Vickie - Dana - Tolliver, Dana - Hodge, Sherri	Parsons, Terry	Blevins, Lenda		[Pas] Foster, James - Nanny, L.C.- Harold - Messenger, Ralph - Williams, Paul	J.M.G.
Spoon, James Paul	Apr 12, 1982	52	Rutledge, Tn			Spoon, James J.	Greenlee, Gertrude		Barbara Lois			Leon			Farrell, Edna (Mother-in-Law)	
Spradlin, Robert Lee	Dec 27, 1986	58	J.M.H.	Knoxville, Tn	Nov 20, 1928	Spradlin, Fred	Robbins, Mary		Randruft, Faye	Army		Sproule, James Jr. [Ne] - Standridge, Jared	Monroe, Reba	[Pas] Willie - [Pas] Young, Paul - Jim - Perkins, Dan - Sheets, Tom - Newcomb, Pete	J.M.G.
Sproles, Velma L.	Apr 20, 1987	74	Knoxville, Tn	Knox Co	Jul 18, 1922	Lindsey, William E.	Thornton, Mary Belle		Sproles, James Earl			Henry	Brooks, Mollie - Minnick, Minnie - Rashberry, Louisville	Lindsey, William M.	Roseburry, Mascot, Tn	
Stallard, George	Feb 5, 1949	80	New Market, Tn	Washington Co, Va		Unk	Unk		Nellie [S]		Brewer, Mrs. Pa	Henry		Prater, Doris [Mack]-Virgil [Ky]-Thurman [Ky]	Doug	Friends Station
Stallard, Nellie M.	Sep 27, 1977	74	S.M.H.		Jan 14, 1898						Brewer, Mary		England, Edna [Ky]	Prater, Doris [Mack]-Virgil [Ky]-Thurman [Ky]	Willie - [Pas] Welch, Mark-Mike - Norton, Dan - John - Franco, Victor - Mauruna, Larry	Fieldens
Stallings, Carl Jr.	Feb 21, 1991	58	U.T.H.	Jeff Co	Sep 21, 1932	Stallings, Earnest Adam	Brock, Mary Lucille		Welch, Deborah		Hodge, Rebecca - Lust, Darlene - Stanl, Davis, Jennifer - Teresa		Norton, Shirley - Pollard, Joan - Deans, Sue	James-Robert		Piney
Stallings, James Roy	Sep 30, 1999	80	U.T.H.	Jeff Co	May 22, 1919	Stallings, Mack	Koontz, Sallie		Largo, Estelle		Campbell, Phyllis & Ben	Gerald D & Wilson J.R. Jr. & Georgia			Pleasant Grove	
Stallings, Leo Maude	Feb 14, 1991	82	J.M.H.	Kodak, Tn	Aug 31, 1908	Henderson, Dennis	Coln, Adri		Stallings, Willie		Nichols, Margie - Prutt, Ruth-Jean	Billy-Ray - Thurman-James - Thomas	Russell, Gertie Mae - Foland, Minnie		Stallings, Louise	Piney
Stallings, Raymond Eugene	Jun 20, 1978		F.S.H.	Tn	Jun 17, 1904	Stallings, Samuel C.			Beatrice H.		Moore, Jean & Don - Sharon, Juanita & Ralph - Paschall, Anne & Marilyn & Dean	Robert Joe - Samuel Fred	Louise		Willie	Piney

Name	Death Date	Age	Place	County	Birth Date	Father	Mother	Spouse	Children / Relatives	Burial
Stallings, Willie Samuel	Oct 14, 1994	89	New Market	Jeff Co	Jun 19, 1905	Stallings, Walter Alex	Cornwell, Elizabeth Virginia	Henderson, Lee M. [D]	Nichols, Margie - Purtt, Jean - [G] Houser, Mrs. Glenn [Va]; Bill-Reg-Thurman Thomas-James; [b-Lee] Foland, Majorie; Son	Pleasant Grove
Stalsworth, Albert [Bud]	Mar 10, 1999		Jeff Co	Tn	Oct 16, 1887	Stalsworth, Joe	Henshaw, Artie	Haworth, Jessie		J.M.G.
Stalsworth, Albert Earnest [Jack]	Apr 9, 1983	65	U.T.H.	Grainger Co	May 20, 1917	Stalsworth, Albert	Howard, Jessie	Kerr, Ruth		J.M.G.
Stalsworth, Charles Oscar	Jul 1, 1997	40	Rutledge, Tn	Jeff City	Sep 25, 1956	Stalsworth, Donald	Costner, Eva	Div	WW 2	J.M.G.
Stalsworth, Jessie	Nov 7, 1976	78	New Market	Grainger Co		Haworth, Euen ?	Campbell, Mollie	Stalsworth, Albert E. [D]	Jack - [G] Stalsworth, Jim; Mann, Blanche - Roach, Mable - Caine, Allagie; Frank-Lewis; [G] Houser, Mrs. Glen [Va]; Vanita; David & Joan	J.M.G.
Stalsworth, Ruth	Dec 17, 1997	78	Morristown, Tn	Dandridge, Tn	Jun 24, 1919	Kerr, Hugh	Wilson, Ella	Stalsworth, Albert Jr.	Houser, Jackie Ann & Glenn [Va]	J.M.G.
Stansberry, Effie Virginia	Dec 14, 1988	84	Strawberry Plains	Grainger Co	Dec 9, 1904	Roach, Ben	Maples, Beatrice	Stansberry, Lilburn R. Sr. [D]	Jim & Linda; Hodge, Trick; Sue - Ed	Strawberry Plains
Stansberry, Lilburn Richard	Jun 11, 1987	86	F.S.H.	New Market	May 24, 1901	Stansberry, Joe	Wright, Flourie	Roach, Effie	Richard, Katherine - Sherman - Trent, Barbara & Ed - Cain, Betty & Bob - Swann, Sue & Steve - Lewis, Leona & Ben - Hogan, Judy & Lonnie - Ray, Mildred [Fla]; Herman-J.W.-Everate-Fred-Ed-Joe-Jr.; Wife - [Pals-G-Sons] Stansberry, Craig-Joe David-Dexter-Travis-Richard, Mitrel	Strawberry Plains
Stansell, Lucille F.	Sep 4, 1999	79	Rockwood, Tn	Gadsden, Alabama	Aug 3, 1920	Foster, Walter	Williams, Parslee	Stansell, Arthur J.K. [D]	Ronald Dean-Art [Nev]; Michelle	City - Shannon, Tn
Stapleton, Amy Lynn	Apr 21, 1983		Knoxville, Tn		Nov 29, 1982	Stapleton, David	Greene, Birdie Jo		David & Kim-Dwight & Demetria; J.A.-George Luke	New Market
Stapleton, Kye Randolph	Apr 7, 1999	66	U.T.H.	Mooresburg, Tn	Jun 2, 1932	Stapleton, R.C.		Mc.Glamery, Marjorie		J.M.G.
Steele, Ernest L.	May 26, 1986	52	W. Va	W. Va	Mar 16, 1934	Steele, W.R.	Milligan, Martha	French, Imogene	Kenneth Peters; Cline, Bonnie - Kissinger, Ruth - Brant, Frances; Oria-Quinton; [Phil] French: Rick-Tom-Fred - West, Carter - Howard - Hanrich, Bill	New Market
Steele, Wilma W.	Jan 27, 1978	72	Tn		Oct 31, 1905	Elmore, John	Fielden, Lara	W	Raymond	New Market
Stein, Frank J.	Mar 3, 1979	57	J.M.H.	Stanton, Pa	Feb 8, 1922	Stein, John	Mies, Dora	Bess	WW 2; Bagley, Dorothy; Edmonds, Nola [D] - Russell, Eula [D] - Collins, Laura [D] - Templeton, Emma - Lyle, Chester - Walker, Dorothy; [Pals] Fral-Jim Longmire, Bill-Denton, Jack-Gates, John	West View

Name	Date	Age	Place	State	Birth										Cemetery
Steward, Jamesena P. [Black]	Jun 19, 1990	20	Dayton, Oh	Tn	Jul 7, 1959	Nance, Raymond H.	Brooks, Mary Elizabeth			Joyce, Elizabeth	Vernon	Hooker, Betty A. - Mary A.	Mae E.	[Pale] Steele, Wayne-Tommy - Wright, John - Oliver, Earnest - George, Thed	West View
Stiner, Hugh Davis	May 28, 1964	40	Jeff Co.	Tn	Mar 12, 1924	Stiner, Hatley G.			Faye W.			Marchant, Mrs. Loyd - Shultz, David G. - Maynard, Mrs. William J. - McColloch, Mrs. Earl	Willie		J.M.G.
Stinson, Gladys O.	May 2, 2000	96	B.H.	Mississippi	Feb 14, 1904	Osborne, James Walton	Lock, Willie		Stinson, Robert E. [D]	Mapes, Beth	Robert E. James W.	Osborne, Lola [D]	John [D]- Richard	Husband	New Market
Stinson, Marion Maybee	Nov 22, 1971		Jeff City	Tn	Jul 28, 1927	Grant, Guy	Woody, Louise		Stinson, Robert E.	Mapes, Chris- Woody-Warren-David					Lynnhurst, Knoxville, Tn
Stipes, Franklin Lee	Jan 15, 1999	72	S.M.H.	Jeff Co	Sep 27, 1926	Stipes, Fred	Cain, Gladys	Tn	Witt, Helen Elizabeth	Navy	Vineyard, Carolyn & Jim - [D] Vineyard, Mrs. Carolyn		Fred Jr. [D]		East View
Stipes, Fred	May 30, 1974	78	Jeff Co	Tn	Jul 28, 1895	Stipes, Mack	Galloway, Charlotte		Cain, Gladys		Fred Jr. [Pa]- Frank				Shaw Plains
Stipes, Gladys Elizabeth	Feb 2, 1982	87	Jeff Co	Tn	Jul 11, 1904	Stipes, Jacob	Oakes, Cora Belle	Tn	Stipes, Fred Sr.	Frank			Son		Strawberry Plains
Stipes, Jack	Feb 15, 1982	93	B.H.	Strawberry Plains	Mar 17, 1888	Stipes, John	Miles, E.		Marble [D]	McCall, Elizabeth [Ohio]	Tom	Morgan, Ellis - McDaniel, Sidley Mae	Whitaker, Clyde	[Pale] Stipes, Laura A.D. - McCall, Charlie - Wayne - Hilliard, James - Whitaker, Clyde	Strawberry Plains
Stipes, John Thomas	Oct 2, 1991	80	Strawberry Plains	Strawberry Plains	Jun 11, 1911	Stipes, Jack	Crowe, Myrtle		McCall, Reba		Lowell T. - Ronald D.- James H.	McCall, Lizzie	Doc [D]- Deddick [D]- J.C. [D]-Frank [D]-Charles [D]-Simmon [Pa]	Willie	Strawberry Plains
Stipes, Reba Viona	Aug 1, 1998	82	Dandridge, Tn	Sevier Co.	Nov 4, 1915	McCall, Frank	Snyder, Hattie Lee		Stipes, John Thomas [D]	Whitaker, Jean - Horner, Louise	Lowell & Jacob - [Mtd] - Hackworth, Mary [Pa]- Langdon, Dorothy	Whitaker, Jean & Clyde - Horner, Louise & Kent [Aai]			Strawberry Plains
Stone, Inez P.	Jan 29, 1987	70	Morristown, Tn	New Market	Aug 29, 1916	Phipps, Raymond	Brandt, Lillian		Stone, Willie W. [D]		Richard A.	Scruggs, Lorene - Phipps, Burnez - Hargood, Marie	Augustilon- William	[Pale] Scruggs, Carl - Roper, Walter - Lindle, Robert- Cunningham, Willis - Phipps, Raymond - Monroe, William - Sims, John	Youngs Memorial
Stoner, Willie Wallis [Col]	Oct 15, 1976	68	New Market	Alabama		Stoner, Willey	Moore, Rosa		Phipps, Inez			Anderson, Naomi [Ala]	Mos ? [Ala]	[Pale] Cunningham, Willis - Brazelton, Gilbert - Simon - Cunningham, Willis - Phipps, Eugene - Agnut, Carl	Youngs Memorial
Stockberry, Fred Tolbet	Jan 21, 1990	79	J.M.H.	Union Co, Tn	May 5, 1900	Stockberry, Sam	Loy, Nola		Mersey, Evelyn		Webb, Sandra	Harold [Kd]- Walter	Nichols, Jamie- Kilcranaick, Mrs. Artie	[Pale] Sanborn, Leon - Scarlett, Neal - Miller, Robert - Byrd, Greg - Watters, Ed - Branch, Joe	J.M.G.
Storey, George Bentley	Apr 13, 1999	98	Jeff City	Pine Bluff, Ark.	Aug 12, 1900	Storey, John Wesley	Malone, Georgia Etta		Essma, Nellie - Elsie [D]	WW 1	Moore, Evelyn - Williams, Georgi- Margaret [D]		Monroe-Reed		Shiloh

Name	Died	Age	Place	Origin	Born	Father	Mother	Spouse	Mil.	Notes
Stott, James Paul	Aug 24, 1994	70	J.M.H.	New Market	Mar 26, 1914	Stott, Alexander Levi	Howorth, Grace Allen	Boolly, Luella [Separated]	WW 2	Carter, Ruth — [Pals] Howorth, Willford-- Northern, Tracy-- Ballinger, Mindi-- Dean - Lindsey, Ted - Owen, David — Pleasant Grove
Strange, Charles William	Oct 6, 1995	58	Morristown, Tn	Dandridge, Tn	Jan 27, 1937	Strange, Earnest	Smith, Paralee	Willinck, Shirley		J.W. Michale — Wright, Lavada — Willie — J.M.G.
Strange, Daniel Briscoe	Oct 11, 1996	62	Knox Co.	Hamblen Co.	Dec 29, 1933	Strange, David M.	Adkins, Lexie	Div	Korea	Darrel W. — Louks, Anna-Pearl- Michale-Stacy- James-Phillip- Tony-Roy — St. Pauls - Morristown, Tn
Strange, Donald Earl	Oct 3, 1991	36	Newport, Tn	Jeff City	Feb 5, 1955	Strange, Dexter	Ward, Sally	Div		Young, Eula Mae — George-Roger- Earnest-David — Shiloh
Strange, Earnest Dexter	Oct 14, 1983	88	Morristown, Tn	Jeff Co	Jun 24, 1895	Strange, Wesley	Edmonds, Rhoda Jane	Partlow [D]	army	Wright, Laudda & Isaac - Atkins, Viola — Julia-Samantha- Kelvin-Donald Jr. — Young, Eula Mae — George-Roger- Earnest-Dexter — Shiloh
Strange, Earnest Douglas [Peanut]	Aug 23, 1999	46	Newport, Tn	Jeff City	Feb 21, 1953	Strange, Dexter Sr.	Branam, Janice [Div]		Army	Roger Dexter Jr. — Young, Eula Mae — [Pals] Strange, Charles-Michale- Jim-David-Robert- Kenneth-Roger- Adkins, Charlie — Coker Hill - Blount Co, Tn
Strange, Janice Marie	Dec 3, 2000	40	B.H.	Georgia	Nov 30, 1960	Branam, Fred	Strange, Ernest [D]			Wright, Loradla- Juan-Bill-Lloyd- Floyd-Gillogly- Harvey — Helton, Addie- Spencer, Charlie- Elmore, Mary Sue — James M.- Harvey — Church Of God - Townsend, Tn
Strange, Paralee	Aug 11, 1979	75	J.M.H.	Jeff Co	Jan 12, 1904	Strange, George	Brooks, Liza	Strange, Ernest		Leroy-Eugene- Juan-Bill-Lloyd- Floyd-Gillogly- Harvey — James M.- Harvey — Church Of God - New Market
Strange, Wendy Michelle	May 28, 1987		Jeff City	Newport, Ne	Apr 1, 1987	Strange, Terry Gene	Dotson, Rebecca Jean			New Market
Stratton, Bessie Mae	Jan 12, 1976	77	J.M.H.	Granger Co		Spoon, George	Greenlee, Mollie			Morgan, Otis & Nadine — Jim — Spoon, Paul- Clyde Jr.- Shorter, Pauline [Neice] — New Market
Sturgill, Ernest Edward	Aug 30, 2000	63	S.M.H.	Wise Co, Va	Feb 14, 1937	Smith, Coon	Tector, Ollie Mae	Div		Ernest E. 3rd & Crystal — J.M.G.
Sullridge, Claude L.	May 13, 1981	75	U.T.H.	Union Co, Tn	Sep 20, 1905	Sullridge, L.T.	Norris, Margaret	Div		Mc Dougal, Lillith — Arthur G. — Bebb, James, Roy — Bebb-James-Roy Sullivan, Nancy-Arnold [Wife]-Arnold, Glenn- Susie-Evelyn — Friends Station
Sullivan, Frank Jerome	Jan 7, 1982	73	Jeff City	Mass.	Nov -, 1878	Unk	Unk			Friends Station
Sullivan, Nancy	Nov 4, 1969	79	Knox Co	Tn	Aug 18, 1890	Arnold, W.B.	Riddle, Leah	W		Winter, Maggie [Pa] — Bert — Sullivan, Nancy-Arnold [Wife]-Arnold, Glenn- Susie-Evelyn — Friends Station
Swann, Harold R.	Apr 13, 1992	65	U.T.H.	Knoxville, Tn	Jul 18, 1926	Swann, John Sr.	Thornton, Dorothy	S		Simmons, Jennie Mae [Sis]	Homer- [Ha]- Robert [half] — Homer — Friends Station
Swann, James Percy	Feb 4, 1994	60	J.M.H.	Knoxville, Tn	Jul 16, 1933	Swann, John	Thornton, Dorothy	S	WW 2	Simmons, Jennie Mae [Sis] — James- Homer [Ha]- Robert [half] — Homer — Tn Vets - Knoxville, Tn
Swann, John Jr.	Dec 8, 1981	57	J.M.H.	Knoxville	Apr 16, 1924	Swann, John Sr.	Thornton, Dorothy	Vicki M.	WW 2	John Runnie — Simmons, Junia Mae- Homer-Robert Leo — [Pals] Hodge, James-Travlish- Gilmer, David- Allsup, Don - Spencer, Lloyd- Gary — West View

Name	Date	Age	Init	Place	Date	Father	Mother	Spouse	Div	Note						Cemetery
Sweet, Ira	Mar 29, 1972	69	J.M.H.	Tn	Jun 6, 1902	Harper, William	Bonnett, Edith	Sweet, Marvin S.			[Step] Ledford, Mrs. Garland C.; W.W. - [Nephew] Harper, Jerry	[Step] Sweet, W.W. - [Nephew] Harper, Jerry				Pleasant Grove
Talamantes, Minnie Louise	Jan 9, 1997	69	F.S.H.	Knox Co	Sep 25, 1927	Mitton, Thomas	Hensley, Sarah Alice	Talamantes, Ray			Mc Kivitt, Paula [Calif] - Matieiro, Tom [Canada]	Hensley, Kenneth [Cal] - Johnstone-Kathleen- Ramona-Beatrice- Ruth [See Child]	Barbara-Margaret- Helleld, John - Lewis, Olllie- Gordon - Hawk, Bob - Daniels, Jim	Hubbard, Bob- [Yr] - Landreth, Gordon- Franklin	Husband - [Pals] Hubbard, Jeff-Rick - Bob - Daniels, Jim	J.M.G.
Talley, Hazel Deloris	Dec 1, 1996	67	J.M.H.	New Market	Apr 6, 1931	Taylor, Cecil R.	Walker, Laura Mae	Talley, Homer [D]			Breeden, Loretta & Bill	Douglas & Cathy	Strange, Arlene- Connett, Betty- Taylor, Eva	Dale		Oakland
Talley, Herman Henry	Aug 4, 1992	84	J.M.H.	Russellville, Tn	Dec 3, 1907	Talley, Joseph	Solomon, Louisa	Seals, Edna		WW 2	Jones, Gladys & Bruce		Dorothy	Bill	National Guard - Muncey, Ava	Shiloh
Tanner, Charles William	Nov 28, 1986	38	U.T.H.	Elmira, Ny	Jun 4, 1948	Tanner, George	Alexander, Reita	Shultz, Mary Ruth Shelton [Div]	unk		Tanner, Renee- Kathleen		Dorothy	Bill	National Guard - Muncey, Ava	Piney
Tapley, Noah	May 29, 1991	71	Hill Haven	Unk	Sep 12, 1919	Unk	Unk	S					Ray, Ruby- Scott, Sarah	Lloyd	Sister	New Market
Tapley, Bonnie Ethel [Black]	Jan 20, 1993	66	Knoxville, Tn	Alpha, Tn	Feb 14, 1904	Lesborough, Grant	Shannon, Hattie	Taylor, Augustus G.					Ray, Ruby- Scott, Sarah	Lloyd	Sister	St. Lukes - New Market
Taylor, Callie M. [F]	Aug 12, 1973	76	J.M.H.	Tn	Oct 16, 1896	Mitchell, Wiley	Campbell, Eva	W		WW 2			[Hr-Law] Taylor, Minnie	Mitchell, W.B. - Farrell, Ethel [1st Cous]	Indian Ridge
Taylor, Carol Ann	Jun 28, 1978				Jun 7, 1978	Taylor, Richard	Brenda						Delia - Starnes, Emma - Pierson, Kathryn - Starnes, Laura - Starnes, Lizzie [Va]		Strange, Jim - Taylor, Gladys - Taylor, Troy [G-Parents] Strange, Earnest - Chamberon, Ellen [G-G-Parents]	
Taylor, Cecil Robert	Aug 3, 1978	70	J.M.H.	Scott Co, Va	Jul 3, 1908	Taylor, Ben	Elam, Alice	Laura Mae			Talley, Dolores - Strange, Arlene - Moody- Connett, Betty - Ballinger, Eva Sue	Dale		Veamard [Va]	Willie	Mill Springs
Taylor, David	Jan 31, 1980	74	J.M.H.	Nc	Oct 6, 1905	Taylor, John	Evans, Margaret	Unk		WW 2		Dale		Veamard [Va]	Willie	North Side - Fayetteville, Nc
Taylor, Frankie Lena	Nov 5, 1999	53	F.S.H.	Knoxville, Tn	Sep 23, 1946	Tatum, Euell Jeptha	Tatum, Eula Amelia	Taylor, Robert E.			Johnson, Rebecca & Rick	Roper, Morgan & Eleanor - Glenn, Robin & Dennis	Vann, Betty- Williford, Barbara	David [D]-John Alfred	[Pals] Roper, Marty - Johnson, Rick - Glenn, Denny-Dennis - Williams, Jack - Burnell, Earl	East View
Taylor, Gladys Pauline	Jul 15, 1982	61		Knox Co	Nov 16, 1920	Rden, Louis	Shepherd, Londis	Taylor, Troy L. [Div]			Gray, Helen - Williams, Faye	Troy-Ronald- Richard-David	Price, Mrs. Clyde	Earl	[Pals] Roper, Marty - Johnston, Rick - Glenn, Danny-Dennis - Williams, Jack - Burnell, Earl [Pals] Price, Curtis - Rden, Nathan-Carl- Randy - Dixon, Leon - Strange, Eddie	Highland Memorial West

Name	Date	Age	Place	Date									Burial
Taylor, Harriet Angelyn	Aug 13, 1992	72	Dandridge, Tn	May 20, 1920	Lane, Hardin Stocton		Sexton, Grace Violet		Taylor, James C. [D]	Clements, Jacquelen [Idaho] Rhinehart, Blaine - Sawyer, Ruth - Buchanan, Deborah	James Andrew [Pa]	Doug - [Pats] Rhinehart, Blaine & Clements Taylor [4&9]	West View
Taylor, James Claude	May 29, 1991	73	F.S.H.	Mar 9, 1918	Taylor, Claude Vaughn		Coffey, Mable		Lane, Harriet	Clements, Jacquelen [Idaho] Rhinehart, Blaine - Sawyer, Ruth - Buchanan, Deborah	James Andrew [Pa]	Norman-Clyde - Huntley	West View
Taylor, Mabel Mae	Oct 3, 1989	69	U.T.H.	Jul 24, 1894	Repass, James Welton		Holbrook, Elizabeth Cordelia		Biddle, Catherine	William-James	Blackwell, Lillian [Sc]	Repass, P.V.-Bill - Miller, Jim - Zoll, Charles - Murphy, Joe - Wheatley, George - Davis, Robert - Wineinger, Ed - Jefferson, R.	New Market
Taylor, Margaret Hedrick	Dec 6, 1988	74	Jeff City	Jan 8, 1914	Arnold, John E. [Elridge]		Walden, Rosa Tranum		Taylor, Troy Lee			Arnold, Gilbert	Lynhurst
Taylor, Mary Billie	Oct 8, 1988	77	Tn	Mar 4, 1911	Lewis, Emmit		Heworth, Susie		Taylor, Robert W.	McCurry, Joan	Westphal, Johnnie	Husband - [Pats] McCurry, Klein - Emmit - McCurry, Jim - Stalsworth, Jim - Kerr, J.R.-Joshua	J.M.G.
Taylor, Myrtle	Mar 19, 1986	69	J.M.H.	Jun 20, 1906	Unk		Unk		S	West, Beulah - Roach, Bonnie - West, Hazel - Stover, Janette - Harbin, Shirley - Rainwater, Rosa		Simpson, Kenneth E. [Nephew]	East View
Taylor, Ora Pearl	May 11, 1985	88	J.M.H.	Mar 27, 1907	Woods, Cleveland		Finley, Ida Pearl		Taylor, William [D]	Paul-William Jr.	Foster, Minnie Jo - Kerr, Carrie - Morery, Mae	Son	Mill Springs
Taylor, Paul	Jan 24, 1983	69	New Market	May 6, 1883	Taylor, W.H.	Tn	Biddle, Mary	Tn		Katherine	W.P.-James H.	Vincent, Miss Eleanmcmll] - Vickers, Mrs. Anna (Chicago)	Robert	Taylor, Mabel [Wife]	New Market
Taylor, Paul Alvin	Jul 22, 1957	72	B.H.	Mar 14, 1925	Taylor, William		Woods, Ora			Paul E.-Steve	Rainwater, Rosie - West, Beulah - West, Hazel - Stover, Janette - Harbin, Shirley - Roach, Lorene	William Jr.	Mill Springs
Taylor, Robert William	Apr 19, 1953	84	New Market	Aug 28, 1908	Taylor, James Lula		Hill, Alice		Lewis, Mary [D]	[Step] McCurry, Joan [Pa]	[Step] McCurry, Jim & Jack [Calif]	Heworth, James [Dau.] - [Pats] McCurry, Clark, Willie - Shelton, Roy - Goins, Hout - Roberts, H.B. Jr. - Lewis, Darrell - Miller, George Jr.	J.M.G.
Taylor, Paul William	Apr 19, 1953	84	New Market	Aug 28, 1908	Taylor, James Lula		Hill, Alice	WW 2	Cross, Virginia				New Market
Taylor, Terry Michael	Jul 15, 1981		Knoxville, Tn	Jul 6, 1980	Ballinger, Terry			WW 2	Hendrick, Margaret	Gray, Helen T. - Williams, Faye	Troy Jr.-Ronald-Richard-David	Riggs, Lorraine - Drew, Toddie - Degeorn, Louise	Ben	Oates - Kodak, Tn
Taylor, Troy Lee	Mar 4, 1991	74	Atlanta, Ga	Nov 1, 1916	Taylor, John Riley		Sizemore, Addie Lena					Troy - [Pats] Gray, Doug-Chuck - Wilson, Paul - Dyer, Gerry	Lynnhurst

Name	Death Date	Age	Place of Death	Birthplace	Birth Date	Father	Mother	Spouse	War/Notes	Children / Survivors	Relatives	Cemetery
Taylor, Virginia	Oct 29, 1993	74	Jeff City		Jun 6, 1919			Taylor, R. Harold		Cole, Ann - Standridge, Rochelle	Ladd, Larry - Eddie	Magnolia - Maryville, Tn
Torgerson, Elizabeth Vienna	Apr 11, 1991	76	F.S.H.	Beaver Dam, Nc	Jun 14, 1914	Andrews, Gilbert	Moss, Mary	Lowe, Mary Ellen [Me]		Lowe, Ann - Standridge, Rochelle [Me]	Ladd, Larry [Uncle] / Willie - [Pink] / Gann, Roy - / Jones, Harold [Uncle]	New Prospect - Webb, Nc / Farris - Knox Co, Ky
Temple, Charley Webster	Jun 6, 1975		Knoxville, Tn		Mar 9, 1919	Temple, C.W.	Jones, Carol		Ky		Brinkley, Jim - Gann, Bill	J.M.G.
Temple, Donald Roger	Sep 22, 1990	39	Jeff City	Hillsborough, Nc	Feb 21, 1951	Templin, Jake	Stapleton, Emma	Underwood, Jane	WW 2	O'Barr, Connie & John	Ronald	J.M.G.
Terrell, Harold Anderson	Aug 17, 1991	71	S.M.H.		Jan 1, 1920	Templin, Joseph Anderson	Hayes, Mary Mae	Roderick, Elsie Mae	WW 2	[Step] Earwood, Patricia [Dd]	Joseph Anderson Edward - Harold Mark	Piney
Terrell, Betty Jean	Apr 18, 1990	55	Oak Ridge, Tn	New Market	Apr 3, 1934	Thomas, John Floyd	Templin, Della		S		Slater	New Market
Thomas, Carl Edward	Jul 21, 1983	34	Knox Co	Tn	Oct 12, 1918	Thomas, Floyd			Tn	Betty Helen - Mary, Mary Ruth & Earl - Elliott, Louise [Dd]	Ed Jr.	New Market
Thomas, Della	Dec 3, 1973	79	Knox Co	Tn	Oct 10, 1894	Templin, William T.	Denton, Lura	Thomas, Floyd [D]		Juanita Wanda - Judy	Napier, Pauline	J.M.G.
Thomas, Irene	Aug 12, 1996	67	J.M.H.	Va	Jun 16, 1929	Thomas, Wesley	Lester, Grace	McCrosky, Floyd	Thomas, Mary Sue		Ex-Husband	Sutler Springs - Chilhowie, Va
Thomas, Ralph Charles	Jan 24, 1974	54	Nashville, Tn	Tn	May 17, 1920	Thomas, Ell S.	Waters, Lura	Helton, Etta Sue	WW 2	Tammie	Thomas, Sue	Tn. Valley Memorial Garden
Thompson, Ina Cecil	Dec 19, 1998	98	Jeff City	Michigan	Jul 24, 1890	Zongker, Henry	West, Lottie	Thompson, Frank W. [D]			Thompson, Wayne E. [Son]	Cremated
Thresher, Flora Myrtle	Jun 20, 1984	89		Jeff Co	Oct 25, 1894	James, Bascom	Nichols, Elizabeth	Thresher, J.C. [D]	Carnes, Hazel - Langston, Elizabeth	Wilson, Ada	Thresher, Wayne E. [Son] / Frazier, Ken -	Piney Grove
Thresher, Charles			Jeff Co		Mar 22, 1906							
Tillett, Genvee Edith	Jun 23, 1978	92	Jeff City	Kodak, Tn		Chesney, Richard N.	Huffaker, Mary	Tillett, John Melvin [D]		Donna	Chester - Roberd-Clary	Woodlawn
Tipton, Donald Alvin	Aug 24, 1981	29	Jeff Co	Dandridge, Tn	Jun 18, 1952	Tipton, Hubert R.	Cate, Martha				Tipton, Hubert [B] - [Father]	Catas - Jeff Co
Tipton, Hubert	Apr 15, 1974	39	Jeff City	Washington Co	Aug 25, 1934	Tipton, George	Herron, Stella	Owens, Margaret	Moody, Debbie	Michael	Ralph - [1/2] Tipton, Oscar	West View

Name	Date	Age	Place	County	Birth Date	Father	Mother	Spouse		Info	Relatives	Siblings	Pallbearers	Cemetery
Tipton, Margaret Sue	Feb 10, 1995	46	J.M.H.	Granger Co	Aug 2, 1938	Owens, Ralph	Kitts, Bessie	Tipton, Herbert [D]		Moody, Deborah T.	Michael	Wagner, Doris Ann - Weber, Ruby - Collins, Willie Mae - Bates, Lorene	Floyd-Everette-Leon-Jim	[Pals] Moody, Faye - Sam - Belinda, Tony - Oakley, Ted - Ritner, Chris - Owens, Jim	West View
Tipton, Sheila	Aug 11, 1975	74	J.M.H.	Washington Co, Tn	Apr 15, 1901	Howren, Jim	Freeman, Addie	W			Ralph-Oscar	Dotson, Lucille		West View
Tolliver, Boyd	May 19, 1988	58	U.T.H.	Claiborne Co	Aug 3, 1929	Howren, Jim	Shelton, Mary	Maples, Edna		Pressley, Ann	Kermit-Lloyd-Herman-Harmon	Ronnie-Steve	Willie - [Pals] Livesay, Kermit - Rombhest, Harold - Howard, Austin - Ballinger, Austin - Don - Greene, Jackie	West View
Tolliver, Herman	Jun 23, 2000	61	New Market	New Market	Oct 24, 1938	Tolliver, Verlin	Shelton, Mary	Div		Humbard, Teresa	Tim-Harmon Wayne[Az]	Kermit-Lloyd-Herman	Tolliver, Mary - Burchett, Jackie [G-McReins]	West View
Tolliver, Jackie Glenn	Mar 7, 1974	19	New Market	Tn	Jan 19, 1955	Tolliver, Herman	Gladys	S			Sandra	Kermit-Lloyd-Herman	Larry-Logan	West View
Tolliver, Mary Florence	May 12, 1977	71		Claiborne Co	Oct 4, 1905	Shelton, William	Moore, Nancy	W			Kermit-Lloyd-Boyd Herman-Harmon	Sharp, Ida	[Pals] Tolliver, Billy-Larry-Ronnie-Lynn - Shelton, Bobby Or Danny - Mc George, Steve - Sharp, Herschel	West View
Tolliver, Robert Dale	Nov 8, 1979	22	F.S.H.	Jeff Co	Sep 15, 1957	Tolliver, Kermit	Northern, Wanda			Crystal Dawn	Debbie-Anita - Haynes, Nancy - Haynes, Karen - Smith, Becky	Billy	[Pals] Hensley, David-Ray - Mills, Darrel - Donnelson, Lowell - Hardin, Gary-Ted - Payne, Steve	West View
Tolliver, Verlin C.	Mar 29, 1971	68	Knoxville, Tn	Tn	Oct 12, 1902	Tolliver, George	Gibbs, Mollie	Shelton, Mary			Boyd-Lloyd-Kermit	Thomas, Georgia - Keck, Mrs. Dewey - Williams, Alice, Cora - Dale [Mich] - Patton, Nora - Williams, Lora - Bates, Flora	Willie - [Pals] Sharp, Herschel - Disels, Ed - Shelton, Wyson - Roy - Mc George, Roy - Lackey, Herbert	West View
Tolliver, Robert Dale	Nov 8, 1979	68	F.S.H.	Jeff Co	Sep 15, 1957		Northern, Wanda				Kermit-Lloyd-Boyd Herman-Harmon			West View
Tolliver, Wanda Margaret	Jun 27, 1998	66	New Market	New Market	Jul 31, 1931	Northern, Harmon	Carter, Leatha	Tolliver, Kermit			Billy	Olvey, Nancy - Smith, Becky - Haynes, Karen - Varner, Anita - Jeffers, Debbie	[Pals] Tolliver, Family	Tolliver Family
Tolliver, William Kermit	Jul 29, 1999	47	F.S.H.	Jeff City	Jun 26, 1952	Tolliver, Kermit	Northern, Wanda M.	Div		Eddington, Amy Michelle	William Jamie	Olvey, Nancy - Smith, Becky - Haynes, Karen - Varner, Anita - Jeffers, Debbie	Tolliver Family - New Market	New Market
Tolliver, Kenneth Lee	Dec 25, 1982	18	Jeff City	Milligan Clinic	Mar 2, 1964	Tolliver, Boyd	Maples, Edna	S			Ronnie-Steve	Pressley, Ann	Ronnie-Steve	West View
Townsend, Sammie	May 4, 1949	1	Knoxville, Tn	Knoxville, Tn	Feb 8, 1948	Townsend, Robert K.	Reynolds, Daisy				Alice-Mary	Pressley, Ann	[Pals] Tolliver, Larry-Jon-Tim - Bill - Foster, Don - Dotson, Darrell	West View
Trapp, Iva Ester Maynard	Jul 14, 1982	68	J.M.H.	Whitley Co, Ky	Mar 18, 1914	Estes, Alfred J.	Deeds, Helen	W		Clark, Carolyn - Newmanger, Marie [Fla] - Sherrod, Maxine	Chow, Dessie [Tn] - Houston, Merle [Va]	Alice-Mary	Townsend, Robert K.-Sam [G-Father]	[Pals] Sherrod, Walter-Donald - Newmanger, Wesley - Loucks, Scott - Corbie, Walter - Corbie, William - Sellers, Dale	Hendrons Chapel

Name	Date	Age	Place	Place	Date	Name		Name							Burial
Trent, Arlin Wilson	Sep 5, 1993	82	J.M.H.	Snowville, Tn	Feb 18, 1911	Trent, Fred O.	Tn	Ballinger, Edith		Howard, Frances	Curtis-Charles-Edgar	McDaniel, Elzi - Kirkwood, Arlie	George-Grant	Willie - [Pals] Trent, Diane-Charles-Tony-Gary - Howard, Doug - Steve	J.M.G.
Trent, Charles T.	Jan 18, 1988	72	Strawberry Plains	Strawberry Plains	Feb 3, 1916	Trent, D.M.		Cook, Alice		Polly	Smith, Sue - Rushing, Patt	D.M. - Tim - Thomas P. - Tony B.	Napier, Arlie - Williamson, Gladys - Erickson, Regina - Miller, Gloria	Thomas-Doy	Willie - [Pals] Trent, Tom - Smith, Rodney - Slip - Bilkie - Sammy-David - Wiggleton, Joe	Strawberry Plains
Trent, Claude G.	Feb 12, 1954	66	Johnson City, Tn	Hawkins Co, Tn	Mar 18, 1887	James, I.C.	Tn	Trent, Ellen	Tn					Trent, Carson	Snowville - Snowville, Tn
Trent, Edith Edna	Jul 25, 1997	82	New Market	New Market	Sep 28, 1914	Ballinger, J.H.		Vineyard, Ada		Trent, Arlie [D]	Howard, Frances & Cornell - [P] Carolyn - Trent, Glenda	Howard, Curtis & Phyllis - Charles-Edgar & Barbara-Harold [D]	Kinder, Della - Whitlock, Hazel - [P] Ballinger, Dorothy	Trent, Claude	Shiloh
Trent, Eugene E.	Jun 30, 196	51	New Market	Tn	Jul 16, 1911	Trent, Claude		Seals, Louvana		Sandra Kay	Amy - Goldschmidt, Richard - Belvidere, Janice & Joe [Pa] - Newton, Rhonda & Roger - Linsley, Alicia & Karen	Jerry-Larry	Morgan, Mrs. G.A. - Gentry, Mrs. W.A. - Wilder, Mrs. Fred - Austin, Mrs. Jewell	Grant	Oakland
Trent, George W.	Oct 4, 1965	74	Rutledge, Tn	Snowville, Tn	Feb 24, 1919	Trent, Fred		Odom, Laura		Talley, Una		Stanley & Cheryl (Fla) Nathan & Iradia	McDaniel, Elzi - Kirkwood, Arlie	Grant	Willie - [Pals] Goldschmidt, David-Eric-Tom - Trent, Danny - Belvidere, Jeff - Jerry	Oakland
Trent, Grant Harvey	Nov 18, 1983	78	Hancock Co.	May 21, 1915	Trent, Fred O.		Odom, Laura Alice		Pruitt, Betty Lucille	Betty Lucille	Lovell-Ronald-George	McDaniel, Elzi - Kirkwood, Arlie	Son - [Pals] Trent, Larry-Carl-Ricky-George Jr. - Griffey, Eddie - McDaniel, Jerry	Pruitt Church - Kocurek, Tn
Trent, Harold Glendon	May 14, 1983	52	Jeff City	New Market	Jul 7, 1940	Trent, Arlie		Ballinger, Edith		Hansel, Glenda		Glenn H.-Dean E.	Howard, Frances T.	Curtis-Charles-Edgar	Trent, Mike-Chris-Tony-Dan - Howard, Steve - Hansel, Jeff	Pleasant Grove - Felther
Trent, Hope Elaine	Oct 2, 1965		J.M.H.	Tn	Sep 30, 1965	Trent, Harold G. - Glenn, James - Wesley		Jernigen, Mary E.	S			Wright, Jamie - Ray-Billy		James	Husband	Trent, Family - Snowville, Tn
Trent, Judy Lee	Dec 24, 1995	41	Jeff City	Jeff City	Jul 12, 1954	Trent, Perry H.				Trent, Perry H.	Russell, Mrs. George - Kirkwood, Mrs. John - Mc Daniel, Mrs. Albert	George (Pa) - Grant-Arlie		Kathy	James	Snowville, Tn
Trent, Laura Alice	May 10, 1971	78	J.M.H.	Tn	Sep 6, 1893		Tn			W					Shiloh
Trent, Lusanna	Oct 8, 1950	61	Kingsport, Tn		May 25, 1889	Seal, Oliver	Tn	Smiley, Rianna		Morgan, Mrs. G.A.	Lovell-Ronald-Bridge	McDaniel, Elza - Kirkwood, Arlie		Trent, Glenda	Snowville - Snowville, Tn
Trent, Martha Caroline	Apr 25, 1997	57	S.M.H.	Jeff City	Apr 24, 1940	Hansel, Lloyd E.		Caruthers, Helen		Chris & Theresa - Lumb, Mary Jayne & Terry		Hansel, Jim & Carolyn	James	J.M.G.
Trent, Rose Lee	Dec 23, 1991	76	B.H.	Snowville, Tn	Dec 6, 1915	Burchett, John		Swiney, Fanny		Trent, Hugh	Chancey, Joan	Gary	Trent, Glenda - Lumb, Mary Jayne & Terry	Lawson, May	Son	Strawberry Plains

Name	Death Date	Age	Facility	Place	Birth Date	Father	Mother	Spouse	Mil.					Narces Grove
Trent, Stella Jane	Dec 30, 1997	80	New Market	Hancock Co.	Apr 15, 1917	Rowe, Timon	Holton, Eva	Trent, Eugene [D]		Lawson, Kay & Jack	Jerry & Frieda [K]-Larry & Jewell	Moles, Nettie		
Trent, Una Mae	Feb 12, 1994	69	U.T.H.	Rutledge, Tn	Sep 4, 1924	Turley, Frank	Watson, Beuna	Trent, George W. [D]		Amy-Godschznell, Jeanette-Belvedere, Janice-Newton, Rhonda-Linsley, Alicia	Stanley-Mathias-Albart [D]	Davies, Hallicksen-Cammon, Ina Pearl-Imogene-Moody, Marilyn	Paul-Glen-Gobschnell, Richard Erick-Thomas-David-Belvedere, Jonah-Bryan	Doug [Frds]
Trujillo, Gilbert Emmet	Jun 16, 1965	28	S.M.H.	Pedro, Columbia	Jun 15, 1937	Trujillo, Robert R.	Helen	Mollie O.					Wife	J.M.G.
Turk, Iva [Black]	May 31, 1999	104	Jeff City	New Market	May 4, 1895	Fain, William	Brazelton, Laura	Helen	1	McFarland, Anna Bell [D]-Chambers, Doris		Baylor, Beulah-Hardin, Mirie	4	Youngs Memorial
Turley, Hubert Dolphia	Sep 28, 1994	85	Morristown, Tn	Dallas, Texas	Dec 27, 1908	Turley, Robert	Stubblefield, Mattie	Harville, Bertha P.		Ellison, Mary Ann-Morgan, Carolyn-Watson, Florine	Amos-Andy-Norman-Donald-Avery-Harold-Ellis	Ellison, Mary Ann-Morgan, Carolyn-Watson, Florence	Amos-Andy-Norman-Donald-Avery-Harold-Ellis	Oakland
Turley, Robert Nelson	Jan 6, 1982	61	F.S.H.	Rutledge, Tn	Dec 14, 1930	Turley, Hubert	Harville, Bertha	Ladd, Kathy		Daughty, Sharon	Don-Dustin	Ellison, Mary Ann-Morgan, Carolyn-Watson, Florence	Wife-Sons	Oakland
Turner, Edith	Jun 18, 2000	93	J.M.H.	Dandridge, Tn	Apr 23, 1907	Phillips, C.A.	Willburd, Vernie	Turner, Guy [D]		Johnson, Ethel-Eslinger, Verna	Turner, Charles			Oakland
Turner, Martha Alice	Mar 28, 1975	82	Dandridge, Tn	Clark Range	Feb 17, 1890	Norman, William H.	Peters, Sarah	Martha Alice			Charles-Ray [Frds]		T.B.	Clark Range-Fentress Co, Tn
Turner, Thomas Phillip	Dec 8, 1967	82	Hillcrest Med. Inst.			Turner, James C. Jr.	Voiles, Nancy	Martha Alice		Charles-Earl-Shade	Charles-Ray [Frds]		T.B.-Turner, Charles	Clark Range-Fentress Co, Tn
Underwood, James Edward	Feb 22, 1998	84	Jeff City	Jeff Co	Mar 7, 1913	Underwood, Elisha Edward	Comte, Gillie Ann	Cannon, Lillie L. [D]		Annie Lou [D]-Higgs, Beth	Thomas & Ann C.-Morrisett, Lillie Mae-George T. & Ann B. [Tr]	Merle, Alice [D]-Morrisett, Lillie Mae [D]-Jett, Laura [D]-Cothran, Juanita [D]-Carter, Mary	Fred [D]-Jess-John [D]-Frank [D]-Granville [D]-William [D]	Son- [Frds] Underwood, Jonathan-Eugene-Higgs, Jeff-Peterson, J.D.-Merle, Harry Jr.-Cox, Jennings
Underwood, Lillie Isabell	Nov 10, 1995	86	Dandridge, Tn	Jeff Co	Sep 4, 1907	Cannon, James E.	Cox, Lou	Underwood, James E.		Thomas E-George Turner	Thomas E-George Turner			J.M.G.
Underwood, Richard Edward	Apr 7, 1994	72	U.T.H.	Luttrelle, Tn	Dec 9, 1921	Underwood, Samuel	Cooper, Kizzie	Cooper, Kizzie	Wilson, Ann	Bryant, Mary		Bryant, Mary	George	U.T. Memphis
Underwood, Tony Haskel	Mar 4, 2000	61	New Market	Jeff City	Oct 14, 1938	Underwood, Fred A.	Bateman, Beulah	Bates, Charlotte	unk	Long, Tammy-Hurst, Debbie & James	Mike & Lisa	Una Lee-Riner, Jane-Williamson, Wanda	Fred E.-Marion	
Valentine, Charles A.	Dec 22, 1944	24	Paris, France		Mar 8, 1920	Valentine, Clinton L.			Army	Jo Elizabeth	Jo Elizabeth	Franklin, Mrs. Earl	William-Walter-Roy-Fred-Leslie-Jessie-C.L. Jr	Valentine, Reg-Clinton L.
Valentine, James Robert	Jun 25, 1990	54	New Market	Sevier Co.	Jan 29, 1936	Valentine, Ernest	Williams, Dona	Appling, Joyce Lawn	Army	Becky Lynn	Robert Wayne [D]-James Michael-Jimmy	Galyon, Rose Lee-Terracino, Rachnad [Frds]	Dean-Kenneth	Mother- [Frds] Haggard, A.C.-Wolf, George-Arnold, H.-Russell, Pat-Mike-Nash, Troy-Jones, M.L.-Morgan, Estelle-Hoard, Joey
Valentine, Robert Wayne	Sep 25, 1979	18	U.T.H.	Knox Co.	Sep 19, 1961	Valentine, James Robert	Appling, Joyce		S	1	Becky	Michel-Jimmy		Manila-Sevier Co.

Name	Date	Age			Birth									Relations	Location
Van Dyke, Martha Ethel	May 11, 1994	88	J.M.H.	Talbot, Tn	Feb 23, 1906	Line, John Bettis	Purkey, Laura Belle	Van Dyke, T.H. [D]				Don & Josephine	Mansell, Helen	Son - [Pals] Parker, Don - Thomas, Carol - Franklin, Cindy - Byrd, Roger - Howard, Jim - New James	Sunderland
Van Dyke, Thomas Haskel	Jan 9, 1981	76	J.M.H.	Talbot, Tn	May 21, 1904	Van Dyke, Andrew	Lucy Ann	Line, Ethel				Dan	Jacobs, Clara	Wife - [Pals] Reposs, P.V. - Ezlinger, Alger - Vance, Arnold - Charles - Traylor, Paul - Haworth, Marshall - Sunch, Lawrence - Parker, Clarence	Sunderland
Vance, Charles Alvin	Mar 27, 1990	56	New Market, Tn	Jeff Co	Jan 8, 1934	Vance, Sam A.	Humbord, Pauline	Wright, Imogene	Cogdill, Debbie	Jeffery		Shoupe, Anna Lou	Roger	Wife - [Pals] Repass, P.V. - Vance, Arnold - Wollord, Darrell - Martin, James - Chandler, Rom	New Market
Vance, Elizabeth E.	Oct 1, 1984	87	U.T.H.	Tn	Mar 16, 1879	Hinchey, Lee	Mary	Vance, J.K. [D]		[Step] Vance, Earnest	Dan		Smith, W. Lee [Son]		New Market
Vance, Fred W. [Fisher]	Mar 19, 1988	49	J.M.H.	Sweetwater, Tn	May 8, 1938	Vance, Paul	Drake, Thelma	Rhodes, Mary Jo			Paul W.-Franklin	Peet, Margaret- Mc Carter, Beth - Dennis, Juanita - Wilhite, Virginia-Ellen - VdZz, Flora	Vance - New Market		
Vance, Gary Stephen	May 20, 1984	30	Talbott, Tn	Jeff Co	Aug 7, 1953	Vance, Jesse James	Cameron, Maybelle	Div	army	Chastity Renee			McDelle Lynn	Father - [Pals] Brewer, Eugene - Smith, Jim-Dave- Walker, Bobby - Pollard, Danilin	J.M.G.
Vance, James Earnest	Dec 17, 1988	58	Jeff Co	Tn	Nov 16, 1911	Vance, James K.	James, Martha	Sellers, Ruth		Ernestine- Breeden, Wilma	Jesse			Wife [Pals] Hubbard, Carl - Hubbard, Arthur - Sellers, Dean- Jessie-J.D.	Friends Station
Vance, James K.	Jun 6, 1965	82	M.C.	Tn	Mar 20, 1873	Vance, Sam	Kennedy, Elizabeth		spanish am			Randles, Eva	C.B.	Vance, Elizabeth [Wife]	New Market
Vance, John D.	Mar 10, 1972	30		Tn	Nov 29, 1941	Vance, Paul		Wanda			Mike	Gary-Dennis- Dwayne--Johnny	William-Fred- Franklin	Wife-Drake, James- Wilhite, Virginia- Edzerkn, Juanita - Mc Carty, Beth - Peet, Margaret - [Alabama]	Vance
Vance, Mae Belle	Aug 21, 1996	69	Morristown, Tn	Jeff Co	May 27, 1936	Cameron, Manuel	Gibbons, Evene			Vance, Jesse J.				Wife- Drake, Thomas - Vance, Elizabeth [G-Parents]	J.M.G.
Vance, Mary Ruth	Dec 27, 1996	77	B.H.	Knox Co	Jun 6, 1909	Sellers, Jessie	Sanders, Mattie	Vance, Earnest [D]						Husband - [Pals] Smith, Jim-David- Pollard, Darwin- Loren, Mike - Mc Ghee, Bob- Housley, Tim Vance, Ernestine- Wilma [Pals] Breeden, Jim John-David-Bill - Vance, Michie- Hubbard, David	Friends Station

Name	Death Date	Age	Hospital	Location	Birth Date	Father	Mother	Informant	Mil.	Relatives 1	Relatives 2	Relatives 3	Relatives 4	Cemetery
Vance, Paul Inman	Dec 14, 1977			Tn	Sep 1, 1907	Vance, Fred	Inman, Elizabeth	Drake, T.	WW 2	Peek, Margaret [Ala] - Mc Carty, Beth [Ala] - Davis, Juanita [Ala] - Willhite, Flora - Willhite, Ellen	Owenby, Paula	Ron	Bill-Fred	Mill Springs
Vance, Paul Lester	Jan 7, 1989	64	Jeff Co	Tn	Feb 22, 1924	Vance, Andy	Major, Biddie	Bunch, Mary Elmo					Heston	Vance
Vance, Pauline E.	Oct 15, 1980	70	New Market, Tn	Jeff Co	Jun 4, 1910	Humbard, Charlie	Elmore, Bertha	Vance, Sam [D]		Anna Lou	Roger-Charles	Carl-Bill	[Pete] Humbard, Charles-Donald-Daugh, Dreama-Holt, Arthur-Courtney, Arthur	New Market
Vaughn, Samuel Alvin	Feb 17, 1982	53	J.M.H.	Tn	Apr 15, 1928	Vance, J.K.	James, Martha			Anna Lou	Charlews A.-William R.-Bobby R Kim-David	Ernest	Vance, Pauline Elizabeth [Wife]	New Market
Vaughn, Robert Franklin Sr.	Jun 22, 1998	55	B.H.	Baltimore, Md	Feb 221, 194	Vaughn, William Patton Sr.	Harrison, Priscilla A.		Air Force	Wooten, Kathy-Lyle, Vicky	Charlews A.-William R.-Bobby R Kim-David	Bill-Tony-Patrick [Cal]	Charles	J.M.G.
Vesser, Frank	Sep 4, 1990	66	S.M.H.	Jeff Co	Oct 17, 1924	Vesser, Walter	Jones, Hattie			Coleman, Alene [Superseded]		Charles		West View
Vineyard, Ada L.	Jul 2, 1978		J.M.H.	Hawkins Co.	Aug 8, 1910	Hensley, Phillip	Shropshire, Hulda	Vineyard, Robert		Looney, Mary - Mc Ghee, Mae - Looney, Christine - Saylor, Hassie Lee - Buff, Esther - White, Ethel	Quisenberry, Alice - Lamplin, Lola - Norris, Mary	Mary-Carmen [Cal]-Cattie-Crews-Kyle-Dana-Jim-Nash, Tilda	Husband	West View
Vineyard, Allen Elmore	Feb 11, 1997	81	Jeff City	Grainger Co.	Jan 30, 1916	Elmore, Mabel Gertrude	Cochran, Hazel Pauline	Vineyard, Robert	Army	Cameron, Joyce & James	Gary & Deb	Cook, Wanda		J.M.G.
Vineyard, Beulah	May 27, 1979	74	J.M.H.	Grainger Co.	Jul 9, 1904	Vineyard, Melton	Davis, Amy	Vineyard, Virgil						Strawberry Plains
Vineyard, Gary Allen	Feb 21, 1999	49	J.M.H.	Jeff City	Jan 25, 1950	Vineyard, Allen	Cochran, Hazel	Sexton, Debra		Cameron, Joyce & James - [In-Law] Sexton, Scott	Travis-Tyler	Cameron, Joyce & James - [In-Law] Sexton, Carla	[In-Law] Sexton, Scott	J.M.G.
Vineyard, Halmon	Dec 2, 1984	64	B.H.	Grainger Co.	Oct 2, 1920	Vineyard, Milton	Davis, Amy	Whitaker, Thelma			Stephen L.-Edgar M.	Acuff, Lucilla-Mitchell, Lula	J.H. Jr.	Moser ?
Vineyard, Hazel	Oct 21, 1996	73	U.T.H.	New Market	Mar 13, 1923	Cochran, Charles	Foster, Minnie	Vineyard, Allen		Cameron, Joyce	Gary	Vineyard, Margaret	Fred-Steve	West View
Vineyard, Henry Frank	Sep 29, 2000	81	Rutledge, Tn	Rutledge, Tn	Mar 21, 1919	Vineyard, Burley	Davis, Ophelia	Maggie Rosetta [D]		Cook, Mary Ruth & Ed - Mc Elhaney, Wanda & Bob - Daniel, Betty & Grady - Bilbrea, Ruby	Collins, Helen - Holt, Mattie	J.D.-Curtis-Ray Dean	Wife - [Pete] Smith, David - Anderson, Mike - West, Bob - Martin, Bob - Starling, Sam - Wilson, W.O. - Gary - [Pete] Repass, P.V. - Cameron, Ellis - Jim - Adams, Dennis - Cochran, James	Grainger Memorial
Vineyard, James Robert	Sep 13, 1992	83	New Market	Grainger Co.	Mar 29, 1909	Vineyard, William Gentry	Davis, Isa Belle	Hensley, Ada [D]		Dyer, Beulah - Collins, Helen - Holt, Mattie		Kinder, Della [Niece]		West View
Vineyard, Johnnie Fennell	Mar 4, 1999	73	F.S.H.	Lee Springs - Grainger Co.	Oct 13, 1925	Vineyard, Clifford	Fennell, Maggie	Mitchell, Betty		Amy [Cal]	David & Teresa-Carl			
Vineyard, Mabel	Sep 14, 1973	84	Knoxville, Tn	Knoxville, Tn	Aug 12, 1889	Elmore, John T.	Fielden, Laura			Craig, Mrs.-Glenn	Allen E.	Steele, Wilma		Indian Ridge

Name	Date	Age	Initials	Place	Date 2					[Niece]	[Nephew]			Cemetery
Vineyard, Maggie	Mar 19, 1972	82	J.M.H.	Tn		Farrell, John		Vineyard, Clifford [D]		Robinson, Mrs. Lucie	Fielden, Eugene			Vineyard, Johnny [Son] - [Pals] Vineyard, J.P. - Nelson, Roy - Nelson, Ed - Ships, Everett - Ferrell, Ralph	Indian Ridge
Vineyard, Maggie Roetta	Jul 1, 1999	88	Rutledge, Tn	Sevier Co						Cook, Mary Ruth & Ed - Mc Elhaney, Wanda & Bob - Daniel, Betty & Cindy - Blakke, Ruby	Jack & Jane [Rel]			Granger Memorial
Vineyard, Marion Franklin	Jul 21, 1967	84	Knoxville, Tn	Granger Co	Feb 25, 1983	Vineyard, Samuel	Elmore, Mabel	Vineyard, Henry		Craig, Mrs. Glenn				Vineyard, Allen R. [Son] - [Pals] Vineyard, Jack - Miten-Helmond - Elmore, Wayne - Jay Branson, Ellis	New Market
Vineyard, Nettie	May 20, 1972		J.M.H.					Vineyard, Elmer Boyd [D]		Bissel, Loretta [M]		Gronostoon, Mamma - Fradkin, Lillian [B]; Ballinger, Grace [B];		Kerr, Hazel [Dau] - [Pals] Watson, Mike - Riley - Mc Clain, Shane - Jennison, Vineyard, Jerry - Charles - Henry - Collins, Richard	New Market
Vineyard, Ruby Marian	Jan 2, 1984	51	Knoxville, Tn	Granger Co	Oct 8, 1932	Watson, Boyd		Vineyard, Ray Dean		Hardin, Brenda	Jimmy		Bobby-Ralph	Husband - [Pals] Hauk, Scott-Jim - Fultz, Nick-Rocky - James -	Shiloh-Granger Co
Vinson, Jack	Aug 22, 1999	73	Knoxville, Tn	Sparta, Tn	Sep 25, 1925	Vinson, Guster	Rice, Maude	Watkins, Sarah	WW 2	Ronald Lynn [M]		Daniels, Pauline - England, Lorene - Golden, Imogene - Gray, Sue			Shiloh
Voiles, Pauline Lucille	Mar 19, 1993	73	S.M.H.	Strawberry Plains	May 7, 1919	Lauderdale, Wilmer	Compton, Ella	Voiles, Alonzo		Bounds, Dorothy		Fultz, Roy James - Samuel			Piney
Wadsworth, Ida Carrene	Nov 16, 1998	74	B.H.	Maulwie, Ga	Jan 25, 1914	West, Ansel P.	Dunn, Ida Carrene	Wadsworth, Lewis [D]			Joe B. Elijah Sr. & Reta	Gentry, Blanche - Walker, Katy	Alexander, Odies - Tyson, [Maudie, Gla] Elsie		Maulwie, Ga
Wagner, Christine Mae	Apr 28, 1989	90	S.M.H.	Jeff Co	May 3, 1989	Sellers, Elbert E.	White, Sally	Wagner, Floyd T. [D]		Sawson, Peggy - Wagner, Evelyn	Le.E.-Ray	Foster, Hazel - Ships, Verna	Henderson F.H. - Edmonds, Dewey		Piedmont
Wahl, Dwight Lewis	Feb 16, 1998	73	J.M.H.	Monroe Co, Ny	May 29, 1914	Wahl, Louis Franklin	Holland, Emma	Collier, Grace		Baker, Marion [Ind] - Francis, Joan [Rel] - Tinsley, Elaine [Pal] - Yannessy, Linda [Wid]	Donald [Pa]	Cuthbert, Anna [M]	Lincoln D.	[Pal] Hatton, Gene - Hubbard, Robert - Collier, Frank-Robert-Allen	J.M.G.
Wahl, Grace	Jul 24, 1995	69	F.S.H.	Jeff City	Feb 21, 1927	Cotter, Frank E.	Cameron, Zelma	Wahl, Dwight [D]		Hall, Gertrude & Herbert - Hall, Edith & Rueil - Sturgill, Betty & Ernest	Buford A.-George W. Jr.	Burchall, Ramona			Slater
Walker, Annie	Mar 3, 1974	76	J.M.H.	Tn	Mar 31, 1897	Strange, George	Moore, Huticha	W				Edmonds, Mae			J.M.G.

Fielden Funeral Home
New Market Jefferson County Tennessee

Name	Death Date	Age	Place	County/Origin	Birth Date	Father	Mother	State	Spouse	War	Relatives	Relatives	Relatives/Children	Survivors/Children	Cemetery
Walker, Brad H.	Mar 11, 1986	76	Jeff City	Hawkins Co.	Mar 16, 1909	Walker, Elbert	Brown, Mary Lou				Marsh, Ella - Kennedy, Marie - Strange, Neddie	Larry H.-L.H.- Howard		[Pala] Walker, Mike-Ron-Don-Bill-John - Parker, Bill-John - Marsh, Tom	J.M.G.
Walker, Buford Andrew	Dec 27, 1976	57	U.T.H.	Jeff Co	Jan 13, 1919	Walker, George	Strange, Annie		Annie M.			Malcolm E.- Clifford, Gertrude- Sturgill, Betty	George Jr.	Willis	J.M.G.
Walker, Claude E. [Col]	May 31, 1963		J.M.H.	Tn	Aug 19, 1886	Walker, Allen	Huff, Sara Ann	Tn	W	WW 2	Susie	Johnson, Ida- Leffy, Okla [Sister]	Husband		Old Mitchell - Blaine, Tn
Walker, Della Ault	Jun 1, 1957	75	Knoxville, Tn	Tn	Jun 20, 1881	Ault, Jerome	Walker, John A.		W			James Wayne [Okla]	Ault, J.A.-A.J.	Husband	
Walker, Edward Dodd Taylor	Apr 5, 1989	71	Richmond - 23221	Tn	Sep 29, 1917	Walker, Marshall Mark	Murray, Gertrude		Div				Roxy-Hazel- Buford-Harold	Sister [Pala] Shafer, Spencer- Tim-Ron-Bob-Dan	Flat Gap
Walker, Elizabeth Georgiana	May 5, 1994	40	U.T.H.	Knoxville, Tn	Sep 27, 1953	Walker, Buford A.	Hawkins, Annie Mae		S		Walker, Andrew	Malcolm- Stanley-Don		Brother - [Pala] Walker, Michael- Ritchie- Stanley- Cawood, David- Donna - Billy, Penny	J.M.G.
Walker, George Washington	Aug 3, 1966	80	New Market, Tn	Tn	May 16, 1886	Jarnigan, Ports	Nooteboom, Adeline				Ann Sarah Elizabeth				J.M.G.
Walker, Georgia [Col]	Mar 31, 1966	79	S.M.H.	Va	Feb 22, 1907	Hawkins, Sam	Carr, Susan				Walker, Porter William [D]	Anna M.	Cash, Dorthy	West View	J.M.G.
Walker, John Adam	Sept., 1969	96	Tulsa, Okla.										James Walker	Brown, Mrs. T.G. [Pa]	[Broken Arrow, Ark.]	New Market
Walker, Joseph Robert	Nov 11, 1991	59	Morristown, Tn	Hamblen Co.	Jan 26, 1933	Walker, Frank W.	Lesper, Aileen		Kay L.	Korea	Shafter, Bobby H.	Tucker, Anna - Watkins, Elizabeth	James-Lynn- John		Hamblen Memorial
Walker, Larry Zane	Jun 14, 2000	52	S.M.H.	Hancock Co.	Apr 1, 1948	Walker, Brad	Davis, Vernie		Case, Agnes		Drinnen, Shirley- Carroll, Linda	Ronnie & Carol[Ne]-Donnie & Pam	Walker, Ellis - Kennedy, Sie - Strange, Neddie	Troy [D]-L.H.- Howard- Cass, Dale & Timmy	West View
Walker, Merna L. [Cindi]	Aug 3, 1980	96	Knoxville, Tn	Tn	Sep 2, 1973				Walker, George W. [D]		Edith - Yohio, Mrs. Herbert	Brown, Mrs. T.G.- George W.- Mrs. Thomas G.	John	Mariey Genevieve [Doug]- Walker, Harold T. [Son]- Brown, Mrs. T.G. [R]	New Market
Walker, Sarah Jane	Oct 4, 1958	82	New Market	Tn	Dec 29, 1875										New Market
Walker, Timothy Clark	Jan 3, 1993	30	Knoxville, Tn	Jeff City	Aug 8, 1962	Walker, George W. Jr.	Clifton, Mary Ruth						Scott	John - Father - [Pala] Clifton, Steve- Sturgill, Ed- Banks, Neal- Lindsey, Arthur- Valentine, Clint- Walker, Stanley	J.M.G.
Wallson, Joe Sanders	Sep 9, 1999	82	Dandridge, Tn	Travis, Tx	Oct 18, 1916	Walker, Joel	Bates, Ellis		Walker, Phyllis G.		Wood, Anne			[Pala] Hamilton, Clifford-Howard- Helms, Bob- Shelly, Fred- Campbell, Pete-Jack	J.M.G.
Walllard, Anna Lee	Jul 24, 1992	80	Morristown, Tn	New Market	Aug 21, 1901	Mc Campbell, Joseph	Moreland, Ella		Walllard, Edgar [D]				Keith		Mc Campbells Chapel
Walters, Oscar N.	Feb 13, 1982	78	S.M.H.	Tn	Oct 25, 1963	Walters, William	Pauline	Tn	Stone, Lillie		Colley, Mrs. G.E.- Fugate, Mrs. W.B.- Carr, Mrs. Arch M.			Children	J.M.G.

Name	Date	Age	Place		Birth Date									Burial
Watkins, Albert G.	Oct 1, 1966	71						Grace		Precd., Mrs. Albert - Frances, Mrs. Vernon [Ch] - Fisher, Mrs. Guttierrez, Richard [Mil] - Ruby [N]	Resend, A.	Pierce, Jeanette - Pierce, Mrs. Tate - Rutledge, Kate	Don [Mch]-Will-Britt	
Watkins, Carl Britt	Jun 9, 1974	74	Jeff Co		Apr 28, 1900	Watkins, Will		James, Elizabeth			Tommy	Rutledge, Kathryn - Pierce, Belle-Fannie	Don [Mch]	New Market
Watkins, Ethel F.	Aug 16, 1978		Morristown, Tn	Tn	Nov 18, 1902	Forster, Marion D.		Scott, Savanah		Watkins, Britt [D]	Bill-Tommy		Wife - [Pds] Corum, Arthur - Griffin, Pete - Loy, Harold - Watkins, Hugh B. Pierce, Owen	New Market
Watkins, Evelyn						Churchman, Clyde				Watkins, Jack			July 13, 2000 - Moved From Hazelton Memorial To West View	
Watkins, Harvey Don	Apr 19, 1975	69	Battle Creek, Mich.		May 30, 1905	Watkins, William B.		Peck, Rachel				[In-Law] Peck, Wilma - Carton, Guanna	Wife - Watkins, Mrs. Harvey	West View
Watkins, Irene [Col]	Aug 15, 1964	69	Jeff City	Tn	Aug 20, 1895	Link		Brownlow, Jess					Husband	Shiloh
Watkins, Juanita	Sep 6, 1961	32	Knoxville, Tn	Jeff Co		Bolen, Raymond	Tn	Whitaker, Ruth	Tn	Watkins, William M.		Bane, Dorothy - Young, Mary R.	George - Wayne-Dexter-Haskell	New Market
Watson, Ann Ruth Harmon	Jul 17, 1981	59	U.T.H.	Bristol, Tn	Mar 2, 1922	Caldwell/Harmon, Hurley		Little, Susie		Watson, Stuart L.	Barbara - Caldwell, Kathy & Bill	Stuart Jr.-Eric	Harmon, Paul Ray-Harmon, Paul Jr. - Mitchell, Bill - Burton, Tim	[Pds] Watkins, Tommy-Harbert-Burton, Tim	Glenwood - Bristol, Tn
Watson, Boyd Ralph	Jun 13, 1992	80	J.M.H.	Rutledge, Tn	Jun 24, 1911	Watson, John Harlin		Mitchell, Vanda Mae		Newman, Lena Mae		Ramsey, Grace - Whaley, Hazel	Fred	Son	Tampico
Watson, Cecil Franklin	Feb 18, 1980	66	J.M.H.	Granger, Co	Oct 11, 1913	Watson, Harlin		Mitchell, Dona	WW 2		Pauline - Belin, Barbara	Bobby & Ella Jean-Ralph & Norma	Ramsey, Grace - Whaley, Hazel	Fred-Boyd	Wife - [Pds] Watson, Carl - Ramsey, Roy-Earl - Bobby - Mc Ghee, Glenn	Tampico
Watson, Claude Calvin	Nov 13, 1970	42	Bean Station, Tn	Tn	Apr 10, 1928	Watson, John		Mitchell, Dona		Bullinger, Edna	Whit, Janice	Darrell	Whaley, Hazel - Ramsey, Grace - Mc Ghee, Stella - Whaley, Hazel	Fred-Boyd-Cecil	Wife	Tampico - Rutledge, Tn
Watson, Coy Wallace	Jan 31, 1968				Aug 21, 1909					Lavone					
Watson, Fred William	Jun 23, 1995	75	Rutledge, Tn	Rutledge, Tn	Mar 23, 1921	Watson, John		Mitchell, Dona		Frances L.	WW 2	Paul-Earl	Whaley, Hazel	Claude-Boyd-Cecil-Fred	Wife - [Pds] Whaley, Cecil - Mc Ghee, Vaughn - Whitt, Jim - Craig - Bobb, Ron	Tampico
Watson, Lena Mae	Aug 20, 1994	79	J.M.H.	Sevier Co, Tn	Jul 19, 1915	Newman, William A.		Sherrod, Florence		Watson, Boyd Ralph [D]		Bobby & Ella Jean-Ralph & Norma		Sons - [Pds] - G. Shird] Harmon - Mc Ghee, Vaughn - Watson, Don - Mc Clain, Steve - Watson, Milo-Dale-Anthony-Rick	Tampico Baptist

Name	Date	Age	Place	Birthplace	Date	Father	Mother	Spouse	Service	Children	Relatives	Relatives	Pallbearers	Cemetery
Watson, Luna Ray	Dec 28, 2000	74	Knox Co	Rutledge, Tn	Mar 29, 1926	Watson, Ernest	Mc Daniel, Frances	Howard, Bertie Joyce		Jerry & Lola Joan Larry & Cynthia[Sc]			Everett [D]	Mill Springs
Watson, Richard David	Sep 15, 1990	59	J.M.H.	Knox Co, Tn	Apr 28, 1921	Watson, Gardner	Davis, Betty	Mary E.	army	Elmore, Angie - Berry, Max.	Cheaney, Eddie - Owen, Mrs. Alvin	William-John	[Pals] Smith, Donnie - Sherlin, John - Sherlin, Larry - Chesney, G.H.- Watson, Don- Eddie-John Kay [Pals] Webb, Richard - Chesney, Jean - Watson, Don- Parker, Bill - Riley, E.J.	Piney
Watson, Roy Newman	Aug 3, 1983	48	J.M.H.	Grainger Co	Apr 27, 1934	Watson, Boyd	Newman, Lena Mae	Profitt, Joyce		Annette	Vineyard, Ruby	Bobby-Ralph		Ebenezer
Watson, Stuart Lansing	Feb 4, 1998	82	B.H.	Bluff City, Tn	Jun 20, 1915	Watson, Samuel Joseph	Lewis, Ross Belle	S		Watson, Barbara - Caldwell, Kathy	Stuart Jr. [Ne]- Eric K.	Tom [Ne]	Mother - [Pals] Richard - Mullins, John Jr.- Mark-Michael - Love, Chad- Overton, Jay- Barrett, Lester / Sister [Pals] Webb, Harold- Ron - Sesson, Ollie, Keith - Griffin, Mark- Chevers, Ralph	Hills Union
Watts, Cleo [M]	Mar 3, 1994	28	Jeff City	Scottsburg, Ind	Apr 13, 1985	Bailey, Clarence - Watts, John N.	Mullins, Alma Sue Bailey	S		Harmon, Mary Anna Ruth- Little, Celene [D]		Newman, Tammy, Lyle, [Step] Baldwin, Vicki - [Step] Bailey, Linda [Sc]	[1/2] Bailey, Jarnigan - [Step] Bailey, Dale [pxd]	Hills Union
Watts, Eura	Apr 7, 1987	78	Knoxville, Tn	Cocke Co, Tn	Apr 22, 1910	Watts, Sam	Luna, Bell	S		Greenlee, Gladys		Fred E.		Rays Chapel - Newport, Tn
Weaver, Henry William	Jul 7, 1972		Johnson City, Tn	Johnson City, Tn	Dec 9, 1888	Weaver, James	Sherly, Nancy Jane	Duane, Mattie		[Nephew] Weaver, Fredric- David-George	Jeter, Nancy	Willie		Friends Station
Weaver, Teresia Lynn	Aug 25, 1997	42	Knoxville, Tn		Apr 7, 1955	Weaver, Rasson Sanford	Mc Nellis, Mildred	Unk	Div		Jackie-Gail-Donna-Callie			Cremated
Webb, George Lewis	Nov 16, 1981	60	S.M.H.	Georgia	Jul 7, 1921	Webb, Cleve	Unk	Green, Eula						Flat Gap
Webb, John Wallace	Feb 9, 1994	84	J.M.H.	Knoxville, Tn	Jan 17, 1910	Webb, Orville O.	May, Bessie	Lawson, Anna Lou	Navy	Harrison, Polly- Brandshaw, Peggy- Brown, Margarine- Owen, Earline- Strange, Patsy	Tammy - [Step] Huddleston, Jumcry	Taylor, Bessie- Hobbs, Evelyn- Garrison, Margaret	Orville-O.L.- Lawson, Carl- Ralph-Harold-Bill- Clarence	Strawberry Plains
Welch, Emily	May 23, 1987	79	S.M.H.	Parrish, Alabama	Jul 14, 1907	Welch, Will	Thomas, Fannie	S		Hensley, Della		Rudesick, Thomas- Charlie-Alvin	Walker Memorial - Jasper, Alabama	
Wells, James Willard	Apr 28, 1989	4m	U.T.H	Tn	Dec 25, 1987	Wells, James	Dyer, Linda	Div					Father - Dyer, Mrs. Troy [G.Mother]	Beech Springs - Sevier Co.
Wells, James Willard	Jan 1, 1996	51	Straw Plains	Straw Plains	Feb 14, 1944	Wells, James C.	Pollard, Linda	Div		Canupp, Lisa - Ramsey, Cindy	Troy	Lisa-Cindy	Robert-Stanley- Steve	Kingsport
Wells, Llinda Margaret	Sep 17, 1994	58	J.M.H.	Kodak, Tn	Mar 16, 1926	Pollard, Monroe	Holt, Jean	Wells, James Carroll		Wells, James Carroll		Jim-Bob-Stanley- Steve	Gidorth, Louise- Sorrell, Bonnie- Lee, Zoda? Husband - [Pals] Foster, Glover - Jarvney, C.- Ballinger, Doyt- Stipes, Lowell- Rodrick, Jerry- Ralph	Beech Springs - Sevier Co.
Werner, Anna Jeanette	Dec 28, 2000	75	Jeff City	Philadelphia, Pa	Mar 31, 1925	Zimmer, William	Orr, Agnes	Werner, Richard Thomas [D]		Pflueger, Barbara [Pa]	Charles & Renee	Robert Jr.-	Samuel [Ch]	J.M.G.

Name	Date	Age					Tn			Pfluger, Barbara	Robert Charles	Stryker, Agnes	Wife	J.M.G.
Werner, Robert Thomas	Feb 1, 1991	67	Philadelphia, Pa	S.M.H.	Jul 25, 1923	Werner, Robert	Rutledge, Tn	Warden, Bessie	Zimmer, Anna J.					
West, Becky Sue	Jun 28, 1980	18	S.M.H.	Tn	Oct 30, 1961	West, Hugh Allen	Tn	Willlock, Deloris	S				Mother - [Pals] Strange, Billy; Mike - Whitlock, Roy-Johnny - Scarlett, Bill	Blue Springs - Rutledge, Tn
West, Dillon Reeves	May 15, 1951	66	U.T.H.	Jeff City	Apr 24, 1885	West, John N.	Tn	Yates, Parthenia	Tn			Morgan, Mrs. O.A. - Griffin, Mrs. W.L.	Neel, Flora [Wife]; Hatcher, Jean [G-Daug - Pal] - Lutz F.H. [Roanoke, Va]	Lynnhurst
West, Fred R.	1965	82	Jeff City	Granger Co					Ng		West, C.I.? [Va]		Morgan, Gladys - Daniel, Anna	Buffalo
West, Glen Haskel	Sep 15, 1972				Sep 25, 1910	West, Gentry		James, Eula					John A. - Charles Harrison	Blue Springs
West, Hugh Allen	Jan 13, 1980	43	U.T.H.	Granger Co	Oct 3, 1936	West, Harrison		Owens, Gladys			R.L.- Hugh Allen Jr.	Willie	West, Evelyn B. [Wife]	Mill Springs
West, James Fredrick	Feb 18, 1994	66	Newport, Tn	Union Co	Sep 21, 1927	West, Charles P.		Stifler, Ida	Marines		[Step] Talley, Richard-Michael		West, Evelyn B. [Col]	Presbyterian [Col]
West, John [Col]	Jul 9, 1950	59	Sc		Dec 24, 1890	Unk		Unk						
West, Mary	Apr 4, 1956	66	New Market	Tn	Jun 1, 1886	Davis, Joseph	Tn	Galpin, Eliza	Tn		C.T. [Va]	Higgs, Prisha	West, Fred R.	Buffalo
West, O.C.	Feb 12, 1996	60	U.T.H.	Tazewell, Tn	Jun 21, 1925	West, Samuel J.		Bunch, Rachel	Div	Mills, Kathy - West, Lisa Kay	Larry - Joey		Hall - Jim - Sam - Pulisa	West Family - Tazewell, Tn
West, Ross Lee [Col]	Jul 24, 1949	45	New Market, Tn		Nov 22, 1903	Unk		Unk		West, John	John Jr.		Doug - [Pals] Mullins, Louise - Hodge, Kenneth - Munzey, William - Hurst, Charles - Snoderly, Vandas	Presbyterian [Col] - New Market
West, Ruth Mae	Jun 27, 1966	43	Jeff City	Tn	Apr 15, 1923	Wright, David W.		Tompkins, Mary M.	Div			Robert [Kir] - Hand - Raymond [Ind.]	Cochran, Betty J. - [Daug]	Mill Springs
West, William Rex	May 29, 1978	48	J.M.H.	Tn	Sep 15, 1927	West, William Rex Sr.		Oates, Amanda	Div			Greenlee, Georgia - Petty, Estelle - Foster, Imogene	Jeny [1/2] Koontz, Anna	Oates - Piedmont
West, Susan Louisa	Oct 8, 1995	82	Jeff City	Granger Co	Apr 12, 1913	Phillips, George H.		Pierce, Mary	Div	West, Paul Allen [D]	Pratt, Betty	McGinnis, Pauline - Roach, Dell	Brady, Edith; Emert-Paul - Doug	Buffalo
Whaley, Earnest	Mar 18, 1995	82	Sevier Co		Nov 8, 1923	Whaley, Jerry		Chibo, Louisa		Jarnigan, Louisa	Cox, Barbara	Paul-Alfred	Fulton, Massie - West, Frances - Royston, Stella - Hurd, Ruby Jean	P.L.- Raymond - Hand - Bernard	Shiloh
Whaley, Horace Lee	Nov 22, 1959	38	Dexter, Oregon	Tn				Whaley, Myrtle	WW 2	LaMore-Mary - Carolyn-Myrna	Jerry	Myers, Doxie - Lockhart, Clara - Cochran, Ellis - Bales, Opal - Pierce, Leola	Whaley, Mary [Wife] - Harvey-Claude	Mill Springs
Whaley, Inez Celia	Sep 20, 1992	90	Gatlinburg, Tn	Tn	Jan 13, 1902	Mc Carter, Thomas C.		Profitt, Martha		Whaley, Aaron [D]		Dials, Eva - Pruitt, Laura	Son	Mansfield Gap; ?
Whaley, Mayford Wayne	Feb 17, 1973		Straw Plains	Tn	Jan 16, 1911	Whaley, Jeremiah		Chibo, Louisa		Bishop, Helen	Jerry	Fulton, Massie - West, Frances - Royston, Mrs. Steller - Hurd, Ruby	Willie	Shady - Straw Plains

Name	Death Date	Age	Place	County	Birth Date	Father	Mother	Status	Mil.	Survivors / Notes		Burial	Code
Whaley, Perry Lester	Jan 20, 1987	79	J.M.H.	Sevier Co	Jan 21, 1907	Whaley, Jerry	Claybom, Louisa	S	WW 2	Felkin, Mossie - Wed., Frances - Royston, Stella - Helfrich, Ricky Jean	Raymond - Hansel - Bernard	Fain - Kodak, Tn	J.M.G.
Whaley, Ricky Wayne	Jun 9, 1983		New Market	Davidson Co	Mar 22, 1969	Whaley, Conley	Kelly, Shelby	S		Whaley, Conley [Father] - [Pall] 24	Terry-Ronald	Fain - Kodak, Tn	J.M.G.
Whaley, Robert Don	Aug 31, 1981	43	Rutledge, Tn	Rutledge, Tn	Dec 19, 1948	Whaley, Raymond	White, Margaret E.			Angela Brandy-Patches	Whaley, Raymond - Whaley, Robert - Dewitt - White, Jack - Beacon - White, Dean - Hebert, Larry		Tampico
Whaley, Ronald Lynn	Jun 9, 1983		New Market	Jeff Co	Jun 15, 1986	Whaley, Conley	Kelly, Shelby	S			Ricky-Terry	Whaley, Conley [Father] - [Pall] 24	Fain - Kodak, Tn
Whaley, Shelby Jean	Jun 9, 1983		New Market	Maury Co	Jan 9, 1946	Kelly, Felix	Kinsby, Howdie	S			Ricky-Terry-Ronald	Leonard - Whaley, Howard-Louise - Buford-Cecil - Raymond Lee	Whaley, Conley [Father] - [Pall] 24
Whaley, Terry Lee	Jun 9, 1983		New Market	Sevier Co	Dec 23, 1957	Whaley, Conley	Kelly, Shelby	S			Ricky-Ronald	Whaley, Conley [Father] - [Pall] 24	Fain - Kodak, Tn
Whaley, Mary Elizabeth	Dec 21, 1993	62	Morristown, Tn	Knoxville, Tn	Aug 25, 1931	Russell, James Alexander	Murr, Bonnie Dean			Ballela, Kathy - Cleta, Tammy			New Market
Whitlock, Blanche	May 8, 1985	84		Jeff Co	Dec 18, 1900	Whitlock, Thomas O.	Ballinger, Ida Bell	Whitlock, James Hale [D]		Weeter, Frances		Daughter	Nances Grove
Whitlock, George Andrew	Apr 18, 1986	85	J.M.H.	Jeff Co	May 25, 1901	Whitlock, Lutford	French, Mahala			Lewis, Ruby - Atkins, Mabel Jo	William E. - L.M.	Son - [Pals] Whitlock, Ralph - Kent - Ray - Leonard, Clifford - Denton, Ernestine - Cain, Preston - Mowery, Robert	J.M.G.
Whitlock, Roy C.	Jun 4, 1986	73	J.M.H.	Jeff Co	Mar 7, 1913	Whitlock, James W.	Britt, Annie			Strange, Shirley- West, Deloris	J.T.	Underwood, Bessie - French, Una Faye - Huffaker, Tina - Messengill, Bernnose	J.M.G.
Whitlock, Ruth	May 1, 1996	80	J.M.H.	Kodak, Tn	Mar 1, 1906	Underwood, Tom	Hodge, Audie	Whitlock, Roy		Strange, Shirley- West, Deloris	J.T.	Husband - [Pals] Strange, Bill - Michael - Whitlock, Ray - West, R.L. - Hugh Allen	J.M.G.
Whitaker, Edna L.	Nov 11, 1997	90	Jeff City	Jeff Co	Jul 23, 1907	Koonce, Frank	Owens, Lena	Whitaker, Enos [D]		Harmon, Mattie - Steen, Jessie	J.T.	Melton-Omer	J.M.G.
Whitaker, Enos Elsell	May 15, 1983	83	J.M.H.	New Market	Apr 1, 1900	Whitaker, Charles	Allsup, Minnie			Steen, Jessie - Harmon, Mattie	Charles-Roland	Woodson, Pauline	Valley View
Whitaker, J.J.	Aug 3, 1980	78	Milligan Clinic	Tn	Sep 10, 1881	Whitaker, Jerry Clay	Tn	Waltz, Sarah	Tn	Coker, Alice	Cato, Radie-Agnes	English, Gertrude - Wright, Dora B. - Witt, Mrs. Jess	New Market

Name	Date	Age	E.S.H.	Taxwell	Birth	Father	Mother	Tazwell	Army				Cemetery
Whitaker, Judge Clayton	Jun 1, 1949										Shuttz, Harriet - Whitaker, Dorothy		Whitaker, Dorothy
White, John Robert	Jul 28, 1990	56	Grainger Co	Memphis, Tn	Sep 13, 1942	White, Ralph	Chestwood, Anagene	Tazwell	Army	Jennifer-Heather - Allerton, Mary - John & Gary		Charles [D] - William & Cathy	J.M.G.
White, Minnie D.	Oct 1, 1989	91	Dandridge, Tn	Talbot, Tn ?	Jan 22, 1898	Dials, George M.	White, Prince			Casey, Virginia	Ralph W. [fv]	White, Ralph W. - Casey, Virginia W.	J.M.G.
Whitehead, Keith Benton	Oct 6, 1971	41	Blount Co	Tn	Jun 5, 1930	Benton, Rodies ?	Bryant, Betty			Pat	Jim-Robert	White, Mrs. David [T4] - Bryan, Mrs. Henry - Me Beth, Mrs. Tom	Whitehead, Charles M. - Kenneth [Pa] - Andy	Grandview - Blount Co
Whitehouse, Betty Jean	Mar 5, 1987	57	Knoxville, Tn	Strawberry Plains	Sep 13, 1939	Solomon, William Henry	Bolin, Ruth			Whitehouse, Melvin	Dailis & Jap [Kr] Allen, Scarlett & James		Pleasant Grove
Whitlock, Bess	Jan 24, 1991	93	New Market	New Market	Jul 9, 1897	Haworth, Jeff	Thomas, Maude Ethel			Whitlock, S.H. [D]	Nathan R. [Fa]	Babcock, Maude - Blackhurst, Gordon - Sears, Blanche - Bachmann, Mary - Whitlock, Charles	Naxcos Grove
Whitlock, Charles S.	Feb 18, 2000	77	Talbot, Tn	Jeff Co	Nov 27, 1922	Whitlock, Herman	James, Bernice	Army	Bunch, Joan	Gary		[Pa] Stephin, Tom - James, Bobby - James, Bobby-Charles - Moods, Larraxe	Naxcos Grove
Whitlock, Dora Bernice	Oct 28, 1975	75	U.T.H.	Tn	Mar 22, 1900	James, Will M.	Staple, Louisa				Charles		John	Naxcos Grove
Whitlock, George Herman	Apr 18, 1967	73				Whitlock, T.O.				Cochran, Mrs. James	Acuff, Joan [Da] [6] Holt, Ginger - Cochran [Arl]			Whitlock, Richard - V.A.
Whitlock, Ida	Jul 4, 1956	83	M.C.	Tn	Mar 1, 1873	Ballinger, William Henry	Clawson, Sarah	Tn		Hepworth, Mrs. Clarence - Hall, Mrs. Rufus [Va]	Charles	Blanche - Hale, Mrs. Rufus	Jack	Naxcos Grove
Whitlock, Otis Hazel	Mar 3, 1998	88	Jeff City	New Market	Nov 21, 1909	Ballinger, John Henry	Vineyard, Ada Myrtle			Howard, Lois & Frank		1	5	Whitlock, S.H.	Naxcos Grove
Whitlock, Spurgeon H.	May 3, 1983	66	Jeff Co	Tn	Jan 21, 1878	Whitlock, T.O.	Ballinger, Ida	Tn		Whitlock, Paul [D]	Edward & June-Ivan	[B-] Lewi Ballinger, Dorothy		Friends (Station)
Whitlock, T.O.	Nov 25, 1970	95		Tn	Dec 26, 1874	Whitlock, Temple	Vineyard, Stelle			Whitlock, T.O.	R.H.	Whitlock, Mrs. Blanche - Hale, Mrs. Rufus		J.M.G.
Whitt, Helmer R.	Aug 12, 1973	57	Jeff Co	Tn	Aug 29, 1915	Whitt, Steers	Mc Cann, Ethel		WW 2	Quinn, Mrs. Laquoite - Kirtner, Patsy	G.M.-S.H.-R.H.	Whitlock, Mrs.	G.H.-Ralph	Whilie
Whitt, Mary Ethel	Jun 1, 1975	83	J.M.H.	Grainger Co	Oct 17, 1892	Whitt, Steers	Mc Cann, Mary	W		Clevenger, Rose - Quinn, Mrs. Laquoite - Widrey, Aileen - Cox, Dorthy	Charles	Clevenger, Rose - Shaple, Virgie - Widney, Aileen - Cox, Dorthy	Willie	J.M.G.
Whitt, Mary Ethel	Aug 12, 1973	57	J.M.H.	Tn	Dec 26, 1874	Whitlock, Temple	Clevenger, Rose - Cox, Dorothy - Widney, Aileen [Mich] - Shaple, Virgie	WW 2		Hale, Mrs. R.S.- J.H. - Whitlock, Mrs. J.H. - Haworth, Mrs. C.E.	R.H.	Clevenger, Rose - Shaple, Virgie - Widney, Aileen - Cox, Dorthy		Naxcos Grove
Whitaker, Brandy Renee	Jul 11, 1977	0	J.M.H.	J.M.H.	Jul 11, 1977	Whitaker, Johnny Lee [Age-24]	Nash, Lois Faye [Age-29]	Jeff Co		White, Helmer Ruben [D]		[1/2] Nash, Brian Lynn	Whitaker, George - Nash, Kory [D-Fathers] - Lunsdorog, Mr. & Mrs.-7 - Nash, Mr.-Stake [D-G-Parents]	Central Point - Grainger Co
Whitaker, Brandy Renee	Jul 11, 1977	0	J.M.H.	Knoxville, Tn	Jul 11, 1977	Whitaker, Johnny Lee [Age-24]	Nash, Lois Faye [Age-29]	Jeff Co				[Fate] Johnson, Roy - White, Larry - Cole, Paul - Kinder, Gene	Whitaker, George - Nash, Kory [D-Fathers]	West View

Name	Date	Age	Place	County	Date	Father	Mother	War	Spouse	Relations	Children	Relations 2	Grand-relations	Cemetery
Whitaker, George Riley Sr.	May 26, 1990	75	J.M.H.	Jeff Co	Jul 27, 1914	Whitaker, Bert Sr.	Rines, Ella	unk	Warren, Nancy	Craig, Mildred - Whitaker, Floria [W.] - Farmer, Mary - Whitaker, Jamie - Murray, Georgia - Brite, Barbara	George Jr.-John	Voiles, Elizabeth - Williams, Mollie - Simmons, Martha		Son - [Pals-G-Sons] Whitaker, Michael - Nash, Bryan - Lewis, Darryl - Brown, Raymond - Tulver, William - Timmy - Russell, Eddie	J.M.G.
Whitaker, Nancy Ann	Oct 26, 1999	83	New Market	Jeff Co	Apr 12, 1916	Warren, Lemmie	Campbell, Mary		Whitaker, George R. Sr.		George Jr.-John	Collins, Calra - Wolfe, Lou - Knight, Elsie	Robert	J.M.G.
Wigginton, Billy Gene	Aug 1, 2000	67	Johnson City, Tn	Mascot, Tn	Sep 13, 1932	Wigginton, Earl Ray	Dix	unk	Bryant, Shirley [Sd]	Billy Gene [Cold] - Bobby - C.D. [Cold]	Rudder, Barbara, Mc Elroy, Ida Mai [Pal] - Neal, Mary	Bruce	[Pals] Phillips, Joe T. - Hickman, Steve - Davis, Steve	Thorn Grove
Wigginton, Earl Ray	Aug 5, 1975	62	U.T.H.	Knox Co, Tn		Wigginton, Joe C.	Dix					Bryant, Shirley Ann	Wigginton, Bobby Ray - Former, Buddy	Thorn Grove
Wigginton, Grace	Oct 4, 1982	65	F.S.H.	Knox Co	Dec 22, 1916	Wigginton, Joe	Pitard, Maude				Joe-Bruce	Neal, Mary	Bruce	Wigginton, Bob - Pedigo, Mike - Eddie - Neal, Bobby	Thorn Grove
Wiles, George Lewis	Jan 12, 1970	75	Severe Co	Tn	Dec 29, 1894	Wiles, J.W.	Lindsey, Caroline	WW 1	Huffaker, Mrs. Hal R.		George Jr.-Hal	George Jr.-Hal	Lon-Hal	Wife	Woodlawn - Knoxville, Tn
Wiles, Hal	Jul 4, 1986	79	J.M.H.	New Market	Aug 2, 1906	Wiles, William	Lindsey, Lucicia	S					[Pals] Pierce, L.E. - Dawk, Ed - French, Curtis - Stelos, Robert - Acuff, J.R. - Wollenbarger, Joe	Friends Station
Wiles, Minnie Alice	Jan 31, 2000	96	Sevier Co	New Market	Oct 9, 1903	Sellers, Robert	Russell, Annie		Wiles, George [D]	Huffaker, Nadine	Robert [D] - George [D] - Hal - D - Wallace [D]			Woodlawn
Willis, Bonnie Clark [M]	Apr 15, 1990	65	B.H.	New Market	Oct 23, 1924	Willis, Shade	Denton, Emma G.	WW 2	Bates, Anna Lorene	Calfery, Linda	Stephen	Poe, Katie	Wagene	Willis - [Pals] Underwood, Tony - Mike - Long, Frank - Warren, L.B. - Hurst, James	
Willis, Charles Oliver	Mar 10, 1979	82	Jeff City	Jeff Co	Apr 19, 1896	Willis, George	Leek, Mary	WW 1	Gertrude	Poe, Katie	Bonnie-Gene	Poe, Katie	Wagene	[Pals] Kelter, James - Underwood, Tony - Bates, Conteser - Jones, Gary - Stines, Max	Friends Station
Willis, Gertrude Emma	Mar 16, 1967	67	New Market	Tn	Mar 21, 1899	Denton, Scott	Link		Willis, C.D. [Shade]	Janeway, Lara [Mon] - Parker, Estelle	Bonny-Guy		Hal-Keel	[Pals] Kelter, James - Underwood, Tony - Bates, Conteser - Jones, Gary - Stines, Max - Husband	Friends Station
Willis, Guy R.	Nov 25, 1978	53	New Market	Tn	Aug 17, 1925	Willis, C.O.	Denton, Scott	WW 2	Willis, C.D. [Shade]	Janeway, Lara W.	Bonny-Guy		Hal-Keel	Husband	Hal-Keel
Willis, Guy Richard	Nov 20, 1978	53	F.S.H.	New Market, Tn	Aug 17, 1925	Willis, C.O.	Denton, Gertrude	WW 2	Janeway, Arlena Elizabeth	Bunch, Laurana W.	Ronnie J.	Poe, Katie	Bonnie	Wife	J.M.G.

Name	Date	Age	Place	Place	DOB	Father	Mother	Spouse	Mil	Children			Mother	Cemetery
Withie, Ronnie Jene	May 1, 1992	39	Morristown, Tn	May 7, 1952		Withie, Guy	Jones, Arlene	Div	unk	Sharland	Richard Wayne	Bunch, Lajuana		J.M.G.
Wilhoite, Harold Rex Sr.	May 31, 1985	42	Wayne Co., Michigan			Wilhite, Ervin		Wilson, Ola			Fred-Rex-Harshel	Hancock, Nola Mae - Platma, Imogene	Wilhoite, Kenneth F. - Utis Mezzanell - Sherman-Burl F.-Billy E.- Mitch J. - Miller, Robert	Holston View
Williamson, Mary E. [Back]	May 28, 1982	47	Dayton, Tn	New Market	Jan 1, 1934	Unk	Deals, Ruth	Williamson, Shirley Van				Deals, Arthur - Walter	[Pete] Campbell,Glynn, Loy Jr. - Imma, Robert - Phipps, Alex - Roper, Walter	West View
Williamson, Robert Eugene	Jun 14, 1982		U.T.H.	New Market	Dec 25, 1950	Williamson, Shirley Van	Deals, Mary	Army				Spelton Ali	Willie - [Pete] Gaza, Don - Korr, John - Huff, Avery, Robert - Phipps, Bobby Joe - Jones, Curtis - Lindsey, Dennis	West View
Willard, Bobbie Joe	Jul 23, 1983	56	U.T.H.	New Market	Aug 4, 1936	Willard, Clyde Otis	Koontz, Addie	Lowery, Virginia		Rainwater, Linda	Dwayne	Mills, Goldie - Parton, Pat Stellino	Mills, Goldie - Stellings, Patricia Ann	Jim	Mc Campbells Chapel
Willard, Jewel Clyde	Apr 14, 1989	54	J.M.H.	Jeff Co	Aug 10, 1934	Willard, Clyde Otis	Koontz, Addie Bell	Div		Debbie-Elaine	Dwayne			Mc Campbells Chapel
Williams, Claude Franklin	Jul 1, 1990	79	Jeff Co	Hawkins Co	Oct 6, 1918	Williams, Edgar	Long, Maude	WW 2		Hoffner, Claudia Sue [D]	Ted Lloyd	Mc Daniel, Katherine[Ca]	Earl [D]-Glenn [D]-George [D]- Marvin-Robert	J.M.G.
Williams, Colbert Carlton	Jan 11, 1994	60	F.S.H.	Dandridge	Mar 12, 1933	Williams, Homer	Woods, Della	Morgan, Sarah	unk	Linda-Terri	James-Ricky Glen -Terry-Dated	Starbin, Lori Renee-Stepton, Shirley Kaye - Smith, Jo Ann	Cleston	New Market
Williams, Dustin Cody	Aug 5, 1996		F.S.H.	F.S.H.	Aug 5, 1996	Williams, Jeff	Singleton, Crystal							Blue Springs
Williams, Erby	Sep 24, 2000	52	J.M.H.	Union Co	Feb 28, 1948	Williams, Robert Milton	Tolliver, Lora Ellen	Union Co		Amanda Victoria	Ross Brian	Collins, Georgette - England, Mildred & - Odie, [Mich]- Johnston, Anna & - Dennis [Ind] - Kevin & Jewell & Jack [Ind]	Hayes [D]- Francis [Mich]	J.M.G.
Williams, Eudie Pearl Foster	Dec 27, 1974	79	Hawkins Co	Nov 6, 1895				Williams, Roy				Ballinger, Louise	James T.-Ralph	Ballinger, Robert	[Pete] Foster, Charles Jr.- Terry, Wagner-Jimmy - Dunsmore, Jack- Tom - Ballinger, Austin	Mill Springs
Williams, George	Jan 13, 1996	87	Jeff City	Ohio	Jan 14, 1878	Williams, Charlie		Ora V.						Nances Grove
Williams, Goldie Irene	Jul 17, 1996	83	F.S.H.	Powell, Tn	Jun 2, 1913	Cooper, Jasper	Dishman, Hester Ann	Williams, Jess [D]				Robert B.		Williams, Walter	Annabelle, Rutledge, Tn

Name	Death Date	Age	Facility	Birthplace	Birth Date	Father	Mother	War	Spouse					Cemetery
Williams, Joes	Nov 25, 1987	79	U.T.H.	Granger Co	Apr 13, 1908	Williams, Melton	Roberts, Ollie		Cooper, Goldie Irene	Robert-Ray-Jim	Vanover, Georgia	Robert-Arch-Hallmer-Gene	Willis - [Pals] Wigglesfoble, Joe - Rines, Bob - Cooper, Len - Smith, Bay - Norman, Harry	Nances Grove
Williams, Mary Ellen	Mar 8, 1982	66	J.M.H.	Sevier Co	Feb 3, 1916	Russell, Harvey	Underwood, Hattie		Williams, George					Nances Grove
Williams, Ora	Aug 9, 1954	76	M.C.	Virginia	Oct 8, 1877	Unk	Unk		Williams, George	Haworth, Ruby - Ruth, Ethel [Shep]	Walter-Roy	Walter [Jude]	Husband	Hill Springs
Williams, Roy	Sep 25, 1981	74	J.M.H.	Tn	Feb 8, 1907	Williams, George	Ora		Foster, Pearl E.	[Shep] Foster, James-Ralph-Grover	Walter [Jude]		Husband	Nances Grove
Williams, Walter	Oct 26, 1981	68	J.M.H.	Peabody	Jan 6, 1913	Williams, George		WW 2	Russell, Mary	Haworth, Ruby			Mill Springs	Nances Grove
Williams, Wanda Faye	Nov 18, 1999	60	Jeff City	Blaine, Tn	Jul 6, 1939	Heatherly, Paris			Williams, Paul E.	Gerald & Karen	May, Sandra	Monroe [D]-John [D]-Don		East View
Williams, Nelmer	Mar 4, 1997	77	J.M.H.	Rutledge, Tn	Jul 22, 1919	Williams, Milton			Storey, Georgia	George & Sharon	Vanover, Georgia-Guy, Vena Mae	L.C. & Bernice [Ice]		Shiloh
Williams, Alma Ruth	Oct 11, 1992	66	J.M.H.	Jeff City	Jun 27, 1926	Burchfield, Cleophas			Staton, Mattie Sue	Gary-Bill [G] Kitt, Derek	Gaz, Mary E.-Spock, Virginia E.-Etherton, Faye		Husband	Ebenezer
Williford, James Philip	Apr 2, 1999	62	S.M.H.	Knoxville, Tn	Aug 7, 1936	Williford, Samuel Taylor			Brock, Irma [D]-Barbara [the]	Bible, Karen & Mark	Blackburn, Judith & Paul		Husband	U.T. Medical - Memphis, Tn
Williford, Perry W.	Nov 13, 1996	86	J.M.H.	Talbott, Tn	Sep 29, 1910	Williford, Abe	Reynolds, Hannah	WW 2	Burchfield, Alma Ruth [D]	Hurst, Ramona	Gary-Bill	Dawson, Aileen	Ray	Ebenezer
Willings, Donald Franklin	Nov 8, 1982	67	J.M.H.	Jeff, Tn	June 3, 1915	Willings, Coy	Stallsworth, Ellie		Hodge, Betty-Jones, Mary	Coy	Mc Daniel, Penny	Bennie	[Pals] Nances, Len-Harold - Foster, Grover - Denton, Dwight-Crowson, Curtis-Stallsworth, Grover Jr.	
Willings, Ollie	Dec 19, 1976	898	Jan 24, 1960	Riggs, Joseph Cleveland [Apr-27]		Riggs, Ollie Jane		W	Largin, Penny	Donald-Bennie		Bennie	Father	Nances Grove
Willings, Patricia Ann	Nov 4, 1983	69	Hamblen Co	Nov 4, 1963	Willings, Coy	Kirkland, Joe Ann [Apr-20]	Tn				[1/2] Willings, Rickey	Father	Nances Grove
Wills, Laura Templin	Dec 25, 1958	87	Cocke Co. Tn	Jan 13, 1871	Denton, David	Penman, Mary		Thomas, Della - [Step] Anderson, Mary - Huston, Hattie	Templin, George - Eugene			Nipper, Pauline [Dwg]	Carter - Valley Home
Wilson, Ault Charles	May 27, 1987	51	Dandridge, Tn; Knoxville, Tn	Mar 8, 1936	Wilson, Everette Garfield	Lovell, Edith	Korea	Bates, Nadine	Guinn, Pete - Howard, Connie	Brown, Mary - Heldemer, Betty Jo - Houser, Flora Mae - Roww, June Marie	W.T.-Ralph-Howard	[Pals] Bates, Donnie-Donnie - Sharp, Mike - Harris, Mike-Chip - Shields, Scott	J.M.G.
Wilson, Carrie	Jan 4, 1952	66	Jeff City	Georgia								J.R. & Sylvia-Don & Mary-Katherine-Roy & Junior-Troy & Ross Lee	Wilson, Homer [Son]	Newport, Georgia
Wilson, Doris Nadine	Jun 23, 1998	58	New Market	New Market	Jun 28, 1939	Bates, James R.	Huffaker, Mary		Wilson, Paul C.	Howard, Connie & Jeff - Guinn, Paula	Sharp, Grace & Nelson - Messersmith, Opal & Bill	Bates, Elizabeth - Lay, Adolie - Foster, Helen		J.M.G.
Wilson, Earl Nathan	Jul 20, 1987	83	Tn	Aug 24, 1903	Wilson, John	Downs, Mary		Bull, Kate	Talbott, Corrie-Hayes, Earlene	Roger [Cal]-Charles Ray	Roy-Ralph-Woodrow		
Wilson, Homer Tait	Jul 29, 1971	62	Gla	Tn	May 23, 1909	Wilson, Oliver	Bowen, Carrie		Gardner, Mattie	Earl Lee-Joe Ray	Hooper, Mrs. Keith [Mich]	Bates, Elizabeth - Lay, Adolie - Foster, Helen	Son	Friends Station

Name	Death Date	Age	Place of Death	Place of Birth	Birth Date	Father	Mother	Spouse	Military	Relatives 1	Relatives 2	Relatives 3	Relatives 4	Relationship	Cemetery
Wilson, James Greig	Apr 26, 1996	74	Jeff Co	Maynum Terrace, Scotland	Jul 17, 1921	Wilson, Stephen Bruce	Greig, Ann	Glenn, Alice Blendeen	WW 2	Lockhart, Lisa - Elizabeth	Pollard, Sarah [England]	Steve [Scotland] - Sandy [Scotland]		Wife	J.M.G.
Wilson, John L.	Jan 29, 1957	82	Knoxville, Tn	Tn	May 28, 1875	Wilson, Joseph, Tn	Tn			Arnold, Mrs. Bert - Loy, Mrs. C.W., Jr. - Bull, Mrs. W.M. Jr. - Bates, Mrs. Jamee - Foster, Mrs. Fred	Tyler, Mrs. Jim - Kerr, Mrs. Ralph - Woodrow-Ralph - Franklin, Mrs. Gray	Earl-Wallace-Woodrow-Ralph-Roy	Ernie-Ed	Wife	New Market
Wilson, Kate	Oct 20, 1990	80	J.M.H.	Wears Valley, Tn	Feb 19, 1910	Wilson, W.M.	Rollins, Belle	Wilson, Earl [D]		Hayes, Earlene - Richardson, Connie	Roger-Ray	Doyal, Connie	Ray	Wife	J.M.G.
Wilson, Lena Grace	Jul 13, 1992	84	J.M.H.	White Pine, Tn	Nov 20, 1907	Williams, Joseph Manley	Pryor, Mary Elizabeth	Wilson, Roy T.						Husband	J.M.G.
Wilson, Lillian Pauline	Aug 25, 1995	60	S.M.H.	Jeff Co	Oct 3, 1934	Elmore, Ottis Cleo	Quilliams, Myrtle Mae	Wilson, Earl [DM]		Chamberlain, Portia Mae - Davis, Jo Ann	Mabrey-Larry [D]			Son	Strawberry Plains
Wilson, Mary E.	Nov 10, 1959	74	Morristown, Tn	Tn	Mar 19, 1885			Wilson, John L. [D]		Arnold, Mrs. Bert - Loy, Mrs. C.W., Jr. - Bull, Mrs. W.M. Jr. - Bates, Mrs. Jamee - Foster, Mrs. Fred	Earl-Wallace-Ralph-Roy			Wilson, Woodrow [Son]	New Market
Wilson, Mary Tresa	Jul 20, 1992	83	New Market	Knox Co	Apr 9, 1909	Jones, Robert	Young, Nellis	Wilson, Wallace [D]		Lee, Frances	Earle Lee-Joe Ray	Merritt, Iva		Aug	Valley View
Wilson, Mattie Marie	Apr 29, 1983	74	J.M.H.	Mineral Co., W. Va	May 30, 1908	Gardner, Porter	Bell, Jennie	Wilson, Homer [D]						Joe	Friends Station
Wilson, Phillip Larry	May 5, 1975		Strawberry Plains		Sep 12, 1955	Wilson, Earle	Elmore, Lillian			Lee, Frances & Fred	Jo Ann - Cook, Porta & Steve	Corum Deana	Wilson, Mrs. Homer [Grandmother] - Elmore, Otha [G-Father] - Wilson, Fairhef / Elmore, Otha [G-...] - Joe Ray [Uncle] - Cook, Justin Allen [Nephew]	Mack	Friends Station
Wilson, Ralph Roland	Nov 25, 1991	83	New Market	New Market	Aug 16, 1928	Wilson, John	Doane, Mary	C'Dell, Mary Elizabeth		John D.	Bates, Elizabeth - Loy, Addie - Foster, Helen			Roy-Woodrow	Valley View
Wilson, Roy Truman	Dec 29, 1996	85	J.M.H.	New Market	Jul 27, 1911	Wilson, John	Doane, Mary	Williams, Grace	Army		Arnold, Mrs. Bert - Bull, Blanche [D] - Bates, Elizabeth - Loy, Addie		Woodrow-Earl [D]-Ralph [D]	Wife	J.M.G.
Wilson, Wallace E.	Nov 30, 1976	70	New Market, Tn	New Market, Tn	Jul 20, 1906	Wilson, John	Doane, Mary	Jones, Mary			Arnold, Mrs. Jessie [D] - Bull, Blanche [D] - Bates, Elizabeth - Loy, Addie		Roy-Woodrow-Earl [D]-Ralph [D]-Wallace [D]	Wife	J.M.G.
Wilson, Zollie	Mar 1, 1976	57	Knox Co. Tn	Knox Co. Tn	Mar 4, 1917	Wilson, E.T.	Whaley, Mary Ella	Kaiser, Mary Jean	Marines	Mc Carty, Theoura [Tx] - Payne, Eldora Brown [Tx] - Wilson, Audrey [Tx] - Wilson, Cordelia [Tx]	Kennedy R. [K]-Allen-David	Charles H.- Woodrow-Jack		Willie	Trundville - Straw Plains, Tn
Wingate, Ruth E.	Jul 16, 2000	87	Jeff City	Grand Isle, Vermont	Jul 22, 1912	Speer, Harold A.	Savage, Mae	Wingate, Norman Cornell [D] - Moody, Clifford L. [D]		Hosea, Ruth & Walter - Wallis, Jesse & Pat [Tx] - [Bri-Lee] Moody, Joyce [Ga]	Moody, Harold T. [D] - Moody, James & Esther	Abele, Helen [D]	Ralph [D] - Kenneth [D] - George & Eleanor - Leo & Joan [Ver]	Wife	J.M.G.
Wingate, Norman Cornell	Apr 6, 1995	77	Medford, Mass	Medford, Mass	Jun 13, 1917	Wingate, Frank	Cornell, Margaret	Speer, Ruth E.		Hosea, Ruth & Walter - Wallis, Jesse & Pat [Tx] - [Step] Wallis, Ruth - Hosea, Ruth	[Step] Moody, James - Harold	Wingate, Catherine		Willie	J.M.G.

Name	Date	Age			Date									
Wise, Carl J.	Aug 18, 1985	61	J.M.H.	Knox Co	May 7, 1924	Wise, Carl William		Dlv			Caughron, Peggy - Perry, Patsy - Taylor, Kathy	Hodge, Mona Mae	Sister [Pek] - Hodge, Gary - Frank - Taylor, Richard - Dlann, James - Bailey, Ken	New Market
Wise, Carl William	Jul 30, 1969	71	J.M.H.	Knox Co	May 7, 1924	Wise, Carl William		Dlv			Duncan, Mrs. Frank [Mrs.] - Bailey, Mrs. James - Beeler, Nora	Dewey-Clifford- J.B. [Red]-George- Carl	Wise, Carl	New Market
Wise, Carl William	Jul 30, 1969	71	U.T.H.	Tn	Aug 8, 1897	Wise, Jim		w			Duncan, Mrs. Frank [Mrs.] - Bailey, Mrs. James - Beeler, Nora	Dewey-Clifford- J.B. [Red]-George- Carl	Loveday, Mrs. Rosa	New Market
Wise, Dewey Franklin	Apr 26, 1987	67	Jeff City	Tn	May 16, 1912	Wise, Jim		Dlv			Loveday, Mrs. Jess - Guinn, Hubert-Dewey, Mrs. Jess - Duncan, Mrs. Frank - Bailey, Mrs. James - Beeler, Mrs. Nora	Hodge, Nora Mae		Cremated
Wise, James W.	Jan 12, 1950	74	Dandridge, Tn	Tn	Aug 1, 1875	Wise, Jim	Tn				Loveday, Mrs. Jess - Guinn, Hubert-Dewey, Mrs. Jess - Duncan, Mrs. Frank - Bailey, Mrs. James - Beeler, Mrs. Nora	Floyd-Carl-Ernest		Trenton
Wise, Lucille	Jul 24, 1959	58	Jeff Co	Texas	Apr 7, 1903	Harp, Joe	Texas				Harp, Susan ? Wise, Carl [Stacy]	Carl J.-Dewey- Clifford-George- J.B.	Clinton	New Market
Wise, Pauline Julia	Nov 8, 1985	72	Jeff City	Rutledge, Tn	May 31, 1923	Bailey, Albert		w			Solomon, Viola	Brooks, James E.- A.C.-T. Leon	Solomon, Lucille - Bradshaw, Ada - Lane, Allelene		Husband	New Market
Witt, Charles Franklin [Pete]	Jan 26, 1998	72	Jeff City	Mascot, Tn	Jun 23, 1925	Witt, John		Dlv			Smith, Ruby		Klein-Mike & Denise-Joe & Lorrie	Bailey, James	Lebanon Cumberland Presby.
Witt, Charles Michael Trinity	May 14, 1976	6m	U.T.H.	Morristown, Tn	Nov 15, 1975	Witt, Charles Michael		S			Lamb, Mary Darlene				Lebanon Cumberland Presby.
Witt, Clarence Everett	Jan 10, 1999	75	Straw Plains	Straw Plains	Sep 16, 1923	Witt, Hubert		Smith, Jean	Army		Campbell, Carolyn			Witt, Charles - Lamb, Mrs. Chester [G-Parents] - Witt, Hubert - Lamb, John - Vetal - Miller, Nina [G-G-Parents]	Cremated
Witt, George Hubert	Dec 13, 1976	78	S.M.H.	Tn	Nov 6, 1898			w	Marines		Gibson, Stella - Lauderdale, Goldie	Clarence-Walter- G.H.[III]	Parrish, Mollie	Billy-Ray-Jimmy	Straw Plains
Wizard, Samuel Berlie	Jul 8, 1959	67	New Market	Tn	Feb 22, 1882	Wolfe, Rue		S				Brown, John [Sheriff, Jeff Co.] - Wolfe, Rue	Pleasant Grove
Wolfe, Ginger Diane	May 27, 1965	9d	Jeff City	J.M.H.		Wolfe, Rue					Wizard, H.A.			
Wolfenbarger, Carl Verlin	Apr 11, 1998	77	F.S.H.	Grainger Co	Dec 13, 1920	Wolfenbarger, Walter		Satterfield, Selda		Howard, Virginia		Rupert, Elizabeth Nell [D]	James Robert & Sheila	Dyer, Edna & Carl - Moody, Waneva & Paul - Harding, Ruth & Fred - Phelps, Grace - Dalton Verona - Winkler, June [Sharp-See Cox]	Mill Springs
Wolfenbarger, Walter	Apr 8, 1998	68	F.S.H.	Jeff Co	Feb 3, 1930	Wolfard, William B.		Riley, Ada M.		Hicks, Anna Jean			Darrell	Brook, Maurice - Hickman, Ollie- Pauline - Riddle, Shirley - Kelner, Dorothy	Harold-Bob			
Wolfard, Everett Odell	Jul 1, 1982	69	J.M.H.	Tn	Sep 13, 1892	Wilson, Joseph		Rawlings, Bell				Denton, Lucyllennon, Mrs. Cleo - Roderick, Leona- Hazel		Kyle, Emma - Franklin, Bessie	Children	Valley View
Wolfard, Frankie	Jul 1, 1982	69	J.M.H.	Tn	Sep 13, 1892	Wilson, Joseph		Rawlings, Bell						Emie	

Name	Death Date	Age	Place	County/State	Birth Date	Father		Mother								Cemetery
Wallard, J.E.	Feb 6, 1950	59	Jeff City	Jeff Co	Dec 10, 1890	Wallard, Joe	Jeff Co	Unk		White, Doris June	Keith, Camellia	Damon, Mrs. Hal - Lawrence, Mrs. Oscar - Roderick, Mrs. Charles	Butt, Mrs. W.M.	Martin, Larry	Wallard, Mrs. Frankie	Valley View
Woods, Earl Ray	Sep 30, 1996	61	F.S.H.	Jeff City	Oct 26, 1934	Woods, Walter C.		Riley, Genevieve Martin		White, Doris June		Rogers-Jim	Shaffer, Mrs. Jess		Willie	Piedmont
Woods, Grant C.	Mar -, 1967	77										Patterson, Cobb - Neal, Frank - Lawrence			Willie	New Market
Woods, Grover C.	Dec 29, 1987	84	U.T.H.	Jeff Co	Jul 2, 1923	Woods, G.C.		Finley, Ida Mae		Melissa - Jenkins, Frankie		Ronnie	Foster, Minnie - Orb - Kent, Carrie - Mowery, Mae	Harold	[Pals] Allen - Jackins, Curtis - Bickton, Steve - Spencer, Ron - Foster, Ken - Damon, Jack	
Woods, Marcie Hartley	Feb 28, 1976	83	J.M.H.	Boone, Nc	Feb 25, 1893	Hartley, Ruben A.		Wilson, Mary E.		w	Harley, Ira - Woods, Harold - [Step] Woods, Grover	Melissa, Eunice [Nd] - Harvey, Minnie [Nd]	Harley, Lindley	[1/2] Woods, Harold	Write - [Pals] Cobb - Curtis - Allen - Jackins, Edd - Howard, Jonny - Anderson, Eugene	Mill Springs
Woods, Walter Cyrus	Jan 23, 1969	91	F.S.H.	Jeff Co	Nov 16, 1897	Woods, Richard Luther	Friends Station	Porter, Rowena		Porter, Mary Ruth [D-1897]		Earl	Carroll, Jessie	T.R. - Hollis-Orland	Son	Mt. View
Wooten, Ada A.	Sep 16, 1994	94	J.M.H.	Jeff Co	Aug 23, 1890	Wooten, Will		Hodges, Sallie Bell	Hodges Switch	S					Wooten, Ada [Sister]	Friends Station
Wooten, Charlie Hodges	Sep 21, 1960	86	Jeff Co	Jeff Co	Feb 22, 1894	Wooten, Will		Hodges, Sally Bell						Wooten, Will	Gardner, Dan W. [Brother]	Friends Station
Wooten, Maggie	Oct 17, 1980	88	Jeff Co	Virginia	Oct 22, 1873	Gardner, Joseph E.	Va	Raney, Clarissa K.	Va	Wooten, E.E. [D]	Navy		Hewitt, Mrs. L.C.	John - Ralph	Gardner, Dan W. [Brother]	Friends Station
Workman, Billy Gene	Nov 11, 1987	60	S.M.H.	Chattanooga, Va ?	May 8, 1937	Workman, Nimrod		Bowens, Mattie		Div	Navy	Deck, Brenda - Margillott, Karen - Workman, Charmell	Billy Gene Jr. [Sc]	Hamilton, Dorthy - Moore, Little Mae - Pearl - Rivers, Doris Anna - Lipsic, Phyllis	Thomas - Charles - James E. - Harvey J. - [Tronnie S. - Bro]	Workman, Nimrod [Brother]	Caledonia
Workman, Mattie Mae	Sep 13, 1996	86	F.S.H.	Ashland, Ky	Feb 8, 1912	Bowens, Thomas		Mallett, Rebecca Anglin		Workman, Nimrod [D]		Hamilton, Dorothy - Moore, Little Mae [Vd] - Mc Neely, Gladys [W. Vd] - Rivers, Doris - Lipsic, Phyllis [Pd]	Tronnie - Thomas [Sc] - James [Pa] - Harvey J. - Charles		Oscar	Bowens, Mattie	Caledonia
Workman, Nimrod	Nov 26, 1994	99	Knox Co	Ispcc, Ky	Nov 5, 1895	Workman, James Harvey		Henrietta Jewell		Bowens, Mattie		Hamilton, Dorothy - Little Mae [Vd] - Mc Neely, Gladys [W. Vd] - Rivers, Doris	White, Laura [W. Vd] - Workman, Gertrude [Vd]	Russell [Vd] - Sid [Pd]	Write - [Pals] Hamilton, Billy - Workman, Billy - Tom - Adam Ester - Brian - Buyers, Charles - Tronnie - Moore, Charles - Carroll, Tom	Caledonia

Name	Date	Age	Place	Birth Date	Father	Mother	Spouse	Relatives	Relatives	Relatives	Notes / Siblings	Cemetery
Workman, Ollie Elizabeth	Jan 3, 1994	74	F.S.H.	Oct 17, 1919	Gilbert, George	Compton, Florence	Workman, Walter	Browning, Ida	Brooks, Bertie		Husband - [Pala] Rickard, Sherman - Brooks, Donald - Dub - Norton, Ron - Gator, Ray	Strawberry Plains
Workman, Roy Edward	Sep 7, 2000	55	S.M.H.	Feb 2, 1945	Workman, Roy Stanley	Brock, Lonnie	Mills, Debbie	Johnson, Debbie Ann & James - Crawley, Lonnie Jo & Danny	Brian & Donna - Danny Ray & Tracy	Willis, Phyllis - Hutchens, Brenda	Jerry	Pollards - Sevier Co
Workman, Roy	Jan 18, 1967	76	S.M.H.	May 21, 1921	Workman, George Arthur	Cook, Jane	Brock, Lonnie	Brenda - Willis, Phyllis	Ray Jr - Jerry	Bailey, Ruby	Roy	Piney
Workman, Walter G.	Feb 18, 1996	77	Jeff Co	Mar 15, 1918	Workman, George	Cook, Jane	Browning, Ada		Bailey, Ruby	Roy		Strawberry Plains
Worthington, Stella Mae	Oct 10, 1986	85	Jeff City	Aug 6, 1901	Bryan, Silas	Gilbert, Ollie	Worthington, John				Worthington, John	J.M.G.
Wright, Alfred	Sep 7, 1970	67	Jeff City	Sep 3, 1907	Wright, Oscar	Maynard, Margaret	Wright, Kattie				Wright, James - [Pala] Wright, J.L. - Mc Bee, Eugene - Bobby - Byrd, Eugene - Reuse - Dandridge, Tn	Lawsons - Dandridge, Tn
Wright, Alfred A.	Dec 9, 1976	65	Cooke Co, Tn	Jul 22, 1911	Wright, John Wesley	Becker, Willie	Bonne Jean	Miss Carolyn Joan - Miss Vickie Gale	William A. - James Herman	Lindsey, Prella - Smicker, Elvis ?	B.J.- Isaac	Rocky Valley
Wright, B.J.	Jul 31, 1982	67	J.M.H.	Jul 30, 1915	Wright, John W.	Becker, Willie	Berry, Dorrity	Eldridge, Roberta W.	Tommy-Ray	Lindsey, Pearlie - Smicker, Elvie	Isaac	New Market
Wright, David	Nov 13, 1969		Tn	Sep 25, 1893	Wright, Albert	Bellinger, Almanda	Tompkins, Mary	Berry, Dorrity				Mills Spring
Wright, Dorothy Arletta	Feb 10, 2000	84	Union Co	Jul 17, 1915	Berry, Frank	Braden, Dora	Wright, B.J.		Ballinger, Marjorie & Ken	Linda - [Step] Wright, Glen & Bobbie-Ray	[In-Law] Berry, Elllie	New Market
Wright, Ernest Jamie 3rd [Black]	Oct 25, 1996	22	U.T.H.	May 25, 1974	Wright, Ernest P. Jr.	Brazelton, Margaret "Shewa"	S		Reagon, Joshua	Wright, Theresa - Hilliard, Stephanie [1/2] Favors, Dawn [Pa]	Brazelton, Gerard [3-Father]	J.M.G.
Wright, Erie	Mar 31, 1986	82	Dandridge, Tn	Jun 28, 1903	Adams, Arch	Cox, Mary	Wright, Wesley J. [2]	Vance, Jean - Chandler, Peggy	Vance, Gary	Jordin, Hattie	Roscoe	[Pala] Vance, Jeff Chandler, Arnold - James - Lindsey, Kermit - Greene, Mike
Wright, George Bee	Jul 29, 1989	45	Knoxville, Tn	Jan 23, 1944	Wright, Bee Jessie	Lindsey, Rhoda Grace Hay			George Bee Jr.	Eldridge, Roberta	Thomas R. - Ray	Mother
Wright, Harold Reese	Sep 19, 1999	60	New Market			Thompson, Mary	Dix	Army	Wright, Jodie [Ind]-Addy [Ind]	Wright, David [Ind]-Robert [Ind] Haynes, Rick [Ind]	Petty, Estelle [Ind] - England, Georgia [Ind] - Wright, Imogene	Robert [IV]	Mill Springs
Wright, Isaac C.	**Jan 30, 1989**	**83**	**New Market**	**Jul 20, 1909**	**Wright, David**	**Thompson, Mary**					**Dewitt**	**Mills Spring**

Name	Date	Age	Place	County	Date	Father		Mother		Spouse	Military				Cemetery
Wright, Isaac Loyd	May 9, 1996	76	New Market	Greene Co.	Jun 6, 1921	Wright, John		Beckner, Willie		Strange, Loweta		Osborne, Shirley - Moody, Janie - Wilson, Linda			Rocky Valley
Wright, J.W. (Dut)	Nov 24, 1982	52	Jeff Ccity	Grainger Co.	Mar 25, 1930	Wright, Alfred		Rhinehart, Kellie		De Vrou, Evelyn			Allen		Lawsons Chapel - Dandridge, Tn
Wright, James	Jun 16, 1994	70	F.S.H.	Dandridge, Tn	May 30, 1924	Wright, Alfred		Rhinehart, Kellie		Dubos, Ada Mae	Army	Byrd, Paulina - Duncan, Frances - Cochrian, F. - Becker, Shirley - Pinkston, Sylvia	J.C.-Steve	Russell, Brenda - Allsop, Sandra	Raymond-Cletis	J.M.G.
Wright, John Arthur	Apr 23, 1982	19	M.C.		Sep 18, 1942	Wright, Wesley J.	Tn	Adams, Eula	Tn						New Market
Wright, Katie	Jun 13, 1995	81	J.M.H.	Jeff Co	Apr 5, 1905	Rhinehart, Richard		Hanox, Martha		Wright, Alfred [D]		Duncan, Frances - Byrd, Pauline - Buchanan, Betty - Faye - Mc Bee, Betty Ray - Buckner, Shirley - Pinkston, Sylvia			Lawsons Chapel
Wright, Lisa Marlene	1995		Ft. Benning, Ga	Ft. Benning, Ga		Wright, James C.									
Wright, Lucille	Jun 27, 1967	73	Jeff City	Knoxlife, Tn	Sep 5, 1923	Mc Falt, Ballard		Mc Clain, Mattie		Wright, W.C. [D]				Wright, Caroline - Minton, Juanita - Be-Lord, Mr. F.H., Dale-Grace	New Gray - Knoxville, Tn
Wright, Mary T.	Oct 31, 1967	87	J.M.H.	Green Cove, Va	Apr 11, 1900	Hart, Will		Unk		Wright, Dave W. [D]		England, Georgia - Petty, Estelle - Hart, Imogene	Robert-Harold		Mill Springs
Wright, Raymond	Jan 2, 1972	46	U.T.H.					Wright, Mary		Wright, Dave W. [D]			Gary W.		Mills Spring
Wright, Wesley John	Dec 27, 1970	69		Tn	Oct 6, 1902	Wright, John W.		Beckner, Willie		Adams, Eula		Green, Mrs. Edgar - Vance, Jean & Charles - Chandler, Peggy & Thomas			New Market
Wrinkle, Mary	May 1, 1962	61	M.C.	Tn	Jan 30, 1891	Wright, W.T.		Kennedy, Margret		Wrinkle, Sam					Friends Station
Wuerdeman, Paul Gustave	Mar 31, 1990		New Market	Claiborne Co, Tn	Aug 12, 1921	Wuerdeman, Gustave		Hertz, Nancy		Mullins, Novella		Mullins, Kathy - Ross, Lisa	Ralph - [Step] West, Larry-Joey		Evans - Tazewell, Tn
Wyrick, Dolores Dean	Jan 6, 1992			Unk		Unk		Unk		Mullins, Kathy - Ross, Lisa			Woods, E.C.	Willie	Bodweiler

Name	Date	Age	Place	Loc	Date	Father		Mother		Spouse					Husband	Friends Station
Young, Eula Blanche	May 12, 1984	51	Jeff Co	Tn	Jun 29, 1912	Ballinger, Charles H.		Bryant, Jessie		Young, Guy	Allsup, Mrs. Bill - Bellamy, Alice	Bill-Robert-Paul-Lynn	Whaley, Mrs. Harvey - [1/2] Ross, Mrs. Vassel - Havely, Mrs. Kenneth	Clarence [1/2] Ballinger, Guy - Donald-Gerald	Arwood, Virgie - Collins, Vyonorgia	Mill Springs
Young, John Andrew	Jan 16, 1972		Jeff Co	Tn	Jan 14, 1972	Young, Frank Clevenger, William		Henson, Linda							Russell, Kevin - Hicks, Tony - Allsup, Gary - Collins, Floyd - Ballinger, Guy	Mills Spring
Young, Mary Ellen	Nov 7, 1967	87	J.M.H.	Tn	Oct 3, 1880			Elmore, —		Young, I.G.		Joe M.				Mill Springs
Young, Paul Guy	May 18, 1984	82	Morristown, Tn	Jeff Co	Mar 19, 1902	Young, William		Pratt, Molly		Ballinger, Eula [D]	Allsup, Doris - Hicks, Alice	Bill-Robert-Paul-Lynn				Mill Springs
Yount, William Floyd	May 4, 1982	42	V.A.-Asheville, Nc			Yount, Mack H.		Lancaster, Virginia		Edna C.	mary	William Jr.-Mack	Stults, Elaine - Johnson, Patricia - Waldies, Elizabeth - West, Emmiens Jean	Tommy	Military	Valley View
Zirkle, Charles Elmer	Jan 30, 1989	82	U.T.H.	New Market	May 1, 1926	Zirkle, Elmer B.		Nance, Muriel		Ellis, Barbara	Jan - Greene, Kristy	Steve			[Pall] Taylor, James - Churchman, Bruce - Cole, Robert-John N.- Sheddon, Glenn- John	J.M.G.
Zirkle, Elmer Bruce	Jun 7, 1983	80	B.H.	Jeff Co	Oct 4, 1902	Perry, Arthur		Brice, Carrie		Nance, Myrle		Charles	Sheddon, Elsie - Churchman, Helen		[Pall] Taylor, Paul - Jones, Leland - Hodges, Edward - Fielden, Eugene	West View
Zirkle, Myrle [F]	Apr 14, 1990	89	J.M.H.	New Market	Aug 17, 1900	Nance, Robert		Loy, Martha		Zirkle, Elmer [D]	[In-Law] Zirkle, Barbara				Zirkle, Bobby E. [Pall] Mitchell, Ted - Jones, Leland - Cole, Robert- John - Coleman, Roe - Bishop, Sydney	West View